Royal Palaces, Residences and Pavilions of India

Royal Palaces, Residences and Pavilions of India

— 13th through 18th Centuries — An Iconographic Consideration

By
Fredrick W. Bunce, Ph.D.
Professor Emeritus of Art
Indiana State University

D.K. Printworld (P) Ltd.
New Delhi

Cataloging in Publication Data — DK
[Courtesy: D.K. Agencies (P) Ltd. <docinfo@dkagencies.com>]

Bunce, Fredrick W. (Fredrick William), 1935-
Royal palaces, residences and pavilions of India. 13th through 18th centuries : an iconographic consideration / by Fredrick W. Bunce.
p. 29 cm.
Includes bibliographical references (p.)
ISBN 8124603561

1. India — Kings and rulers — Homes and haunts — Designs and plans. 2. India — Kings and rulers — Homes and haunts — History. 3. Royal houses — India — Designs and plans. 4. Palaces — India — Designs and plans. 5. Dwellings — India — Designs and plans. 6. Pavilions — India — Designs and plans. 7. Architecture, Domestic — India — Designs and plans. I. Title.

DDC 725.170 954 2

ISBN 81-246-0356-1
First published in India in 2006

Published and Printed by:
D.K. Printworld (P) Ltd.
Regd. Office: 'Sri Kunj', F-52, Bali Nagar
New Delhi-110 015
Phones: (011) 2545-3975; 2546-6019; *Fax*: (011) 2546-5926
E-mail: dkprintworld@vsnl.net
Website: www.dkprintworld.com

Contents

Contents (Continued)

List of Plates

List of Plates (Continued)

List of Plates (Continued)

List of Plates (Concluded)

List of Figures

List of Figures (Continued)

List of Figures (Continued)

List of Figures (Concluded)

List of Figures (Concluded)

Abbreviations

AH	A.B.M. Husain, *Fatehpur-sikri and its Architecture*
AM	Anisha Shekhar Mukherji, *The Red Fort of Shahjahanabad*
AP	Amjad Bohumil Prochazka, *Architecture of the Islamic Cultural Sphere*
BD	Bruno Dagens, ed. & trans. *Mayamatam, Treatise of Housing, Architecture & Iconography*
CA	Catherine B. Asher, *Architecture of Mughal India.*
CJ	C.G. Jung, *Maṇḍala Symbolism*
CS	C.M. Villiers Stuart, *Gardens of the Great Mughals*
EG	Ernst Grube, et al, George Mitchell (ed.) *Architecture of the Islamic World: Its History and Social Meaning*
EH	E.B. Havell, *Encyclopaedia of Architecture in the Indian Subcontinent*
EK	Ebba Koch, *Mughal Architecture: An Outline of Its History and Development 1526-1858.*
FWB	Fredrick W. Bunce, *The Iconography of Plans: A Study of the Influence of Buddhism and Hinduism on Architectural Plans of South and South-east Asia.*
FWB 2	Fredrick W. Bunce, *Numbers, Their Iconographic Consideration in Buddhist and Hindu Practices.*
FWB 3	Fredrick W. Bunce, *Islamic Tombs in India: The Iconography and Genesis of their Design*
GC	George Coedès, *The Indianized States of South-east Asia.*
GG	Godfrey Goodwin, *A History of Ottoman Architecture*
GM	George Michell, *The Royal Palaces of India.*
GM 2	George Michell, ed., *Architcture of the Islamic World.*
GM 3	George Michell, *The Vijayanagara Courtly Style.*
GT	G.H.R. Tillotson, *Mughal India.*
GT 2	G.H.R. Tillotson, *The Rajput Palaces: The Development of an Architectural Style, 1450-1750.*
HC	Henry Cousens, *Bijapur and Its Architectural Remains: With a Historical Outline of the Adil Shāhi Dynasty;*
HS	Henri Stierlin (ed.), *Architecture of the World: Islamic India.*
HS 2	Henri Stierlin (ed.), *Architecture of the World: India.*
IS	Issam El-Said and Ayse Parman, *Geometric Concepts in Islamic Art*
JP	Jose Pereira, *Islamic Sacred Architecture: A Stylistic History*
KC	K.A.C. Creswell, *A Short Account of Early Muslim Architecture*

Abbreviations (Conclued)

KR	K.V. Soundara Rajan, *Islam Builds in India.*
MA	Mohammad al-Asad, et al. Martin Frishman and Hasan-Uddin Khan, eds. *The Mosque: History, Architectural Development & Regional Diversity.*
MC	Manekshah Sorabshah Commissariat, *A History of Gujarat: Including a Survey of its Chief Architectural Monuments and Inscriptions.*
MN	M.A. Nayeem, *The Splendour of Hyderabad : The Last Phase of an Oriental Culture* (1591-1948 AD)
MS	Margaret Sevcenko, ed., *Theories and Principles of Design in the Architecture of Islamic Societies*
MW	Mohammad Waliullah Khan, *Lahore and its Important Monuments*
PB	Percy Brown, *Indian Architecture* (*Islamic Period*).
RH	Robert Hillenbrand, *Islamic Art and Architecture.*
RH 2	Robert Hillenbrand, *Islamic Architecture: Form, Function & Meaning*
RHo	Rima Hooja, "Of Buildings and Books: The Theory and Practice of the Architect Mandan," *Marg: A Magazine of the Arts*
RM	Rustam Mehta, *Masterpieces of Indo-Islamic Architecture*
RN	R. Nath, *Fatehpur Sikri and its Monuments.*
RN2	R. Nath, *History of Mughal Architecture.*
RN3	R. Nath, *History of Sultānate Architecture.*
RN4	R. Nath, *Indigenous Characteristics of Mughal Architecture.*
RS	K. V. Soundara Rajan, *Ahmadabad.*
RS 2	K. V. Soundara Rajan, *Islam Builds in India*
SC	Stephen Carr, *Archaeology and Monumental Remains of Delhi.*
SG	Satish Grover, *Islamic Architecture in India*
SN	S. A. A. Naqoi, *Humayun's Tomb and Adjacent Buildings*
SS	Shehbaz H. Safrani, *Golconda and Hyderabad*
TC	Thomas Crump, *The Anthropology of Numbers.*
VM	Vettam Mani, *Puranic Encyclopaedia*
VS	Vibhuti Sachdev and Giles Tillotson, *Building Jaipur: The Making of an Indian City.*

Introduction & Iconography:

Beginnings

Ratios and Proportions
Basic Plans

Physical Iconography

The Palace
Axiality
Symmetry/Asymmetry
Orientation
The High Place
The Labyrinth

Implied Iconography

"By the Grace of God"
Dynasty
Royal Accoutrements
Power
Defensive
Property — Religious/Cultural

Introduction

The vast area of India consists of an equally vast number of geographically isolated regions. The broad, rolling plains that are seen in North or South America or northern Asia which spread for hundreds, even thousands of square kilometers, are not seen in the subcontinent. Numerous ranges, hills, plateaus, escarpments, and rivers crisscross the land creating sundry isolated, though contiguous, geographical enclaves, regions, lands — some smaller, others larger. Within these polities, assorted peoples and diverse tribes established themselves and sought dominance.

Countless petty states rose and fell, each vying for power and dominance and leaving their aesthetic stamp upon the land they tyrannized. Indeed at times the map of India was as bewildering in its ever-changing complexity as the map of nineteenth century Germany! Nearly from A to Z, from Ahmadnagar to Vijayanagara, certainly from Abdul Kasim to Zorowar Singh, hundreds of states existed at one time or another, with thousands of rulers. Many rulers were vastly influential politically and fewer were of note due to their aesthetic contributions to the land and peoples they controlled.

Empires also emerged, flourished and sunk into political oblivion. The Delhi Sultanate, the Empires of Vijayanagara and the Mughals coalesced the aesthetic and iconographic direction of this diverse land seemed unified to a point, but that was never to be! This added to the incredible mix, the diversity of styles and approaches that are the hallmark of India's architecture and art. Where else can one find such diversity as seen in the *Gol Gumbaz* of Bijapur, the *Tomb of I'timad-ud-daula* at Agra, the later additions to the *Temple of* Śiva *and* Mīnākṣī at Madurai, the *Govind Mandir* at Datia or the *Jami' Masjid* at Delhi which were all begun within a quarter century of each other and each singular in every way!

The numerous petty states that arose, coupled with the introduction of Islam stirred up this cultural stew. The second major Indo-European invasion — the Afghani-Turko Muslims — likewise added to this diverse cultural broth. The benefit India accrued, culturally from these petty states, the empires, the introduction of Islam and the second Indo-European invasions is enormous; monumental.

As civilizations developed throughout history certain traditions were established which later became codified into rules or laws. Conquerors invaded and brought with them their own cultural imperatives. They amalgamated those beliefs with the beliefs of the conquered peoples that did not infringe upon their core convictions. No less so with the civilization of India. In the second millennium BCE rapacious light skinned Indo-Europeans (aka Aryans) began to invade from the north and west. Their aggressive, efficient armies easily subdued the local populous of the Indus valley — i.e. the Dravidians. They conquered and displaced the established dark skinned Dravidian groups and, in time, instituted a caste system as a means of further subjugation and control of the subdued population. The Dravidians fled to the south. There they prospered and were to establish their own civilization, once more.

This system, this imposed caste system was based in part on colour (Ind.: *varṇa* = caste = colour) as well as the individual's position within the society — e.g. brāhmaṇa were priests, kṣatriya were warriors and kings, vaiśya were herdsmen and/or involved in trading and commerce, and śūdra were those who worked with their hands and served the higher castes.

Caste became an integral part of Vedic beliefs and was furthered by Hindu practices as well. Strictly speaking, unlike the other major

Introduction (Continued)

world religions, one cannot become a Hindu — i.e. assuming a caste position. If a Hindu ruler married a woman outside the Hindu pale, the position of their offspring was always considered highly suspect. If the said ruler was provided with an only son from this out-of-caste union, his right to succeed his father was in grave peril indeed. Generally, in that case, the line would move laterally to an acceptable Hindu candidate.

Caste became a powerful tool over the millennia. Laws were established, based upon caste, that included all manner of human activity and economic intercourse. As stated, marriage was only expected within the castes. Between the castes, it was severely frowned upon. A man of a higher caste could marry a woman of a lower caste and retain his caste designation. However the children of this union were "mixed caste" and generally did not retain the caste standing of their father. On the other hand, if a woman married beneath her caste, she was considered as a *bête noire*.

Laws were promulgated that dealt not only with social status and the types of work allowed for the castes, but, later, the types of houses or dwellings and their location within a city or town. These "laws" were inviolable and applied to every member of society. These codifications which applied to a structure are to be found in the *Mayamatam* and the *Manasara*.

Another great invasion came to India. This time it was religion oriented — i.e. Islam — but the invaders were again Indo-Europeans. In 1173 CE, Prince Muhammad of Ghur, an Afghani conquered much of northern India. His general, Qutb-ud-din Aibak conquered Delhi in 1206 CE and declared himself the first Sultān of Delhi. By the sixteenth century there was a strange mixture of Islamic, including Mughal, and Hindu states throughout the subcontinent (See: **Appendix A, Plates 102-107**). Each ruler established a capital with citadel or fort (Indic: *kotila* or *garh mahal*) and residential structures. From Afghanistan, Iran and Turkey, various invading Islamic rulers brought with them customs and requirements for their residences. Some brought architects/ builders, however, most utilized the indigenous *sthapati*s for their constructions. What emerged is a wonderful amalgamation, a cross-cultural pollination and/or adaptation of the Hindu and the Islamic worlds.

Much of this amalgamation can be seen in the remarkable tombs of Islamic India. However, what is truly outstanding are the palaces, pavilions and residences of the ruling class. Religion and ethnicity may have separated them — i.e. Hinduism and Islam; Indo-Europeans (*aka Āryans*)-Hindu, or Dravidian-Hindu, or Afghani, or Iranian, or Turk — but as rulers they sought the same. Whether *mahārājā, rājā, nawāb, nāyaka, nizam, rao, rāya* or *sultān* each viewed themselves and their residences with a degree of 'sameness.'

Each ruler possessed similar needs demanded by his assumed position. Each considered their person unique, inviolable. Each felt a need to elevate themselves and their family further into the hallowed halls of rule. One way in which this was accomplished was through the construction of citadels — places of protection from their foes as well as residences. Further, the building of palaces, pavilions of pleasure and other residences, in a concrete way, established and underlined their royal status. But, these constructions were no mere whim. They were needed. They were demanded by their status.

These buildings, these palaces, pavilions of pleasure and other residences assumed iconic importance and proportions. The plans of these structures reveal the multilayered requirements of rule and become iconographic representations of rule.

'The Palace,' 'Ratios and Proportions,' 'Basic Plans,' 'Axiality,' 'Symmetry,' 'Orientation,' 'The

Introduction (Continued)

High Place,' 'The Labyrinth,' '"By the Grace of God,"' 'Royal Accoutrements,' 'Defensive,' and 'Property — Religious/Cultural' are twelve iconic qualities seen to be common threads connecting these palaces, pavilions of pleasure and other residences within the Hindu and Islamic worlds of India. Each of these twelve is important individually and as an interconnecting web applying to rule. Each become iconographic elements. They are further considered as either physical iconography or implied iconography. Physical Iconography is exemplified in various aspects such as: the palace, axiality, symmetry/asymmetry, orientation, the high place and the labyrinth. Implied Iconography is denoted by concepts such as: "By the Grace of God," dynasty, royal accoutrements, power, defensive and property — religious/cultural.

The palaces (*garh mahal*), pavilions and residences herein were chosen as they represented the group, the period and the locale. It was not the desire of this author to include every palace, pavilion or residence of note. Indeed, the number of these structures worthy of consideration within India is truly staggering! Therefore, there are, undoubtedly, examples which many feel should have been considered and which were not.

Iconography

Beginnings

Ratios and proportions and basic plans may be seen as the most elemental form of iconography as they apply to plans. One may observe the plan of the *Govind Mahal* at Datia (See: **Plates 44-46**) and surmise that the ruler was a Hindu with the status of a king (*rājā*) not an emperor (*Mahārājā*) and that he came from the warrior (kṣatriya) and not priestly (brāhmaṇa) caste. This all can be gleaned from the plan. Further, more esoteric evidence may be found in the ratios and proportions of many of the structures. The Hindu *śilpa śāstra*s were the handbooks of the *sthapati*. With the influx and the invasions of Islam, this strong tradition was utilized by numerous Muslim rulers to varying degrees.

Ratios and Proportions

In the construction of a building within the Hindu tradition, whether temple or residence or palace, once the plan has been decided upon, then there are complicated procedures that included ratios and proportion. The following lengthy quote deals with those considerations as they apply to a temple plan. However, they are equally applicable to a dwelling (Note: where the term "temple" is found, insert the term "dwelling").

From the simplest temple to the most elaborate in size certain proportions were established to which adherence was mandatory. Basically, this proportion was found in the ratio between the height (**H**), the width (**W**), and/or the depth (**D**) of the structure. For example if that ratio was one to one (1:1):

$$\mathbf{H} \div \mathbf{W} = 1.00$$

the resulting structure fell under the *Śantika* type or class of temple. These ratio/types vary as to the size of the temple — e.g. the *Śantika* is the ratio for large structures whereas the *Abdhuta* with a ratio of 2:1 is for small buildings:

$$\mathbf{H} \div \mathbf{W} = 2.00$$

This ratio is further delineated by which unit (**H** or **W**) is used as the basis for the ratio. If the height (**H**) is the basis then the delineation is referred to as *Sthānaka* — e.g. *Śantika Sthānaka* or *Abdhuta Sthānaka*. If, on the other hand, the width (**W**) is the basis then the delineation is referred to as *Āsana* — e.g. *Śantika Āsana or Abdhuta Āsana*. Finally, if the depth (**D**) is the basis then the delineation is referred to as *Śayana* — e.g. *Śantika* or *Śayana* or *Abdhuta Śayana*. There are, therefore six different computational variations regarding height, width and depth:

$$\mathbf{H \div W \quad W \div H \quad D \div W}$$
$$\mathbf{W \div D \quad D \div H \quad H \div D}$$

The various parts of a structure may also be utilized in establishing ratios. However, there is one which appears to be more important than the others — i.e., the ratio between the height of the base (**HB**) and the height of the temple (**H**). Atmadi notes that in the works within his purview, one ratio stands out — i.e. the relationship of the base to the height. This ratio appears to be a constant one to eight (1:8):[1]

$$\mathbf{HB} \div \mathbf{H} = 1/8\ \mathrm{H}$$

Regardless of whether the height of the structure is divided into divisions other than eight, the resultant ratio is 1:8. For example: if the height (**H**) of the building is divided into twelve modules, the height of the Base (**HB**) is 1.5 of the whole, or:

$$1.5\ (\mathbf{HB}) \times 1/12\ \mathbf{H} = 1/8$$

These ratios were not merely theoretical standards, they were proportions and rules which for both the Hindu and the Buddhist had cosmic implications that were applied to civilizations outside the confines of Mother India.[2]

Importance of Site

Where a temple is to be erected, the locale is also of major importance. Consideration is given to construct a temple upon a high place as noted above, however that is not a prime consideration. The plot of land under consideration must be clean, clean of any of the darker vocations of mankind — i.e. it may not have been used for burial or cremation purposes, it may not have been used as a dump for refuse, it may not have been an abattoir, or a locale in which any sort of violence (murder, rape, war or pillage) had occurred. (This was mandatory for temples and highly desirable for dwellings as well.) The area of the temple is then outlined and the orientation is established. After offerings and ritual cleansing by the priest, the land is then ploughed and corn is planted, to grow and ripen. After the crop has matured cows are allowed to graze upon the plot for two days, further cleansing and sanctifying it. It is after this that the *Vāstu Puruṣa Maṇḍala* is drawn on the ground.

Rules of Size, Duration and Caste[3]

The size of the *maṇḍala*, and, therefore, the temple is not arbitrary, but, must conform to a series of arithmetic computations, each based upon the preceding calculation. The results of these 'cosmic' related calculations, if auspicious in their results along with the proportions and ratios, will result in a temple that is not only aesthetically pleasing but also one which possess a viable time-space harmony.

When the *Vāstu Puruṣa Maṇḍala* is drawn on the ground, numerous calculations have already been made which must yield positive results. The construction of a temple, a terrestrial manifestation, is undertaken with the idea that the earth is imperfect. Only The Absolute, the *brahman*, represented by the square, is perfect. Therefore, the various calculations, which always include a division component, are so devised as to result in a remainder. It is the remainder which guides the *sthapati* and establishes the proper proportions. It is the remainder which ultimately represents the terrestrial in the lengthy and complex process of "design."

The primary calculations undertaken in the consideration of the possible construction of a temple are six in number. Each relates to each other as well as the whole and the resultant computations must conform to a number of variables. Time and space both play a vital part in the calculations. These foundational reckonings are:

1. A set of calculations pertains to the width of the temple, the remainder of this calculation is called *vyaya:*

$$\mathbf{W} \times 9 \div 10 = \text{whole \# (remainder} = \textit{vyaya})$$

The integer ten is cosmic in its make-up (1 + 2 + 3 + 4 = 10) and represents perfection or completeness.

2. The next formula affirms the length (**L**) of the temple, the remainder of this calculation is called *riksha*:

$$\mathbf{L} \times 8 \div 27 = \text{whole \# (remainder} = \textit{riksha}).$$

The remainder determines under which star or planet the temple is to be constructed. Twenty-seven is the number of stars recognized by the Hindu astronomers. If, for some reason, the temple is to be built under a particular star, then the **L** must be adjusted until the *riksha* falls within the index number of the star.

3. This formula is linked to the second in that the length of the temple is the determinant factor, the remainder of this calculation is called *āya*:

$$\mathbf{L} \times 8 \div 12 = \text{whole \# (remainder} = \textit{āya}).$$

The integer twelve in this figuring is related to the signs of the Zodiac, an important consideration in Hindu practice as well as Buddhist.

4. The circumference (**C**) is affirmed by the fourth calculation, the remainder of this calculation is called *vara*:

C x 9 ÷ 7 = whole # (remainder = *vara*).

Seven in this formula refers to the seven days of the week and the *vara* is the day that the construction should commence — one is Monday and so forth. If for some reason the *vara* falls on an inauspicious day, then there must be adjustments made.

5. The fifth also relates to the fourth in that the circumference is involved, the remainder of this calculation is called *tithi*:

C x 9 ÷ 30 = whole # (remainder = *tithi*).

This remainder refers to which day in the calendar month that the construction of the temple should begin. Thirty in this formula refers to the days in a calendar month. And,

6. This, the last of the primary calculations is related to the orientation of the temple, the remainder of this calculation is called *yoni*:

W x 3 ÷ 8 = whole # (remainder = *yoni*)

The remainder is the manifestation of the phenomenal sphere, the world. For example, in arriving at the orientation of the temple, the width (**W**) of the temple is multiplied by the perfect number three and divided by the auspicious eight — the eight directions of the compass. Since a remainder of zero (0) could result, the eight directions are numbered from zero to seven. Zero representing the east (See: **Figure 1**). Of course the east is the most favoured orientation with the west being acceptable, but less auspicious. Virtually every other orientation is considered to be inauspicious. The remainder is known as the *yoni* and that denotes the orientation. For example:

7 (**W**) x 3 = 21 ÷ 8 = 2 (5 remainder)

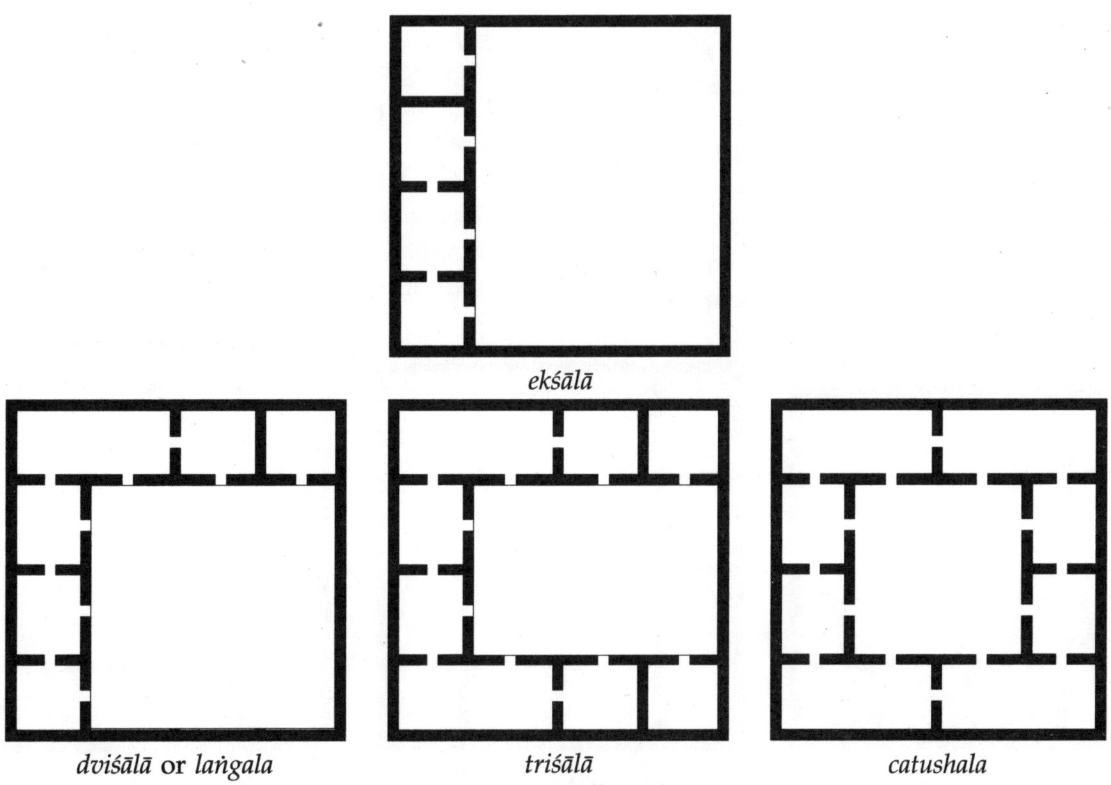

Figure 1 — Dwelling plans

Iconography (Continued)

Since the remainder is five (north-west), an inauspicious orientation, the calculations must be made again with certain adjustments along the way until an auspicious orientation is achieved.

"There are other computations that are made only after these basic six are accomplished. One curious formula relates to the duration of the temple's life and is related to the planets:

> **L** x **W** x 27 ÷ 100 = duration
> 21 x 7 x 27 = 3969 ÷ 100 = 39 (69 remainder)

In this instance the temple will stand for sixty-nine years. It is to be noted that no temple, utilizing this calculation, would stand for more than ninety-nine years.

"Caste has always been important in India since the *Vedic* period. This too has a formula:

> L x W x 9 ÷ 4 = whole # (remainder: caste)
> 21 x 7 x 9 = 1323 ÷ 4 = 330 (remainder: 3)

This calculation would indicate that the temple with these dimensions would be built by a vaiśya."[4]

Complex as these numerous considerations may have been, the results were not left up to the layman, but were the province of the architect-builder, the *sthapati*. He, with reference to the major treatises — e.g. the *Manasara* and/or the *Mayamatam* — would make all the necessary calculations and follow, where applicable, the wishes of his patron in the design and size of the house.

Basic Plans

There are four acknowledged plans for residential dwellings — i.e. *ekśālā*,[5] *dviśālā*,[6] *triśālā*,[7] and *caturśālā*[8] (See: **Figure 1**). Within the *Mayamatam*, each plan may have two or more variations. These variations are based upon the number of gables that the structure of a particular plan may have. The *Mayamatam* provides for one further dwelling plan — i.e. the "royal palace."[9] This plan is described and shown with a double court and described as a *caturśālā* plan with a *triśālā* plan attached, creating the double courtyard.[10] Additionally, there are a number of variations within the *caturśālā* plan(s) that do not include a roof-line variation. These variations include entrance(s), their locations and size — e.g. the *sarvatobhadra* (five types), the *vardhamāna* (seven types), and the *nandyavarta* (five types). A number of these sub types are relegated to specific castes — e.g. the *nandyavarta* (first type) is suitable for all castes, but for the vaiśya and śūdra castes the entrance *must* be oriented towards the east; the *nandyavarta* (fifth type) is suitable only for brāhmaṇas and kings. These were not the only considerations.

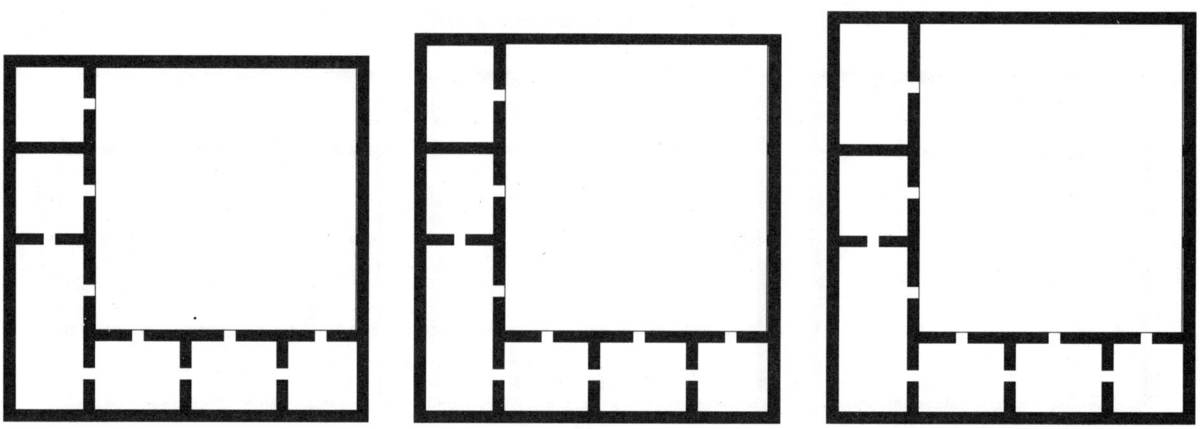

Figure 2 — *dviśālā* or *laṅgala* plan, indicating proportions for brāhmaṇa (left),

Iconography (Continued)

Other caste designations regarded the height of a dwelling also to be considered. By observing the number of storeys of a dwelling, one could ascertain the occupant's caste. A brāhmaṇa's dwelling may reach the height of six- and one-half storeys; a kṣatriya's home can be no taller than five-and one-half storeys, whereas a vaiśya's dwelling shall be four storeys and no higher, and a śūdra can only construct a home of two-and one-half storeys or less. Additionally, the proportion of the ground plan was strictly prescribed — i.e. length to width. A brāhmaṇa's home was the only dwelling which could be square, *en plan*. The length of a kṣatriya's and vaiśya's dwelling in proportion to its width may be no less than one-and-one-eighth the width. Finally, the length of a śūdra's home may be no less than one-and-one-fourth the width (See: **Figure 2**).

Those beyond caste — i.e. the ubiquitous untouchables and those non-Hindus who lived within their midst were not allowed to construct a house within these four established, inviolable plans. There were also some anomalies within this system. The size of the dwelling did not necessarily denote caste. For example, a vaiśya of great wealth may live in a home that was considerably larger than that of a brāhmaṇa who had limited means. Of course, the location of the house — i.e. the quarter of the city or town — as well as certain proportions and number of storeys allowed were always the determining factor.

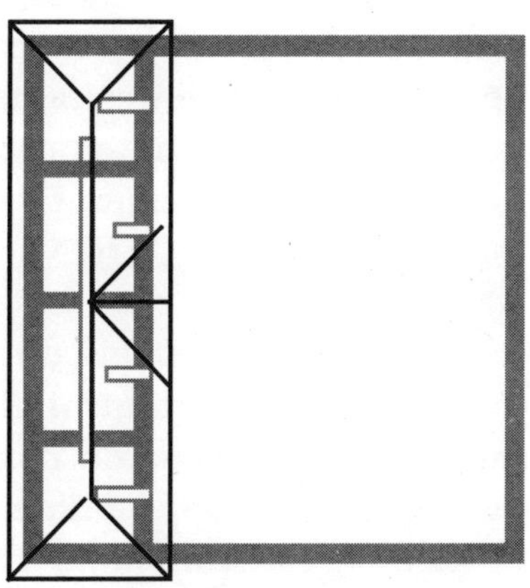

maulika type A (1 gable)

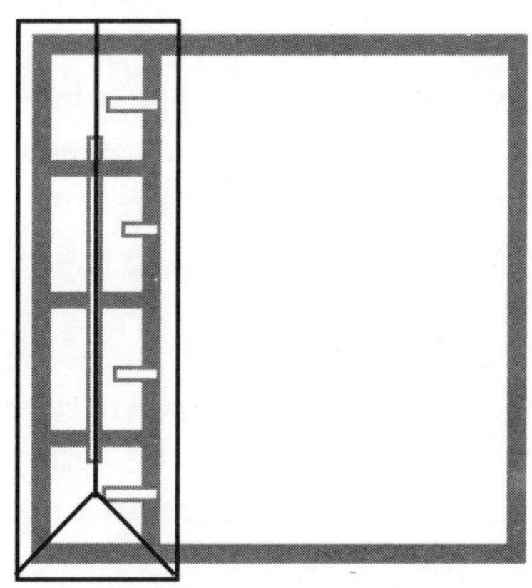

maulika type B (1 gable)

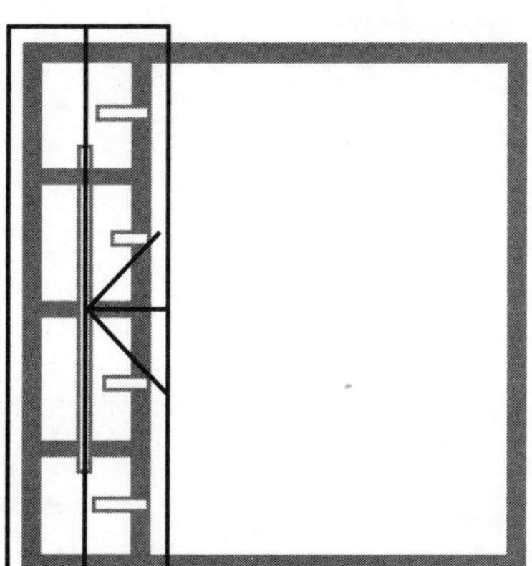

svāstika type (3 gable)

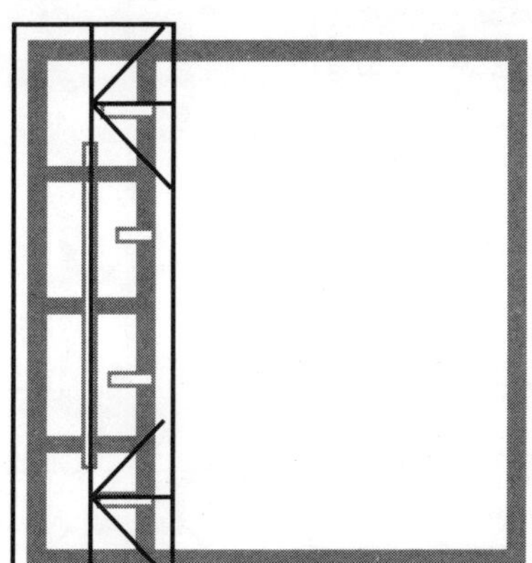

caturmukha type A (4 gables)

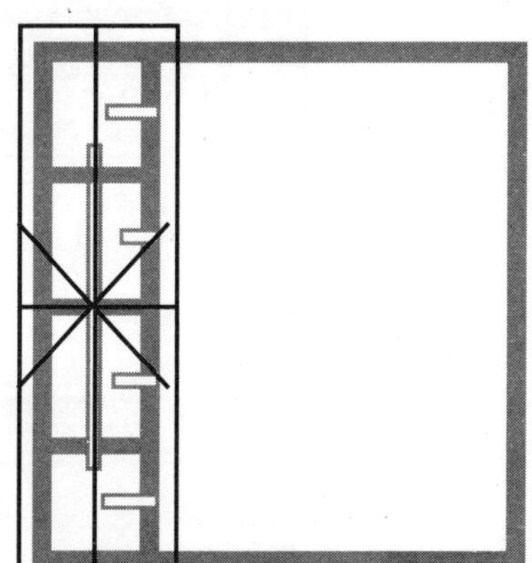

caturmukha type B (4 gables)

Figure 3 — *ekśālā* roof plan types

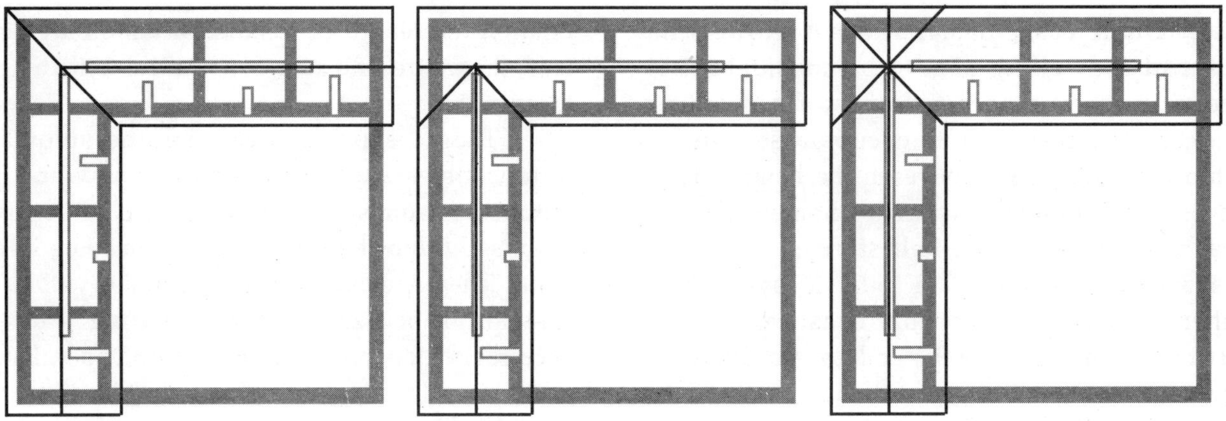

dandavaktra type (2 gables) *svāstika* type (3 gables) *caturmukha* type (4 gables)

Figure 4 — *dviśālā* or *laṅgala* roof plan types

As has been stated, the four basic plans — i.e. the *ekśālā, dviśālā* or *laṅgala, triśālā* or *śūrpa,* and *caturśālā* — possessed certain roof-line configurations. The *ekśālā*, or the dwelling with a single unit, as well as the other four basic plans, possessed an entrance that was oriented towards the South for a brāhmaṇa, towards the West for a kṣatriya, towards the North for a vaiśya and towards the East for a śūdra. This basic *ekśālā* plan indicates five variations for the roof-line (See: **Figure 3**). The first — i.e. the ***maulika* type A**[11] — is shown with a single gable in the centre of a hip roof's length. This placement follows the general, but not exclusive, Indian predilection for symmetry and balance. If, on the other hand, the confusing description found in the *Mayamatam*[12] is followed, it would appear that ***maulika* type B** is the alternative. However, this option is less than desirable as the roof-line is thereby asymmetrical, a state of affairs that the Indians find generally loathsome and inauspicious. The third variation is called the ***svāstika* type**. The roof-line of this type is made up of three gables. One on either end and one in the center. The central gable corresponds to the location of the main portal and may extend outward, in the appropriate direction, to form a portico. The ***caturmukha* type A** is the fourth

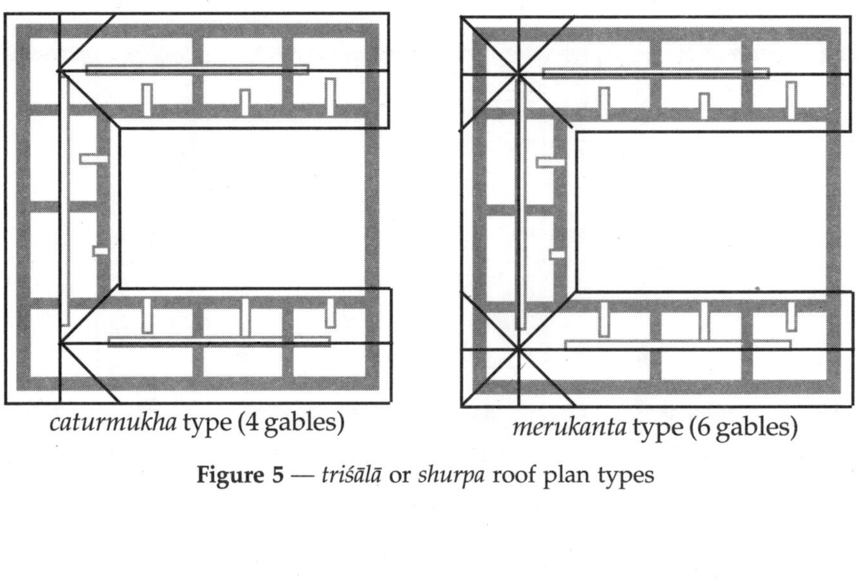

caturmukha type (4 gables) *merukanta* type (6 gables)

Figure 5 — *triśālā* or *shurpa* roof plan types

Iconography (Continued)

variation. Here, it is seen that *caturmukha* (literally: four heads) is a type in which the simple gable-roof is punctuated with two gables facing the fore court.[13] ***caturmukha* type B** indicates the variation.

The basic plan which included a second unit placed at right angles to the first, forming an "L" is the *dviśālā* or *laṅgala* (plough share) plan. Three simple roof-line variations occur (See: **Figure 4**). First, the ***dandavaktra* type** in which the two gabled roofs intersect forming a 'hip.' The second variation has three gables and is seen in which one of the units is made up of a gabled roof (2) and the second gabled roof intersects, but does not form a gable at the intersection. This type is known as the ***svāstika* type**. Finally, the ***caturmukha* type** in which the plan is seen with four gables formed by the intersecting and overlapping gabled-roofs.

The *triśālā* or *shurpa* (literally a winnowing basket) is composed of three wings in the form of a block "C." It is the type with the least variations within the various plans. Merely two variations occur in this plan (See: **Figure 5**). The ***caturmukha* type** with four gables and the ***merukanta* type** with six gables. It is interesting to note that although this plan would easily allow for a two-gable type, it is not an option in the *Mayamatam*.

The *caturśālā*, with four units forming an inner courtyard, is that plan which exhibits the most variations. The first three variations apply to roof-lines that are on the same plane — i.e.

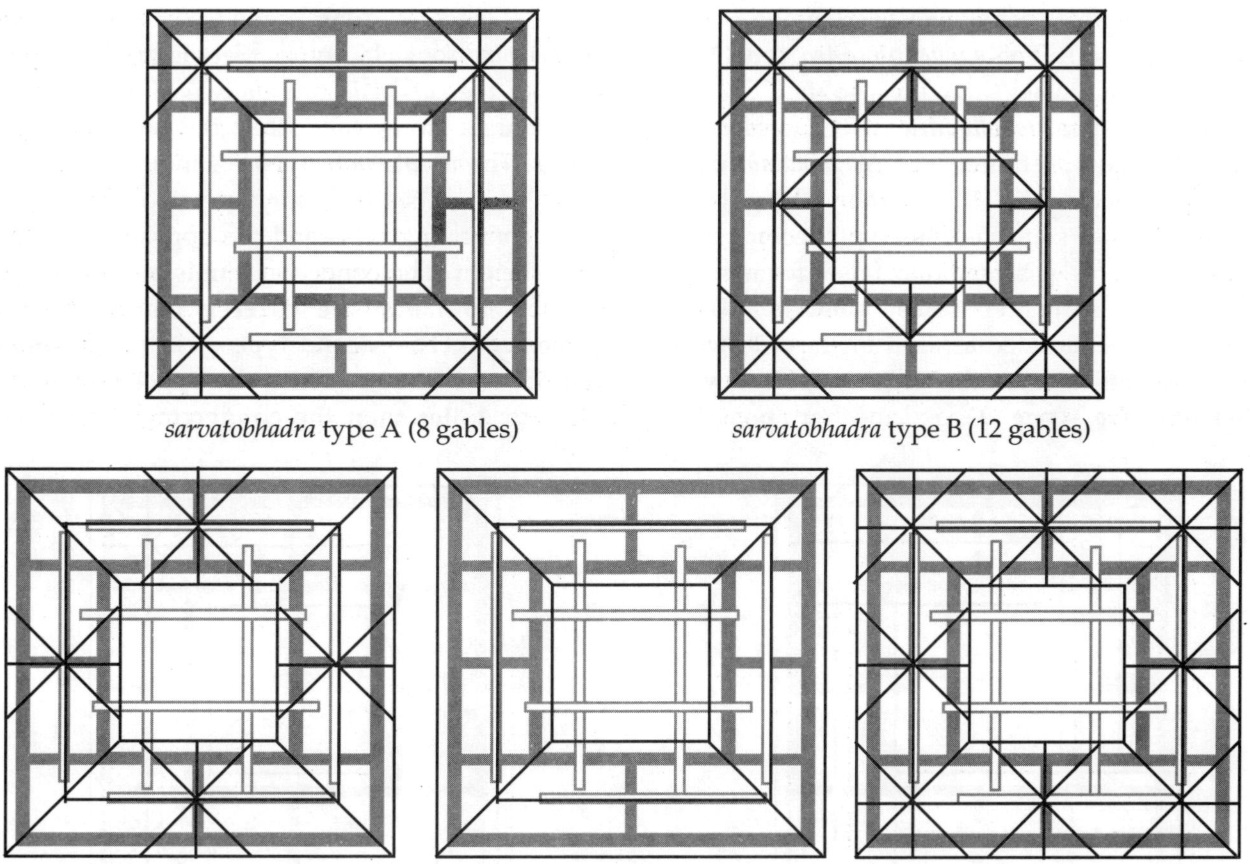

sarvatobhadra type A (8 gables)

sarvatobhadra type B (12 gables)

sarvatobhadra type C (8 gables)

sarvatobhadra type D

sarvatobhadra type E (16 gables)

Figure 6 — *sarvatobhadra* roof plan types

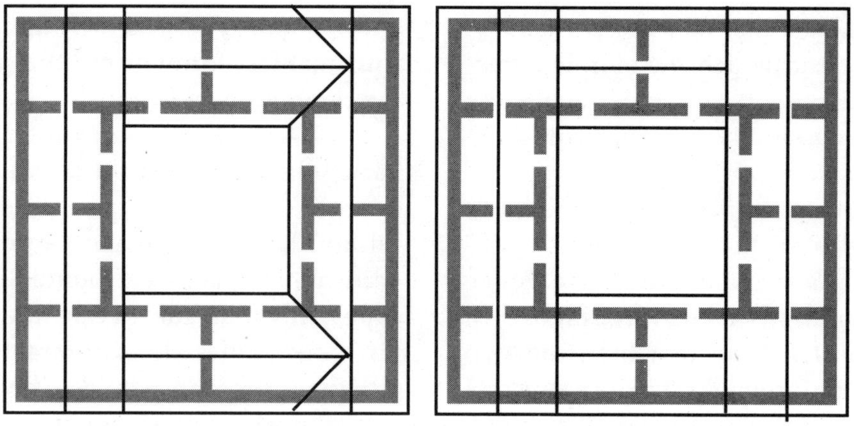

vardhamāna type A (4 gables) *vardhamāna* type B (4 gables)

Figure 7 — *vardhamāna* roof plan types

the ridge-lines are all the same distance from the ground (See: **Figure 6**). The first type — i.e. the ***sarvatobhadra* type A** — exhibits eight gables formed by the intersecting and overlapping of the four gabled-roofs. The ***sarvatobhadra* type B** is said to be composed of twelve gables. On the other hand, the ***sarvatobhadra* type C** presents a problem of interpretation. The *Mayamatam* does not state specifically the number of gables. However it does state that this type is composed of "hipped roofs with median false dormers."[14] This author interprets these "median false dormers" to be situated as seen in "*sarvatobhadra* type C (8 gables)" seen in **Figure 6**. However, ***sarvatobhadra* type D** is another possible variation. Finally, the ***sarvatobhadra* type E** is composed of sixteen gables, a natural extension of this roof-line type.

A second plan type is noted as the *vardhamāna* roof plan types (See: **Figure 7**). In this form of the *catuśālā* one or two of the opposite wings are a storey taller than the two connecting wings. The ***vardhamāna* type A** indicates that one of the wings is taller, forming two gables. The other connecting units and the opposite are of the same height. The connecting units merge into the parallel unit and the latter is composed of a gabled-roof. The second type — i.e. ***vardhamāna* type B** — is that in which the opposite units are a storey taller than the connecting units. Each

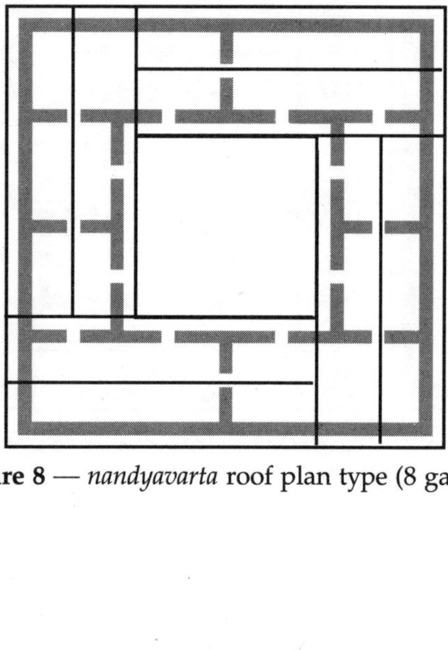

Figure 8 — *nandyavarta* roof plan type (8 gables)

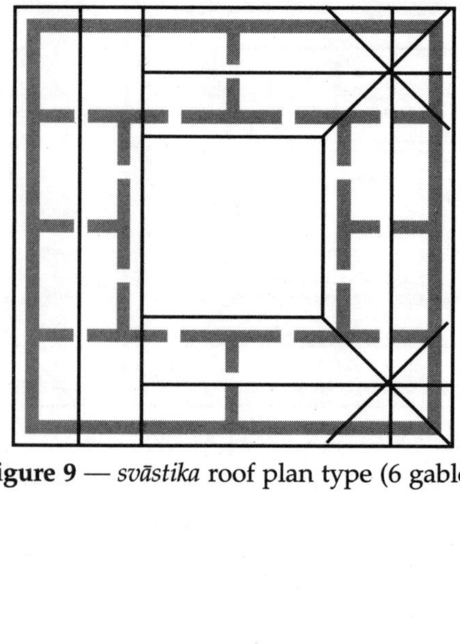

Figure 9 — *svāstika* roof plan type (6 gables)

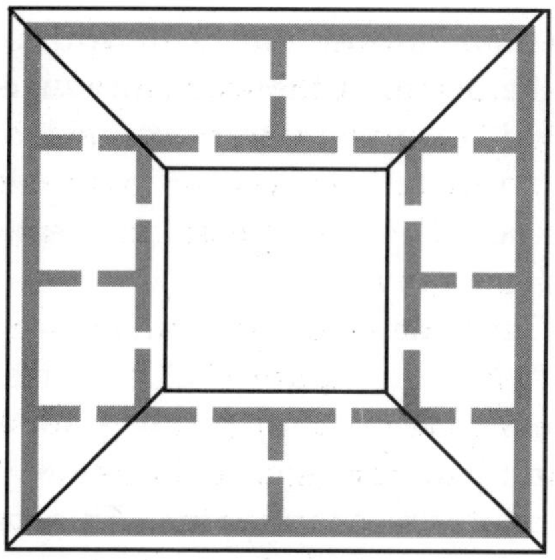

Figure 10 — *rucaka* roof plan type

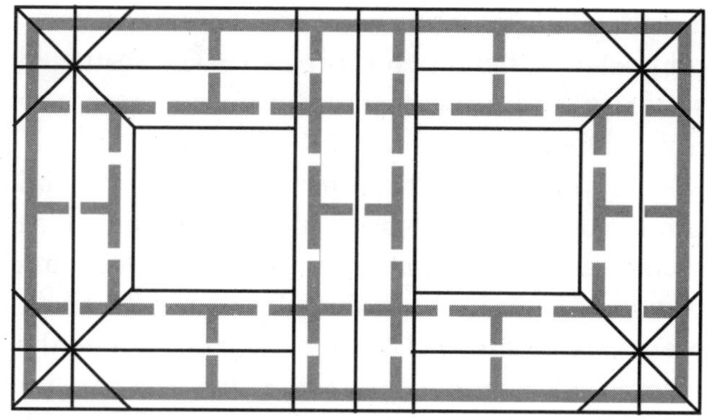

Figure 11 — seven unit house roof plan type (10 gables)

of the taller units are covered by a gabled-roof.

A further variation is seen in the ***nandyavarta* roof plan type** (See: **Figure 8**). Here the four gabled-roof units abut each other. The result is a broken roof-line with eight gables, four of which are masked. The result is similar to the plan of the *Neak Pean*, Angkor, in which a *svāstika* is seen to be the basic design element (See: **Appendix A, Plate 71**). However, the *Mayamatam* is confusing in describing this type. It states that "A court is to be built above a court and an outward room constructed above an outward room!"[15] However it is stipulated that this plan type is suitable for a temple, brāhmaṇa or king.

The *svāstika* roof plan type is that plan in which one of the elements is taller than the others and is covered by a gabled-roof (See: **Figure 9**). The lower storeys are covered by gabled-roofs which intersect and overlap, creating six gables. It is noted that if this plan is to be utilized by either a vaiśya or Śūdra, it must face east.

The final *caturśālā* plan is the ***rucaka* roof plan type** (See: **Figure 10**). This is the most 'democratic' of all the roof plans as it is said: "According to the sages, all that is fitting for the four classes is fitting too for gods and brāhmaṇas whilst what is fitting for the vaiśya is fitting for the śūdra."[16] It may be utilized by all, including a temple. However the restriction as to the location of the main entrance remains.

The above sections all refer, of course, to

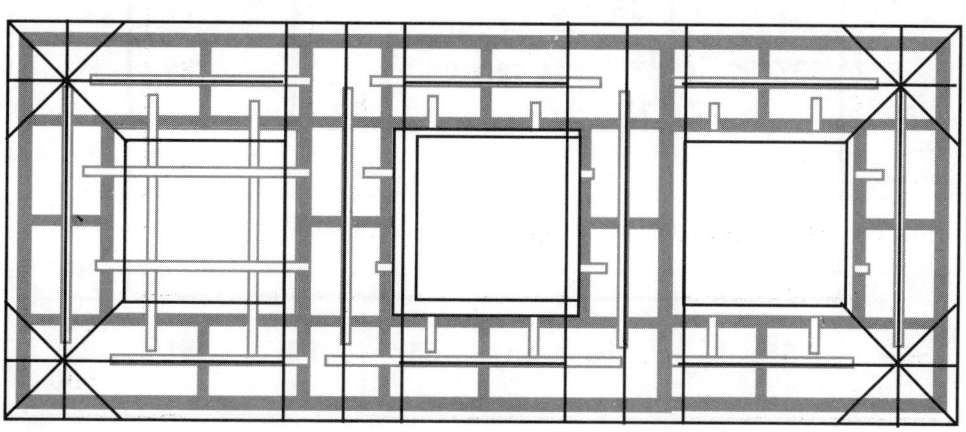

Figure 12 — ten unit house roof plan type (12 gables)

dwellings of the four castes. On the other hand a completely different and somewhat less restricted set of rules applies to the design and size of a royal dwelling.

The first two plans are variations and combinations of the above four basic plans. One such variation-combination is called the seven unit plan (See: **Figure 11**).[17] In this plan two of the above plans are combined into a hybrid — i.e. the *caturśālā* and the *triśālā* or *śūrpa* plans. The *triśālā* is appended to the *caturśālā* creating a dwelling with two courts. The resulting roof plan creates ten gables. This particular plan is a basic plan for a royal dwelling in which there are two courtyards. One is the domain of the women (wives) of the household. As a basic unit for a palace, this is the simplest plan. However, it does indicate, as does the next plan, the fact that frequently palaces are rectangular, *in toto*.

A final variation-combination is seen in the ten unit plan (See: **Figure 12**).[18] In this plan an additional *triśālā* or *śūrpa* plan is added to the seven unit plan creating a roof line with twelve gables and three courtyards. This particular structure is reserved for rulers. Here the rectangular quality is extended even further.

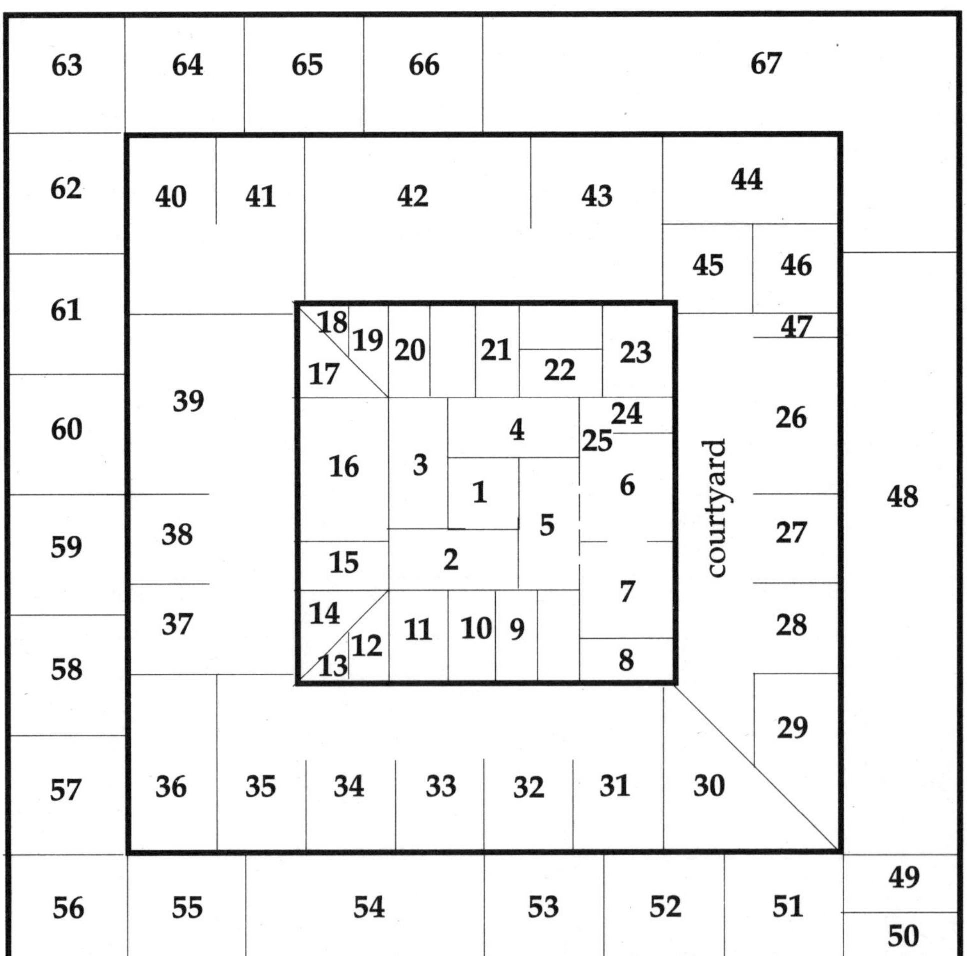

Figure 13 — a small royal palace with three enclosures

Iconography (Continued)

On the other hand, the *Mayamatam* describes a "plan for a small palace" which is cross-axial (See: **Figure 13**).[19] Of course, "small" here is a relative term. This palace possesses three concentric enclosures and each area is specifically denoted. These special areas for the inner enclosure are: 1)[20] the altar of *Brahmā*, 2) the King's quarters, 3) a theatre, 4) the Queen's quarters, 5) the entrance pavilion, 6) a courtyard, 7) the "bull stable" (Ind.: *vṛtta*) (possible a Śiva shrine), 8) store or treasury, 9) guard house or entrance, 10) dance hall, 11) stable, 12) confinement house, 13) reception pavilion, 14) ablution room, 15) store for salt and spices, 16) *śaṅkarālaya* ("pleasure house"), 17) residential area, 18) nursemaids and chamberlains' quarters, 19) young girls' quarters, 20) infirmary, 21) masseuses quarters, 22) bath, 23) shrine, 24) dining room, and 25) reception hall — all of which are for the direct and private support of the ruler. The designated areas in the middle enclosure are: 26) store of musical instruments and royal paraphernalia, 27) almsroom, 28) "water for charity," 29) grinding stone and fuel depot, 30) stable, 31) gate and armory, 32) kitchen, 33-34) commander-in-chief's quarters, 35) fakir's and conjuror's quarters, 36) buffalo stables, 37) almsroom, 38) reception hall, 39) baths, 40) tank, 41) young girls' and wet nurses quarters, 42) artists' quarters, 43) quarters for hunchbacks, dwarfs and barren women, 44) nurses quarters, 45) well, tank and flower garden, 46) honoraria room, and 47) almsroom. The areas of the outer enclosure are: 48) school, 49) main kitchen, 50) stable for cows, 51) store for salt, 52) elephant's stable, 53) painting gallery, 54) condiment's store, 55) fuel depot, 56) alms' store, 57) wrestler's quarters, 58) lodging, 59) crown prince's and *purohit*'s quarters, 60) assembly house (Ind.: *indraśālā*), 61) deer shed, 62) donkey and camel stable, 63) reservoir and lotus pond, 64) horses' stable, 65) elephants' stable, 66) initiation and confinement area, and 67) gardens, tank and assembly area.

It is interesting to note the use and frequency of certain areas. Stables (nine) dominate this small palace plan and are to be found in the three enclosures. Various stores

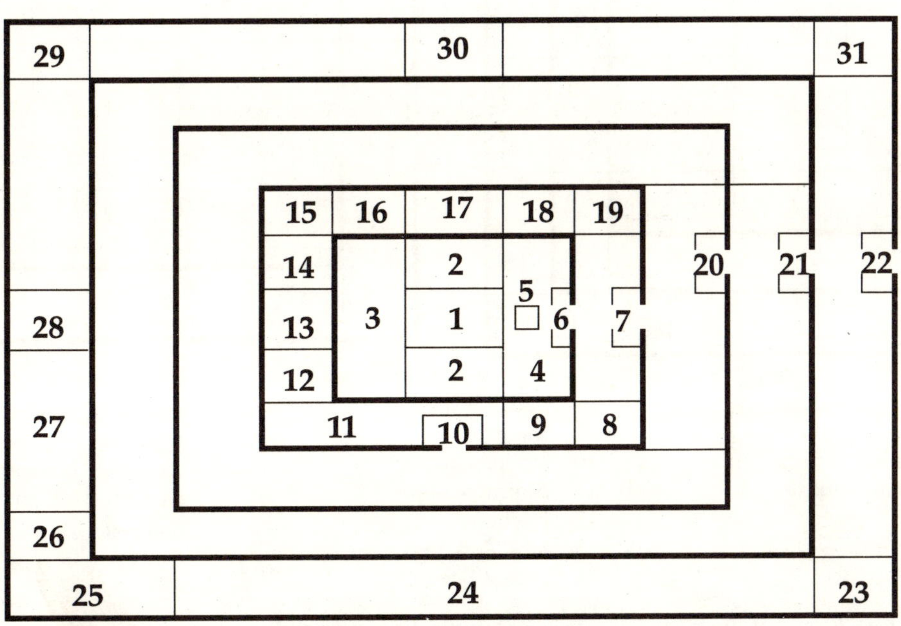

Figure 14 — *Saubala* palace

Iconography (Continued)

(five) are also found in all three areas as are tanks and/or reservoirs for the storage of water. In the middle and outer enclosures are to be found four areas which are the quarters of individuals who entertain. Here it is interesting to note that barren women are excluded from the inner enclosure and are quartered with dwarfs and hunchbacks.[21] Areas for alms (four) also make up an important segment of this "small palace." Baths, also, figure prominently within these enclosures.

An axial palace, the rectangular *Saubala Palace*[22] is described in some detail in the *Mayamatam* (See: **Figure 14**). It is considered to be a palace appropriate to a *cakravartin* or emperor, the highest of six rulers.[23] As with the "small royal palace," it consists of numerous areas, but is singular in its five, concentric compounds. The inner compound holds: 1) the altar of *Brahmā*, 2) the Queen's ceremonial quarters, 3) the emperor's ceremonial quarters, 4) the inner courtyard, 5) the coronation pavilion, and 6) the gateway into the inner compound. The second compound consists of: 7) a gateway leading to a courtyard, 8) the kitchen serving the inner compound, 9) the treasury, 10) a second gateway for the serving areas, 11) women's quarters, 12) the theater, 13) emperors quarters, 14) *purdah* room (*zenānā*), 15) pool (tank), 16) Queen's quarters, 17) ceremonial area (*tulabhara* & *hemagarbha* ceremonies), 18) imperial storehouse and elephant stable, and 19) tank and latrines. The third and fourth compounds consist of: 20) & 21) gateways leading to a courtyard. The rest of these areas are not designated. One may assume that these areas, as with the "small palace," contain spaces and/or rooms which support the two central compounds and their layout is of no substantial or cosmic importance. The outer compound is made up of: 22) a gateway leading to a courtyard, 23) offices and the main

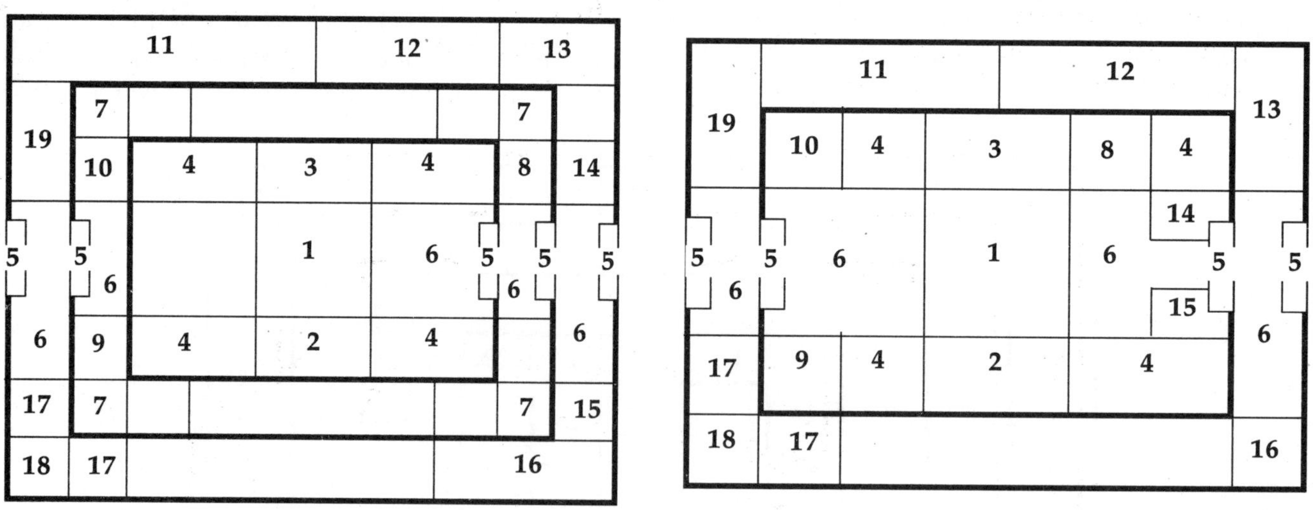

1 Shrine to Brahmā
2 King's quarters
3 Queen's quarters
4 hall with annexe
5 gate
6 courtyard
7 hall
8 bath tank
9 theatre
10 singers quarters
11 dining hall(s)
12 kitchen
13 tank & baths
14 Durga Shrine
15 reviewing stand
16 treasury
17 women's quarters
18 women's śālā and garden
19 *śaṅkarālaya*

Figure 15 — Palace of the *narendra* or *padmaka*, indicating conjectural arrangements (two variations)

kitchen, 24) exercise areas, 25) "King's dwellings," 26) an annexe, 27) women's quarters (females attached to the court, but not concubines or wives), 28) *śaṅkarālaya* ("pleasure house"), 29) tank, garden and hermitage, 30) ceremonial area (*tulabhara* & *hemagarbha* ceremonies), 31) Śiva temple, and areas which are not designated, but appropriate to this compound.

There are two more palaces considered in this important chapter of the *Mayamatam* — i.e. the palace of the *narendra* or *padmaka,* and the palace of the *adhirāja*.[24] Unfortunately, the descriptions are extremely ambiguous and only that of the palace of the *narendra* or *padmaka* offer anything that comes close to being able to illustrate this structure (See: **Figure 15**).[25]

These "Basic Plans" are, of course, Hindu-based, stemming from the *śilpa-śāstras*. The Muslim invaders, including the Mughals, were not constrained to observe these forms. Yet, many of those Muslims who entered India as conquerors availed themselves of the indigenous *sthapati* and craftsmen that abounded in this great land — e.g. the Mamluk Dynasty, the Tughluqs, the 'Adil Shahi, the Muzaffarid Shahi, etc. A few rulers abandoned the *sthapati* in favour of their own, imported craftsmen, exclusively. The palaces of their homelands were often a foundation for those of their newly conquered domains. Many of these would have fit easily within the moulds of those found in the *Mayamatam* and *Manasara* — e.g. the *Kasr Kharana* (*c.* 710 CE) of Amman, Jordan (See: **Appendix A, Plate 56**); the *Palace of Ukhaydir* (a. 750 CE) of Ukhaydir, Iraq (See: **Appendix A, Plate 58**); the *Kasr Amman* (a. 750 CE) of Amman (See: **Appendix A, Plate 57**).

Physical Iconography

Iconography, as it is interpreted within this study, falls within two basic categories — i.e. physical and implied. Physical iconography revolves around the structure and includes: the palace, axiality, symmetry/asymmetry, orientation, the high place and the labyrinth.

The Palace

The palace alone — the structure is an iconographic device. It denotes the locale of a ruler, and often the seat of rule or power. Its very existence connotes the supposed or inferred fact of the conferral of Divine acceptance upon the one who resides within.

The *Mayamatam* devotes a whole chapter "Royal Palaces."[26] In this *śilpa śāstra* four types of structures are considered — i.e. "a small palace," a "palace of the *narendra*" or "padmaka," the "*Saubala* Palace," and "the *adhirāja* palace." These palaces have been dealt with in detail in the section entitled: "Iconography: Basic Plans" above.

Beyond the ideal palace plans considered in the treatises of Hindu India there are other elements which later became incorporated in royal residences — e.g. see the preceding "Ratios and Proportions." Many of these ideas were introduced to the Muslim invaders of India by *sthapatis* and indigenous workmen employed to raise forts and palaces.

One of the important considerations in the daily life of a ruler was related to the religious rite known as *darśana* in which the deity was revealed. This concept was translated to the secular and the ruler would show himself every morning as a temporal equivalent of the rite. This served two objectives. First, it symbolized the meeting or melding of the human with the royal or divine world. Secondly, by showing himself the ruler assured that he was alive and the continuity of his rule continued, uninterrupted. Therefore, an architectural device was required. Frequently, it was merely a balcony of the royal residence fronting a public square. Later, particular areas or buildings were designed such as the *diwān-i ām* or *sabhā*. These places where the ruler exhibited himself became a feature found in many palace complexes. Also, for more private audiences the *diwān-i khās* was developed. All these accoutrements were architectural manifestations of the divine right of rule.

Indicated in the preceding figures (See: **Figures 13-15**) are areas set aside for the women of the royal household — i.e. the *harem* or *zenānā*. Therefore, in palace architecture, the zenānā was of particular importance. It was carefully guarded and often times was quite large.[27]

The possession of elephants was an exclusive royal prerogative throughout South and South-east Asia. It became an iconographic device signifying the ruler's dominion over the animal world within his realm — a royal prerogative. Therefore, stables were constructed to house the royal elephants and his horses as well. Not only did elephants symbolize royalty, frequently, the size of these stables was seen as a manifestation or icon of the ruler's power and status. Many palaces displayed vast stables.[28] Whether or not, in actual and real terms, the size of the stable corresponded with the ruler's power is not the question. They were a regal and potent icon.

Parallel with the royal elephants and horses a space of necessity developed — i.e. a large open parade ground (Indic: *maidān*). The *maidān* served three purposes. First, it was an area in which the elephants, horses and troops of the ruler could parade and train. Second, it often was connected with the *diwān-i ām* for public audiences.

Finally, it was an area which exhibited the ruler's power and where lavish spectacles could be staged to underline his wealth and position. It is interesting to note that in *qilā* or citadels which were upon tall, but limited plateaus, the *maidān* took up an inordinately large space. The royal residences were cramped into multistorey structures.

Nonetheless, the very existence of a palace is in itself an iconographic device. As an icon of rule, the palace was *de riguer*. It denotes a ruler of some importance, a person elevated in station above those surrounding folk. Further, areas within palace compounds became standardized and, likewise, became iconographic necessities of a palace.

Axiality

Within virtually all of the major structures found within India, a form of symmetry, balance or axiality predominates. Whether the orientation of the plan is axial, cross-axial mirror cross-axial, rotating axial or multiple perpendicular axial (See: **Appendix D, Plates 108-112**), the majority conform. Few complexes or structures within India disregard these forms of axiality, or exhibit multiple non-perpendicular axiality (See: **Appendix D, Plates 113**).

Is it mere balance that man seeks? Certainly there is sufficient evidence to the fact that primitive man did not seek axiality in all cases. He constructs his shelters as they are needed with apparent disregard for the symmetrical axiality of the individual units or of the total. It becomes apparent in early civilizations that certain important buildings were aligned either north-south or east-west. Is it, therefore, a direction sought by "civilized" man? And, if so, what does it signify? Does it imply some cosmic ideal or direction?

Iconography (Continued)

As has been stated, the *Mayamatam* and the *Manasara* were treatises within which a strict code for the design and construction of dwellings was outlined. There are numerous examples of both Hindu and Islamic palaces in India which conform or vary somewhat from the norm suggested in these treatises. If a palace does not conform to the cross-axial ideal of the *Mayamatam* or *Manasara*, it then does conform, in part, to the strict axial ideal — i.e. a symmetrical balance — that is derived from these manuals (See: **Figures 11, 12 & 14**).

The ideal may be cross-axiality, but frequently ideals are difficult to achieve — e.g. geographical exegencies may not allow it. Axiality, a form of symmetry is somewhat easier to attain and may be just as pleasing (See: **Figure 16**). The attainment of axiality is a practice not entirely confined to the Indian subcontinent, nor to the time under consideration. The Egyptian *Temple of Amen-Re* at Karnak (*c.* 1500-1280 BCE) is essentially axial (See: **Appendix A, Plate 62**). The *Palace of Bulkawara* (*c.* 850-860 CE) constructed by the Abbasid al-Mutawakkil possesses a major axis and numerous lesser axes (See: **Appendix A, Plate 66**). So too is the much later *Ziza Palace* of Palermo (See: **Appendix A, Plate 72**). This structure is particularly interesting as it was erected by the Christian King, Roger I, soon after the Moors (Muslims) were driven out of Sicily. This palace — i.e. the *Ziza Palace* — is essentially based upon Islamic prototypes.

A clear feature of the palaces and other royal or aristocratic pavilions in India whether Hindu or Islamic is their abiding commitment to a form of axiality (See: **Plates 1-60** within the body and the greyed arrows which indicate axiality). A cross axial plan may not always be employed, but an axial plan would almost always

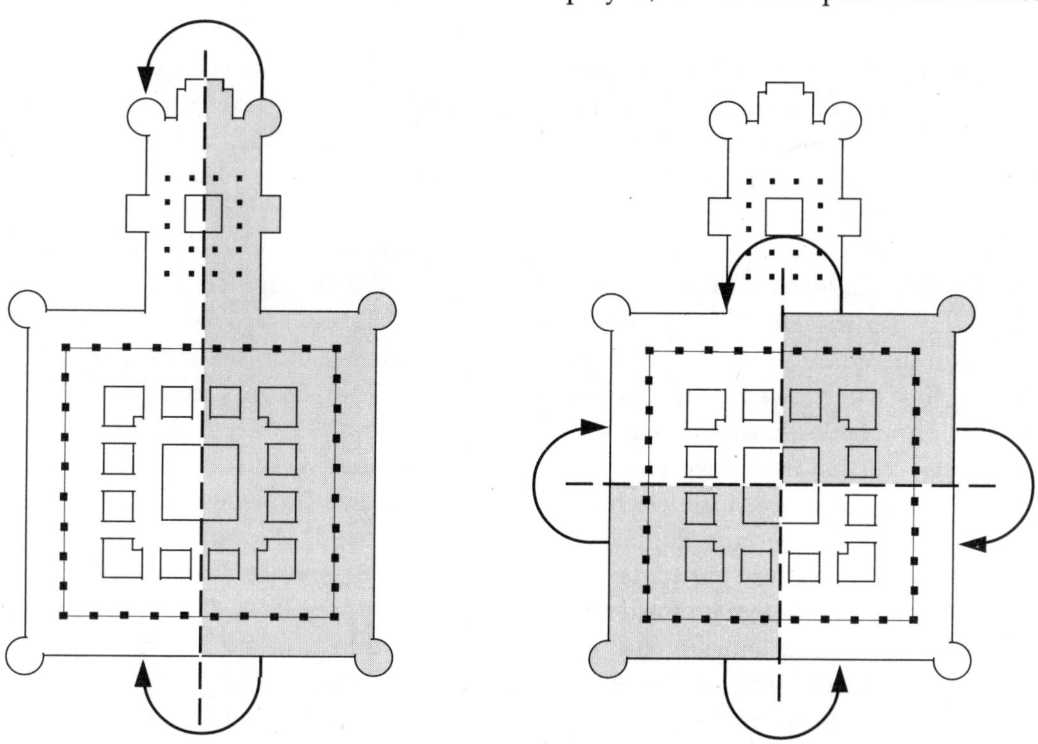

a. axial alignment **b.** cross-axial alignment

Figure 16 — *Amar Vilās* and *Baḍī Mahal, City Palace,* Udaipur, indicating: **a.** axial alignment, including the *Amar Vilās* and *Baḍī Mahal* (left); and **b.** cross-axial alignment of the *Amar Vilās* (right)

be utilized in its stead (See: **Figure 14**), particularly for the most important structures of the *garh mahal* complex. The *Shahjahanabad* (*Lāl Qilā*, Delhi) (See: **Plates 50-51**) utilizes an axial plan as the basis for the whole. The axis starts at the *Lahore Darwāzā* and runs through the *Raṅg Mahal*. To the north and south run complementary axes — i.e. the northern arm housing the imperial stables and the southern arm leading to the *Delhi Darwāzā* — creating multiple perpendicular axiality. The large complex of the Jats of Bharatpur at Deeg (See: **Plates 56 & 57**), bears the undeniable axial basis for its design. Running from the *Keshav Badon* in the east through the *Gopal Bhawan* on the water's edge in the west and bisecting the garden, the whole hangs on this axis. A complementary axis runs north to south connecting the *Nand Bhawan* and the *Kishan Bhawan*. Again, a multiple perpendicular axiality is achieved

In nearly every royal complex there appear evidences of axiality or multiple perpendicular axiality. India is not alone in this predilection — i.e. the very frequent implementation of either a cross-axial or axial or multiple perpendicular axial plan as seen in **Plate 65** or **Plate 67**. But cross-axiality does assume something more than a mere preference in this land.[29]

Cross axiality possesses implications of cosmic dimensions for the Hindu. Cross-axiality is frequently seen in square plans. To the Hindu, the square implies the heavenly, the celestial sphere which is immutable. A square is a square even though it may vary in its dimensions. In this immutability it is associated with the Divine, the celestial sphere. The square became the preferred shape of many Hindu temples, particularly the *garbhagṛha* or the *sanctum sanctorum* of a temple.[30] Nonetheless, the Hindu did employ the circle in temple plans from time to time. However, these temples are more an aberration than a norm, and, interestingly enough they were dedicated to the Lord Śiva.[31] The Buddhists, on the other hand, saw the circle as the manifestation of the immutable cosmic shape.[32] It, too, is cross-axial in its strictest sense and is, likewise, immutable. A circle is a circle, regardless of its diameter. The circle is sparingly employed, at best, in Hindu and Islamic India. An exception is the circular pavilion of the *Gul Mahal*, on the *Jag Mandir*, Udaipur (See: **Plate 48**). Indo-Islamic tombs, on the other hand, are almost always cross axial, employing the square and octagon (See: **Plates 75, 80 & 81**).

There are also numerous examples of cross-axiality in early Muslim residences or palaces outside of India. A salient example is the Umayyad palace near Amman, known as: *Kasr Kharana* (See: **Plate 63**). In this structure the ground plan not only indicates a predilection for cross axiality, but also demonstrates the concept of *hasht bihisht*. Similarly the cross-axiality of the *Kasr Amman* is unrelenting (See: **Plate 64**) in its exactitude.

The cross-axial square with its implication of cosmic, celestial perfection was, of course, a Hindu ideal. But, it was seen by many to be limiting as a basic plan for a royal palace. The axial plan with its implied balance often was employed or preferred.

The square was utilized by the Indo-Islamic architects and employed in a large number of their structures. European architects, on the other hand, were generally less inclined to employ a square, cross-axial plan. There are exceptions. The 15th and 16th centuries, of course, held a number of cross-axial plans. Brunelleschi's *Santa Maria degli Aṅgeli* (abandoned), Florence (See: **Appendix A, Plate 77**), B. Ramante's *Proposed New St. Peters*, Rome, (See: **Appendix A, Plate 79**) are salient examples of ecclesiastical application, as well as Palladio's *Villa Rotunda* (See: **Appendix A, Plate 82**), a residence. However, these examples were more indicative of the sixteenth century's architectural-philosophic quest of squaring the circle, or circling the square. And, these types of plans do not appear in any great number in other periods of European architectural history.

Numerous secular Indo-Islamic structures also tended to display cross-axiality — e.g. the *Chhatta Chowk* and *Musamman Burj*, Shahjahanabad (See: **Plate 50**); the *Farah Bagh*, Ahmadnagar (See: **Plate 39**), and the *Diwān-i-Khās* and *Anup Talao* (*Char Chaman*), Fatehpur Sikri (See: **Plates 27** & **26**). Palaces tended to be axial, rather than cross-axial. However there are notable examples of cross-axial palaces — .e.g. the *Gujari Mahal* of Gwalior (See: **Plate 13**) and the *Govind Mandir* (*Bir Singh Judeo Mahal*) of Datiya (See: **Plate 44**) — both of which were constructed by Hindu rulers.

In plans, particularly dwelling plans that are not square (See: **Figures 11** & **12**, and **Plates 35, 84** & **85**), the square is still an integral element whether doubled or tripled as indicated in the *Mayamatam*, or other additional multiples. This is particularly true in the royal palaces and/or pavilions of India — e.g. the *Jahāz Mahal*, Mandir (See: **Appendix A, Figure 88**), consists of five squares in a row, and the *Rāja Mahal* (*Chandragiri Palace*), Tirupati, employs three squares (See: **Figure 91**).

Traditionally, the Islamic *masjid* tended to be rectangular (See: **Appendix A, Plate 76** [bottom]). However the basic plan of the *Masjid-i-jami*, Delhi, is square (See: **Appendix A, Plate 83**), although the whole is axial rather than cross-axial. On the other hand virtually all the Indo-Islamic tombs were cross-axial, whether based upon a square — e.g. the *Tomb Ghiyas-ud-din Tughluq I*, Tughluqabad, the *Tomb of Firuz Shah Tughluq*, Delhi, the *Sayyid Usman Rausa*, Usmanpur (See: **Appendix A, Plate 75**) — or an octagon — e.g. the *Tomb of Sher Shah*, Saseram, or the *Tomb of Isa Khan*, Delhi (See: **Appendix A, Plate 80**) — or a *muthamman baghdadi* design — *e.g.* the *Tomb of Humayun*, Delhi, or the *Tāj Mahal*, Agra (See: **Appendix A, Plate 81**) — the cross-axis dominated these plans, unrelentingly.

There are numerous Muslim palace complexes which exhibit axiality or cross-axial — e.g. the *Palace of Ukhaydir* (a. 750 CE), Ukhaydir, Iraq (See: **Appendix A, Plate 65**), the *Kasr Kharana* (*c.* 710 CE), Amman, Jordan (See: **Appendix A, Plate 63**), the *Bulkawara Palace* (*c.* 850-860 CE), Samarra, Iraq (See: **Appendix A, Plate 66**), the *Diwān-Khās & Pavilion of Abdul al-Rahman III, Palace* (Detail) (*c.* 936 CE), Cordoba, Spain (See: **Appendix A, Plate 67**) or the *Çinili Kiosk* (*c.* 1473 CE), Istanbul, Turkey (See: **Appendix A, Plate 76** [top]). But, axiality, or cross-axiality did not always appear within Islamic architecture. One of the largest Islamic palace complexes is the famous Ottoman *Topkapisaray*, Istanbul (See: **Appendix A, Plate 85**). Unlike many other Muslim palaces, the *Topkapisaray* is not completely axial in any of its aspects, but maddeningly asymmetrical — i.e. multiple non-perpendicular axiality. It is a conglomeration of various structures seemingly built without consideration of the whole or a symmetrical, or axial, arrangement. This disregard for axiality may be seen in the Temple of Śiva and Mīnākṣī, Madurai (See: **Appendix A, Plate 74**). It consists of numerous structures constructed over a period of years which appear haphazard and 'anti-' axial. However, there is a strong predilection towards multiple perpendicular axiality in this vast complex within its individual elements.

The various palaces and pavilions of India, whether Hindu or especially Muslim, all demonstrate a concern for axiality. This may well be due to the centuries of strictly prescribed design to which the Buddhist and Hindu India ascribed. However, the design history of Islam also indicates a preference for axiality, even cross-axiality.

Axiality is a balanced design which by its very concept and form represents balance and/or stability. It is an inherent, implied concept, an implicit iconographic device. On the other hand, cross-axiality not only implies balance, it denotes cosmic perfection, divine harmony. Within the various royal complexes of India, examples of axiality are to be found and therefore especially axiality and/or cross-axiality are seen as iconographic representations of balance and harmony and all that this implies to rule. Therefore axiality is seen as iconic of balance, stability and harmony, particularly as applied to the Divine.

Symmetry/Asymmetry

There appear to be numerous instances in which an apparent haphazard, asymmetrical plan may have been employed in a palace or palace compound. However, this almost always is a result of construction by various rulers over an extended period of time, each ruler feeling compelled to leave his imprint on the preexistent structures of his predecessors. This, too, is not the sole practice of Indian rulers.[33] Udaipur's *City Palace* is a clear example of this seemingly eclectic arrangement (See: **Plate 38**). The *Lakṣmī Chowk* and the *Tripolia* of the ground level, and *Amar Vilās* and the *Bodi Mahal* of the second level together are clearly axial, while the *Bodi Mahal* alone is cross axial. Started in 1614, the *City Palace* saw construction continuing until well into the 18th century. However, if one studies this and other plans carefully, one becomes aware of a number of the areas which possess a clear, axial plan and some which are cross-axial.

Tillotson views asymmetry as a stylistic development. " . . . It is evident that the irregularity is in some measure the result of a deliberate attempt at picturesque informality. . . . Rajput use of symmetry . . . is rather the result of the architects having uncharacteristically obeyed some of the prescriptions of the *śilpa-śāstras*."[34] Nonetheless, he does acknowledge that the various rulers added on to the existing *garh mahals*, in part, to assert their divine right and a concrete place in history. This was frequently accomplished in an apparent haphazard manner, often times completely abandoning or even cannibalizing preexistent structures for their own, new constructions. Where a *garh mahal* may look asymmetrical, *in toto*, there are, nonetheless, strictly axial elements to be found in each. Additionally, the locales of many of the Indian *garh mahals* — i.e. frequently upon high, uneven, rocky plateaus — are such that symmetry may be difficult to achieve or maintain.

Orientation

Within Hindu practice, the generally preferred orientation for a temple was East to West — i.e. from the sun to the moon, from light to darkness signified by the *garbhagṛha*, the womb.[35] The exception is a funerary or memorial temple which is oriented west to east. The West is the realm of the dead. A prime example of this orientation is to be found in the famed *Angkor Wat* (See: **Plate 70**) which possesses the West to East alignment and is considered to be the mortuary temple for King Suryavarman II.

As has been stated above, the orientation of a structure other than a temple, even a palace, was of some consequence. For the Hindu rulers, proper orientation was imperative and it was based upon caste. If the ruler was of the brāhmaṇa caste, his palace faced towards the South. A kṣatriya ruler's dwelling was oriented towards the West. A vaiśya and śūdra, should they find themselves as rulers would possess palaces that faced North and East, respectively. The famous *Govind Mandir* of Bir Singh Ju Deo is oriented west to east, the proper orientation for a kṣatriya ruler.

Mughal rulers find their palaces oriented: South to North at *Fatehpur Sikri*,[36] West to East at the *Jahangiri Mahal* of Agra's *Red Fort*, and West to East at the *Lāl Qilā* or the *Shahjanahanabad* (the Red Fort of Delhi). It is obvious that the Mughal rulers were not as concerned about the "cosmic orientation" that ruled the Hindu princes' choice. Their concern seemed to be based more upon the alignment of the whole as it applied to its defensible position. Indeed, the same may be said of the palaces of the other Islamic rulers of India — i.e. orientation was not based on class (caste), but was based on other considerations.

Orientation may not have been strictly due to caste. There is, in some *garh mahals*, an apparent desire to "orient" the various structures — i.e. to place all the structures within a complex on a single axis or on the same alignment. The *Bulkawara Palace* (See: **Appendix A, Plate 66**) of Samarra, Iraq, may not be axial or even mirror axial, but it is strictly orientated north-east — south-west. *Vijayanagara's* vast compound appears nonaligned, but this is the fault of the erratic girdle walls. Nonetheless, virtually all of the buildings are oriented north-south, or, in the case of the temples: east-west (See: **Plate 3**). The majority of the *Bidar Qilā & Mandir* are orientated north-south (See: **Plate 9**). Udaipur's *City Palace* (See: **Plate 38**) may not be symmetrical, but virtually all the buildings of this complex are orientated on the north-south axis. On the other hand, the impressive *Meherangarh* at Jodhpur, constructed over centuries by the Jodha Rajputs of Marwar, is maddeningly eccentric in its multiple non-perpendicular axiality (See: **Plate 11**). The ridge upon which the *garh mahal* is constructed runs generally, north to south, but the conglomeration of structures springing up across its surfaces appears as a tossed salad! Even the erratic *Topkapisaray* of Istanbul is not as confused.

Generally, smaller residences within India tended to be orientated towards a point of the compass. It is interesting to note that most of the pleasure pavilions were oriented East-West. This may well have been to avail themselves of the suitable light that this orientation provided.

Therefore, the iconographic concept of orientation by caste is to be applied only to those palaces which were originally constructed by Hindu rulers. To apply this concept to the Indo-Islamic rulers is fraught with danger and is in many cases simply not applicable. Generally, however, orientation of a *garh mahal* on a specific compass axis is seen throughout India with regularity.

The High Place

On earth, the king, or the rājā, or the Mahārājā, or the sultān dwelt in an earthly representation of the heavenly home — i.e. *Mount Meru* or *Mount Sumeru* of the Buddhists and/or *Mount Kalaisha* of the Hindu — and often it was a palace built upon high ground. The high ground not only mimics the celestial palaces in their location, it also provides for very real and a defensive protection of the royal personage. A high place possesses obvious defensive capabilities. Many palaces were part of larger forts situated on an easily defended hill or outcropping. This is obvious. However, there is another consideration regarding a high place. The theological implication of a high place is intertwined with its defensive nature. The concept relates to something that is important and needs to be protected against the onslaught of those who would destroy the cosmic mandate.

Religions, universally, have placed great importance upon a high place, a physical area that is close to the god(s). In both Buddhism and Hinduism, the concept of the 'high place' is an important iconic consideration. *Mount Meru* (*Sumeru*) or *Mount Kailasha*, the centre of the world, is venerated by both religions. It is the locus of the world, the home of the gods. *Mount Kailāśa* which is reputed to be the home of the Lord Śiva is also venerated by the *Vajrayāna Buddhists* of Tibet and is second in importance to *Mount Meru*.

Concrete representation of this concept, the holy mountain, finds varying forms in both faiths and also in the varying cultures of the area. The high point, the holy mountain becomes real in the myriad architectural representations.

The Christian West places great emphasis on the physical location of a church upon a high point or place. In Medieval Europe, particularly in important cities the high point(s) were utilized for the building of edifices of the two great powers — the church (spiritual) and the castle (temporal). Within the Judaic tradition, the high place is auspicious — Mount Sinai where Moses received the Commandments and the Tower of Babel where the unbelievers built an edifice to approach the deity, are also examples. The Christ Jesus utilized a high place in his famous '*Sermon on the Mount*,' and went to the garden of Gethsemane to pray. The latter has traditionally been depicted as an elevated area, a mount. The deity exists, lives above, on high and the human attempts to approach that point either physically, spiritually or symbolically. Therefore, major shrines are built or established upon high ground or geographical prominences — e.g. the *Swayambhu-nātha* of Kathmandu; the shrine of *Murugan*, Batu Caves, Kuala Lumpur; the shrine to *Venkateśvara* (*Bālājī*) of the Tirupati Hills, Andhra Pradesh; *Borobudur* of Java; or even the modern *National Cathedral*, Washington, D.C.

In a number of instances where natural prominences do not exist, artificial mounds or terraces are created to accomplish the same end — e.g. the *Kandariya Mahadeo* of Khajuraho, the *Bakong* of Roluos; the *Chedi Wat Phukhao Thong*, Ayutthaya; or the *Chandi Sewu* of Prambanan. To approach the mount physically, therefore, becomes not only a cultural imperative but a religious imperative as well, one without exception.[37]

The hill even figures prominently in the Islamic faith. For example, the Nabi Mohammad spoke to his followers on the mountain known as *Jabar Rahmah* during one of his numerous persecutions. It becomes for Islam a sermon that is parallel in importance and locale to the *Sermon on the Mount* for the Christians. In addition, it is believed that the Nabi Mohammad ascended to Paradise from a high place now enshrined in the *Dome of the Rock* (*Qubbat as-Sakhra*), Jerusalem.

What applies to a Buddhist or Hindu temple may be applied to a Hindu or Islamic fort/palace. The high place applies to a temporal ruler. His domicile is elevated as befits his position in life. It is near the celestial regions and, therefore, he is as well. He is, "by the Grace of God," the anointed one and he merits a dwelling that is the earthly parallel to the abode of the gods.

Not only are many of the palaces built on a high place, they are frequently further, physically elevated from the surroundings. The impressive Ottoman *Topkapisaray* at Istanbul, was not only constructed upon a long promontory, it possessed pavilions and other structures that were further artificially elevated (See: **Appendix A, Plate 85**). The palace built by a Hindu prince, the *Govind Mandir* at Datiya was elevated further above its locale, placed upon an imposing foundation. The pleasure pavilion known as the *Jahāz Mahal* at Mandu was also constructed far above the maddening crowd on its own artificially elevated plinth.

With the regular and constant use of the cannon, thick walled ramparts placed upon an easily defended hill became less and less feasible as well as more and more costly. Royal residences sprang up which were more residential and less fortified, yet, often, retaining vestiges of the fort. Nonetheless, the main elements of these dwellings tended to be constructed upon a raised, artificial terrace or plinth. Both the *Nand Bhawan* and the *Kishan Bhawan* of the complex of Jats of Bharatpur at Deeg are constructed upon an elevated terrace to which limited access is allowed.

It is difficult to separate the theological and philosophical concept of a high place from that of one that is easily defendable. In truth, the high place both as a theological concept and as a defensive locale for a temporal ruler must be defended! It is not just a right to defend the "anointed one," it is philosophically required, mandated. Both concepts assume major consideration in the iconography of the palace.

The Labyrinth

A further requisite found in the square ideal (See: **Figure 13**) and within most of the axial palaces is the fact that the personal apartments of the ruler are found buried deep within labyrinthine passages or connecting rooms. The labyrinthine character of many of the palaces is not a feature that is solely within the province of a palace.

The labyrinth is seen by many as a symbol of a sacred nature. In numerous and ancient religions, vast and elaborate temples were raised for the Divinity. The *sañctum sañctorum*, the *Holy of Holies* was often buried deep within the confines of the temple and access to this area was severely restricted. In most cases this restriction was to high priests and/or the ruler. The *Temple of Amen-Re*, Karnak, Egypt (See: **Appendix A, Plate 62**), is an early example. Here, the shrine to *Amen-Re* is buried deep within and the very sacred place, the supreme sanctuary is minuscule in size compared to the whole. Numerous temples of south and south-east Asia — i.e. the various Indianized States — display this proclivity for the labyrinth. Foremost are: the *Ānanda* of Pagan, Burma (See: **Appendix A, Plate 69**), the *Bayon* of Angkor Thom (See: **Appendix A, Plate 73**) and in Madurai, India the vast Temple of Śiva and Mīnākṣī (See: **Appendix A, Plate 74**). These three temples — the first and second Buddhist, and the third Hindu — indicate varying degrees in their elaboration of space, structures, passageways to the point of absolute confusion. The *Bayon* and the *Ānanda* were conceived and constructed by single rulers, whereas, the *Temple of* Śiva and Mīnākṣī was constructed over a period of time — i.e. the 13th through the 17th centuries CE — by different rulers. Nonetheless, the labyrinth reigns in most cases of large temples. Certainly the *Topkapisaray* presents a labyrinthine plan that is rivalled by few. Since many of the Sultāns of India found their genesis within the bosom of the Ottoman Empire, it is understandable that they, too, would have adapted their palaces in a like manner (See: **Appendix A, Figure 85**).

The labyrinth in the West is best exemplified in the fabled Palace of Minos in which the equally fabled Minotaur was found. This mythic beast was housed in the labyrinth. The *"Palace of Minos"* (*c.* 1600-1400 BCE) at Knossos, Crete, may well be the source of this fable. Its confines are composed of numerous corridors, rooms and staircases, creating a bewildering maze (See: **Appendix A, Plate 61**). Another palatial structure which contains labyrinthine qualities is the *Palace of Bulkawara* (*c.* 850-860 CE) (See: **Appendix A, Figure 66**) and the *Palace of Ukhaydir*, Iraq (See: **Appendix A, Plate 65**).

The labyrinth serves three purposes. First, it insulates the royal person from close contact with the hurly-burly activities of the daily life of common folk. Second, such a physical isolation underlines his royal and exalted position and cosmic association. He is elevated, he is protected, he is separated both physically and ideologically. The ideal, as shown in **Figure 13,** indicates a triple layering. The inner area being the exclusive domain of the ruler and his queen. The middle area is reserved for those who contribute to the direct support/functions of the ruler and act as a guarded buffer to the inner royal precincts. Finally, the outer area, also support for the ruler, but of a more mundane, daily nature. This tripartite sectioning also possesses certain iconic implications. The number three is seen as the first masculine number and possesses certain cosmic and hallowed implications appropriate to the exalted position of the ruler.[38] A final and more real consideration of this ideal plan is that the labyrinthine access to the royal person insulates and protects him from would-be assassins or persons who would do him harm and compromise the cosmic mandate.

Numerous plans herein indicate that the private apartments of the rulers are arrived at through a circumlocutory series of passageways, rooms and alleys. For example, the royal apartments of the Travancore Mahārājāh, Martanda Varma in *Padmanabhapuram* near Kanyakumari, is buried deep within the third of four compounds, and in the second storey of a relatively small structure (See: **G** (*Upparika Malika*), **Plate 59**). Additionally, the apartment of Akbar at *Fatehpur Sikri* is found deep within the warren of buildings and in a structure that is not particularly imposing or ostentatious (See: **J** (*Khwabgah*), **Plate 26**). Further, in order to gain access to the royal precincts of the *Rāj Mahal* at Amber, it is necessary to travel through a series of narrow passageways that veer first right, then left and right again in a dizzying series of 90⁰ turns.

The physical isolation of the ruler via a series of rooms and/or passages from the common folk is inextricably wrapped in the necessity of protecting the royal person. In addition, many of the thick interior walls possessed secret, inner passageways by which ingress or egress may be obtained from the rooms that they serviced. This was accomplished with relative ease, thereby, allowing the ruler the ability to come and go, or escape at will, as exemplified in the *Rājā Mandir* (See: **Plates 19 & 20**).

The protection of the ruler was accomplished by a labyrinth of hallways and passages. It was a necessity. This is not merely an Indian necessity, but one that is found throughout the various cultures of the world.[39] Again, the labyrinth not only underlines the ruler's cosmic mandate — i.e. "by the grace of God" — it also physically isolates and, therefore, protects his person.

Implied Iconography

Implied iconography is concerned with more abstract concepts as are embodied in or imbued by the structure of the ruler — e.g. "By the Grace of God," dynasty, royal accoutrements, power, defensive/offensive and property-religious/cultural.

"By the Grace of God"[40]

Much of the iconography of a palace is obvious. It is a dwelling, but more, a dwelling for one of high even hallowed social rank, the home of one with royal status, a ruler, the anointed one. The Mughals brought with them to India their own royal lineage as well as the privileges that their rule had assumed in their culture(s). But, they were not the first kings or rulers!

One might ask, "Who were the first kings or rulers?" Certainly, the answer is buried deep within human prehistory. Within the animal kingdom there are numerous examples in which a leader develops and takes control. Amongst the primates, an individual, particularly a male, assumes dominance within a group. This individual guards and maintains the particular group or society — i.e. the group's (and his) status, territorial integrity and movement. Generally, amongst the primates the dominant male reserves the right to mate — *le droit de seigneur* — but not exclusively.[41]

Certainly at one point within the evolution of mankind an individual arose within a group or tribe who clearly possessed the necessary mental and physical qualifications to lead and, tangentially, at a later date, to protect. In the most primitive societies he was most probably an individual of great strength, an accomplished fighter and/or hunter. He obviously was one whom the other members of the society or group acknowledged and were willing to follow — a headman, a chief, a leader. At some point, the process of gather and the development of agriculture became most important. As the group expanded numerically and incorporated more and more areas, the efficacy and efficiency of employing a leader of some permanence, female or male, became apparent and/or desirable. Also, at some point, it was seen necessary to institutionalize this process or this rule. Probably, a council or a smaller group of the whole may have gathered to choose the one who could lead — i.e. one who possessed the necessary abilities to oversee the larger group. Or, a clearly dominant individual may have merely asserted herself/ himself — i.e. as in the animal world — and assumed that position of leader.

Again, as in the animal world, when a society grew and developed certain members of the group assumed particular roles for which they were suited — i.e. as hunters, or gatherers, or artisans, or defenders, etc. Further, as a society developed and grew, often these roles became codified or institutionalized for the apparent or perceived benefit of all. They were passed down from father to son or mother to daughter and seen as a natural progression. These various roles were often placed within a rigid hierarchy, a hierarchy which is not an exclusive human characteristic or domain.[42] With the invasions of the Kurgans ("Aryans") from the north and east the peaceful, agricultural based society that appeared around the Mediterranean and India was replaced by unrelenting patrism and male rule.

This was to affect India, as well. The installed priestly group, or brāhmaṇa caste, assumed the highest level. The installed warrior group, or kṣatriya caste was second in the hierarchy. It was from these two upper castes in India, particularly the kṣatriya, that the rulers were normally but not always drawn. All others were relegated to either the installed vaiśya or installed śūdra castes. European societies also developed a class system — e.g. England or Russia. Early in the Indo-Islamic culture the Ghaznavid Dynasty and the Ghurid Sultanate were reluctantly accepted as rulers by the indigenous Hindu, as the Ghaznavids and the Ghurids had come from a ruling class, albeit outside of India proper. However, the elevated commander-in-chief, one Qutb-ud-din Aibak, of the Slave or Mamluk Dynasty was considered an anathema as he as well as a number of other Sultāns of that dynasty rose from non-ruling classes. Indeed, Qutb-ud-din Aibak was of decidedly peasant origins.

As the position of leader became developed and codified it assumed certain benefits — e.g. wealth, power and an exalted position not being the least of these. Obviously there were those outside the position of rule, or caste, or class who coveted this role, who desired to rule and accrue for themselves the benefits of that elevated position. If they were strong enough, or possessed the ability to gather together the requisite number of supporters they could challenge the ruler, depose him or break away and form a new group.

Rule as a God-given right — e.g. "by the Grace of God," or the "Mandate of Heaven," or "*Bhāgvat kṛpā se*," or "*dengan keizinan Nya* (*Allah*)" — became an accepted norm somewhere in the dim light of the history of man. This was, one might say, a natural progression in the genealogy of rule. A codified system developed by which rule was seen to be ordained by a higher power. The ruler assumed rule through cosmic acceptance and, therefore, was placed in that position which was beyond the reach of common folk. In India, the great epics — i.e. the *Mahābhārata* and the *Rāmāyaṇa* — were seen as possessing the requisite basis and rites for the elevation of an individual to the rank of a ruler. In the West, Biblical history, particularly the elevation of King Saul, was the historical and cosmic basis for kingship, particularly in the Judeo-Christian west.

The elevation to kingship allowed the individual the right to make certain decisions that might seem unacceptable to the general public, but after all, he, or in some cases, "she," was the ruler "by the Grace of God."[43] The near-hallowed aspect that rule ultimately assumed is underlined by the fact that in Thailand, historically, when a ruler was deposed and/or assassinated, he had to be placed within a velvet bag and bludgeoned to death with a sandalwood club. Such was the fate of Taksin, King of Thon Buri, who was deposed by Chaophrāya Chakri, King Rāma I, in 1782.[44] This was required so that his sanctified blood did not touch the earth. Earlier, the Khmer elevated their ruler to the level of a god — i.e. the *devarāj*. Whether one is to interpret the term as the "god who is king" or the "king who is a god" is not a consideration herein. Suffice it to say that a human being, a ruler was elevated so high that even his humanness came into question. So exalted, so elevated was the Khmer kings, that for a commoner to look upon their face was to invite death, swift and sure.[45]

At one point the institution of rule became the endowment, the prerogative of a particular family or a specific group — "by the Grace of God" or the "Mandate of Heaven." In most societies and cultures the right to rule assumed certain hereditary components. This was true in Asia, however the law of primogeniture as practised in Europe was not universally practised in the East. The king or emperor would generally designate his successor although not necessarily the first born son, but almost certainly a family member. In India, for example, the heir to the throne often succeeded to that position by battle or subterfuge. Aurangzeb, not the first born, became the Heir Apparent after battling and killing his claimant brothers, all of whom wanted the imperial throne for themselves. The fact that Shah Jahan did not interfere was not entirely due to his diminished capacity, but was in part an established custom in the Mughal court as well as the parent Turkish, Afghani and Persian courts. It was a prime example of the survival of the fittest!

In some kingdoms the Heir Apparent would assume certain prerogatives and may even be regarded as a co-ruler and possess his own court,[46] although, in the Mughal court, the Heir Apparent was closely supervised, even guarded, and his role was clearly subservient to that of the emperor.

Rule in Asia was seen, generally, as the province of the male. This is not too unusual a state of affairs in a patristic culture which dominated the whole of Asia, although male rule was not exclusively the case. There have been a number of women in the long history of Asia who ruled, and ruled most effectively.[47] In ancient Egypt, with the exception of Queen Hatshepsut and possibly Queen Nefertiti, men ruled, but their mandate of rule came from the female line. Hence, it was not uncommon for a pharaoh to marry a close female relative so as to legitimize his right to rule. Nonetheless, generally the history of man has seen a clear preference to male rule over female.

As a normal occurrence, there were numerous times throughout the history of Asia when rule was imposed from without a particular society or culture. Expansion, invasion, conquest from without brought with it a new line of rulers, new ideas, new blood, new energy. Often the indigenous culture seemed to prevail or even dominate the invading or conquering reign, but always there is to be seen the influence of the conquerors seeping to the top like cream.[48]

There was a common thread that appears to apply to all rulers — i.e. that moment when they assume kingship or rule, that moment when their rule is accepted and granted by the Almighty or the Cosmic Being, that single moment when they "by the Grace of God" become king or queen. It is not the placing of a crown or jewelled turban upon the head that imparts the right to rule — not all rulers throughout the world wear a crown, in the Western sense. The crown, or turban is a mere symbol which comes after the fact. In virtually all ceremonies when a human is elevated to the position of rule, whether it be king, *Nawāb, Nāyaka, Nizam, Rājāh, Rāya, Sultān*, or *Emperor*, it is the process of anointing that is the critical element, the transitional moment that transforms the individual from a normal, common human being to that of a divinely ordained ruler.[49] Prior to Indo-Islamic rulers, the Hindu ruler's elemental ceremony to assume rule was ablution (Ind.: *abhiṣeka*). Without this primal rite a king was simply not a king! *Abhiṣeka* also was an assumed and an important process by the Indo-Islamic rulers as they were elevated to rule. The bejeweled turbans that the Indo-Islamic rulers wore were but a symbol of their elevation after being anointed, and, further, a symbol which they borrowed from the earlier Hindu rulers of India.

As the institution of kingship developed and grew, it assumed all manner of paraphernalia that, symbolically, were attached to the office — i.e. a sword, shield, crown or turban, royal elephant, sun symbol — not the least being a dwelling that reflected the ruler's exalted status — i.e. the palace, the *garh mahal*. The palace itself possessed elements which were equated with rule. The *hāthī pol* or *Ganesh pol*, a ceremonial, major gateway which was decorated with elephants is an element that is found in not only gates (Indic: *pol*) of the Rajputs, Nāyakas and other non-Muslim rulers, but also in the royal compounds of Islamic rulers as well. The *chatrī*, the royal emblem in the form of an umbrella, finds its architectural equivalent in the *chatrī* — i.e. a pavilion consisting of a domed roof supported by slender columns — a hallmark of many Indian palaces and forts. It is seen as symbolic of celestial power.

In the Buddhist Hindu faiths, the deity resided on *Mount Meru* (aka: *Sumeru*) or *Mount Kailasha*. There they live in lavish and spectacular splendour in their cosmic dwellings as befit a cosmic ruler.

In any case, it may be argued that the right to rule is an artificial concept. It was assumed to legalize the claim. The "right to rule" was legitimized in virtually all cultures by "by the Grace of God," or the "Mandate of Heaven," or "*Bhāgvat kṛpā se*," or "*dengan keizinan Nya* (*Allah*)."

Dynasty

The *garh mahal* may be seen, also, as an iconographic statement of dynasty.[50] In order to underline the seemingly artificial "Right to Rule," the passing of this "right" or position to a designated family member was seen as a necessity. A dynasty was assumed and established.

Of course, an heir was apparent! The ruler hopefully insured this by supplying a male offspring. Although in both Hindu and Muslim ruling houses, primogeniture was necessarily practised, nor was it in Asia in general.[51] Heirs could be drawn from scores of sons and/or other close relatives. The Thai King Rāma IV (Mongkut) (r. 1851-1868), brother of King Rāma III (Nangklao), came to the throne late in life, having been a monk/patriarch until his ascension to the throne. He married a number of women and in the seventeen years of his reign fathered, among others, thirty-nine sons.

Iconography (Continued)

A dynasty not only buttresses the "right"; it also establishes a certain continuity that was seen as necessary. This continuity was viewed in the light of the future. Further, a peaceful or fruitful reign was also seen as part of the "right's" mandate and continuity. If, for some reason, the "right" was withdrawn by the Cosmic Being, the result was often seen to be exemplified in protracted war, flood, famine and pestilence. If the "right" or "mandate" was lost, then it was acceptable for some-one to overthrow or conquer the "rightful" ruler and assume that "right" or "mandate" for himself. Thus, a new dynasty was established.

Royal Accoutrements

There are numerous items that are worn or held by a ruler in India that are to be classified as "regalia" — i.e. jewelled turban or crown, sword, shield, umbrella, fly whisk, etc. However, there regularly appears within the various *qilās*, *mandirs*, and/or royal compounds of India architectural structures which assume the status of royal iconography — i.e. accoutrements of rule.

Bathing tanks (variously called: *birka, haud, fisqiya, saqaya, sihrij*) appear within most royal enclosures not only of the Hindu rulers, but the Muslims as well. Sometimes they are to be found with their own walled compound (See: **Plate 3 — O & P**), or they may be found within their own walled enclosure (See: **Plate 3 — R; Plate 14 — C**). Bathing was a regular, daily procedure for all castes. Generally, the lower castes bathed in rivers or streams, publicly. Rulers also bathed regularly, but there were specific times, festivals etc., in which they ritually bathed. The green chlorite, geometric bathing tank of Vijayanagara (See: **Plate 3 — O**; see also: **Appendix A, Plate 93**) adjacent to a large rectangular tank would have been a most dramatic locale for the Rāya of Vijayanagara to have performed the required ablution. The *Water Pavilion* (*hammam*), Kumatagi (See: **Plate 18**), would have been no mere public bathing tank. Its design indicates royal privilege and also a locale for more sensual delights.

Similarly, the appearance of large and/or elaborate stables for the housing of royal elephants as well as horses becomes an iconographic device as well. Since only a ruler could own an elephant and horses were considered, in most areas, a prerogative of a ruler, stables are, therefore, not unlikely to be elevated to the lecel of some grandeur, but also an accoutrement. If a stable to house a horse and/or elephant denotes royalty, then it follows that the larger the stables, the more elaborate their structure, the greater the ruler! The stables of *Vijayanagara* (See: **Plate 5**), Gingee, *Fatehpur Sikri* (See: **Plate 16 — U**), or *Shahjahanabad* certainly are fit for a king, or emperor.

If one is a ruler, he possesses elephants, horses and armed retainers. Then, it would follow, that the ruler would need to inspect these possessions on a regular basis. Within the various *qilās* where stables occur, large parade grounds also are to be found, and also a ceremonial platform or reviewing stand (See: **Plate 3 — C [2]; Plate 14 — E**). Therefore, a reviewing platform, likewise, assumes royal iconographic status (See: **Plate 14 — F**).

The palace is a royal icon, so too is the gate(s) by which one gains entrance. Not only are these gates a defensive addition, they are frequently adorned with carved, stone elephants — i.e. named *hāthī pol* or *Ganesh pol* (See: **Plates 6 — B; 12 — A**; and **95-101**). Therefore, a gate on which carved elephants may be found are employed to announce a royal compound and, hence, are to be considered as a royal icon as well.

Finally, from early in the history of Indian ruling families *darbārs* and/or *darśana* was a regular requirement. The ruler regularly showed his person to the assembled. This played several

Iconography (Concluded)

roles. First, it indicated that he was still alive and, indeed, ruling. Second, it may have had certain connections with the sun and its power, particularly with the Mughals. Therefore, often a suitable venue was needed, the *Diwān-i-Ām* or even a simple balcony where he could present his person on a regular basis.

Power

As one of the ultimate tools of rule, power, might or force is frequently deemed not only necessary, but a virtual gift. Palaces or citadels are statements of power.[52] Frequently, a throne or state is coveted by a powerful usurper or conqueror. In order to achieve that end — i.e. taking what is coveted — armed conflict usually results. It is the one who wields power most effectively that is the ultimate victor in any conflict. Once the rule has been established, without exception a *garh mahal* is raised as a concrete statement or manifestation of the ruler's power and might, as well as a means to sustain that power.

These demonstrations of power often continue when a line of rule is unbroken. This may occur in the construction of completely different palaces or *garh mahals* by each subsequent ruler as seen in the Bundelkhand. Or, a fortified palace my be expanded by the addition of *mahals* or *vilas* to an existing complex by subsequent rulers as seen in the *City Palace of Udaipur*.

The exception to this proclivity is when a ruler does not live long enough to start and/or complete his signature addition. Such is the case with the Sultān Mallu 'Adil Shah (r. 1534-1535) of Bijapur. Or, the construction my be halted by conquest as seen with the Bahmani Sultān Kalim-Allah Shah (r. 1525-1527) who was conquered by the Mughal Zahir-ud-din Muhammad Babur, King of Ferghana, "the Great Mughal" (r. 1526-1530).

The immense, overwhelming imperial power of Akbar, The Great was attested by the substantial fortified additions to the *Lāl Qilā* of Agra. This statement of Akbar' power was completely cemented by the raising of the impressive *Fatehpur Sikri*. Nothing transmits power on a relatively permanent basis than an impregnable, lavish *garh mahal*.

However, with power over successive generations, it has been seen in virtually every civilization that the later rulers tend to take this attribute for granted, with often disastrous results. The power established by Babur, consolidated by Akbar and expanded by Jahangir and Shah Jahan was not understood by Aurangzeb and, consequently the rapid, seemingly irreversible decline of the Mughal Empire in India. Not only does power need to be taken, it needs to be understood, it has to be wielded effectively, and, it must be defended effectively. This often requires a person, a ruler of exceptional abilities.

Many rulers who had attained great power and/or wealth, demanded, as part of their royal prerogative, absolute obeisance from their subjects. The overawed common man often saw their liege lord as akin to divinity.

Defensive

An iconographic aspect of virtually all of the palaces, residences and pavilions of this period is to be seen as one of the side issues or results of rule — i.e. greed which ultimately breeds paranoia; regnal paranoia. There is an obvious antidote when dealing with the covetousness of other rulers: build where access to your person and possessions are easily defendable; preferably so impregnable that few would have the temerity to mount an attack. Hence, particularly amongst the Rajputs, *garh mahals* and *qilās* were constructed on plateaus or outcroppings or islands where access was difficult and in such a way as to maximize the terrain. A further necessity was a regular and sustained water source — i.e. tanks, cisterns and/or wells — to maintain the viability of the citadel in case of siege. Yet, impressive as the location of many of these *garh* palace/forts, these *garh mahal*s were, this did not seem to placate the concerns of those rapacious "neighbors." Few, if any, of these impressive, mighty fortified citadels ultimately protected those who dwelt within.

Defensive locale was reinforced by a *garh mahal* designed in such a way that even direct access to the ruler was met with numerous and daunting physical impediments and difficulties — i.e. narrow stairways, twisting halls with several right angle turns, doors wide enough for only one person, numerous connecting rooms, multiple entrances and exits, and always guards. Few rulers lived without this concern — i.e. ultimately for their personal safety — which insidiously invaded the minds of every one of them — paranoia of rule. This paranoia often extended to and/or was directed towards members of the immediate family, and with good reason. Many Emperors, Sultāns and Rājas were overthrown by their sons or brothers — e.g. the famed Shihab-ud-din Shah Jahan of *Tāj Mahal* fame was deposed by his son Muhiy-ud-din Aurangzeb and spent the rest of his days in confinement, however luxurious. Brothers fought brothers for the right to rule — e.g. again, Aurangzeb defeated and killed his favoured elder brother, Prince Dara Shikoh, as well as disposing of Prince Shah Shuja and Prince Murad Baksh in his quest for the throne; all this while deposing his father.

Frequently, palaces or residences were constructed for the heir apparent away from that of the ruler, but close enough to keep tabs on him — e.g. the *Kanwar Pade* at Chittor (See: **Plate 10 — I**) or the *Vikramaditya Mahal* at Gwalior (See: **Plate 12 — I**) — yet, close enough so that the ruler's many spies could quickly communicate any flagrant indiscretion and swift, punitive action could be taken. This did not always fulfill its purpose or intent.

Again, the locale as well as the private apartments of the ruler had to be easily defended. No expense, time or design was spared. Doubtless, this obsession arose from the fact that many of the rulers themselves had usurped the throne, even from a family member. Therefore, they were constrained to assiduously protect themselves, defend their persons from like actions.

Property — Religious/Cultural

The *zenānā* became an important part of later *garh mahals*. Early in their existence within Hindu citadels, the *zenānā* was not developed as a distinct area or unit. Women, as important members or property of the ruler, had to be protected from the vagaries that may be encountered with public exposure, from offensive actions or sights. When they did go into public, they were veiled, conveyed in curtained sedan chairs and heavily protected. Within the palace, they apparently had much more freedom to move about at will. Still, any social intercourse with men other than the ruler and the neutered eunuchs was severely limited. Private associations with any male outside the immediate family were forbidden. Their strict isolation, virtual imprisonment came later as a partial result of Muslim influence.

Within the later traditions of the Hindu world and as a result of Muslim practice and beliefs, women were sheltered, protected, isolated and/or "imprisoned." This practice is ancient and appears to find its basis in two concepts. First is in the fact that women, particularly wives and daughters, are the property of the patriarch. This concept of property also extended to the sons as well.[53] Part of the wealth of the patriarch was in the family

— i.e. direct members of his genetic family and the wives of his male progeny. It was vital that the offspring of his son's wives spring from his genetic pool. Therefore, they were protected, secluded, insuring that any offspring be from the patriarch's gene bank.[54] The concept of property was absolute! Therefore, if a woman was violated — i.e. raped — or willingly participated in extramarital or premarital relationship, this was considered a violation, debasement and lowered the value of the property of the patriarch, particularly if a child evolved. Even today, in some cultures, this occurrence is sufficient grounds for divorce and/ or the imposition of death upon the woman, even in the case of forcible rape.

Second, if a woman appears in public she must be veiled. This is a secondary means of protecting the property and to protect the woman from the public. Further, it involves the concept that men are inherently uncontrollable sexual beings. The mere sight of a woman, attractive or not, would so inflame their passions that the obvious result would be to forcibly impose themselves upon the hapless woman. In some countries a scarf or other form of head wear may be worn leaving the face exposed.[55] The idea that women could also be sexual beings was not even considered.

The protection of the women from anyone but the royal person was not only a concept of property, but, more importantly, the maintenance of royal sexuality and the divine rite. Hindu theology links rejuvenation to nature, and that to sexuality, and that to the deity, and that, finally to the ruler as divinely ordained. For a ruler to produce many children was seen as divine acceptance and blessing not only of the royal person but of his subjects as well. Vast harems were seen as an icon of the potency of the ruler, symbolically if not actually.[56]

In the *garh mahal,* or the dwellings of noble or wealthy men (patriarchs), this protection of property could be carried one step further — i.e. isolation in a *zenānā*. Virtually every later *garh mahal,* regardless of the size or political importance of the ruler possessed a *zenānā*. In some cases they were vast and possessed several residences, pavilions, gardens and bathing tanks exclusively for the benefit of the women of the court or household. Less wealthy would have areas of their residence set aside for their wives and daughters — i.e. rooms within the house or a floor or upon the roof space for their isolation. The poorer would not have this luxury. However, their womenfolk would have always been veiled in the presence of males outside of the family circle.

Therefore, the presence of a *zenānā*, or a floor of a residence, or room(s) becomes an iconographic device denoting property. It is applicable to Hindu and Muslim residences, alike.

Qilā, Garh Mahal or *Mandir*

What is a citadel? The Indian fortified residences are referred to by various generic terms — i.e. *qilā, garh mahal* or *mandir*. Both *qilā* and *garh* are variously defined as a fort or citadel — i.e. a highly defensible structure with thick high walls and often rudimentary structures for protection, sleep and food. A *garh mahal,* as used by Michell (GM) refers to a pavilion, apartment or residence that is, or lies within a fortified area, or fort, or citadel. On the other hand, a *mandir* generally refers to a temple. However, it may, under certain circumstances, refer to a palace

Iconography (Concluded)

or royal residence.

Conclusions

We may take for granted elements like a sceptre, orb, crown or bejeweled turban in considering the iconography of rule. A palace, too, may appear to be a manifest element of rule. However, it seems that the plans of palaces, especially those found within the Indian subcontinent are replete with iconic content heretofore not considered. Therefore, iconographic considerations appear to involve every aspect of a fortified palace (*garh mahal*). They may be as general as the *Ratios and Proportions* that a *sthapati* uses or even the *Basic Plans*. Both physical and implied iconography appears to be central in the construction of a royal palace, residence or pavilion.

The *Palace, Axiality, Symmetry/Asymmetry, Orientation*, the *High Place*, and the *Labyrinth*, areas of physical iconography, may appear obvious, but in combination with the implied forms — i.e. "*By the Grace of God*," *Dynasty, Royal Accoutrements, Power, Defensive* or *Property* — *Religious/Cultural* — they weave a web of interlocking importance and are of a distinct revelatory nature.

Neither architectural details of the palaces' or pavilions' elevations, nor stylistic considerations are a concern here. However, the intricacies of these elements may also be viewed as symbolic of the owner's status.

The following plans indicate, in varying degrees, these perceived iconographic concerns. The royal palaces, residences and pavilions, herein, were selected as they appeared to be prime examples of their type scattered from the mid 14th Century to the late 18th century CE — i.e. a span of four-hundred plus years.

Palaces, Residences and Pavilions

Hauz Khās, Delhi

(a. 1290- b. 1388 CE)

The *Hauz Khās*,[57] as the later *Kotla Firuz Shāh* was constructed originally as a pleasure pavilion or series of pavilions for the royal family of the Delhi Sultanate. The original, the first structure was built by Sultān 'Ala-ud-din Muhammad Khaljiz (r. 1296-1316) (See: **Appendix B** [Delhi]) the third of the Khaljiz Sultāns of Delhi. It was a favorite place of relaxation for the latter members of the Khaljiz Dynasty and their families. The *Hauz Khās* was also highly favored by the subsequent Tughluqs as well. Sultān Firuz Shāh Tughluq (r. 1351-1388), the fourth of the line, left his mark by having constructed a mosque along the southern bank of the tank. He also erected his tomb in the south-east corner connecting it with the a madrasa along the eastern and southern flanks of the tank (See: **Figures 17 & 18**).

Initially conceived as a place of relaxation and as a retreat for the royal family, much of what is applicable in the consideration of the design of a royal palace is forgotten or ignored here in lieu of its use. Although extensive in its scope the *Haus Khas* does not contain the labyrinthine hallways or remote chambers that one would expect to find in a royal palace. Rather, all structures and areas are generally one room or one space deep, and all look out upon or have access to the water area of the whole. This openness presages later pavilions, such as the later Mughal pleasure pavilions — i.e. the *Farah Bagh* and the *Shāhi Bagh*. This allowed unhampered movement to and from the various areas of the *Hauz Khās* not only by the royal family, but also of the cooling breezes blowing off the surface of the water.

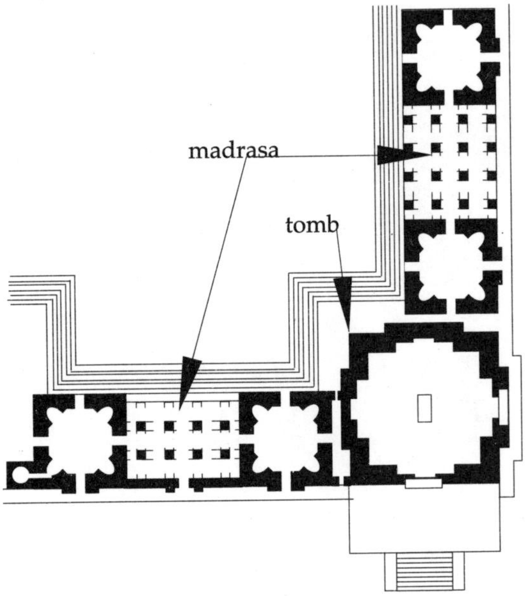

Figure 17 — *Haus Khas* (detail), showing *Tomb of Firuz Shāh* and madrasa

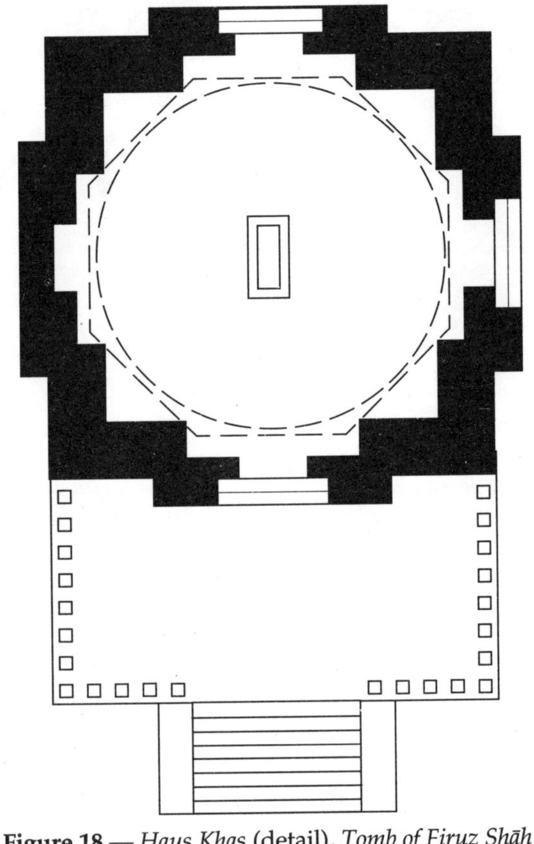

Figure 18 — *Haus Khas* (detail), *Tomb of Firuz Shāh* (plan, with *suffa*)

Legend for **Plate 1**

- **A** Main Pavilion
- **B** Pavilions
- **C** Tank
- **D** Madrasa
- **E** Mosque
- **F** Tomb of Firuz Shāh

Plate 1 — *Hauz Khās*, ground plan (partial), indicating axis

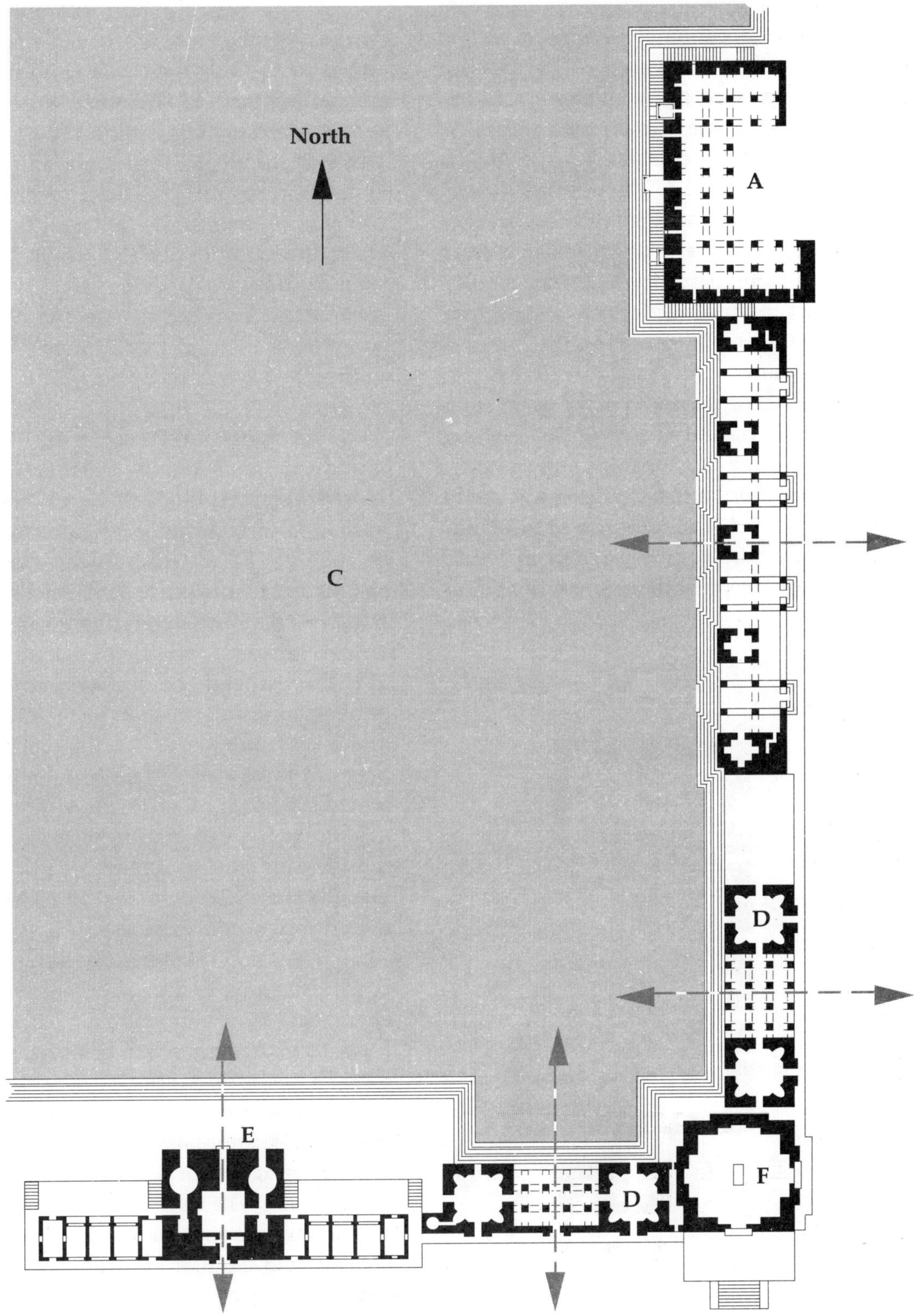

Yet, the major pavilion towards the north (See: **Plate 1 — A**) is cunningly designed so that any entrance from the water's edge — i.e. the west — must be accomplished by mounting a series of steep stairs leading to the western entrance (See: **Figure 19**). The design of this massive pavilion is elegant and essentially axial. The eastern 'façade' of this pavilion is opened and a court-like space, a *maidān* was the main feature. This 'court' was surrounded on three sides by a double arcade which not only presented a pleasant perspective, its roof created a cool interior as the breezes wafted off the water.

To the south of the main pavilion were a series of covered, partially walled spaces that bordered on the water and open on the opposite façade. Here a certain amount of privacy could be sought from the rest of the court or royal family. Gardens and fountains would have been found along this eastern façade adding to the delight of the whole.

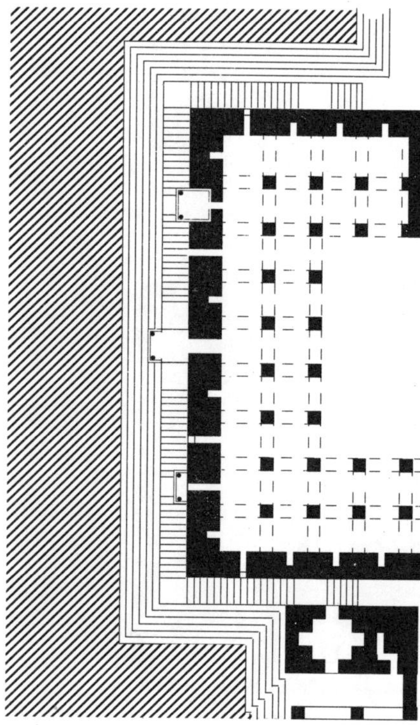

Figure 19 — *Haus Khas* (detail), showing the northern (main) pavilion

This was a period, not unlike subsequent Mughal times, when assassination was a real threat to the sultān as well as to members of his immediate family. Therefore, unrestricted access to the enclosure containing the various pavilions was not to be allowed. And, entry to this royal compound would have been severely curbed and the whole would have been, most certainly, surrounded by protective walls or moats. This would have allowed relative freedom of movement for the royal family within the compound without fear of harm or observation, giving them a rare opportunity for a relaxed sojourn.

As mentioned above, the Tughluqs also found this pleasure site most commodious. The Sultān Firuz Shāh Tughluq obviously found it such a suitable location as to construct his tomb in 1389 CE. In addition to the tomb proper, he also had constructed a madrasa composed of two wings — i.e. one extending from the west, the *qibla* of his tomb and one to the north (See: **Figure 17**). The attachment or abutment of a tomb to other sacred buildings — in this case a madrasa, along with the *masjid* (to the west) — had long been a practice of rulers throughout the Islamic world. It brought to the entombed, by way of proximity, an association with sacred teachings that he may not have been able to accomplish in his lifetime, thereby assuring or buttressing his hoped entry into Paradise.

The tomb is constructed upon a *suffa* with a porch extending to the south (See: **Figure 18**). This alignment — i.e. with the main entrance, here with a porch extending south and the *mikhrab* in the west or towards Mecca — is typical of Mughal tombs. It is the extended and elaborated porch that is most interesting. It provides a plaza-like space in front which acts as a ceremonial access to the interior. The form of the tomb is relatively simple and massive in appearance. The walls are battered and the plan is a simple *triratha* plan. The dome rests upon an octagonal drum (See: **Figure**

20). The tomb of his predecessor — i.e. Ghiyas-ud-din Tughluq Shāh I (r. 1320-1325) — is ostensibly the same in plan and similar in elevation (See: **Figure 21**) but without benefit of the extended porch.

The construction of a tomb within or near an area of relaxation and/or repose was not unheard of during this period. Certainly it would bring attention to the deceased and, thereby, increase his spiritual munificence. The Muslims believed that burial adjacent to a mosque, madrasa or the tomb of a saint would somehow elevate the spirit of the deceased, much in the same way the merit was sought by the Theravada Buddhists.

As a royal retreat, the *Hauz Khās* was relatively simple, especially when compared to later imperial pavilions and gardens. Yet its design was eminently suitable for its purpose. Laid out along a tank, the form of the *Hauz Khās* conformed to its situation, its locale. At a time of imminent turmoil, this quiet area must have been a soothing garden for troubled minds. Neither a high place, nor a labyrinth, it nonetheless exhibited royal characteristics in the axiality of the major structures and with the inclusion of a tomb and madrasa the whole exhibits all the hallmarks of a royal compound for the Sultāns of Delhi.

Figure 20 — *Haus Khas* (detail), *Tomb of Firuz Shāh* (elevation)

Figure 21 — *Tomb of Ghiyas-ud-din Tughluq I* (elevation & half plan)

Kotla Firuz Shāh, Delhi

(a. 1351)

The construction of the *Kotla Firuz Shāh*[58] is attributed to the Sultān Firuz Shāh (r. 1351-1388) (See: **Appendix B** [Delhi]) of the Tughluq Dynasty and a member of the Quarauna Turk tribe. As an Indo-Islamic structure, it is deeply indebted to Hindu tradition. Built in the then city of Ferozabad (aka Firuzabad), now part of Delhi, the *Kotla* is not a palace, but believed to have been a pleasure pavilion for the royal family. As such it is conceptually related to the *Hauz Khās.*

The fourth Tughluq, Sultān Firuz Shāh was a general of some repute. In fact he was elevated to the Sultanate in no small part as a result of his army. As all the members of the Tughluq Dynasty, the Sultān was a builder of no mean accomplish-ments and helped to develop sound agricultural practice in his realm. The *Kotla Firuz Shāh* is one of the few structures built during his reign which survives, though in a somewhat ruined state.

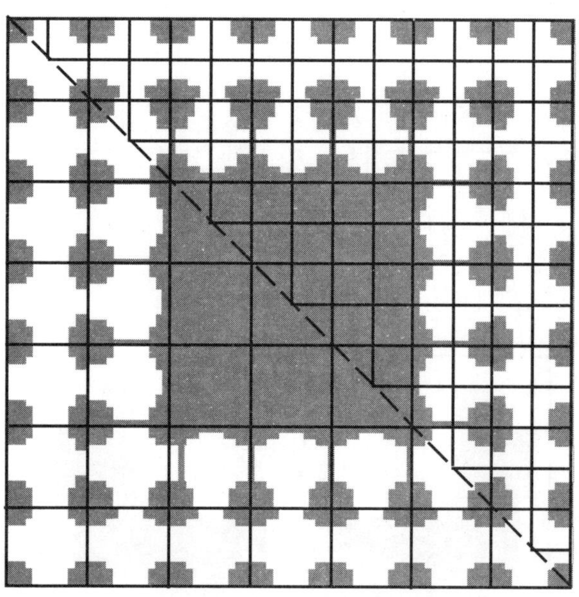

Figure 22 — *Kotla Firuz Shāh* , 1st level indicating a *Bhadramahasana Maṇḍala* (above) and a *Sthandila Maṇḍala* (below)

Constructed upon and around a natural promontory the Kotla appears to have been used as a place of retreat from the hot summer days of Delhi as well as the cool nights. Its open design allowed for the circulation of air through the numerous chambers. Additionally the solid core acted as a natural cooling device (See: **Figure 23**). This core retained its cool temperature during the day, slowly heating up so that during the cool night it would afford some degree of warmth — a natural flywheel effect not unlike a shallow cave — i.e. an ecologically sound device. This arrangement would allow the court a place of relaxation affording some degree of comfort both day and night.

As stated above, this Indo-Islamic structure owed much to Hindu tradition. Hindu architecture was based on architectural treatises (*śilpa-śāstras*) — e.g. the *Mayamatam*[59] and the *Manasara*. In both the square grid, the *maṇḍala* was used as the design basis for important structures and dwellings, particularly temples.[60] The square design of the *Kotla Firuz Shāh* with its regularly spaced divisions is a clear indication of a *maṇḍala*-based plan. It is apparent that either a *Sthandila Maṇḍala* or a *Bhadramahāsana Maṇḍala* was employed (See: **Figure 22**). The *Sthandila Maṇḍala* would appear to be more auspicious as its divisions mirror the days of the week. Islam, as the Hindu faith, was strongly influenced by astrology and numerology. The numerals seven and forty-nine figured in both 'sciences.'[61] Seven is a masculine number. It is often considered as the number of creation and perfection, as well as natural law. This numeral is a most sacred number and mystical being made up of the spiritual three (3) (masculine) plus the practical four (4) (feminine). Forty-nine is also a masculine number. This integer is a sacred numeral whose √ is the equally sacred seven. It is further auspicious in its make up. Nonetheless, the *Kotla Firuz Shāh's* cross axiality is apparent. An obvious influence of pre-existent Hindu practices.

Plate 2 — *Kotla Firuz Shāh*, plan, 1st, 2nd, 3rd & 4th storeys, indicating axis

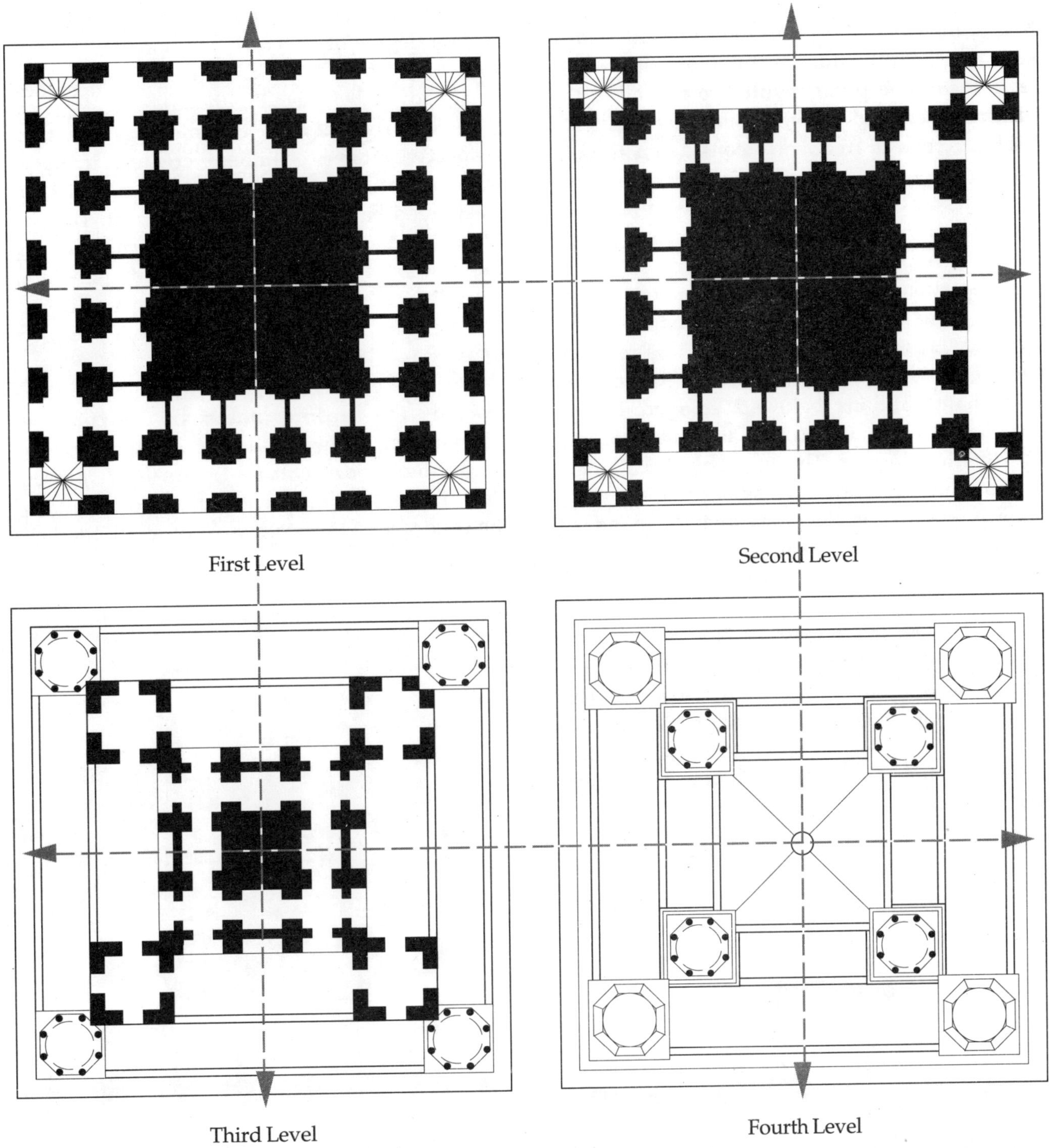

Kotla Firuz Shāh (Continued)

Although the plan is relatively simple in design, there is one element that the Sultān Firuz Shāh apparently added to the topmost level — i.e. a *stambha*, a pillar reputed to be one of the hundreds erected by the Buddhist Emperor Aśoka. Aśoka is frequently considered to be a *cakravartin* — i.e. a universal monarch, a monarch who rules by and within the precepts of Buddhist doctrine, and later accepted as a concept by the Hindu. The pillar or *stambha may* be seen as a representation, an icon of the *axis mundi*.

In so erecting this pillar upon the *Kotla*, Firuz Shāh associates himself with this revered, ancient, Buddhist universal monarch (*cakravartin*) who many Indians believed enjoyed Divine acceptance. It is but one other attribute of kingly rule that he assumed. This may have been added to show his dominance over the predominantly Hindu realm, or he may have added it acknowledging the greatness of this ancient Indian ruler, or also as a subtle means of placating his Hindu peoples, or all three.

The erection of the *Kotla Firuz Shāh* facility, although not a palace, upon a promontory underlines its association with the ruler. The implication of a high, elevated location along with the Aśokan *stambha* underlines the royal quality of this structure. Certainly, during the bright days and cool nights cloth may well have hung over the external and internal openings affording a certain degree of privacy. Additionally, the rock core would have acted as an ecological flywheel as already noted (See: **Figure 23**).

The repetition of the openings and their respective inner chambers creates, if not a labyrinth, at least plethora of spaces in which the ruler could have rested or found retreat. Thereby, he achieved a degree of protection from those who might want to visually intrude or to do him harm. In addition, the disposition of these spaces is such that he could have easily moved from one place to another.

The orientation of the *Kotla Firuz Shāh* is towards the cardinal points of the compass. Whether or not there had been a 'main entrance' established is difficult to discern in its present state. Probably, a main entrance could have faced the residence of this stronghold of which the *Kotla Firuz Shāh* was a part.

The symmetry of the *Kotla Firuz Shāh* is obvious (See: **Figure 24**). Such symmetrical

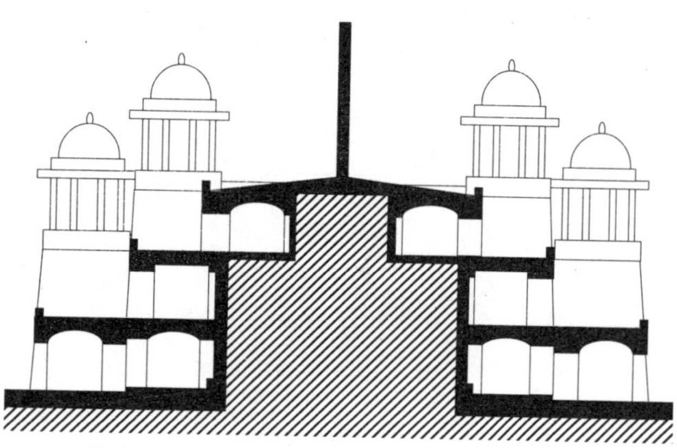

Figure 23 — *Kotla Firuz Shāh,* sectional view indicating rock core

Figure 24 — *Kotla Firuz Shāh,* proportional elevation and half plan (1st level)

pavilions were long the vogue among the rulers of the Islamic world. Within its labyrinthine courts, the famed *Topkapisaray* posses a number of symmetrical pavilions for the retreat of the Ottoman emperor (See: **Appendix A, Plate 85**). The palace complexes of Iran also exhibited such small symmetrical pavilions. Yet, here in the *Kotla Firuz Shāh* the symmetry marches from the lowest to the highest level to the beat of pre-existent Hindu *maṇḍalas*. That is not to say the *Firuz Shāh* was devoted to Hindu architectural forms, it is apparent that the *sthapati* who oversaw this pavilion was thoroughly schooled in the precepts of both the *Manasara* and the *Mayamatam*.

Yet there are also obvious Islamic design components as well. The application of a ninefold division, a *Pīṭha Maṇḍala* (See: **Figures 25 & 26**) This division refers to the eight rivers of the Islamic Paradise that flow through that desired place of supreme happiness and peace. Numerous Mughal tombs employ this concept in their designs.[62] It is little wonder that the same design concept is applied also to the *Kotla Firuz Shāh*, a bit of sought-after paradise on this earth. The fact that the *kotla* appears to be more fortification than place of relaxation says much of the period in which it was constructed.

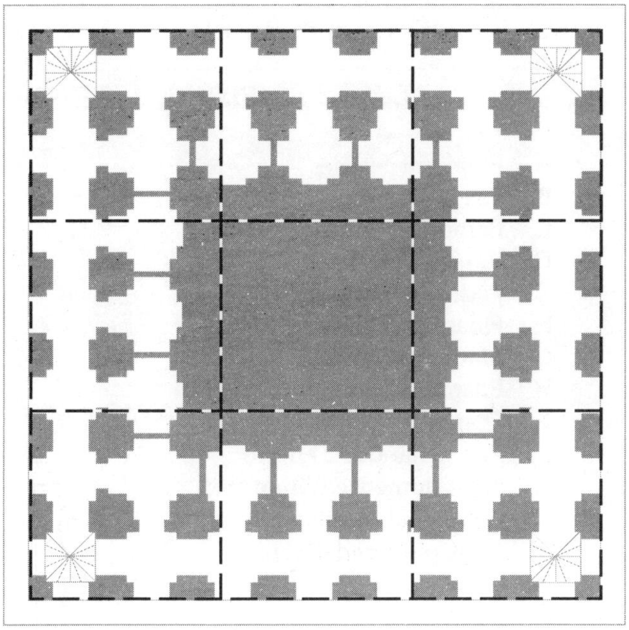

Figure 25 — *Kotla Firuz Shāh,* indicating nine-fold division over 1st level

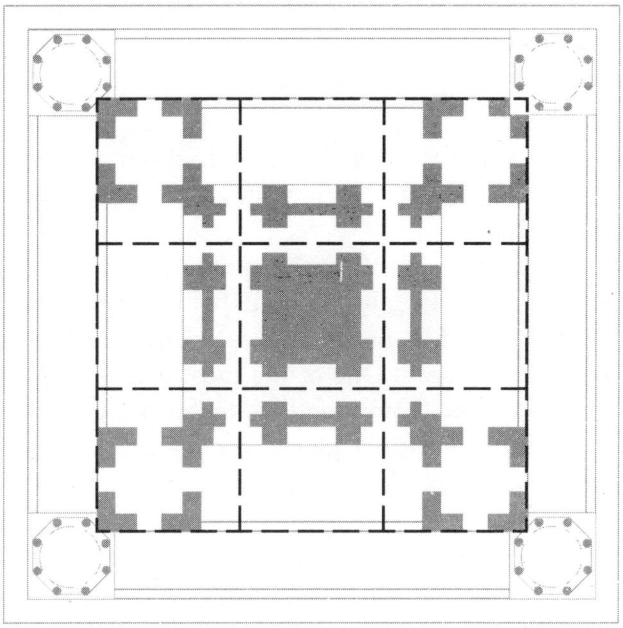

Figure 26 — *Kotla Firuz Shāh,* indicating nine-fold division over 3rd level

Vijayanagara Qilā, Vijayanagara

(a. 1350 - b. 1565 CE)

The Sangamas in the mid-fourteenth century established a Hindu empire with its capital known as *Vijayanagara* — i.e. literally "the victorious serpent" — on the Tungabhadra river near the border between present day Andhra Pradesh and Karanataka. Steadily the Sangamas built their empire (c. 1336-1485 CE) to the point that the Hindu Rayas of Vijayanagara became the powerful force to be reckoned with in southern India. In the year 1485, the Saluvas, then the Yuluvas established their dynasties and were to reign at Vijayanagara until the invasion and defeat by the Muslims in 1565.

During this latter Saluva Dynasty, Vijayanagara saw unparalleled growth and brilliance, particularly during the reigns of Krishnadevaraya (r. 1510-1530 CE) (See: **Appendix B** [Vijayanagara]) and his successor Achyuta-devaraya (r. 1530 — 1542 CE). At this time the *Vijayanagara Qilā*[63] with its *mandir*s and other royal structures became a showplace of southern India, rivalling the northern Mughal court with all its brilliance and architectural grandeur. Isolated in the hilly terrain of the western Ghats and within an easily defensible locale Vijayanagara grew and prospered.

In 1565 CE Vijayanagara was attacked, defeated, sacked and razed by the combined forces of the Muslim Sultanates to the north and was left to decay. One of the most extensive and elaborate royal compounds is today but a ruined shadow of its former glory. The residential areas fared the worst. Apparently, they were constructed with a combination of wood and stone. The wooden areas suffered the most — i.e. they were torched, a normal practice meted out to the vanquished. The temple areas fared somewhat better.

For over the two-hundred plus years of its existence, the *raya*s of Vijayanagara engaged in construction. Primarily, they raised palaces and ceremonial structures — i.e. platforms, undoubtedly for viewing — and walls. Then there were numerous temple complexes constructed. The temple central to the Vijayanagara *Raya*s was the *Rāmachandra Temple* (aka *Hazara Rāma* ["One thousand *Rāmas*"]) in the centre of the main complex (See: **Plate 3 — J**). Yet there were others: to the north and west was a sacred centre in the now modern day Hampi; to the north and east rose the impressive *Viṭṭhala Temple* complex (See: **Appendix A, Plate 86**); and to the east of the main complex two smaller temples — i.e. the *Mādhava* and *Ellamma Temples.*

Consisting of a series of interlocking, overlapping, defensible, enclosing walls and moats, the *Vijayanagara Qilā* with its royal compound(s) and substantial army was a place of some security. Due to its relatively long existence, there does not appear to be a coherent plan; certainly not as found in *Fatehpur Sikri*, the *Lal Qilā* of Agra or *Shāhjahanabad,* Delhi. Rather, the complex is a series of walled enclosures, generally

Legend for **Plate 3**

A	Elephant Stables
B	Pavilion
C	Parade Ground
D	Vaulted Pavilion
E	Padma Mahal
F	Floating Mahal
G	Madhava Temple
H	Ellamma Temple
I	Domed Watchtower
J	Rāmachandra Temple
K	Nine-domed Pavilion
L	Octagonal Pavilion
M	100-Columned Pavilion
N	Great Platform (Mahavanami Platform)
O	Geometric Tank
P	Great Tank
Q	Octagonal Fountain
R	Square Water Pavilion
S	Residences (?)
T	Zenānā (?)
U	Platforms (?)

Plate 3 — *Vijayanagara Qilā, Central Compounds*

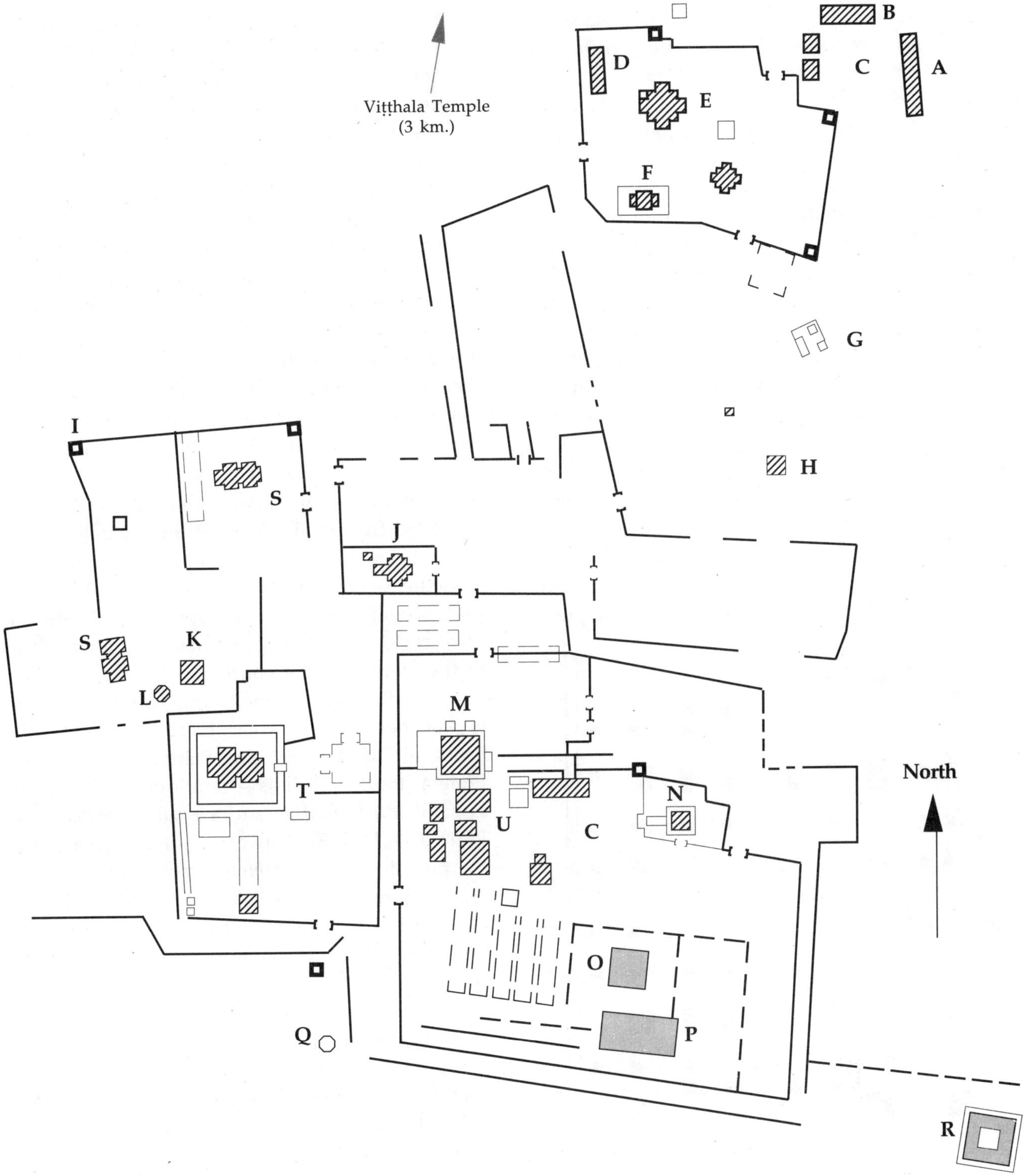

attached one to the other. Apparently, the main royal centre revolves around the *Hundred-columned Pavilion* and the *Great Platform* (See: **Plate 3 — M & N**). Directly to the west of the *Great Platform* is a large open space, a parade ground (?), and to the west of this space are three foundations which some see as smaller viewing platforms (See: **Plate 3 — U**). Within this large compound are two tanks — i.e. a large tank (See: **Plate 3 — P**) and a smaller, geometrically planned square tank (See: **Plate 3 — O**; see also: **Appendix A, Plate 93**). The latter is constructed of green chlorite and is a spectacular example of architecture which, happily, has not suffered the ravages of time to any great extent.

To the west of this large complex are three, smaller, adjoining compounds (See: **Plate 3 — K, S & T**). Again, there are those who view these compounds as residential in nature. The southernmost (**Plate 3 — T**) appears to hold all the requirements of a *zenānā*. It is totally walled, isolated from the others, possesses what appears

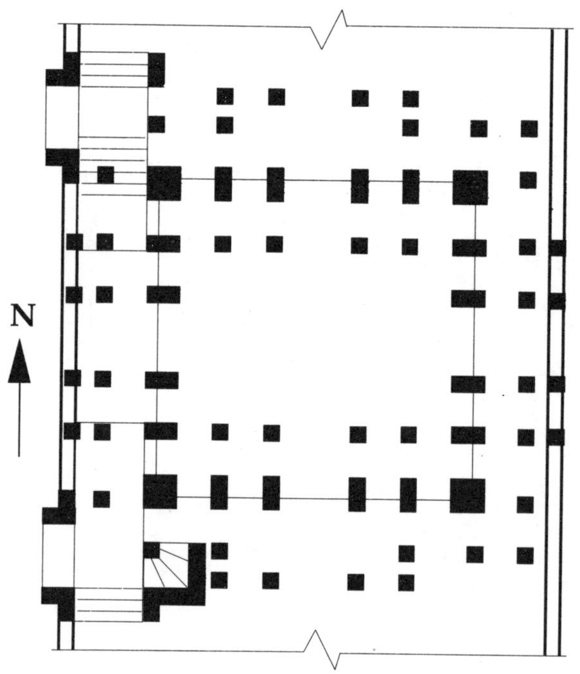

Figure 27 — *Elephant Stable,* second storey (musician's pavilion)

to be a large foundation for some type of structure (a *mahal*?), and limited access and an element which resembles a tank. All of these features would be found in a *zenānā*.

Another structure deserves comment. It is the *Square Water Pavilion,* sometimes known as the *Queen's Bath*[64] (See: **Plate 4** [bottom]). Located to the south-east of the large compound, this bath appears isolated and without surrounding, protective walls. This tank with a surrounding, compartmented pavilion is quite elaborate and commodious. If, indeed, this was the Queen's bath, it is most unusual. It seems an unlikely candidate for the Queen for two salient reasons. First, the fact that it is set apart from any of the other walled compounds and stands in the open, makes it suspect to be labelled as a bath for the women of the court. Second, their royal persons were protected from prying eyes of the menfolk within securely walled areas, guarded by eunuchs. Nonetheless, its architectural detail, including the plan, would make it an appropriate candidate if it were enclosed within appropriate wall for the bath of the women of the court.

To the north of the large, central compound is another walled area. Here one finds the beautiful *Padma Mahal* (See: **Plate 3 — E;** See also: **Plate 4** [top]) as well as several other buildings — i.e. a *Vaulted Pavilion* and a *Floating Mahal* (See: **Plate 3 — D & F**). This compound is adjacent to the famed *Elephant Stables*, a rectangular *Pavilion* (See: **Figure 28**) and a *Parade Ground* (See: **Plate 3 — A, B & C**). Some view this enclosed area as a residence of one of the later *rayas*, while others see it as the compound of a general due to its proximity to the *Elephant Stables* (See: **Plate 5**; see also: **Figure 27**).[65] It may even have been the compound for the heir apparent. However, the presence of three strategically placed guard towers make it unlikely as the residence for a general of Vijayanagara. Certainly such security arrangements are more in keeping with the person of the *raya* or his designated heir than a mere general.

Plate 4 — *Padma Mahal* (top), *Square Water Pavilion* (bottom)

(See: **Plate 3**)

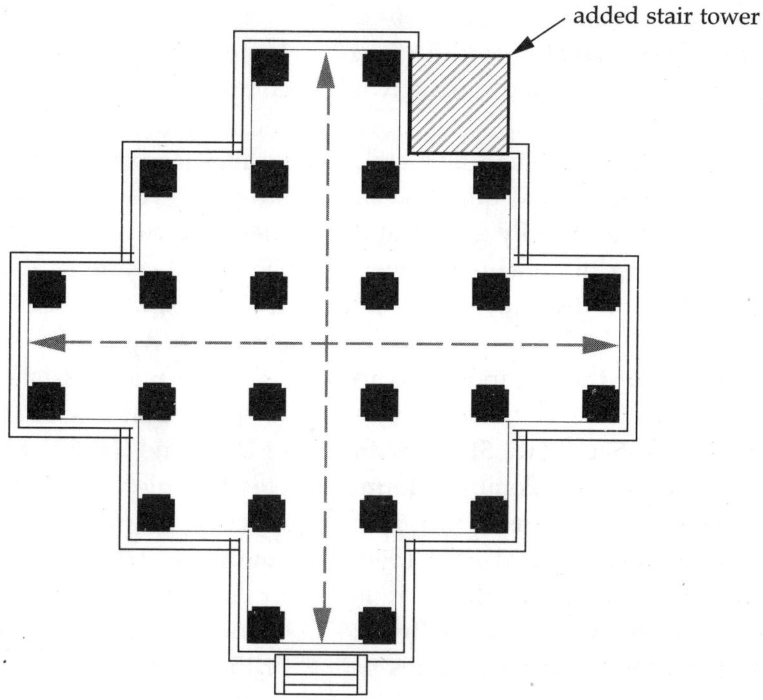

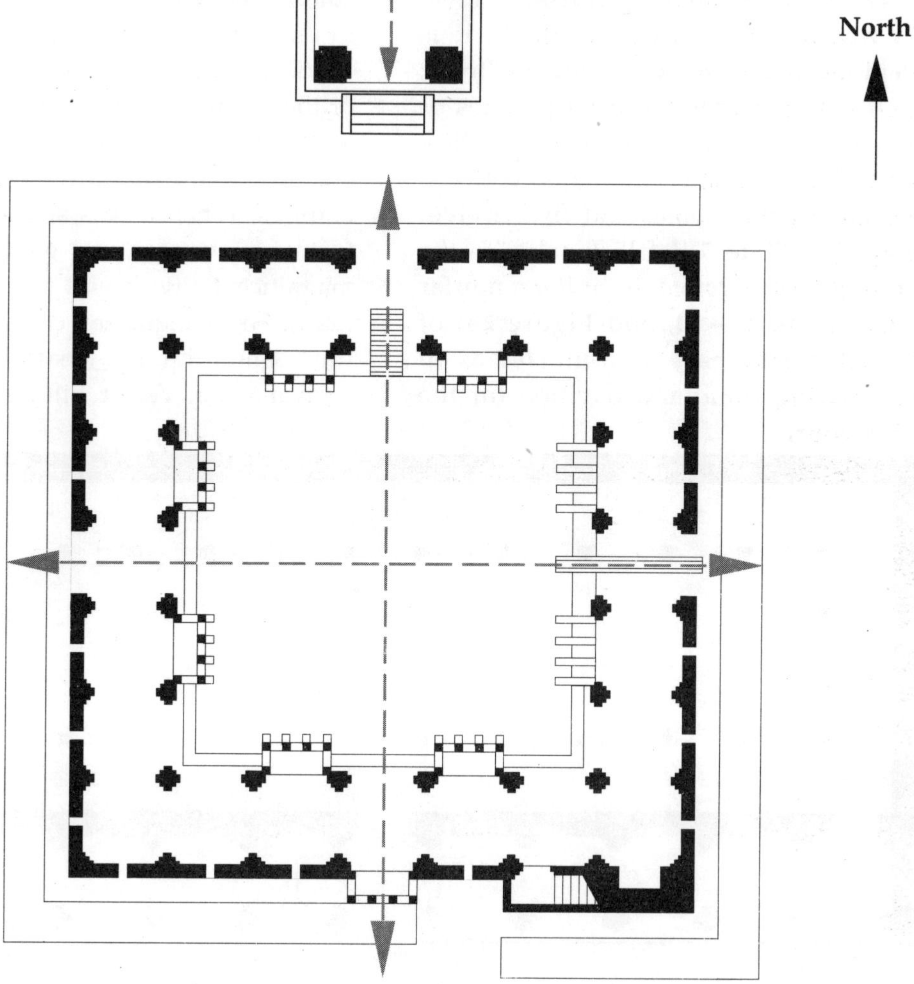

Vijayanagara Qilā (Concluded)

Nonetheless it is within this compound that the wonderful *Padma Mahal* is found (See: **Plate 4** [top]). Cross axial, *en plan*, and raising two storeys, it sits in quiet grandeur. The only element that mars its pristine simplicity is a stair tower which, due to its material and quality, can only be assumed to have been hastily added at a later date. Yet, disregarding the nocuous tower, the *Padma Mahal* is one of the glories of the *Vijayanagara Qilā*.

Directly to the east of this compound is to be found another wonder of the *Vijayanagara Qilā* — i.e. the *Elephant Stables* (See: **Plate 5**). As with the *Padma Mahal*, it is in relatively complete form. Ten domed spaces flank a central area which rose three storeys. This elevated central area (See: **Figure 27**) was an open pavilion which, it is believed, held musicians and/or drummers (Indic: *nakkar khana*) who performed during parades or martial manoeuvres on the *Parade Ground* (See: **Plate 3 — C**). The ten domes alternated between five traditional circular domes and five twelve-sided domes (See: **Plate 5** [left]). Finally, to the north of the *Parade Ground* is a Rectangular Pavilion (See: **Plate 3 — B,** and **Figure 28**) of singular design. It may have been utilized as an elaborate reviewing stand and pavilion for the ruler and his court.

As has been stated, the royal city of *Vijayanagara* consisted of secular — i.e. royal compounds — and temple compounds. Although the *Rāmachandra Temple* compound and the two smaller temples to the east of the main compound are part of/or are adjacent to the *Vijayanagara Qilā*, there are two other important complexes. First, the sacred centre at Hampi, to the north and west; and the *Viṭṭhala Temple* complex to the north and east (See: **Appendix A, Plate 86**).

During its existence Vijayanagara had been the proverbial thorn in the backside of the Muslims of Delhi and later the Great Mughals. *Vijayanagara Qilā* that glorious royal, Hindu, capital city of an equally glorious empire; an empire that ran contiguous with the Muslim and Mughal Empires to the north, an empire that was equally lavish in its riches and buildings fell victim to defeat. The brilliance of its court, the vast riches that foreign ambassadors noted and its presumptuous daring on the fields of battle taunted the northern empires. When it was subdued, two centuries of festering vengeance was let loose on this magnificent city. It was not only sacked — it was razed! Few vanquished cities in India had suffered the ignominious treatment meted out to Vijayanagara. Yet, it still shines!

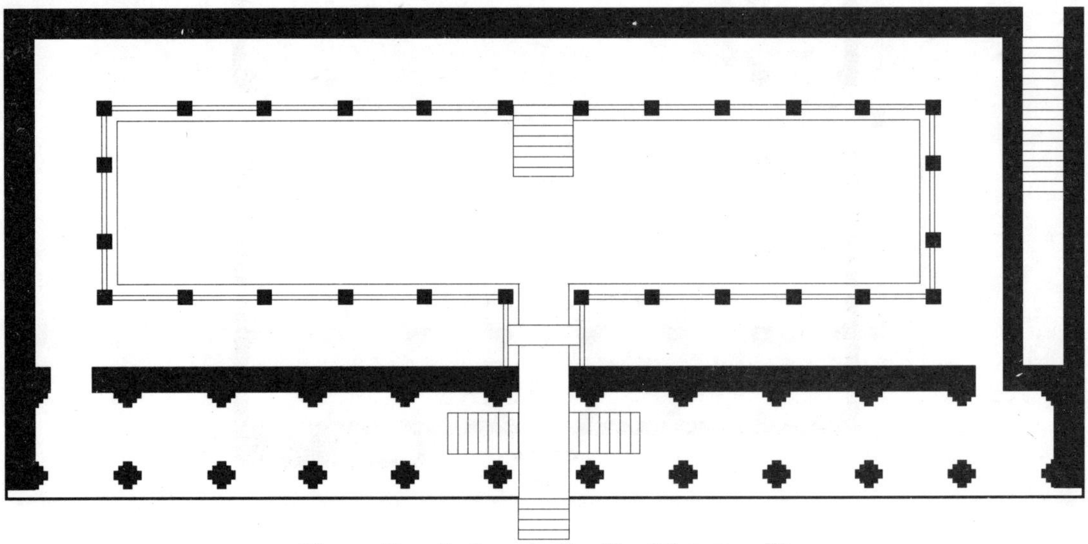

Figure 28 — *Rectangular Pavilion* (**Plate 3 — B**)

Plate 5 — *Elephant Stables,* Domes & Plan (right)

(See: **A, Plate 3**)

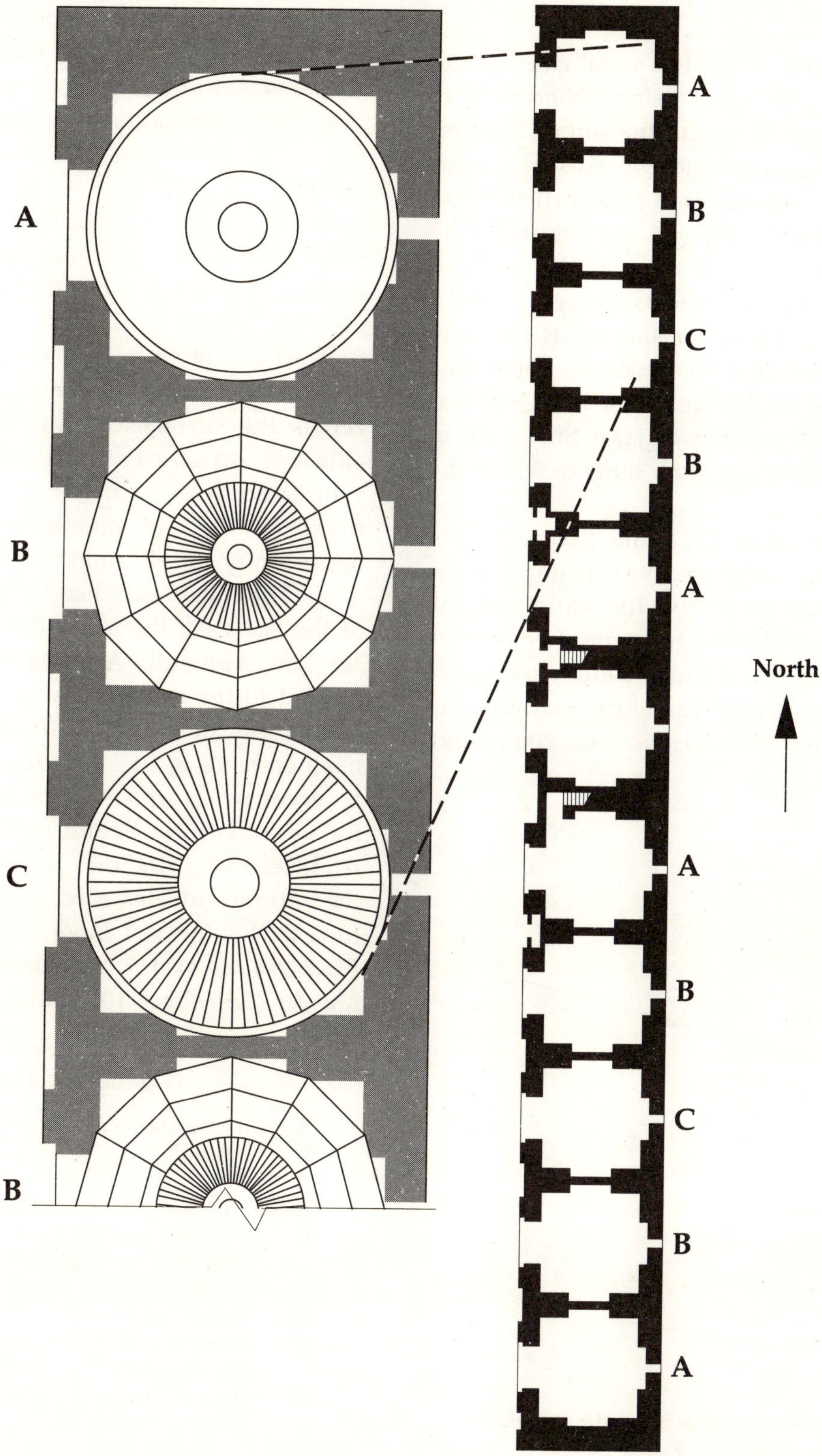

Shadiabad, Mandu

(a. 1410 CE)

Maṇḍu, one of the two royal cities of the Malwa Sultanate, the other being Chanderi, was the most extensive. It was to the son of the first Sultān of Malwa, Husam-ud-Din Hushang Shāh (1405-1435) (See: **Appendix B** [Malwa]) that the initial construction of the *qilā* is attributed. The Sultanate was continually at war with its neighbors — i.e. Gujarat, Chittor and Gulbarga. Mandu afforded what was then considered at the time an impregnable location for the royal capital. The Malwa Sultanate finally succumbed to Qutb-ud-Din Bahadur Shāh of the Gujarat Sultanate in 1531, and later Bahadur Shāh quickly fell to the great Mughals.

Like the *Bidar Qilā,* the *Shadiabad*[66] of Mandu occupied a high and vast plateau — i.e. some twelve square miles. Its walls ran the perimeter of this plateau for some twenty-five miles. Scattered over this wide area were mosques, *madrasas* and residences dedicated to pleasure — i.e. a typical Islamic royal compound.

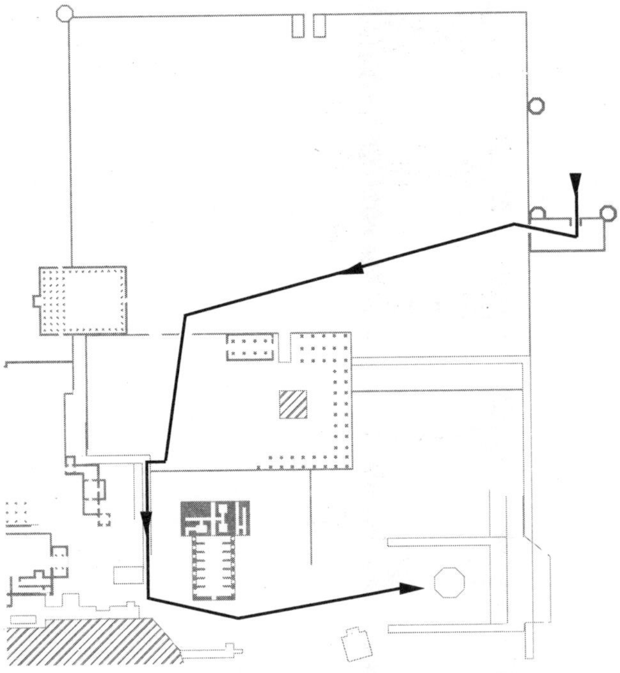

Figure 29 — *Shadiabad Mandir,* indicating path from the *Tripolia*

The main residential compound was situated at the northern border of this plateau — the *Shadiabad*.

Two artificial lakes, tanks — i.e. the *Kaphur Talao* and the *Munja Talao* — dominate this complex (See: **Plate 6 — K & L**). They serve multiple purposes. First, they afforded the *garh mahal* with water, much needed in the event of a prolonged siege. Second, they offer the residents pleasing visual prospects during the brilliant festivals and other relaxed times. Third, the warm breezes are cooled somewhat as they wafted across the surfaces of the tanks and into the adjacent structures particularly during the protracted dry season. And, last, they offer the royal family and members of the court an opportunity for ablution.

The major entrance to the complex proper of the *Sadiabad*, the *Hāthī Pol* (See: **Plate 6 — B**; see also: **Appendix A, Plate 98** [upper right]), is located to the east of a large, open court. Large open areas such as this directly attached to the main entrance is a feature frequently encountered. It serves two purposes. First as a parade ground for various festivals and military-style parades. And, secondly, it allows an unimpeded access to the entrance for defensive purposes by the inner forces. This form of inner defense is seen in the *Bidar Qilā and Mandir* (See: **Plate 9**), *the Rānā Kumbha Mandir* (See: **Plate 10**), among others. Access to

Legend for **Plate 6**

A	Delhi Darwaza
B	Hāthī Pol
C	Outer Court
D	Mosque of Dilwar Khan
E	Palace of Baz Bahadur
F	Palace of Gada Shāh
G	Hiṇḍolā Mahal
H	Lal Mahal
I	Jahaz Mahal
J	Inner Court
K	Munja Talao
L	Kaphur Talao

Plate 6 — *Shadiabad Mandir*, main compound

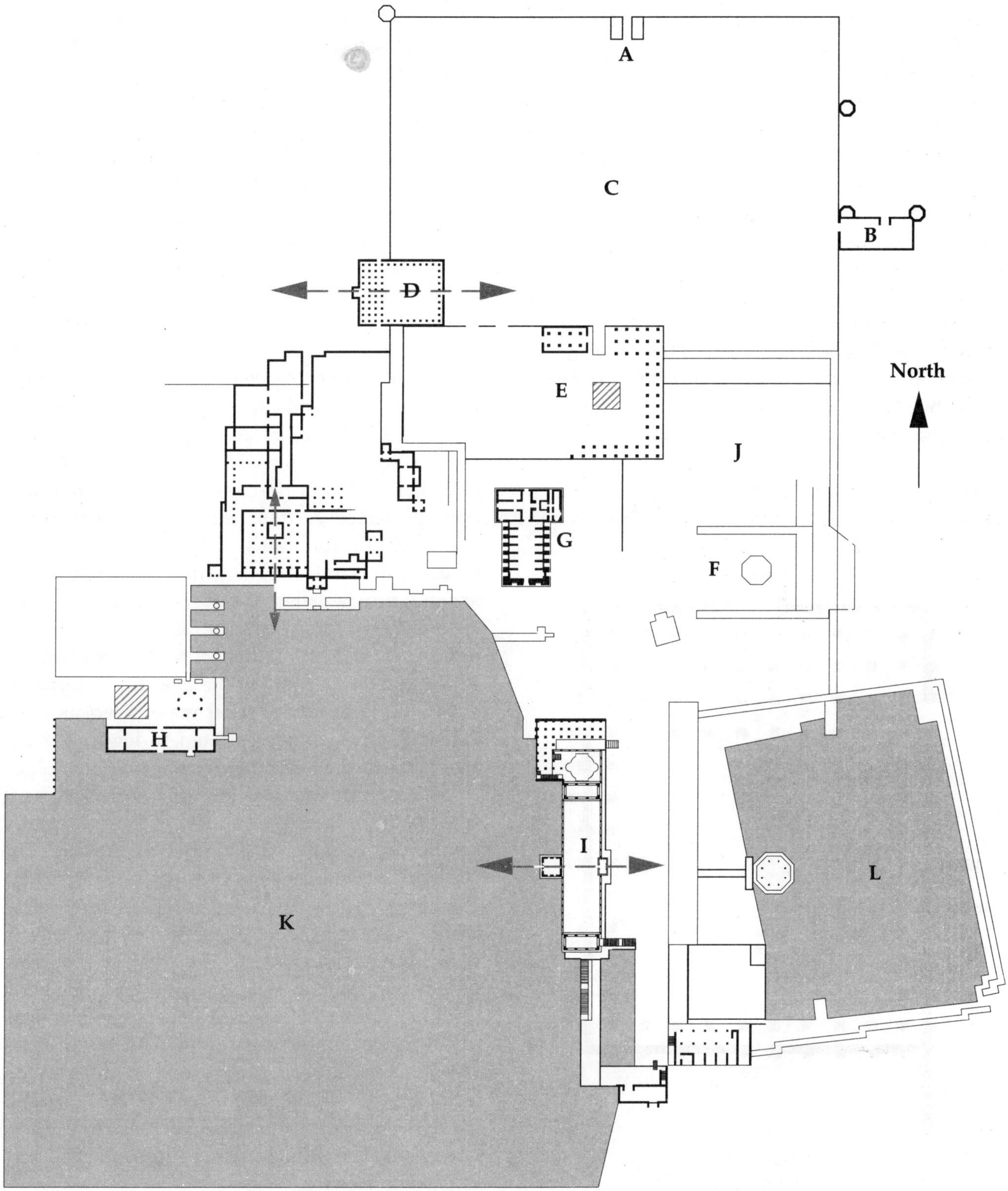

this court is not direct as is seen in the *Rānā Kumbha Mandir tripolia*, but any guest, or enemy must make a 90^0 turn — another defensive design.

Access to the private residential areas of the *Shadiabad* were also protected (See: **Figure 29**) by various gates and passageways. As with all royal residences, there is a circumlocutory route that must be followed in order to gain access to the royal apartments.

The *Shadiabad* possesses several structures of some importance — i.e. the *Jahāz Mahal* (See: **Plate 7**), the *Hiṇḍolā Mahal* (See: **Plate 8**), and the *Mosque of Dilwar Khan* (See: **Figure 30**). The latter — i.e. the *Mosque of Dilwar Khan* — is dedicated to Hushang Shāh's predecessor and father, the Afghani noble, Dilwar (aka: Dilavar) Khan Ghuri. It is opposite the *Hāthī Pol* and its main entrance faces onto the vast, open parade area. The mosque is rather typical, *en plan*, consisting of a square open court surrounded by a covered colonnade and four ranks of ten columns towards the *qibla*. The main entrance, as stated, gives way to the outer court (See: **Plate 6 — C**), and there are two lateral entrances which open on to public areas — i.e. one to the north and the other to the south, the royal enclosure.

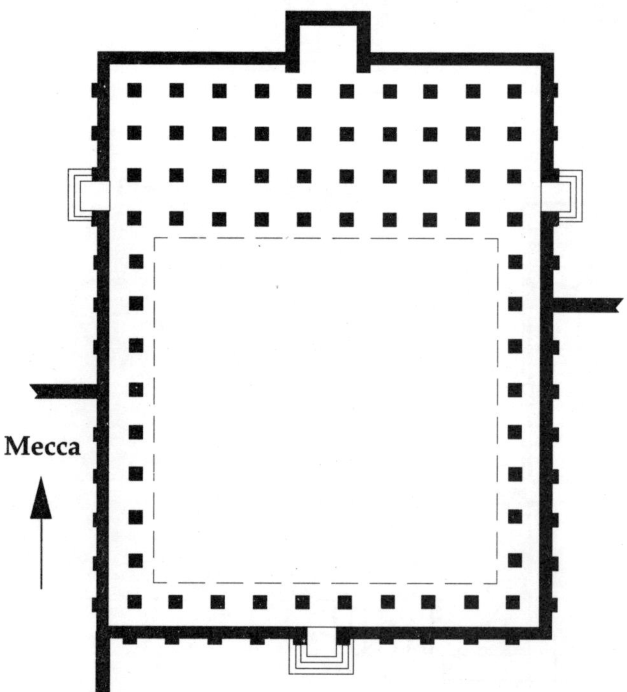

Figure 30 — *Mosque of Dilwar Khan* plan, *Shadiabad Mandir*

The *Jahāz Mahal*

The *Shadiabad* is noteworthy because of its varied structures, not the least being the *Jahāz Mahal* (See: **Plate 7**). The "Ship Palace," a translation of *Jahāz Mahal*, is unique in many aspects. Being constructed on the large reservoir, the *Munja Talao*, and adjacent to the smaller *Kaphur Talao*, this pleasure palace appears to float upon the surface of the tank in glistening beauty. We have long heard of the joys the Mughals found in their perfected gardens, shimmering waterways and bubbling fountains. Yet, here, tucked away from imperial Delhi, a glittering example of architecture worthy of any court or capital is encountered in this complex. Its construction was ordered by the fifth Sultān of Malwa, Mahmud I, Khalji (r. 1436-1469 CE) of the new Khalji Dynasty, c. 1460 CE The *Jahāz Mahal* was raised as if its construction was necessitated to legitimize the ascension to the Sultanate of this new line.

The *Jahāz Mahal* is strongly horizontal as it sweeps from north to south with low steady rhythms of openings and decorative borders. The pleasure palace consists of a series of open air chambers on the first level reserved for private bathing and relaxation. These spaces give way to either the *Munja Talao* to the west or a narrow garden and the *Kaphur Talao* to the east. Sheltered from the sun within these chambers, the members of the royal family were treated to the breezes which blew across the reservoir during the incredibly hot dry months as well as being shaded from the unremitting sun. Such luxury when others toiled ceaselessly in the sun soon gave way to utter indolence.

Plate 7 — *Jahaz Mahal, Shadiabad Mandir,* terrace level plan

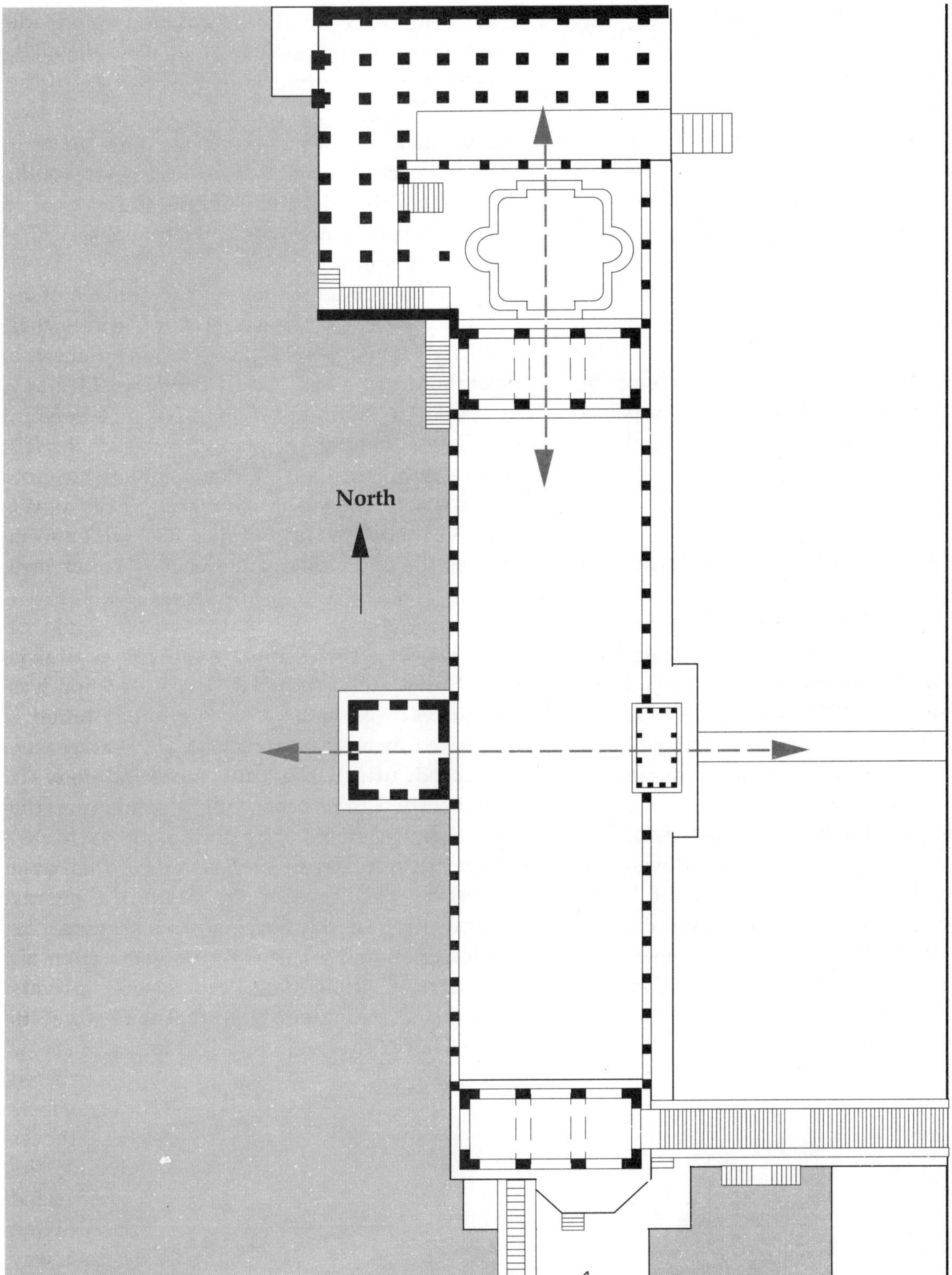

Shadiabad Mandir (Concluded)

The upper level, an open terrace, was punctuated on either end with rectangular pavilions, a domed, square pavilion jutting over the reservoir and opposite a small, square-domed kiosk. Here, raised above the hurly-burly and where the gentle breezes of the evening could cool, the sultān could pursue all manners of pleasure.

Later Khalji sultāns constructed similar pleasure pavilions across the vast plateau of Mandu's *qilā*. The *Jahāz Mahal* even caught the eye of the Mughal emperors, particularly after they absorbed Malwa into their vast empire. Jahangir was so smitten with this pleasure palace that he spent considerable sums for its upkeep.

The *Hiṇḍolā Mahal*

The *Hiṇḍolā Mahal* ("Swinging Palace") is opposite in its ponderous aspect to the elegant *Jahāz Mahal*. It squats to the north and west of this graceful pleasure palace (See: **Plate 8**). Constructed during the reign of Husam-ud-Din Hushang Shāh (c. 1425) its massive scale[67] contrasts with the more delicate neighbor — i.e. one distinctly masculine the other decidedly feminine.

It is suggested that the *Hiṇḍolā Mahal* was constructed as an audience hall where the sultān might hold public *darbārs*. Certainly the large, arched area would have been most suitable for this purpose. The double storied transverse form opens onto this open hall via a smaller arched opening on the second floor as well as a connecting cruciform space on the ground level. On this lower level were a number of smaller, connected spaces. On the second storey were two rooms. One was large with a double row of columns and a small balcony looking out onto the large vaulted space. The sultān may well have held his *darbār* from this elevated, second storey location and the second storey could well have served as his private space.

The ponderousness of the *Hiṇḍolā Mahal* certainly gives the impression of unremitting stability. This would have been eminently desirable for the new Ghuri Dynasty (1392-1436 CE). Like a sentinel, a massive presence, it dominates this part of the *qilā* and *mandir*. If it was to impress, it surely does. A necessity of a new dynasty expressed iconographically in this massive, laboured structure. The *Jahāz Mahal* implies the other side of the coin — i.e. relaxed, elegant and given to earthly pleasures.

It seems that within a short span of time this Sultanate produced two incomparable structures. Nonetheless, various excesses insinuated themselves and the Malwas were soon corrupted, utterly. Not any more indolent nor self-absorbed than other rulers of many of the Indian petty states. The Sultanate of Malwa wallowed in excess to such an extent that when they were challenged by the might of the Great Mughals, they quickly succumbed. It was after but a brief one-hundred-thirty-nine years from the establishment of the Malwa Sultanate — at first a vibrant and strong entity — that it breathed its last — "not with a sigh, but a whimper!"

Plate 8 — *Hiṇḍolā Mahal, Shadiabad Mandir,* plan first storey (top) & second storey (bottom)

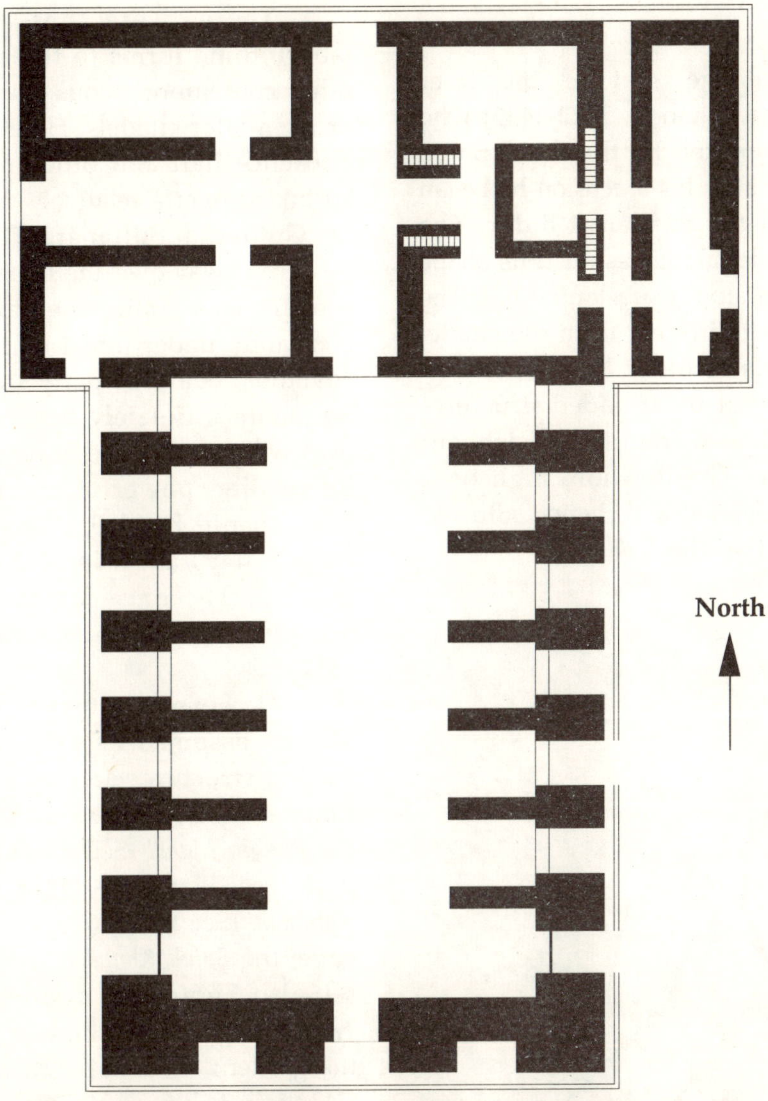

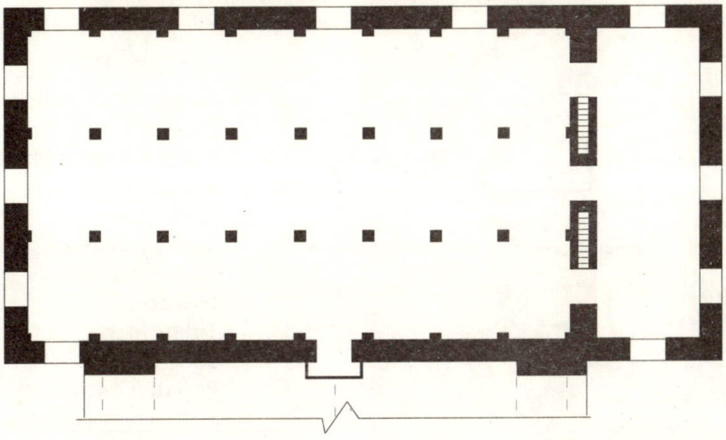

Bidargarh, Bidar

(a. 1424 CE)

Bidar became the seat of the later Bahmani Sultān Ahmad Shah (r. 1422-1435) who was subsequently displaced by the Barid Shahi Dynasty in 1492. Soon after his ascension he began new construction on the citadel at Bidar. The *qilā* had before his undertaking assumed its shape and defensive position atop a substantial hill. The *Bidargarh*[68] is somewhat different from the citadel with their *garh mahal*s of other Muslim Indian rulers. Here, the rulers at Bidar added structures which were often separated from their neighbour by a goodly distance. The location, high on a plateau was easily defended and, hence, allowed for this separation within the *Bidargarh*.

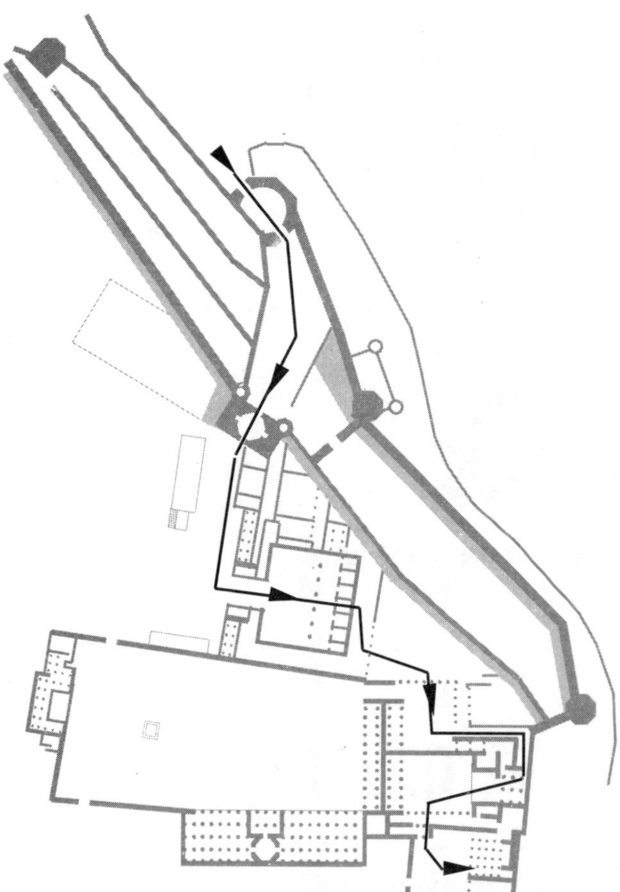

Figure 31 — *Bidar Kotila and Mandir*, indicating path from the *Gumbad Darwaza*

There were not the interconnected, labyrinthine forms to the areas that are seen in other contemporaneous strongholds or of earlier, or even later citadels. Here the royal apartments, audience hall and other regal structures were sprinkled over a relatively vast area. The Bahmani or Gulbarga Sultanate (1347-1527) had held powerful sway over the Deccan prior to 1489. Their power was imposing although they were constantly under threat by smaller, neighbouring, covetous, bellicose petty states. As the Bahmani Sultanate ultimately began to crumble from its own weight and love of luxury it was supplanted by smaller, powerful and even brilliant states: first, Bijapur in 1489, then Ahmadnagar in 1490, Berar in 1490, Bidar in 1492, and finally, Golconda in 1512. The once famous Bahmani Sultanate breathed its last under Kalim-Allah Shah (1525-1527).

However, by that time, the *Bidargarh* had already assumed its shape and disposition. The earliest structures are: the *Gumbad Darwaza* (See: **Plate 6 — A**), to the south-west and adjacent is the *Rangin Mahal* (See: **Plate 6 — B**); the grand *Lal Bagh* (See: **Plate 6 — D**) or ruby garden with the *Hammam* (See: **Plate 6 — E**) bordering its northern edge; the *Solah Khamba Masjid* (See: **Plate 6 — C**; see also **Figure 34**) dominates to the west; the *Tarkash Mahal* (See: **Plate 6 — F**) to the south of the garden; and the *Gagan Mahal* (See: **Plate 6 — G**), again to the south and butting the defensive

Legend for **Plate 9**

A	Gumbad Darwaza
B	Rangin Mahal
C	Solah Khamba Masjid
D	Lal Bagh
E	Hammam
F	Tarkash Mahal
G	Gagan Mahal
H	Diwān-i Ām
I	Takht Mahal
J	Stables
K	Parade Ground

Plate 9 — *Bidar Kotila & Mandir*, plan (partial)

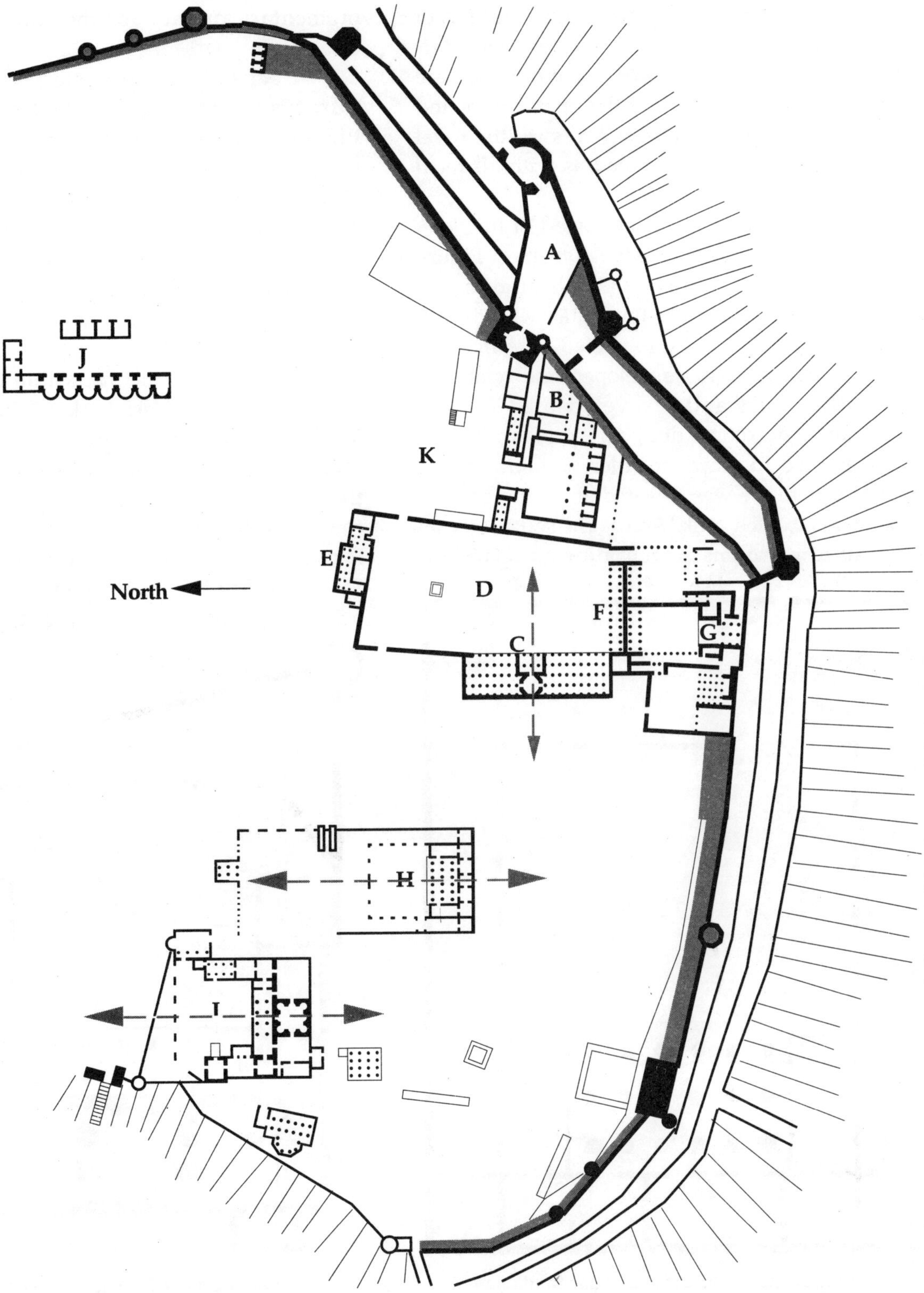

wall. These seven areas are the earliest section of the *Bidargarh*. Together, they create a rather far-flung assemblage of structures, some of which are labyrinthine in character, but the open courts and gardens seem to predominate. Access to the royal apartments was severely limited as with all regal residences (See: **Figure 31**).

Several hundred feet to the west of the *Solah Khamba Masjid* rises the *Diwān-i Ām* (See: **Figure 32**; see also: **Plate 6 — H**), the hall of audience within the *Bidargarh*. Here the sultān would hold public *darbār*s and daily expected *darśana*. The reception area is highly developed and relatively vast with a substantial covered area for the supplicants. A colonnaded, raised area allowed the assembled to view the ruler without getting too close. Here, he was elevated above the masses as befits his exalted rank. Across the southern wall are a suite of rooms which allowed space for momentary privacy for the sultān during these often trying *darbār*s.

Again to the west and north of the *Diwān-i Ām* sits the *Takht Mahal* (See: **Figure 33**; see also: **Plate 6 — I**), a royal residence of the *Bidargarh* with an impressive throne hall. Here the sultān would hold private audiences. This residence was completely surrounded by its own high, defensible wall, and there were rooms available for the sultān's personal use. Access to the whole of the *Takht Mahal*, of course, was limited and carefully guarded.

A singular structure within the *Bidargarh* is the *Solah Khamba Masjid* (aka: "The Sixteen Pillar Mosque," *Jami Masjid*) (See: **Figure 34**; see also: **Plate 6 — C**). It is noteworthy due to the fact that the columns employed to support the roof are round,[69] rather than square as was the custom in Hindu/Islamic India. Additionally, the plan of the *Solah Khamba Masjid* is rectangular — i.e. the length being three-and-one-half the depth. Although

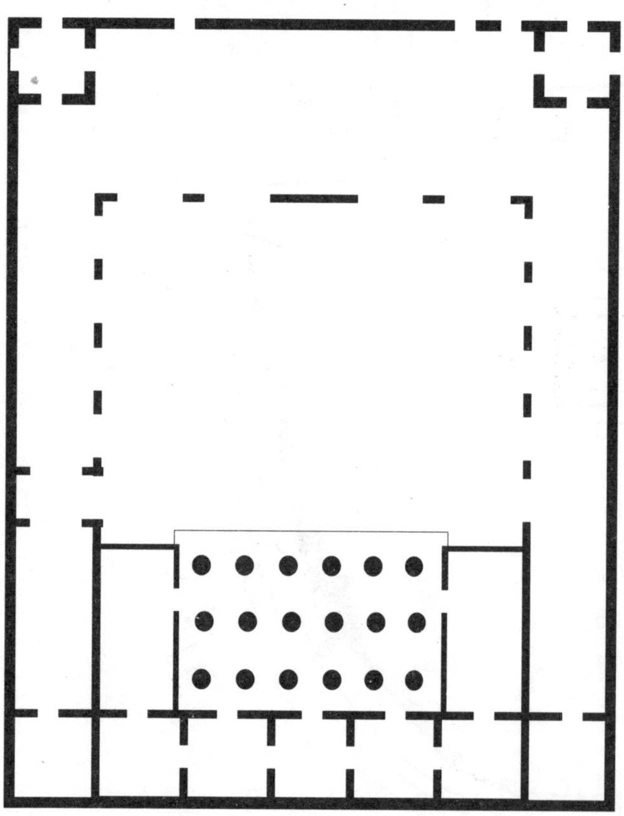

Figure 32 — *Diwān-i Ām*, Bidar Kotila

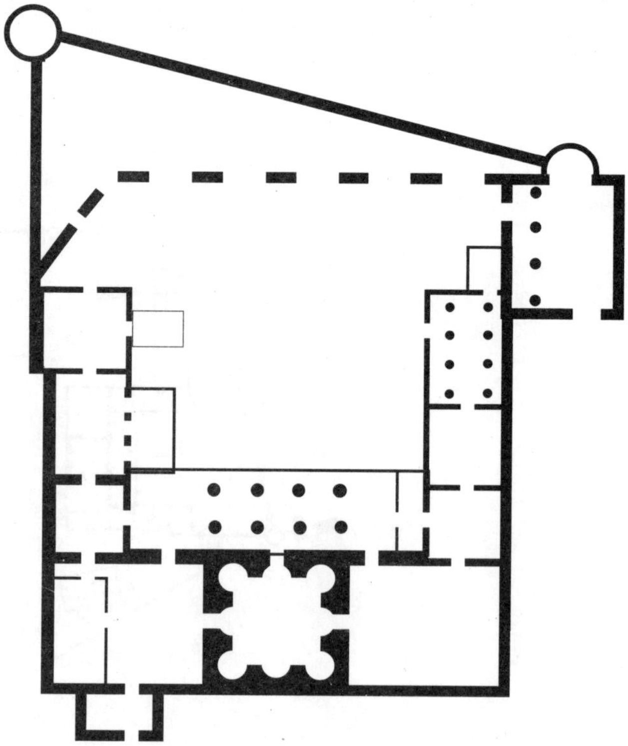

Figure 33 — *Takht Mahal, Bidar Kotila*

this shape would not have been common in Delhi and its environs, it is frequently seen in Gujarat and the Deccan.

With the exception of the earliest part of the *Bidargarh* — i.e. the *Rangin Mahal* and the structure immediately to the west — the later constructions tended towards a multiple perpendicular axiality, particularly a north-south orientation. The exception is, of course, the *Solah Khamba Masjid* which is oriented towards Mecca.

Certainly, the *Bidargarh* with its vast area was not as easily defended as citadels which were more compact or with high defensive walls rising from higher escarpments. An assault from several directions would have spread the defenders too thin and would, ultimately cause its breach and downfall. The reason that it lasted as long as it did was that its army, in the early years, were well trained, highly mobile and committed warriors. An attacking force would have been met on an open field of battle where the disciplined Bidar forces would have predominated. In the later years complacency took over the Barid Shahi Dynasty and the rulers felt more comfortable ensconced in their vast fort, the *Bidargarh,* and attended by their courtiers. Ultimately, this was an unwise position.

Now the *Bidargarh* is in ruins. Immense power and an overweening predilection for the good life ate away at the fabric of this state. A sad demise for a once great state and its capital.

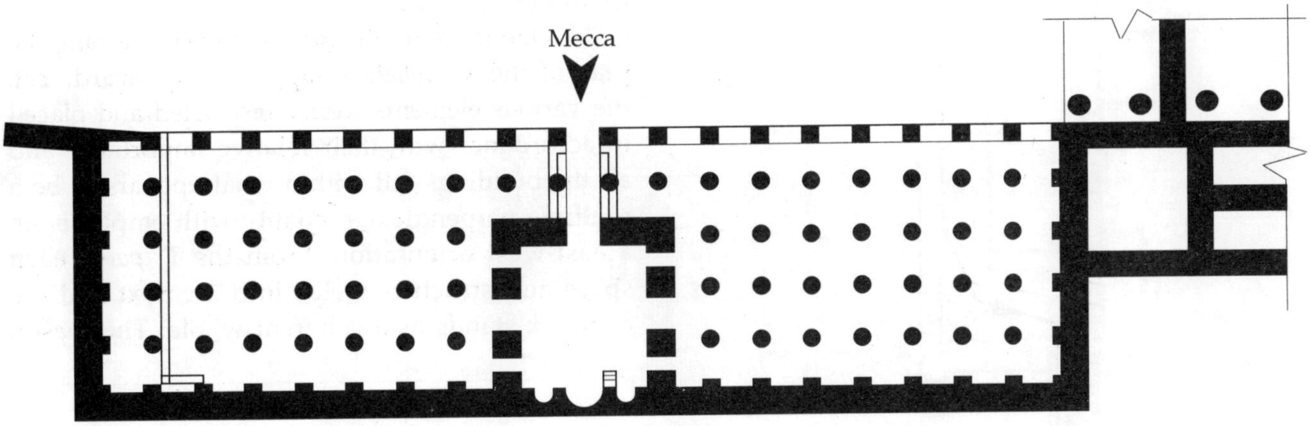

Figure 34 — *Solah Khamba Masjid, Bidar Kotila* indicating orientation

Kumbhalgarh, Chittor

(a. 1433 CE)

Situated atop an imposing hill, the *qilā* of Chittor, initially constructed by Bappa Rawal, was considered virtually impregnable. If an invader wished to proceed into the Rajputana states of the west then Chittor had to be taken. The original citadel was vastly enlarged and developed by Kumbhakarna Singh (r. 1433-1468). The *garh mahal* bears his name — i.e. the *Kumbhalgarh* (aka *Rana Kumbha Mandir* or *Kumbhalmer*) — as a fitting tribute to this Sisodia Rajput ruler.

The *Kumbhalgarh*[70] of Chittor is rather typical of the general layout found in the design of palace architecture throughout most of India. It, as most, consists of a series of structures — i.e. residential areas, stables, audience halls, a large open courtyard, often a subsidiary courtyard for the harem, an imposing gate, all enclosed within a substantial, defensible wall. Indeed, the palaces of the Indian rulers, whether Muslim or Hindu, whether Sultān or Mahārājāh, until the nineteenth century, were always heavily fortified residences much in the same mould as Medieval European castles. Here life was lived in varying degrees of opulence, but always with the sword of disaster hanging low.

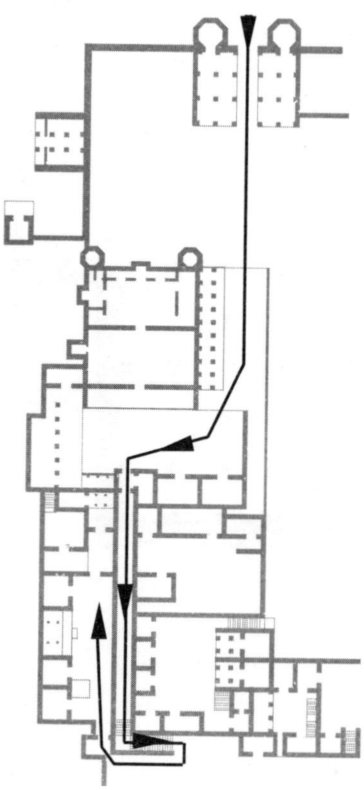

Figure 35 — *Kumbhalgarh,* indicating path from the *Tripolia*

The *Kumbhalgarh* was at one point in Rajput history a most important site being controlled by the powerful and ancient Sisodia Rajputs. Prior to the sixteenth century, Chittor was the capital of this most powerful state — i.e. Mewar. However, power, or seats of power are often challenged. So too was Chittor. In the sixteenth century this well-designed and apparently easily defendable fort was sacked — not once but twice — i.e. in 1535 by Gujarat under the leadership of Bahadur Shah, and in 1567 by The Great Mughal, Akbar.[71] As the last great outpost of Rajput independence and defiance against the Mughals it was finally abandoned in favor of Udaipur and time has taken its toll on this once grand site.

Due to its locale and the uneven terrain, the plan of the *Kumbhalgarh* appears haphazard. Yet, the various elements were constructed and placed in accordance with their relative importance and all the buildings fall within what appears to be a multiple perpendicular axiality with emphasis on a east-west orientation. From the *Tripolia*, each space and structure melds into the next and the complex stands as a coherent whole. The reason

Legend for **Plate 10**

A	Tripolia
B	Elephant Stables
C	Outer court
D	Sabhā
E	Reception area
F	Inner Stables
G	Residential suites
H	Zenānā Court
I	Kanwar Pade residence

Plate 10 — *Kumbhalgarh*, ground plan (partial)

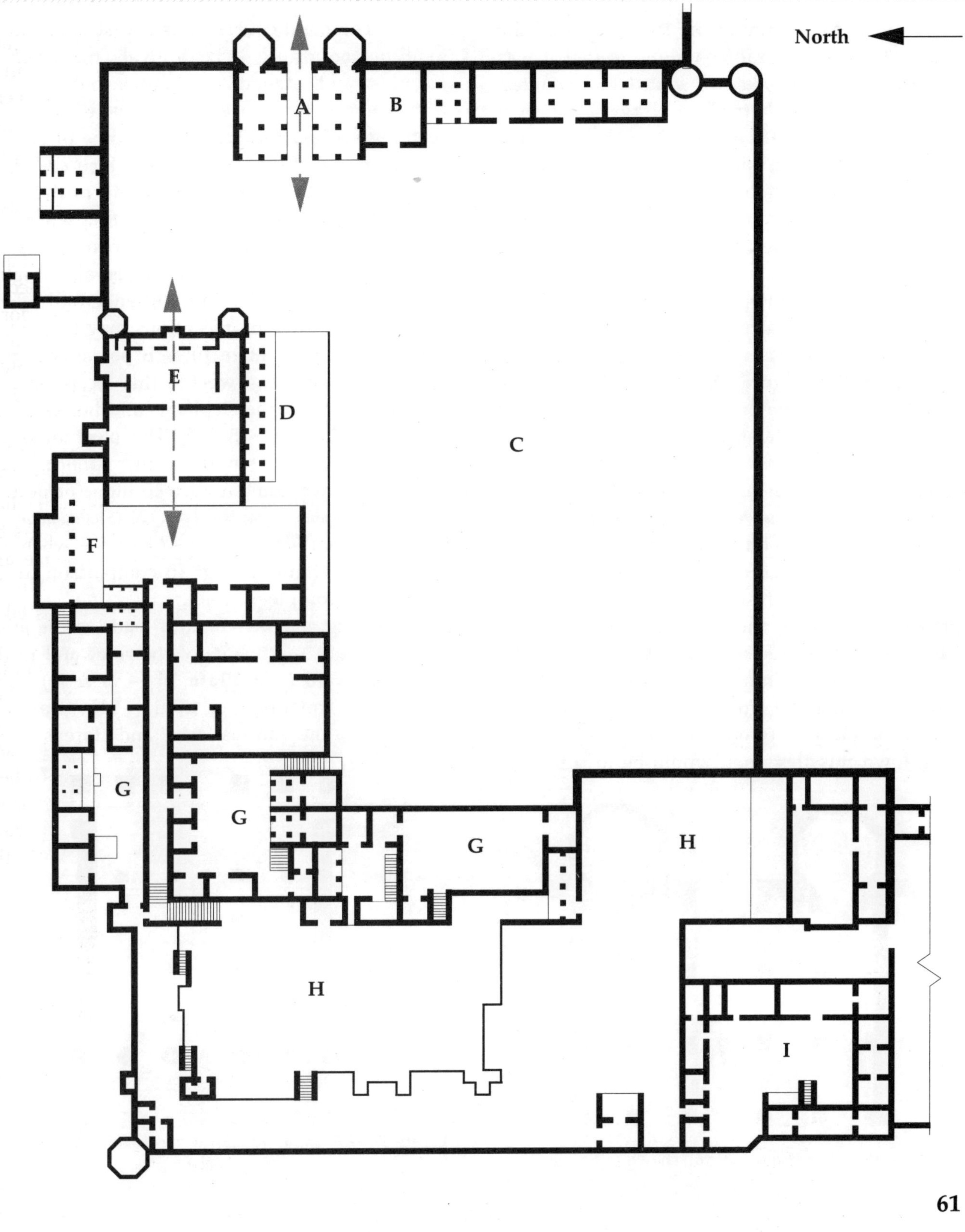

for this is to be found in the fact that the *Kumbhalgarh* is also rather unique in that it was designed by a single, known *sthapati*, the architect Mandan *putra* Kehetra.[72] A large courtyard dominates the plan of the *Kumbhalgarh*. An audience hall with an open pavilion for more public *darbārs* is adjacent to this court to the north — i.e. the *sabhā nivās* or *Diwān-i-Ām*. As one moves back, into the inner recesses, residential suites flow one into the other and at the back, the most remote area is the *zenānā*, the place for the women of the court. The royal apartments are deep within the *Kumbhalgarh* and any ingress or egress was closely monitored (See: **Figure 35**).

The main gate of the complex, as usual, is an easily defensible structure (See: **Figure 36**). Nonetheless, the *tripolia* of the *Kumbhalgarh* must be arrived at by passing through a series of other gates as the *Kumbhalgarh* is but one of several palace complexes found within the easily defended Chittor Qilā. Further, the *tripolia* of the *Kumbhalgarh* is interesting in that it follows the principle found in the *Propylaea* of the famed Athens's *Acropolis* (See: **Figure 37**). As in Athens, here a ramp leads into the courtyard (See: **Plate 3-B**) and is flanked from raised platforms from which the palace's troops can easily defend and rain down missiles upon would-be invaders.

The main courtyard is a vast area, suited to all manner of use — i.e. festivals, mass *darbārs*, parades and staged or mock battles. The *Kumbhalgarh* structure proper is a series of seemingly unrelated structures, some of several stories and all at different levels, which add to its labyrinthine character. To the north of the main courtyard is an open loggia, the *sabhā* where the ruler may sit for a public *darbār* or to review his troops, etc. (See: **Plate 10 — D**; see also: **Figure 35**). This is attached to an audience hall where more formal, intimate receptions may be held — *Diwān-i-Khās* (See: **Plate 10 — E**; see also: **Figure 38**). To the north and west of this reception area are the stables for the elephants and horses of the ruler (See: **Plate 10 — B & F**). This most important area is relatively small in the *Kumbhalgarh*, especially when comparing it to other palaces — e.g. the *Lāl Qilā*, Agra; the *Lāl Qilā* (*Shahjahanabad*), Delhi; *Fatehpur Sikri*, or *Gingee Mandir* — where the stables are relatively large in comparison to the size of the complex.

A long, narrow corridor leads to the areas of the private apartments of the ruler and to the *zenānā* beyond (See: **Plate 10 — G & H**). The private apartments vary in size, elevation and complexity. The various levels and storeys create

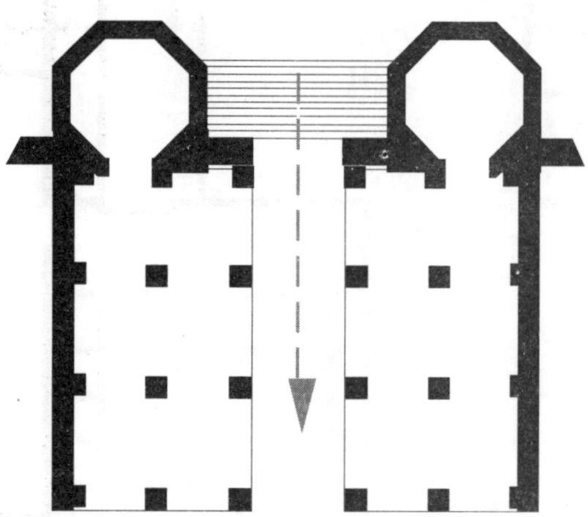

Figure 36 — *Kumbhalgarh*(detail) showing the *Tripolia*

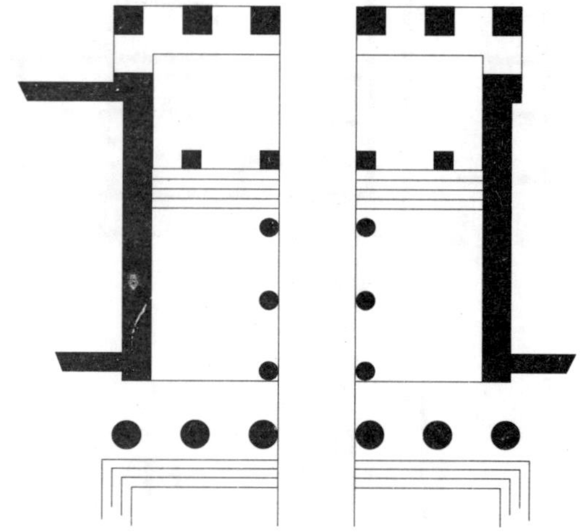

Figure 37 — *Propylaea* (detail), *Acropolis*, (5 c., BCE) Athens, Greece

a labyrinth of sorts. The most interesting aspect of the whole complex is the elaborate courtyard of the *zenānā* (See: **Plate 10 — H**). There are various extensions, stairs and levels elevated over what must have been a refreshing garden. This eclectic plan with its different levels would have made the confinement in this area more bearable.

The coherent design of the *Kumbhalgarh* is doubtless due to the hand of a single architect — i.e. Mandan *putra* Kesetra. Nonetheless, it also indicates something of the ruler Kumbhakarna Singh and the indomitable spirit of the Sisodia Rajput.

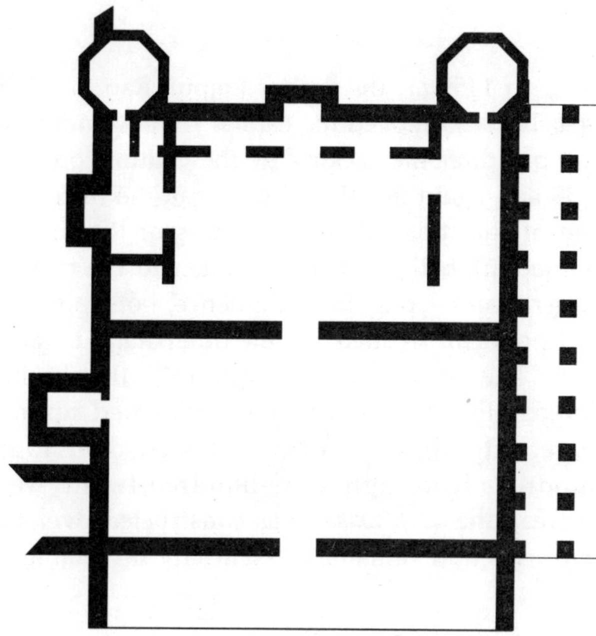

Figure 38 — *Kumbhalgarh* (detail) showing the *Sabhā* (right) and reception area (left)

Meherangarh, Jodhpur
(a. 1459 CE)

In 1459 CE, the Rathor Rajput, Rao Jodha (r. 1438-1489 CE) moved his capital from Mandore to Jodhpur after the sacking by the Chittor forces in 1438 and again in 1453. Thus began the history of one of the most notable capitals of Rajputana. Named after Rao Jodha, Jodhpur and the citadel, *Meherangarh,*[73] rose to prominence, both physical and political, rivalled by few other Rajput states.

The move of the capital to the highly defensible hill was fortuitous. Perched upon a huge outcropping which was well over four-hundred feet high (one-hundred-twenty-five metres), the *garh mahal* was constructed over the centuries and remained essentially inviolable to outside attack and/or sacking. But, it was not outside attack that Jodhpur had to fear. The obstreperous Mahārājā Jaswant Singh I (r. 1638-1678 CE), a thorn in the side of the Empire, died without apparent issue. Quickly the Emperor Aurangzeb absorbed Jodhpur into his troubled domain and Jodhpur remained without a ruler and subservient to the Empire until 1707. The Mahārājā Ajit Singh (r. 1707-1725 CE), having been *in utero* at the time of his father's death, reassumed the throne when Aurangzeb expired and this line continued to modern times.

As with all *garh mahal*s, whether Hindu or Muslim, there were well defined areas of access (See: **Figure 39**). The *zenānā* of the *Meherangarh* is one of the largest areas within the complex. This is not unusual. Frequently, rulers were away from their capital for long periods of time and the constant, onerous ceremonial duties that were required while in residence were considerable. Therefore, suitable and expansive areas were needed for the enjoyment and daily

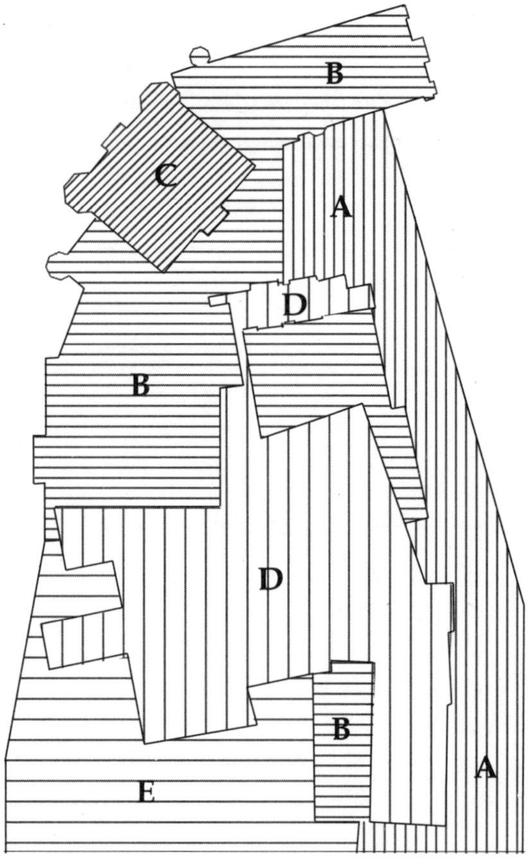

Figure 39 — Distribution of areas, *Meherangarh,* Jodhpur; public areas (**A**), limited access areas (**B**), restricted (**C**), *zenānā* (**D**), and, attendents and military (**E**)

Legend for **Plate 11**

A	Fateh Mahal
B	Phul Mahal (Sileh Khana below)
C	Shish Mahal
D	Umaid Vilas (Daulat Khana below)
E	Daulat Khana Chowk
F	Sardar Vilas
G	Mardānā Deodhi
H	Khabka Mahal (Dipak Mahal)
I	Khabka Mahal Chowk
J	Chandan Mahal
K	Jhanki Mahal
L	Singar Choki Chowk
M	Approach Ramp
N	Khasa Deodhi
O	Moti Mahal
P	Moti Mahal Chowk
Q	Zenānā Residences
R	Suraj Pol
S	Zenānā Residences
T	Zenānā Chowk
U	Zenānā Mahal
V	Temple
W	Zenānā Deodhi

Plate 11 — *Meherangarh,* Jodhpur, plan (partial) indicating multiple-non-perpendicular axes

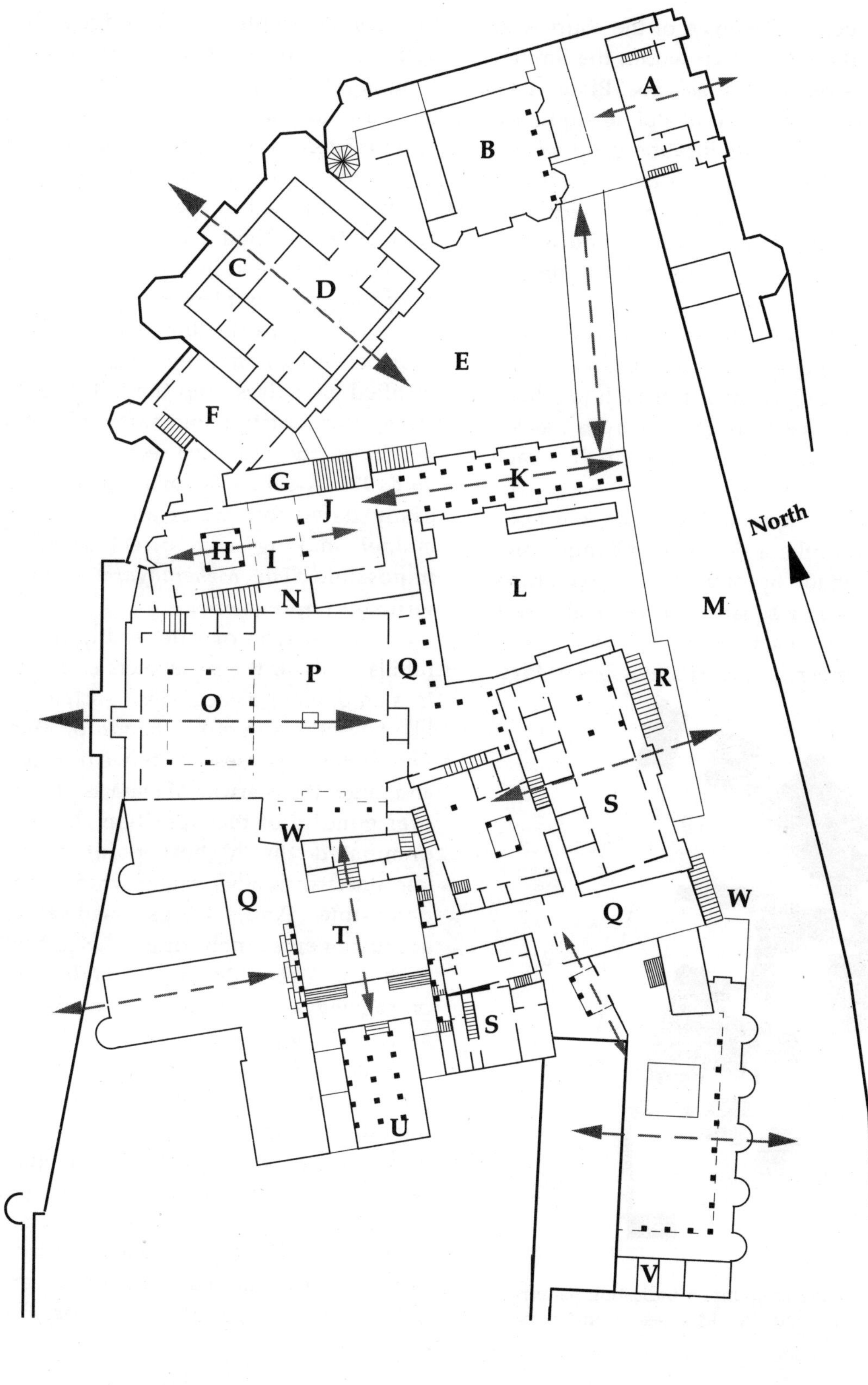

lives of the sequestered women of the court who did not follow the ruler. Deep within the limited access areas was the *Moti Mahal* (See: **Plate 11 — O**) which served as the Hall of Public Audience — i.e. the *Diwān-i Ām*.[74] Its location deep within the *chowk*s, *mahal*s and byways of the *Meherangarh* typifies this citadel. Stables and servants' residences were to be found to the south and not as extensive as those found in Vijayanagara or Bidar.

Direct access to the personal apartments of the *Mahārājā* is impossibly difficult. Unlike others, there is no direct, exterior access or path to follow. Rather, one must pass through numerous *chowk*s, buildings, stairways and rooms to finally reach the ruler's quarters.

Neither based upon a single axis, nor upon multiple perpendicular axes, Jodhpur's impressive *Meherangarh* is made up of a series of structures and courts typified by squares and rectangles each with their own orientation as well as a bewildering number of quadrilaterals (See: **Plate 11**). The assemblage is a hodgepodge with no apparent reason. It is asymmetrical with a vengeance![75] The pattern of *mahals*, *vilas*, pavilions, terraces, balconies and *chowks* (See: **Figure 40**) is more related to the way ancient cities developed — e.g. the warren of ways, byways and alleys of Delhi as opposed to the more ordered design of New Delhi — than a consistent variation on a theme such as seen in the *City Palace* of Udaipur or of the grid city plan of Jaipur.

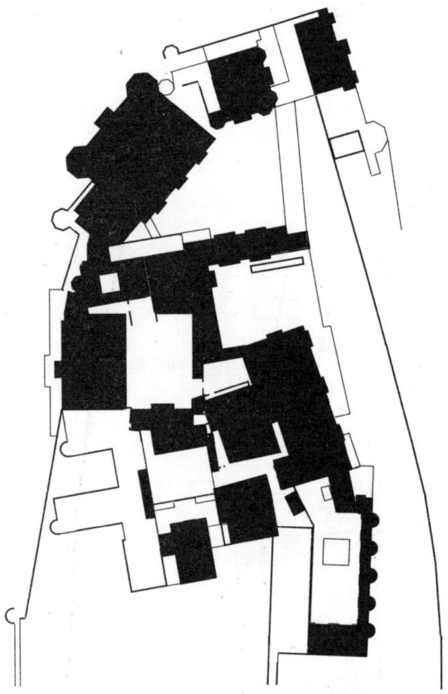

Figure 40 — *Meherangarh*, Jodhpur, indicating pattern of buildings, terraces and chowks as seen from above

Yet, as disorienting as it is the *Meherangarh* is, nonetheless, a most impressive *garh mahal*, well fortified as it rises atop the hill (See: **Figure 41**). Here, the fortifications are one of the most developed and extensive seen in India (See: **Plates 96 & 97**). A series of fortified, well placed and easily defensible walls and bastions gird the citadel making any direct attack virtually impossible. The *Meherangarh* of Jodhpur was virtually impregnable.

As an icon of rule, Jodhpur's *garh mahal* fulfills many of the parameters established earlier. It is an opulent palace which sustained a dynasty like few others in either Hindu or Muslim India. The dynasty possessed its weak rulers, but, by and large, the Marwar Mahārājās of Jodhpur were ever mindful of their position. The *Meherangarh* dominated the highest point in the valley, unconnected to other ridges which made it highly defensible. And, it possessed all the other accoutrements, including a large *zenānā* along with a bewildering conglomeration of passageways and *chowks* that made it worthy of an abode for a great ruler. On the other hand, Jodhpur's *garh mahal* assiduously avoided the basic plans so fundamental to the Hindu *śilpa śāstra*, including a strong preference towards axiality and symmetry. Its eclecticism, its apparent repudiation of accepted standards, its architectural design confusion is also manifest in the bewildering titles assumed by the rulers of this state — i.e. in order, they were entitled: the 1) Raos, 2) Rājās, 3) Sawai Rājās, 4) Mahārājās,

Meherangarh, Jodhpur (Concluded)

5) Mahārājā Dhiraj Mahārājās, 6) Raj Rajeshwar Saramand Raj-hai Hindustan Mahārājā Dhiraj Mahārājās, 7) Raj Rajeshwar Mahārājā Dhiraj Mahārājās, & 8) Raj Rajeshwar Mahārājādhiraj Shri of Jodhpur (See: **Appendix B**).

Nonetheless, it is to be noted that this citadel stood and still stands. Its rulers, with the exception of the brief period during Aurangzeb's reign, continued to sit upon the royal *gaddi* of Marwar until the dissolution of the Princely States in 1948. And, the *Meherangarh* continued to grow well into the twentieth century. It was and is a viable force in this part of India.

It cannot be said that the reason for its continued viability is due to its eccentric plan. Nor can it be seen to be due to a long line of relatively able rulers. Jodhpur had its dissolute and weak rulers sitting on the *gaddi*. Its locale and defenses made it virtually impregnable for its time. This was fortuitous for the Rathors.

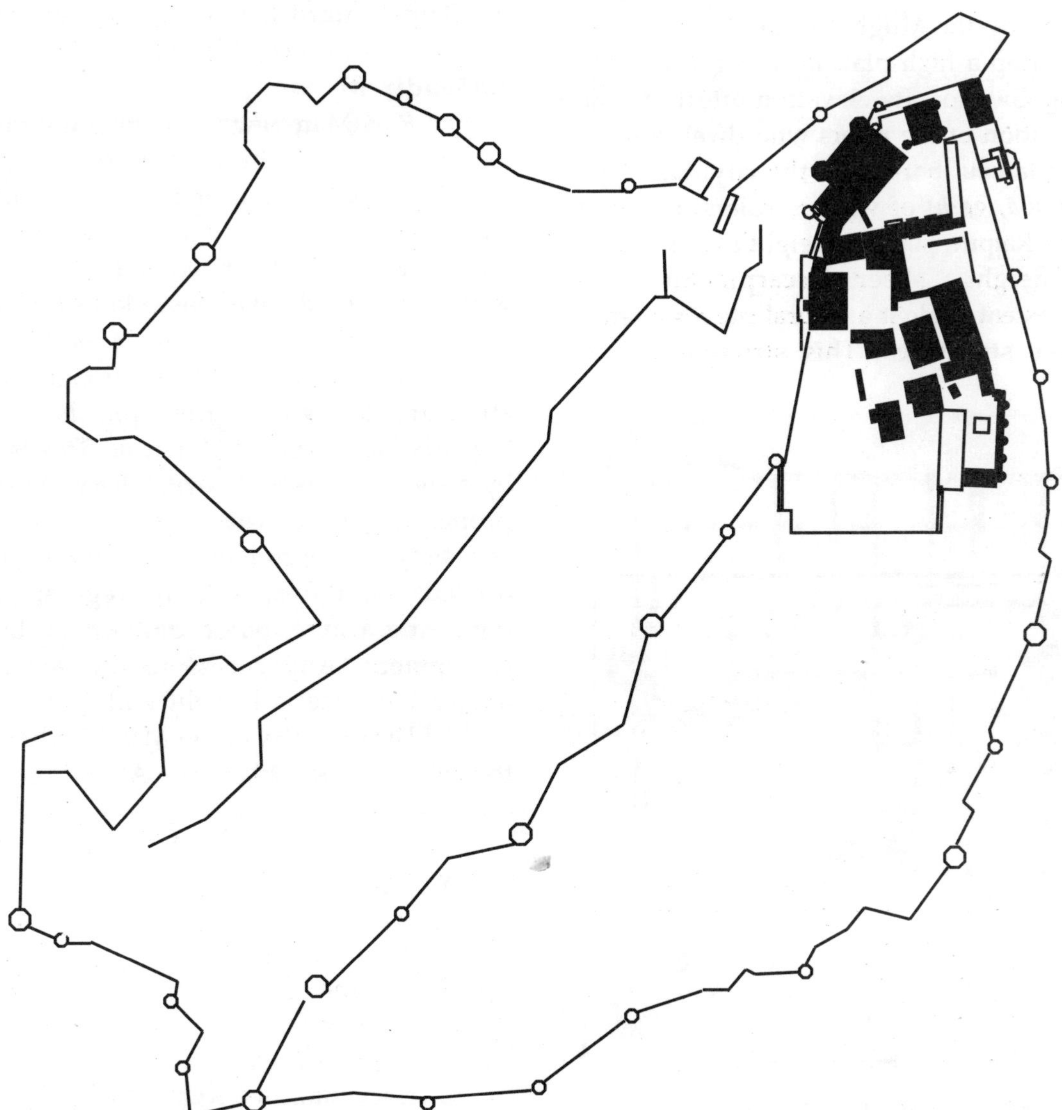

Figure 41 — *Meherangarh,* Jodhpur, indicating the complete primary and secondary fortifications

Mān Mandir, Gwalior

(a. 1486 CE)

Rājā Man Singh Tomar (r. 1486-1516 CE), the most celebrated and powerful of the later Tomar Rajputs, constructed a fortified citadel which was and is known throughout the land. The *Mān Mandir*,[76] also referred to as *Chit Mandir* (painted palace), is acknowledged as one of the most heavily fortified fort/palaces of its period in India. It is also one of the most beautiful — even coveted by the Mughal Emperor. The *Mān Mandir* sits atop a high plateau in regal majesty, overlooking Gwalior. Its elevation attests to the elevated position of the rulers who dwell within.

This plateau, bordering the city, had held forts (Ind.: *qilā, garh*) of various rulers, many of whom were Rajput, since the eighth century. Its location, height, sheer escarpments and treacherous ascent made it a natural site for a series of defensive structures. This stronghold was captured and amalgamated into the Delhi Sultanate, during its most vibrant period, in the thirteenth century. In 1398 the older fortress and surrounding lands were retaken by Rājā Bir Singh Deo (r. 1486-1516), a Tomar, and the kingdom rose to glorious heights. This Rajput dynasty lasted a bit more than one-hundred years when it again fell, after the reign of the mighty Rājā Man Singh Tomar, this time to the Great Mughals. It was not to be re-inhabited by the Rajputs until the eighteenth century by the Sindha (Scindias [Shinde]) Dynasty (See: **Appendix B**).

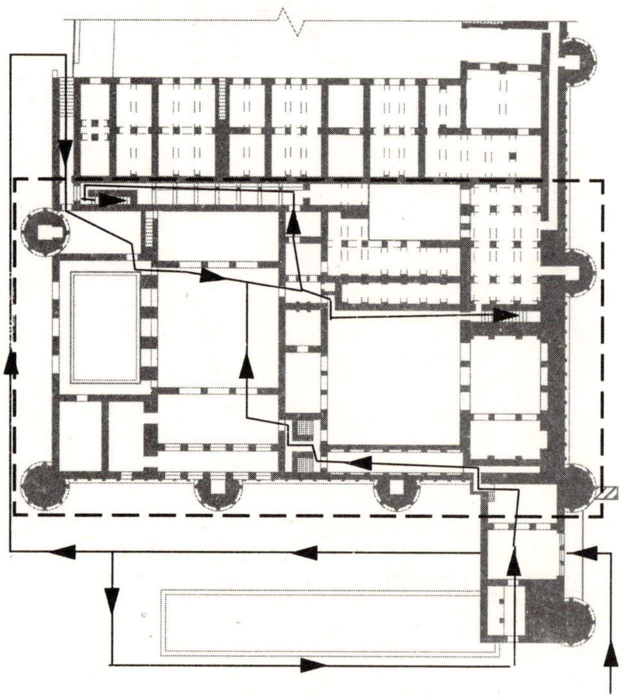

Figure 42 — *Mān Mandir*, indicating paths from the *Hāthī Pol* & the Royal quarters of the *mandir* (— — —)

Rājā Man Singh is known not only as the driving force behind the re-emergence of Gwalior's political and military ascendancy of this early period, he is also known as an important patron of the arts, particularly music. Little wonder he would have caused to be built a palace/ fort of such distinction as the *Mān Mandir*.

Access to this *mandir* is through a large gate structure known as the *Hiṇḍolā Pol*, found towards the base of the plateau. This is followed by a steep ascent with switch-backs to the palace proper at the top. The hallmark of this complex is a series of round towers topped with open, domed pavilions set at regular intervals bordering a long, outer wall which defines the escarpment. Any access to the *mandir* by an aggressive force is fraught with peril.

Direct access to the *Mān Mandir* is through the *Hāthī Pol* (See: **Plate 12 - A**) and up a ramp to

Legend for **Plate 12**

- A Hāthī Pol
- B Ramp
- C First Court
- D Second Court
- E Reception
- F Private areas
- G Servents and Retainers
- H Principal Entrance
- I Vikramaditya Mahal

Plate 12 — *Mān Mandir*, main level plan (partial)

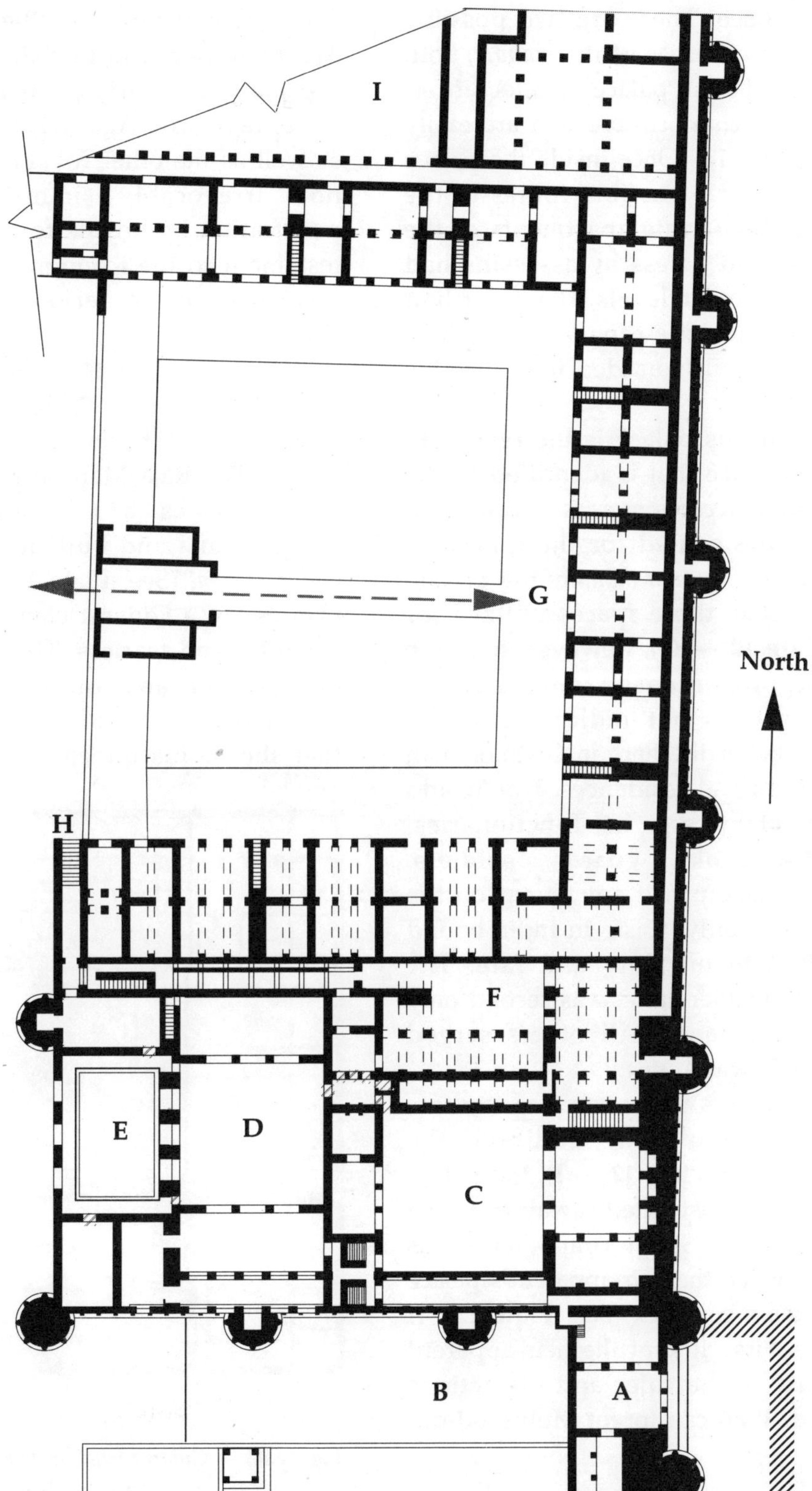

the level of the palace. There are two possible entrances into the royal areas of the *mandir*, both are in keeping with Indian palace architecture — i.e. they are rather circumlocutions and are easily defended (See: **Figure 42**). Once inside the palace there are, again, several possible routes to the upper floors and the private apartments of the Rājā. If any unwanted access by assassins had been gained to the lower levels, the ruler had any one of several paths of escape, each of which would have been heavily guarded to assure his safety.

Of interest in this palace is the relatively small, two storied space that is identified as the royal quarters with its reception areas as compared to the large area designated for the retainers. Normally, in Indian *qilās cum mandirs* the private areas are smaller than those spaces utilized for support (See: **Plate 12 — G**), however, here the private areas are, proportionally, much smaller. Nonetheless, this does not indicate that the retainers had any better life here in Gwalior than in any other of the royal residences. Nor would the numbers of retainers — i.e. functionaries, maids, eunuchs, cooks, guards, soldiers, gardeners, etc. — have posed any threat on the royal person or his family. Caste in India bound each, inextricably, to his duty and fate. The kṣatriya, the warrior/ruler caste, was second only to the priestly brāhmaṇas. All others served without question. It was *karma*.[77]

Nonetheless, access to the royal apartments was physically difficult. In addition the *Vikramaditya Mahal* (See: **Plate 12 — I**), the palace of the successor, was constructed away from the apartments of Rājā Man Singh Tomar. This was generally the case when the heir-apparent's palace was part of the main complex (See: **Plate 12**). It served a purpose. First, it kept the heir apparent in close proximity to the ruler and his actions closely monitored. Who can forget Muhiy-ud-din Aurangzeb?

The beauty and elegance of the *Mān Mandir* were not lost on the Empire. Babur found the *qilā* particularly pleasing and he spent time there, regularly. Again, it is noteworthy that this, as well as the other royal *qilā* and/or *mandir* was not irrevocably immune from ultimate penetration by hostile forces. Yet, it stands as a testament to the iconographic necessity of royal residences of the period.

Gujari Mahal

(1510 CE)

The Rājā Man Singh Tomar took for one of his wives a Gujarati by the name of Mriganayana and built for her a residence, the *Gujari Mahal* (See: **Plate 13**).[78] Mṛganayana was a princess of a Gujarat clan whom, it is said, was beautiful and fearless. The Rājā, upon seeing her desired her and offered to marry her. She accepted his offer of marriage with the proviso that she be his queen and that he provide her

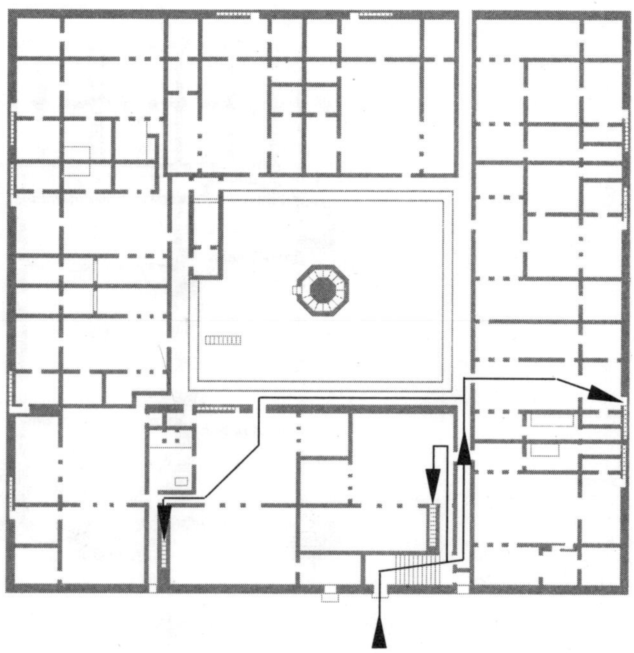

Figure 43 — *Gujari Mahal*, indicating but three paths from the south entrance

Plate 13 — *Gujari Mahal*, ground plan

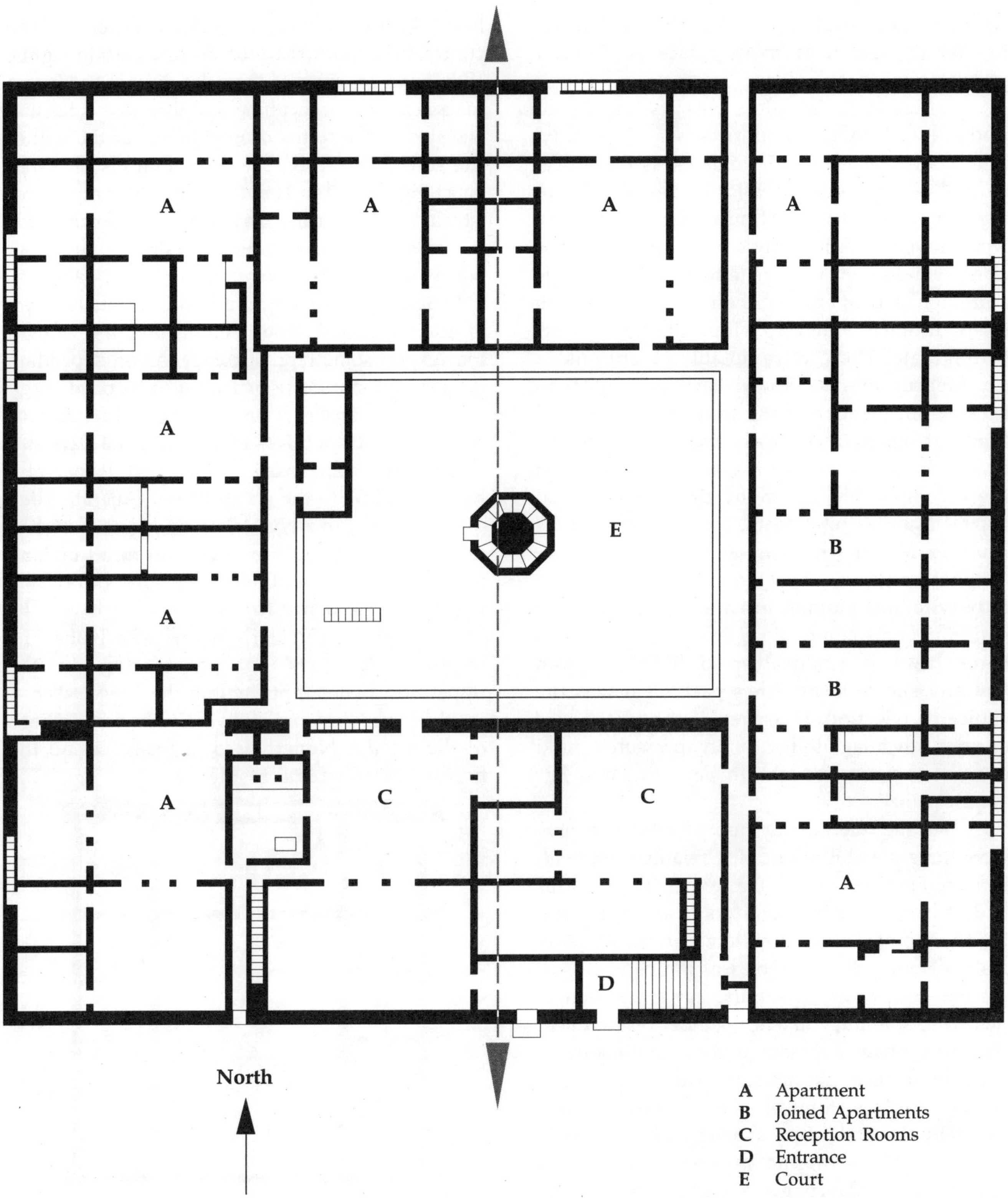

A Apartment
B Joined Apartments
C Reception Rooms
D Entrance
E Court

with an appropriate residence. He constructed for her the *Gujari Mahal*, a palace of singular importance.

Marriage for rulers was seldom based upon "love," in the modern sense. Generally, union between man and woman was a political as well as economic necessity or desirability for royal matches. To the Hindu and the Muslim, women were and, in many cases, still are "second class," subservient to their fathers until marriage and then a property of their husbands. Even today, ultimate authority within the family rests in the male. There were notable exceptions — e.g. Mehrun-un-nisa, known later as Nur Jahan became not just one of the wives of the Mughal Emperor Jahangir, but was elevated to hold the title of Empress, and of course, who can forget the incomparable Arjumand Banu, also called Hazrat Mumtaz-uz-Zamani, best remembered as Mumtāz Mahal who was taken as wife by the Mughal emperor, Shah Jahan and became not only wife and mother, but was the emperor's confidant and companion, companion even in battle. It was generally accepted that if a woman had any choice in her life's partner, it was the choice of rejection. However, if the match was of great advantage to her family, pressures could and often were brought to bear to force her acquiescence.

For the ruler, or any man of substance, here were three possibilities in their relationships with women. First was to take the woman as wife. This had obvious economic and political advantages for the woman and ultimately her family. Any male offspring of this union was in line to rule or assume control of the family. For the Muslims, there was one impediment — under *Shariah* law, a man may have only four wives at any one time. The Hindu rulers did not suffer such a restriction. Nonetheless, the status of wife was elevated and, generally the first wife was paramount. Secondly a ruler, Hindu or Muslim, may have any number of concubines. Concubinage, particularly in Asia, had certain prestige. It was entered into contractually and the woman had certain rights. If the wife or wives of the ruler did not produce a male heir and a concubine did, then that child was elevated to the status of next-in-line at the will of the ruler. Certainly, the most famous of Asian concubine was Tsu Hsi, the Dowager Empress of China. Finally, a ruler may take any woman as his mistress for however long he desired — an Asian equivalent of the European *droit du seigneur*, although, not applying to a bride. Generally, there is no contractual arrangement. But, the woman may expect some type of compensation depending on her status or caste or length of "service."

The construction of a residence for Mriganayana doubtless may have been part of a "prenuptial," contractual arrangement. It may also have been due to the status of the Gujarati wife/ queen, or she, like Nur Jahan or Mumtāz Mahal, may have captured the heart and mind of Man Singh Tomar. Nonetheless, he did build this impressive residence for her.

What is particularly noteworthy is that the *Gujari Mahal* was not constructed on the uppermost plateau, but within the *Hiṇḍolā Pol* — i.e. the lower gate, but still within the fortifications of the *mandir*. Nonetheless, it possesses all the necessities of a royal residence.

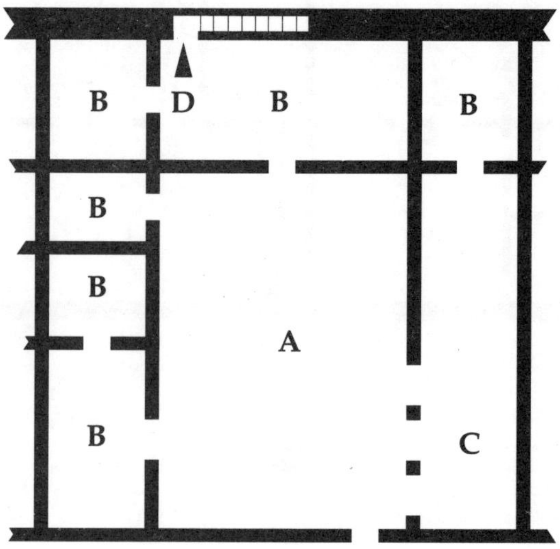

Figure 44 — *Gujari Mahal*, indicating a typical apartment

Mān Mandir (Concluded)

As with any royal structure, admittance to the inner recesses is severely restricted physically (See: **Figure 44**). Based upon a plan that is referred to as a *mardānā* design,[79] the spaces of the *Gujari Mahal* are formed around an open court (See: **Plate 13 — E**) where the residents may move about unseen by the outer world. Here, the court is supplied with a tower which may have served for the enjoyment of the women or for an area of privacy. The outer wall of the *Gujari Mahal* is thicker, without windows and fortress-like, appropriate to a structure reserved for women. The residence is made up of nine apartments (See: **Plate 13 — A & B**) on the ground floor with numerous rooms, each separate from the other, but all opening onto the central court. Two of these nine apartments are joined by a connecting door (See: **Plate 13 — B**). Typically, the apartments possess six or eight rooms — i.e. a reception room (See: **Figure 44 — A**) with smaller rooms (See: **Figure 44 — B**) leading off this area, one of the rooms with an arcaded opening (See: **Figure 44 — C**) and a stairway (See: **Figure 44 — D**) concealed in the wall of every apartment and leading to the second storey. It is to be noted that none of these apartments have windows facing out, but only openings facing the inner court. There are two other stairways. These lead from the reception areas of the ground floor (See: **Plate 13 — C**), again to the second storey. These two suites possess two other rooms or spaces with an arcade opening on to the main area. Neither has a private room as do the apartments. The design of the *Gujari Mahal* with its thick outer walls, overhanging eaves and the absence of large windows is such that the internal rooms would have been somewhat cooler than the outside.

The *Gujari Mahal* may have been built for Mriganayana, but, obviously, its design suggests that it also served as a *zenānā*. Each wife or concubine would have had an apartment of their own, complete with room(s) for their personal retainers. It is also noteworthy that with the exception of the two eastern, connecting apartments, all others are relatively similar implying some equality of those who would have occupied these suites. The rooms of the second storey are similarly disposed.

Finally, the *Gujari Mahal* has something to say of the relationship between husband and wife in India during this period. Whether Hindu or Muslim, it is apparent that there were relationships in which the woman possessed some power or status beyond being a mere possession. Additionally, it is also apparent that there were men in India, rulers whose make-up was such that they either allowed or were compelled to share some of their power with a wife/companion. The results of these unions have ultimately produced spectacular results — e.g. the *Tomb of I'timad-ud-daula*, the *Tāj Mahal* and the *Gujari Mahal.*

Gingee Mandir, Gingee

(a.1490 CE)

Home and fortress of the northern *nāyakas* during and after Vijayanagara's rule, the Gingee *qilā* is composed of a triangular fortress — i.e. anchored by three hills which are: Krishnagiri to the north which is the most developed, Rājagiri to the west, and ChandRāyandurg to the south (See: **Appendix A, Plate 96**). These triangular-spaced hills are high, difficult to ascend, and well fortified rocky escarpments. The *garh mahal* and its compound sets within a series of walls nestled between these three, tall outcropping, and all buried within the Eastern Ghats. Once it gained independence, the *nāyakas* of Gingee reigned supreme during the 16th and 17th centuries in this region.

Around the year 1490, the Vijayanagara Rāya Krishnadeva named Tubaki Krishnappa: Nāyaka (governor) of Gingee. He became known as Krishnappa I. Although Gingee had been a fortified centre as early as 1240 CE, it was during the rule of Krishnappa I that the present layout of the *garh mahal* was established. Later, it was re-fortified under the Maratha Chatrapati Śivaji and again Gingee assumed major importance.

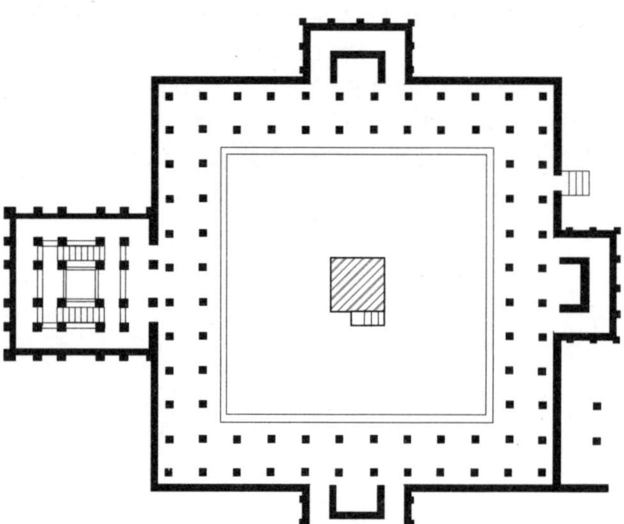

Figure 45 — *Kalyāṇa Mahal*

During the later reign of Vijayanagara and when this great empire was coming under attack from the northern Muslim Sultanates, Gingee declared its independence and there the *nāyakas* ruled. Also, the provinces of Thanjavur (Tanjore) and Madurai (See: *Nāyaka Mandir*, following) declared their independence from Vijayanagara. For a brief period, after the downfall of the Maratha Confederation, Gingee again assumed its independence under Rājā Sarup Singh (r. 1691-1714). But it was short lived. Rājā Sarup Singh's son, the young Rājā Desingh in 1714 did battle with the Nawāb of Arcot and was killed. Gingee as an independent state ceased to exist. Constant war and time has not treated Gingee well. All that remains of the powerful *qilā* are a few partially intact structures and many ruins.

The royal compound of the *nāyakas* of Gingee did not compare in scope or luxury to Vijayanagara its political and aesthetic antecedent. Nonetheless, it possessed its own greatness. Protected on a raised valley, guarded by three elevated fortress hills the *Giṅgee Mandir*[80] developed.

The *Gingee* complex consisted of a number of stately buildings. Certainly the most impressive, and relatively complete, is the *Kalyāṇa Mahal* (See: **Plate 14 — B**; and **Figure 45**). The *Kalyāṇa Mahal* is considered to have been reserved for the women of the court — i.e. the *zenānā*.

Legend for **Plate 14**

- **A** Gate
- **B** Kalyāṇa Mahal
- **C** Bathing Tank
- **D** Stables & Quarters
- **E** Parade Grounds (chowk)
- **F** Reviewing Platform
- **G** Royal Residence
- **H** Retainers' Quarters
- **I** 'Gymnasium'

Plate 14 — *Gingee Mandir*, main palace compound (partial)

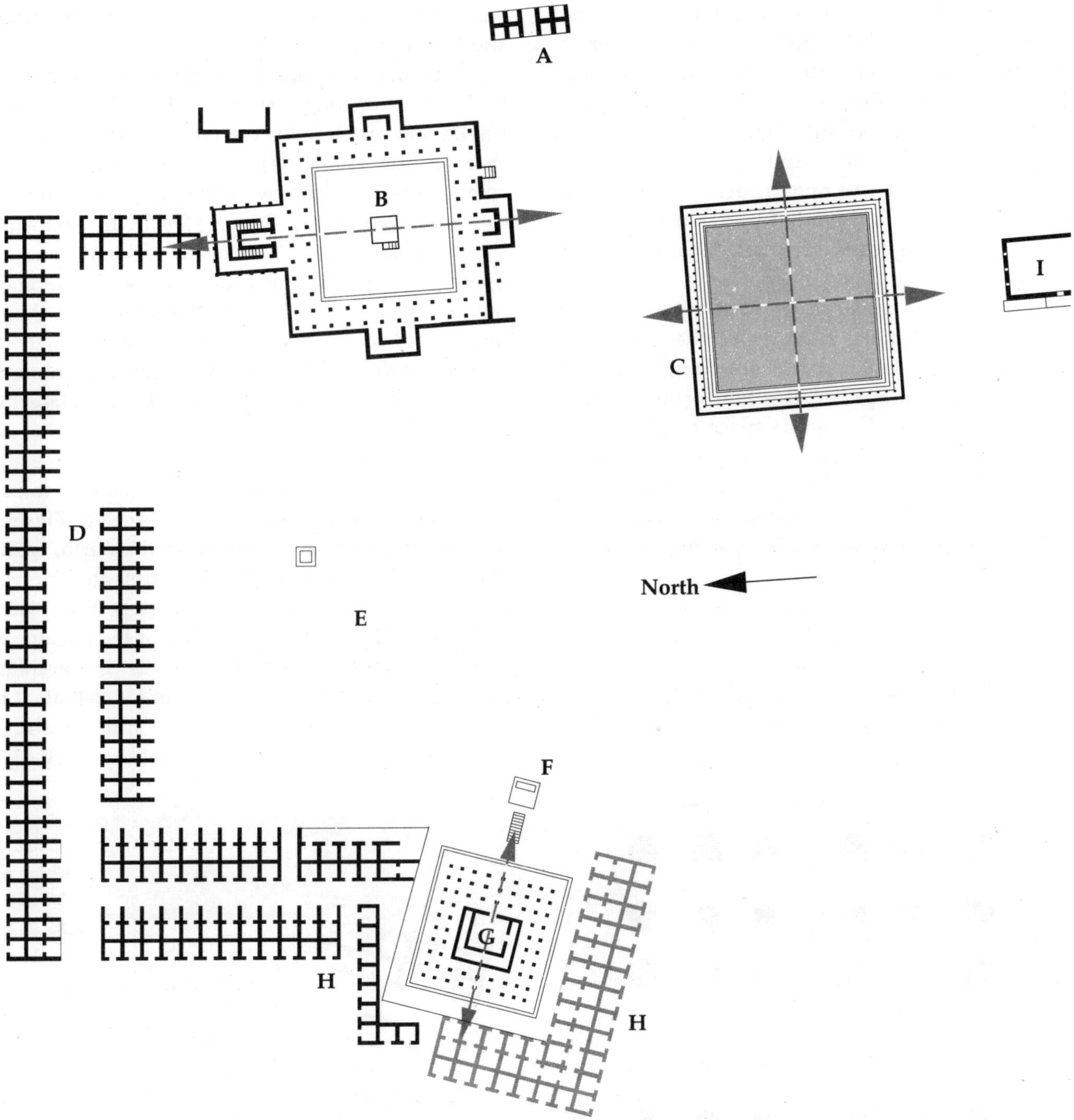

Basically square *en plan* with extensions to the north, east and south, and a six storey tower to the west. The outer wall of the first storey has but a single opening — i.e. an entrance on the south wall. This would effectively shield the prying eyes of all males and protect the women within the *zenānā*. An open court dominates the central portion, surrounded by what may have been apartments for the women. Finally, a small tank rests in the centre of the court. Above the first storey, the tower is faced on its four sides with arched openings from which the women of the court could look out without being observed (See: **Figure 46**). Further, this multi-storey tower would have provided ample space on the upper floors for the privacy and security of the *nāyaka*. A final space appears above the sixth, full storey. This is capped by a pyramidal form. This space, this room was only accessible by a single narrow stair from the sixth floor — a suitable trysting site for the *nāyaka*.

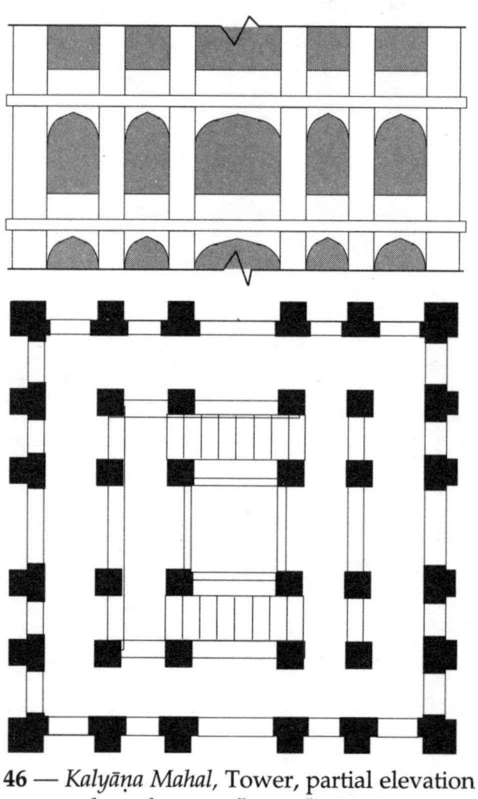

Figure 46 — *Kalyāṇa Mahal,* Tower, partial elevation (top), plan of upper floors (bottom)

To the north and west of the *Kalyāṇa Mahal* are a series of long structures thought to be the stables and quarters for the retainers of the *nāyaka* (See: **Plate 14 — D**). As with many royal compounds, these are by far the largest structures, *en toto*, found in the *Gingee Mandir*. In part, the *nāyaka's* hold on the power of the region depended upon a substantial armed force. These stables and quarters could have housed the force with their horses and elephants. The stables and quarters, with the *Kalyāṇa Mahal* bracket a large open area — i.e. the parade grounds or *chowk* (See: **Plate 14 — E**).

West of the *Kalyāṇa Mahal*, on a rise of ground is found a ruined structure thought to be the royal residence (See: **Plate 14 — G**; & **Figure 47**). The *mandir* is surrounded on the north, west and south with additional compartmented ruins, probably additional Retainer's Quarters (See: **Plate 14 — H**; & **Figure 47**). At the base of the rise upon which the *mandir* rests and to the east is a granite platform — a reviewing platform (See: **Plate 14 — F**). It would have been easy, and certainly dramatic for the resplendent *nāyaka* to regally

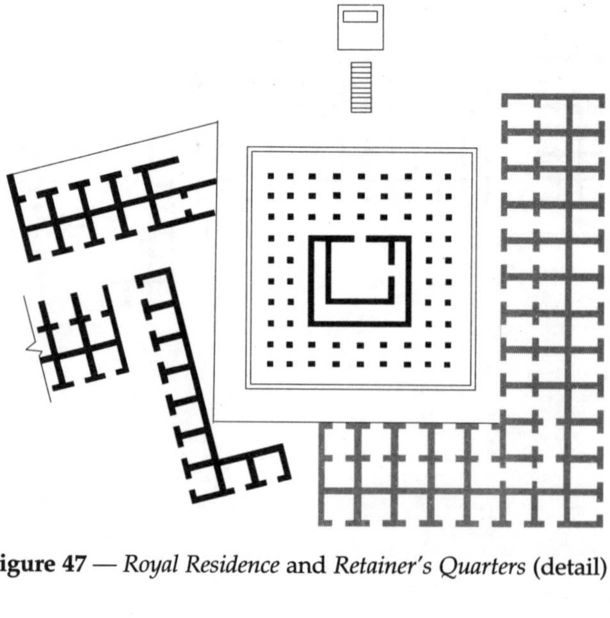

Figure 47 — *Royal Residence* and *Retainer's Quarters* (detail)

process down the stairs from his residence to the platform to observe his troops. This type of 'reviewing stand' was popular in Vijayanagara (See: **Plate 3 — N**).

To the south of the *Kalyāṇa Mahal* is to be found a large bathing tank (See: **Plate 14 — C**; & **Figure 48**). This tank is cut out of the surrounding rock and surrounded by a covered colonnade. Access to this area is limited and once entrance was gained, one could walk down the dramatic, encompassing steps to the cooling water. Bathing was not the sole prerogative of the royal or wealthy. In India at this time, unlike Europe,[81] bathing was a daily occurrence even for the lower castes. It was not merely a physical cleansing, but it possessed religious, ritual significance as well. However, the tanks that are found within the royal compounds of India emphasize the elevated station of the ruler. He need not process to a river or stream to cleanse his person in public.

There are other buildings and traces of structures scattered across this compound. To the south of the large bathing tank is a building identified as a gymnasium (See: **Plate 14 — I**). Similar structures are found up on the Krishnagiri.

A *qilā* of a lesser ruler, a lesser state, the *Gingee Mandir* is, nonetheless, a compound of no mean value and/or size. It emphasizes, in part, the wealth of Medieval India and the numerous rulers who governed this vast subcontinent.

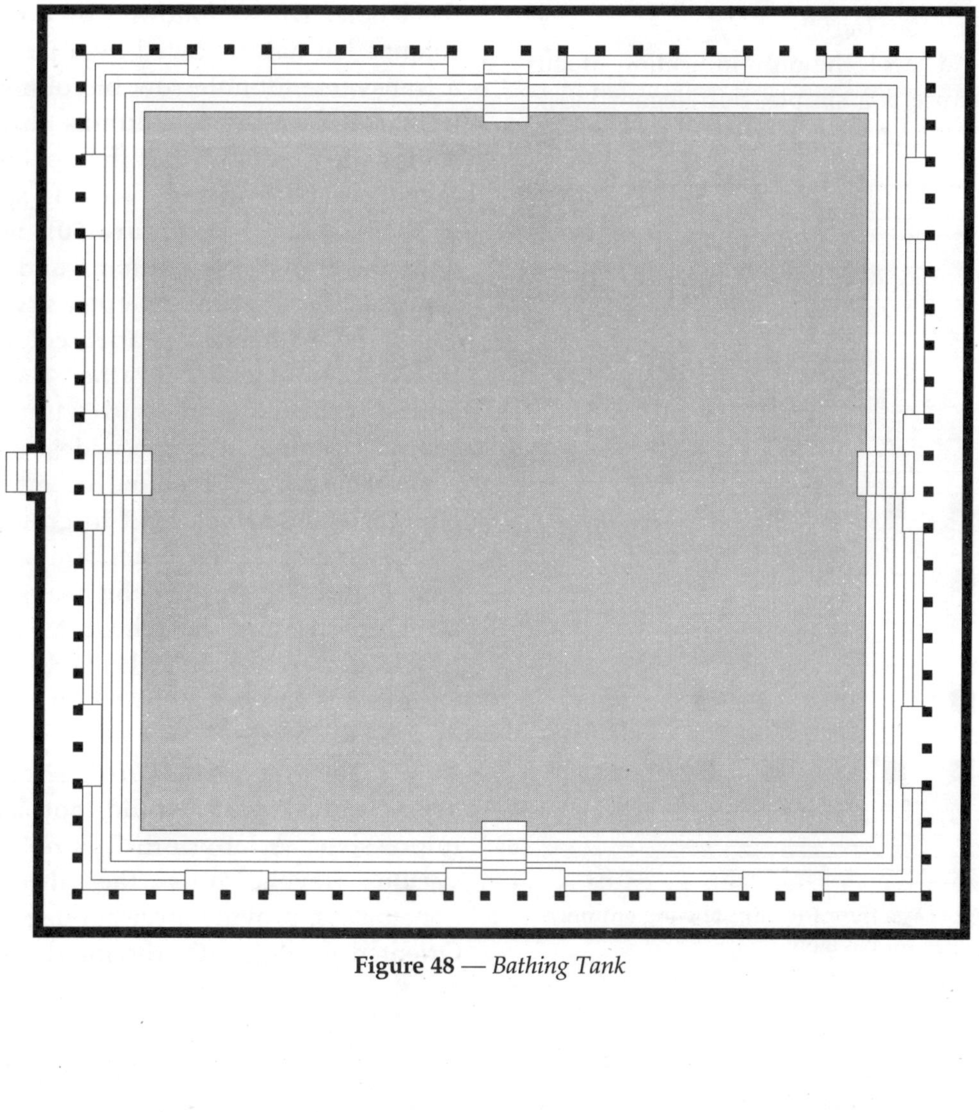

Figure 48 — *Bathing Tank*

Wav Dādā Harir (Baoli Bai Hari), Asarwa

(1499 CE)

Gujarat possesses a number of singular architectural achievements — i.e. wells. Wells which take on an architectural character of their very own. They are not merely simple engineering endeavors which allow for the drawing of buckets of water, but relatively vast architectural endeavours in their own right. These wells (Ind.: *baoli, bauli*) offered considerable relief from the incredibly high temperatures of western India throughout the 'oft prolonged dry season.

During the reign of Nasir-ud-Din Mahmud Shah I Beghara (r. 1459-1511 CE) such a well was constructed near the royal city of Ahmadabad in Asarwa and is now referred to as the *Wav Dādā Harir* or the *Baoli Bai Hari*.[82]

At ground level, the only indication of this elaborate structure is a simple, but elegant kiosk. Square, *en plan*, and surmounted with a dome, this structure sits atop a broad stepped base (See: **Figures 49**; see also: **Plate 16**). Its aspect indicates both Hindu and Islamic influences.

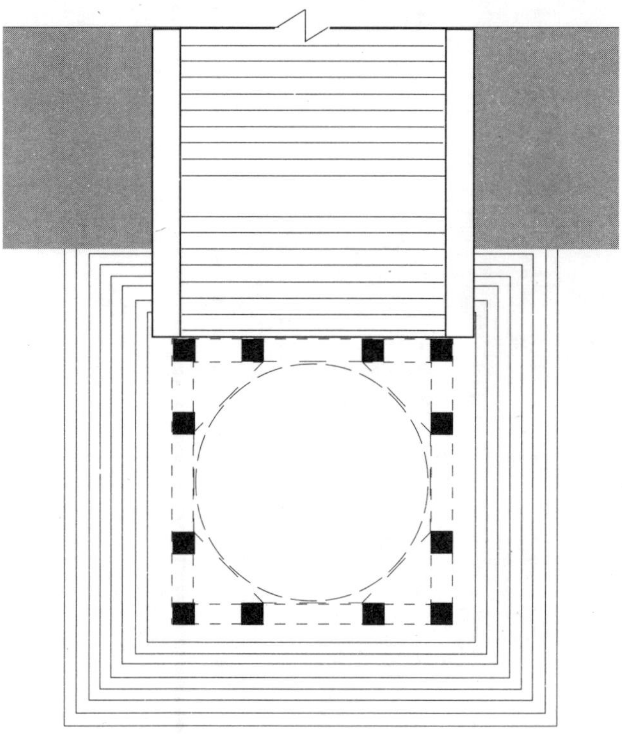

Figure 49 — *Wav Dādā Harir* (detail), showing entrance pavilion

The remaining portion of the *Wav Dādā Harir* is a long, narrow space which descends to the level of the well proper. First, from the entrance pavilion is a broad stairway which moves downwards in two, short flights to a square colonnaded hall, a second double flight stair again descends to the next level and this time to a narrow rectangular space, finally, another broad stairway descending in two, short flights. This third staircase ends in a broad, square colonnaded hall, a mirror of the first. Next is a somewhat larger square space with a double row of columns, transverse to the axis of the whole. This is followed by a repeat — i.e. a colonnaded hall followed by a larger space with a transverse, double row of columns. The halls with the transverse columns differ from the colonnaded halls in that they open upwards to the levels above giving a soaring spatial element to these areas (See: **Figure 50**). Both the halls with the transverse columns and the first two spaces without columns open skyward.

These repeated spatial/colonnaded areas finally culminate in a rather elaborate space. Bounded by columns and with an octagonal central opening, it is the widest of the internal areas. This square is bounded, left and right, by circular stairs which lead to ground level. The whole gives a rather cruciform appearing plan (See: **Figure 51**). Beyond this main space appears a circular chamber which holds a walkway around its circumference and the well in the centre. Overhead is an opening by which buckets on ropes may be lowered.

The *Wav Dādā Harir* is strongly axial. An asymmetrical plan would not have been as impressive. A labyrinth it is not, however the various levels plus the three entrances, nonetheless, provide a certain degree of security. Oriented north/south, the interior of the well is

Plate 15 — *Wav Dādā Harir* (Baoli Bai Hari), ground (left) & upper level (right) plan

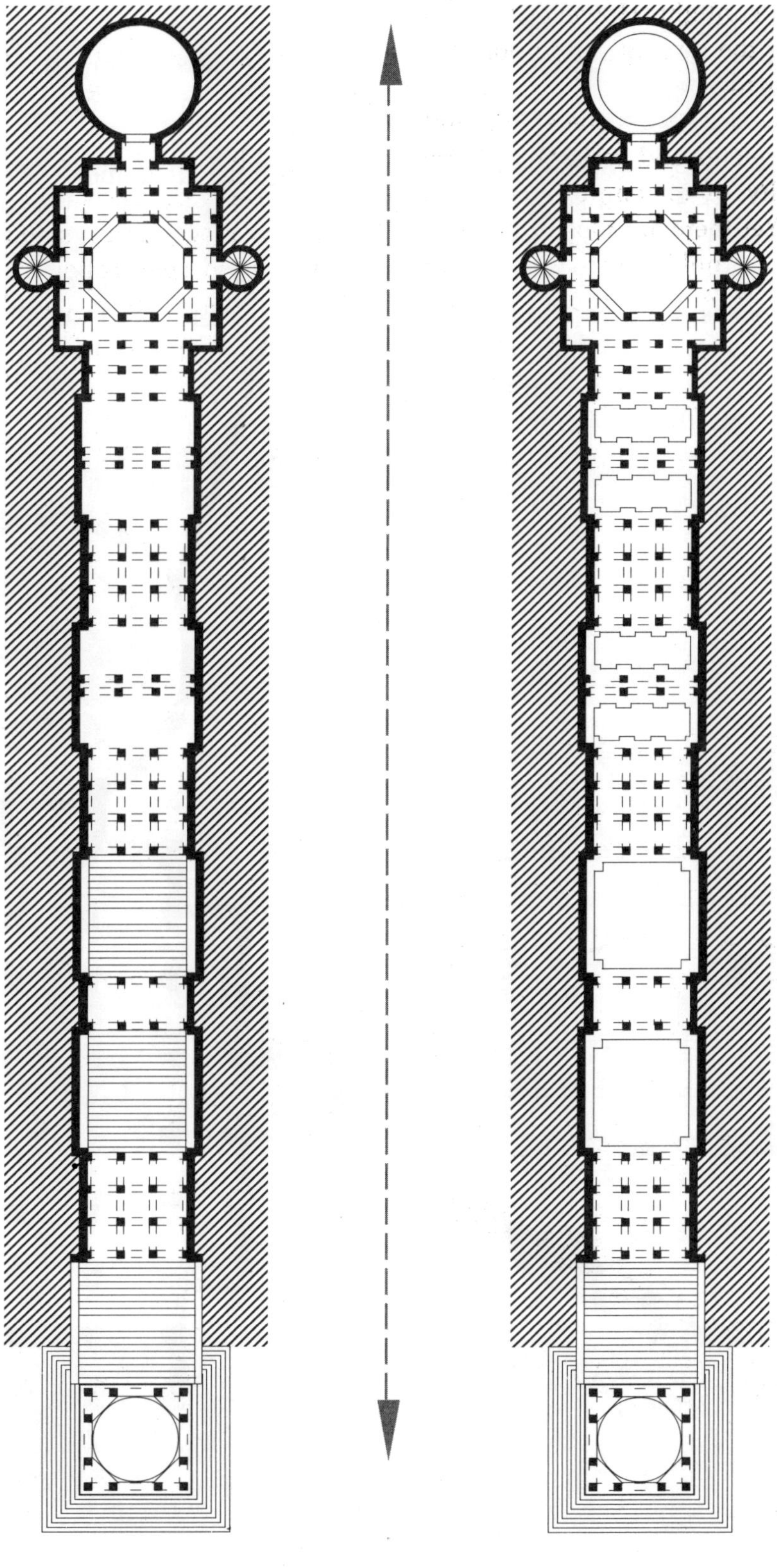

affected by the noon sunlight. However, during the hottest portion of the day, the afternoon, the interior is cast into shade.

The *Wav Dādā Harir* from the standpoint of concept, spatial elements and certainly artistry is a structure worthy of an emperor, even a *Mahārājāh* or sultān. Yet there are those who state that it is a "famous . . . public well" which had been "built at the expense of pious Hindus and dedicated to public service."[83] To think that any ruler, pious or wealthy man of this time and locale, whether pious Hindu or Muslim would have lavished such expense for the public is amusing! Most men of high position and/or caste were more concerned about their own desires, even excesses than to be concerned with the "public." It is more likely, as Grover attests that these were pleasure sites for the royal and wealthy. Places of luxurious idleness where the rulers could seek relief from the blazing sun.[84] Places where they could lounge in lavish indolence amidst architectural wonders. Anything resembling even a fleeting concern for the common man as a reason for the construction of these *baoli* is ludicrous, unthinkable.

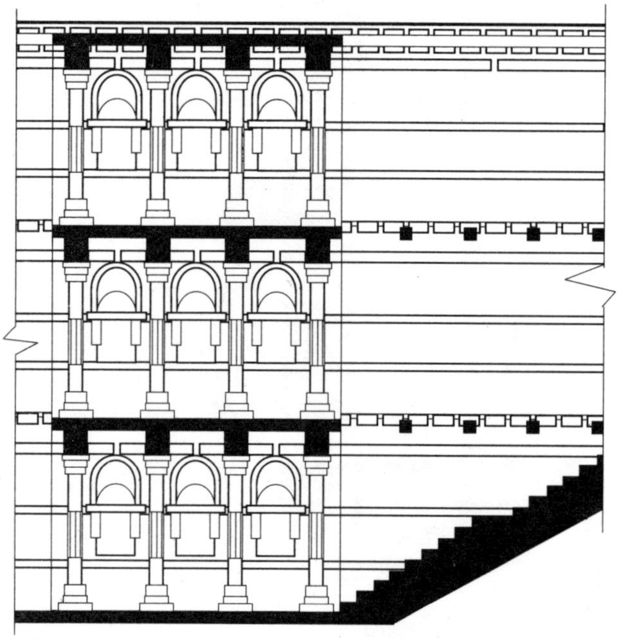

Figure 50 — *Wav Dādā Harir* (detail), showing interior elevation (proportional)

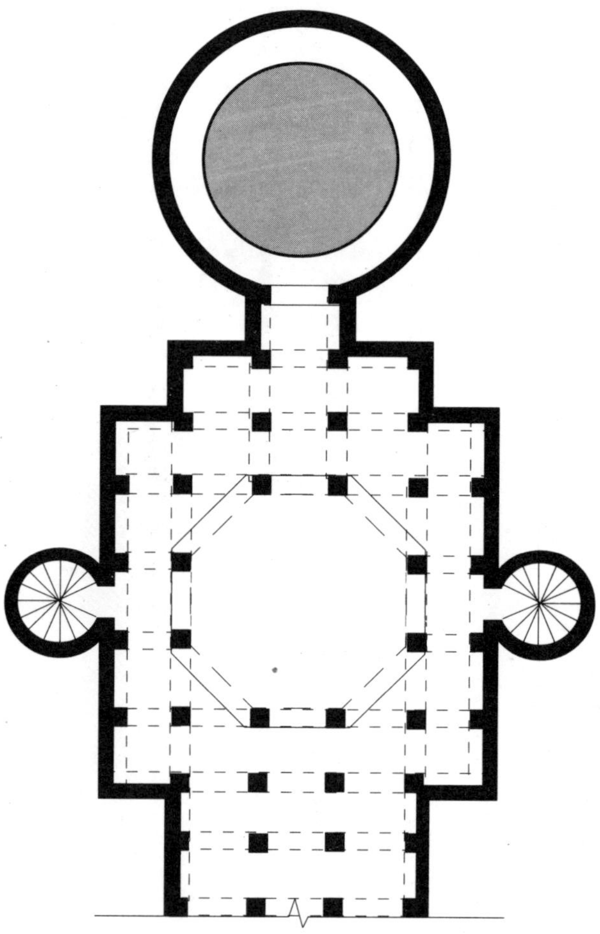

Figure 51 — *Wav Dādā Harir* (detail), showing lower level with well

Plate 16 — *Wav Dādā Harir*, entrance kiosk elevation (proportional) & half-plan

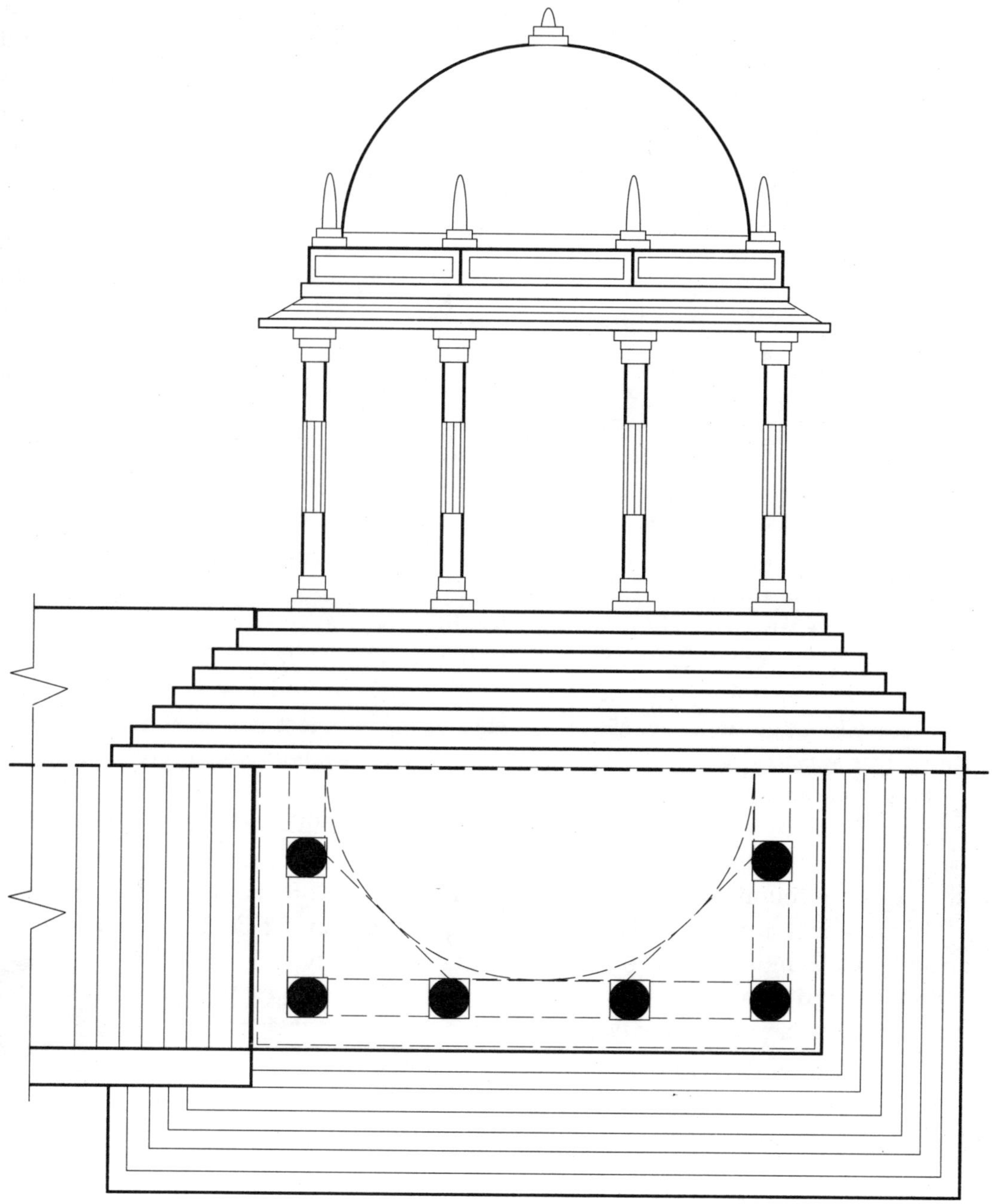

Aināpur Mahal

Aināpur (*c.* 1500-1550 CE)

The *Aināpur Mahal*,[85] a short distance to the east of Bijapur, is an example of a noble residence, albeit on a smaller scale than others. Residences and pavilions constructed by wealthy nobles of India proliferate. They tend to follow the same conceptual designs of the royal residences and pavilions. Unlike the *Daulat Kothi* (See: **Plate 55**) with its more open plan, the *Aināpur Mahal* has inclosed rooms — i.e., without direct access and/ or windows to the exterior — on the ground floor. Above the ground floor rooms is an enclosed terrace (See: **Plate 17** [bottom]) suitable for the women of the house, while over the covered verandah is a higher terrace where members of the immediate household could rest and/or relax.

This small, elegant residence reflects a format that is seen in many of the *mahal*s of Bijapur — i.e. three arched openings which define a roofed space or verandah.[86] Here two narrow arches flank a wider, central arch (See: **Figure 52**). This form is also seen in a number of the royal structures as well — e.g. the *Gagan Mahal* (**Plate 22**) and the *Saṅgat Mahal*.

A wide covered verandah includes the width, while a space, a porch, enclosed on three sides, sits back and is flanked by the three rooms. From this porch entries are found that lead into the three rooms. Off the southern room is another space, an extension of a single storey which appears to have been utilized as a *hammam*.

An unusual feature of the *Aināpur Mahal* is the fact that there are mirrored stairways leading to the roof-terrace (See: **Figure 53**). This adds to the axial quality of the ground floor, but seems to be a waste of space. Certainly either the northern or southern stairways would have provided ample means of ingress and egress to this upper area. The fact that numerous means of access to an area provide different ways to 'escape' cannot be overlooked as a security consideration. What was demanded by the ruler was assumed by the lower members of the nobility as well, apparently. In addition, since the '*hammam*' is located in the south, this may have been the exclusive province of the women of the household. Therefore, the southern stairway would also have been for their exclusive use.

Unlike the *Daulat Mahal*, the *Aināpur Mahal* possesses three door ways which lead to the outside — i.e. either directly or to the covered porch. The exception being the central room which has five doorways — i.e., one leading to the porch, two (one each) leading to the northern and southern room and two (one each) leading the stairways. This fact is somewhat unusual.

The *Aināpur Mahal* is an example of a smaller residence of a minor royal or noble person. It exhibits many features which are requisite for royal, noble and/or upper class/ caste members of Bijapur society. Further, they also possess many of the features of royal Mughal pleasure pavilions.

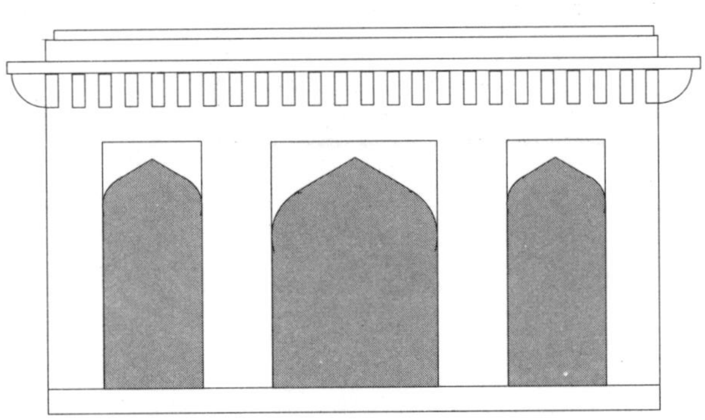

Figure 52 — *Aināpur Mahal*, proportional elevation

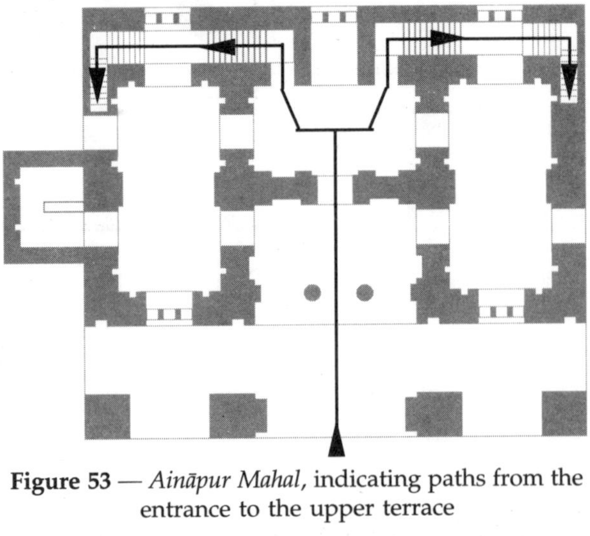

Figure 53 — *Aināpur Mahal*, indicating paths from the entrance to the upper terrace

Plate 17 — *Ainãpur Mahal*, ground & upper storey plan

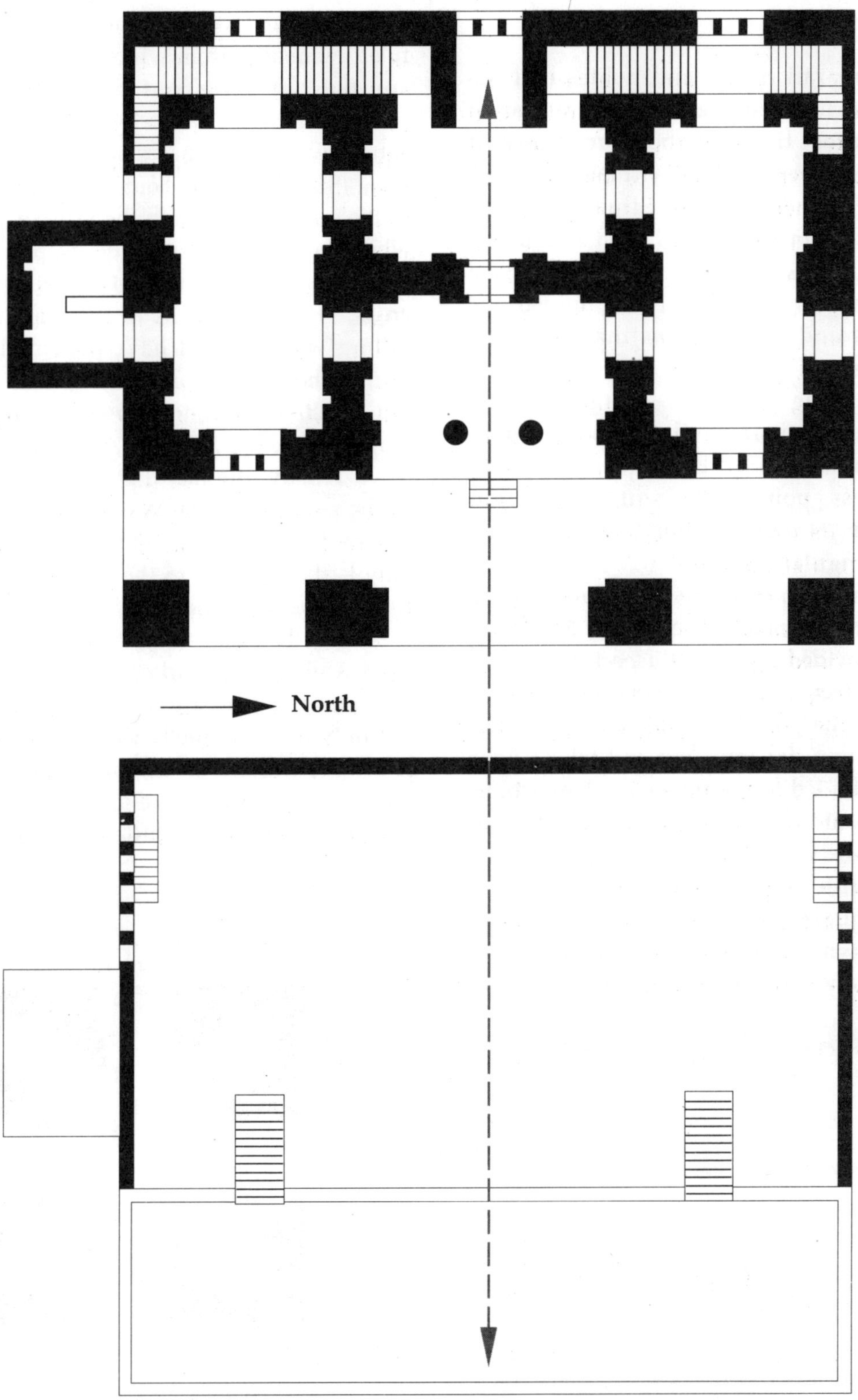

Water Pavilion (*Hammam*)

Kumatagi (*c.* 1500-1550 CE)

The Gujarati royals and nobles had the *Wav Dādā Harir* for their pleasure and relaxation during the hottest times of the year. Those of Bijapur had the Water Pavilion[87] (Arabic: *hammam*) of Kumatagi for their delight. Situated east of Aināpur the area apparently had been a favoured retreat for the nobles and the court. There, a lake provided an ample water supply for the various tanks, cisterns and/or *hammams* that are to be found in this small town.

Chief among these is a tank which surrounds a rectangular pavilion, and a square pavilion further surrounded by a square tank with a single access point. The square pavilion surrounded by its own smaller tank sets it off from the rectangular pavilion.

Within the main entrances of the rectangular pavilion are three fountains (See: **Figure 54**). These would have provided a pleasant aspect and sound for those who frequented this *hammam*. Internal spaces, behind the portals would have provided a degree of privacy for lounging and taking light meals. Two stairs led to the upper level, which, in the evening, would have provided a cool place as the night breezes wafted across its surface.

Facing this rectangular pavilion is a multistorey square pavilion. This rests in the middle of its own watery moat and accessible by a single causeway opposite that of the main tank. The topmost level provided an internal cistern, filled manually, from which thin streams of water spurted out, over and down the sides of the pavilion into the tank. *En plan*, this structure is square with eight spaces springing from a central point (See: **Figure 55**). Four of the spaces give access to the outside and are in the form of a Greek cross, while the other four provide deep, low-lit spaces for retreat and are in the form of a St. Andrew's cross. The thick walls of this pavilion, plus the falling water would have provided a cool spot during the hottest part of the day — i.e., a simple but effective air condition system related to that employed in the *Lāl Qilā*, Agra (See: **Figure 66**).

Finally, the fact that there is limited access to the environs of the Water Pavilion attests to its inherent use by noble and/or royal patrons. Not only is the entrance to the whole limited, but also to the square pavilion.

For the Muslims, particularly those who came from Afghanistan, Turkey and Persia, water — i.e. the sound of running water and its sight — was not only of an aesthetic value, it referred also the rivers of Paradise.[88] In truth these pleasure pavilions were an attempt to create in an otherwise relatively hostile environment a little bit of Paradise.

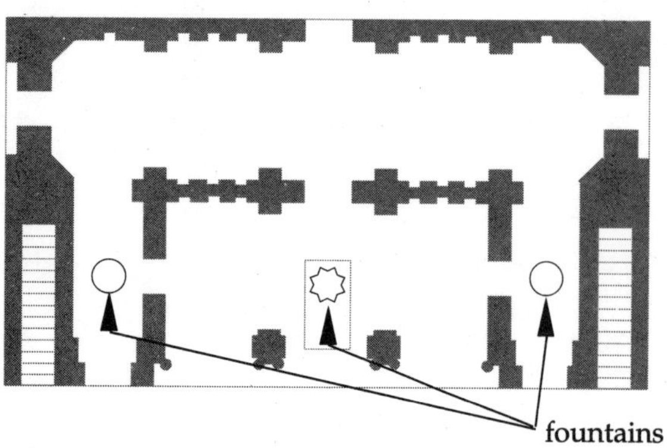

Figure 54 — *RectangularPavilion*, indicating fountains

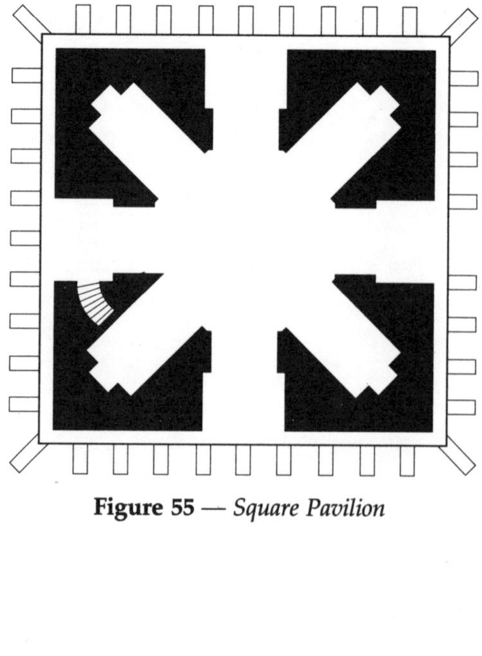

Figure 55 — *Square Pavilion*

Plate 18 — *Water Pavilion (hammam)*, ground plan

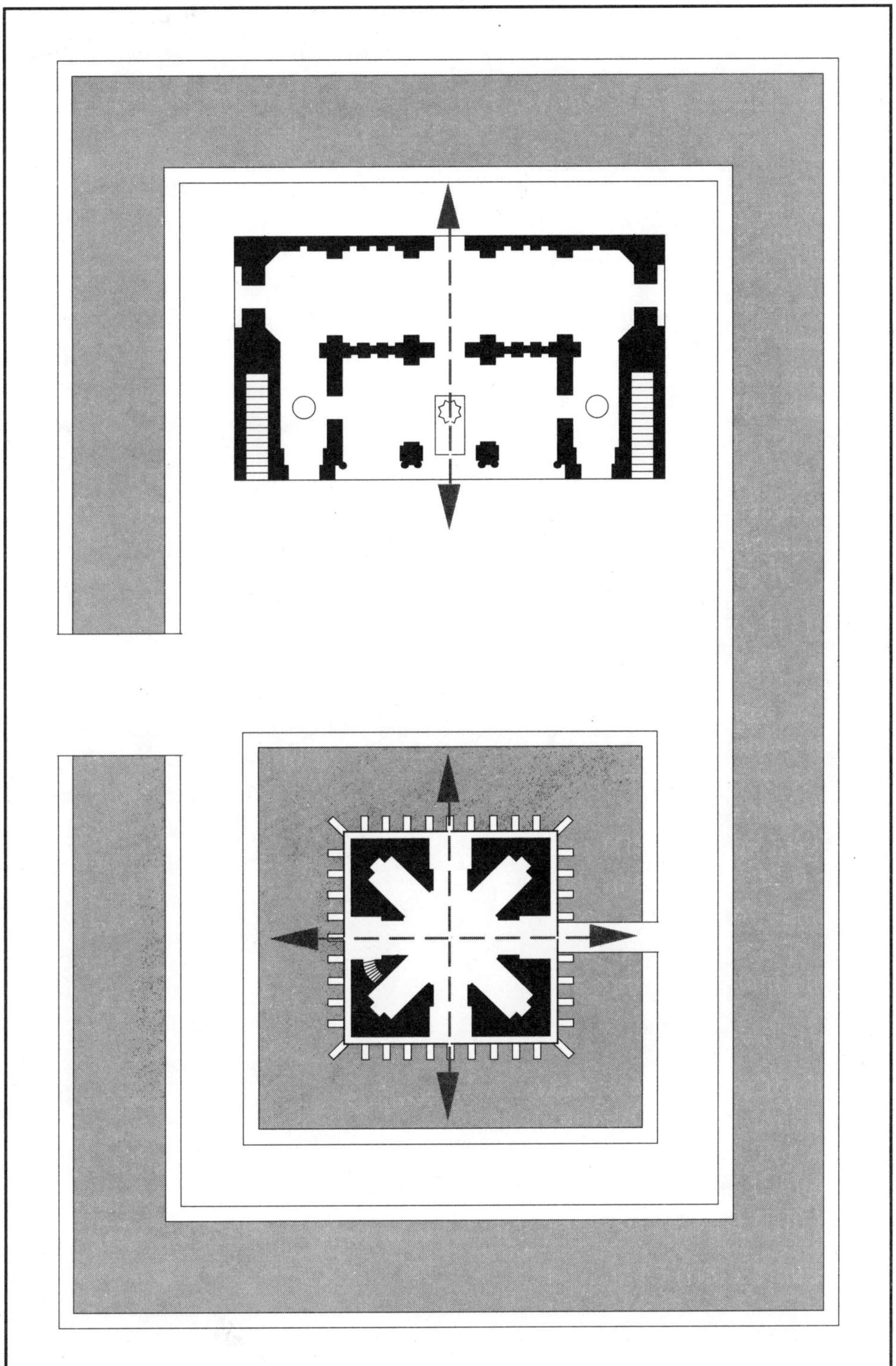

Rājā Mandir

Orchha (a. 1554 CE)

Orchha (Orcha), one of the important Rajput kingdoms' capitals, was established by Rāja Rudra Pratap Singh Bundela (r. 1501-1531 CE). The impressive *qilā* was constructed south of Jhansi on an island in the Betwa. The steep banks of the island, its rocky outcropping and the surrounding river made this area an excellent site for the erection of a strong citadel. The Bundela Rajputs were conscientious builders and unlike other Rajput rulers they did not add on to an existing *garh mahal*, but constructed individual residences at different locales within the citadel. Over the years several remarkable and separate *garh mahals* were raised by these *rājās* in their *qilā* (See: **Figure 56**).

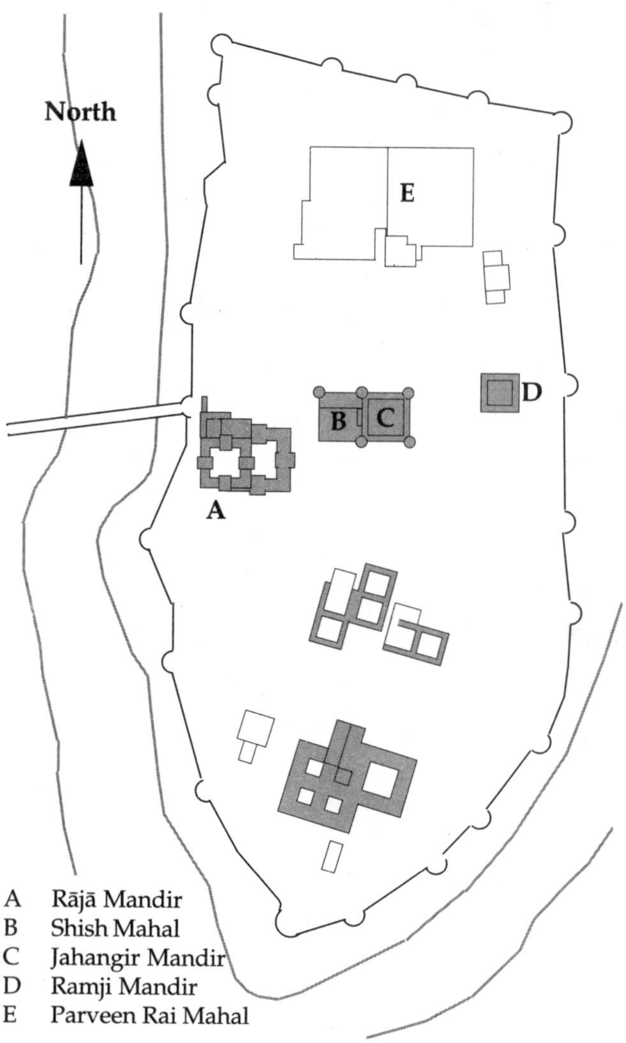

Figure 56 — *Orchha Kotila*

The first *garh mahal* was the *Ramji Mandir* (See: **Figure 57**). The second of the impressive residences to be erected — i.e. the *Rājā Mandir*[89] — was begun by Rājā Madhukhar Shah (r. 1554-1577 CE). He developed an unfortunate enmity with the Mughal Emperor, Akbar the Great, and was "relieved" of his throne. Some fourteen years later Rājā Ram Shah (r. 1591-1605) acquiesced to the suzerainty of the Empire, showed them proper respect and regained the Bundela patrimony. It was he, the Rājā Ram Shah, who completed the *garh mahal* started by his recalcitrant father.

The *Rājā Mandir*[90] supplanted the older *Ramji Mandir*[91] as the residence of the Bundela Rājas. Based upon a traditional Hindu plan (See: **Plate 21** [bottom]), the *garh mahal* is essentially square as was that of the previous royal residence — i.e., the *Ramji Mandir*. A square court is one of the hallmarks of the Bundela *garh mahals* as well

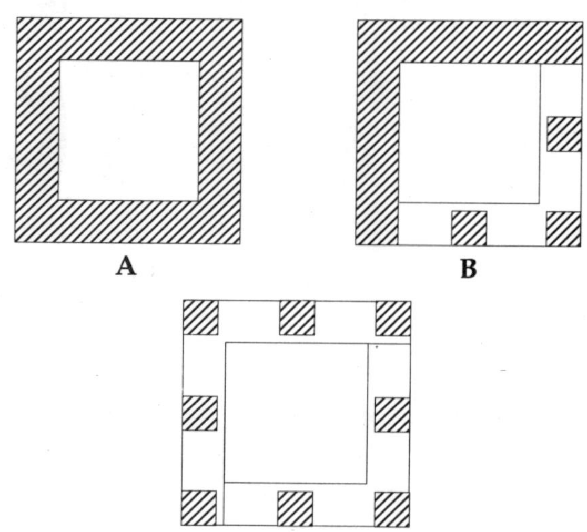

Figure 57 — *Ramji Mandir*, indicating internal space on the **(A)** 1st storey, **(B)** 2nd storey and **(C)** 3rd storey

Plate 19 — *Rājā Mandir*, plan 1st storey

(a. 1554 CE)

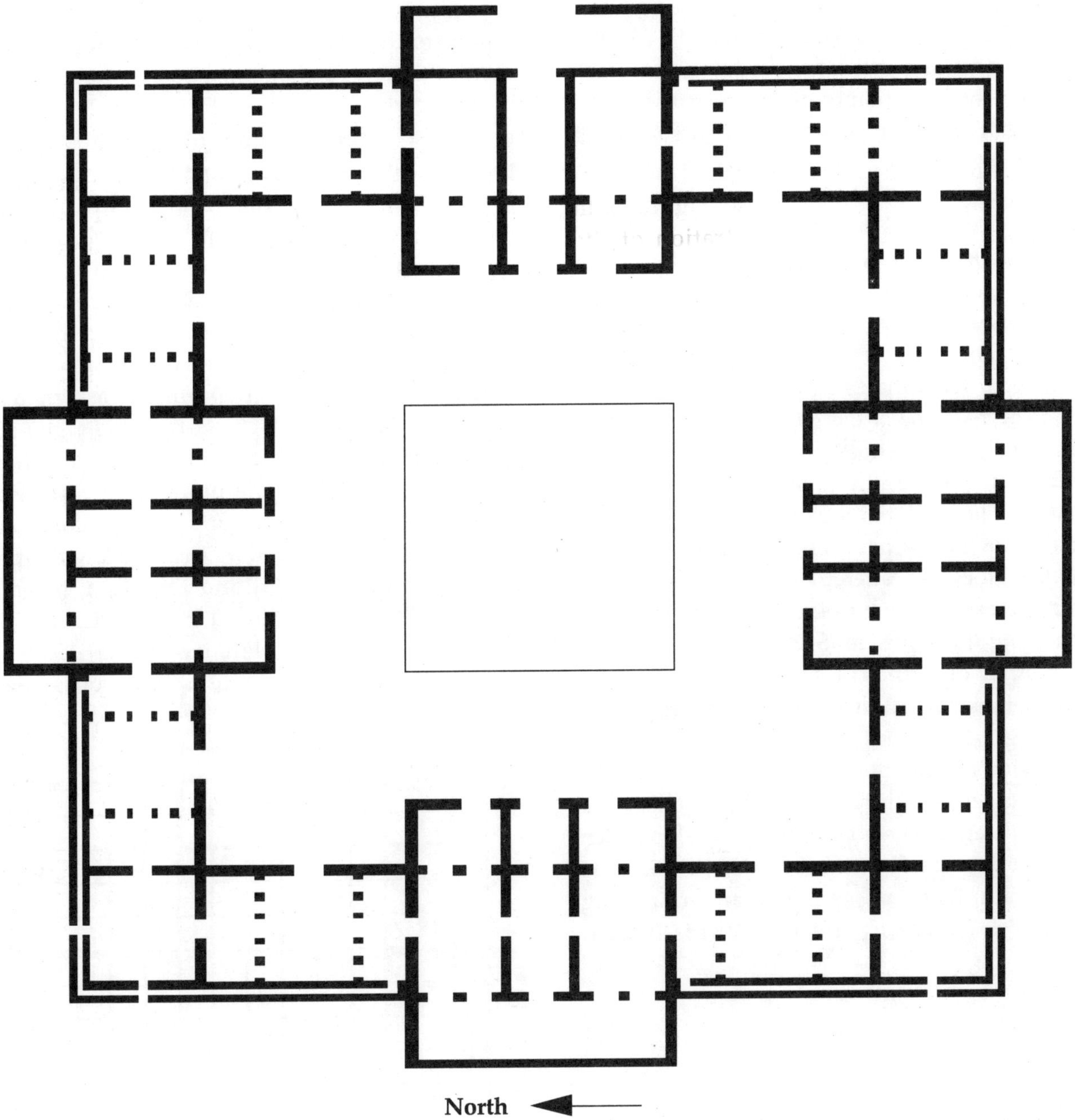

as their close adherence to ancient Hindu models noted in the *śilpa-śāstras*. Here, in the *Rājā Mandir*, square forms bisect each of the sides of the block and at the cardinal points of the compass. They extend from the exterior into the court creating an interesting and pleasing variation on a square, *chatuśāla* plan (See: **Plate 19**; see also: **Figure 1**). In keeping with a *garh mahal*, penetration of the exterior walls of the *Rājā Mandir* was kept at a minimum, particularly in the first storey. On the upper storeys balconies punctuate the exterior prospects. The same is accomplished within the court as well (See: **Plates 19** & **20**).

The roof line of the *Rājā Mandir* is the least interesting of the whole ensemble. Unlike the neighbor at Orchha, the *Jahangir Mandir* or the *Govind Mandir* at Datia, this *garh mahal* possesses no major towers or pavilions to break the main geometric block. An attempt was made to relieve this uninteresting line by placing thirty-two small *chatrīs* along the top edge (See: **Plate 21**), but they were neither of sufficient scale nor of variation in size to make a real difference (See: **Appendix A, Plate 89**). However, since the Bundela rulers were obviously indebted to the *śilpa-śāstra*, one would suspect that these small adornments hold some significance. There are nine *chatrī* along each face. Nine is a perfect number whose š is 3 as well a number possessing an imposing formation. It is called perfect since it is formed from three, and nine always reproduces itself when multiplied with any number. It is a magnification of that most sacred number, and by association and as a derivation from three, nine also becomes one of the most sacred numbers. It is the last whole number before the commencement of the compound numbers. Nine denotes completion, perfection, force, wisdom, silence and when associated with three it connotes space. It is associated astronomically with the planet Mars (*Mangala, Kuja* or *Angaraka*). As the second most powerful odd number (the square of the sacred three), nine is assigned the puissant planet, *Mars*. Thirty-two — i.e. the total number of *chatrī* — is also an important integer. Thirty-two is a feminine number, is considered by some to be a perfect number. As a compound number it is associated with the planet Jupiter (*Brihaspati* or *Guru*) (3) and the Moon (*Soma* or *Chandra*) (2). When reduced it produces five and, therefore, the planet Mercury (*Budha*) (5).[92]

The *Rājā Mandir* of Orchha possesses a

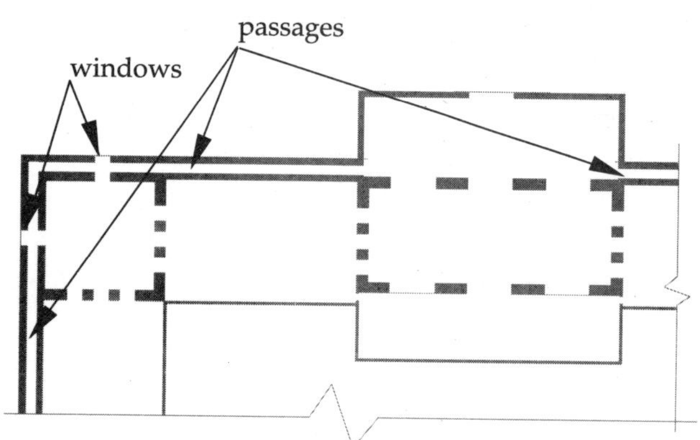

Figure 58 — *Rājā Mandir*, indicating the wall passages

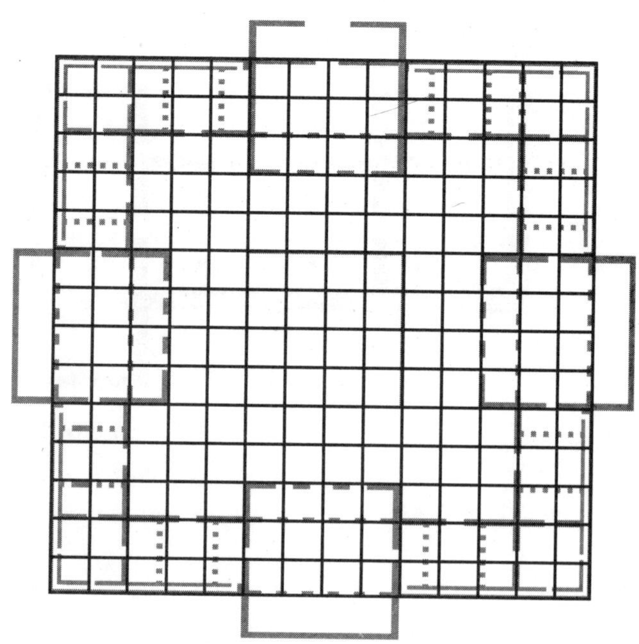

Figure 59 — *Rājā Mandir*, indicating a *Bhadramahasana Maṇḍala*

Plate 20 — *Rājā Mandir*, plan 2nd storey & 3rd storey
(a. 1554 CE)

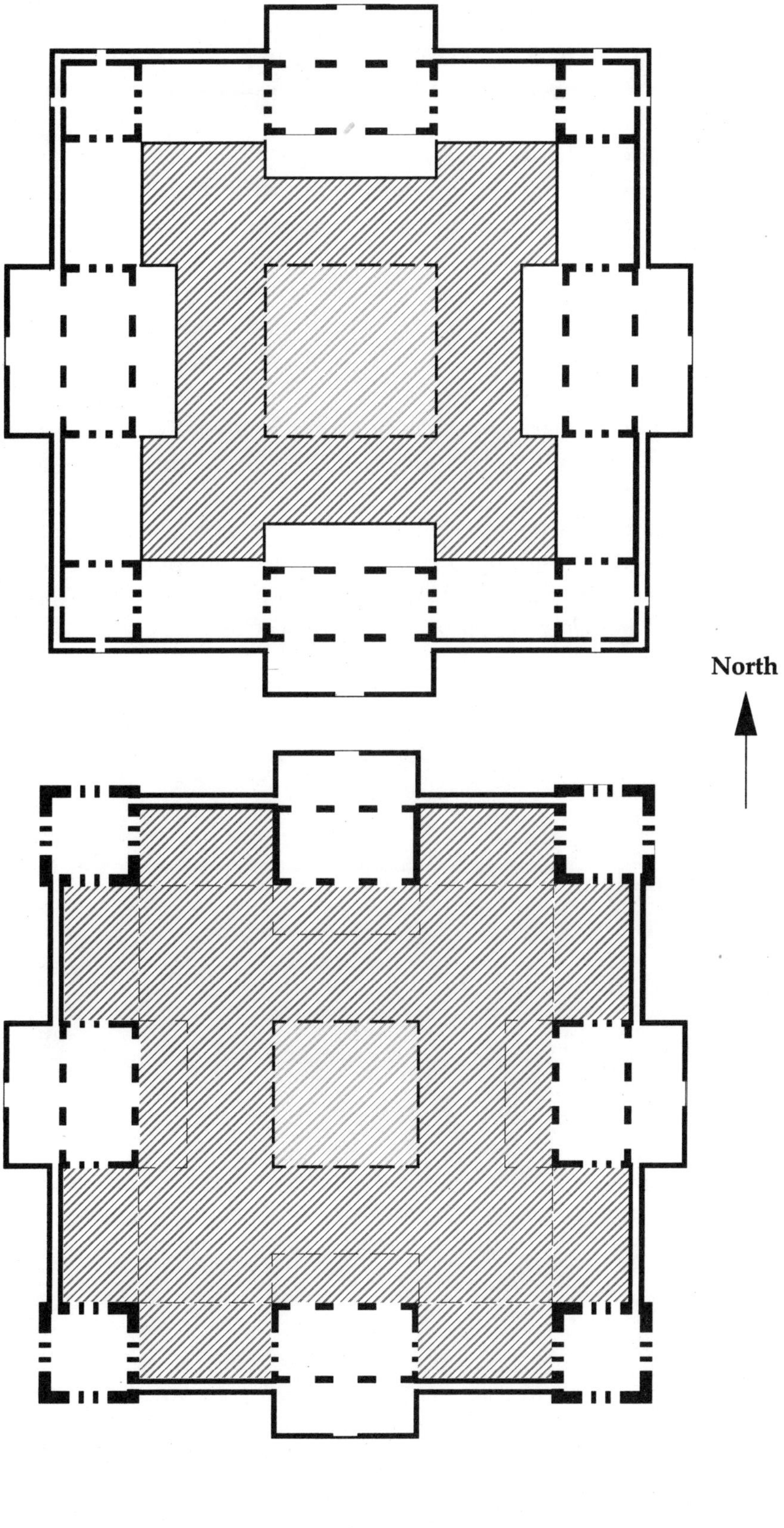

Rājā Mandir (Concluded)

singularly interesting feature. In virtually all residences of India during this period, whether Hindu or Muslim, rooms flowed one into the other. Hallways were at a minimum, if they existed at all. Apparently this is also the case with this *garh mahal* — i.e., rooms flowing on into the other — with the exception that hidden or placed within the exterior walls of the major block are narrow passageways which connect these spaces (See: **Figure 58**; see: also **Plate 20**). Hidden passages were not unheard of in Indian residences of the royal or noble families of this period. However, here in Orchha the passages appear not so much to be hidden — i.e., a security precaution — as to be installed as a convenience.

Since the Bundelas adhered to established Hindu *śilpa-śāstra* design, one is tempted to see whether a *maṇḍala* is applicable to the plan of the *Rājā Mandir*. Indeed, if a *Bhadramahasana Maṇḍala* is placed over the ground plan of this *garh mahal* a near perfect fit appears to be achieved (See: **Figure 59**). There may be other equally cogent examples (See: **Plate 21** [bottom]).

The *Rājā Mandir*, the second of the Bundela's output is a residence of no mean import. It served as an extension of the *Rāmji Mandir's* plan and ultimately was to culminate in the impressive *Govind Mandir* of Datiya. The variation on the square plan is interesting, indeed. Likewise, the incorporation of passages placed within the outer walls indicate the lengths to which the Bundelas allowed themselves to experiment. The *śilpa-śāstras* may well have been the genesis for their plans, but their variation is what is noteworthy.

The *Rājā Mandir* adheres to virtually all of the iconographic principles associated with those who rule. It is 'a' and 'the' *Rājā Mandir*, the King's palace, and as such it is a most apt example.

Plate 21 — *Rājā Mandir*, plan, roof line (top) & floorplan based on Hindu ideal (bottom)

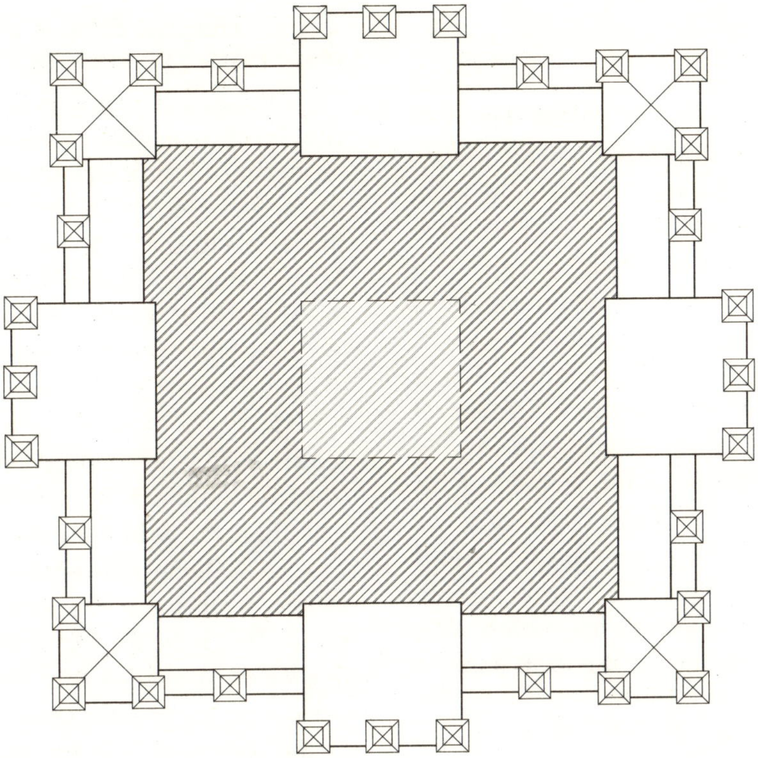

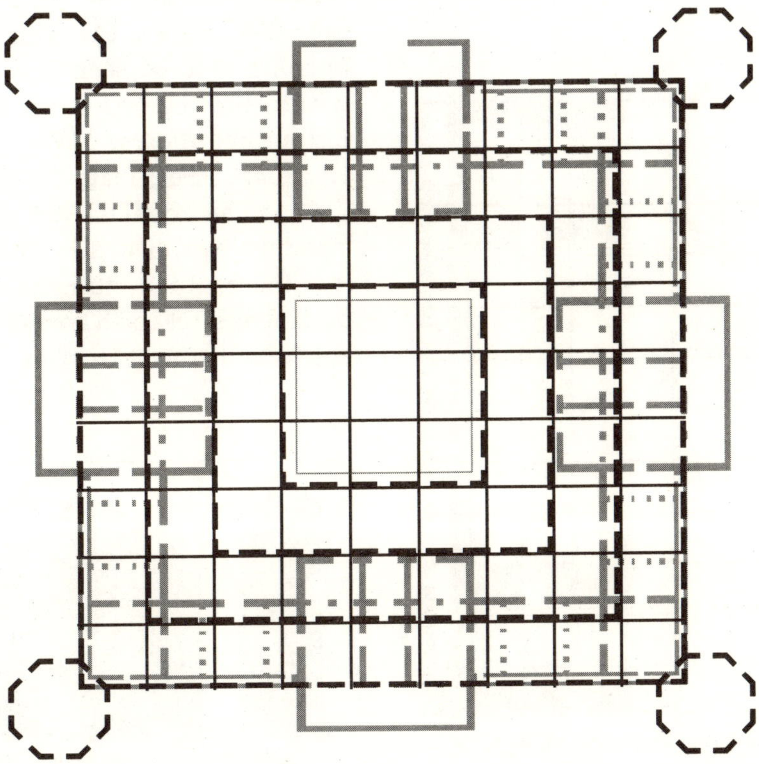

Gagan Mahal

Bijapur (1561 CE)

Built during the reign of Sultān Ali 'Adil Shah I (r. 1557-1580 CE), the *Gagan Mahal*[93] stands within the impressive Bijapur citadel (Indic: *qilā*). It is believed that when this stately *mahal* was constructed, it served a dual purpose — i.e., as a location for the sultān's *darbār* on the lower level and as his residence on the second storey.

The disposition of the rooms of the second storey is no longer known. However, it certainly would have contained rooms for the sultān and a separate suite for the women of his court. Doubtless there would have been windows and/or balconies, suitably screened, that would have looked down onto the main floor below. In addition there were two staircases which lead down to the first storey; one, in the east, exits to the outside and may have been for the use of the women. Nonetheless, they afforded easy ingress and egress to the second floor; an obvious security device.

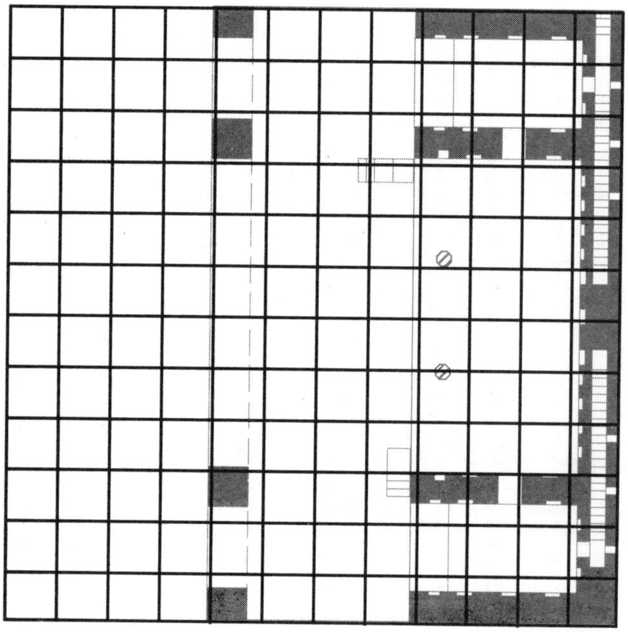

Figure 60 — *Gagan Mahal*, indicating a *Deśiya Maṇḍala*

The first floor is divided into four areas (See: **Plate 22**). First, the broad northern space runs the full width and nearly half the depth of the structure. This area was suitable for the gathering of supplicants for the daily *darśana* of the sultān. Second, a raised central space, a stage in the south that was half the width of the *Gagan Mahal*. It provided a suitable expanse for the enthroned sultān and his advisors. Finally, there are two other southern areas, flanking the central space. These smaller areas offer access to the central space as well as access to the staircases leading to the second storey and are open towards the north. Together, these two areas were less than the width of the central platform.

A distinctive feature of the *Gagan Mahal* is to be found in the triple arched, northern façade.[94] If a *Deśiya Maṇḍala* is superimposed over the *mahal*, it is seen that its depth — i.e. front to back — is eight *pada* (See: **Figure 60**). The width of the central arch is six *pada* and that of the side areas, including the supporting piers, is three *pada* (See: **Figure 61**). This type of triple arched opening is to be seen in a number of structures within the region — e.g. the *Saṅghat Mahal* of Bijapur, the *Aināpur Mahal* (See: **Plate 17**) and the *Feria Bagh* (See: **Plate 39**) of Ahmadnagar.

The royal *Gagan Mahal* rests within a standard established by the Adil Shahi. Further, it adheres to a number of the iconographic parameters set forth earlier in this study as they apply to a royal structure.

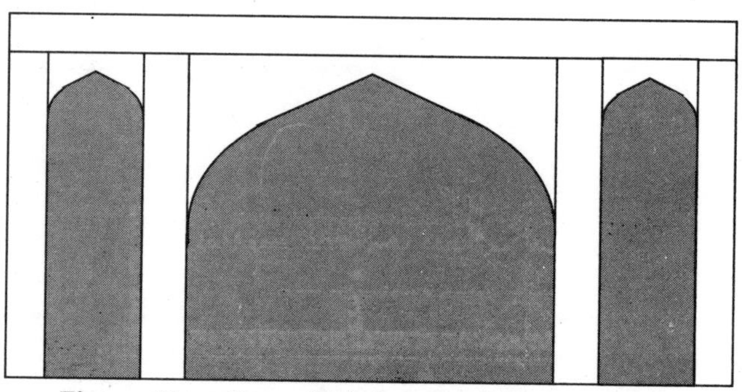

Figure 61 — *Gagan Mahal*, proportional elevation

Plate 22 — *Gagan Mahal*, ground plan

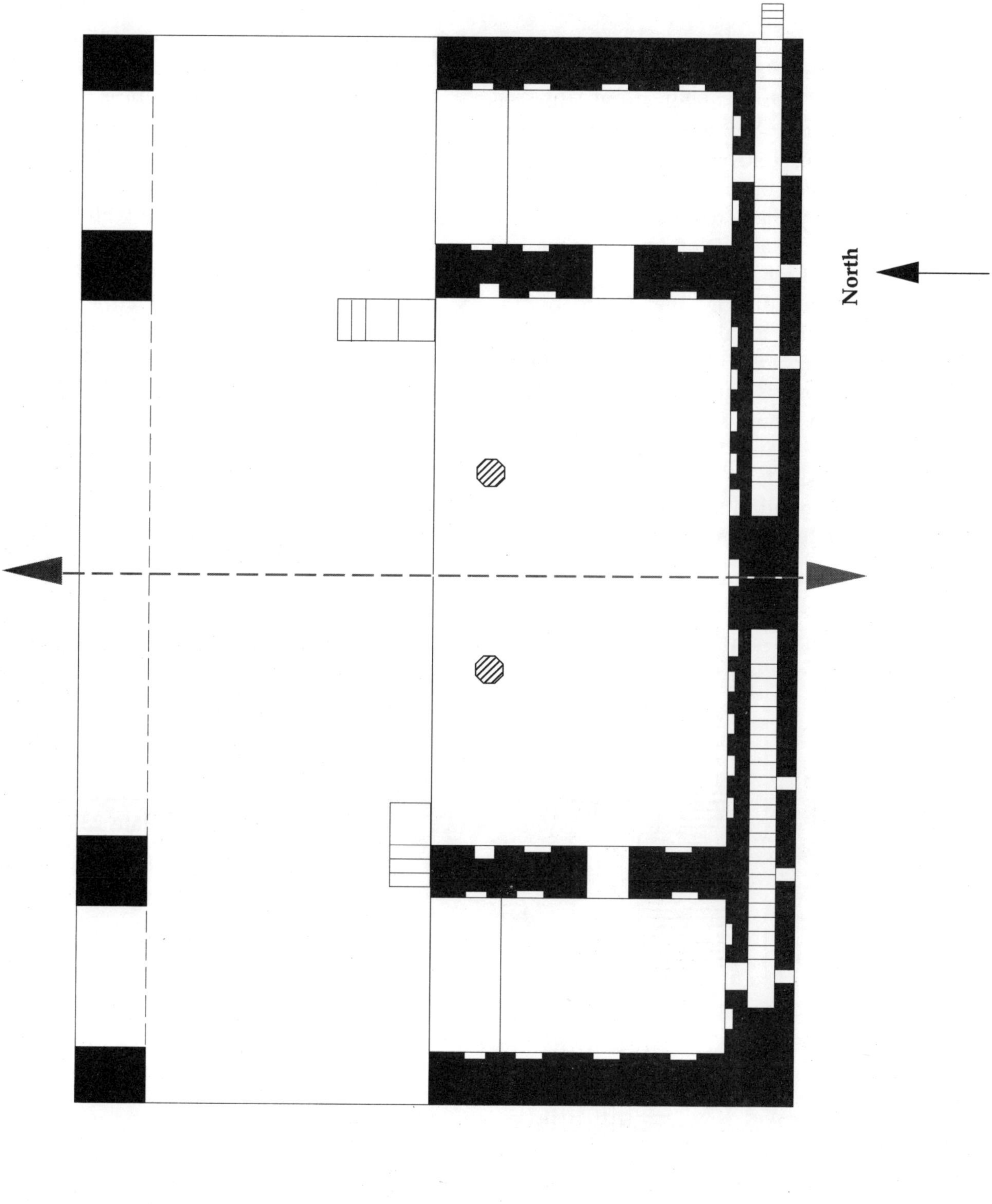

Lāl Qilā (Red Fort)

Agra (1565-a. 1600 CE)

Of course Agra is known as the site of one of the world's great architectural triumphs — i.e. the *Tāj Mahal*. Yet, within this very same city stands a second structure of no mean note — i.e., the *Lāl Qilā*[95] or the *Red Fort* — also built predominantly by the Mughals.

The present *Lāl Qilā* of Agra was the first of the major Mughal citadels in India. Its construction was during the reign of the inveterate builder, Jalal-ud-din Muhammad, Akbar the Great (r. 1556-1605 CE), who preferred Agra to Delhi for his capital. The new citadel was constructed upon the foundations of an older *kotila* built by Sher Shah's son Salim Shah. It was a natural site for a fortification and Akbar built a strong foundation upon which others added. *Lāl Qilā* then felt the imprint of Akbar's son and grandson — i.e., the emperors Jahangir and Shah Jahan. It remains today a superb example of a fortified residence in India, a fully developed and conceived *garh mahal*.

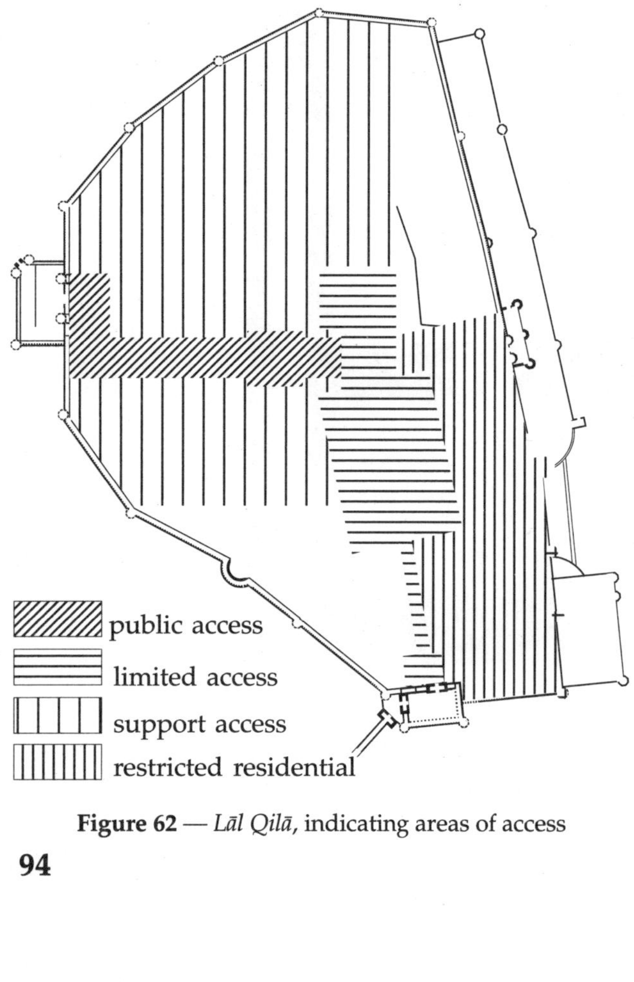

Figure 62 — *Lāl Qilā*, indicating areas of access

The citadel was constructed on the banks of the Yamuna, flowing to the east of the fort and upon a rise of land. Its fortifications consisted of enormous, thick, double walls surrounded by a deep dry moat along the south, west and north perimeter of *Lāl Qilā*. The deep dry-moat and the double walls provided a defense which could not be easily breached without appalling loss of personnel. The eastern aspect was similarly fortified and was provided additional protection by the Yamuna. Its massive construction made this *qilā* virtually impregnable and a secure residence for the imperial family.

The internal area of *Lāl Qilā* at Agra consists of three areas which supported the residential area (See: **Figure 62**). A public area where merchants set up their shops — i.e. the *Minar Bazaar* (See: **Plate 23 — K**) — and the common folk could enter lay to the east of the *Hāthī Pol* (See: **Plate 23 — N**). An area of limited access, which included the *Diwān-i Ām* (See: **Plate 23 — H**) ran north to south and was connected

Legend for **Plate 23**

- **A** Amar Singh Darwāzā & Akbari Darwāzā
- **B** Akbari Mahal
- **C** Jahangiri Mahal
- **D** Anguri Bagh
- **E** Khass Mahal
- **F** Musamman Burj
- **G** Diwān-i Ām Courtyard
- **H** Diwān-i Ām
- **I** Macchi Bhavan
- **J** Diwān-i Khās
- **K** Minar Bazaar
- **L** Naginā Masjid
- **M** Moti Masjid
- **N** Hāthī Pol
- **O** Delhi Darwāzā

Plate 23 — *Lāl Qilā* (Red Fort), Agra, plan (partial)

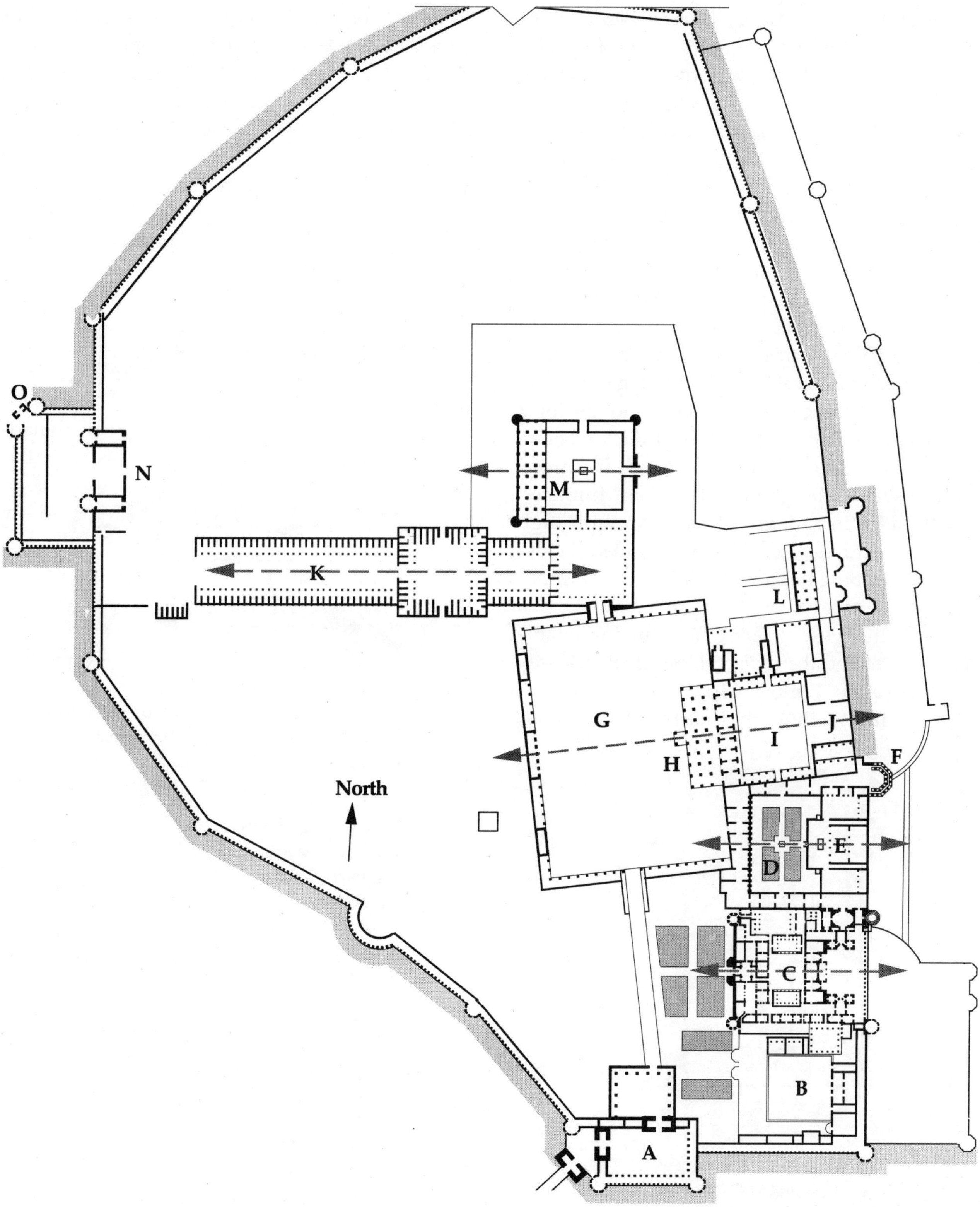

to the *Amar Singh Darwāzā* & *Akbari Darwāzā*. A third area reserved for the retainers of the imperial family and the military was by far the largest and occupied an area to the west and north of the *qilā*. Finally, the residential area of the imperial family, secure and developed for their needs, lay to the east and south.

Any access into the citadel was further fortified and offered obvious resistance to any invading forces — in particular, the *Amar Singh Darwāzā* & *Akbari Darwāzā* (See: **Plate 23 — A**) which were so designed that any entrant had to negotiate a 45° turn, then a 90° turn through three narrow, fortified, easily defended gates (See: **Figure 64**). These gates were wide enough for a single elephant and each possessed thick wooden doors which had to be breached if forced entrance was to be gained. This then funneled the would-be intruders onto a ramp with high walls at its entrance, also easily defended, before access could be gained to the level of the inner fort.

To the west of *Lāl Qilā* is the formidable *Delhi Darwāzā* and the *Hāthī Pol* (See: **Plate 23 — N & O**; see also: **Figure 63**). Here entrance is primarily gained through a narrow gate similar to those found in the *Amar Singh Darwāzā* and the *Akbari Darwāzā*. Immediately, a right turn of 45° is required as one then proceeds through a relatively narrow space created by a barrier wall. Then two 90° left turns must be negotiated into a wider, but, also easily defended small court. Finally, a third 90° turn to the right and through the final defensive position, the *Hāthī Pol*. One then enters the public area, flanked by the inner

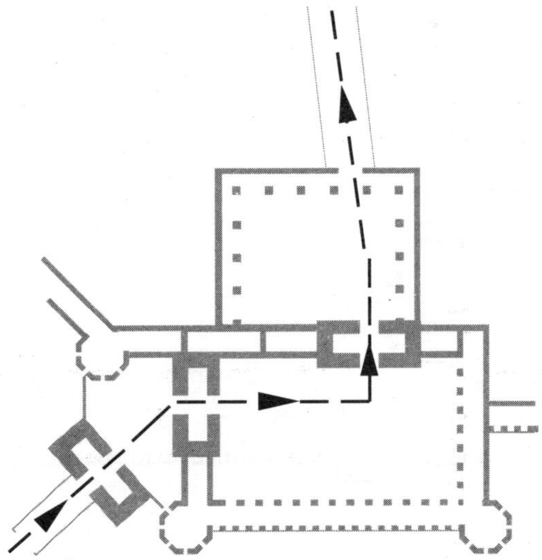

Figure 64 — *Amar Singh Darwāzā & Akbari Darwāzā, Lāl Qilā*, Agra, indicating entrance path

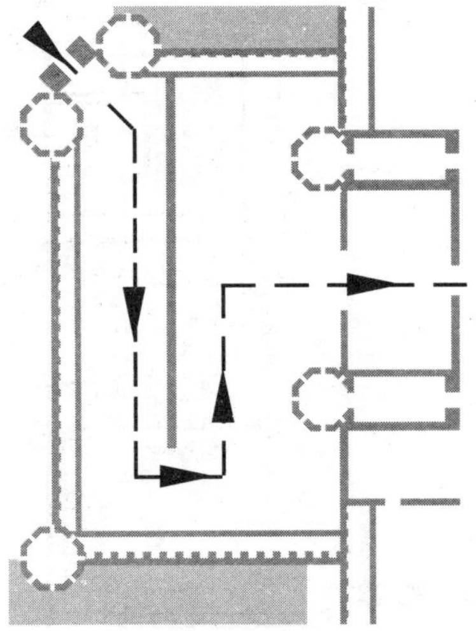

Figure 63 — *Delhi Darwāzā & Hāthī Pol, Lāl Qilā*, Agra, indicating entrance path

Legend for **Plate 24**

A	Amar Singh Darwāzā
B	Akbari Darwāzā
C	Akbari Mahal
D	Jahangiri Mahal
E	Anguri Bagh
F	Khass Mahal
G	Bangaldar Pavilion
H	Musamman Burj
I	Diwān-i Ām
J	Macchi Bhavan
K	Diwān-i Khās
L	Hammam
M	Minar Bazaar
N	Naginā Masjid
O	River entrance

Plate 24 — *Lāl Qilā* (Red Fort) (detail), residential areas

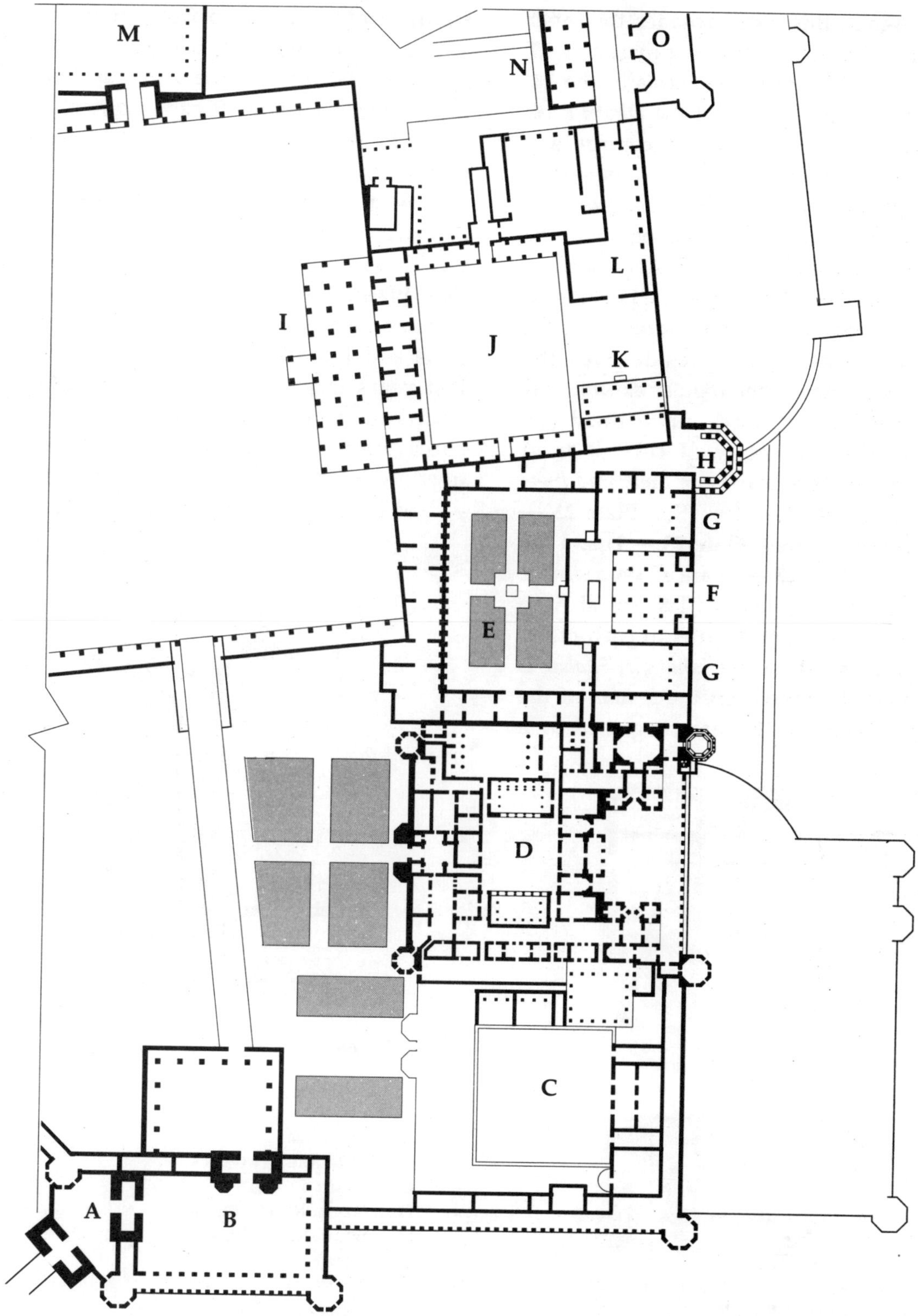

Lāl Qilā (Red Fort) (Continued)

cantonment. Again, this gate provides the inner reaches of the *qilā* with sufficient protection.

By far the largest enclosed area of the *Lāl Qilā* at Agra is the open court and the *Diwān-i Ām* (See: **Plate 23 — G & H**). Here the populous could gather at specified times for the ceremonial and lavishly splendid *darbār*s of the emperor. The *Diwān-i Ām* is a covered colonnaded pavilion, the eastern portion of which is the western wall of the *Macchi Bhavan* (See: **Plate 24 — J**). Here, from an intricately carved balcony, the emperor would appear, exhibit himself and preside over the *darbār*. As has been noted, the regular *darśana* was not only a rite, but, in part, underlined the importance of the continuity of rule. It is of interest to note that the *Diwān-i Ām Courtyard* (See: **Plate 23 — G**), the *Diwān-i Ām* (See: **Plate 23 — H**), the *Macchi Bhavan* (See: **Plate 23 — I**) and the *Diwān-i Khās* (See: **Plate 23 — J**) are all on a similar axis. The rest of the structures of *Lāl Qilā* at Agra are on a different axis, but parallel to each other.

The areas north of the *Jahangiri Mahal* is believed by some to have been the *zenānā* of the *Lāl Qilā*, Agra. Access to this area is gained by a small unobtrusive doorway on the north-east section of the *Jahangiri Mahal* (See: **Figure 65**). This *zenānā* would include: the 1) *Anguri Bagh* — i.e. a formal *bagh* called the "Grape Garden" (See: **Plate 24 — E**) — 2) the *Khās Mahal* — i.e. a typical pleasure pavilion, roofed and supported by many narrow pillars (See: **Plate 24 — F**) — 3) the *Bangaldar Pavilion(s)* — i.e. two rectangular pavilions with bulging Bengali (Bangla) roofs (See: **Plate 24 — G**) — and 4) the *Musamman Burj* — i.e. a large, octagonal tower, open on the top level and the area where Shah Jahan spent his last years imprisoned (See: **Plate 24 — H**). In addition, the *Macchi Bhavan* — i.e. an enclosed court with two storeys of apartments on its north, west and south sides (See: **Plate 24 — J**) — and the *Hammam* (See: **Plate 24 — L**) may well

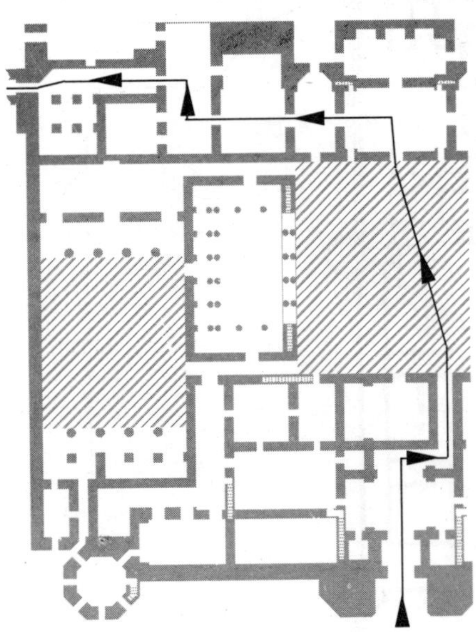

Figure 65 — *Jahangiri Mahal, Lāl Qilā*, entrance area indicating access path to the *Anguri Bagh*

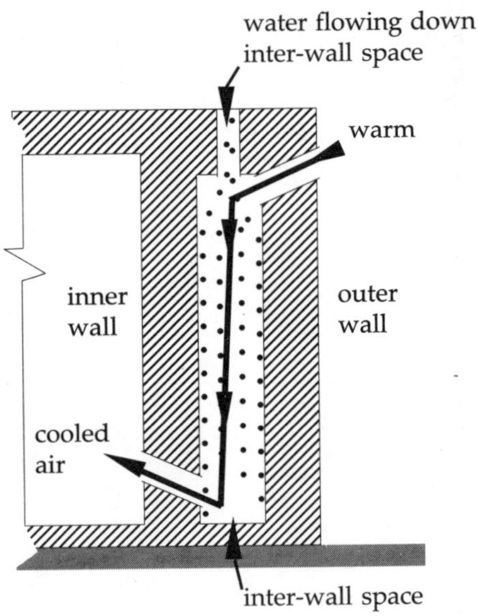

Figure 66 — Cooling system employed in *Lāl Qilā*,

Legend for **Plate 25**

- **A** Entrance
- **B** Octagonal Towers
- **C** Court I
- **D** North Reception Hall
- **E** South Reception Hall
- **F** Court II
- **G** Court III
- **H** Octagonal Pavilion

Plate 25 — *Jahangiri Mahal, Lāl Qilā*, plan, ground floor

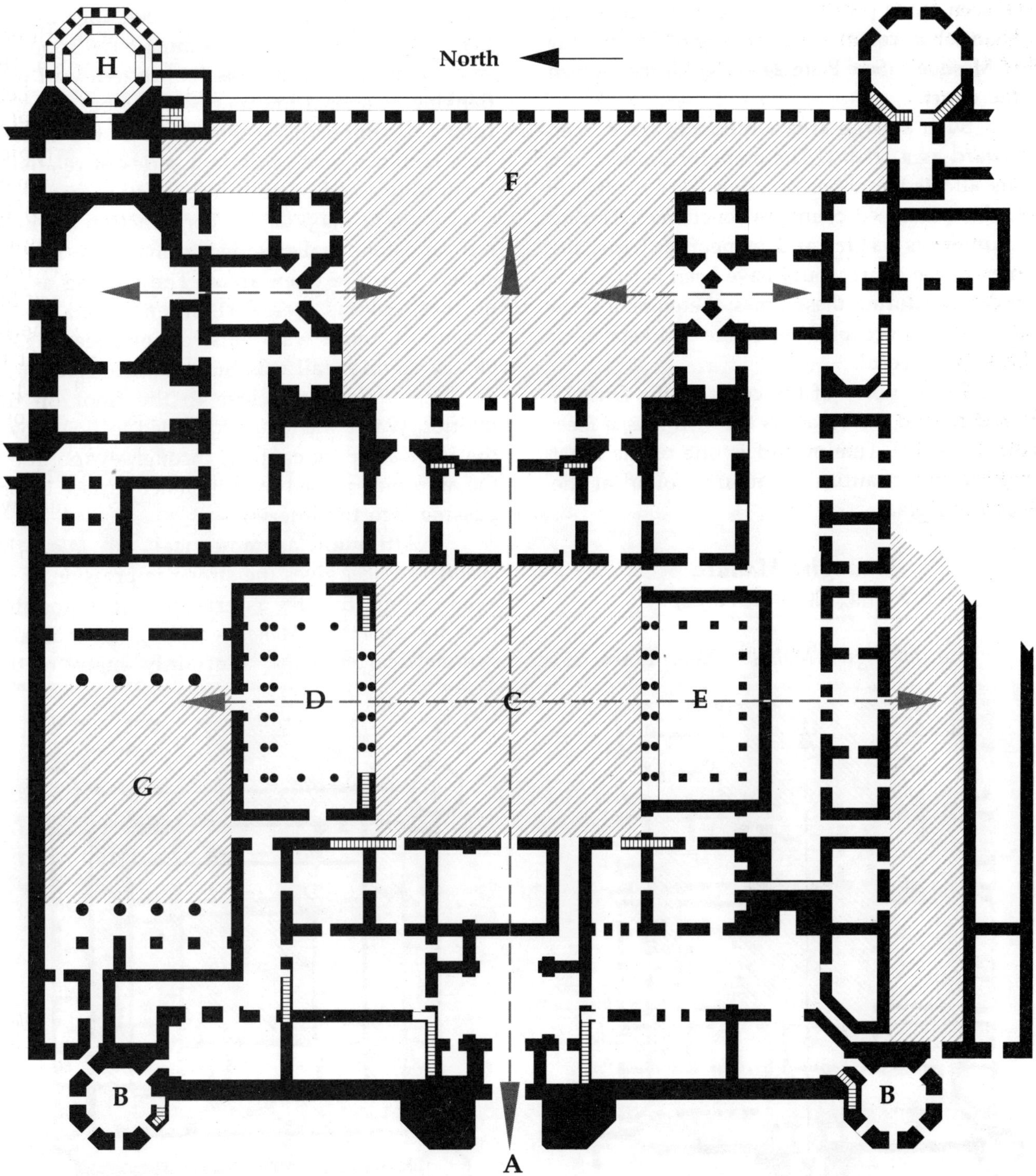

have been made part of the *zenānā* at a later date as Shah Jahan constructed the *Naginā Masjid* (the "Bird Mosque") (See: **Plate 24 — N**) for the women of the court.

Such a large area would not have been untoward as a *zenānā*. The emperor, in addition to his allotted number of wives under Islamic law, also possessed countless concubines. During his numerous battles and inspection trips, the women of the court would have been left to their own devices during these times; therefore, a large *zenānā*, in part, occupied their time and kept them relatively peaceful.

To the north of the court of the *Diwān-i Ām* and beyond the bazaar is the *Moti Masjid* (See: **Plate 23 — M**). This masjid is one of the most complete and beautiful structures found at the *Lāl Qilā* of Agra.

Jahangiri Mahal
Lāl Qilā, Agra (1570 CE)

The *Jahangiri Mahal*[96] (See: **Plate 25**) presents a rather relatively complete idea of how the total *garh mahal* at Agra must have appeared in its original state. Its massive western wall with flanking octagonal towers possessed but a single, relatively unobtrusive entrance in the centre. This entrance gives way to a series of relatively small rooms and open courts. Small rooms, open courts, wide *chajjā* and a construction of thick, red sandstone walls tended to make the interior cooler than the open areas. The cooling aspect of these rooms was further enhanced by an ingenious, outer wall construction (See: **Figure 66**). A double wall was built with louvres high on the outside and close to the floor on the interior. Water was then channeled to flow down the interior space cooling, through evaporation, the air which passed over its inner surface before passing into the interior.

Although asymmetrical, *in toto*, the *Jahangiri Mahal* gives the strong impression of an axial design. Stierlin asserts that it is possible that the *Jahangiri Mahal* was originally axially symmetrical, *en plan*.[97] Certainly, many of the

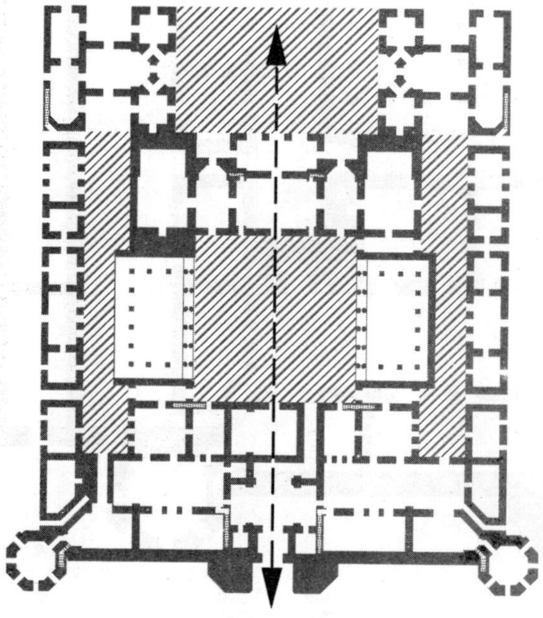

Figure 67 — *Jahangiri Mahal, Lāl Qilā*, Agra, indicating possible symmetrical plan

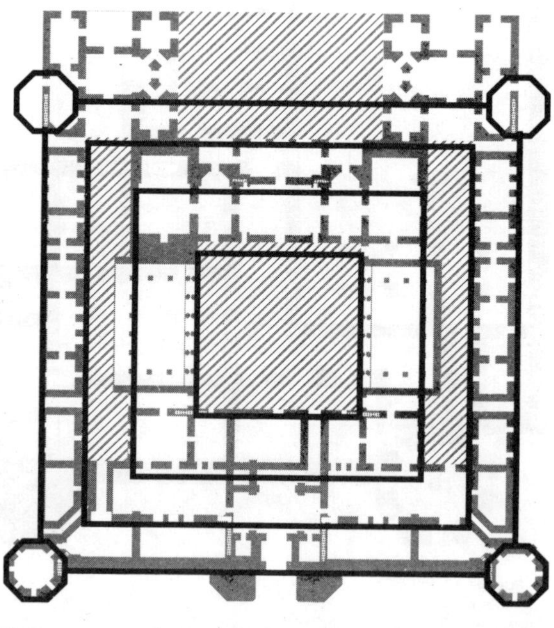

Figure 68 — *Jahangiri Mahal, Lāl Qilā*, Agra, possible symmetrical plan with cross-axial implications

spaces, rooms and passageways south of the east-west axis are duplicated to the north making this assertion a real possibility. Such axiality would not be revolutionary in the least and would provide a most pleasing design (See: **Figure 67**). Additionally, he asserts, again with some visual evidence, that the internal divisions harken to a Hindu plan (See: **Figure 68**). Indeed there are a number of rooms and spaces found south of the axis that are mirrored to the north. This would appear to make this assertion most plausible.

If a symmetrical design was the basis, why then the deviation? Certainly, by the supposed time of its construction, Akbar was already involved in the realization of *Fatehpur Sikri*. This complex, sophisticated ruler appeared to be a person concerned with detail. Was it to accommodate the ruler's wish that certain changes seem to have been made in this plan?

Further, Stierlin asserts that the distribution of rooms within the interior, lend themselves to a "Persian" arrangement. Again, if the symmetrical arrangement is used, as seen in **Figure 69**, then this too has great merit. It must also be noted that this arrangement is also applicable to the present plan as well. The division of the internal space into: 1) entrance area, 2) reception area, 3) library area, and 4) zenānā appears to make perfect sense. However, the *Jahangiri Mahal* was neither a solitary palace within this *garh mahal*; nor, apparently was it the first to be constructed. Why then would this division, including a *zenānā* be employed? There was apparently already a rather complete harem.

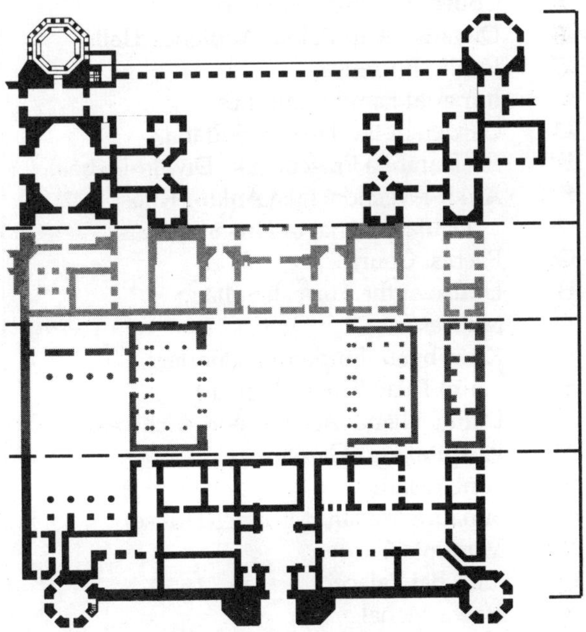

Figure 69 — *Jahangiri Mahal, Lāl Qilā*, indicating division of "Indian and Persian" areas according to HS

There are those who view the *Jahangiri Mahal* as being the *zenānā* of the *Lāl Qilā*. The solitary western entrance in a windowless wall is one of the reasons for this assertion. In addition it is also noted that there are few other means of ingress or egress from this complicated space. Interestingly enough, these are also arguments that may be applied to a *mardānā*. There are few means of direct access to the residential areas of any *garh mahal*. The single western entrance is not a compelling reason to label this area as a *zenānā*.

Agra's *Lāl Qilā* is one of the three great Mughal Imperial *garh mahals*. Constructed upon an uneven site, it indicates not only an accommodation to the site, but also a tendency towards axiality. All structures except the *Diwān-i Ām* and its courtyard, the *Macchi Bhavan*, the *Diwān-i Khās* and the *Naginā Masjid* (See: **Plate 23**) are on the same axis. The areas/structures mentioned immediately above are on a perpendicular axis to the eastern wall of the citadel where they meet.

Neither eccentric nor unusual in its total plan, *Lāl Qilā* of Agra exemplifies the requirements of a *garh mahal*. Further, it underlines the iconic nature of its existence and of the great Mughal dynasty. It acts as a counterpoint to the *Tāj Mahal* around the bend on the sacred Yamuna.

Fatehpur Sikri

(*c.* 1569 -1585 CE)

Fatehpur Sikri[98] stands as a magnificent monument to Akbar the Great. It exemplifies all the iconographic parameters of a royal residence set out in the "Introduction." As a palace compound, it reigns above the majority of royal residences, *garh mahal* of India for its coherent design. The fact that this complex, particularly the imperial compound with its many elements, was conceived and constructed by a single and purposeful individual — i.e., the Mughal Emperor Jalal-ud-din Akbar (r. 1556-1605 CE) — accounts for its cohesive design.

In toto, Fatehpur Sikri is neither axial nor symmetrical although buildings within the imperial compound tend to be oriented north-south. Yet, as will be seen, numerous buildings within the complex adhere to strict axiality, even cross-axiality. From the spacious public court of the east to the massive stables in the west, each area melds one into the other, yet are distinct unto themselves (See: **Figure 70**).

Built upon a ridge with a river to the west, *Fatehpur Sikri's* separate buildings seem to flow one into the other. No single structure dominates the whole in either size or scale. Neither are there massive escarpments with towering walls directly connected to and protecting the *garh mahal*. The walls surrounding *Fatehpur Sikri* proper are well away from the royal compound, and, in truth, are far less imposing than those surrounding the *Lāl Qilā* of Agra (See: **Figure 71**). In this feature, *Fatehpur Sikri* seems to be related to, or as Mughal counterpart of, the famous Loire chateau *Chambord* of François Iere — i.e., a *chateau* rather than a *donjon*, a place of elegance and peace where one might relax rather than a fortified *donjon*.

That is not to say that *Fatehpur Sikri* was not a secure residence. There were numerous

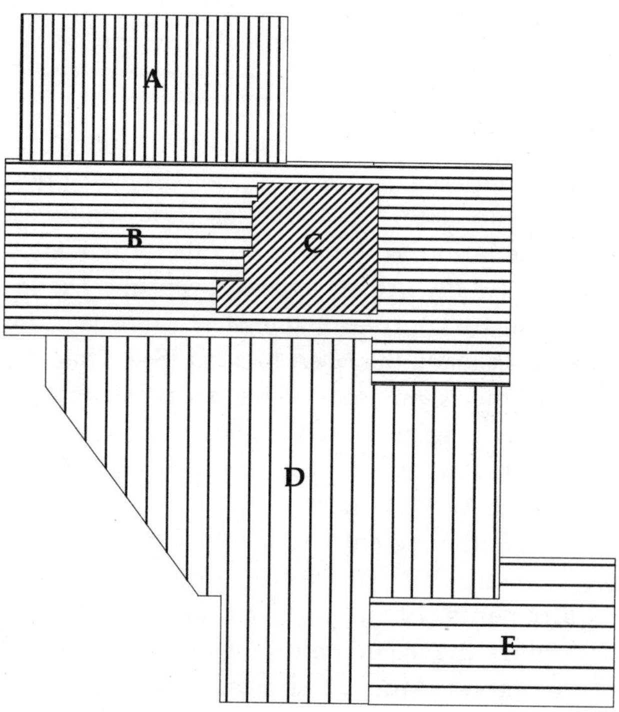

Figure 70 — Distribution of areas, ***Fatehpur Sikri***; public areas (**A**), limited access areas (**B**), restricted (**C**), *zenānā* (**D**), attendents and military (**E**)

Legend for **Plate 26**

A	Court of Public Audience
B	Diwan-i-'Am, Public Audience Hall
C^1	Public Entrance
C^2	Imperial Family Entrance
D	Garden of the Turkish Sultāna
E	Ekastambha Prasada (aka Diwān-i-Khās)
F	Ānkh-i-Michoni (aka Ānkh-i-Khās, Daulat Khānā) or Diwān-i-Khās
G	Pachisi Court
H	House of the Turkish Sultāna
I	Madrasa
J	Khwabgah, Emperor's Quarters
K	Anup Talao (Char Chaman)
L	Daftar Khānā (Admin. and Archives)
M	Hospital and Garden
N	Pañch Mahal
O	Sunahrā Makān (Miriam's House)
P	Miriam's Garden
Q	Jodh Bai Palace
R	Hawa Mahal
S	Naginā Masjid
T	Birbal Bhavan (House of Raja Birbal)
U	Stables for Camels and Horses
V	Hammam

Plate 26 — *Fatehpur Sikri*, plan of royal compound

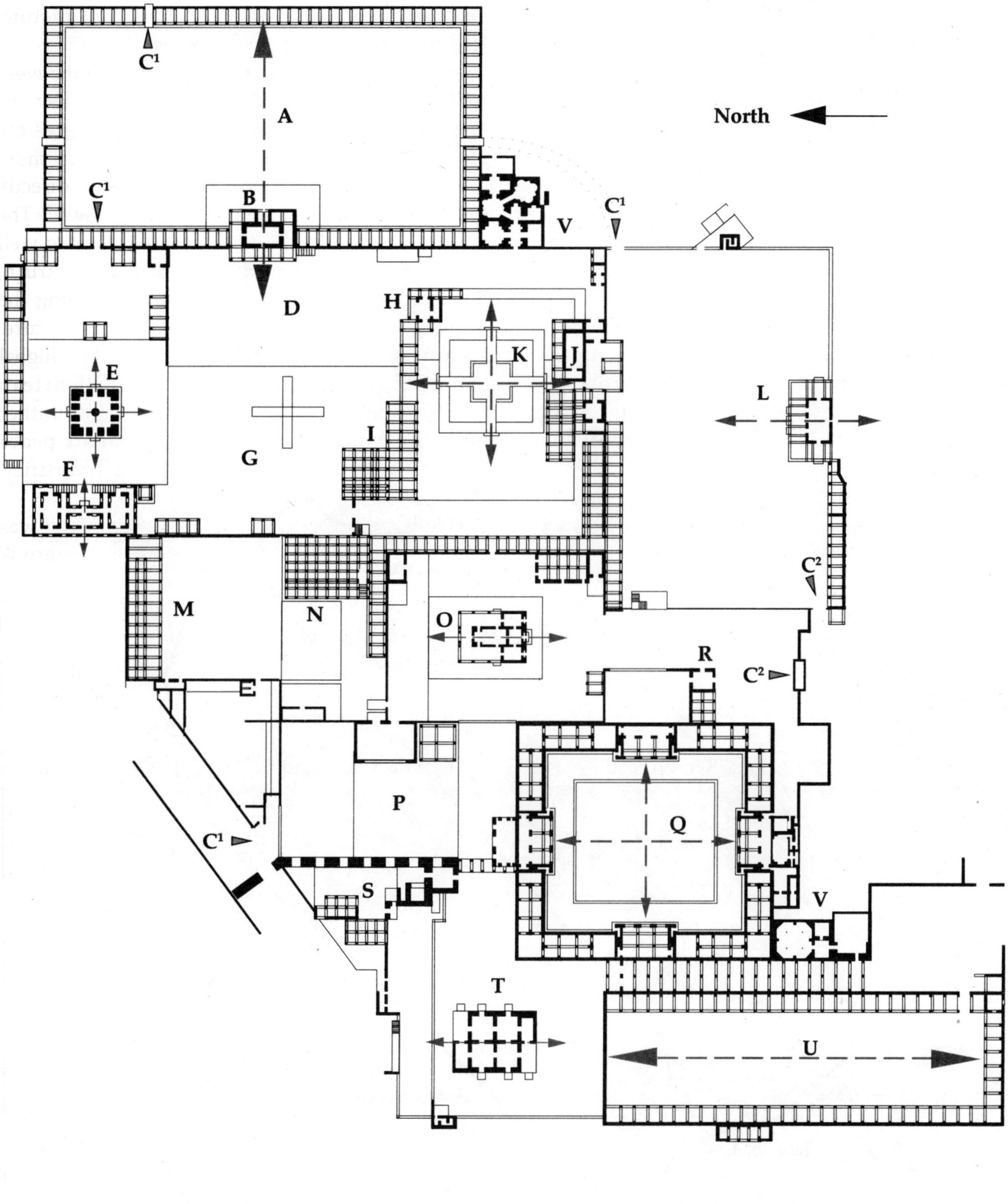

security measures employed, but they did not dominate the design or external aspect of this *garh mahal*, but were inconspicuously incorporated into the whole complex. The path that one must take to arrive at the emperor's private quarters was no less devious than other residences (See: **Figure 72**). In this case, the vast open areas that one had to cross were easily defendable, and, further, a number of paths in which the emperor could exit in haste, if need be, are to be found.

Nonetheless, the disposition of the royal compound and the girdle wall which enfolds *Fatehpur Sikri* is dramatically different from the *Lāl Qilā* of Agra citadel or even *Shahjahanabad* of Delhi. Additionally, the girdle wall supports no less than nine gates (Indic: *darwāzā*), an unusual feature for a citadel. Likewise, the imperial compound possesses a number of entrances which were for the public (See: **Plate 26 — C[1]**), as well as several for royal access alone (See: **Plate 26 — C[2]**). The number of gates (Indic: *darwāzā*) found in the *Lāl Qilā* (See: **Plate 24**) of Agra and the *Shahjahanabad* of Delhi (See: **Plate 50**) were far less; amounting to two or three.

Such apparent disregard for traditional fortifications of *Fatehpur Sikri* may be seen as an implication of power. Akbar may have felt so secure in his domination of and hold on the empire that he did not find traditional citadel fortifications necessary. Indeed, should an invading force threaten the person of the

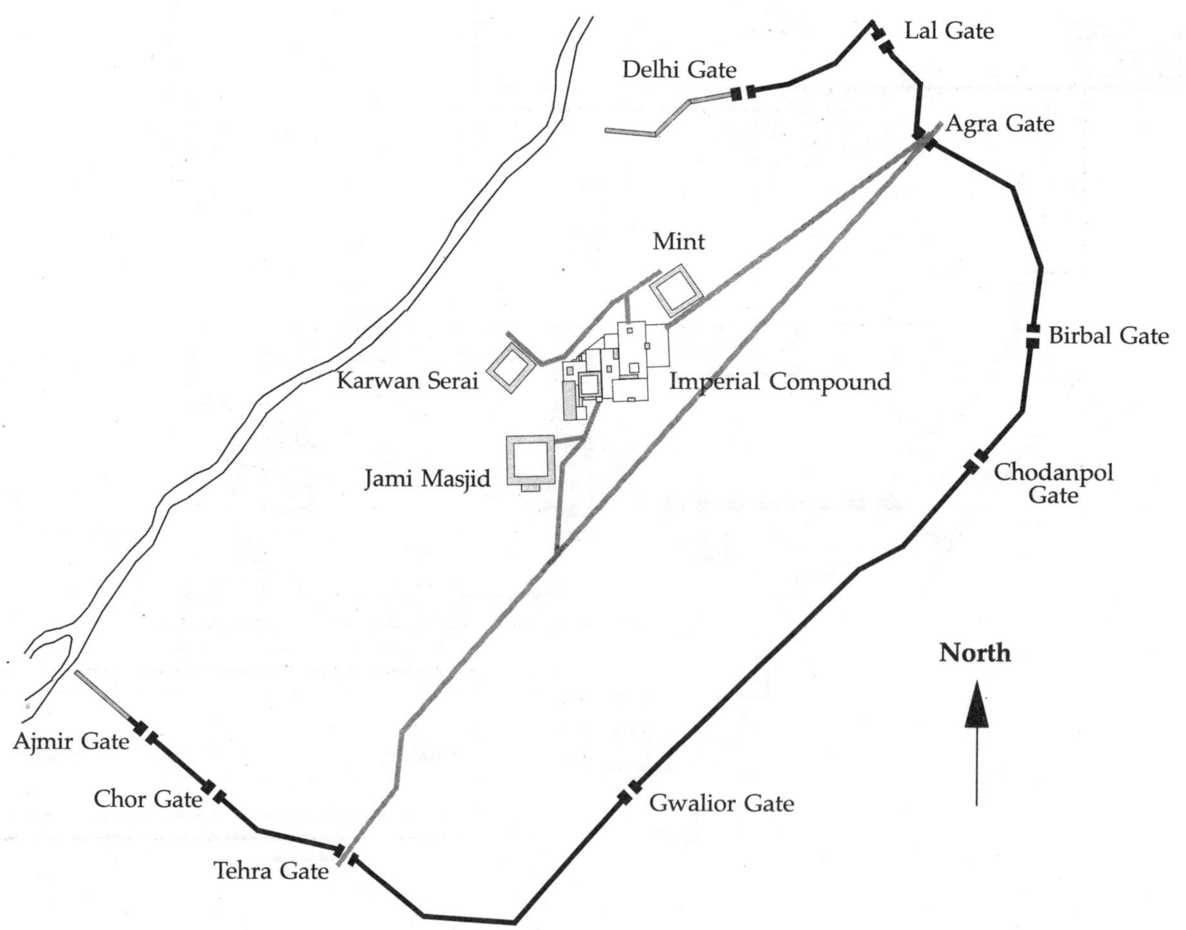

Figure 71 — ***Fatehpur Sikri***; indicating girdle wall and imperial environs

emperor, *Lāl Qilā* at Agra was but a short distance away — easy access in times of peril.

However, that aside, *Fatehpur Sikri*, as noted by many scholars, is a *garh mahal* of numerous axes (See: **Plate 26**). Grover describes *Fatehpur Sikri* as a town which possesses "symmetry around multiple axes."[99] The multiple axes here are: multiple, perpendicular axes.[100] The whole is aligned to the cardinal points of the compass as are each building or structure within the imperial compound. The impressive *Jami Masjid*, to the south and west, also follows this alignment (See: **Figure 71**). On the other hand the *Mint*, to the north and east, and the *Karwan Serai*, to the south and west, are oriented differently — i.e., not to the cardinal points of the compass. Within the imperial compound the buildings tend to be of similar height — i.e., one or two storeys in height — with the exception of the *Pañch Mahal* (See: **Plate 26 — N**).

Axially aligned buildings predominate within the Imperial compound of *Fatehpur Sikri*. The important axial buildings include: the *Diwān-i-Ām* (**B**), the *Ānkh-i-Michoni* (aka *Ānkh-i-Khās, Daulat Khānā*) or *Diwān-i-Khās* (**F**), the *Daftar Khānā* (**L**), the *Sunahrā Makān* (**O**), the *Birbal Bhavan* (*House of Rājā Birbal*) (**T**), and the stables (**U**). Cross axial buildings and structures are evident in: the *Ekastambha Prasada* (aka *Diwān-i-Khās*) (**E**), the *Anup Talao* (*Chār Chaman*) (**K**), and to some extent the *Jodh Bai Palace* (**Q**). Actually, the *Jodh Bai Palace* is mirror cross-axial rather than axial (See: **Appendix D, Plate 104**). It is to be noted that nearly all the axial buildings are oriented north to south, with the exception of the *Diwān-i-Ām* (**B**) and the *Ānkh-i-Michoni* (aka *Ānkh-i-Khās, Daulat Khānā*) or *Diwān-i-Khās* (**F**) which are oriented east to west.

Various other *garh mahals* possessed many of the elements found in *Fatehpur Sikri* — i.e., public areas, *mardānā*, *zenānā*, stables, etc. However, few exhibit a strict adherence to the cardinal points of the compass as their sole axes, or any variation, thereof. There is, as always, an exception — i.e., the *City Palace of Udaipur* (see: **Plate 38**) and the *Suraj Mal Mandir* of the Jats of Bharatpur at Deeg (See: **Plate 56**).

The similarity in height of the structures, the utilization of the same building material and the strict alignment to the cardinal points of the compass of the imperial compound are all part of the cohesive quality of *Fatehpur Sikri*. As a capital of an empire, it was most innovative in its design. However, there was a single flaw that was to cause the magnificent *Fatehpur Sikri* to be abandoned within two decades — i.e., water.

The water supply during the rainy season was more than adequate for the imperial household and the builders. But, as the population grew, it became evident that the water supply during the dry season was not near enough to sustain what the growing population required. Therefore, this innovative city with its incomparable imperial compound was abandoned! This was a setback for Akbar the Great. Yet for posterity it was fortuitous as its abandonment, in part, preserved it for our contemplation and enjoyment.

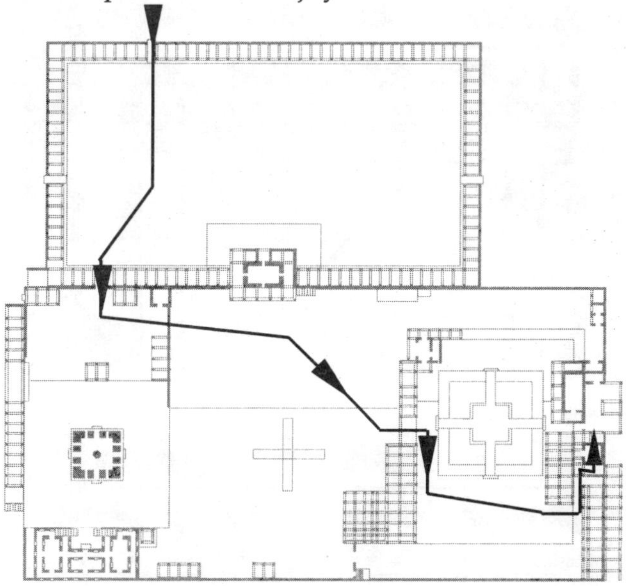

Figure 72 — *Fatehpur Sikri*, indicating path from the public entrance to the *Diwān-i-Ām Court* to the *Khwabgah*

Diwān-i-Khās (aka *Ekastambha Prasada*) *Fatehpur Sikri* (a. 1569 CE)

The so-called *Diwān-i-Khās* of *Fatehpur Sikri*, or the *Ekastambha Prasada*[101] ranks as one of the most elegant and symmetrical designs in the architectural history of mankind. Located to the west of the *Diwān-i Ām*, resting upon a shallow podium, the *Ekastambha Prasada* is essentially orientated south towards the *Pachisi' Court* (See: **Plate 26 — E**).

It was originally assumed that this was the *Diwān-i-Khās* where Akbar could hold private audience for a limited number of people. Normally, the *darśana* may have been held in the *Diwān-i Ām*, but it was to the *Ekastambha Prasada* (aka *Diwān-i-Khās*) that special audiences for high ranking courtiers and foreign nobles or diplomats **could** have been given. However, Nath asserts that the *darśana* was performed on the uppermost storey of the *Pañch Mahal*.

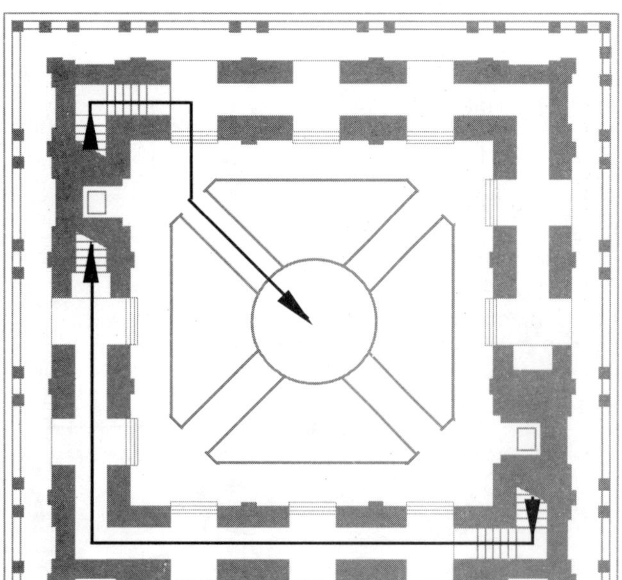

Figure 73 — *Diwān-i-Khās* (*Ekastambha Prasada*), *Fatehpur Sikri*, second storey plan indicating possible routes

The performance of the *darśana* would have given the opportunity for pomp, majesty and untold elegance to have been displayed. This would have provided the assembled, common folk and courtiers with a view of the majesty of the imperial person. It, doubtless, was a spectacle few forgot. However, the *Ekastambha Prasāda* (aka *Diwān-i-Khās*) provided a different venue, and in some cases and a more impressive view of the emperor's presence, iconographically. In reality, it is a political stage designed to impress!

The *Ekastambha Prasāda* (aka *Diwān-i-Khās*), compared to many of the other buildings at *Fatehpur Sikri* was small in comparison and unique. It consists of a two storeyed space interrupted by a surrounding balcony, and four bridges to the central throne area, creating the second storey. Square and cross-axial, *en plan*, the first storey consists of four doorways set at the cardinal points of the compass. Flanking each door was a window with elegant *jālīs*, and in the centre a massive support column for the "throne" above. Just within the entrance ways of the east and west façades were stairways set within the thick walls leading to the second storey. This level is essentially more complex that the lower level. As one would have alighted on this level one would have found themselves in a narrow corridor that bordered two sides of this storey (See: **Figure 73**). One route would have led to a second stairway ascending to the roof level, while the second possible route would have led to the "throne" in the centre. On each façade of the *Ekastambha Prasāda* (aka *Diwān-i-Khās*) there are three openings, corresponding with those on the first storey. The flanking openings may have had *jālīs*, but the central one probably did not. This would have permitted sufficient light into this upper storey to fully illuminate the "throne" area (See: **Plate 27**; see also: **Figure 74**).

The lack of security here can be seen as a non-issue for the second storey. The narrow 'bridges,' a mere two feet four inches wide, would

Plate 27 — *Diwān-i-Khās* (*Ekastambha Prasada*), plan 1st & 2nd storeys

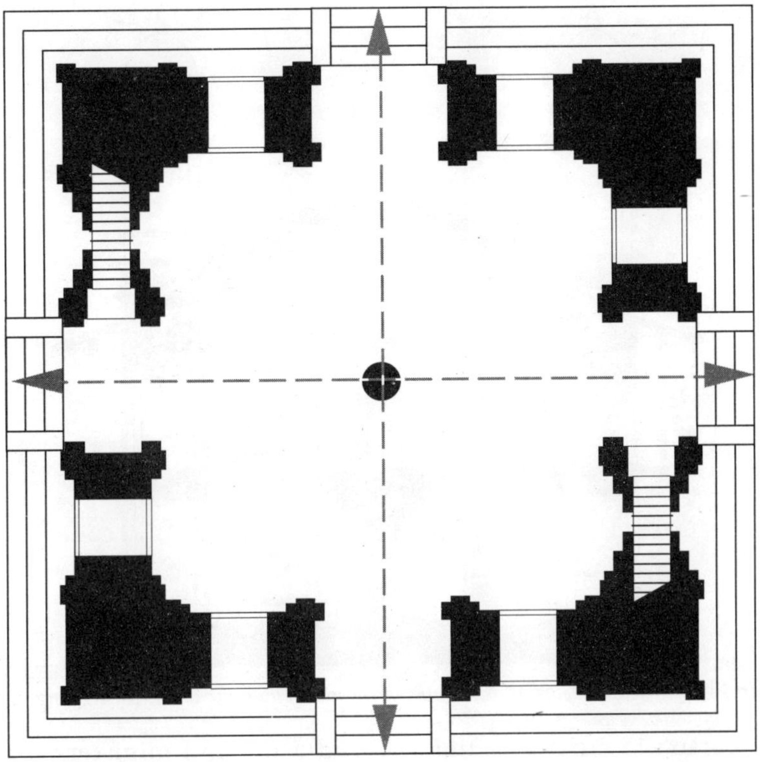

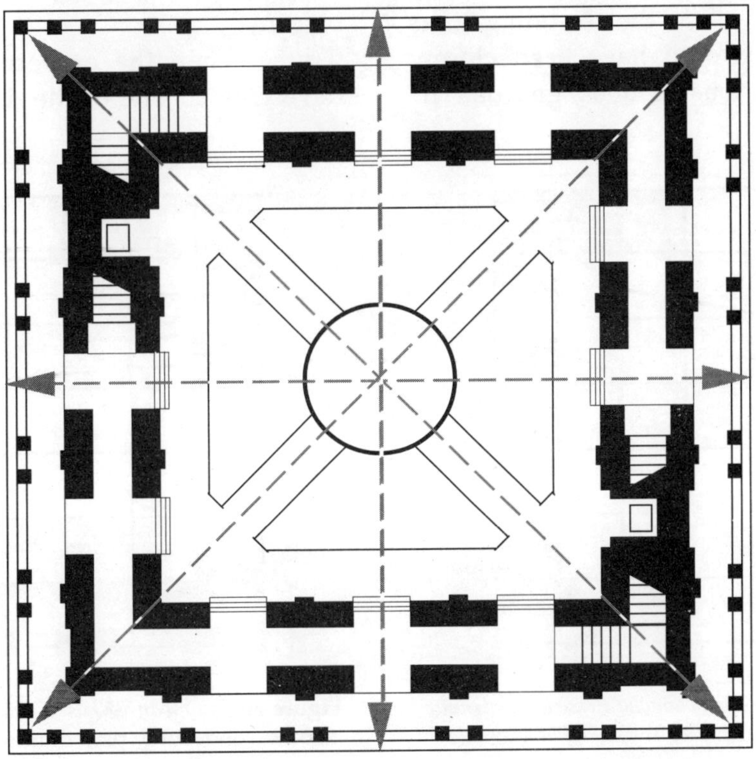

Figure 74 — *Diwān-i-Khās (Ekastambha Prasada), Fatehpur Sikri,* indicating section

have allowed but one person to cross at a time. One might well imagine that the entrances to these four bridges as well as the ascending stairs to this second level would have been closely guarded by his most trusted body guards. His advisors and ministers may probably have been relegated to the lower floor or the surrounding balcony.

When the emperor entered, he would have crossed one of the diagonal bridges to the

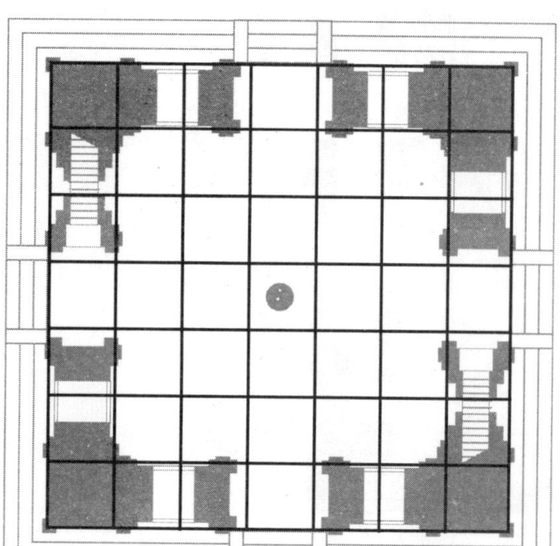

Figure 75 — *Diwān-i-Khās (Ekastambha Prasada), Fatehpur Sikri,* first storey plan indicating an *Sthandila Maṇḍala*

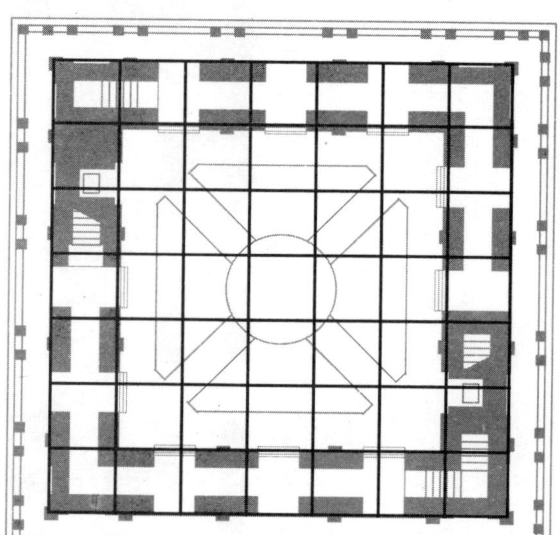

Figure 76 — *Diwān-i-Khās, (Ekastambha Prasada) Fatehpur Sikri,* second storey plan indicating an *Sthandila Maṇḍala*

central, circular "throne" or *gaddi*. Seated upon cushions, the person of the emperor would have been obscured from most of those gathered beneath. Yet, his voice would have been heard by everyone as it resonated off the surface of the four-sided, domelike ceiling above his head. Here the emperor, physically elevated, isolated, exalted by locale emphasizing his imperial status, is presented to the gathering below. Iconographically and in reality, his voice descends from the cosmos as he spoke, seated, visually obscured, upon the elevated *ekastambha*, the *axis mundi* of his empire. His physical presence noted only by his disembodied voice. The effect within the *Ekastambha Prasāda* (aka *Diwān-i-Khās*) must have been stunning, even startling, certainly impressive!

A *Sthandila Maṇḍala* of forty-nine square *pada*, seven on each side, is seen to comfortably fit over the floor plan of the first storey (See: **Figure 76**). Similar results occur when the same *maṇḍala* is superimposed over the second storey (See: **Figure 77**). Numbers here begin to assume

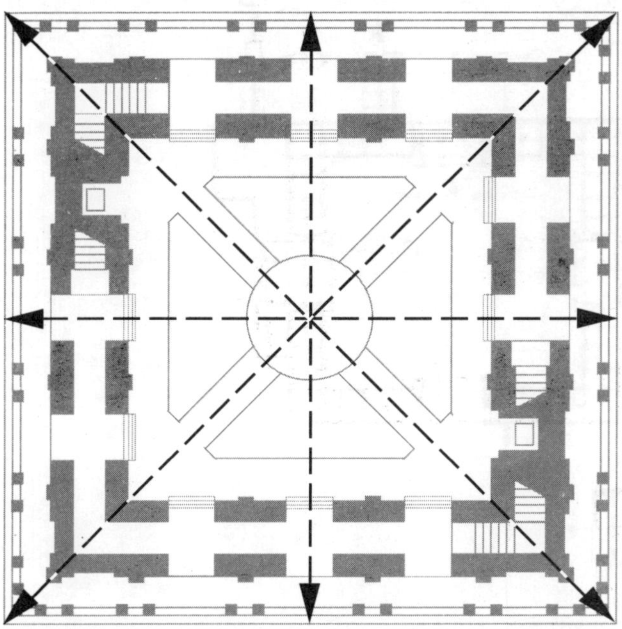

Figure 77 — *Diwān-i-Khās (Ekastambha Prasada), Fatehpur Sikri*, indicating cardinal and intercardinal axes

some cosmic importance. Forty-nine, a masculine number, is a sacred numeral whose š is the equally sacred seven. It is further auspicious in its make-up. As a compound number it is associated astronomically with the planet *Rāhu* (the ascending node of the moon) (4), the planet Mars (*Maṅgala, Kuja* or *Aṅgāraka*) (9). When reduced it produces four and, therefore, the planet *Rāhu* (the ascending node of the moon) (4). On the other hand, seven, a masculine number, is often considered as the number of creation and perfection, as well as natural law. It is a most sacred number and mystical being made up of the spiritual three (3) (masculine) plus the practical four (4) (feminine). Seven is associated astronomically with the planet *Ketu* (the descending node of the moon). It may be represented as heptagon as in the *Sharabha Yantra*, a seven-petaled lotus (Ind.: *sapta-dala padma*) as in the *Matsya Yantra*, a diagram which connotes endlessness.[102]

Finally, there arises another consideration which further underlines the implied character of the emperor. This is to be found in the orientation of the *Ekastambha Prasāda* (aka *Diwān-i-Khās*). Not only is the *Ekastambha Prasada* (aka *Diwān-i-Khās*) orientated towards the cardinal points of the compass, the use of the diagonal bridges of the second storey also connect this structure to the intercardinal points as well (See: **Figure 77**). There is no other building or structure within this imperial complex to which this double orientation can be applied. This would seem to point to the omnipotent power that a ruler wished to have associated with his being. Akbar the Great's wide ranging intellect embraced many divergent philosophies and theologies, his conquests were equally far reaching and his empire was relatively secure. It would appear that the including of the cardinal and intercardinal points of the compass becomes an iconic representation not only of the emperor, but the empire as well.

The use of an *ekastambha* was not unique to Akbar the Great or to the Muslims. Aśoka raised numerous pillars which may be seen as serving the same purpose. Further, the *Kotla Firuz Shah* (See: pp. 40-43, & **Figures 23 & 24**) also made use of a 'unitary pillar,' but in an assumed way. Finally, the 'stem' or *devata kotuva* (Sinhalese) of a typical *stūpa* was also, iconographically, seen as an axis — i.e., *axis mundi* — connecting the terrestrial with the celestial (See: **Appendix A, Plate 94**). However, a 'commemorative' or 'symbolic' pillar is not architecture — i.e., architecture as the art or science of designing and constructing a building, or the enclosing of space. The *Ekastambha Prasada* (aka *Diwān-i-Khās*) at Fatehpur Sikri is! Nonetheless, the employment of an ekastambha upon which the Emperor **may have** sat would have, iconographically, placed Akbar at the centre of the world, the *axis mundi.*

The Zenānā
Fatehpur Sikri (a. 1569 CE)

The *zenānā* of *Fatehpur Sikri,* like so many other similar areas within the *garh mahals* of Indian citadels, both Hindu and Muslim, is extensive and occupies a large portion of this imperial complex (See: **Plate 26**; see also: **Figure 78**). As has been stated, often times the *zenānā* is the most developed area of a *garh mahal.* The ruler frequently spent great amounts of time away from his capital in conquest, state visits, or residing in other, less formal *mahals* of his realm. It would have been inefficient and impractical for a ruler to transport all his wives and concubines during his many travels. Certainly, his "favorites" would have accompanied him as he moved about. Therefore, the *zenānā* of his

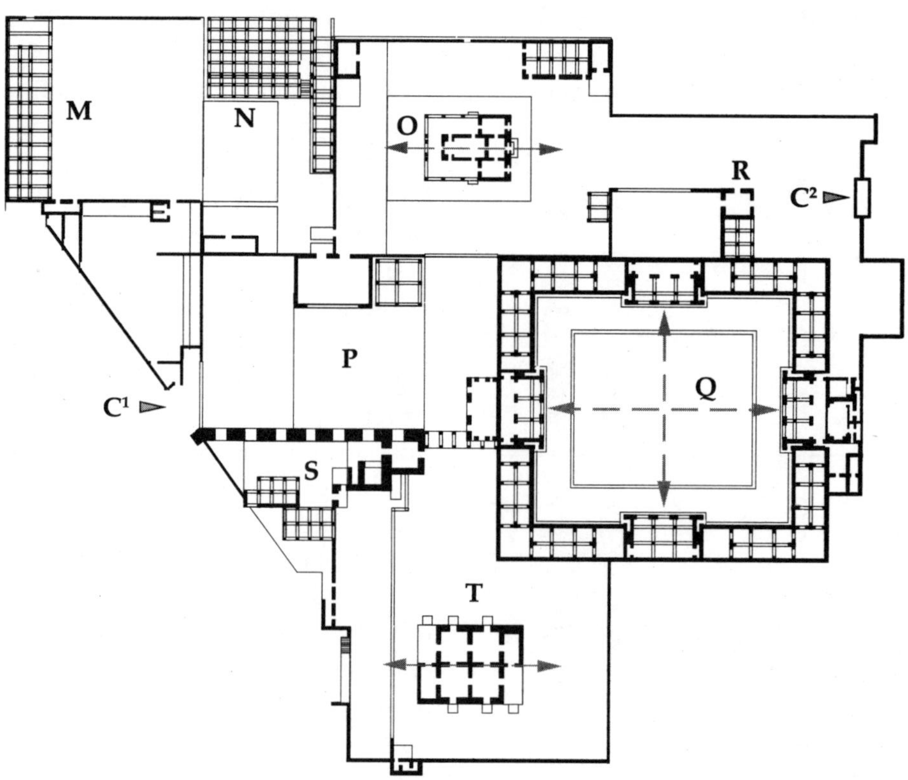

Figure 78 — *Zenānā, Fatehpur Sikri* (designations are the same as seen in **Plate 26**)

capital was developed, in part, to accommodate all his wives and concubines, and to provide those who were in semipermanent residence suitable means to wile away their considerable free time.

The *zenānā* of *Fatehpur Sikri* is most important as it holds several buildings of some note — e.g., the *Birbal Bhavan* (the *House of Raja Birbal*) (See: **Plate 26 — T;** see also: **Figure 78 — T**), the *Jodh Bai Mahal* (See: **Plate 26 — Q;** see also: **Figure 78 — Q**), the *Sunahrā Makān* (aka *Miriam's House*) (See: **Plate 26 — O;** see also: **Figure 78 — O**), and the *Pañch Mahal* (See: **Plate 26 — N;** see also: **Figure 78 — N**). Each one is unique in design, plan, detail and scope. Three of them — i.e., the *Birbal Bhavan*, the *Jodh Bai Mahal* and the *Sunahrā Makān* — were most probably residences within the *zenānā*, while the *Pañch Mahal* was a pavilion of pleasure and observation.

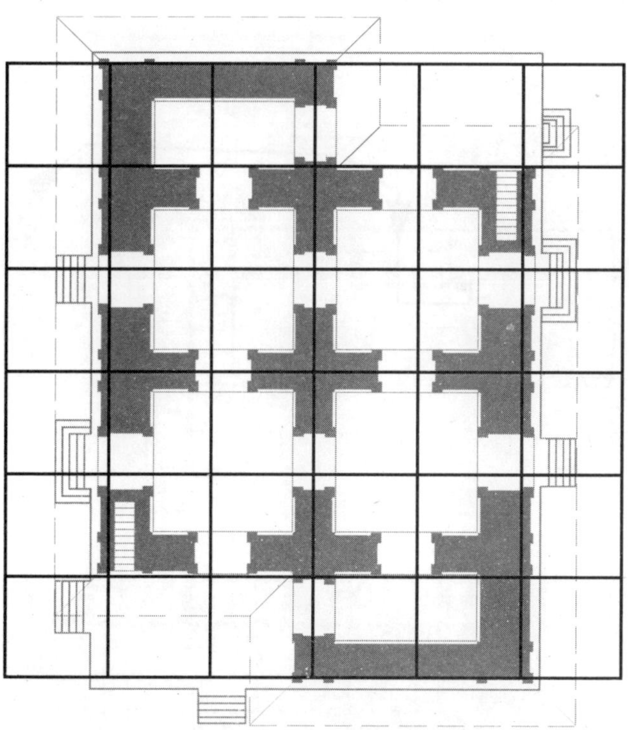

Figure 79 — *House of Raja Birbal, Fatehpur Sikri,* indicating an *Ugrapitha Maṇḍala*

Within the *zenānā* there were gardens, fountains and *hammam* for the women. Their life was closely regulated, guarded, but their environs were such as to ameliorate their confinement.

Birbal Bhavan
(House of Raja Birbal)
Fatehpur Sikri (*c.* 1572 CE)

The *mahal* most frequently identified as the *Birbal Bhavan* (*House of Raja Birbal*),[103] is small in scale compared to many of the other buildings in the ensemble of *Fatehpur Sikri* (See: **Plate 26 — T;** see also: **Figure 78 — T**). Yet, it is one of the most important architecturally and from the standpoint of design it is unique.

Set deep within what is recognized as the *zenānā*, the *Birbal Bhavan* (*House of Raja Birbal*) is one of the few examples of rotating axiality (See: **Appendix D, Plate 105**) and indicates the variations that may be achieved in an axial plan. It is believed that this residence was designed and constructed for one of the important wives of Akbar as it lies within the recognized *zenānā* of the *garh mahal* (See: **Plate 26 — T**) and separate from the other structures.

The first storey consists of four square rooms with two narrow, rectangular rooms serving as vestibules (See: **Plate 28**). These two small rectangular rooms each lead out onto their own porch or terrace and are lit only by the entrance door. Two of the rooms possess two windows, while those with the attached vestibule have but a single window. The whole of the first storey is protected by a deep *chajjā* which, coupled with the thickness of the masonry wall, would provide a cooler interior than the unprotected outside. Within the thick, outer walls are two staircases leading to the second storey. Here are two additional, domed rooms, each with two doors leading to the two terraces and both connected to each other at the corners.

Additionally, each of these second storey rooms indicate a window and another doorway leading to a small balcony. Doubtless, these rooms served as sleeping chamber(s) elevated so that they could benefit from the evening breezes wafting through the multiple openings.

Since the *Birbal Bhavan* is not square, a square *maṇḍala* is not altogether applicable. However, it is interesting to note that if an *Ugrapīṭha Maṇḍala* is superimposed over the plan, certain propitious conjunctions appear to occur (See **Figure 79**). First, the width of the "house" is approximately four *pada* wide. Second, each of the four rooms of the first storey fall within four square *pada* — i.e., a *Pechaka Maṇḍala*. Third, together, these four rooms fall within sixteen square *pada* — i.e., a *Mahāpīṭha Maṇḍala*. Finally, the narrow vestibules are two *pada* long and one wide.

The fact that the *Birbal Bhavan* (*House of Raja Birbal*) does not conform to any of the known "Basic Plans" (See: pp. 8-13) is not untoward. This *garh mahal* was, after all, constructed by and for a Muslim ruler, and one who possessed an active and far ranging aesthetics. It is a pleasing and unique addition to an already remarkable complex of imperial buildings — a complex that mirrored the wealth and intellectual range of Akbar the Great.

The *Birbal Bhavan* provides easy ingress and egress to both its first and second storeys as any royal residence must provide. Furthermore, it provides both common areas for entertainment — i.e., the lower storey — and intimate areas — i.e., the second storey — for more personal entertainment.

Jodh-Bai Mahal
Fatehpur Sikri (a. 1569 CE)

The *Jodh-Bai Mahal* (aka *Jodha Bai Mahal*),[104] set within the *zenānā*, appears to dominate this area by its size and scale (See: **Plate 25 — Q;** see also: **Figure 78 — Q**). It differs from the other two important buildings of this part of the complex — i.e., the *Birbal Bhavan* (See: **Plate 25 — T;** see also: **Figure 78 — T**) and the *Sunahrā Makān* (ākā Miriam's House) (See: **Plate 25 — O;** see also: **Figure 78 — O**) — in that it is completely enclosed with only a single entrance and with no windows facing outwards in the first storey and only several small windows with *jālī* on the second storey (See: **Plate 29**). It is a typical *zenānā*.[105] Direct access to this area of the *zenānā* is via either one of the royal portals or through one of the narrow gates from the *mardānā*. The only entrance into the *Jodh-Bai Mahal* is found on the east face of the edifice, protected by a deep porch with suitable security (See: **Figure 80**).

The main feature of the *Jodh-Bai Mahal* is a large courtyard, surrounded by rooms and four pavilions projecting from the cardinal points of the compass, and four domed, corner rooms at the intercardinal points. The rooms flow one into

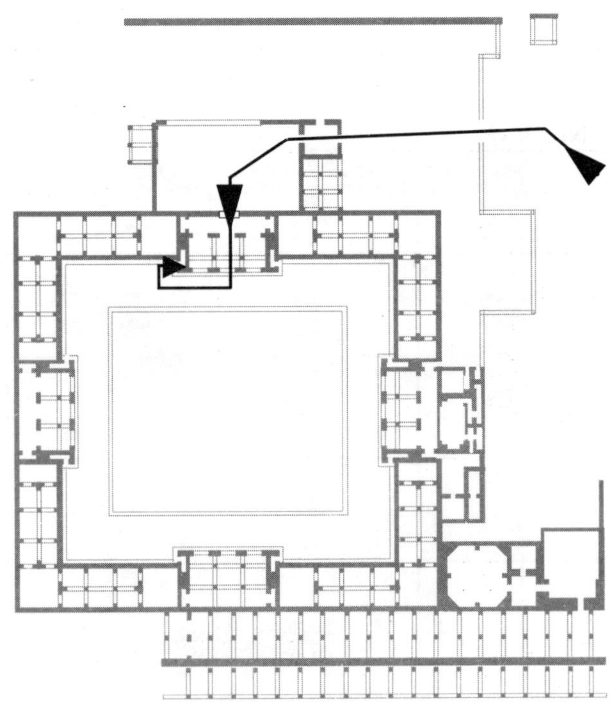

Figure 80 — *Jodh-Bai Mahal, Fatehpur Sikri,* indicating path from the private entrance

Plate 28 — *Birbal Bhavan*, plan, 1st & 2nd storeys

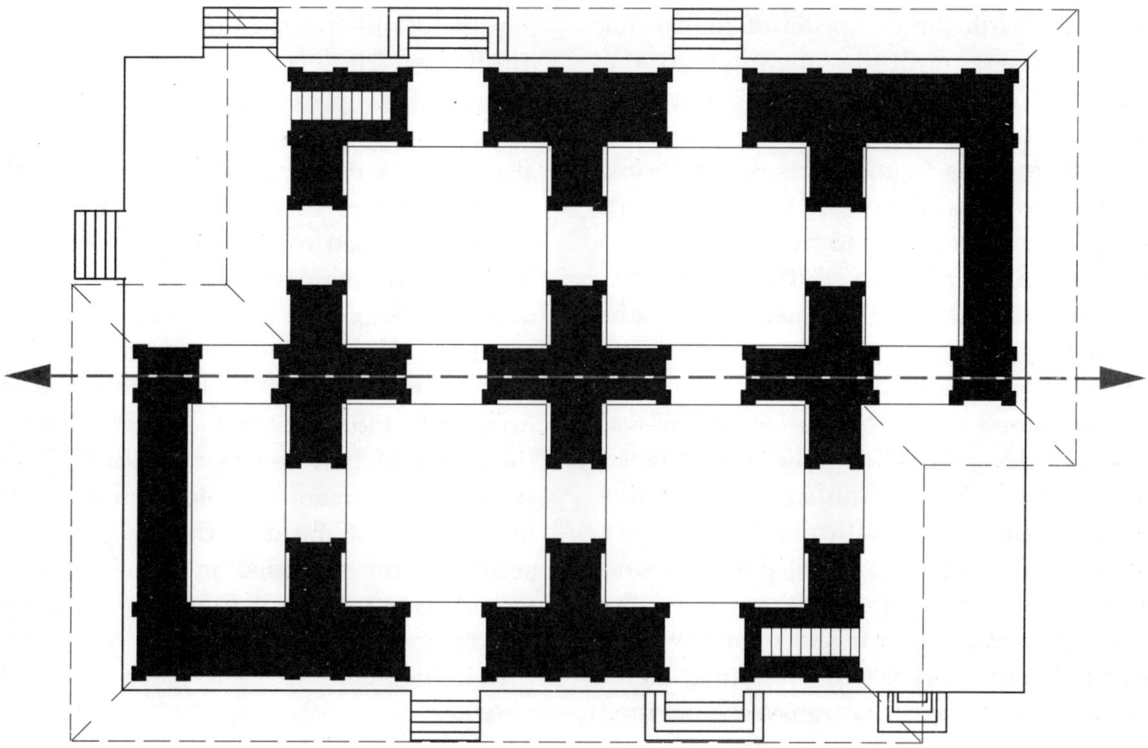

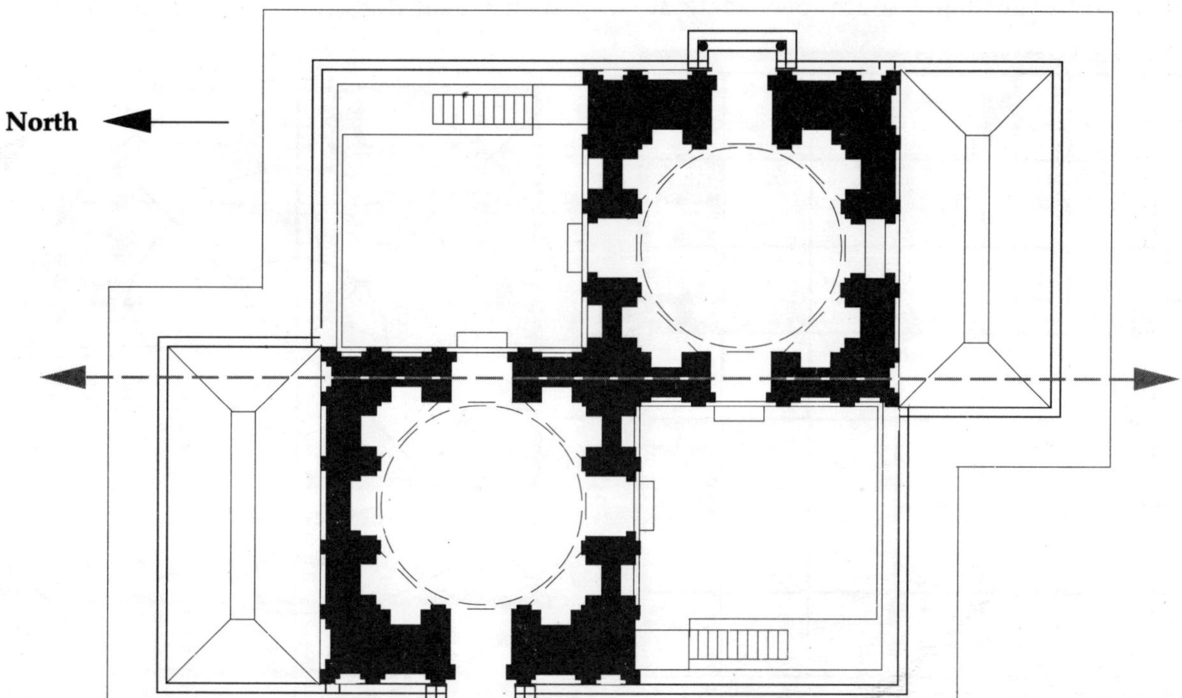

the other, and, with the exception of the corner rooms, all possess multiple openings to the courtyard. The only variation is to be found in the rooms of the cardinal pavilions. They are entered only from the façades of these pavilions. The cardinal pavilions of the east, west and north all possess two staircases leading to the second storey. The exception is the southern pavilion. Here the areas that in the other three would have been stairways are now narrow passageways leading to the *hammam* and other private areas.

The second storey of the *Jodh-Bai Mahal* is, by its very design, considerably more private. As noted above, access is limited. Once on this level, one is confronted with eight subsidiary structures: four over the cardinal pavilions and four domed rooms at the corners — i.e., the intercardinal points. The east and west pavilions are identical, consisting of two projecting, eight-columned *śālās* attached to a transverse pavilion with five openings towards the court and wide openings to the north and south (See: **Plate 30**). Similarly, the north and south pavilions are duplicates. They consist of two *chatrī* over the corners of the projections and an enclosed space or room with a single door. These two rooms also possess two narrow windows in the ends. At the corners of the second storey are four identical, domed rooms. They all possess narrow doorways on the east-west axis as well as on the north-south axis. In addition each has two small windows, facing outwards with *jālī*.

The rooms of the first storey would have provided more formal spaces. Due to the thickness of their walls and *chajjā* these areas would have been a cooler refuge during the hottest part of the day. On the other hand, the second storey provided an area for strolling and would have been cooled by the evening breezes. In addition, the open *chatrī* and *śālās* would have provided a cool space to sleep during the hot weather.

The design of the *Jodh-Bai Mahal, en plan*, is such that it does not conveniently conform to a

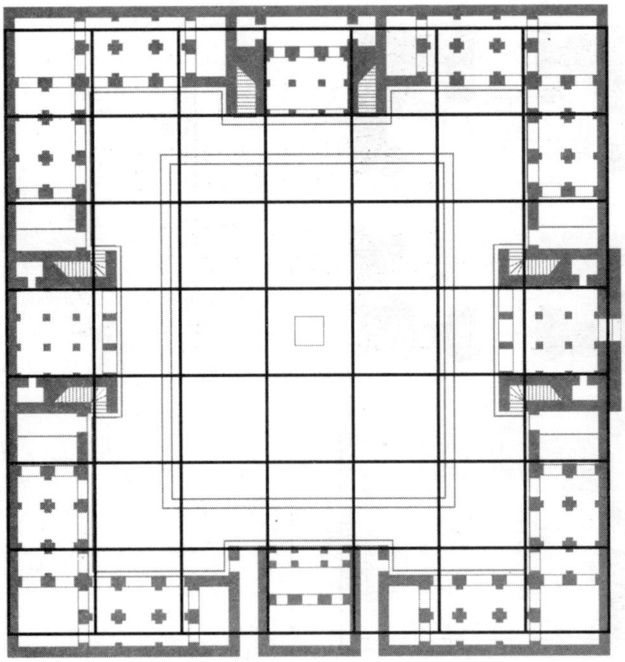

Figure 81 — *Jodh-Bai Mahal, Fatehpur Sikri,* with *Sthandila Maṇḍala*

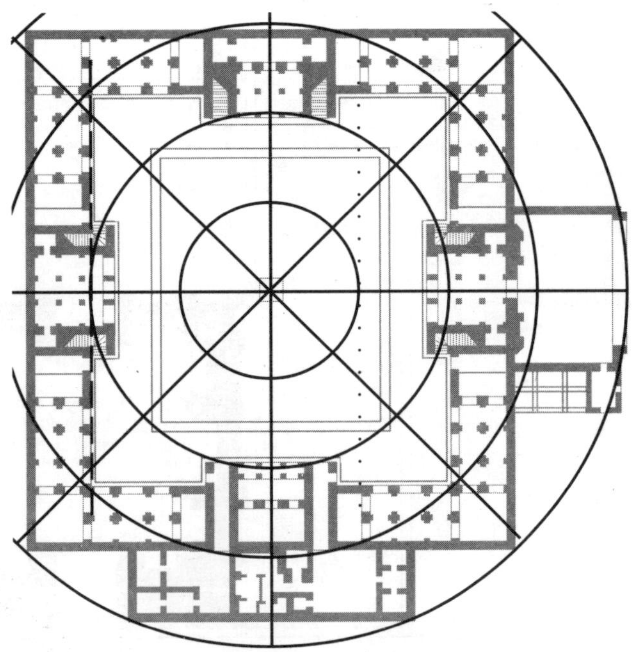

Figure 82 — *Jodh-Bai Mahal, Fatehpur Sikri,* with circular *Maṇḍūka Maṇḍala*

Plate 29 — *Jodh-Bai Mahal*, plan, 1st storey

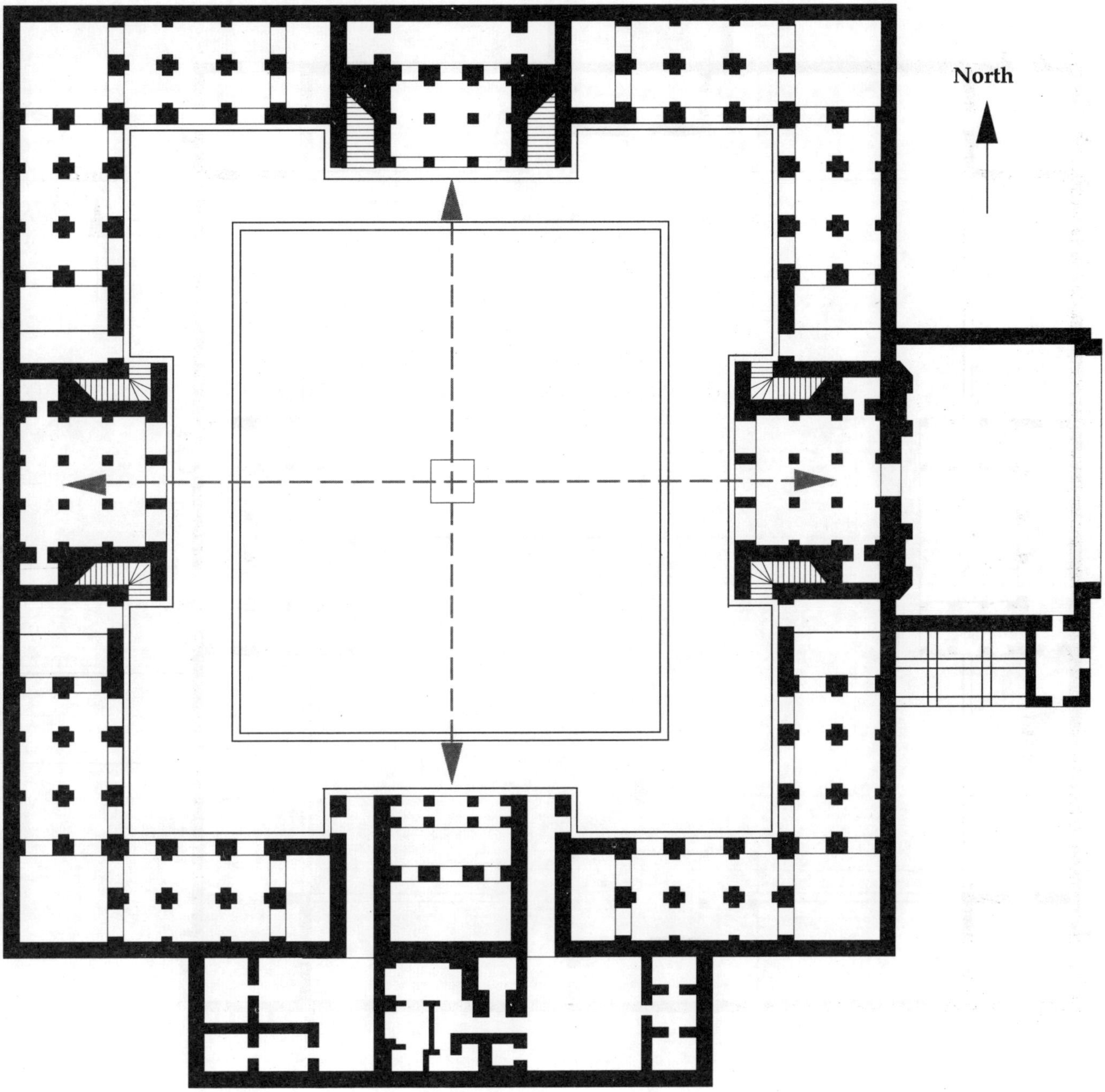

Plate 30 — *Jodh-Bai Mahal*, plan, 2nd storey

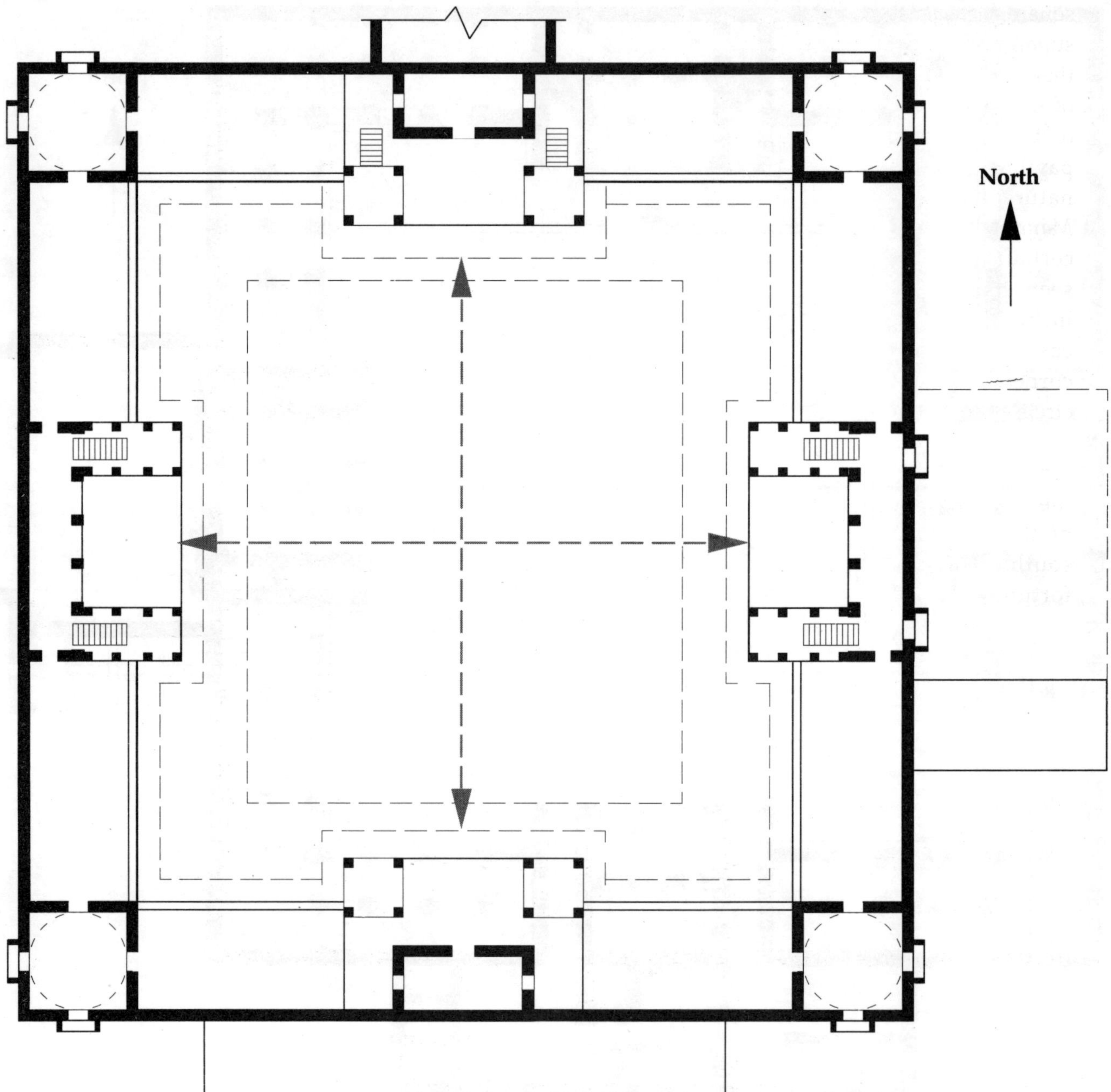

square *maṇḍala*. However, if a *Sthandila Maṇḍala* is superimposed over the first storey plan, it is seen that the width of the rooms fall within the width of one *pada* (See: **Figure 81**). Similarly the width of the main spaces of the projecting, cardinal pavilions are all one *pada* wide. The rectangular nature of the plan might suggest a circular *Maṇḍūka Maṇḍala* (See: **Figure 82**). Here, too, certain conjunctions are interesting. First, it is seen that the outer ring enfolds the whole, including the *hammam* and entrance area to the east. Next, the second ring bisects the inner corners of the court. Third, the penultimate circle touches the east and west extremity of the court (See: **Plate 30** [dash line]) and bisects the corners of the north and south pavilions. Finally, the inner circle is equal to the inner dimension of the two rooms, each on the north and the south. These conjunctions may be simply fortuitous, but they are interesting!

It is known that Akbar the Great was not interested in applying strict *śilpa-śāstra* dimensions to his city; nonetheless, the strict axiality of many of the structures indicate a reliance on these treatises. The *Jodh-Bai Mahal* is not the least amongst these buildings which may have found their genesis in Indian architectural treatises.

Sunahrā Makān (*Miriam's House*)
Fatehpur Sikri (a. 1569 CE)

The *Sunahrā Makān* or *Golden House*[106] is the smallest of the residential structures within the *zenānā*. It is generally accepted that this building was constructed for Bibi Miriam-uz-Zamani (ākā Maryam) the Goan, Christian wife of Akbar the Great. The fact that Akbar took for a wife a Christian indicates the pantheistic nature of this ruler.

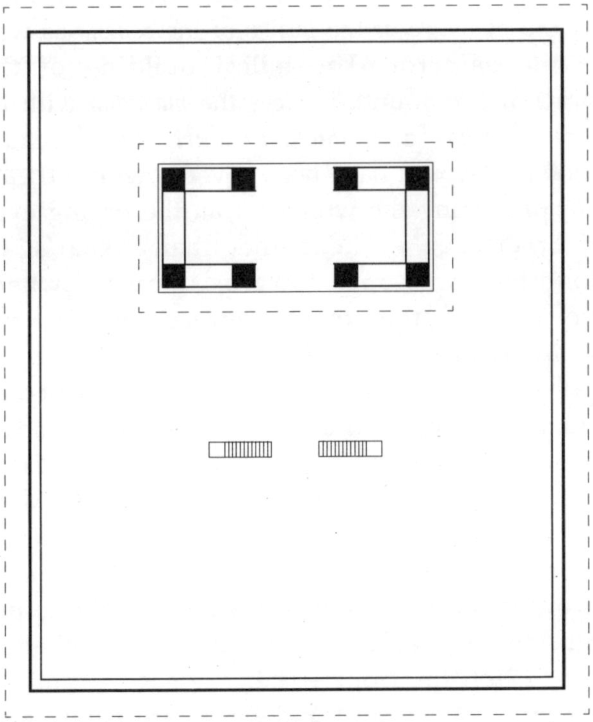

Figure 83 — *Sunahrā Makān, Fatehpur Sikri,* 2nd storey plan

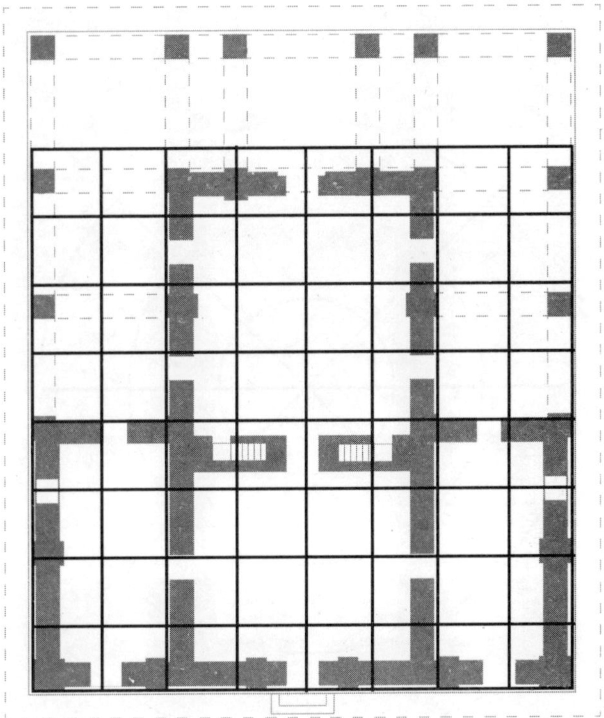

Figure 84 — *Sunahrā Makān, Fatehpur Sikri,* with *Maṇḍūka Maṇḍala*

This residence consists of four rooms on the first floor in the form of a Tau cross (See: **Plate 31**). Each of the rooms has doorways exiting to the exterior as well as internal connecting doors. The north room is surrounded by a deep porch on three sides. From the southern side of the north room are two staircases leading to the roof terrace. There, a narrow *śālā* rests (See: **Figure 83**).

The interior details are sumptuous, belying the simple, austere exterior. The thick walls, wide *chajjā* and narrow openings would have provided a cool retreat, especially in the north room. Similarly, the *śālā* of the upper terrace would have given a place of retreat and privacy as well as an alternate location to sleep during the warm nights.

Again, as with the *Jodh-Bai Mahal*, the *Sunahrā Makān* does not lend itself to a square maṇḍala. If a *Maṇḍūka Maṇḍala* is superimposed, it is seen that the north room falls within the four central *pada* (See: **Figure 84**). The dimensions of the southern extensions — i.e., the eastern room and the western room — are also four *pada* in width. When a circular *Maṇḍūka Maṇḍala* is laid over the plan certain conjunctions become apparent (See: **Figure 85**). The second ring defines the length of the residence, approximately. On the other hand the third ring seems superfluous, while the inner circle defines the width of the northern room.

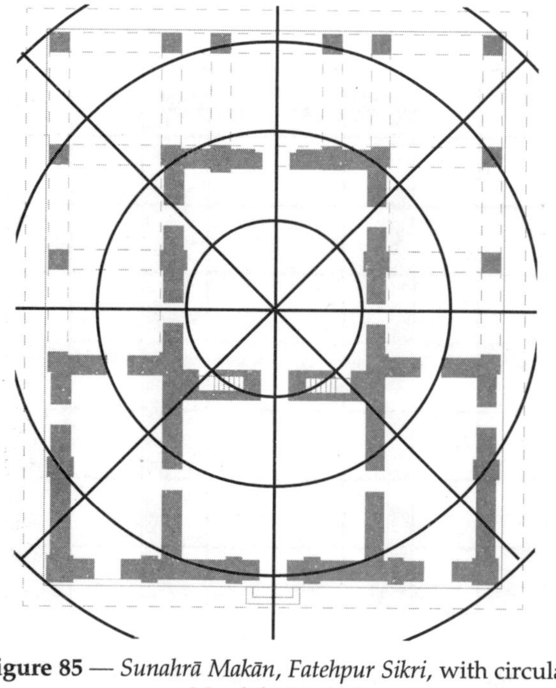

Figure 85 — *Sunahrā Makān, Fatehpur Sikri,* with circular *Maṇḍūka Maṇḍala*

The sometimes-used-term, the "Golden House" is an apt name for this small, elegant residence. The cruciform plan, in the shape of a Tau cross — i.e., a "**T**" form — would have been appropriate for the Christian wife, Bibi Miriam-uz-Zamani.

Pañch Mahal

Fatehpur Sikri (a. 1569 CE)

The *Pañch Mahal*[107] is not a residence, but a pavilion, a structure that must have been built for the pleasure of the ladies of the *zenānā* as well as the emperor. The tallest building of the imperial compound, it faces the *mardānā* with its *Diwān-i-Khās* and *Pachisi Court*. This façade, doubtless would have been covered with intricate *jālī*, protecting the women from the prying eyes of other men — i.e., other than Akbar's. It, doubtless, was open towards the west, where the rest of the *zenānā* spread out to the compounds outer wall.

The first storey consists of forty-eight squares, punctuated at their corners by slender, elegant, supporting columns. The third rank of columns from the north and that from the west are doubled presenting, *en plan*, an interesting variation. These double rows were obviously incorporated to support the weight of the upper four storeys and do not mar the total aesthetics. In addition the front — i.e., the east — rank of columns on the third and fourth storey are also doubled. Again, this is obviously for additional stability of the structure.

Plate 31 — *Sunahrā Makān* (Miriam's House), ground floor plan

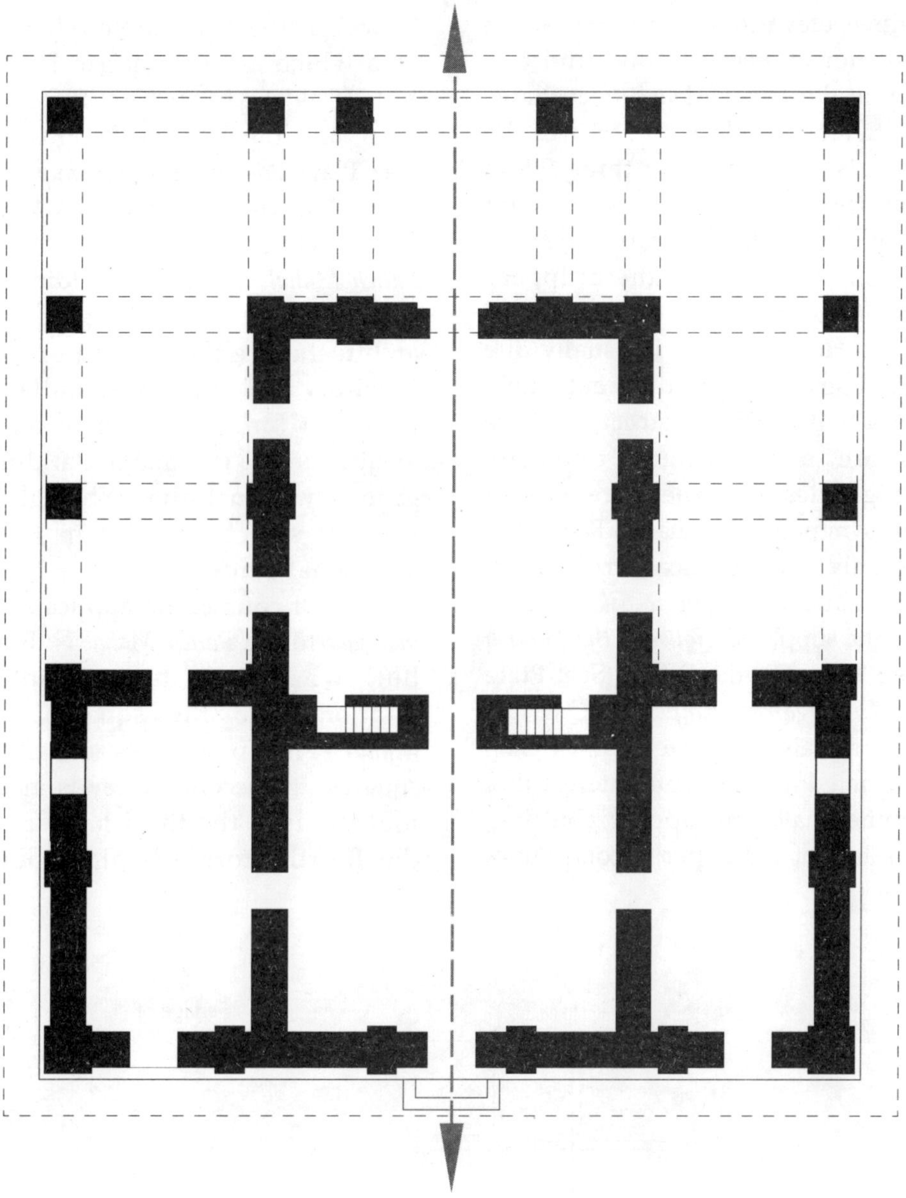

Fatehpur Sikri (Continued)

From neither elevations — i.e., east-west or north-south — nor *en plan* can one find any type of symmetry in the *Pañch Mahal* (See: **Plates 32 & 33**). If one attempts to place an arc over the stepped storeys, it is seen that only three floors can conform. In this respect it is somewhat eccentric. In many of the plans of *garh mahal*s in India, both Muslim and Hindu, there appear some elements of asymmetry, or structures which are not axial. However, this is usually due to the adding-on of structures by different rulers over the years. If a building is constructed where its dimensions are not infringed upon by geographical exigencies or other preexistent edifices, it will be symmetrical, usually. The *Pañch Mahal* is not the only asymmetrical structure in the Imperial compound of *Fatehpur Sikri*. Other structures such as the supposed *House of the Turkish Sultāna* (See: **Plate 26 — H**), the *School* (See: **Plate 26 — I**) and the *Khwabgah* or *Emperor's Quarters* (See: **Plate 26 — J**) are also asymmetrical, *en plan*.

It is to be noted and of some interest that all of these asymmetrical plans appear abutting, or in the *mardānā* area of the imperial compound. However, there are three other structures in this area which are symmetrical — i.e., the *Ānkh-i-Khās* (*Daulat Khānā*) (See: **Plate 26 — F**) which is axial, and the *Ekastambha Prasada* (*Diwān-i-Khās*) (See: **Plate 26 — E**) and the *Anup Talao* (*Chār Chaman*) (See: **Plate 26 — K**) both of which are cross-axial.

This concern with the asymmetry of the *Pañch Mahal*, and other buildings, is not meant to imply that it was a foreign feature to Indian architecture, either Hindu or Muslim. Both the Muslims and Hindus of India had exhibited a penchant for axiality, cross-axiality or mirror-axiality in all the major buildings of these two groups within India. When it does occur in a solitary structure built in 'one throw,' it is somewhat unusual.

Of course, the application of a traditional *maṇḍala* to the *Pañch Mahal* is thrown to the wind! But, what does become interesting is the relationship of the "squares" within the *Pañch Mahal*. The first storey consists of forty-eight squares, the second storey is made up of twenty-four squares, the third has eight squares, while the fourth storey displays but three and the

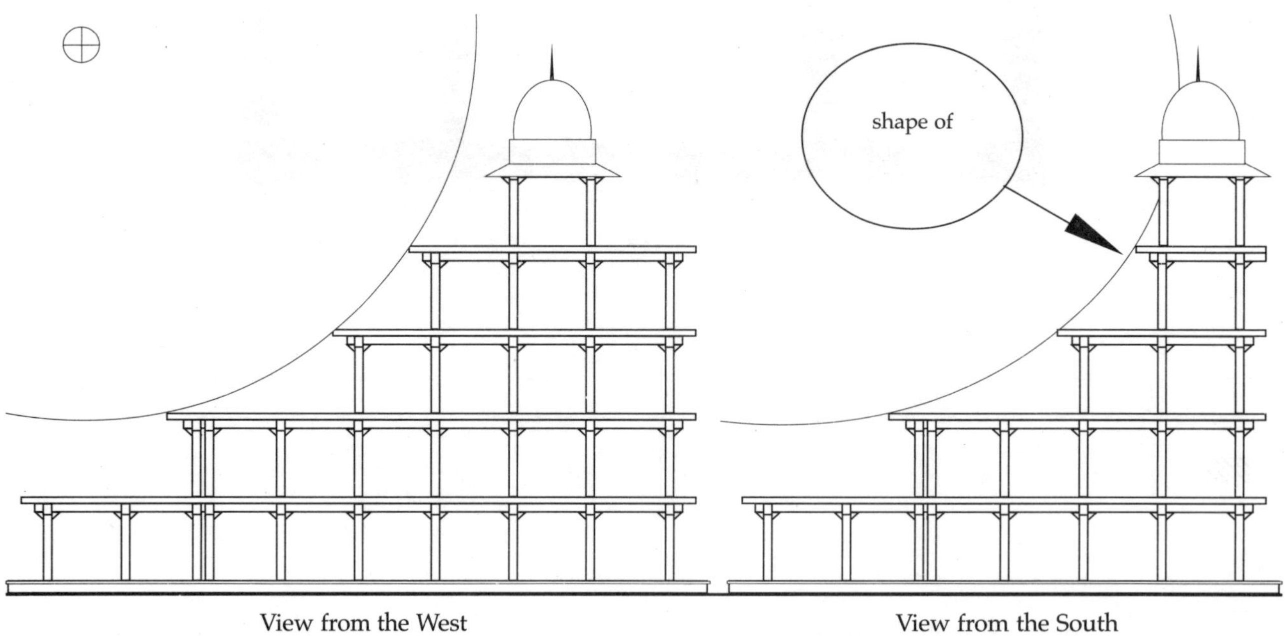

Figure 86 — *Pañch Mahal, Fatehpur Sikri,* simplified elevations with arc and oval

Plate 32 — *Pañch Mahal*, 1st storey plan

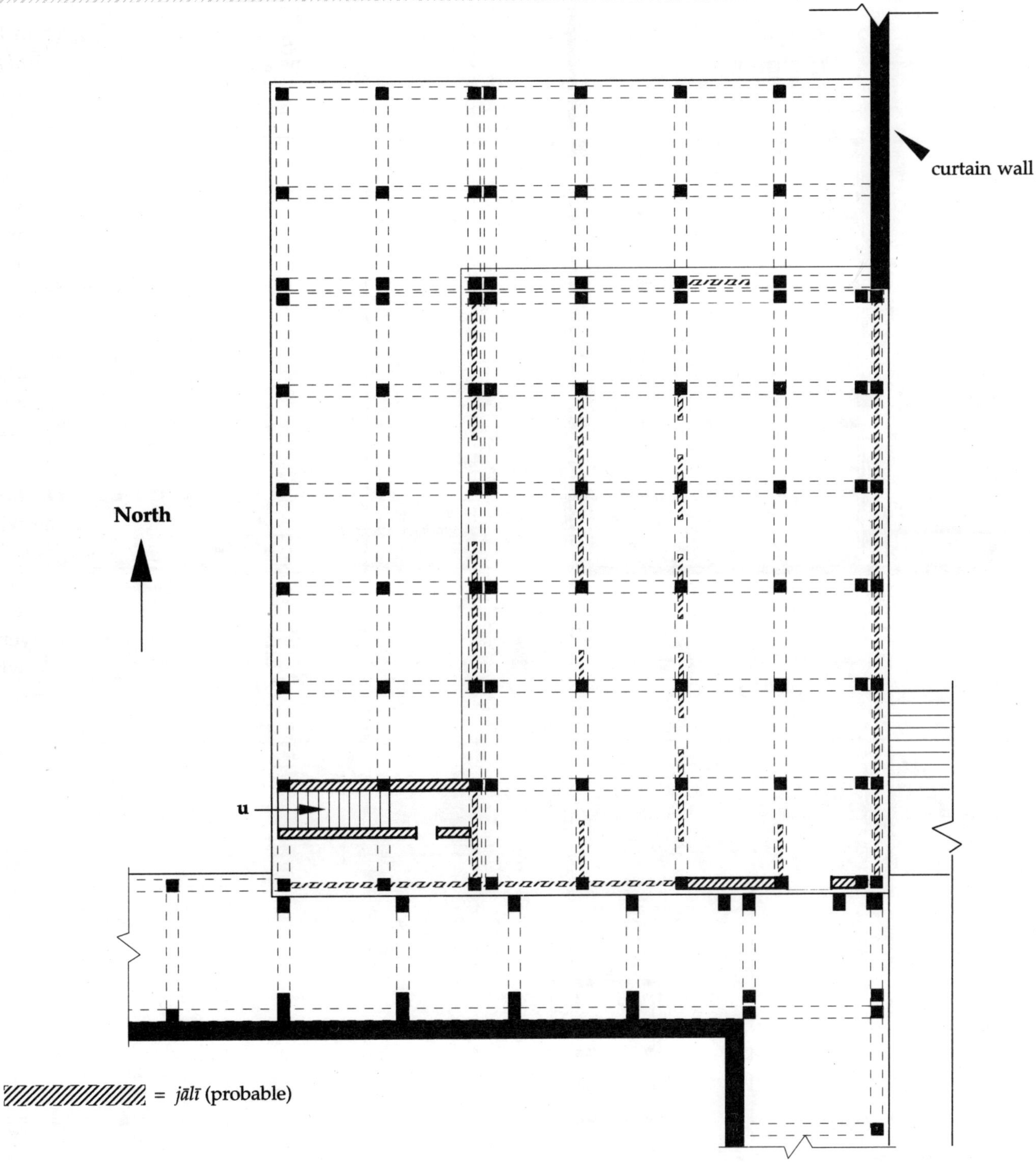

Plate 33 — *Pañch Mahal*, plan, upper storeys

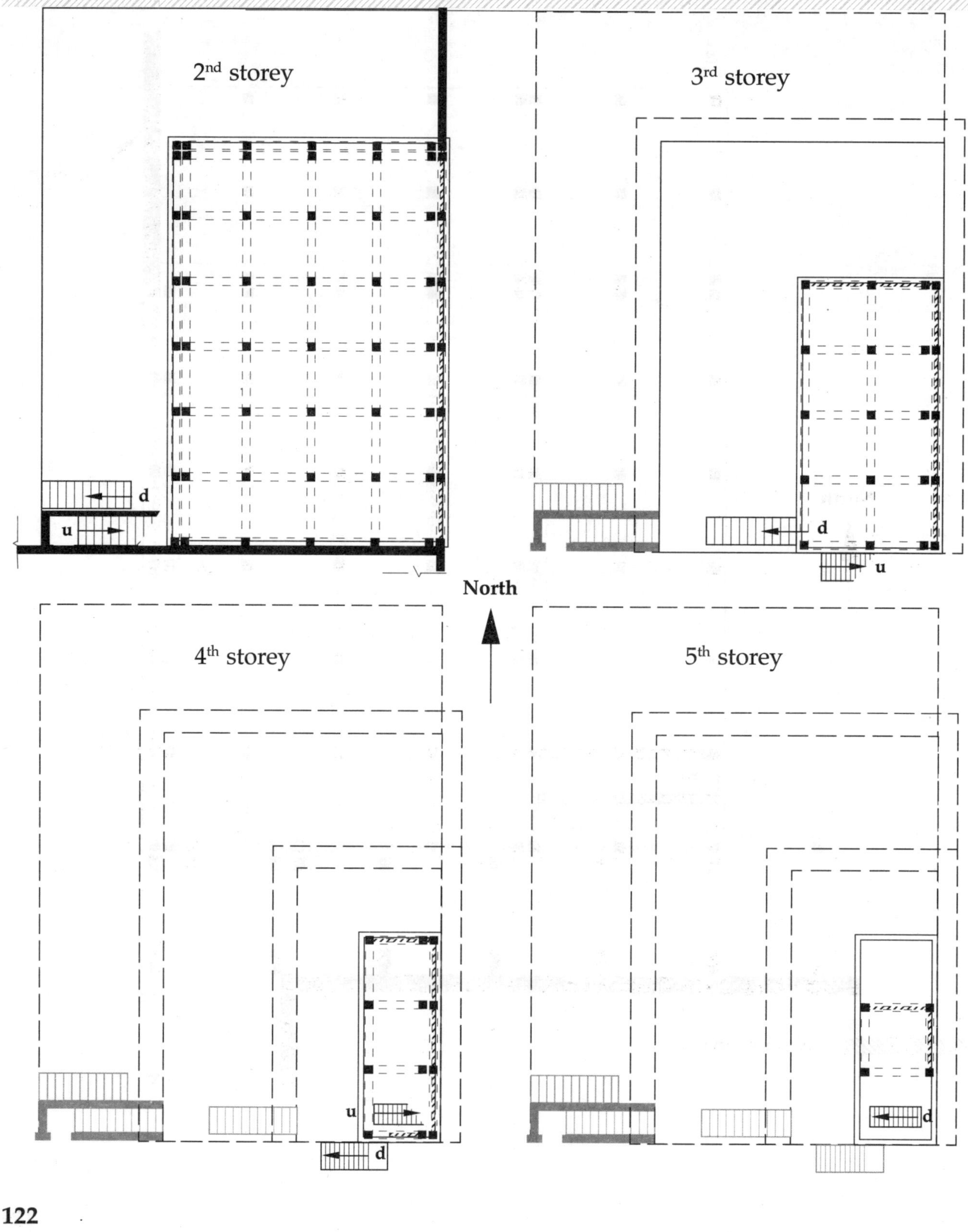

uppermost storey consists of one square (See: **Figure 87**). There are a total of eighty-four squares within the five storeys, and also there are a total of eighty-four columns on the first storey. The numerals: forty-eight, twenty-four, eight, three and one, all possess certain symbolic significance. Both the Hindu and the Muslims paid great heed to numbers, numerology and astrology as they saw them all intertwined with some cosmic significance. Is it possible that a key to the *Pañch Mahal* lies in the numbers?[108]

Forty-eight, a feminine number, denotes mystical completeness. Forty-eight's association with the cosmic number twelve, which comprehends all numbers lower than itself, is propitious. As a compound number it is associated astronomically with the planet *Rāhu* (the ascending node of the moon) and the planet Saturn (*Śani*). When reduced it produces three and, therefore, the planet Jupiter (*Bṛhaspati* or *Guru*).

Twenty-four, is also a feminine number and denotes totality and the combination of two opposites — i.e., 2, represented by the Moon, and 4, which represents *Rāhu*. Twenty-four is a cosmic number and is considered a lucky number as well. As a compound number it is associated with the Moon (*Soma* or *Chandra*) and the planet *Rāhu* (the ascending node of the moon). When reduced it produces six and, therefore, the planet Venus (*Śukra*).

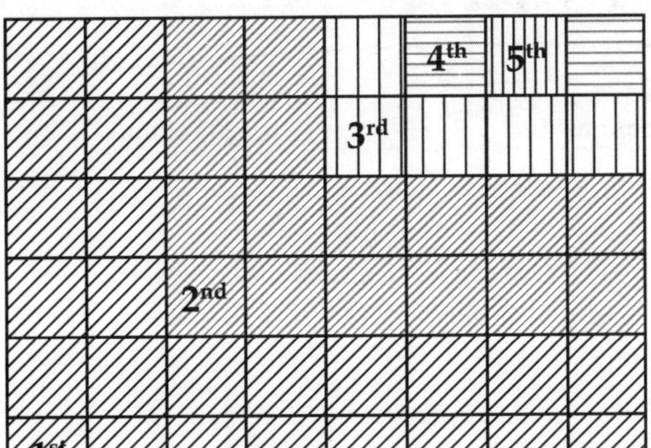

Figure 87 — *Pañch Mahal, Fatehpur Sikri*, diposition of the floors upon the grid

Eight is a most sacred number within both the Buddhist and the Muslim faiths. It denotes perfection, good fortune, and on the divine plane: justice and balance between attraction and repulsion, positive and negative. This integer as even, is representative of motherhood. It is auspicious in its make-up being an evenly even number and the first cube number. Eight is associated astronomically with the planet Saturn (*Śani*). The even (feminine) eight is assigned to a powerful and often fierce masculine planet. This may be a referent to: "justice and balance between attraction and repulsion."

Three is considered to be the first masculine (odd) number and therefore has certain precedents as a vivifying force. As an odd number, three is a male symbol and further represents the idea, principle, day, light, right hand and the Sun. It is the most sacred number within the Hindu faith and a number which likewise possesses great significance in Buddhism. It consists of unity plus diversity which equals perfection. As such, the numeral three denotes perfection, the trinity and the divine family, consisting of father, mother and child. The integer three is associated astronomically with the planet Jupiter (*Bṛhaspati* or *Guru*). As the first masculine number (odd), the powerful and sometimes fierce planet/deity is an apt symbol.

One is generally considered neither an odd nor an even number. It is seen as an absolute, and as an absolute, it is beyond all, therefore divine. It denotes the first principle, The Absolute One, The Primordial One, Allah, *Brahmā*, *Devī*, *Ādi-Buddha*, *Buddha Sāmanta-Bhadra* and God. It is the source, the monad and 'non-dualism' (Ind.: *advaita*). Further it represents unity, spiritual balance, the divine sign of universal life.

However, there are those who consider it as an odd number and as such it is a male symbol. One is associated astronomically with the Sun (*Ravi* or *Sūrya*).

Then, there is eighty-four. This integer is a feminine number which denotes auspiciousness in its make-up. This numeral represents eight in the four corners of the world, and, more importantly, the perfect life of man. As a compound number it is associated with the planet Saturn (*Śani*) and the planet *Rāhu* (the ascending node of the moon). When reduced it produces three and, therefore, the planet Jupiter (*Bṛhaspati* or *Guru*). It would seem to appear of considerable importance that this numeral, eighty-four, is repeated — i.e., the total number of squares on all five levels, and the total number of columns on the first level.

It is of further interest to note that in the *Pañch Mahal* the totals of the first three storeys are feminine — i.e., forty-eight, twenty-four and eight — and the last two storeys are masculine — i.e., three and one. Since one connotes the Absolute, it is but a short step to associate this number with the Emperor. Doubtless there were times in which he sat under the *chatrī* of the fifth storey, elevated above all. The fourth storey may well have represented the imperial family — i.e., Akbar, his queen and heir. After all, *Fatehpur Sikri* was chosen after Akbar received a prophecy there that he would soon produce an heir for his earthly empire.

That leaves the five storeys of the *Pañch Mahal*. Five, a masculine number which is created from the first masculine number — i.e., three — and the first feminine number — i.e., two — and, therefore, to many represents love, the union of the masculine and the feminine. An apt icon when applied to Akbar, his wife and heir. This important integer represents the natural man. It is revolutionary and reduces all to the meaningful through its magical/mystical power.

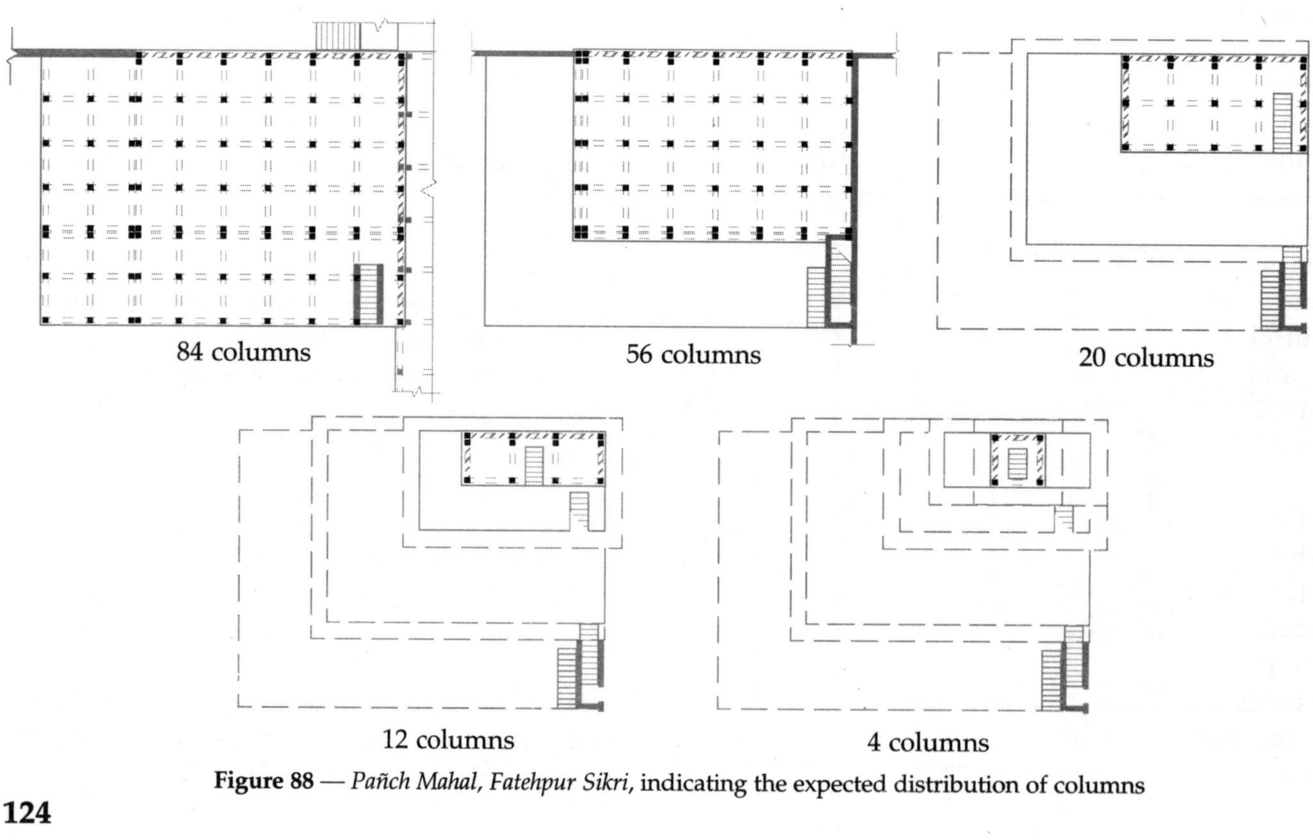

Figure 88 — *Pañch Mahal, Fatehpur Sikri,* indicating the expected distribution of columns

Five denotes magical properties, mental activity, intelligence, and the natural elements both positive and negative — e.g., the pentagram positive or pentagram negative (upward or downward pointing). Five is associated astronomically with the planet Mercury (*Budha*) who is personified as seated upon a lion, the king of beasts. Again as an odd, masculine number five is assigned this masculine and powerful planet.

Finally, one ought to consider the total number of columns on the five levels. Due to the intervening curtain wall, the first storey, as noted, has eighty-four columns. The second storey with fifty-six columns, the third has twenty, while the fourth and fifth possess twelve and four, respectively (See: **Figure 88**). This totals one-hundred-seventy-six expected columns — i.e., acknowledging the six replaced by the curtain wall. One-hundred-seventy-six is not in and of itself a number recognized to have acknowledged significance. However, if one takes the sacred four and double it, then double it again, the result is: four, eight and sixteen. Then if one takes eleven — i.e., the mystical number of universal energy — and double it, then double it again, the result is: eleven, twenty-two and forty-four. The result of multiplying four with forty four is: one-hundred-seventy-six. The same result appears when twenty-two is multiplied by eight and eleven by sixteen. Do the arcane treatises of India or the Muslim world contain some mystic significance in one-hundred-seventy-six?

Are the interpretations of these numbers and the many ways that they can be applied to Akbar, and/or the emperor specifically, merely fortuitous? Possibly! However, nothing then was undertaken without serious consideration of the various aspects of the ratios and proportions of a structure and its association with the cosmos — i.e., numbers, astrology and orientation — even with the Muslims.

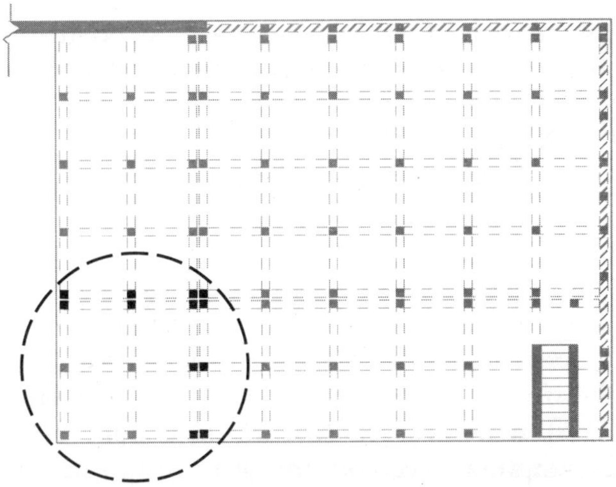

Figure 89 — *Pañch Mahal*, 1st storey, indicating unnecessary duplication concern

Nonetheless, the *Pañch Mahal* is a building of intriguing aspects. It is noted by scholars that Akbar wanted to avoid the slavish adherence to the *śilpa-śāstra*s of the indigenous *sthāpati*s as well as Islamic predilections in the possible quest or affirmation of his own pantheism. Is this the answer to the eccentric design of the *Pañch Mahal*?

Yet, there are other attractions. The employment of the double rows of columns on the first storey plan and their duplication on the second storey may be attributed to structural and/or design necessities. However, why were they extended to the northern and western edges of the first storey (See: **Figure 89**). Further, why were they employed in the third and fourth storeys in the manner seen (See: **Plates 32 & 33**) — i.e., on the east side of these two floors — when structural requirements did not require their employment? Was this purely for design reasons? Finally, why were wide *chajjā*s used only on the second and third storeys and not on the first and fourth?

The *Pañch Mahal* is certainly one of the most recognized buildings of the imperial complex at *Fatehpur Sikri*, not only because of its height, but also because of its grace and elegance. It is an erratic design, but in this lies its charm. It is not an easy structure to understand, and, also in this too lies its charm.

Diwān-i-Khās (aka Ānkh-i-Michoni, Ānkh-i-Khās, or Daulat Khānā) Fatehpur Sikri (a. 1569 CE)

The structure generally known as the *Ānkh-i-Michoni*, *Ānkh-i-Khās*, or *Daulat Khānā*, but proposed by R. Nath[109] as the *Diwān-i-Khās*, is to the west of the *Ekastambha Prasada* (aka *Diwān-i-Khās*). It would seem that this is an appropriate assumption since both this structure — i.e., the *Diwān-i-Khās* (aka *Ānkh-i-Michoni*, *Ānkh-i-Khās*, & *Daulat Khānā*) — and the *Diwān-i-Ām* are oriented towards the east (See: **Figure 90**). The alignment of the *Diwān-i-Ām*, towards the east is underlined by the fact that the massive *Court of Public Audience* is to the east. R. Nath asserts that this orientation is due to the fact that Akbar the Great "worshipped the Rising Sun every morning."[110] Frankly, the operative and highly problematic term in this source is "worshipped." Akbar the Great may have been extremely broad minded, philosophically. He may have been more open to accepting and/or acknowledging many and various philosophies than any other Indian Muslim ruler. However, it is inconceivable that his theology was anything but Muslim. He may have seen in the Sun a manifestation of The Divine, *Allah*. He may have performed certain rites — i.e., *jharoka-darśana* — but, to see in these acts the worship of the Sun (*Surya*) is dangerous. Even the recitation of the *Surya-sahastra-nama* does not, necessarily belie sun worship. He may have been an iconoclast of sorts or even heterodox — i.e., acknowledging various philosophies and faiths, accepting the painted images of people and animals, the inclusion of Quaranic verses upon tombs — but he was first and foremost, born and died a Muslim. *Allahu akbar! Ashhadu Allah illa ha illallah wa, asy hadu anna Muhammad darro sululloh.*

That aside, the proposal of the *Ānkh-i-Michoni*, or *Ānkh-i-Khās*, or *Daulat Khānā* as the *Diwān-i-Khās* has some merit (See: **Plate 34**). The three pavilions stand upon a low podium and are encircled by an arcade. The whole is aligned towards the east as is the *Diwān-i-Khās*. No other major or important structure there is so aligned.

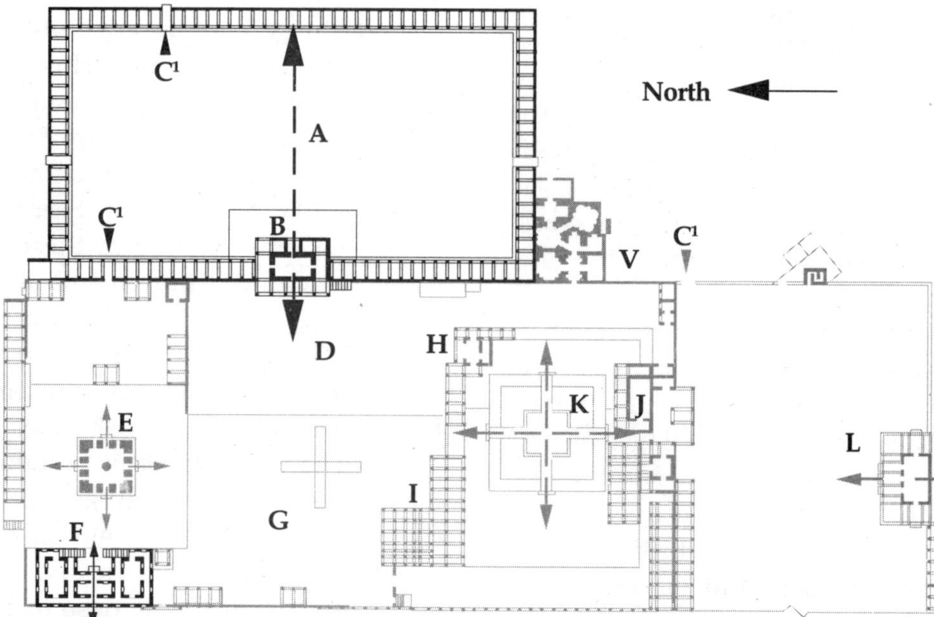

Figure 90 — *Diwān-i-Khās* (aka *Ānkh-i-Michoni*, *Ānkh-i-Khās*, & *Daulat Khānā*) & *Diwān-i-Ām*, indicating similar alignment

Plate 34 — *Diwān-i-Khās* (ākā Ānkh-i-Michoni, Ānkh-i-Khās, or Daulat Khānā)

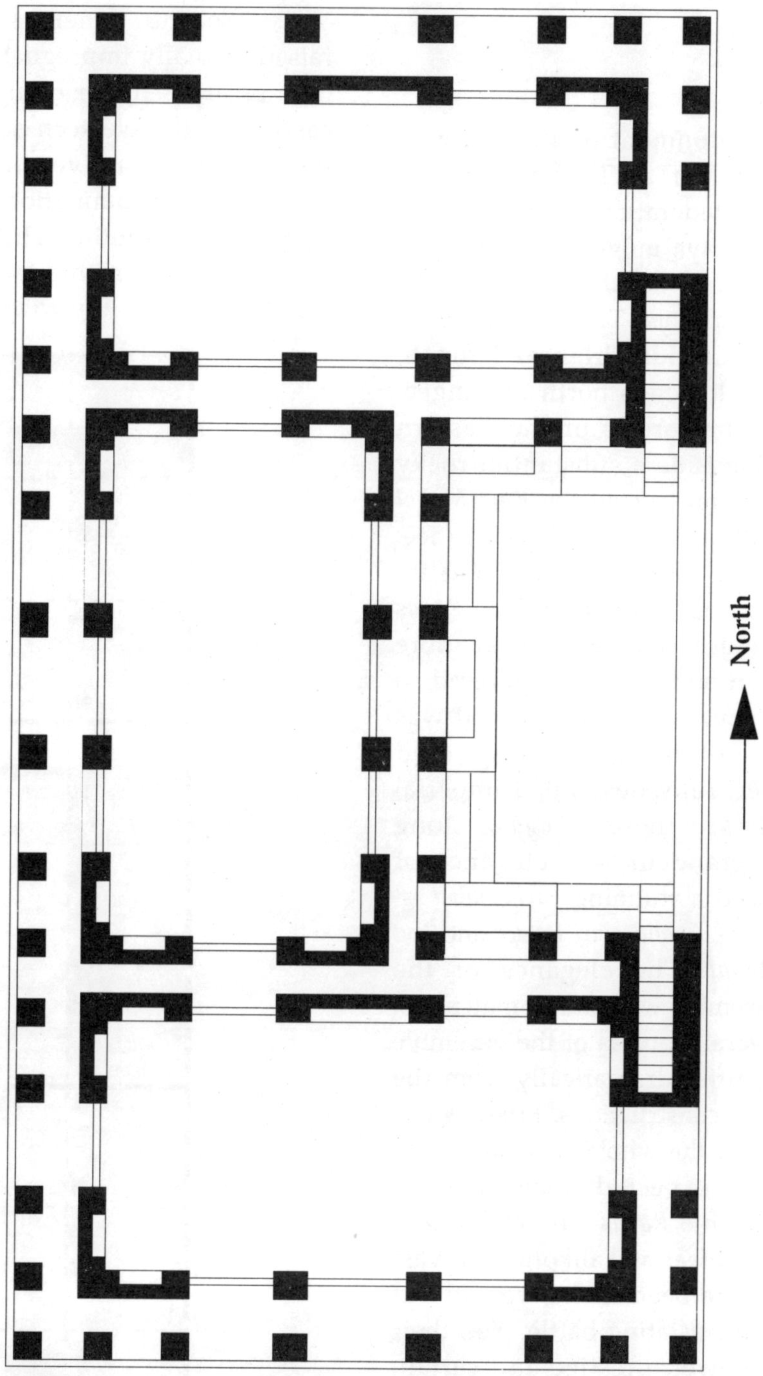

Chandragiri Palace (*Rājā & Rānā Mahals*)

Tirupati (a. 1565 CE)

After the abandonment of *Vijayanagara* subsequent to the defeat at Talikota by the Deccan Sultanates' confederation in 1565 CE, the *Tuluva Rāya* Sadashivaraya moved his capital of the diminished empire south and east to Penukonda. The *Saluva Rāya*, Tirumala I, again moved — this time to Chandragiri, near Tirupati, one-hundred-fifteen kilometers north of Gingee. There, deep within the forests of the Eastern Ghat and nestled alongside a substantial rocky outcropping, the *Rāya* constructed the *Rājā Mahal* (See: **Plates 35 & 36**)[111] and the *Rānā Mahal* (See: **Plate 37**). Defeated by the combined Muslim forces, the proud and once supreme *Saluva Rāya*s built their new capital ensemble on a far more diminished scale than had been encountered in the vast, imperial *Vijayanagara*. This capital was but a mere shadow of the glory, scope and splendor of the older, fully developed imperial capital. Nonetheless, these *Rāya*s, long accustomed to the grandeur and elegance of *Vijayanagara* , produced a stunning *garh mahal* — i.e. the *Rājā Mahal* or the *Chandragiri Palace* and the attending *Rānā Mahal*. The elegance of the *Chandragiri Palace* ensemble was and is matchless.

There are several features of the ensemble at Chandragiri that differ dramatically from the previous *Saluva* palace constructions. First, as has been stated, the scale of the whole is considerably smaller. That is to be expected since the once supreme and indomitable *Rāya*s suffered a near mortal blow in their defeat at Talikota. The vast resources that had once been theirs was all but wiped away in that devastating battle. Yet, their name, their former power, prestige and certain substantial capital allowed them to reconstruct a scaled down *garh mahal* of considerable beauty and sophistication of design.

Second, whereas the Rajputana rulers raised virtually impregnable bastions situated on high escarpments or easily defended hills — i.e., castles, in the western sense, that were second to none in this universal genre — the scope of *Vijayanagara*'s domination as well as their power and might in southern India was such that their defense rested in this fact alone. They were, in truth, an empire. *Vijayanagara* was fortified — i.e.,

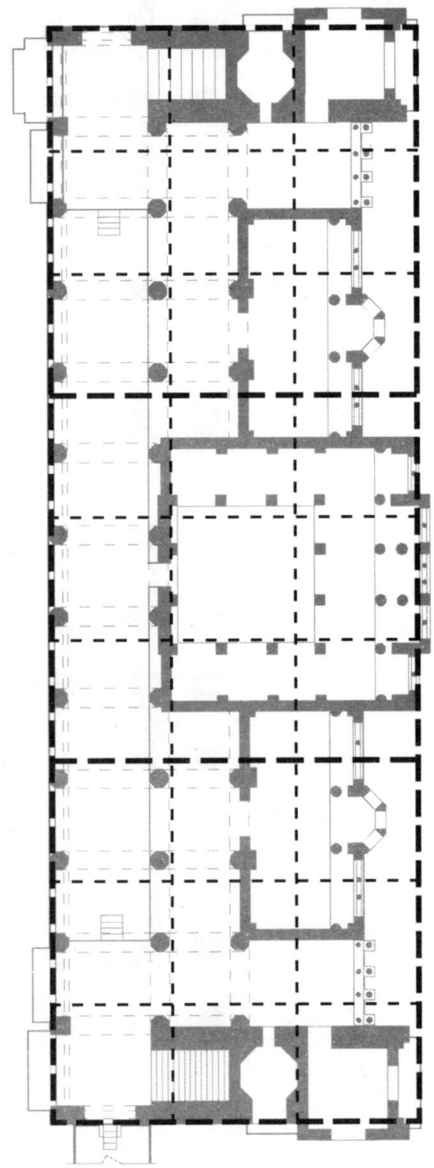

Figure 91 — *Rājā Mahal*, Chandragiri, indicating three square proportion with triple division

Plate 35 — *Rājā Mahal*, plan, ground floor

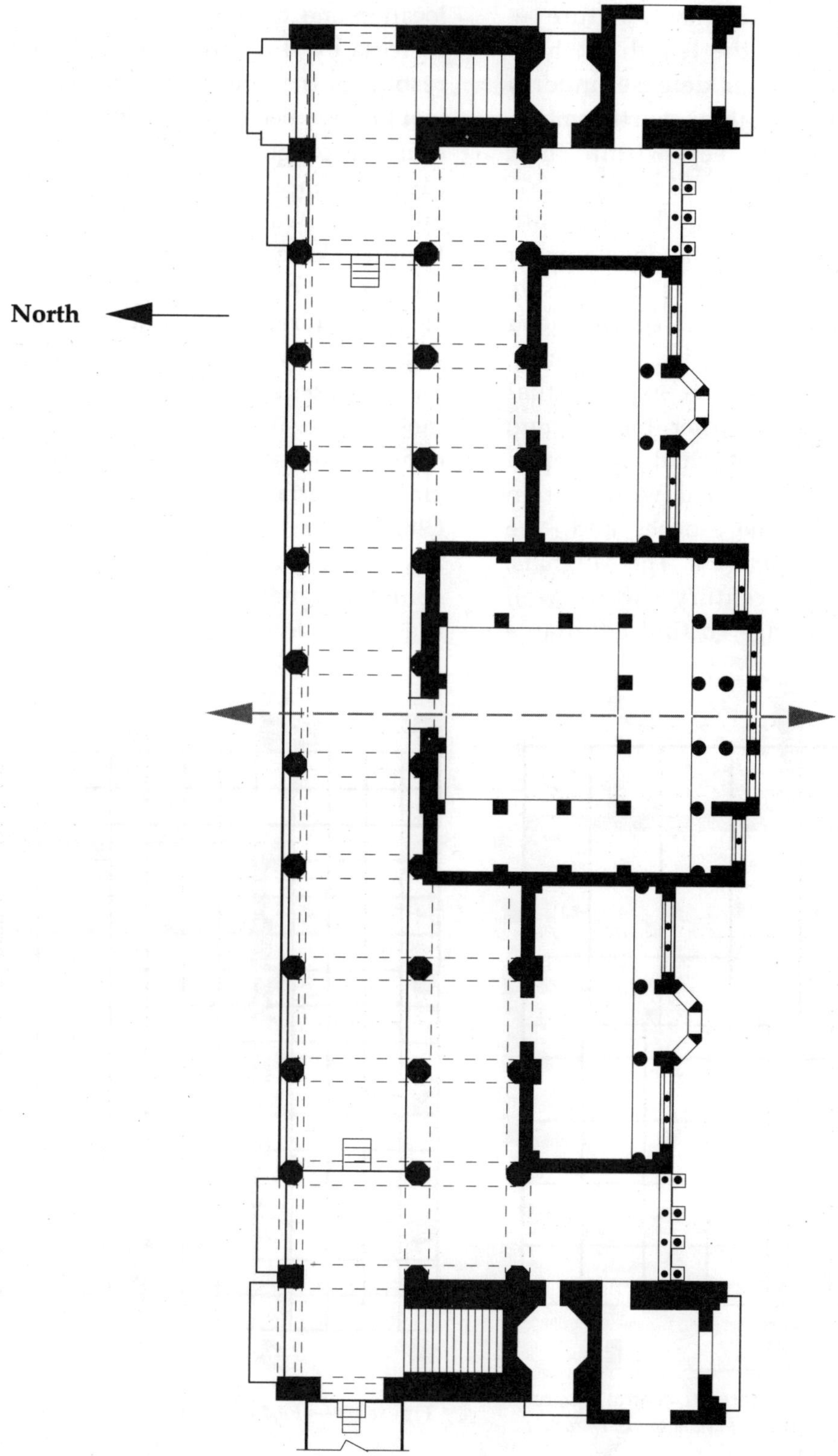

surrounded by walls of a defensive nature — but the locale, height and the length of these walls would have made their defense under a concerted siege impracticable. Furthermore, their capital city nestled deep within their domains, was in itself a defense of sorts.

Third, by the middle of the sixteenth century in India, as in Europe, the development of weaponry, particularly cannon as an offensive device neutralized and/or obviated the need and/or efficacy for thick defensive walls and/or fortifications and the extreme expense that their construction entailed. Further, the Tughluq and Lodi Sultanate of Delhi had developed imperial proportions and gazed with certain covetousness towards the south and the incredible wealth of *Vijayanagara.* The Mughals, by the mid sixteenth century, were well established and expanding. To find a suitable location and to endeavor to raise an impregnable fortress by this late date and with the limited resources that the *Saluva Rāyas* now possessed would have been vainglory. The time to mount a building program suitable to defend against the Mughal Empire and/or the combined Muslim Sultanates was unfeasible. Few *garh mahals* or Hindu kingdoms had the geographical advantage of impregnability against modern siege warfare. One possible exception was the impressive *Meherangarh* at Jodhpur (See: the *Meherangarh*, **Plate 11** & **Figure 41**) — one of the most impressive citadels in India — which could conceivably stand up under the might of the empire. Certainly, the hilly region surrounding Chandragiri did not offer that singular advantage. Therefore, as with the builders of the contemporaneous French *chateaux* of the Loire, the *Saluva Rāyas* took the expedient route and

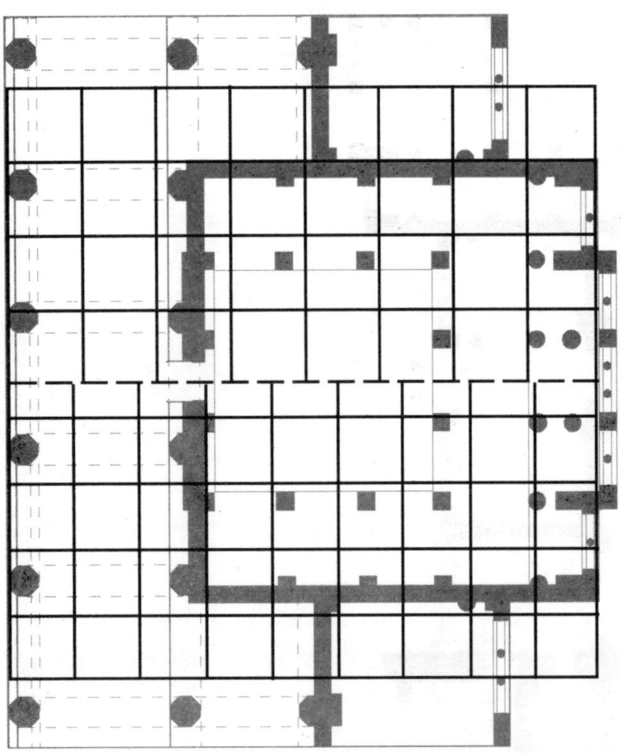

Figure 92 — *Rājā Mahal*, Chandragiri, central square with *Maṇḍūka Maṇḍala* (top) and *Paramaśayika Maṇḍala* (bottom)

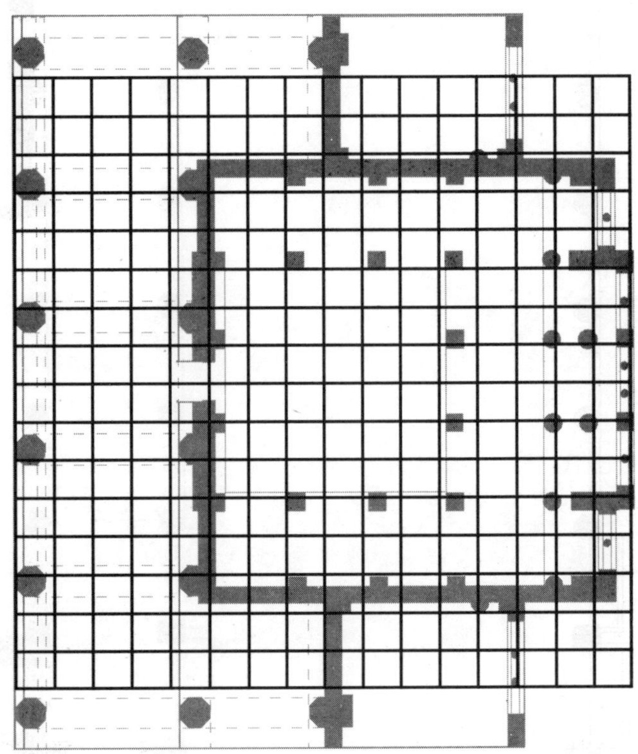

Figure 93 — *Rājā Mahal*, Chandragiri, central square with *Triyuta Maṇḍala*

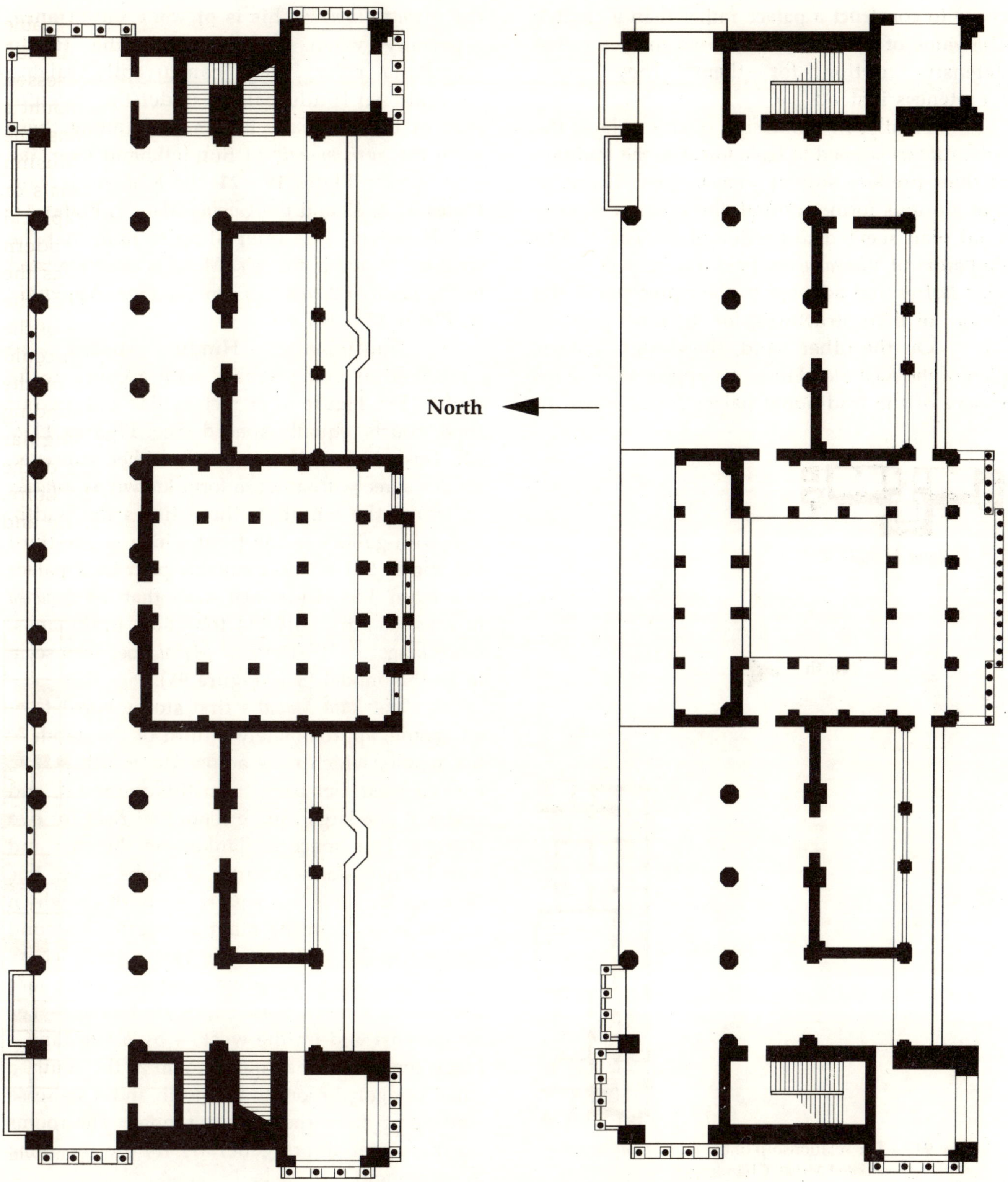
North

chose to construct a palace rather than a citadel. The value of the latter had ceased to be a viable defensive option for them. They chose remoteness instead.

Finally, in the design of this palace, the *Saluva Rāyas* seemed to have forsaken the tradition of their predecessors at *Vijayanagara*. There, at that glorious former capital, the square or cross-axial plan seemed to predominate. The Hindu Emperors of *Vijayanagara* paid due respect to the *śilpa-śāstras* and adhered to their precepts in the design of their structures, for the most part.

On the other hand, the design and/or plan of the *Rājā Mahal* does not appear to conform to any of the traditional palace forms noted in the *Mayamatam*.[112] This is of some importance, especially when in the north the Hindu Rajputana rulers were concurrently raising conventional Hindu palaces under the watchful eyes of the Mughals. Paramount among these were the *garh mahals* of Bundelkhand (See: the *Rājā Mandir*, **Plates 19 - 21**; the *Jahangir Mandir*, **Plates 42 & 43** and the *Govind Mandir*, **Plates 44-46**). However, it is interesting to note that the southern façade of the *Rājā Mahal* is closely related to the *Jahangir Mandir* of Orchha (See: **Appendix A, Plates 87 & 90**).

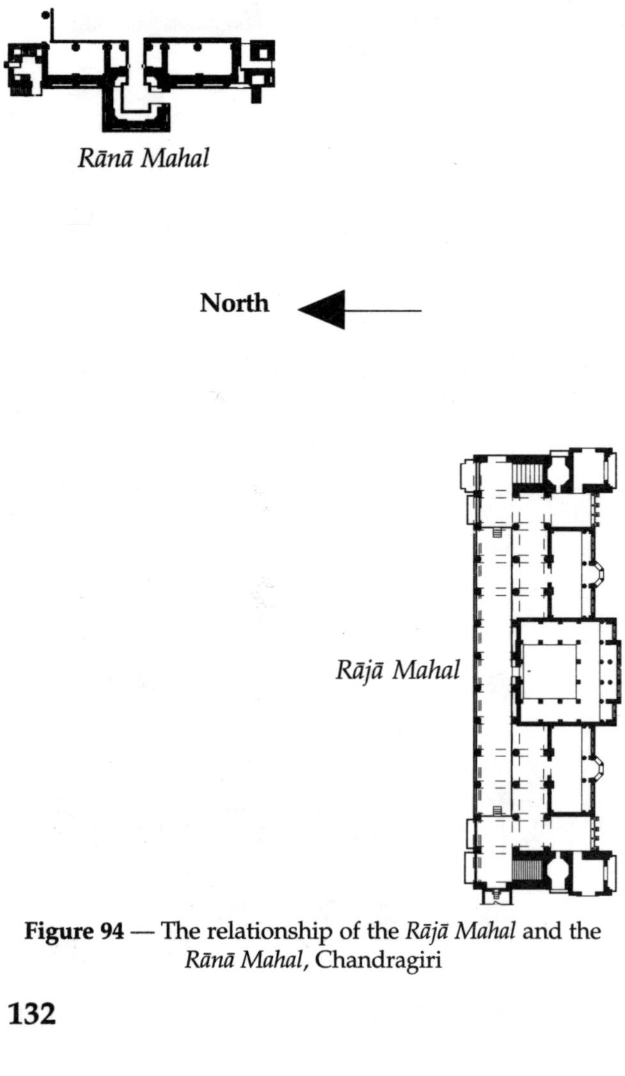

Figure 94 — The relationship of the *Rājā Mahal* and the *Rānā Mahal*, Chandragiri

Traditionally, Hindu palaces are conceived as being square with a court in the centre (See: **Figure 6**) or rectangular with two or three courts, equally spaced (See: **Figures 11 & 12**). This *garh mahal* conforms to neither. However, it does agree with a house form known as *daṇḍaka* in which the length is three times the width, and with gallery in the front which is one-third the width. But is this a suitable plan for a palace of a *Rāya*? The *Mayamatam* states that "all *daṇḍaka* houses . . . are suitable for gods, brāhmaṇas, (and) kings. . . ."[113] The *Rājā Mahal* does then seem to fit this model (See: **Figure 91**).

The *Rājā Mahal*'s first storey consists of an arcade, approximately a third of the depth of the whole, which runs across the width — i.e., east to west. Set back from this verandah and centered is a large square room that rises for two storeys. This space is flanked on the east and west by two identical suites of rooms — i.e., one rectangular and one square — both of which are set back from the main arcade by a second vestibule, the width of the two rooms. These suites each have numerous windows which face southward. Finally, these suites are bound — i.e., on the east and on the west — by a substantial block consisting of a square room at the south, a small octagonal room to the north and a staircase leading up from the main verandah. The rooms on the upper floors generally follow the same arrangement.

Plate 37 — *Rānā Mahal*, Chandragiri, plan

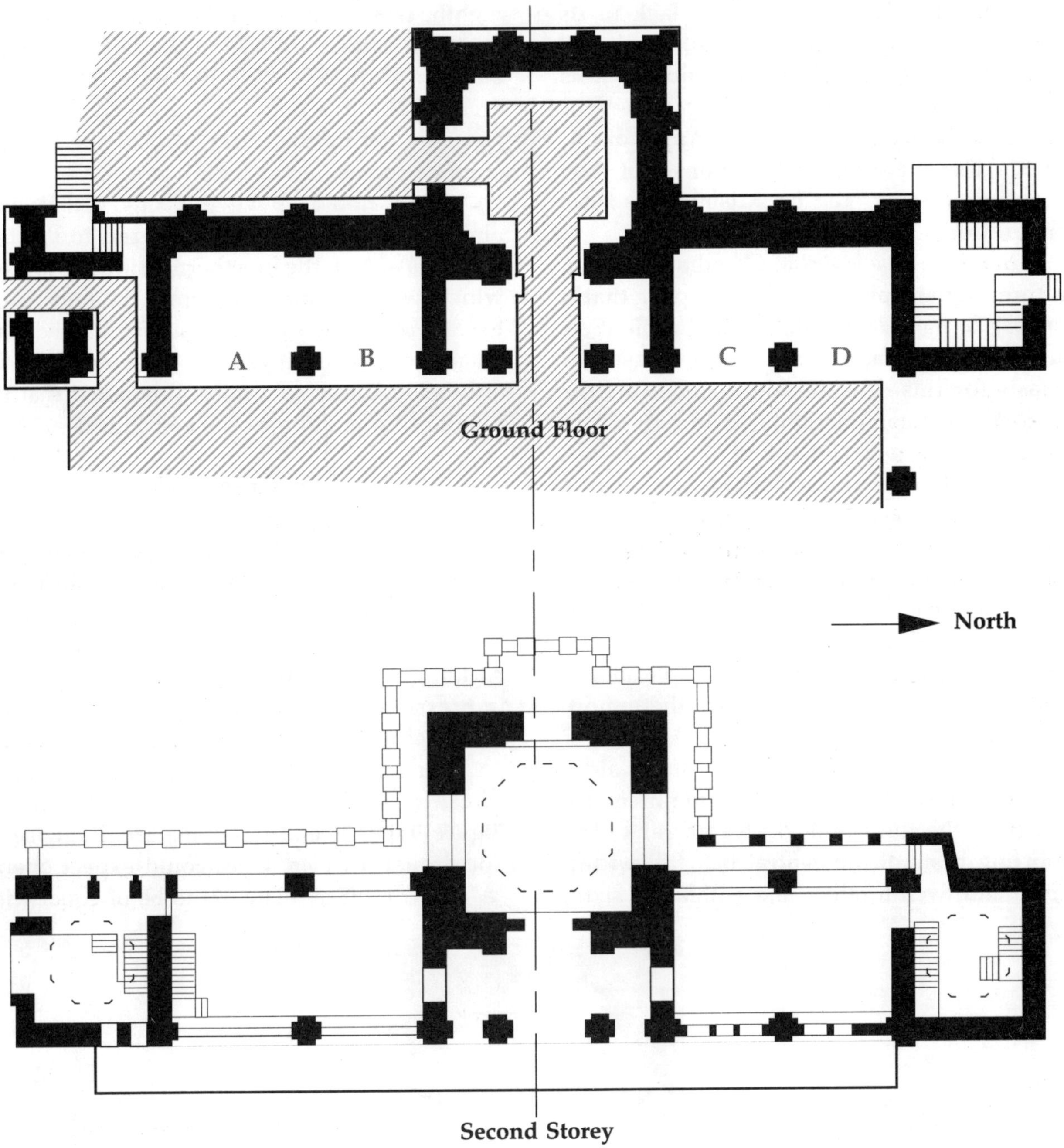

What the *Rājā Mahal* might lack in its conformity to known palace models based upon the *śilpa-śāstras*, it more than makes up for in its strict axiality. The eastern half of the *garh mahal* is mirrored in the western half (See: **Appendix A, Plate 87**). There are minor variations, but they are so minor as to be dismissed from consideration.

Since the *Rājā Mahal* at Chandragiri is seen as a three-square plan, it would appear that a *Paramaśayika Maṇḍala* would be applicable (See: **Figure 91 & 92**). The central square is used as the basis for this consideration. However, the most fortuitous conjunction(s) is to be seen in the fact that the piers of the main arcade fall squarely within their respective *pada*(s) — that is all! A *Maṇḍūka Maṇḍala* is interesting only in as much as the width of the central square is defined by the line between the first and second ranks. Again, that is all. Therefore, it would seem that neither the *Paramaśayika Maṇḍala* nor the *Maṇḍūka Maṇḍala* are unreservedly applicable to the *Rājā Mahal* (See: **Figure 92**). Are there more viable alternatives?

A *Triyuta Maṇḍala* does offer more possibilities (See: **Figure 93**). The main square falls within the third and fourteenth rank. The supporting piers of the central hall fall within the fifth and twelfth ranks, and within the sixth, eighth, tenth and twelfth files. The piers of the northern arcade are within the first file of *pada* and the fifth file holds the piers of the inner arcade. The line between the eighth and ninth *pada* file define the outer wall of the southern suite of rooms.

As noted above the *Rājā Mahal* seems almost antithetical when compared to the three *garh mahals* of the northern Hindu Bundelas, which were roughly contemporaneous — i.e., the *Rājā Mandir*, the *Jahangir Mandir*, and the *Govind Mandir*. However, if each of these northern *garh mahals* is reduced to a third, it is noted that their relationship is quite close (See: **Figure 117**).

The *Rānā Mahal*

The *Rānā Mahal*, "the palace of the queen," on the other hand, presents two intriguing problems — e.g., asymmetry in the face of apparent symmetry, *en plan*, and the podium. Although the plan and elevation give the impression of symmetry, it is essentially asymmetrical. The western block is not centered on the north-south axis, but is set slightly north of centre (See: centre line, **Plate 37**; see also: **Figure 95**). The end pavilions are, likewise, are not similar, *en plan*. One would expect opening "A" and "D" (See: **Plate 37**) to be of equal width,

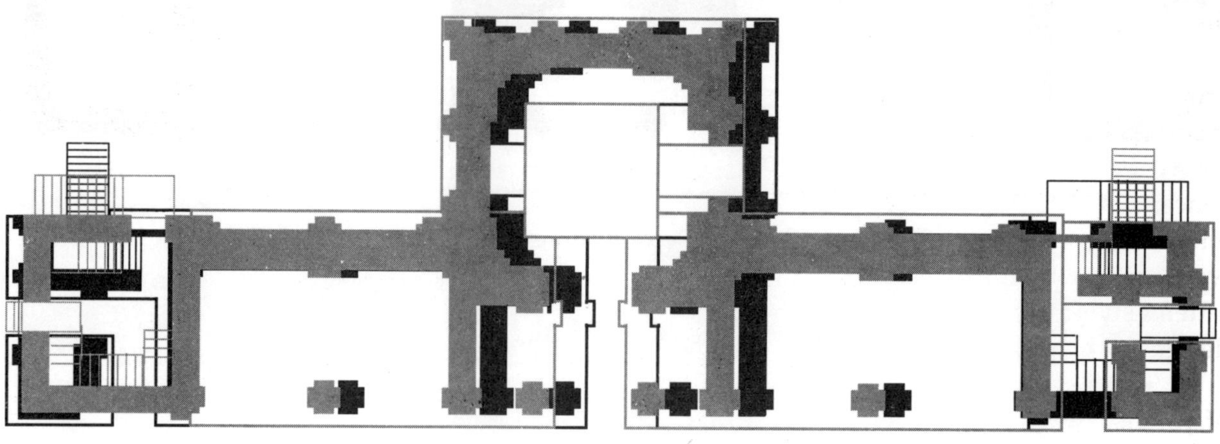

Figure 95 — *Rānā Mahal* indicating the deviation from axial symmetry

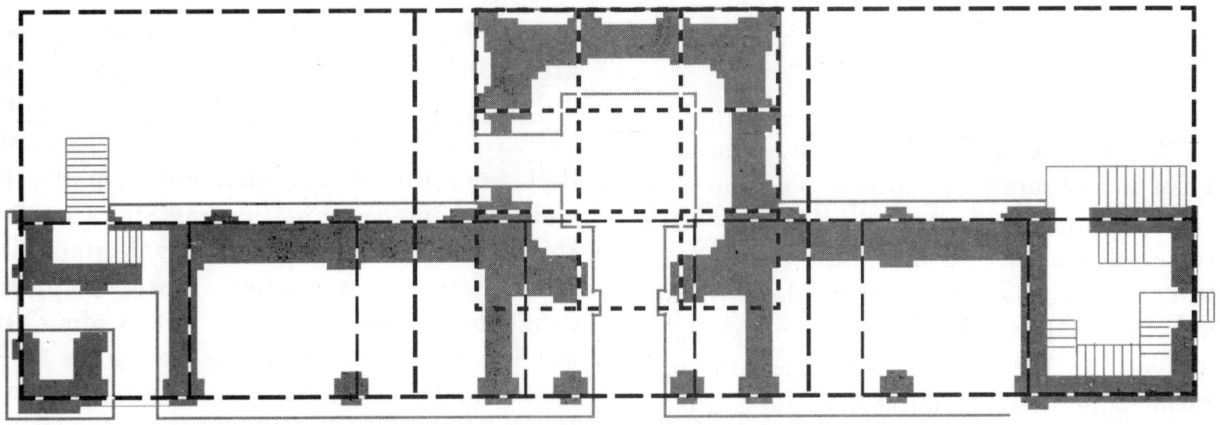

Figure 96 — *Rānā Mahal*, indicating possible divisions

and the same may be expected of openings "B" and "C." Not so! As a matter of fact, openings "B" and "D" are close to the same width, *en plan*. Furthermore, the overhang or balcony to which one has access from the central openings (doorways) on the second storey extends from the south-eastern corner of the northern pavilion, across the front and half way across the eastern facade of the southern pavilion. Nonetheless, the eastern façade of the *Rānā Mahal* is most intriguing.

The *Rānā Mahal* consists of two levels on what would be considered the ground floor plan. The eastern spaces — i.e., those bracketed by the openings "A" and "B," and "C" and "D" — and the northern pavilion, as well as portions of the western pavilion are on one level, on what appears to be a podium. The remainder of the ground floor is approximately two metres lower (See: darkened areas, **Plate 37** [top plan]). This would seem to imply that the *Rānā Mahal* had been conceived of as a monumental gate in which the entrance to the rest of the ensemble interior wended its way through this lowered portion — a defensive measure. Would this have been the design for a *zenānā*?

The second storey is divided into a series of rooms, flowing one into the other and three staircases leading to this level. Certainly, the upper level would lend itself to the quarters for the *Rānā* with adequate, multiple means of ingress and egress. But, what of the lower level? It is suggested that either the deep eastern spaces of the ground floor — i.e., the southern or the northern — with their wide arched openings could well be utilized for the *Rāya's darśana*.

Finally, due to the eclectic design of the *Rānā Mahal*, it is difficult to view this structure as adhering to any of the standard design forms. The whole does fall within the *daṇḍaka* plan, as does the *Rājā Mahal*, previously noted (See: **Figure 96**). Similarly, a *Piṭha Maṇḍala* — i.e., a *maṇḍala* composed of nine *pada* — has certain applicability to the western pavilion. However, the above noted deviations make any firm application of traditional design parameters extremely problematical.

Upon the diminution of their rich and considerable empire, the *Saluva Rāyas*, in the construction of the *Rājā Mahal* (*Chandragiri Palace*) had obviously not lost their appreciation of either the grand or the elegant. This *garh mahal* and its attendant *Rānā Mahal* were not on the scale of *Vijayanagara*. However, what they lacked in size, they made up for in refinement, grace and elegance. The *Rājā Mahal* (*Chandragiri Palace*) was a fitting cap-stone for this once powerful dynasty.

City Palace, Udaipur

(a. 1567 CE)

Udaipur, a city of legend, a city of beauty, a city of incomparable palaces — i.e., the *City Palace,*[114] the *Jag Nivās* and the *Jag Mandir* — is a fairly recent Rajput capital. After the sack of Chittor, the Sisodia Rajput Rāja Udaya (Udai) Singh, who ruled over his vassals from 1537-1572 CE, moved to the west of his domain and established the new capital at Udaipur ("Udai's city") where he reigned for a short time (r. 1567-1572).[115]

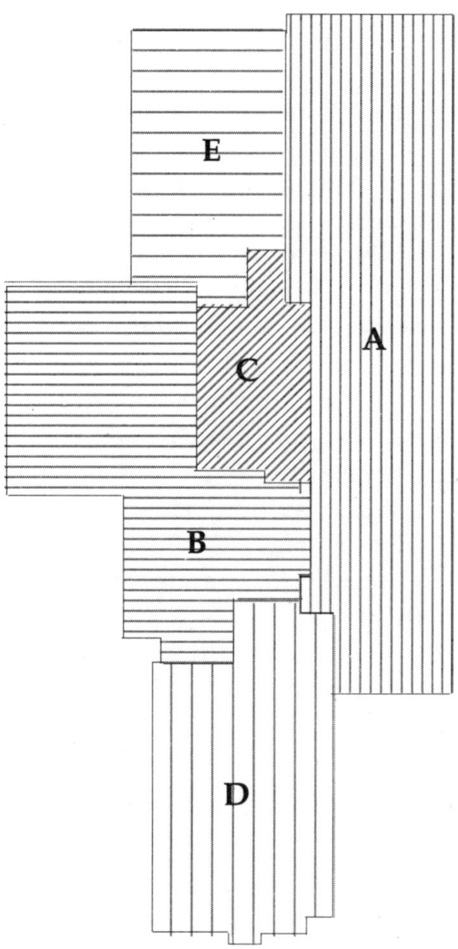

Figure 97 — Distribution of areas, *City Palace,* Udaipur; public areas (**A**), limited access areas (**B**), restricted (**C**), *zenānā* (**D**), attendents and military (**E**)

For four hundred years this *garh mahal* grew under almost constant, even incessant building projects of one *rājā* or another. Constructed upon a hill with high escarpments that were further fortified with equally high walls and imposing battlements, the *City Palace* stands as an example for a royal citadel. One would expect a rather loose, haphazard conglomeration of buildings and to some extent this is true. However, unlike the Rathor Rajputs to the north at Jodhpur, the Sisodia Rajputs of Udaipur employed multiple perpendicular axiality in their *garh mahal* thus creating a complex assemblage of structures, but one which hinged upon the north-south axis. These additions, over the years, imparted a kind of massive regularity, a purposeful progression, as they proceed from the *Lakṣmī Chowk* northwards to the *Badi Pol* (See:

Legend for **Plate 38**

A Badi Pol
B Tripolia
C Mahendra Sabhā
D Baḍī Mahal
E Amar Vilās
F Manek Chowk
F[1] Stables
G Karan Nivās
H Shila Khana
I Sabhā
J Moti Chowk
K Toran Pol
L Sūraj Pol
M Lakṣmī Chowk (zenānā)
M[1] Zenānā apartments
N* Badi Chatur
O* Mor Chowk
P* Rajya Angan Chowk
Q* Kanch-ki Burj
R* Chitram-ki Burj

= Level 4

*See: **Figure 98**

Plate 38 — *City Palace*, Udaipur, plan (partial)

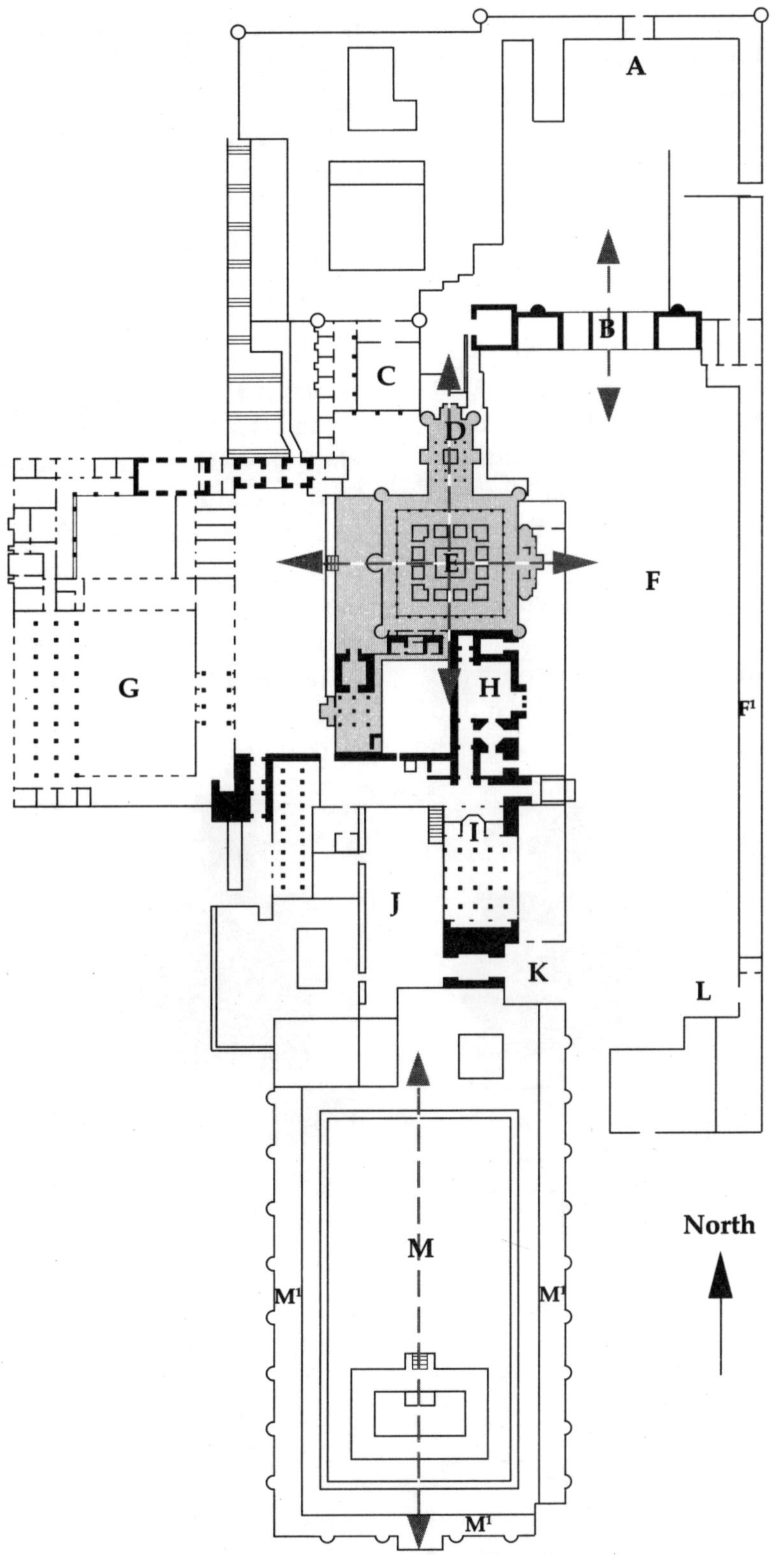

Plate 38). This arrangement is not unlike the Sisodias' former capital at Chittor. One might state that the influence of Mandan *putra* Kshetra was even felt in Udaipur.

As in all *garh mahals*, there were areas for the public, restricted areas as well as a *zenānā* (See: **Figures 97**). Access to the inner reaches of the *garh mahal* is severely restricted, particularly enter to the areas of the upper region (See: **Figure 98**). This is in keeping with the security of the ruler from untoward intrusions or danger. Gate after impressive gate must be passed before entering the palace proper. This grand labyrinthine approach could not help but to instill in all those who entered the exalted position of the ruler. Then access to the upper regions is achieved only via a series of staircases and ramps which would be easily defended.

The *City Palace* consists of a large courtyard known as the *Lakṣmī Chowk* at the southern end of the citadel (See: **Plate 38 — M**). To the north is one of the entrances into the *garh mahal* proper — i.e., the *Toran Pol* (See: **Plate 38 — K**). There are several storeys which contain various apartments and the royal residence until the uppermost level. The *Amar Vilās* and the *Baḍī Mahal* is to be found there (See: **Plate 38 — D** & **E**). The *Amar Vilās* provided the rājā with a luxurious garden atop his *garh mahal*. These areas rest upon a rocky outcropping that is encased by the lower reaches of the *garh mahal* (See dark grey areas: **Figure 98**).[116] To the east of the *garh mahal* and along its whole length is the *Manek Chowk* (See: **Plate 38 — F**) and the stables (See: **Plate 38 — F^1**). Here the sumptuous and elaborate celebrations and/or parades befitting the ruler's position could be staged. The *chowk* was also suitable for the rājā's splendid *darbārs* and *darśanas*. In the east wall of this *chowk* is the *Sūraj Pol*, one of the principal entrances to the citadel (See: **Plate 38 — L**). Private audiences with the ruler were held in the formal *Sabhā* (See: **Plate 38 — I**).

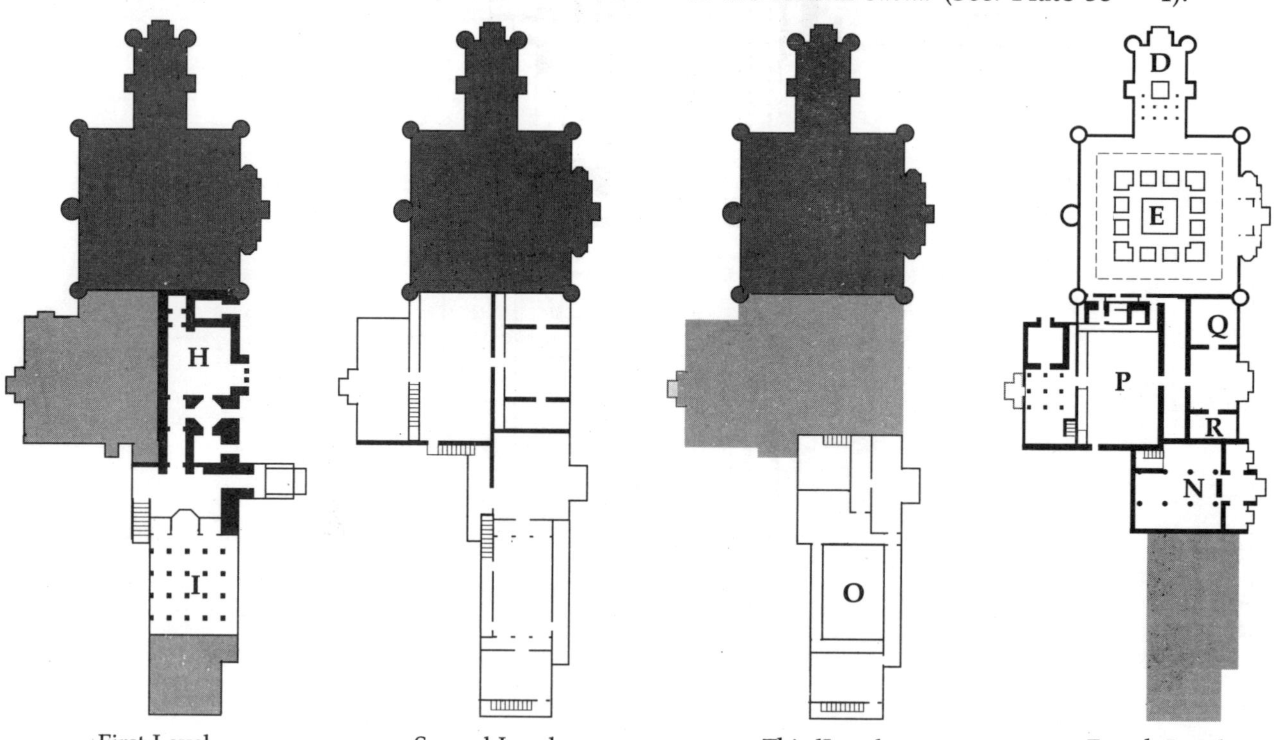

Figure 98 — *City Palace*, Udaipur, indicating the four levels

City Palace, Udaipur (Concluded)

The multiple perpendicular axiality allows for some degree of flow from one area to the other. However, the employment of a *maṇḍala* to most of the structures is pointless. Nonetheless, the *Amar Vilās* does conform to a *Paramaśayika Maṇḍala* (See: **Figure 99**). The first, second and third ranks and files define the *bagh*. Further, the four circular bastions at the corners conform to an ideal suggested by the *śilpa-śāstras* and exemplified in the *Jahangir Mandir* of Orchha, the *Govind Mandir* of Datia (See: **Figure 100**). This was also the plan that the Muslim sultāns and Mughal emperors also employed from time to time — e.g., the mausoleum of Nasir-ud-Din Muhammad, known as the *Tomb of Sultān Ghari*, Delhi (1231 CE); the *Tomb of Jalau-ud-din Mohammad Shah (Eklakhi)*, Pandua (1430 CE); the *Tomb of Jahangir*, Lahore (1627 CE); and the tomb of Sultān Muhammad 'Adil Shah, *Gol Gumbaz*, Bijapur (1626-1656 CE).[117] This adherence to a Hindu model may well have been due to their employment of indigenous *sthapati*.

The Sisodia Rajputs continued in Udaipur what had been for them an architectural heritage of regal grandeur. They constructed not only the magnificent and sumptuous *City Palace*, but also two more notable *mandirs* on the islands of the lake where they built their capital. There may have been larger *garh mahals*, there may have been more elaborate palaces, but none in India were more regal or elegant or beautiful than the *City Palace* of Udaipur.

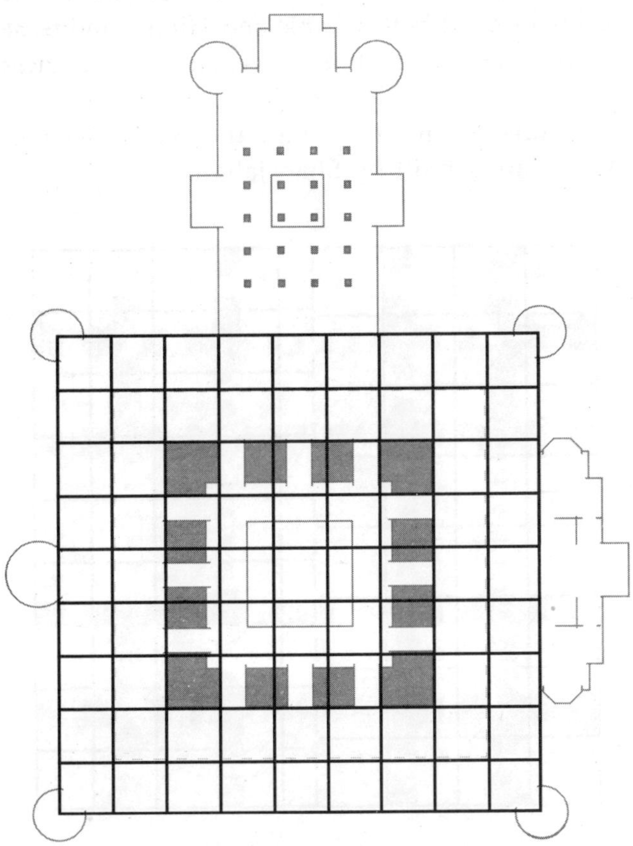

Figure 99 — *Amar Vilās, City Palace*, Udaipur (detail), indicating a *Paramaśayika Maṇḍala*

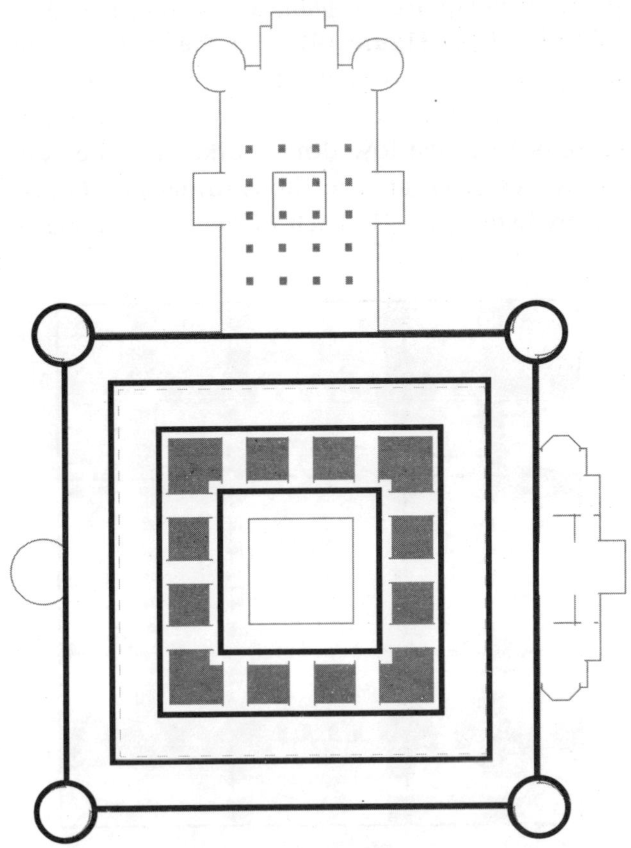

Figure 100 — *Amar Vilās, City Palace*, Udaipur (detail), indicating a *śilpa-śāstra* ideal

Farah Bagh (*Feria Bagh*)

Ahmadnagar (c. 1583 CE)

The *Farah Bagh* (aka *Feria Bagh*)[118] is a prime example of a pleasure pavilion. These pavilions were not meant to be permanent residences, but provided the builder with a suitable and pleasant place to relax away from the rigours of courtly life. The *Farah Bagh* was constructed by the aristocratic courtier Salabat Khan during the reign of Akbar the Great and far south of the Imperial court. There, it is supposed, Salabat Khan would have been able to relax well away from the stress of his position, if even for a short time.

The *Farah Bagh* exhibits the requirements of a rather traditional pleasure pavilion, not unlike those of Persia — e.g., the *Hesht Behest* of Isfahan (See: **Appendix A, Plate 92**). Here, the pavilion is square, *en plan*, and exhibits a nine-fold plan (See: **Figure 101**). For the Muslims, the iconography of this plan refers to the eight rivers surrounding Paradise. The central area rises two storeys to a shallow dome. Likewise the four vestibules orientated to the cardinal points also are two storeys high. Each of the internal spaces are fronted by deep vestibules, thereby protecting them from the direct glare of the sun and creating a cooler interior. Set within the thick masonry walls, narrow stairways lead to the abbreviated second storey. The spaces found here would have provided ample space for more pleasurable and private activities. The numerous windows and the large open areas all provided the unimpeded passage of the cooling breezes, particularly in the evenings. Five bubbling fountains also added to this Sybaritic atmosphere.

The square plan would seem to imply the utilization of a *maṇḍala*. The utilization of the nine-fold plan appears to favor a *Paramaśayika Maṇḍala* over a *Maṇḍūka Maṇḍala* (See: **Figure 102**), although the latter is not without merit.

The elegantly designed and conceived *Farah Bagh* mirrors the needs of noble India and seems to meld both Islamic and Hindu traditions in its plan. Built by a nobleman, the courtier Salabat Khan , it nonetheless reflects imperial pavilions of India — e.g., the *Shahi Bagh* of Ahmadabad built by Shah Jahan.

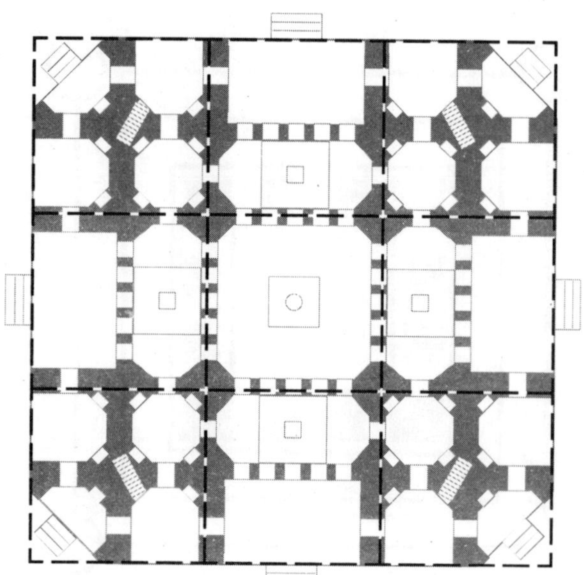

Figure 101 — *Feria Bagh*, indicating nine-part division

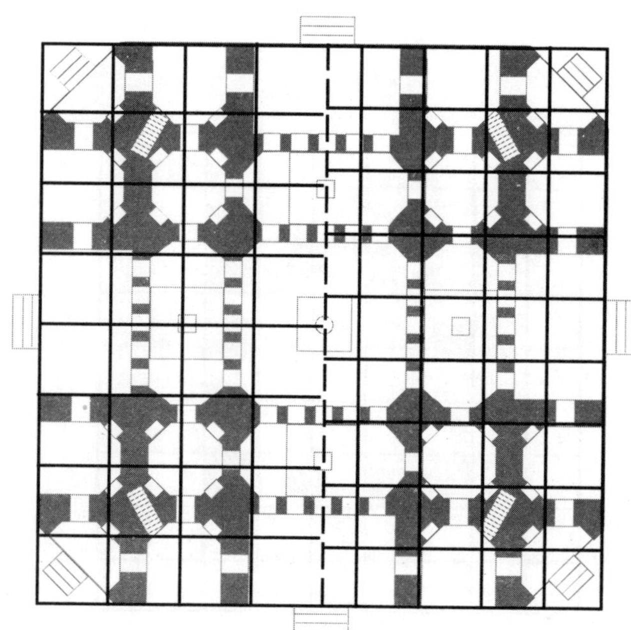

Figure 102 — *Feria Bagh*, indicating *Maṇḍūka Maṇḍala* and *Paramaśayika Maṇḍala*

Plate 39 — *Feria Bagh*, ground floor plan

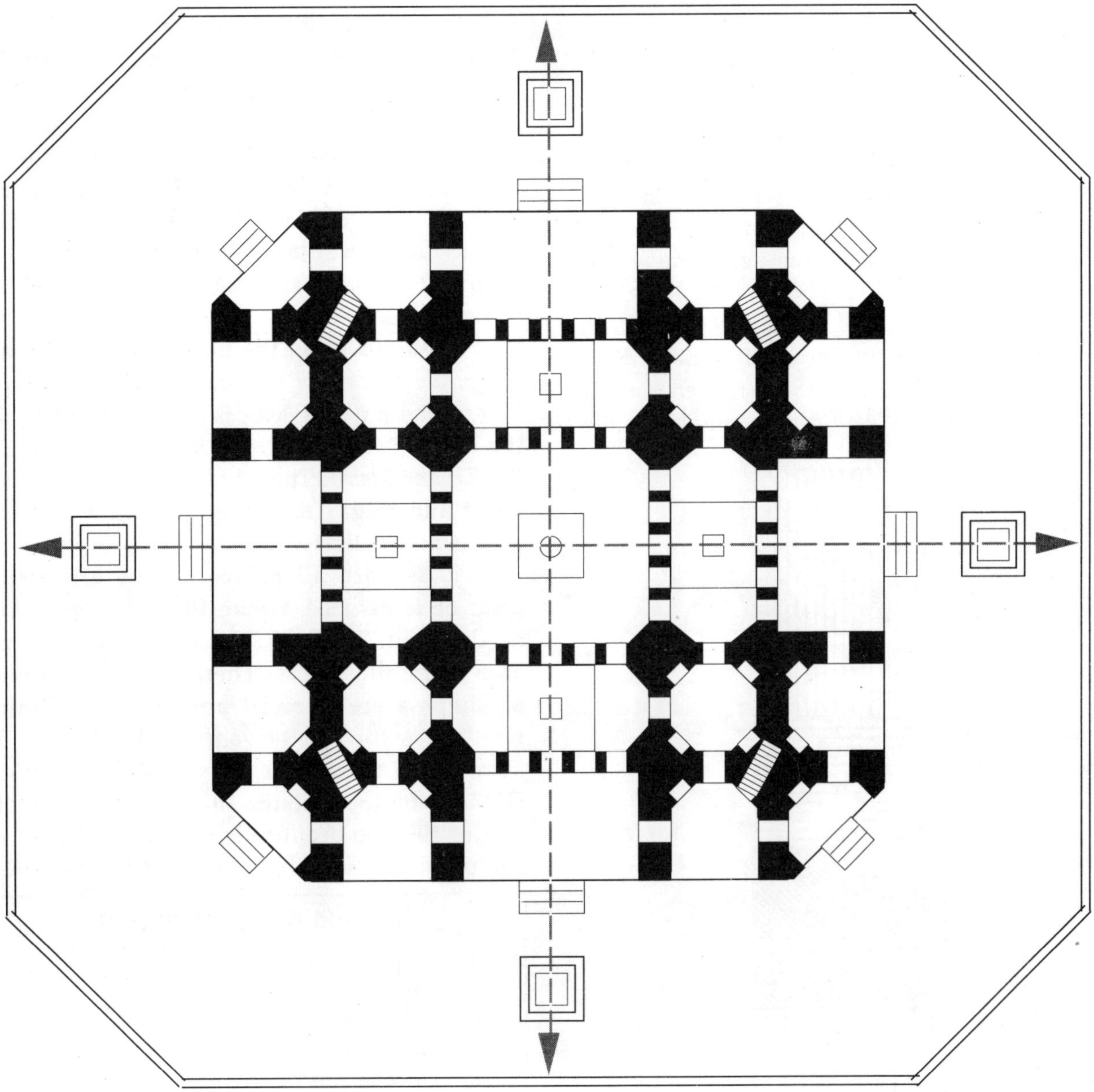

Rāj Mahal

Amber, (a. 1592 CE)

The Kachwaha Rajputs had established their capital at Dhundar in 967 CE. There they remained and ruled until 1150 when they moved their headquarters to Amber. This city was the Kachwaha capital until it was again moved to Jaipur in 1727 by Sawai Jaya Singh II (r. 1700-1743 CE). A formidable citadel was constructed, the *Jaigarh* during the early period in Amber. Rāja Man Singh I (r. 1592-1615 CE) then began construction on a new *garh mahal*, completing the

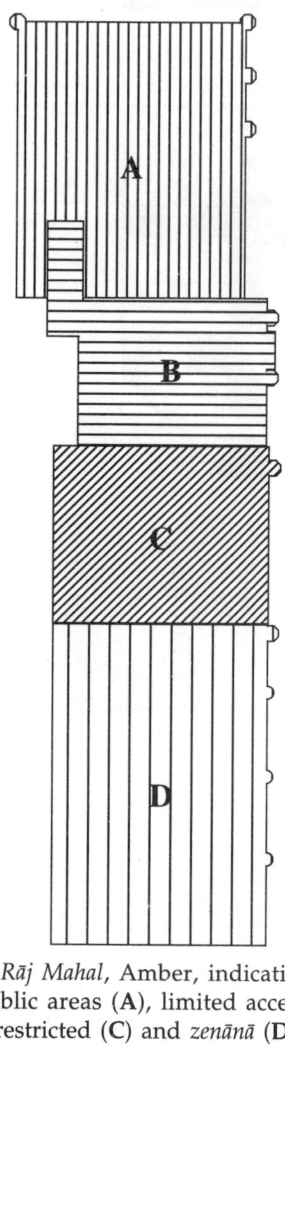

Figure 103 — *Rāj Mahal*, Amber, indicating distribution of areas: public areas (**A**), limited access areas (**B**), restricted (**C**) and *zenānā* (**D**)

area that is now utilized as the *zenānā* of the *Rāj Mahal*.[119] The reign of Mirza Rāja Jai Singh (aka Jaya Singh I) — i.e., 1622-1667 CE — saw the construction of the second and third major areas: the *Residential Chowk* (See: **Plate 40 — I**) and the *Diwān-i Ām Chowk* (See: **Plate 40 — F**). The spacious *Jaleb Chowk* (See: **Plate 40 — A**) was an addition by the Rāja Sawai Jaya Singh II (r. 1700-1743 CE), completing what is essentially the *garh mahal* as it now stands.

Raised upon the northern end of a high ridge, the *Rāj Mahal* is subject to the topography. The northern *Jaleb Chowk* is somewhat lower than the *Diwān-i Ām Chowk*, the *Residential Chowk* and the *Zenānā Mahal*. The whole dominates this high point and reigns over the city below radiating power and majesty.

As with all palaces, there are distinct areas of access (See: **Figure 103**). The *Rāj Mahal* is no different. The *Jaleb Chowk* was essentially an area of public access. There, a limited number of shops were allowed and it also contained residences for the servants and military. The *Diwān-i Ām Chowk* was the site of the impressive *Diwān-i Ām* (See: **Plates 40 & 41 — E**: see also: **Figure 105**). So beautifully designed, elegant and sumptuous was this pavilion that it was brought

Legend for **Plates 40 & 41**

- **A** Jaleb Chowk
- **B** Sūraj Pol
- **C** Chand Pol
- **D** Singh Pol
- **E** Diwān-i Ām
- **F** Diwān-i Ām Chowk
- **G** Temple of Sila Devi (lower)
- **H** Ganesh Pol
- **I** Residential Chowk
- **J** Sukh Nivās
- **K** Jai Mandir
- **L** Jess Mandir (above)
- **M** Chowk of Zenānā Mahal
- **N** Baradari Pavilion
- **O** Zenānā Mahal

Plate 40 — *Rāj Mahal*, Amber, plan (partial)

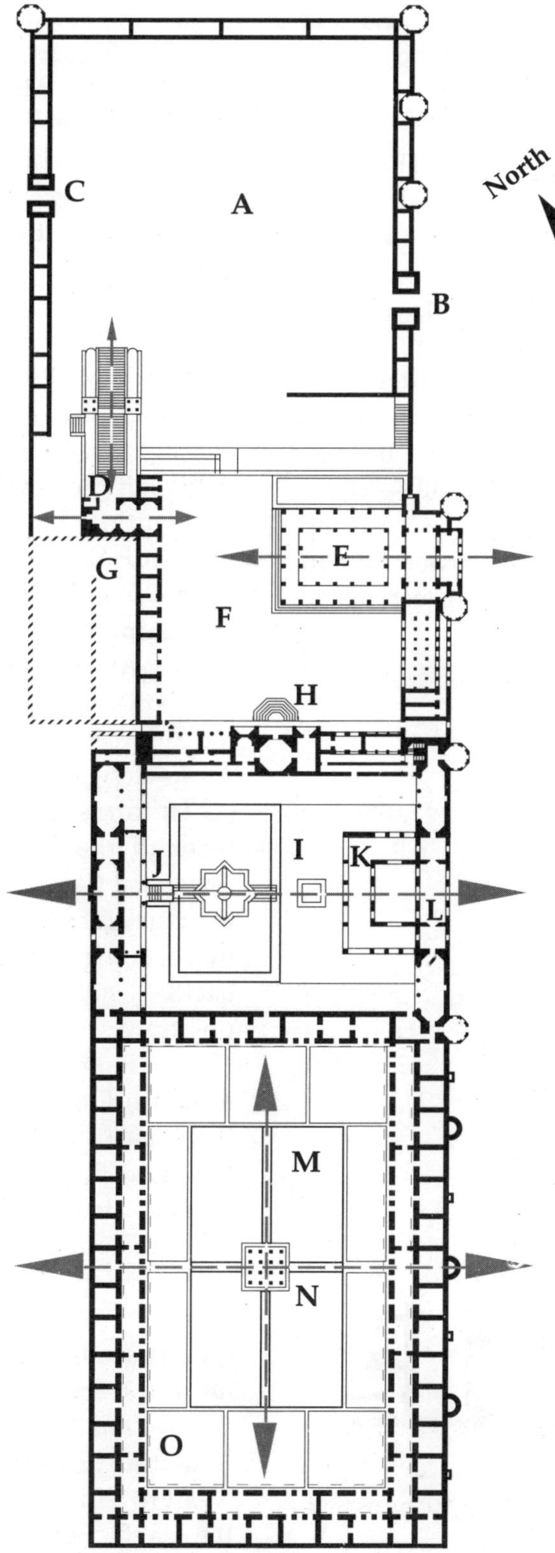

to the attention of the Emperor Jahangir who was reported to have been quite envious. In the middle of the southern façade of the *chowk* was another elegant feature — i.e., the *Ganesh Pol* (See: **Plates 40 & 41 — H**: see also: **Figure 104**). This gate allowed access into the private residential area of the *garh mahal*. The *Residential Chowk* contained the *Sukh Nivās* (See: **Plates 40 & 41 — J**), the *Jai Mandir* (See: **Plates 40 & 41 — K**) and the *Jess Mandir* (See: **Plates 40 & 41 — L**) above the preceding. These elegant rooms overlooked a formal garden with a fountain in the form of an eight-pointed star. From this locale there was even more limited access to the *Zenānā Mahal* (See: **Plate 40 — O**) — the women's quarters of the *Rāj Mahal*. Consisting of suites bordering a developed garden and in the centre of which was a pavilion of sixteen pillars

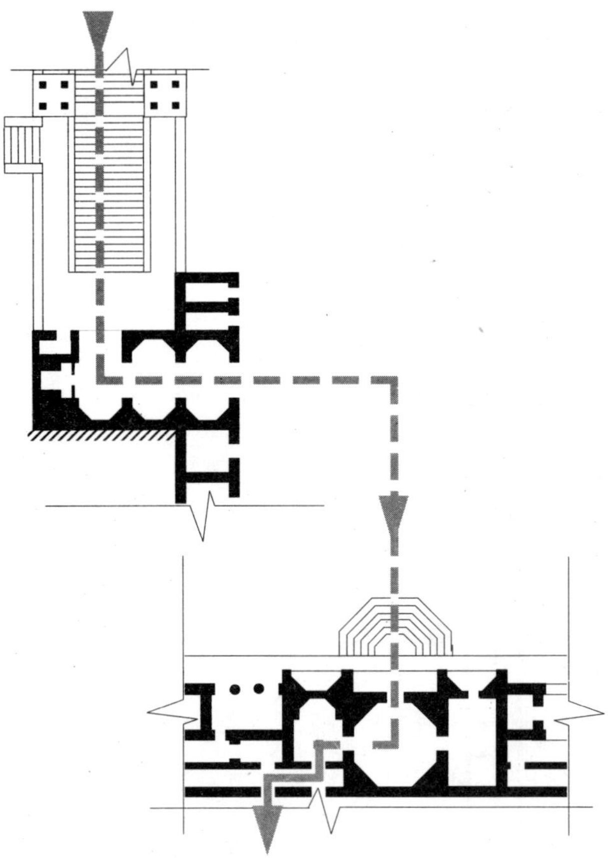

Figure 104 — *Rāj Mahal*, Amber, indicating 90⁰ turns thru *Sūraj Pol* and *Ganesh Pol*

— i.e., the *Baradari Pavilion* (See: **Plate 40 — N**; see also: **Figure 107**) — the *zenānā* is the largest area of the *Rāj Mahal*. The larger, comparative size and well developed nature of the women's quarters is not unusual in the later Hindu and Muslim *garh mahals* — the exceptions being the *mandirs* of the Bundelas (See: **Plates 19-20 & 42-46**).

From the *Jaleb Chowk* to the *Zenānā Mahal*, the *Rāj Mahal* follows a single axis — i.e., roughly north-south. Within the whole complex various buildings are oriented east-west — e.g., the *Diwān-i Ām*, the *Sukh Nivās* or the *Jai Mandir*. Although the whole appears to be axial, it must, in truth, be described as a multiple perpendicular axial ensemble (See: **Plate 41**). The *Rāj Mahal* is in the same tradition as the *City Palace* of Udaipur.

As can be observed the access to the residential area — i.e. the *Residential Chowk* — of the *Rāj Mahal* was not only circumloucutious, but it was designed in such a manner that there were six 90⁰ turns to be negotiated from the *Sūraj Pol* through the *Ganesh Pol* before entry into the *Residential Chowk* (See: **Figure 104**). Many of these turns required any possible interlopers to pass by several guard rooms, thereby presenting their backs — not an acceptable nor an advantageous position.

From the *Jaleb Chowk*, one would have to mount a long stairway to the elevated *Diwān-i Ām Chowk*. Immediately upon passing through the *Sūraj Pol* one would be confronted with this elegant structure of red sandstone and white marble across the *chowk*. Essentially it is a columned pavilion, open on three sides. The outer ranks of pillars are doubled and quadrupled at the corners. This is obviously more for aesthetic value than structural as the *Diwān-i Ām* (See: **Figure 105**) is but a single storey. Essentially, there are six 'groups' across the western side, or narrow end, and eight along the length. Set in, the depth of an inter columnar

Plate 41 — *Rāj Mahal*, Amber. plan detail,
Diwān-i Ām Chowk and *Residential Chowk* indicating axes

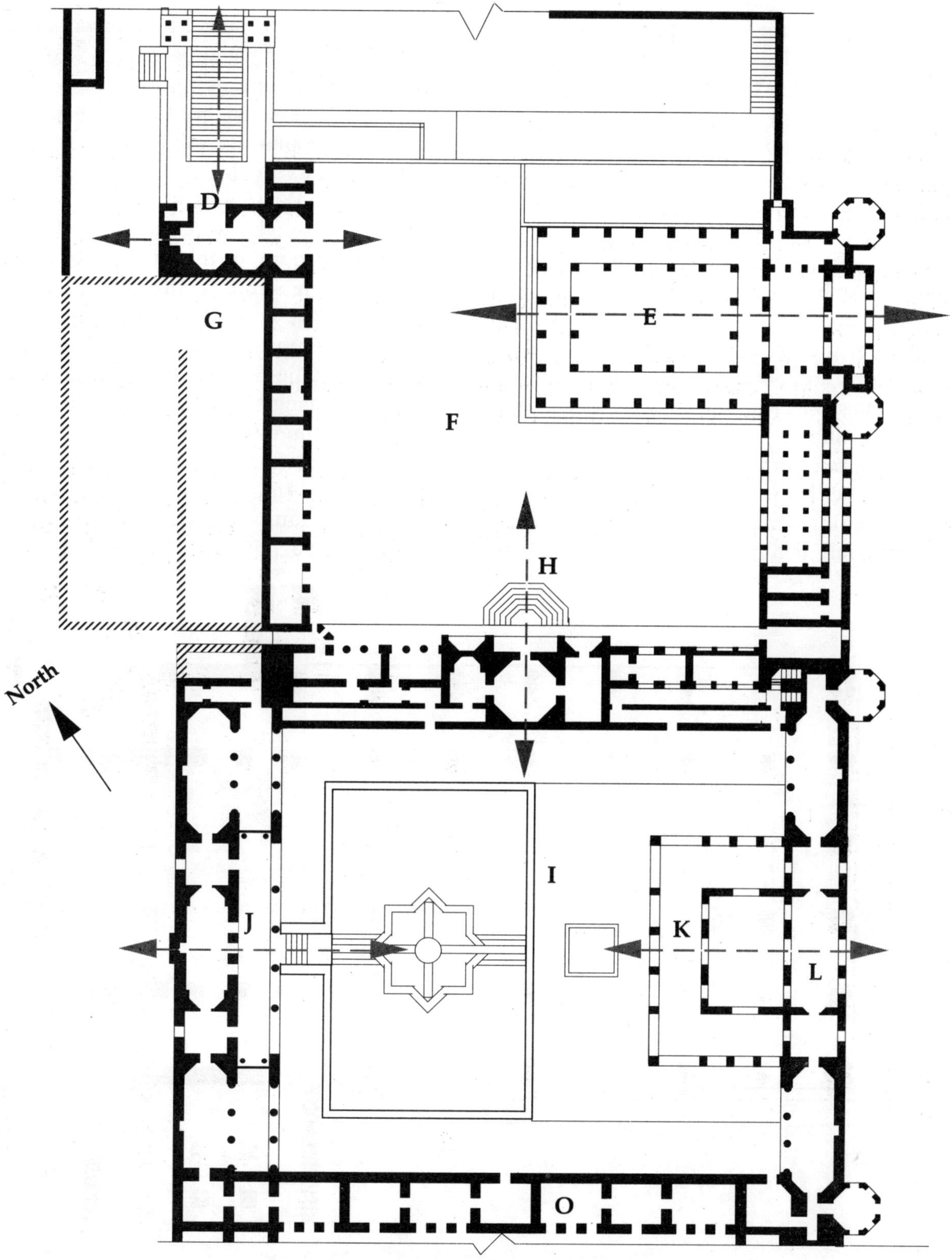

space is a single rank of columns — i.e. four columns by six. This allows fifteen "bays" of unimpeded space in the centre of the structure. At the eastern end of this space is a raised, vaulted dais, then a triple arch, followed by a rectangular space and then five windows opening onto a vista of Amber.

The *Diwān-i Ām*, as has been noted, was one of the jewels in the crown of the Kachwaha Rajputs of Amber. It is a rectangle with the *gaddi* situated in the centre of the narrow side. This differs from the imperial *Diwān-i Āms* at Agra, *Fatehpur Sikri* and *Shahjahanabad*, where, they are all rectangular, but with the *gaddi* set in the centre of the long side.

One can but imagine: it would have been most dramatic that during a *darśana* or *darbār*, the triple opening might have been draped concealing all behind it. The central curtain would have been pulled back or raised and there the rājā would have appeared, backed by the sun light of the five windows. His luxuriously dressed, bejeweled body is framed as if by a dazzling nimbus. He would then regally proceed onto the dais to slowly take his seat upon the royal *gaddi*. What a sight!

Those who were unable to stand beneath the stone canopy of the *Diwān-i Ām* would have found ample space in the chowk. All this was meant to awe. From the bustle of the *Jaleb Chowk*, the long climb up to the *Sūraj Pol* and then the elegant pavilion — one can well understand the envy of Jahangir of this Kachwaha building and the rājās who built it.

Zenānās are generally quite spacious, so too here in Amber as well. Frequently they are built over long periods of time and began to sprawl in various directions. However here in

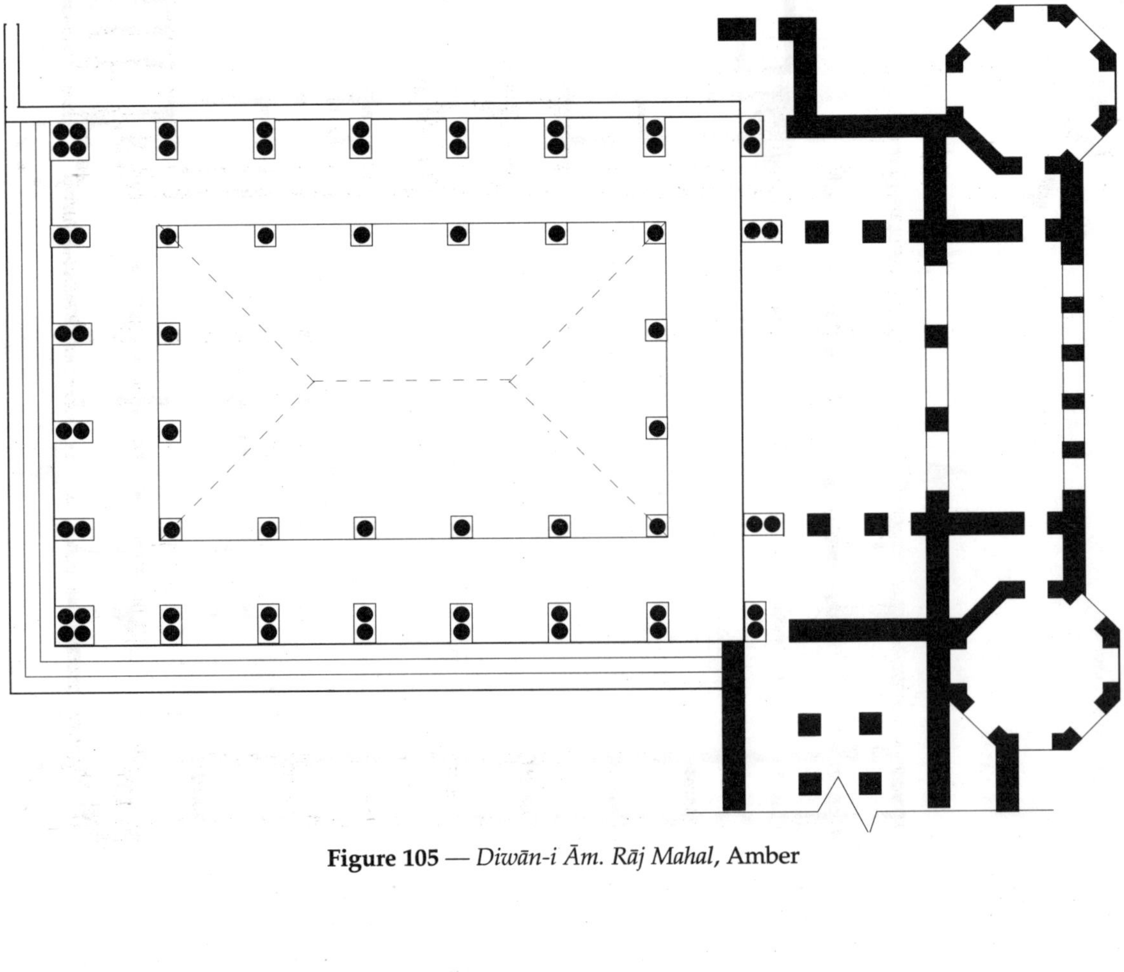

Figure 105 — *Diwān-i Ām. Rāj Mahal*, Amber

the *Rāj Mahal* the *Zenānā Mahal* is quite regular, spacious and strictly rectangular (See **Plate 40**; see also **Figure 106**). As has been noted, it is thought that the present *Zenānā Mahal* was the main section of an early Kachwaha rājā. It consists of a large courtyard with sectioned arcades behind which are the various apartments. The *mahal* contained a second storey with balconies facing the court for access. During a later period, some of the arcade was sealed off and *jālīs* were inserted. Along the eastern outer wall were circular battlements and balconies overlooking the valley below.

The court was sectioned and a garden was planted for the delight of the women. In the centre a sixteen pillar *śālā* was erected — the *Baradari Pavilion*[120] (See: **Figure 107**). It is of interest to note that neither a *Maṇḍūka Maṇḍala* nor a *Paramaśayika Maṇḍala* is applicable to the plan of this small pavilion. However a *Sthandila Maṇḍala* of forty-nine *pada* is eminently applicable (See: **Figure 107**). Forty-nine is a masculine number, is a sacred numeral whose √ is the equally sacred seven. As a compound number it is associated astronomically with the planet *Rāhu* (the ascending node of the moon) (4), the planet Mars (*Maṅgala*, *Kuja* or *Aṅgaraka*) (9). When reduced it produces four and, therefore, the planet *Rāhu* (the ascending node of the moon) (4).[121]

From south to north, roughly, marches the impressive *Rāj Mahal*. Its four courts not only define the *garh mahal*, they also act as a calendar of construction of this important Kachwaha Rajput palace. Of all the structures, the elegant *Diwān-i Ām* is the most noteworthy and exhibits the height of design. Although Amber was superseded by Jaipur as the Kachwaha capital, the *Rāj Mahal* still reigns supreme as a most impressive *garh mahal*.

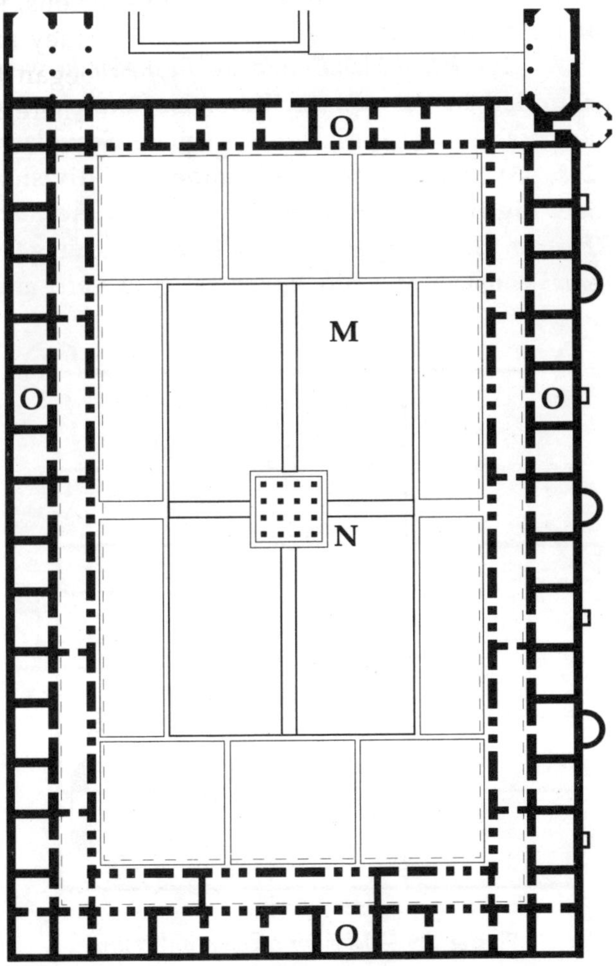

Figure 106 — *Zenānā Mahal. Rāj Mahal*, Amber

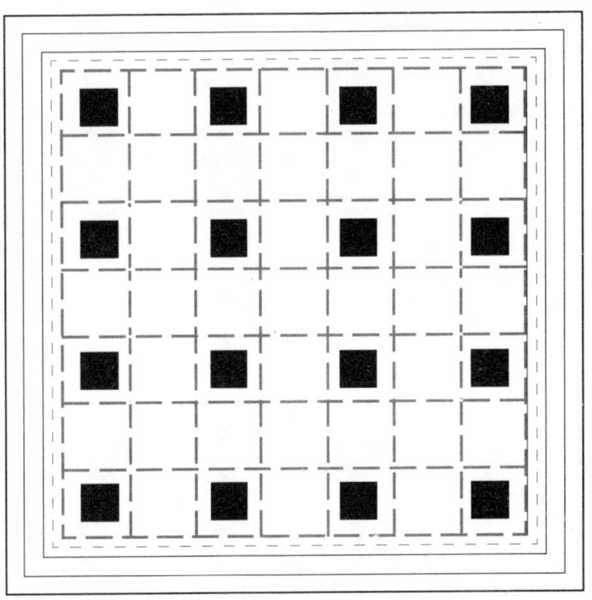

Figure 107 — *Baradari Pavilion. Rāj Mahal*, Amber with *Sthandila Maṇḍala*

Jahangir Mandir (*Jahangiri Mahal*)

Orchha (a. 1605 CE)

The sophisticated, cunning and ambitious Rājā Bir Singh Ju Deo (r. 1605-1627 CE), son of the Rājā Madhukhar Shah (r. 1554-1577 CE), ascended the Bundela throne after his elder brother Rājā Ram Shah was deposed by the Mughal Emperor Jahangir. As a prince of Bundela, Bir Singh Ju Deo had earlier supported the then Prince Salim — i.e., Jahangir — in his assertion of his imperial inheritance. Bir Singh Ju Deo fell under the wrath of Salim's father, Akbar the Great, who sought to imprison the rash Bundela prince. But, the prince managed to evade capture and the subsequent wrath of the emperor. He bided his time. Then Emperor Akbar died and his friend, Salim, became the Emperor Jahangir. In thanks for his loyal support the emperor elevated Bir Singh Ju Deo to the *gaddi* of Bundela, setting aside his luckless elder, brother, the Rāja Ram Shah (See: **Appendix A**).

The newly elevated Bundela king soon began a remarkable building program — remarkable for this small Rajputana polity. His first architectural endeavor was the construction of the *Jahangir Mandir*[122] at Orchha (See: **Figure 108**). The name of this *garh mahal* indicates the obvious! This was the third of the noteworthy *garh mahal*s of this citadel. As with his predecessors he went to the ancient *śilpa-śāstras* for his inspiration.

The *Rāmji Mandir* and the *Rājā Mandir* were grounded in the square. Likewise, the plan of the massive *Jahangir Mandir* was square (See: **Plates 42 & 43**) and conforms to a nine-part division (See: **Figure 109**). Related, *en plan*, to the *Kasr Kharana* (See: **Appendix A, Plate 63**), this *garh mahal* consists of a block, central courtyard and

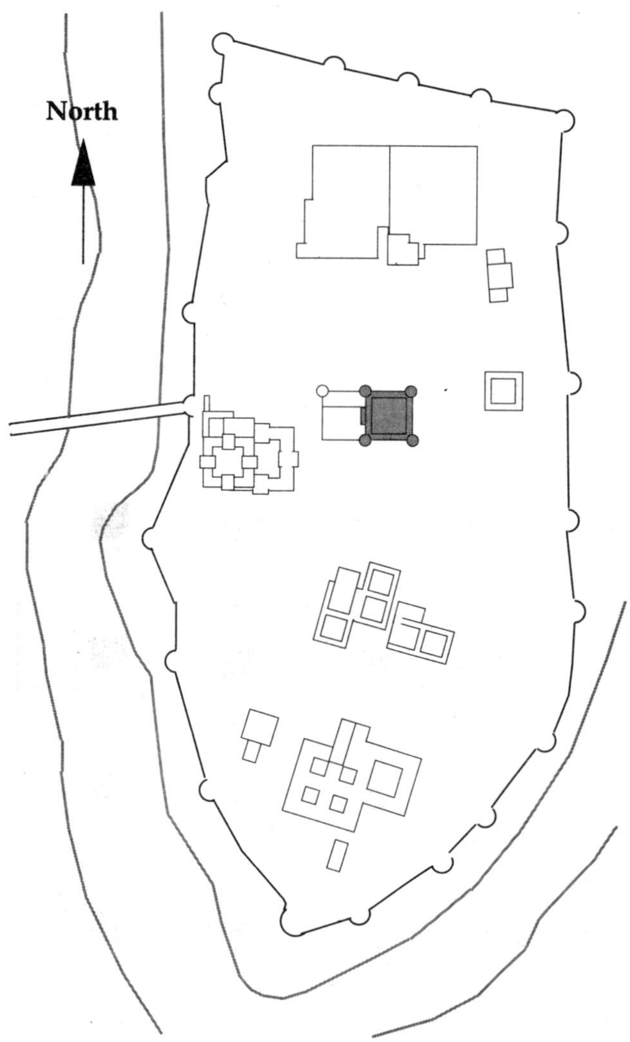

Figure 108 — *Orchha Qila*, indicating *Jahangir Mandir*

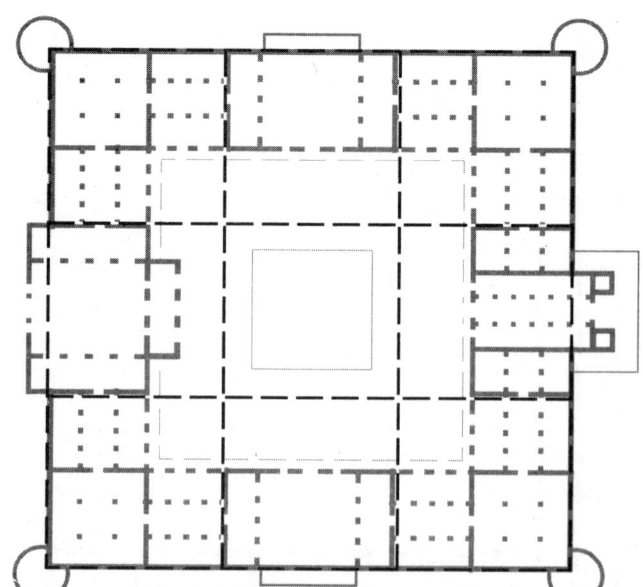

Figure 109 — *Jahangir Mandir*, indicating nine-part division

Plate 42 — *Jahangir Mandir*, plan 1st & 2nd storey

(a. 1605 CE)

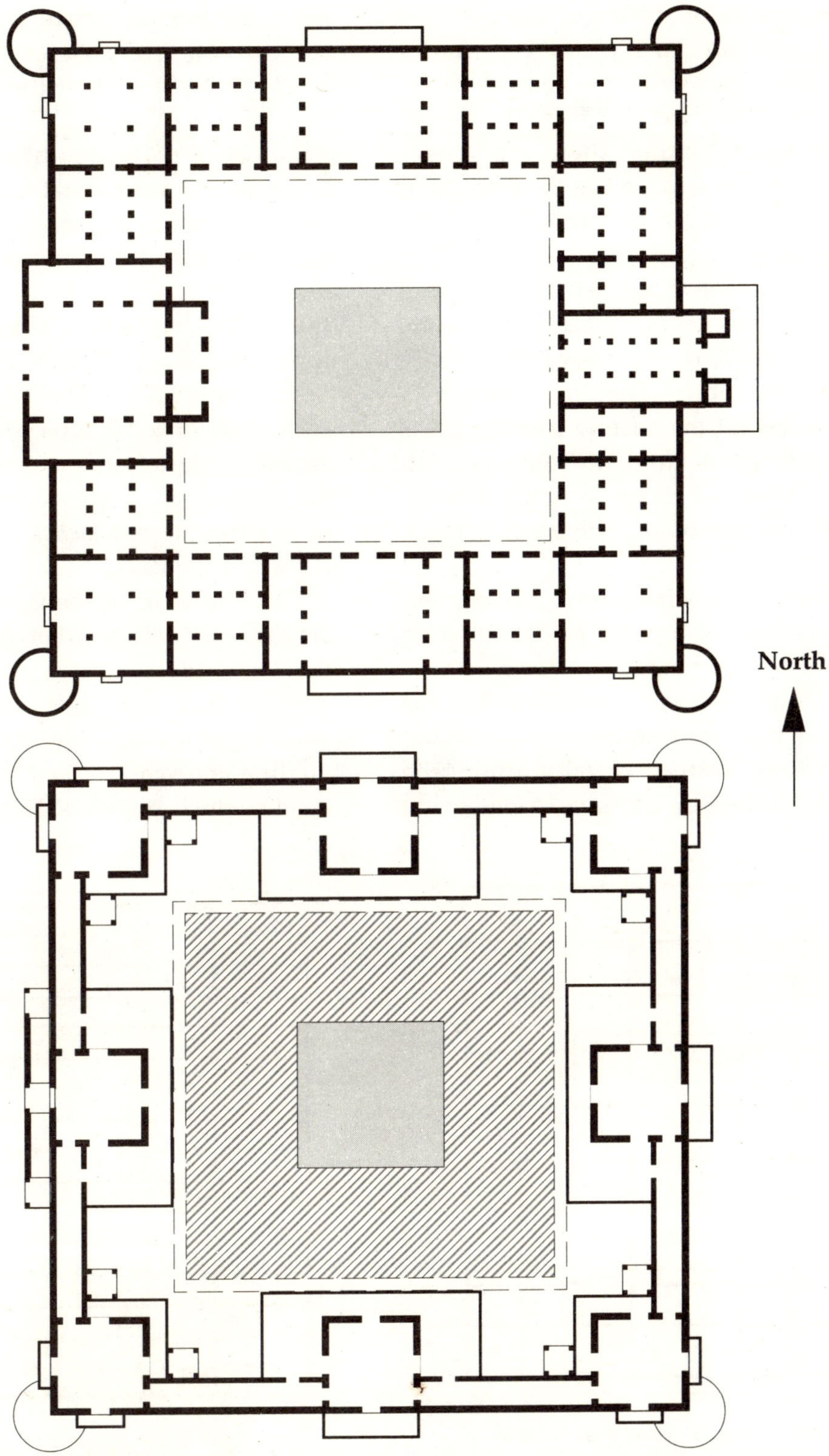

towers on the corners of the lower storeys. The rooms of the first storey, with the exception of the corner rooms, open onto the central court. Each subsequent storey recedes from the court so that on the second storey there are square rooms at the corners and at the intercardinal points. Access is gained to these rooms by narrow passageways against the outer wall or wooden balconies corbelled against the outer wall and around the rooms proper. *Chatrīs* punctuate the internal corners and rise above this storey (See: **Plate 43** [bottom]). The third storey is similar, *en plan*, except the narrow passage gives way to balconies connecting the corners with the central pavilions (See: **Plate 43** [top]). Finally, a narrow walkway surrounds the whole on the upper level.

The effect of the whole, from the exterior, gives the impression of a massive block rising into the sky (See: **Appendix A, Plate 90**). In actuality, the *Jahangir Mandir's* interior belies the exterior. Rather than four storeys of connected rooms, one storey resting equally upon the subsequent one, defined by the area of the central court, the internal space steps back, towards the outer wall. The area of the second storey is substantially less than the first, and so forth to the uppermost storey. This fact is lost on those who would view this block from the exterior. The result is quite theatrical. The exterior of the *Jahangir Mandir* suggests something that does not exist, but it does impart an impression of power and mass.

The imposition of a *Paramaśayika Maṇḍala* upon the plan indicates its ultimate suitability (See: **Figure 110**).[123] The *Triyuta Maṇḍala*, related to the *Maṇḍūka Maṇḍala*, possesses a number of cogent conjunctions as well (See: **Figure 111**). The application of the standards of the *śilpa-śāstra* to this Hindu *garh mahal* continues the tradition of the Bundelas.

The third of the impressive *garh mahals* of Orchha, the *Jahangir Mandir* continues that regal line. It builds upon the traditions of the *Rāmji Mandir* and the *Rājā Mandir* and is only overshadowed by Rājā Bir Singh Ju Deo's last building endeavor — i.e., the magnificent *Govind Mandir* which reigns at Datia.

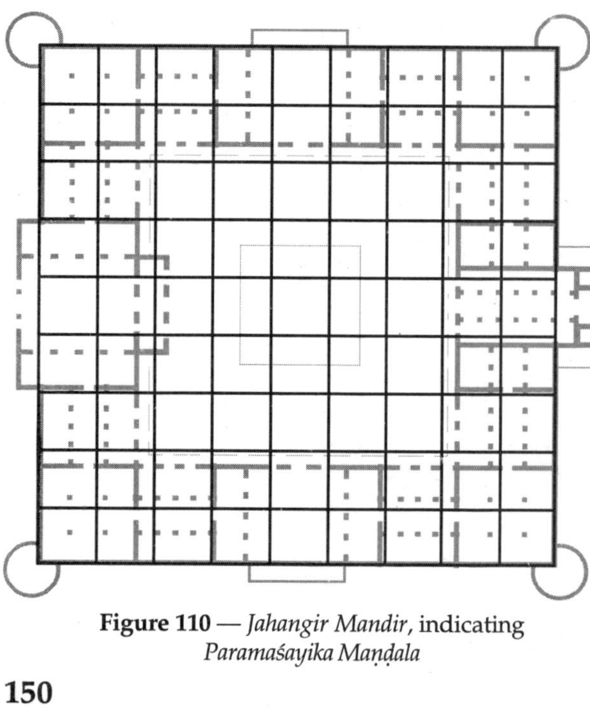

Figure 110 — *Jahangir Mandir*, indicating *Paramaśayika Maṇḍala*

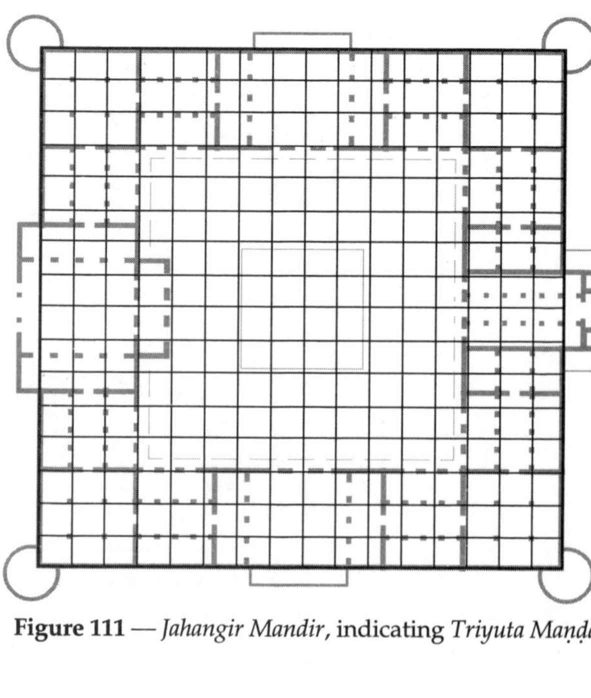

Figure 111 — *Jahangir Mandir*, indicating *Triyuta Maṇḍala*

Plate 43 — *Jahangir Mandir*, 3rd storey & roofline plan

(a. 1605 CE)

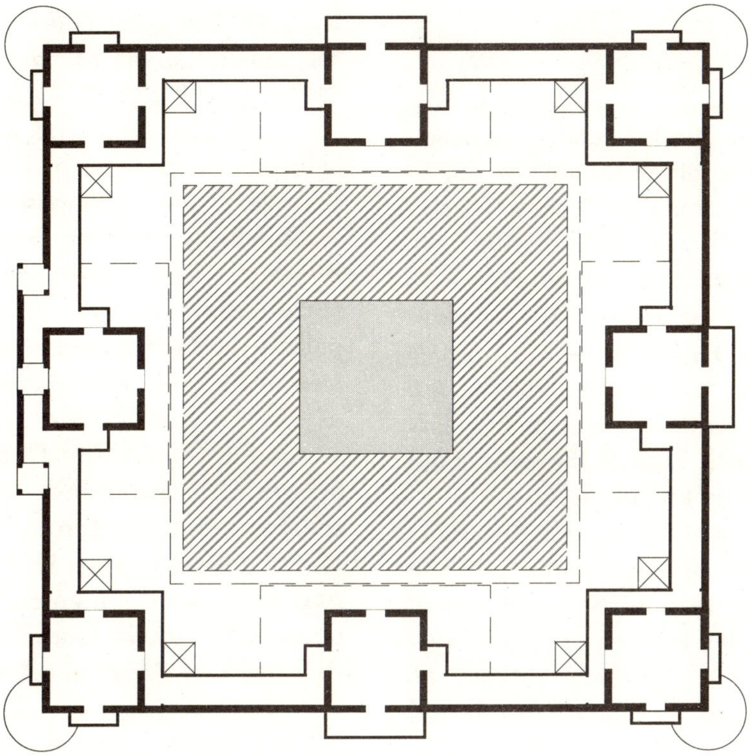

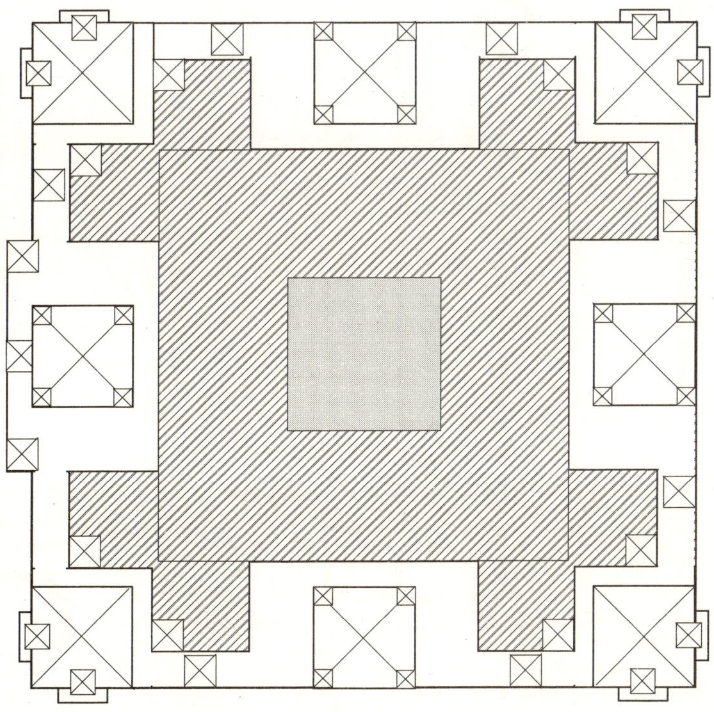

Govind Mandir (*Bir Singh Judeo Mahal*)

Datia (a. 1620 CE)

The kingdom of Bundelkhand, established by the Rājā Rudra Pratap Singh Bundela (r. 1525 - 1531 CE), found its main capital in Orchha. There a vast *qilā* was constructed on an island with three notable *mandirs*: the *Rāmji Mandir* (See: **Figure 56 — D**), the *Rājā Mandir* (See: **Figure 56 — A**) and the *Jahangiri Mahal* (See: **Figure 56 — C**). This *qilā* was somewhat unique as the pre-existent *garh mahals* were not added onto by subsequent rulers as is seen in other citadels. Each of the three stand as historical briefs of this kingdom.

Yet it was not at Orchha that the most famous Bundelkhand palace was to be constructed. That honor fell to the small city of Datia, some fifteen miles to the north and west of Orchha. There the Rājā Bir Singh Ju Deo (r. 1605-1627 CE) constructed what is often referred to as the last great Hindu (Rajput) Palace — i.e., the famed *Govind Mandir* (aka: *Bir Singh Judeo Mahal*) (See **Plates 44, 45 & 46**).[124]

A year before his death Rājā Bir Singh Ju Deo gave a portion of his lands to a favored, younger son, Bhagawan Deo, in effect establishing another petty kingdom with a Bundela line. This included Datia, the surrounding area and, of course the magnificent palace, the *Govind Mandir*. Certainly, Bir Singh Ju Deo must have remembered his own usurpation of the Orchha throne from his brother and wanted to avoid any fratricidal confrontation between his own sons. Apparently, the heir to the Bundelkhand throne at Orchha, the Rājā-to-be Jhujhar Singh (r. 1627-1635 CE) accepted this partition with equanimity, thus avoiding a potentially bloody feud. Nonetheless, it appears that the Rājā Bhagawan Deo did not occupy the *Govind Mandir* (aka: *Bir Singh Judeo Mahal*) building, instead, another *garh mahal* was constructed for his own purpose. Essentially, this magnificent

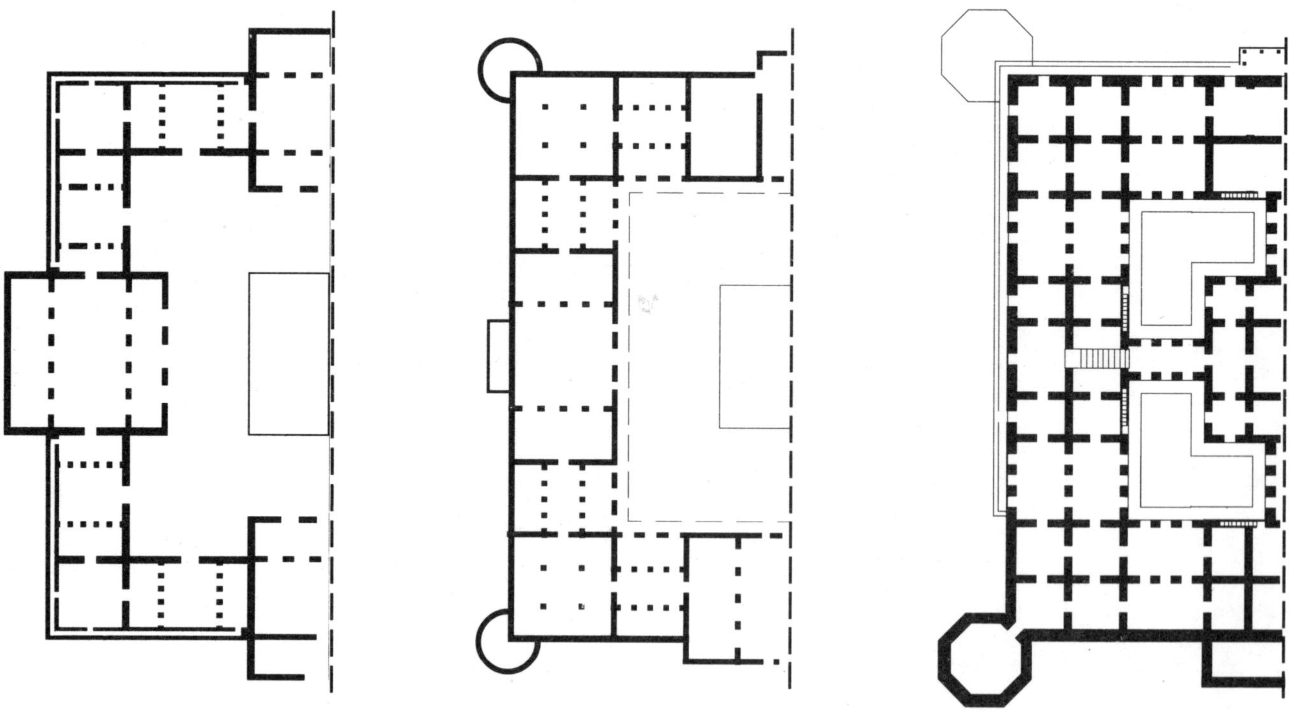

Figure 112 — the *Rājā Mandir*, the *Jahangir Mandir* and the *Govind Mandir* (left to right), half-plan comparison

Plate 44 — *Govind Mandir* (*Bir Singh Judeo Mahal*), plan 1st storey

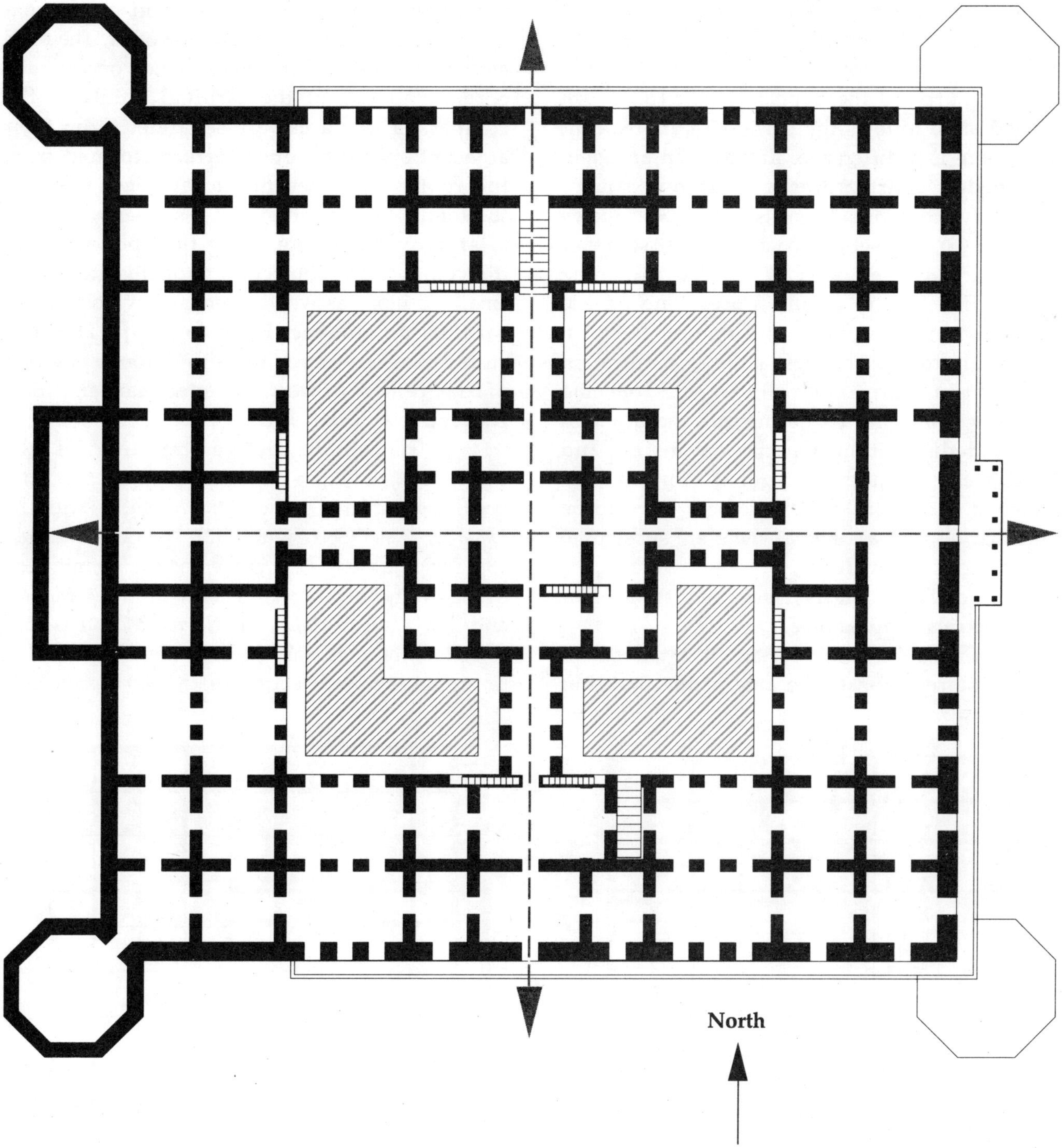

mandir was never utilized for the purpose for which its costly construction was undertaken.

Consisting of an immense block with a central courtyard the *Govind Mandir* (*Bir Singh Judeo Mahal*) follows the earlier traditions. But, here there is a difference. Rather than an open, unimpeded courtyard, a five storey, square secondary block rises from its centre (See: **Plates 44, 45 & 46**), a novel approach. The first storey of the central 'tower' area is divided into nine rooms, five on the second storey, one on the third, five on the fourth and one on the fifth and final storey. The first storey of the main block consists of rooms on all four sides, opening onto the court. Each side mirrors the other in size and disposition. On the north-west and south-west corners octagonal towers are attached. Apparently these towers were to be mirrored on the east side as there are substantial foundations in evidence, but they were never completed. This anomaly gives the plan a rather asymmetrical appearance.

Unlike the *Jahangiri Mahal*, this *garh mahal's* second storey repeats the area of the first, but with variations of the disposition of internal spaces. Again each side reflects the other. The third storey consists of eight areas — i.e., one at each corner and one at the cardinal points of the compass. These areas are separated from their adjacent spaces by open terraces formed from the roofs of the second storey (See: **Plate 45** [bottom]). The fourth storey essentially presents a large terrace surrounding the open space of the court. In the four corners of this storey are small pavilions as well as similar pavilions at the cardinal points (See: **Plate 46** [top]). The fifth storey is reserved for the single-room pavilion of the central tower, as noted earlier (See: **Appendix A, Plate 91**).

The Hindu design tradition of the Bundela *rājās* began with the *Rāmji Mandir*, and continued through the *Rājā Mandir* and the *Jahangiri Mahal* (See: **Figure 112**). The *Govind Mandir* (*Bir Singh Judeo Mahal*) is seen as the culmination of this regal heritage. As with the *Rājā Mandir* and the *Jahangiri Mahal*, the *Govind Mandir* is seen to reflect the nine-part division (See: **Figure 113**), an apparent predilection of the *garh mahals* of

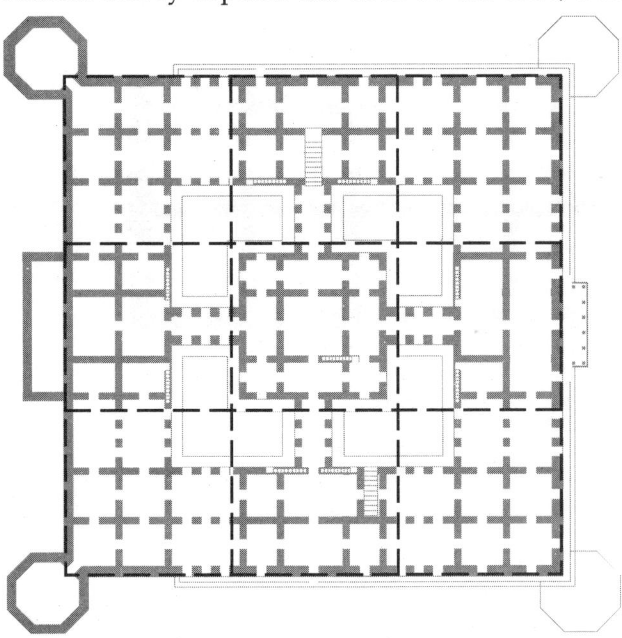

Figure 113 — *Govind Mandir*, showing nine-part division

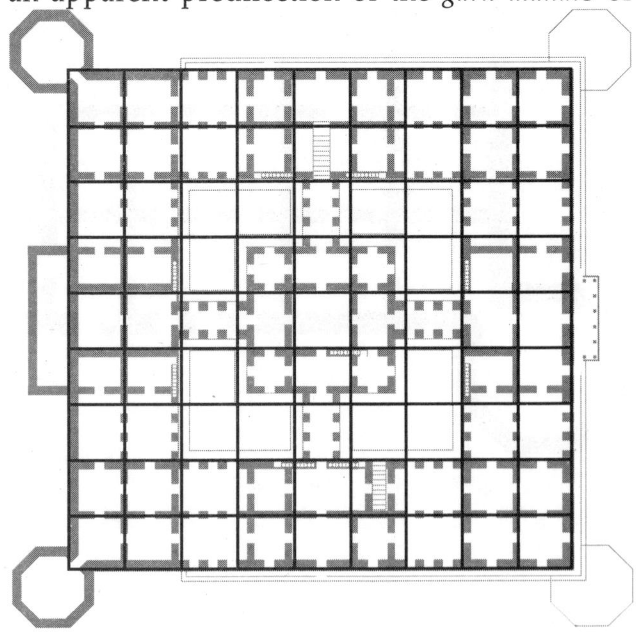

Figure 114 — *Govind Mandir*, indicating *Paramaśayika Maṇḍala*

Plate 45 — *Govind Mandir (Bir Singh Judeo Mahal)*, plan, 2nd & 3rd storeys

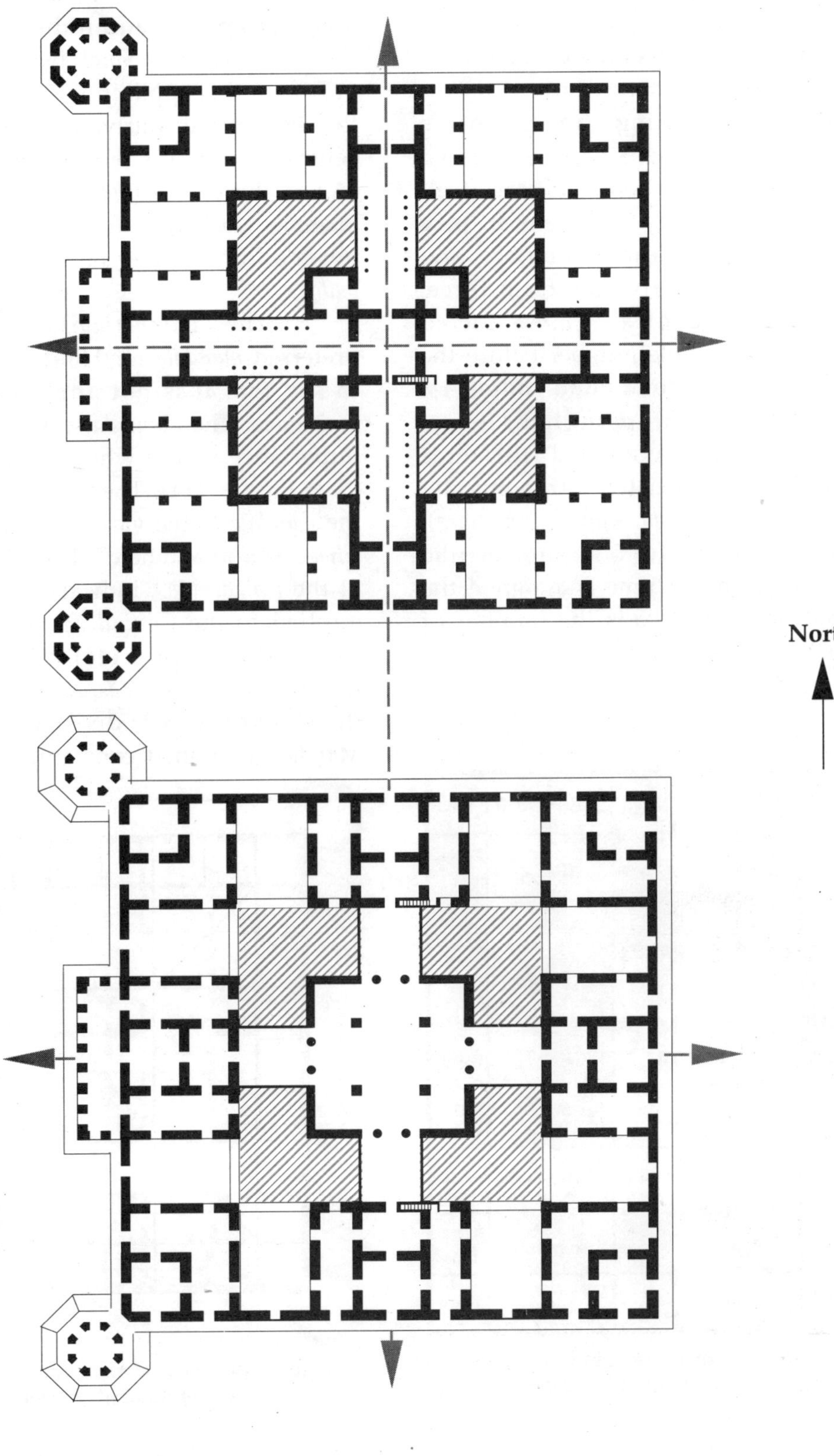

Orchha. This places emphasis upon the sacred number nine and is further underlined by the number of rooms of the first storey of the central tower. Nine is a perfect number whose Ü is 3 as well a number possessing an imposing formation. It is called perfect since it is formed from three and nine always reproduces itself when multiplied with any number. It is a magnification of that most sacred number, and by association and as a derivation from three, nine also becomes one of the most sacred numbers. It is the last whole number before the commencement of the compound numbers. Nine denotes completion, perfection, force, wisdom, silence and when associated with three it connotes space. It is associated astronomically with the planet Mars (*Maṅgala, Kuja* or *Aṅgaraka*). As the second most powerful odd number (the square of the sacred three), nine is assigned the puissant planet, *Mars*. It also is the number of *pada* in a *Piṭha Maṇḍala* and is the smallest form of a magic square.[125]

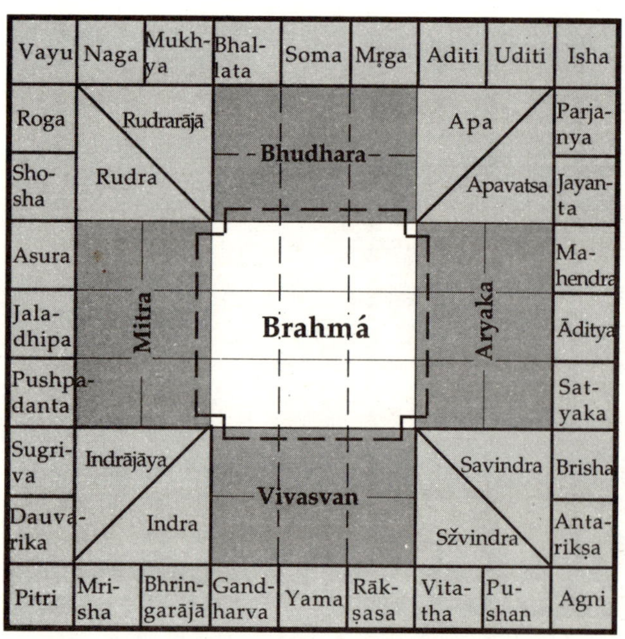

Figure 115 — *Paramaśayika Maṇḍala,* indicating the *padadevatas* according to the *Mayamatam*

It is observed as well that a *Paramaśayika Maṇḍala* applies admirably to the plan of the *Govind Mandir* (*Bir Singh Judeo Mahal*) (See: **Figure 113**).[126] In this application, the width of the rooms that border the courtyard are two *pada* wide. The central tower falls within the central nine *padas* — i.e., the *brahmásthāna*. Finally, the uppermost room — i.e., that found in the centre of the tower's fifth floor — falls within the centre most *pada*.

The *Paramaśayika Maṇḍala* was the preferred *maṇḍala* for Hindu temples. That is not to say that it is not applicable to a palace or residence. The *maṇḍala* was a diagram of cosmic importance within which various deities reigned (See: **Figure 114**). The assignment of the *pada* of the *maṇḍala* to the various deities varied from one *śilpa-śāstra* to another.[127] The *Mayamatam's* division of the *padadevatās*, indicated in **Figure 115**, when applied to the *Govind Mandir* produces similar results (See: **Figure 116**). Whether the *Manasara*, the *Arthaśāstra*, the *Vāstuśāstra*, or the *Mayamatam*, the eighty-one *pada* division of the *Paramaśayika Maṇḍala* remained constant.

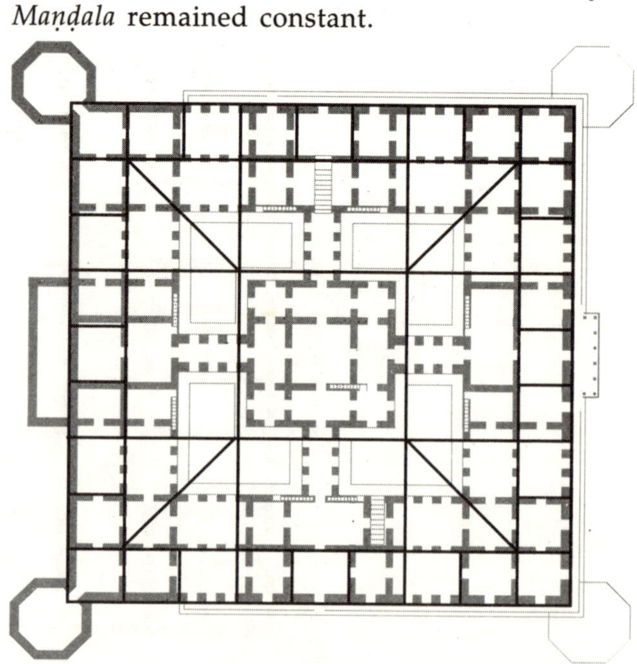

Figure 116 — *Govind Mandir,* indicating *Paramaśayika Maṇḍala* with *padadevata* division after *Mayamatam*

Plate 46 — *Govind Mandir* (*Bir Singh Judeo Mahal*), plan, 4th & 5th storeys

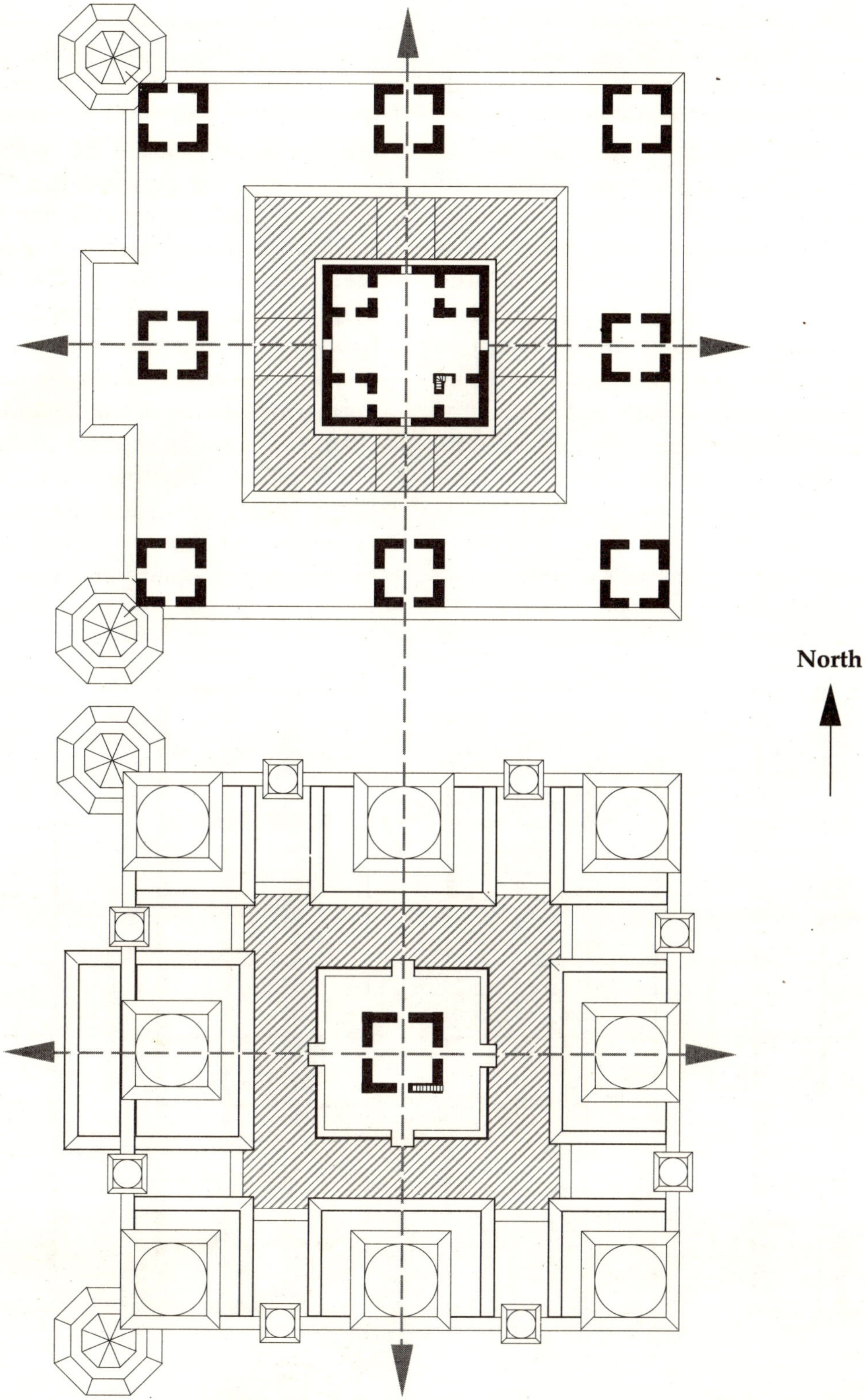

The *śilpa śāstras* also suggest certain plans for the layout of a city. The *Govind Mandir* (*Bir Singh Judeo Mahal*) may also be seen as a microcosm of a city based upon the aforementioned ninefold plan. The original plan for Jaipur is a prime example. There nine squares were established in the form of a *Pīṭha Maṇḍala* — i.e., a *maṇḍala* of nine *pada*. The central square was reserved for the palace compound of the ruler and the various quarters were traditionally assigned to the four castes. Here at *Govind Mandir* the same seems to apply. The royal apartments are to be found in the central tower-block and the rest of the compound occupies the outer ranks. The high, elevated central tower block may also have additional cosmic implications. The high *śikhara* or tower of Hindu temples is a visual referent to Mt. Sumeru, the home of the gods. The towering central tower block at *Govind Mandir* would seem to represent this cosmic locale.

An interesting comparative relationship is seen when the ninefold division is made. If one third of that division — i.e., a three fold division — is compared between the *Rājā Mandir*, the *Jahangir Mandir* and the *Govind Mandir* and with the *Rājā Mahal* (*Chandragiri Palace*) (See: **Plate 35**) the design relationship is quite close (See: **Figure 117**). Granted, the *Rājā Mahal* is not a square plan, however, within the confines of a three-fold division, the relationships are unmistakable. The northern vestibule of the *Rājā Mahal* (*Chandragiri Palace*) falls within a third of the whole length. The depth of the rooms in the *Govind Mandir* (*Bir Singh Judeo Mahal*) are one-third as well. The extensions, pavilions of all four are closely related to the central square and they all terminate in

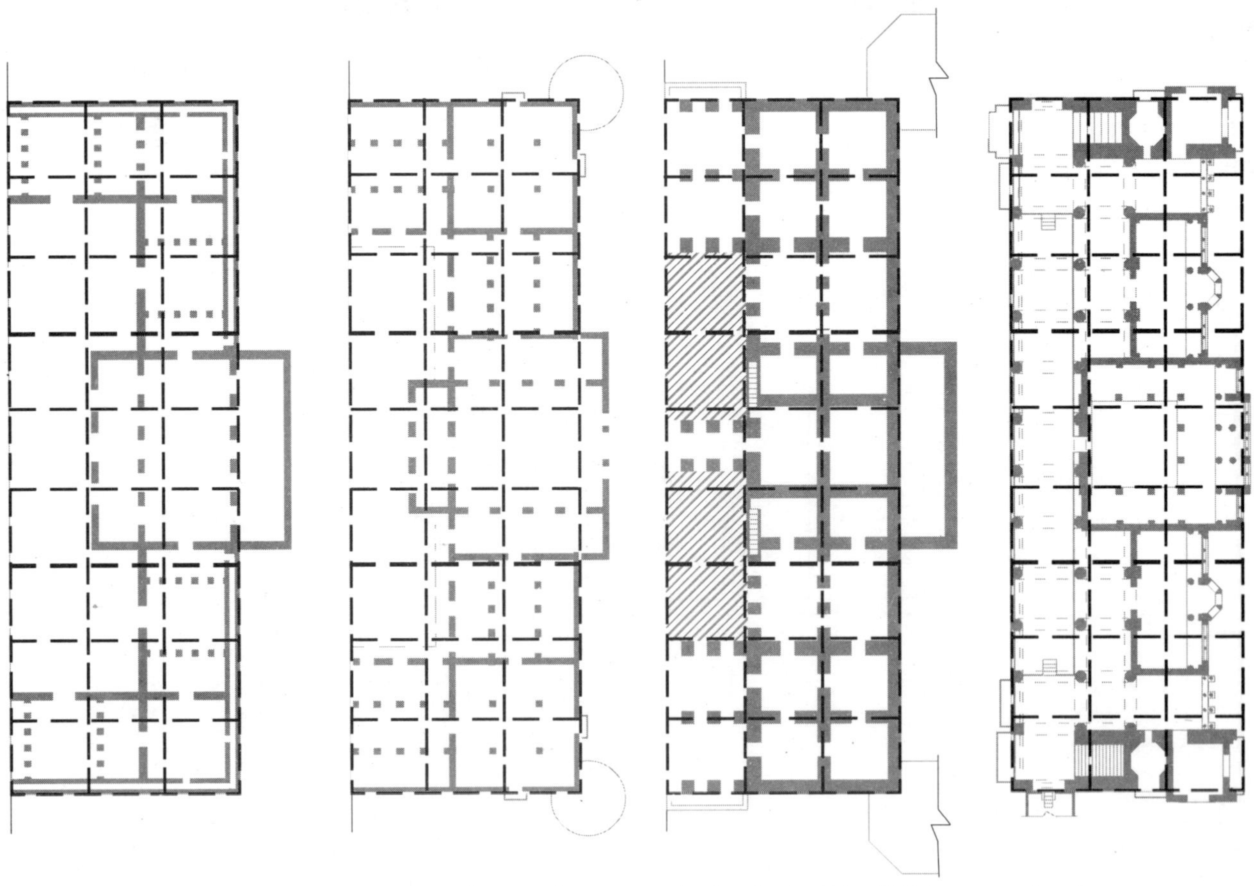

Figure 117 — the *Rājā Mandir*, the *Jahangir Mandir*, the *Govind Mandir* (third plans) and the *Rājā Mahal* (*Chandragiri Palace*) (left to right) indicating a three-part plan comparison

two-thirds. There are of course discrepancies, but the relationships seem apparent.

Finally, it is of interest to note that in both the *Govind Mandir* and the earlier *Jahangir Mandir*, the Hindu ideal, based upon the *Paramaśayika Maṇḍala*, is most applicable (See: **Figure 118**). In particular the *Govind Mandir* appears to be the closest. It would emphasize as many scholars state that the *garh mahal*s of Orchha, and Datia, find their design genesis in ancient *śilpa śāstra* texts.

It has been noted that in the three *garh mahal*s of the Bundelas, considered herein, there does not appear to be a well defined *zenānā*. In the other *garh mahal*s of India, there have been well defined, separate and often extensive quarters for the women of the court — e.g., *Lāl Qilā* at Agra, Fatehpur Sikri, or Vijayanagara. The plan of this *garh mahal* is such that any part of it could have been closed off with *jālī*s to provide a suitable *zenānā*. Or, the third and fourth storeys would have made an adequate space for the women. Their ingress and egress could have easily been such as to insure their privacy. On the other hand, early Hindu practice was to protect the women of the court from the "public" — i.e., seeing untoward events, actions or offensive areas. The women of the ruler were viewed as delicate, sensitive, often well educated and intelligent beings whose 'sensibilities' needed to be protected. Therefore, generally, they did not go out into public unless heavily veiled and well protected. The idea of separating physically the women of the court from the supposed prying, lecherous gazes of men came later and is seen as a Muslim influence. Therefore, it may have been that the three *garh mahals* — i.e., the *Rājā Mandir*, the *Jahangir Mandir* and the *Govind Mandir* — merely followed older Hindu practices and the women were allowed to roam with relative ease and within expected guidelines.

The *Govind Mandir* is a cap-stone, not only of Bundelkhand royal residence architecture, but of the Rajputana as well. It seems fitting that the "last great Hindu (Rajput) Palace" should be constructed within this tiny kingdom. But it did have a glorious lineage.

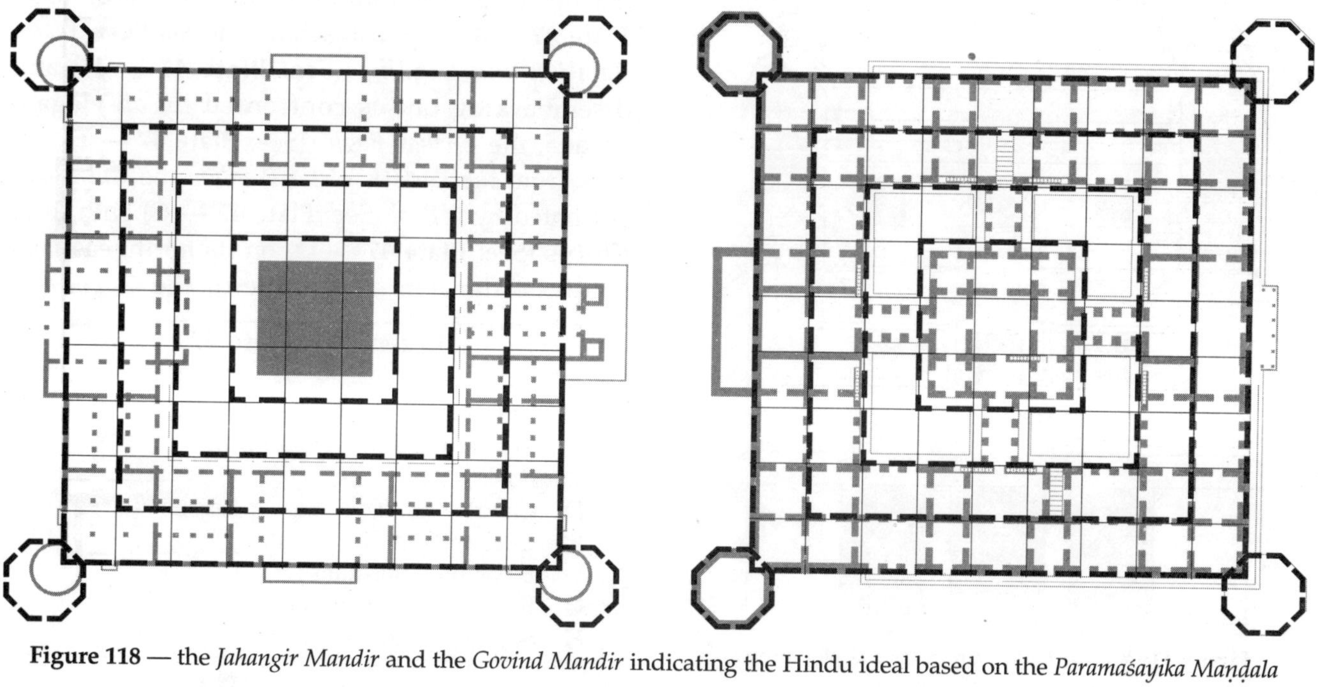

Figure 118 — the *Jahangir Mandir* and the *Govind Mandir* indicating the Hindu ideal based on the *Paramaśayika Maṇḍala*

Jag Mandir

Udaipur, (*c.* 1620-1652 CE)

Udaipur had been established as the capital city by the Sisodia Rajputs after 1567 CE The artificial Lake Pichola upon which the city bordered was the site of two beautiful and exotic isle retreats: the *Jag Nivās* and the *Jag Mandir* each on separate islands. The former has achieved fame as the Lake Palace Hotel, while the latter, equally elegant has remained relatively untouched by the commercialism that affected the former.

At the time of the initial construction on the island by Karan Singh (r. 1620-1628 CE) (See: **Appendix B**), the state had achieved a degree of permanence having been in Udaipur since 1567. It is said that Karan Singh built the *mandir*, in part, as a refuge for the Prince Khurram, later to be known as Shah Jahan, who was in revolt against his father, the Emperor Jahangir. It was during the time that Karan Singh acted as an emissary to the Imperial Mughal Court that friendly relations were founded between the two courts. This amicable association between the two states was further cemented when Shah Jahan ascended the Peacock Throne.

Figure 119 — *Gul Mahal*, proportional elevation

By the time Rājā Jagat Singh I (r. 1628-1652 CE) completed the *Jag Mandir* during the early part of his reign, Udaipur was relatively stable politically. This was due, in part, to the good auspices of the Imperial Mughals. Therefore, the massive ramparts that characterize the *City Palace* of Udaipur were not employed at *Jag Mandir*. In truth, the lake provided a measure of security, but if a force wanted to take this remote pleasure pavilion, it would have had little trouble.

The central feature of the *Jag Mandir* (See: **Plate 47**) is the *Gul Mahal*[128] (See: **Plate 48**). Although there are other pavilions on this island the *Gul Mahal* reigns. The retreat is approached from the east and one is greeted by the many columned *Eastern Water Pavilion* (See: **Plate 47 — G**) which are flanked by eight massive white marble elephants standing in the water (See: **Plate 47 — F**). Upon reaching the *Southern Water Pavilion and Landing* (See: **Plate 47 — H**) and disembarking one is confronted by an elegant garden, the *Chahar Bagh* (See: **Plate 47 — E**). Set back from the *Eastern Water Pavilion* the *Gul Mahal* is fronted by a *Pool* (See: **Plate 47 — C**) with three *Chatrīs* (See: **Plate 47 — D**) on its north, east and south border. On either side of the *Gul Mahal*

Legend for **Plate 47**

- **A** Gul Mahal
- **B** Residential and Support Suites
- **C** Pool
- **D** Chatrī
- **E** Chahar Bagh
- **F** Elephant Guardians
- **G** Eastern Water Pavilion
- **H** Southern Water Pavilion and Landing

Plate 47 — *Jag Mandir*, plan (partial)
(a. 1620 CE)

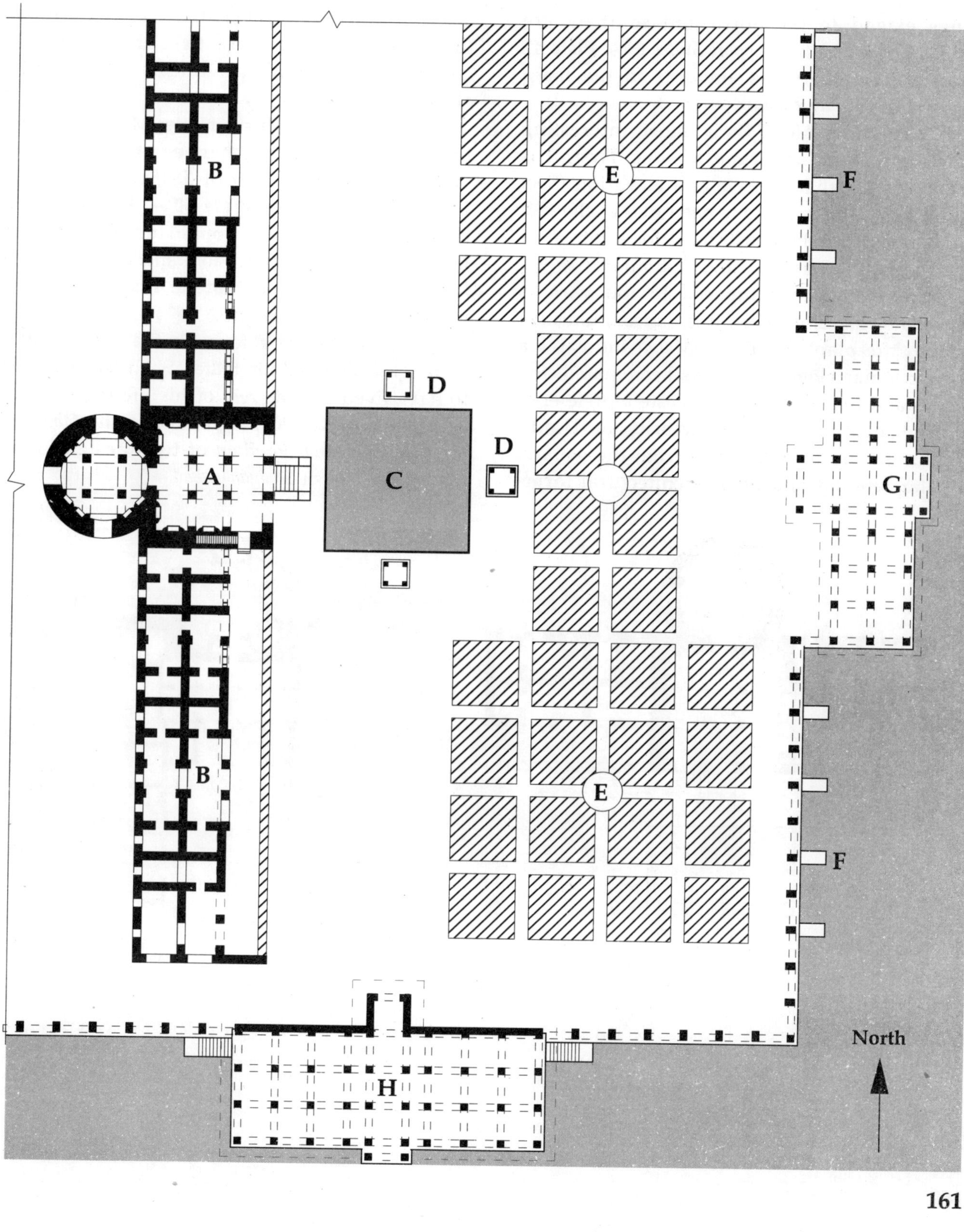

Jag Mandir (Concluded)

wings extend to the north and south where various *Residential and Support Suites* (See: **Plate 47 — B**) are located. This amounts to the main prospect of the *Jag Mandir*.

The *Gul Mahal* is a most interesting structure for two important reasons. First, it is essentially Mughal in style and elevation (See: **Figure 119**). This may have been due to the fact that it was primarily constructed for a retreat of a Mughal Prince and Emperor-to-be. Nonetheless, when compared to the various elements of the *City Palace*, it is, indeed, unusual. Second, the plan of the *Gul Mahal* indicates a major circular element. As has been stated, the *sthapati* and the *śilpa śāstra*s indicate a preference for the square. The vast majority of Hindu structures tend to be derived from the square. Circular temples and other architectural forms are rare indeed, however, there are exceptions (See: **Appendix A, Plate 68**). Therefore, this circular form coupled with its Mughal-like elevation is noteworthy.

An aspect of further interest is to be seen in the design similarity between the *Gul Mahal* and the *Musamman Burj* of *Shahjahanabad* (See: **Figure 120;** see also: **Plate 50 — L**) built some twenty years later. One would surmise that Shah Jahan's stay in Udaipur, more specifically on the *Jag Mandir* was such that he may have been influenced by its design.

A final irony is found in the fact that after Aurangzeb deposed his father, Shah Jahan is said to have lived out the rest of his life imprisoned, as it were, in *Lāl Qilā*, Agra, and in the *Jahangiri Mahal's Octagonal Pavilion* of twin design to the *Musamman Burj* of *Shahjahanabad.*

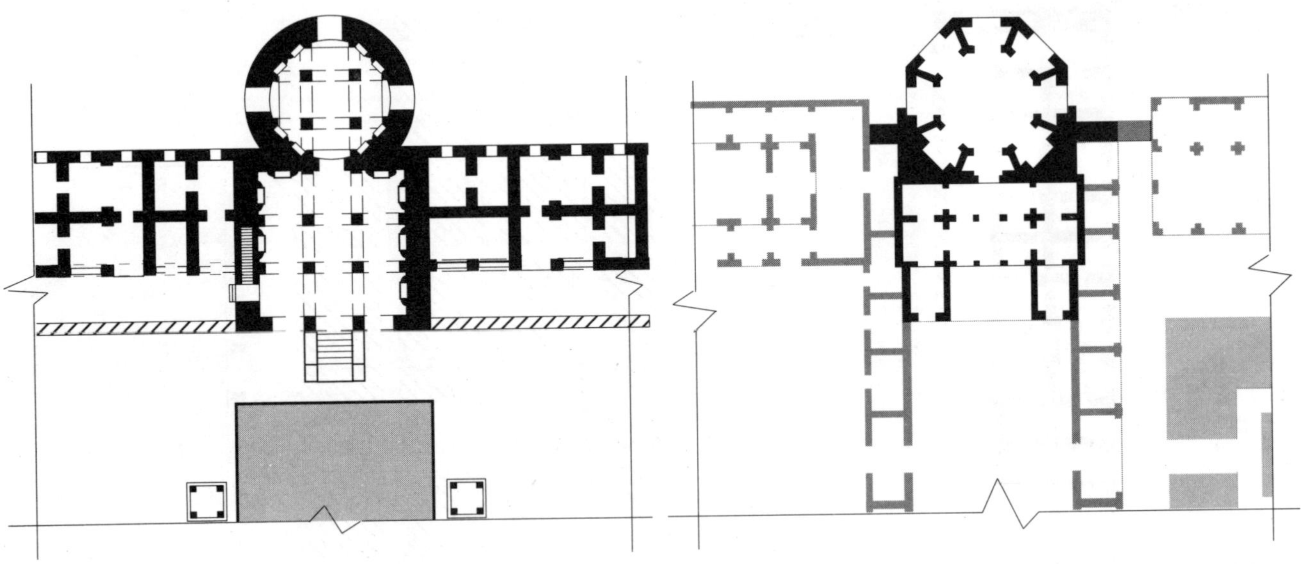

Figure 120 — *Gul Mahal* (a. 1620), *Jag Mandir*, Udaipur, (left) & *Musamman Burj* (a. 1639), *Shahjahanabad*, Delhi (right) indicating design similarities

Plate 48 — *Gul Mahal*, plan (partial)

(*c.* 1625-1628 CE)

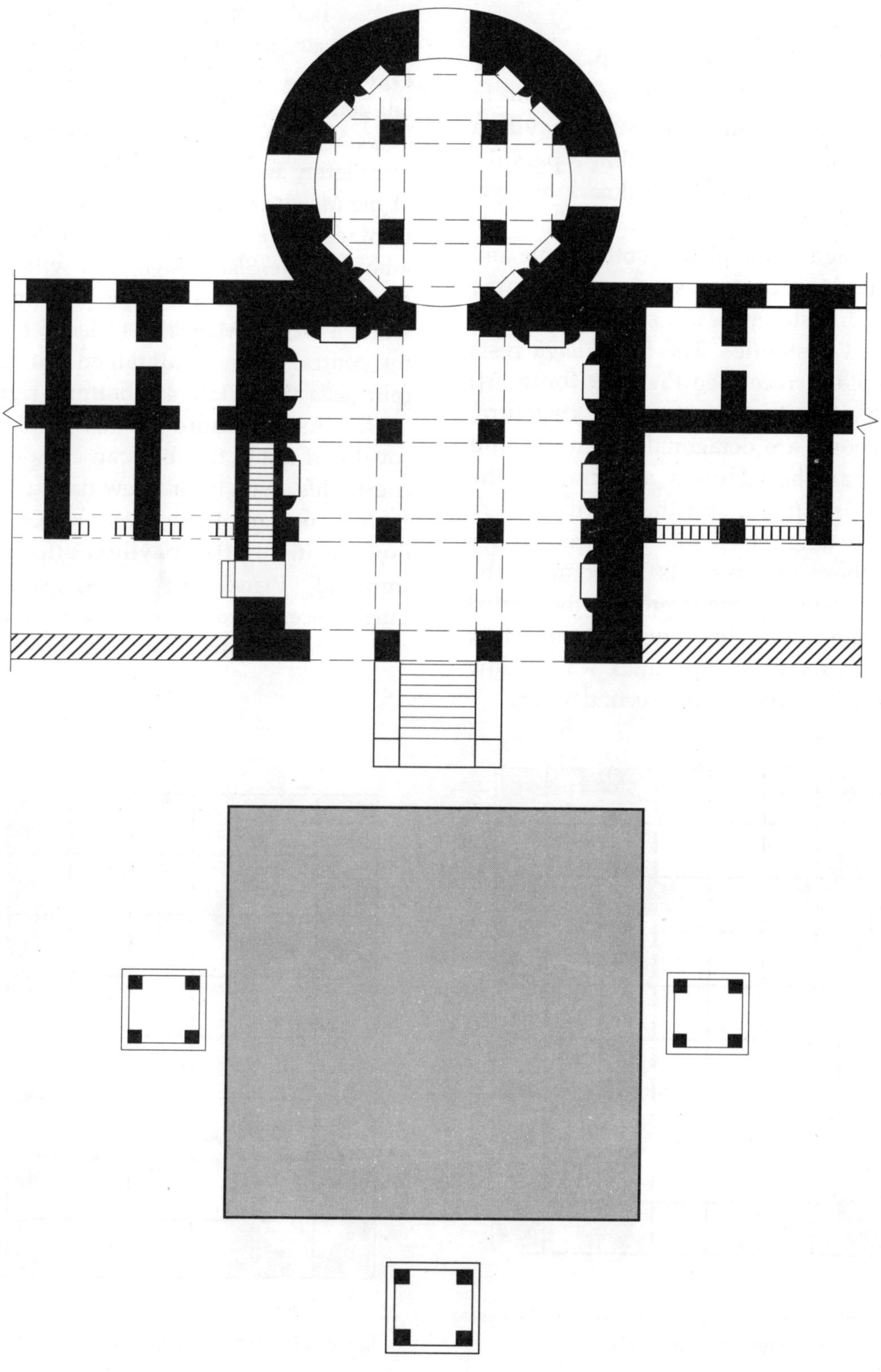

Shahi Bagh

Ahmadabad, (*c.* 1623 CE)

While still an Imperial Prince, the Emperor-to-be, Shah Jahan spent some time in Ahmadabad and in the delightful pavilion known as the *Shahi Bagh*.[129] Set within a parklike garden this pavilion stands as a hallmark of royal pleasure palaces.

The design of the plan is both simple and elegant, consisting of two storeys with nine spaces in the first storey — i.e., seven rooms and two developed vestibules. The *Shahi Bagh* rests upon an ample terrace (See **Plate 49** [bottom]) acting as a pedestal presenting this structure. The corner rooms are octagonal, the north and south rooms are based upon an octagon, the central space is square, and the vestibules are essentially rectangular with redented inner corners. Niches and indents punctuate the internal walls adding to the interest of the spatial divisions as the rooms flow one into the other. Two staircases, set within the thick walls allow both ingress and egress to the second floor.

Both a *Paramaśayika Maṇḍala* and a *Maṇḍūka Maṇḍala* are seen to be applicable in degrees (See: **Figures 121 & 122**). The eight perimeter spaces fall generally within the outer two ranks and files of *pada* in the *Paramaśayika Maṇḍala*, but rest completely within the equivalent ranks and files of the *Maṇḍūka Maṇḍala*. When a *Maṇḍūka Maṇḍala* is placed over the podium, it is seen that the whole of the *Shahi Bagh* falls within the sixteen central *pada* (See **Plate 49** [bottom, left]). But, when a *Deśiya Maṇḍala* is placed over the same, the central room is contained within the central four *pada* (See **Plate 49** [bottom, right]).

As a pleasure pavilion, a place where the royal and noble families can escape the rigors of courtly life, even if for a few days a year, the *Shahi Bagh* is an example *par excellence*. One can imagine how positively this pavilion affected the young Imperial Prince of taste, sensitivity and intelligence. It was a most commodious residence during his sojourn from the Imperial court.

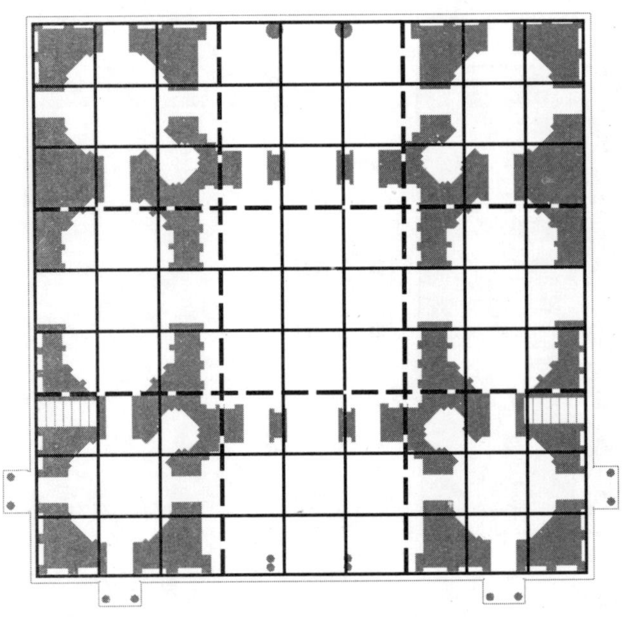

Figure 121 — *Shahi Bagh*, indicating a *Paramaśayika Maṇḍala* with the nine-part division

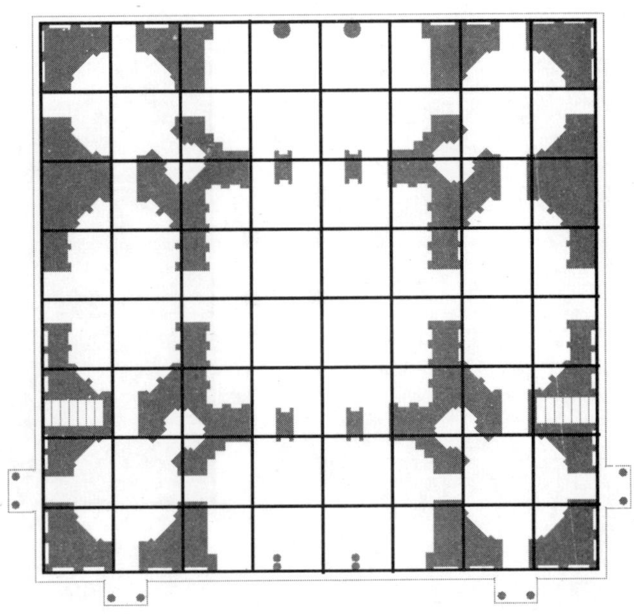

Figure 122 — *Shahi Bagh*, Indicating a *Maṇḍūka Maṇḍala*

Plate 49 — *Shahi Bagh*, plan, ground floor and with terrace (with *Maṇḍūka Maṇḍala* [left] & *Deśiya Maṇḍala* [right])

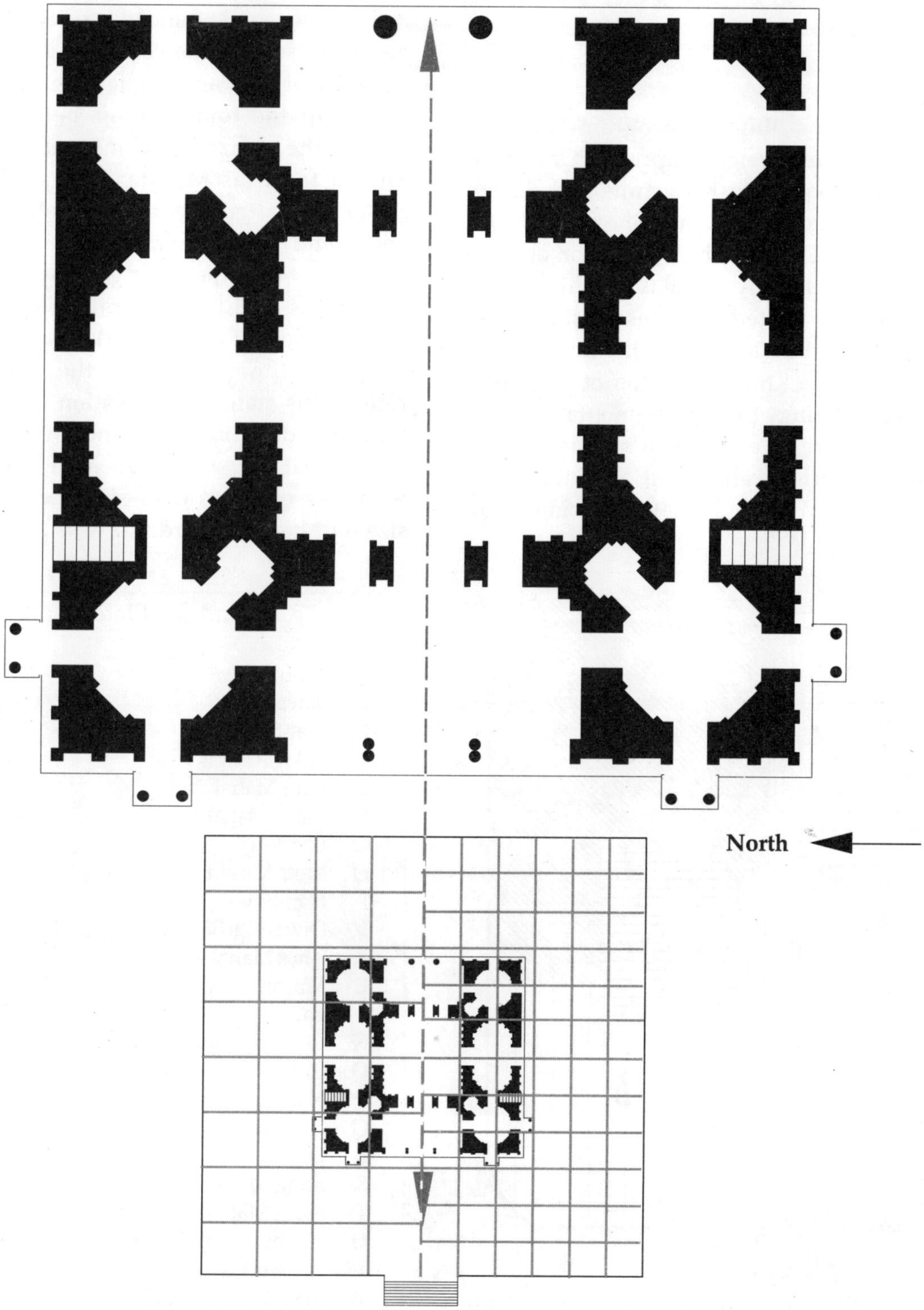

Lāl Qilā, Shahjahanabad

Delhi (1639-1648 CE)

Among the building programs of Shah Jahan, the *Tāj Mahal* reigns supreme. One often forgets or overlooks that his genius and design acumen later influenced the magnificent *Lāl Qilā, Shahjahanabad* of Delhi.[130] Shah Jahan forsook the *Purānā Qilā* started by Humayun, his great-grandfather, and started the construction, a bit farther north on the Yamuna, of his own citadel in 1639 CE. It is ". . . the conception of one mind executed according to requirements of one authority."[131] Here, the Emperor's concern was "to produce a perfect refinement of contour and decoration (rather) than . . . new experiments in structural design."[132]

The single minded quality of Shah Jahan's aesthetics seen in the construction of the *Lāl Qilā, Shahjahanabad* is another facet of the person who had built the tomb for his beloved Arjumand Banu, the Hazrat Mumtaz-uz-Zamani, best known to all as Mumtāz Mahal. The *Lāl Qilā, Shahjahanabad* is a synthesis of elegance in stone, space and refinement.

As with the other *garh mahals* of India, the *Lāl Qilā* is divided into rather precise areas of access (See: **Figure 123**). Each serves and supports the person of the Emperor. Each reflects his status and position. It is to be noted that here the *zenānā* is of nearly equal size with the restricted, imperial area. Generally the women's quarters over-shadow the *mardānā* in size, but here the gardens — i.e., the *Mahtab Bagh*

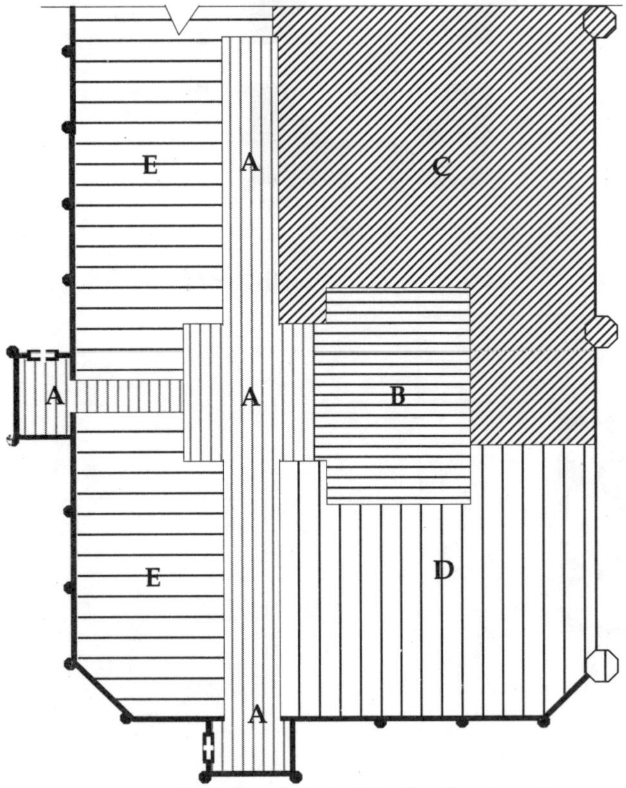

Figure 123 — *Shahjahanabad*, Delhi, distribution of areas: public areas (**A**), limited access areas (**B**), restricted imperial area (**C**), *zenānā* (**D**), attendants and military (**E**)

Legend for **Plates 50 & 51**

- **A** Shah Burj
- **B** Sawan
- **C** Mahtab Bagh
- **D** Bakhsh Bagh
- **E** Hira Mahal
- **F** Zafar Mahal
- **G** Bhadon
- **H** Moti Masjid
- **I** Hammam
- **J** Diwān-i Khās (with Peacock Throne)
- **K** Khās Mahal
- **L** Musamman Burj
- **M** Lahore Darwāzā
- **N** Chhatta Chowk
- **O** Chowk Hawd Nahr
- **P** Naqqār Khānā
- **Q** Chowk Diwān-i Ām
- **R** Diwān-i Ām
- **S** Raṅg Mahal Bagh
- **T** Raṅg Mahal
- **U** Mumtaz Mahal (Chotta Raṅg Mahal)
- **V** Zenānā Garden
- **W** Residence (zenānā)
- **X** Rastah Dilhi Darwāzā
- **Y** Dilhi Darwāzā

Plate 50 — *Shahjahanabad* (*Lāl Qilā*), plan (partial)

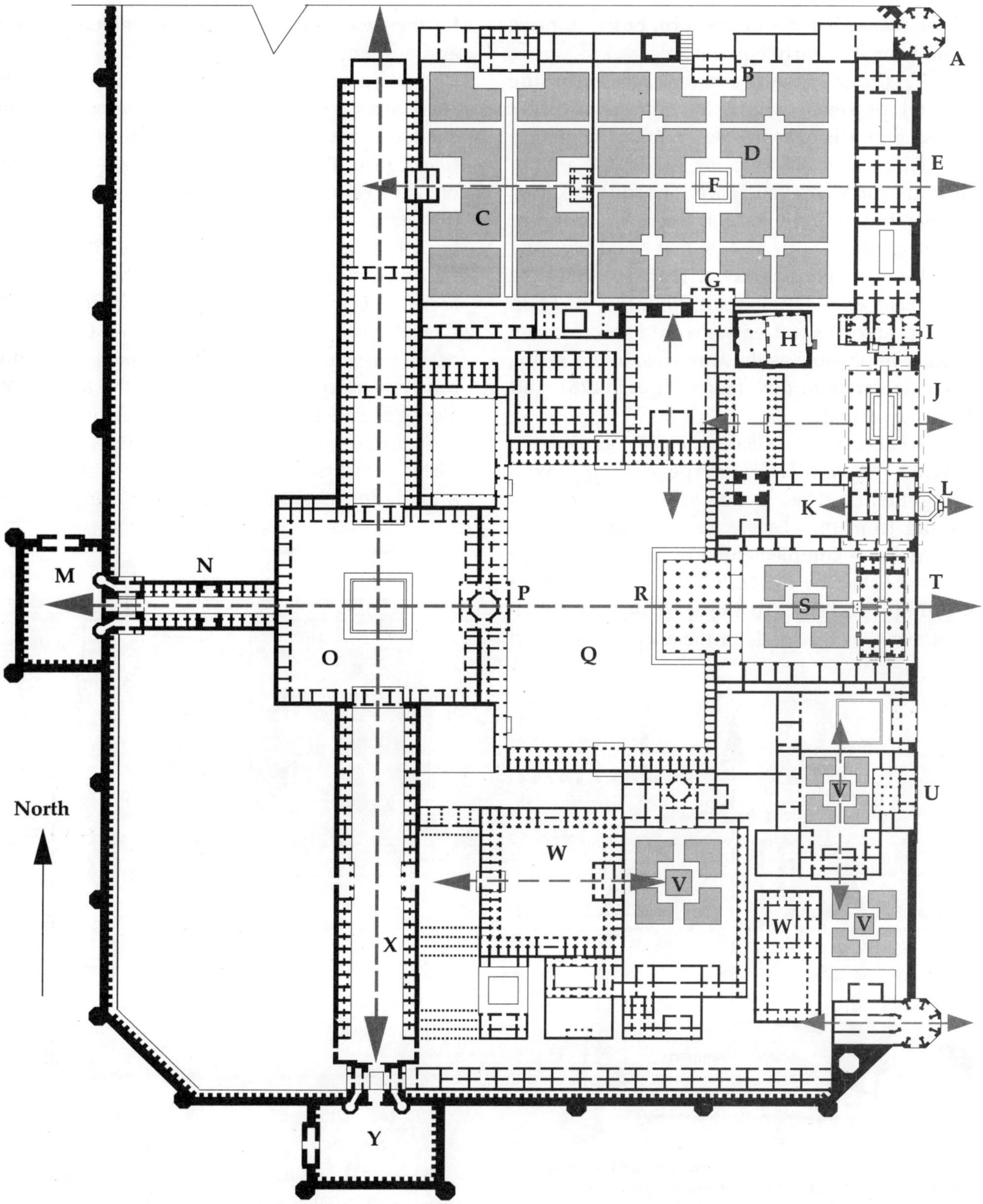

and the *Bakhsh Bagh* — in the north of the *mardānā* account for its nearly equal size.

As one would assume access to the imperial presence would have been severely limited and all measures were taken to insure the ruler's safety. Enter to the residential area of the Emperor was even more labyrinthine than in other Indian *garh mahals*. Even the entrance into the citadel was by a route that could be easily defended (See: **Figures 124 & 125**). To attain the *Musamman Burj* or the *Shah Burj*, two of Shah Jahan's favorite retreats, would have been virtually impossible as the way was, by necessity, quite circumlocutious (See: **Figure 125**) and heavily guarded.

The *Lāl Qilā, Shahjahanabad*, as is seen, presents a multiple perpendicular axial arrangement. The primary east-west axis running from the *Lahore Darwāzā* through the *Raṅg Mahal* is complemented by the north-south axis established by the *Delhi Darwāzā* (See: **Plate 50 & Figure 124**).[133] To the west of this north-south axis was the locale of the ancillary, support for the *garh mahal* — i.e., stables, military barracks and servant quarters.

Entering the *Lahore Darwāzā* one encounters a broad, vaulted avenue with regular, enclosed spaces on either side. This is the *Chhatta Chowk* (See: **Plate 50 — N**), the main market area of the *garh mahal*. Here the most notable merchants brought their exotic wares, and it was here that the visitors to the *Lāl Qilā, Shahjahanabad* had their first glimpse of the riches of this *garh mahal*. This avenue empties into a large *chowk*, the *Chowk Hawd Nahr* (See: **Plate 50 — O**) with the main north-south axis in the form of another broad avenue known, in part, as the *Rastah Delhi Darwāzā* (See: **Plate 50 — X**). Proceeding east, one passes under a multistorey structure, the *Naqqār Khānā*, which served as a ceremonial gateway and a locale for musicians employed during the daily

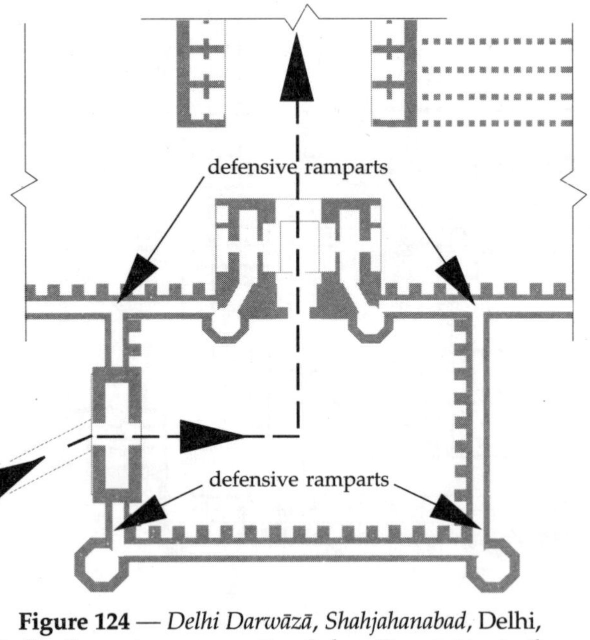

Figure 124 — *Delhi Darwāzā, Shahjahanabad*, Delhi, indicating entrance security, *Lahore Darwāzā* is similar

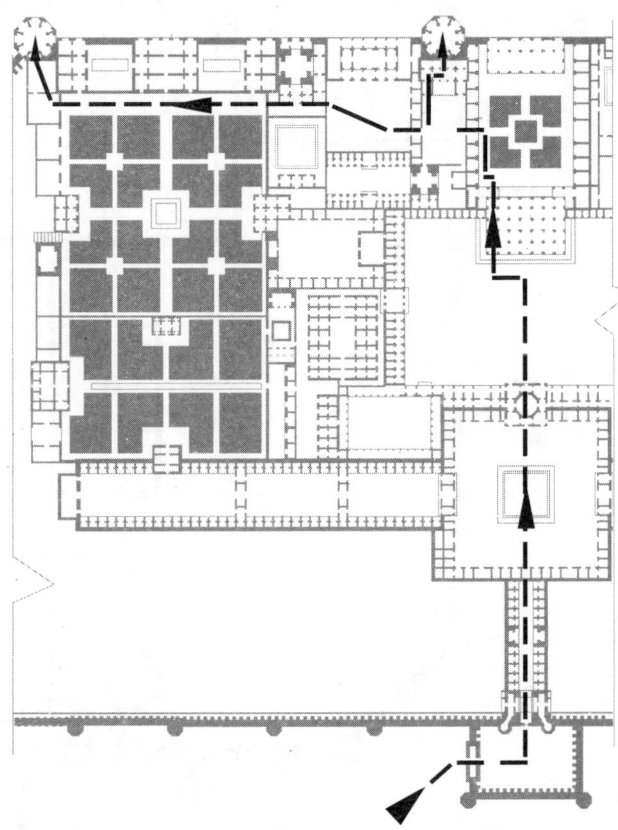

Figure 125 — *Shahjahanabad*, Delhi, indicating entrée to imperial apartments from *Lahore Darwāzā*

Plate 51 — *Lāl Qilā, Shahjahanabad*, plan (partial) indicating east-west axis and imperial north-south axis

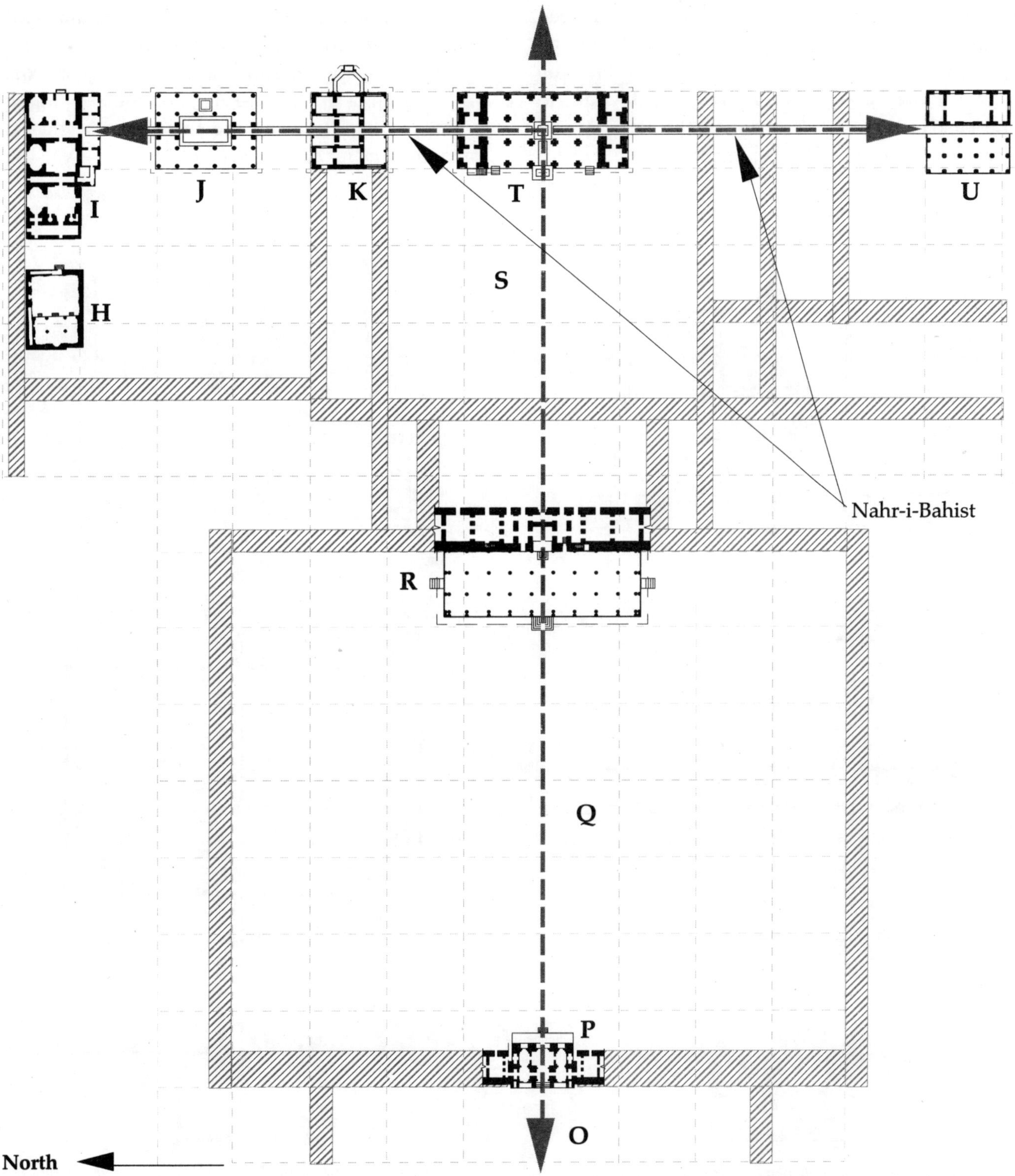

darśana (See: **Plate 50 — P**) and into another open court, the *Court of the Diwān-i Ām* (See: **Plate 50 — Q**) with the Hall of Public Audience (*Diwān-i Ām*) (See: **Plate 50 — R**; & **Figure 132**). Beyond, to the east is a garden/forecourt, the *Raṅg Mahal Bagh* (See: **Plate 50 — S**) and finally, the *Raṅg Mahal* (See: **Plate 50 — T**) on the east side of the *garh mahal*. This axis — i.e., from the *Lahore Darwāzā* to the *Raṅg Mahal* — is of prime, ceremonial and iconic significance (See: **Figure 126**).[134]

This line establishes the east-west axis. To the south of the *Diwān-i Ām* and the *Raṅg Mahal* is the *zenānā*. Here too are to be found several gardens (Indic: *bagh*) (See: **Plate 50 — V**), the

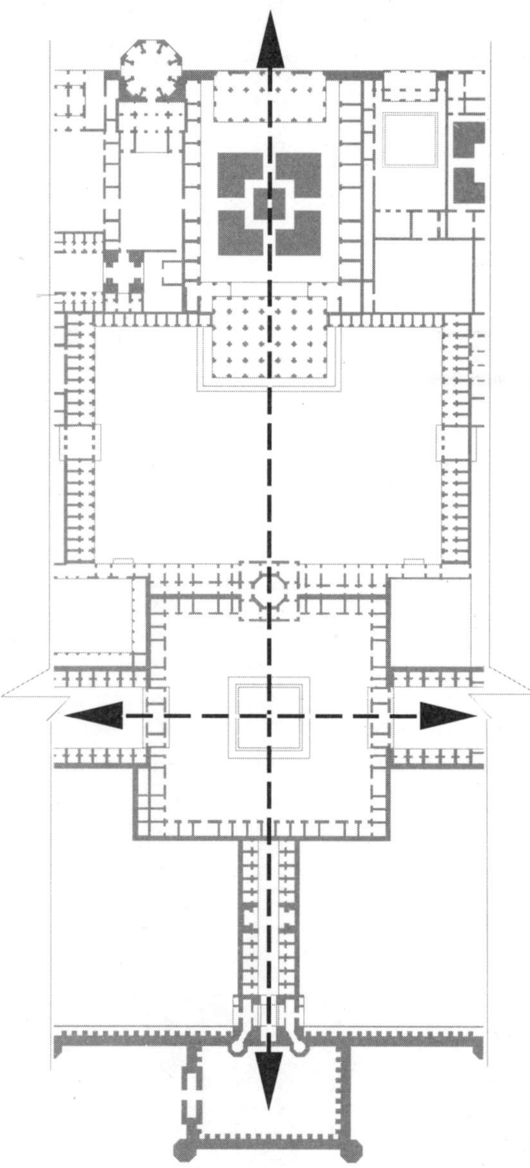

Figure 126 — *Shahjahanabad*, indicating axes from *Delhi Darwāzā* and *Lahore Darwāzā*

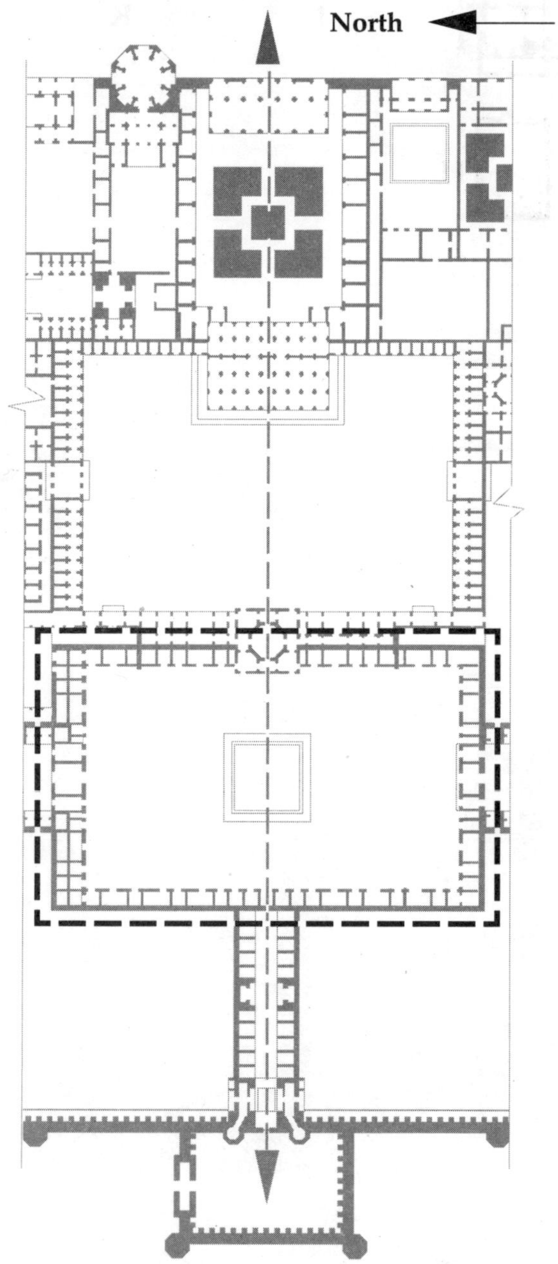

Figure 127 — *Shahjahanabad*, indicating rectangular *Chowk Hawd Nahr* as favoured by A. Mukherji

Plate 52 — *Lāl Qilā, Shahjahanabad*, Imperial Pavilions indicating Type

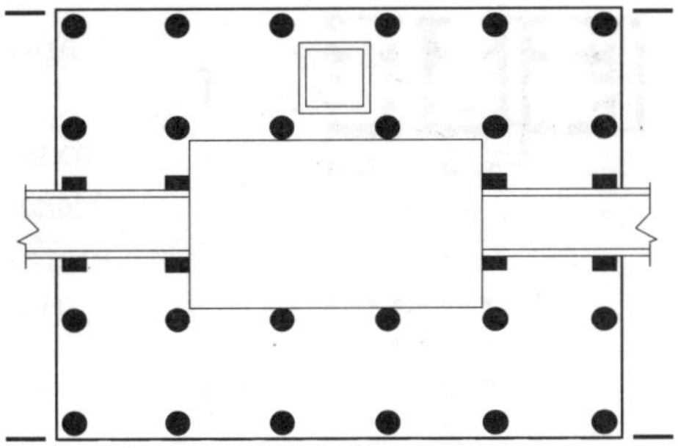

Type A - *Diwan-i-Khās*

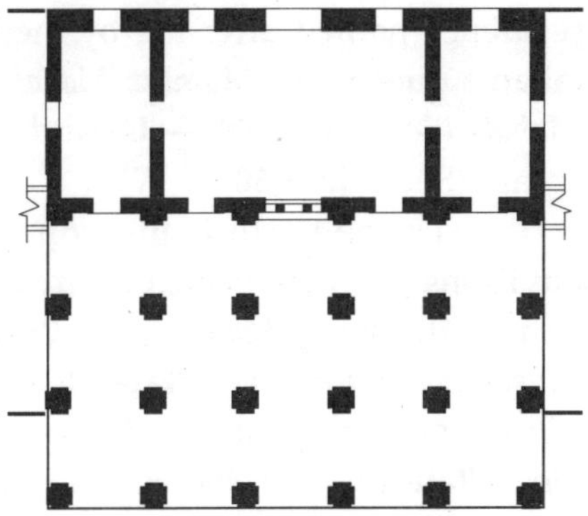

Type B - *Mumtāz Mahal*

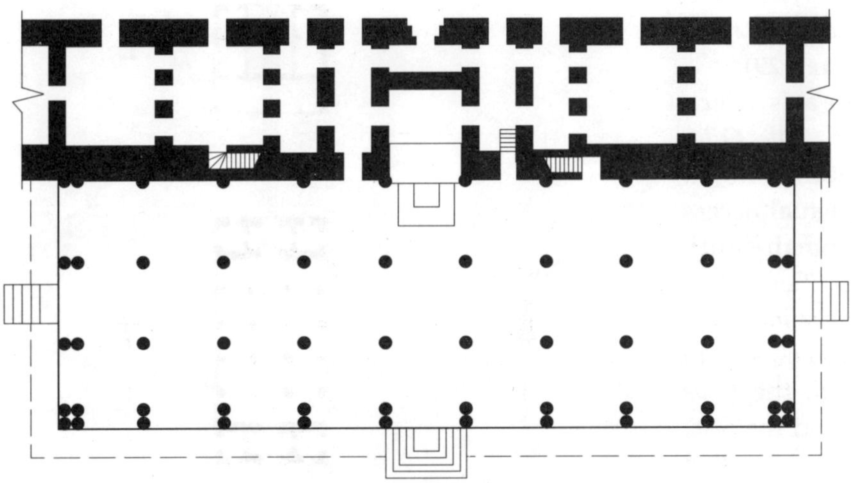

Type C - *Diwān-i-Ām*

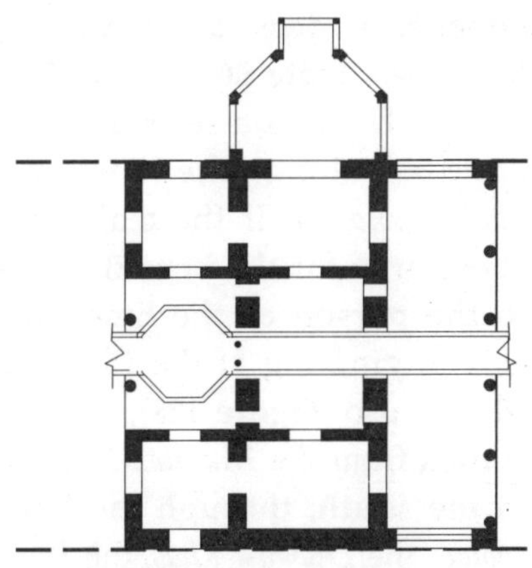

Type D - *Khās Mahal*

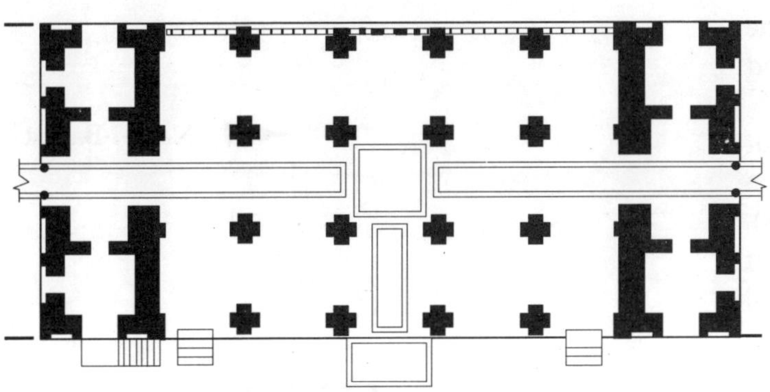

Type E - *Raṅg Mahal*

North ←

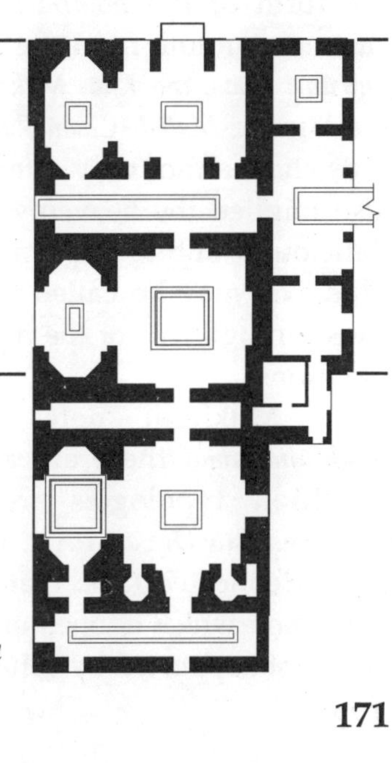

Type F - *Hammam*

residence named after the by-then-deceased Shah Jahan's queen, the *Mumtāz Mahal* (aka *Chotā Raṅg Mahal*) (See: **Plate 50 — U**) and other residential areas (See: **Plate 50 — W**).

To the north is the imperial precinct and pavilions with its principal areas and structures — i.e., the *Raṅg Mahal* (See: **Plate 50 — T**), the *Musamman Burj* (See: **Plate 50 — L**), the *Diwān-i Khās* where the fabled Peacock Throne rested (See: **Plate 47 — J**), the *Hammam* (See: **Plate 50 — I**), the *Moti Masjid* (See: **Plate 50 — H**; & **Figure 131**), the *Shah Burj* (See: **Plate 50 — A**) and the imperial gardens: the *Mahtab Bagh* and the *Bakhsh Bagh* (See: **Plate 50 — C & D**; & **Figure 129**).

There is a second north-south axis which appears along the east wall of *Lāl Qilā, Shahjahanabad*. If the main east-west axis noted above was for the benefit of visual/actual access to the person of the Emperor, the north-south axis originating at the *Delhi Darwāzā* (See: **Plate 50**; see also: **Figure 128**), was exclusively imperial. It runs from the *Mumtāz Mahal* (*Chotā Raṅg Mahal*) in the south, through the *Raṅg Mahal*, the *Khās Mahal*, the *Diwān-i Khās*, the *Hammam*, and the *Shah Burj* (See: **Plate 51**). Not only is there an implied connection, there is a very real connection in the form of the *Nahr-i-Bahist* — i.e., a water channel running from the *Hammam*, through the *Diwān-i Khās*, the *Khās Mahal*, the *Raṅg Mahal*, and the *Mumtāz Mahal* (*Chotā Raṅg Mahal*) to the south. This channel not only offered visual delight, but also implied the heavenly river of Paradise — a deliciously subtle implication (See: **Figure 128**). This axis may be called the Imperial axis as it runs through five of the most important Imperial pavilions.

Mukherji notes that in *Lāl Qilā, Shahjahanabad* there are a number of different "pavilion typologies" represented.[135] If one includes the *Diwān-i-Ām*, then there may be six types delineated (See: **Plate 52**). The first type is a pavilion which is open on four sides, composed of a roof supported by columns. The *Diwan-i-Khās*

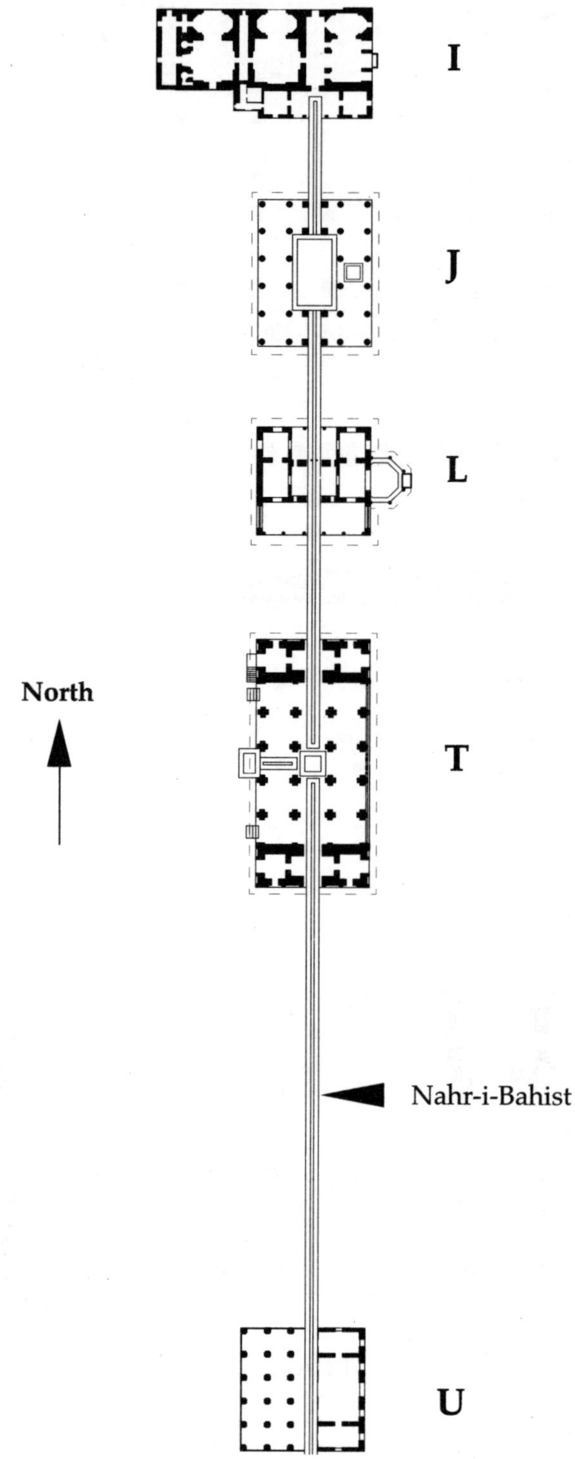

Figure 128 — *Shahjahanabad*, indicating axis from the *Hammam* to the *Mumtaz Mahal* with the *Nahr-i-Bahist*

would exemplify this type — i.e., **Type A** (See: **Plate 52**). A second type may be seen in the *Mumtāz Mahal* — i.e., **Type B**. Here a narrow rank of rooms is fronted by a deep, open, roofed portico which is supported by a number of ranks of pillars. A third type — i.e., **Type C** — is exemplified by the *Diwān-i-Ām*. Here a columned, roofed, open on three sides area abuts a wall, and elements of the pavilion are to be found on the other side of this intervening wall. **Type D** may be described as a pavilion in which one face is open and columned. The *Khās Mahal* represents this type. It is to be seen that the east and west walls of the pavilion extend to include this pillared, southern portico. The fifth type — i.e., **Type E** — is seen in the *Raṅg Mahal*. This pavilion is open on two opposite sides, but with two room ensembles bracketing this open pillared area. Finally, the sixth type is exemplified by the Imperial *Hammam* — i.e., **Type F.** This pavilion is

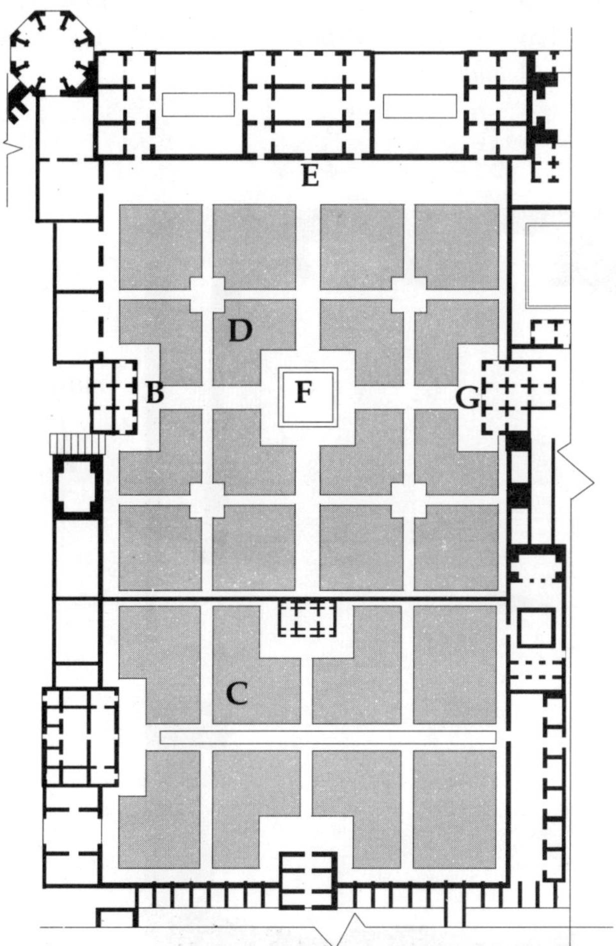

Figure 129 — *Shahjahanabad, Lāl Qilā, Bakhsh Bagh* (D) & *Mahtab Bagh* (C)

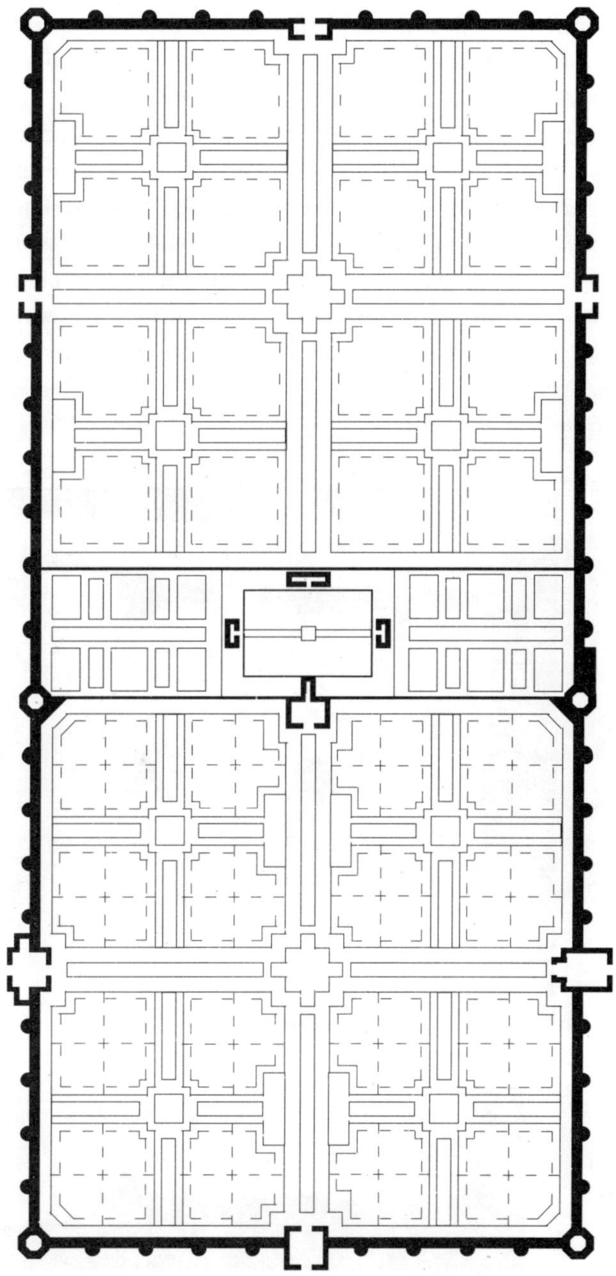

Figure 130 — *Shalimar Bagh*, Lahore, 1634 CE.

open on one side, but with rooms bracketing this open, columned portico. From the *Mumtāz Mahal* in the south to the *Hammam* in the north, and including the *Diwān-i-Ām*, the imperial axis exhibits these variations on "pavilion typology."

From one carefully designed structure to the next quiet elegance predominated. Sumptuous detail was played off against quiet surfaces or magnificent prospects. The eye is constantly delighted by colour, or detail, or pattern, as well as the flow of space, sometimes restricted, sometimes confined, sometimes expanding, but always exciting in its variety. The *Shahjahanabad* was not only a visual delight, it was also a kinetic feast of varying and interconnected spaces.[136] More *chahar-bagh*s were employed here than in nearly any other *garh mahal* in India — i.e., six in all.

The *Mahtab Bagh* and the *Bakhsh Bagh* (See: **Figure 129**) dominate the space of the imperial north-east section of *Lāl Qilā, Shahjahanabad*. Oriented east-west they are completely walled in creating an extremely private space for the delight of the Emperor. The relationship between these gardens and the *chahar-bagh* exemplified in the *Shalimar Bagh* of Lahore (See: **Figure 130**), also built by Shah Jahan, is obvious. Here, in the *Bakhsh Bagh* based upon the *chahar-bagh* concept is anchored by the *Hira Mahal* (See: **Figure 129 — E**) in the east, the *Sawan* to the north and the *Bhadon* in the south (See: **Figure 129 — B & G**). In the centre a tank with the *Zafar Mahal* (See: **Figure 129 — F**). Within the *Zafar Mahal* the Emperor may have sought additional privacy. To the west is the *Mahtab Bagh*.

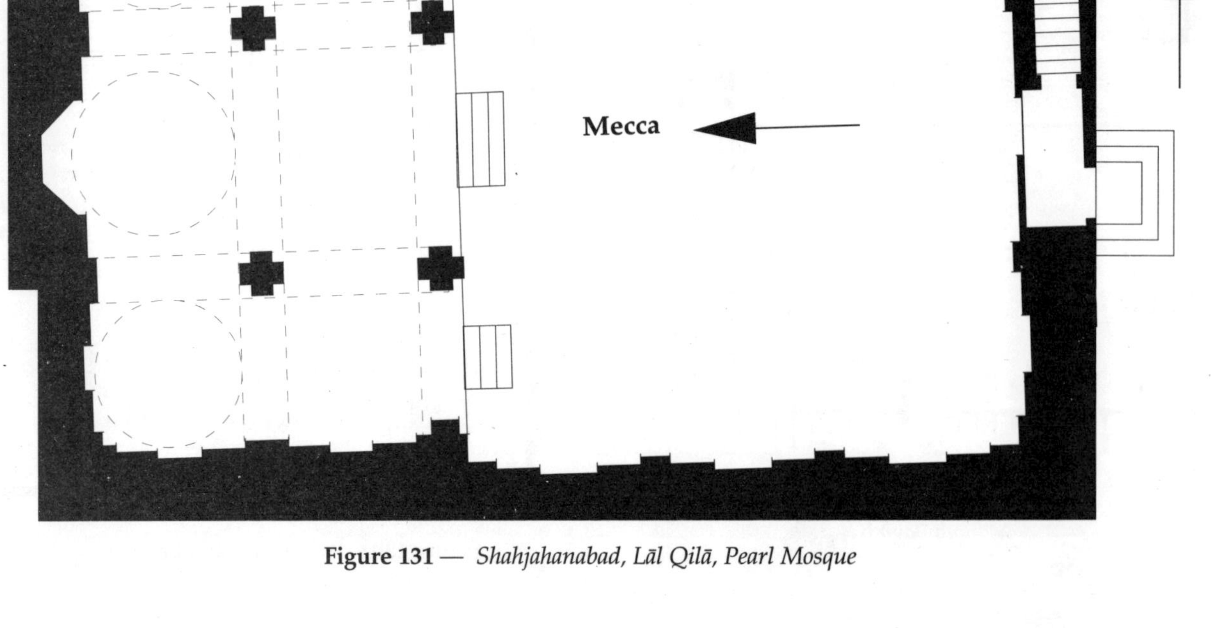

Figure 131 — *Shahjahanabad, Lāl Qilā, Pearl Mosque*

Lāl Qilā, Shahjahanabad (Continued)

The strict *chahar-bagh* division of the *Bakhsh Bagh* is countered by the rectangular plan of the *Mahtab Bagh*. Smaller and rectangular, it may be seen as mirroring the central part of the *Shalimar Bagh* of Lahore (See: **Figure 130**). Such gardens were primarily for delight and pleasure, nonetheless, the *chahar-bagh* possessed potent iconography for the Mughals — i.e., it was a bit of Paradise on earth.[137] Here within the confines of the *Lāl Qilā, Shahjahanabad*, the Emperor possessed his little bit of paradise.

There are two structures that merit special consideration: the *Moti Masjid* (*Pearl Mosque*) and the *Diwān-i Ām*. As if in further evidence of his lack of filial piety and wanting to leave a mark on his father's *garh mahal*, the Emperor Aurangzeb attached his name to the *Moti Masjid*, completed circa 1659 (See: **Figure 131**).[138] It is west of the *Hammam* and the chamber is oriented towards Mecca which accounts for its being set askew within the surrounding walls that are oriented north-south. Small, but elegant the *masjid* consists of an open court and a covered, domed area. Adjacent to the *Hammam* (See: **Plates 50 & 51**) it allowed but a few steps for the Emperor to enter after his ritual ablution. Built of the finest white marble, from whence its name is derived, the *Moti Masjid* is one of the most notable constructions of *Lāl Qilā, Shahjahanabad*.

Meant to be the centerpiece of the area of limited access (See: **Plate 50 & 51, & Figure 132**), the *Diwān-i Ām* dominates the court, the *Chowk Diwān-i Ām*, and the *Naqqār Khānā*. To the east of the *Diwān-i Ām* is a *chahar-bagh*, the *Raṅg Mahal Bagh*, and the *Raṅg Mahal*, a pleasure pavilion. Like so much of *Lāl Qilā, Shahjahanabad*, the *Diwān-i Ām* is neither revolutionary nor evolutionary (See: **Figure 132**). Rather, it is a synthesis of much of what had gone before — i.e., at *Lāl Qilā* of Agra, or Fatehpur Sikri, and even the *Sayyid Usman Rauza* of Usmanapur, Gujarat. Here is an open pavilion with ten,

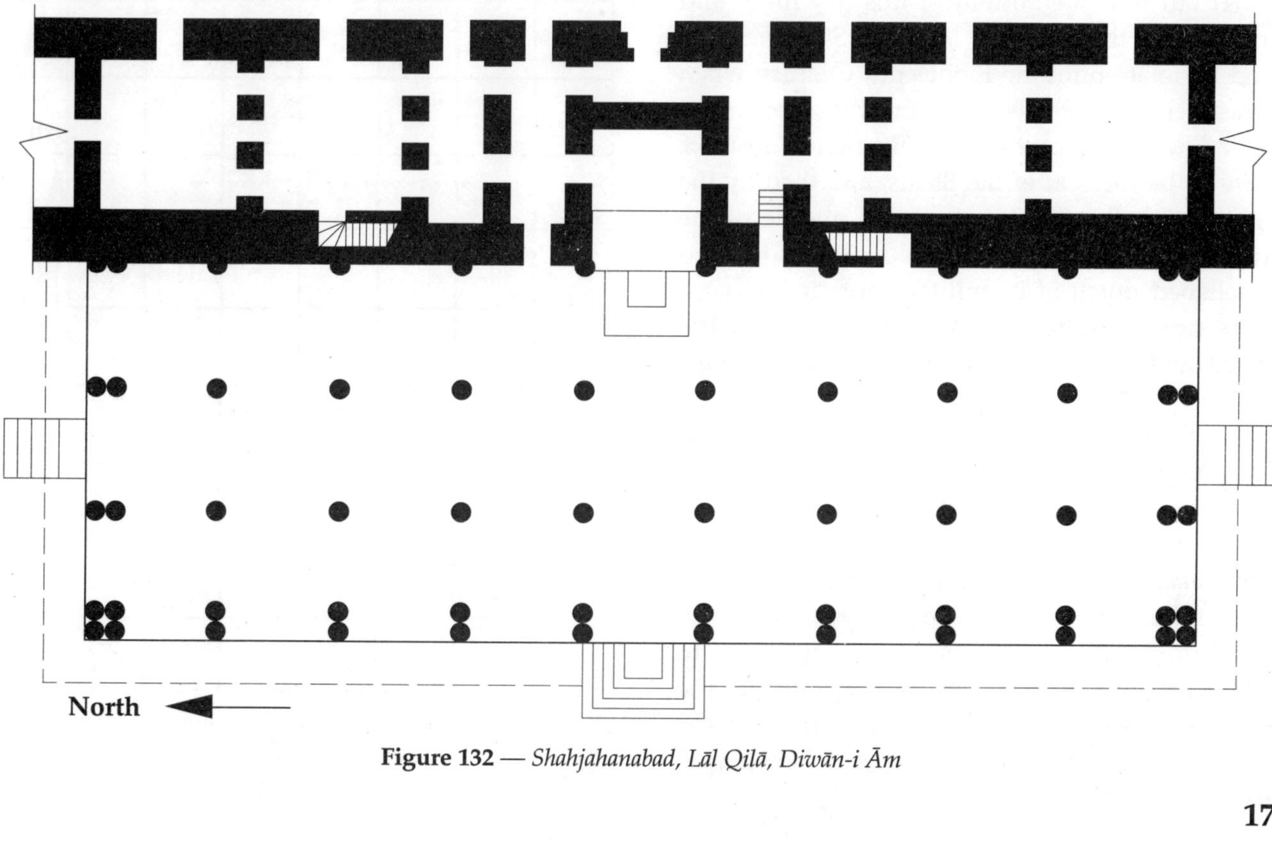

Figure 132 — *Shahjahanabad, Lāl Qilā, Diwān-i Ām*

doubled columns across the front, three bays deep to a dividing wall. This depth is the same as is to be seen in the *Diwān-i Ām* of *Lāl Qilā* (Red Fort) at Agra (See: **Plate 24 — I**). Centred against the back wall, is a raised, canopied throne upon which the Emperor heard the petitions of his vassals. Entrance to the *gaddi* was achieved via a room whose floor corresponded with the level of the *jharoka*. This opening, doubtless, would have been curtained allowing for the maximum, dramatic effect as the regally dressed Emperor made his entrance for the daily audience — i.e., *darśana*.

Although not set upon a high promontory, *Lāl Qilā, Shahjahanabad* was nonetheless secure due, in part, to the power and might of the Mughals. Surrounding the inner areas was a tall, massive curtain wall with regularly spaced bastions. To the north and east ran the river. A deep, wide dry moat encircled the curtain wall on the west and south providing an additional defensive buffer. There is some evidence that a channel was further cut into the bottom of this dry moat and connected to the Yamuna. *Lāl Qilā, Shahjahanabad* stood inviolate until the Eighteenth Century when it was twice sacked. First by the Persians under Nadir Shah who carried off the fabled *Peacock Throne* to be the seat of the Shahs, and then by the Afghans. Finally, the British, in the middle of the Nineteenth Century, captured this site and demolished much of its military area to the west of the north-south axis as well as most of the zenānā and the structures north of the east-west axis.

Finally, although Shah Jahan was Muslim, it seems possible that the *maṇḍala*s so ingrained in the *sthapati*'s traditions might find their way into the design of the *Lāl Qilā, Shahjahanabad*. Since the time of Akbar the Great, the Mughal Court had been steeped in Hindu tradition, particularly as it is applied to architecture. Three *maṇḍala*s were applied to the east-west axis from the *Chowk Hawd Nahr* to the *Raṅg Mahal*. The grid utilized by A.S. Mukherji[139]

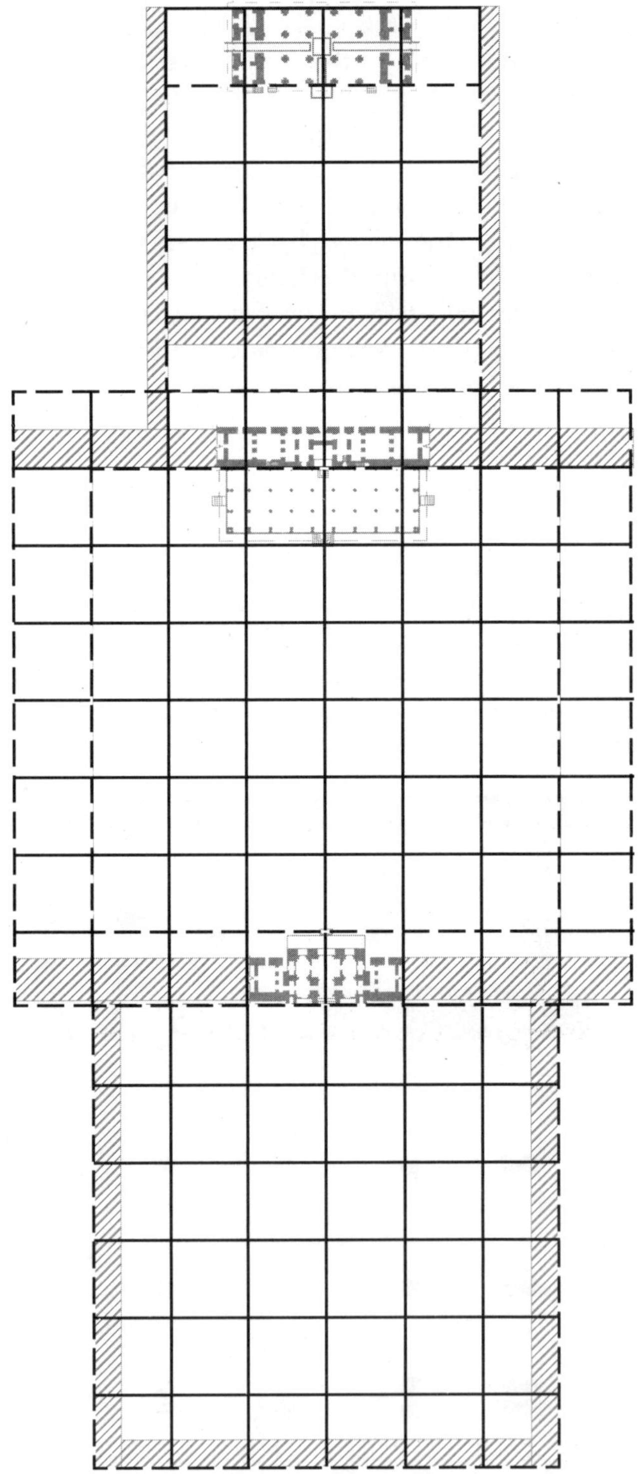

Figure 133 — *Shahjahanabad*, Application of grids to the east-west axis

Lāl Qilā, Shahjahanabad (Concluded)

provides the genesis of this approach (See: **Figure 133**). As indicated in "Note #133" and seen in **Figure 133** the *Chowk Hawd Nahr* consists of a square of thirty-six *pada* — i.e., an *Ugrapīṭha Maṇḍala*. On the other hand the *Chowk Diwān-i Ām* does not conveniently fit within a square. However, if one adds to this rectangle the ranks within which the *Diwān-i Ām* rests as well as the *Naqqār Khānā*, then a square of sixty-four *pada* is formed — i.e., a *Maṇḍūka Maṇḍala*. Finally, the forecourt, including the *Raṅg Mahal* consists of sixteen pada — i.e., a *Mahapīṭha Maṇḍala*. This forecourt was formed on the western edge by a range of small columned spaces. However, if the *Mahapīṭha Maṇḍala* is lowered one rank, it then touched the eastern border of the *Maṇḍūka Maṇḍala* and the western edge of the *Raṅg Mahal*. The progression of numbers — i.e., four, six and eight; or sixteen, thirty-six and sixty-four — are highly symbolic not only within Islam, but to the Hindus as well.

With the dethronement and subsequent death of Shah Jahan, little of real note was constructed by the Mughals. Aurangzeb's bigotry and lust for power was paralleled with neither any real aesthetic need nor talent. His reign marked the beginning of the sure and steady decline of the Mughals into ignominious oblivion. The *Lāl Qilā, Shahjahanabad* also stands, in its present state today, as a testament to the exigencies of war and to the extent to which a conquering nation mutilates the cultural heritage of the defeated peoples. Yet, *Lāl Qilā, Shahjahanabad*, still reigns as a testament and the synthesis of what had been begun during the reign of Shah Jahan's great-grand-father, Humayun, and carried on by his grandfather, Akbar the Great, and his father Jahangir — i.e., the Great Mughals.

Daulat Kothi

Bijapur (*c.* 1626-1656 *c.* CE)

The Sultanate of Bijapur, governed by the 'Adil Shahi was a realm of architectural brilliance — e.g., the *Ibrahim Rauza* (1615 CE), the *Gol Gumbaz* (1626 CE), the *Afzal Khan Tomb* (1659 CE), and the *Ali II Tomb* (1672 CE). Their architectural splendour was matched by their political vigour. Though small by prevailing standards, the vigorous sultanate grew and dominated their region. Breaking away from the once powerful Bahmani Sultanate in 1489, Bijapur quickly flourished.

"As with many of the noble families of Islamic India, the 'Adil Shahi came to their position out of distress. Upon the death of Sultān Murad II of Turkey, his eldest son set about assassinating all his younger brothers. One of these brothers, Yusuf Adil Shah, was spirited away by his mother and sent to Persia. Later, he went to the court of the Sultān of Bidar where he proved his bravery, allegiance and was awarded the governorship of Bijapur. In 1489 he declared himself Sultān of Bijapur, thus fathered one of the most interesting and dynamic sultanates in India, albeit Turkish in origin."[140]

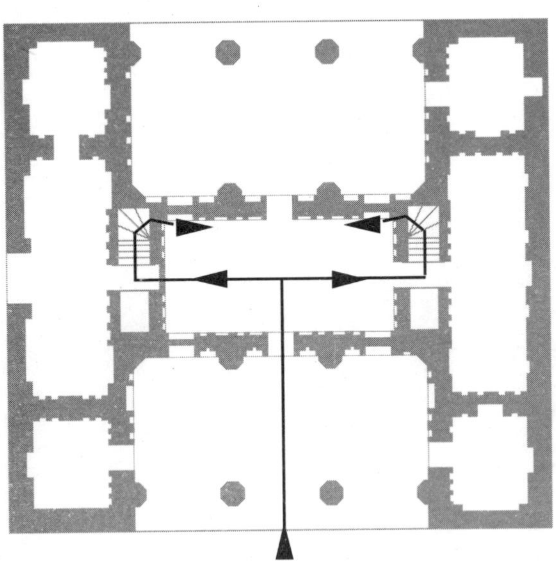

Figure 134 — *Daulat Kothi,* indicating path from the entrance to second storey

The *Daulat Kothi*[141] is an example of Bijapur's development. Reputed to have been built during the reign of Sultān Muhammad Adil Shah (r. 1626-1656 CE) this small 'palace' doubtlessly housed a nobleman or minor member of the royal family. It most certainly would not have been constructed for the ruler as it possesses none of the major elements usually associated with the residence of a ruler, nor does it possess the scale or size. On the other hand, its design, size and quality of detail places it above the possibility of the common man of the period. However, the fact that this residence is nearly mirror cross-axial, *en plan*, reflects the abiding love of balance and its inherent implications.

En plan, this residence is in the form of an "H." The *Daulat Kothi* consists of two storeys punctuated by a wide, deep, pillared entrance front and back. This entrance, this space exhibits two, free standing columns and six engaged columns per side. This area,[142] enclosed on three sides and under a common roof serves as a traditional court as well as an impressive entrance. There are no internal hallways, rooms lead one to the other. On the ground floor all but one room opens onto the outside. These openings, these doorways are the only source of natural light for the interior with the exception of the central reception area — i.e., the cross arm of the "H." Thick walls aid in keeping the interior cool during the heat of the day. Narrow, enclosed stairs on either side of the central reception area, in the passage to the extended arms, are the only access to the second storey (See: **Figure 134**). The plan exhibits limited access to the private areas of the upper storey.

The *Daulat Kothi* stands as an example of Bijapur and India's Muslims' adaptation of the traditional Hindu plan in its mirror cross-axiality and it near-square plan. As the residence of a noble or minor royalty, it follows many of the elements of a ruler's abode.

Plate 53 — *Daulat Kothi*, ground plan & 2nd storey

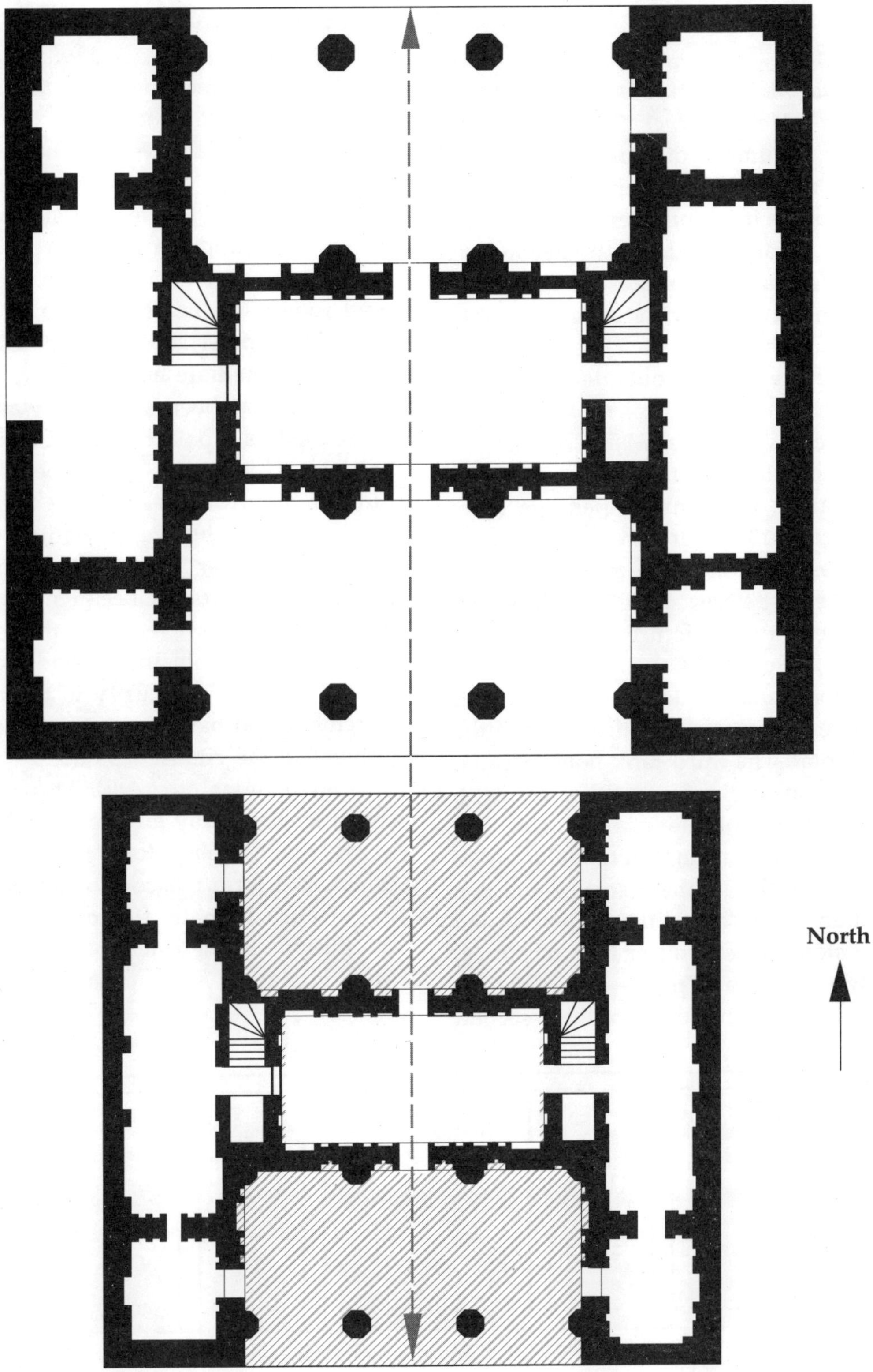

Athar Mahal (*Dad Mahal*)

Bijapur (*c.* 1646 CE)

The *Athar Mahal*[143] (āka: *Dad Mahal, Ashar Mahal, Mubārak Mahal, Athar Sharif*) is most interesting for a number of reasons. First, its original use is somewhat obscured, even confused, although it is considered to be ". . . typical (of a) Bijapur palace."[144] Second it possesses many features of 'palaces' paradigmatic of this sultanate, but with some notable exceptions. And, third, for such a supposedly important structure, it rests outside the citadel wall(s).

Facing east, the *Athar Mahal* consists of boxlike form facing a large tank with an arched faṛade. But, rather than three openings (See: **Plate 54** & **Figure 135**), here are five. Moving from east to west there are three ranks of rooms or spaces on the first storey. First, a space which runs the width of the structure as well as the height. Second, five spaces — i.e., two square spaces to the north and two to the south flanking a rectangular central space — which are half the height of the total. The third rank holds a room at the north and one at the south, the same width as the square rooms of the second rank, but somewhat deeper and a long rectangular room in between. Within the southern small room is a staircase leading to the second floor. The division of the second storey spaces mirror the first storey, but with only two ranks of rooms deep. Further, there are windows and balconies on this second storey which look down into the broad eastern space.

The plan of the *Athar Mahal* is eminently suited for a Palace of Justice (*Dad Mahal*). The supplicants could have presented their petitions to the sultān as he was enthroned within the central porch of the second storey. As a Palace of the Relic (*Mubārak Mahal* or *Athar Sharif*), the sacred relic was ensconced in the upper north west room. Finally, as a Palace of the Court, the *Athar Mahal* possessed ample spaces for the Sultān and his immediate entourage.

As has been stated, it was said to have been used as a palace of the Court for a period of time. This seems rather peculiar as it was outside the protective wall of the citadel. Even though, with a bridge or viaduct connected the back of the *Athar Mahal* to the citadel proper, it seems unlikely to have been employed as a palace of the Court. However, with the multiple access routes to and from the second storey it would provide adequate security to the *mahal*. It most certainly could have been utilized as a ceremonial adjunct to the citadel's palaces.

Although , the *Athar Mahal*, most probably constructed initially for use as a *Dad Mahal* or as a *Mubārak Mahal*, does follow the standard established for a palace or residence in this most important sultanate. It provides a glimpse into the lifestyle of the rulers of this Southern Indian Muslim state.

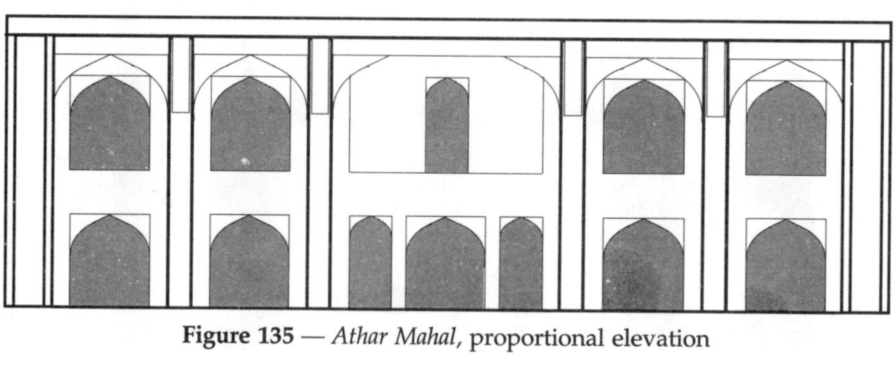

Figure 135 — *Athar Mahal*, proportional elevation

Plate 54 — *Athar Mahal*, plan, first (top), second (bottom)

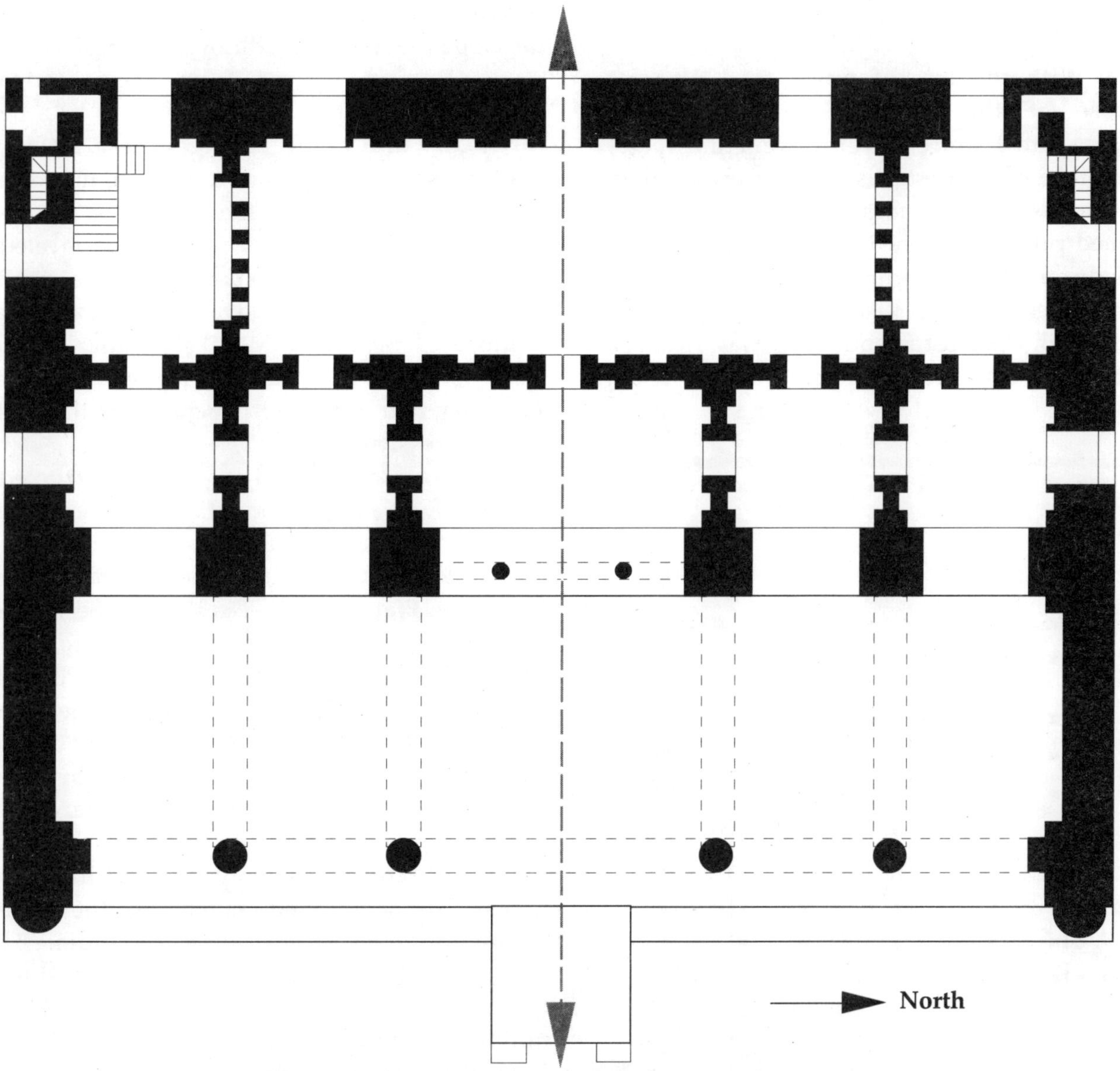

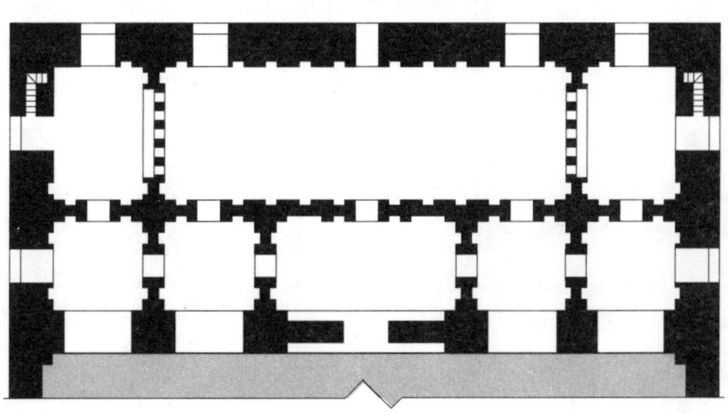

Nāyaka Mahal

Madurai (*c.* 1650 CE)

With the loss of power and ultimate collapse of the vast and incredibly rich Vijayanagara Empire, several exuberant, petty states broke off and established their own realms. The *nāyaka*s or governors of the various areas assumed rule and retained the title. The Nāyakas of Madurai, of the Thirumala Nāyaka Dynasty, based its genesis upon Vishvanatha (r. 1529-1564 CE) although the most famous ruler was Tirumala (r. 1623-1659 CE) (See: **Appendix B**). Their realm provided all that could be desired and they developed fabulous wealth over a period of time.

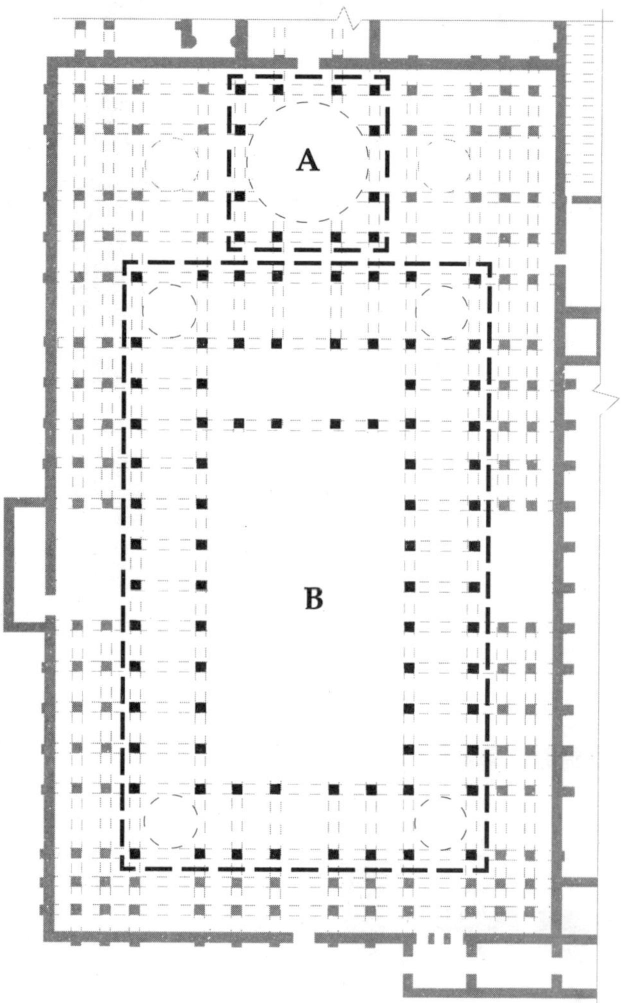

Figure 136 — *Nāyaka Mahal, Darbār Hall* indicating contiguous areas (— — —), throne area (**A**) & central court (**B**)

Having sprung from the wondrous Vijayanagara Empire, there seemed to be a need for luxury and pomp amongst these Nāyakas. Madurai was so situated as to provide the former, and the *Nāyaka*s saw to the latter. The members of the Thirumala Nāyaka Dynasty were inveterate builders. They were responsible for a goodly amount of the impressive and equally vast Temple of Śiva and Mīnākṣī (Indic: *Mīnākṣī Sundareśvara*) at Madurai (See: **Appendix A, Plate 74**). They had a distinct penchant for the grand and impressive.

Tirumala is said to have constructed a large palace complex at Madurai, the *Nāyaka Mahal*.[145] All that now remains is the impressive *Darbār Mahal* (*Darbār Hall*) and the *Nṛtya Sabhā* (*Dance Hall*) (See: **Plate 55**). The *Darbār Hall* (See: **Figure 136**) is a long rectangular structure. It is essentially divided into two areas — i.e., the throne area (See: **Figure 136 — A**) and the central court (See: **Figure 136 — B**). The throne or *gaddi* sits beneath a dome which is supported by twelve pillars — i.e., four on each side. This area may have been used for private audiences as, doubtless, screens and drapes would have been extensively employed much as they were throughout the *garh mahal*s of India. This arrangement — i.e. four pillars on each side or face — recalls the *baradari* form utilized by a number of Hindu rulers (See: **Figure 107**). The *Inner Court* was originally roofed and vaulted, providing a large unimpeded space within the massive *Darbār Mahal* (*Darbār Hall*). This *Inner Court*

Legend for **Plate 55**

A	Inner Court
B	Throne Area
C	Nṛtya Sabhā (Dance Hall)
D	Baradari (Pavilion)
E	Maidān

Plate 55 — *Nāyaka Mahal, Darbār Hall, Nṛtya Sabhā & Maidān*, plan, ground floor (partial)

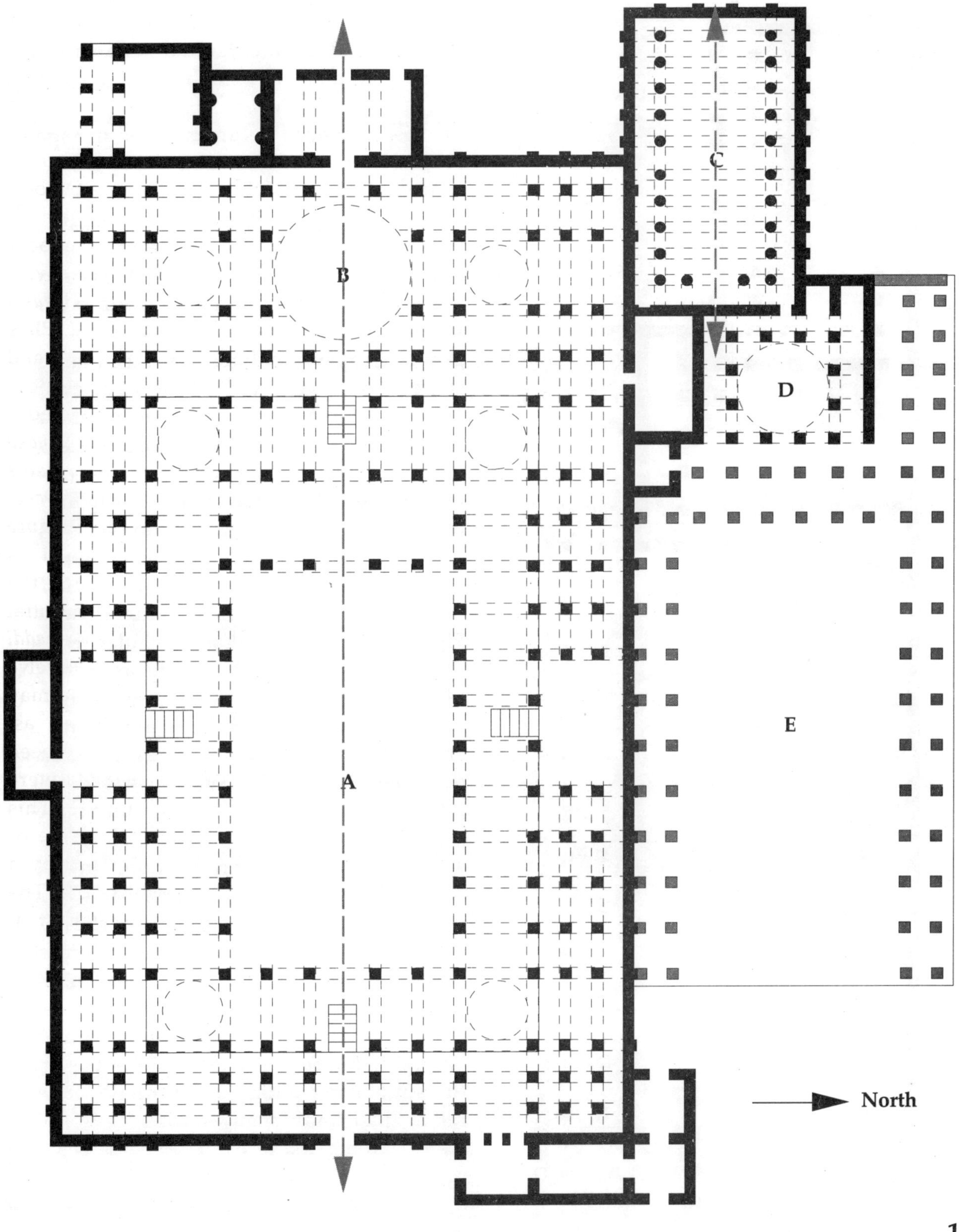

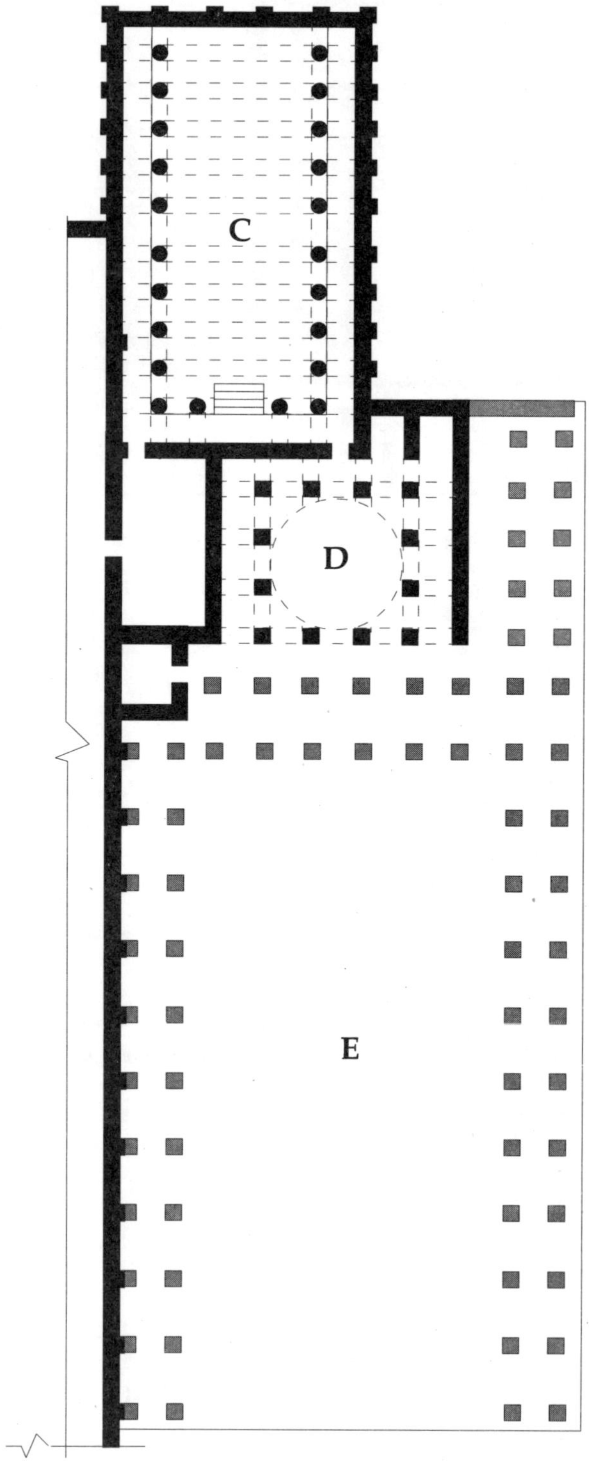

Figure 137 — *Nāyaka Mahal, Nṛtya Sabhā* (**C**), *Pavilion* (**D**) and *maidān* (**E**)

consists of a space encircled by thirty-two columns and a wide vaulted aisle surrounded by forty columns. Outside these two spaces, the rest of the *Darbār Mahal* consists of rows and files of closely spaced columns. This arrangement, obviously, gives special emphasis upon these two spaces.

The hallmark of this structure is its immense size and the fact that it is almost completely enclosed. Prior to the construction of the *Darbār Mahal* (*Darbār Hall*) here in Madurai, similar structures — i.e., *Diwān-i Ām* — were generally open pavilions that faced large open spaces (See: **Plates 10, 23, 26 & 40** as examples). Not so here in Madurai. The Nāyakas of Madurai, for some reason chose an enclosed space, similar to those encountered in cooler climes, especially in Europe where the climate was far more intemperate than in southern India.

The *Nṛtya Sabhā* is to be found to the north-east of the *Darbār Mahal* (*Darbār Hall*) and connected along part of its southern wall (See: **Figure 137 — C**). It follows a similar rectangular plan as its larger neighbor. Here, as in the *Darbār Mahal*, the central space is repressed with a raised aisle around the north, east and south sides. Smaller than the *Darbār Mahal*, the *Nṛtya Sabhā* is, nonetheless, equally lavish in its detail and possesses a clerestory which illuminates the interior.

A similar feature is found in both the *Nṛtya Sabhā* and the *Darbār Mahal*, that is, they both possess unusually and uncharacteristically thick pillars which support the upper structure. This gives both areas a rather heavy look, unlike the more airy appearance of other Indian pillared halls, whether Hindu or Muslim. In addition, like the earlier *Solah Khamba Masjid* of the *Bidargarh* the supporting pillars of both halls are round rather than traditionally square.[146]

To the east of the *Nṛtya Sabhā* is a domed pavilion which is enclosed on three sides and open to the east (See: **Figure 137 — D**). Again

Nāyaka Mahal (Concluded)

four pillars are seen across the face and the same along the other three aspects. As with the *Throne Area* of the *Darbār Mahal*, this disposition would seem to recall the *baradari* form.

To the east of this pavilion is a large open space which is enclosed by a double rank of columns (See: **Figure 137 — E**). This open area is of considerable size and may have served as a *maidān*; an area where entertainments, ceremonies and military parades could have taken place. The pavilion to the west may well have served as a locale where the Nāyaka could have sat upon his *gaddi* as he observed and was observed. All the extant structures of the *Nāyaka Mahal* are oriented east to west. This would have been in keeping with the preferred orientation suggested in the *śilpa śāstra*.

These three spaces of varying, but considerable size, are all that remain of the once great *garh mahal*. These areas — i.e., the *Darbār Mahal*, the *Nṛtya Sabhā* and the *Maidān* — were essentially ceremonial areas and would have been larger than the *mardānā* and the *zenānā* areas individually. Nonetheless, these latter residential areas and that which would have included the private residence of the Nāyaka would have to be substantial. Doubtless their plan would have been such as to offer suitable security to the Nāyaka. As was stated earlier, the Nāyakas of Madurai built on a scale that may be characterized as imperial. The *Nāyaka Mahal* of Madurai would have been a *garh mahal* of impressive size and design in its entirety.

Deeg-garh (Garden Palace)

Deeg, (1722-1763 CE)

After the intolerant bigot, Aurangzeb took the imperial throne, the might and glory of the Mughals began to slip rapidly and irrevocably into decline due also, in part, to his ineptitude. In the early part of the eighteenth century the Jats, a group from the Hindu agricultural caste, coalesced and rebelled. This they did so after the Emperor Aurangzeb seized and destroyed a particularly important Hindu temple in Mathura. The Jats grew in numbers and furore. In time, through a series of decisive military actions, the Jats had established themselves as a force to be reckoned with in an area north and west of Agra. Unable to control their expansion, the Emperor along with the Rajputs tried to capitalize upon an enmity that had developed between the Jats of Sinsini and those of Thun in hopes of weakening them. That was not to be! The Jat leader Badan Singh (r. 1722-1733 CE) (See: **Appendix B**) of Sinsini emerged as the overwhelming winner in the clan warfare and quickly absorbed his Thun rivals. This was neither what the emperor nor the surrounding Rajput rulers had expected. Badan Singh was then awarded the cities of Thun and Deeg in hopes of placating any further expansion. He was soon declared Raja of Deeg under the auspices of Amber who wanted a peaceful neighbour to the north-east. It is to be noted that rulers may emerge from any caste, although most of the Rajputana rulers were kṣatriya.

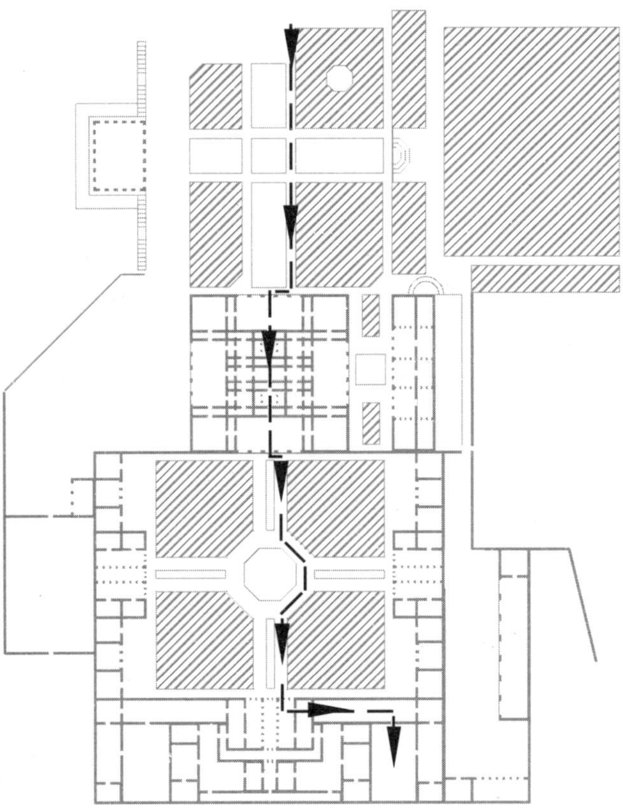

Figure 138 — *Sūraj Bhawan, Sūraj Bagh & Hardev Bhawan, Bagh Mahal*, Deeg, indicating path from *Singh Pol*

Thus, in the centre of Rajput territory a vibrant state arose which was neither part of any of the Rajput clans, nor of the ruler/warrior caste. Thun and Deeg were ruled by erstwhile farmers who assumed the title Thakur and, as stated, were elevated to the position and title of Raja, and later Mahārājā. After a stay in Deeg the Jats moved their capital to the more easily defendable Bharatpur (City of the West). There

Legend for **Plate 56 & 57**

A	Singh Pol
B	Temple
C	Nand Bhawan
D	Sawan Bhawan
E	Gopal Bhawan
F	Keshav Badon
G	Gopal Sagar
H	Rup Sagar
I	Bhadon Bhawan
J	Kishan Bhawan
K	Sūraj Mahal
L	Tank
M	Sūraj Pol
N	Purānā Mahal
O	Sūraj Bagh
P	Hardev Bhawan
Q	Shish Mahal

Plate 56 — *Deeg-garh* (*Garden Palace*), plan

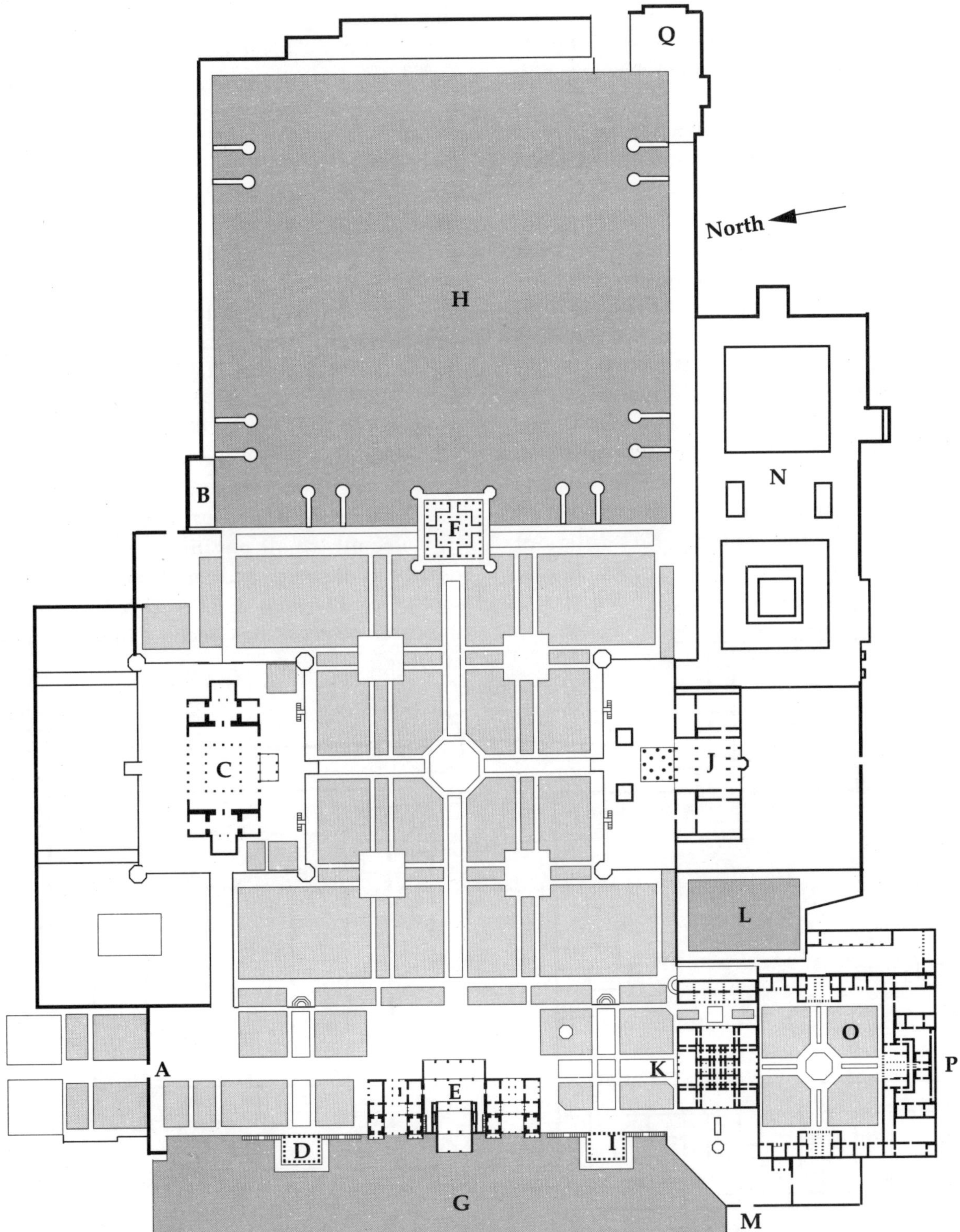

an impressive citadel had earlier been constructed and was further reinforced by the Jats. It became one of the most impregnable citadels in the region. But it was at Deeg that the Jats of Bharatpur finally constructed their most lavish *garh mahal* — i.e., the *Deeg-garh* (*Bāgh Mahal* or *Garden Palace*).[147]

Neither impregnably fortified (See: **Figure 138**) nor located in a particularly strategic site, the *Deeg-garh* grew from the relatively modest *Purānā Mahal* of Badan Singh (See: **Plates 56 & 57 — N**) to a *garh mahal* of some size and considerable beauty, not to mention luxury. It became for the Jats of Bharatpur a haven, a retreat from the rigors of the more heavily fortified and confined palace at Bharatpur, much in the same way that the *Hauz Khās* was constructed by the Delhi Sultān 'Ala-ud-din Muhammad Khaljiz as a retreat or the *Jag Mandir* for the contemporary rulers of Udaipur. It also was an obvious manifestation of their power and wealth.

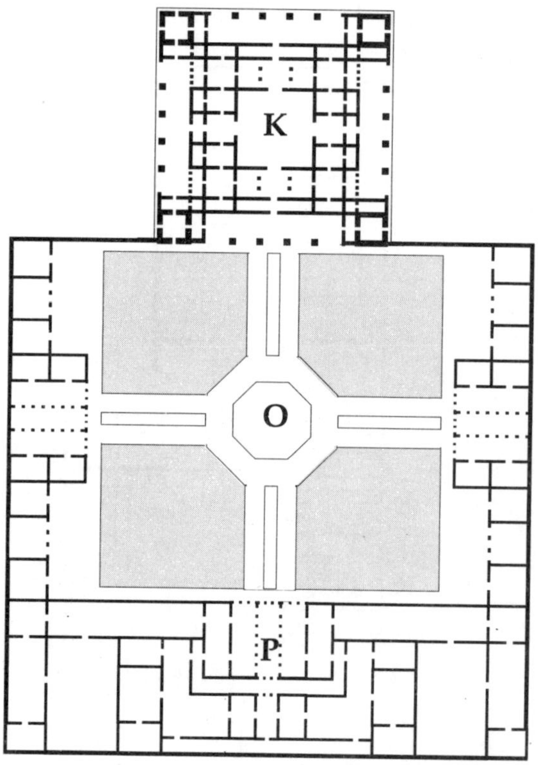

Figure 139 — *Sūraj Mahal* (**K**), *Sūraj Bagh* (**O**) & Hardev Bhawan (**P**)

More a pleasure palace than a true *garh mahal*, the *Deeg-garh* was bracketed by two large tanks or reservoirs — i.e., the smaller *Rup Sagar* to the east and the larger *Gopal Sagar* to the west (See: **Plates 56 & 57 — H & G**). The Raja Badan Singh constructed the *Purānā Mahal* (See: **Plates 56 & 57 — N**) soon after his elevation to the *gaddi*. It was the Raja Suraj Mal (r. 1733-1767 CE) who contributed the most impressive number of buildings and gardens in the whole complex — i.e., the large formal garden (*bagh*) in the centre, the *Nand Bhawan* (See: **Plates 56 & 57 — C**) to the north, the *Kishan Bhawan* (See: **Plates 56 & 57 — J**) to the south, the *Keshav Bhawan* (See: **Plates 56 & 57 — F**) to the east on the *Rup Sagar* and the *Gopal Bhawan* (See: **Plates 56 & 57 — E**) in the west on the *Gopal Sagar*. The *Gopal Bhawan* is flanked by two elegant, small pavilions — i.e., the *Sawan Bhawan* to the north and the *Bhadon Bhawan* to the south (See: **Plates 56 & 57 — D & I**). This vista of the three *bhawans* has become the most famous at Deeg.

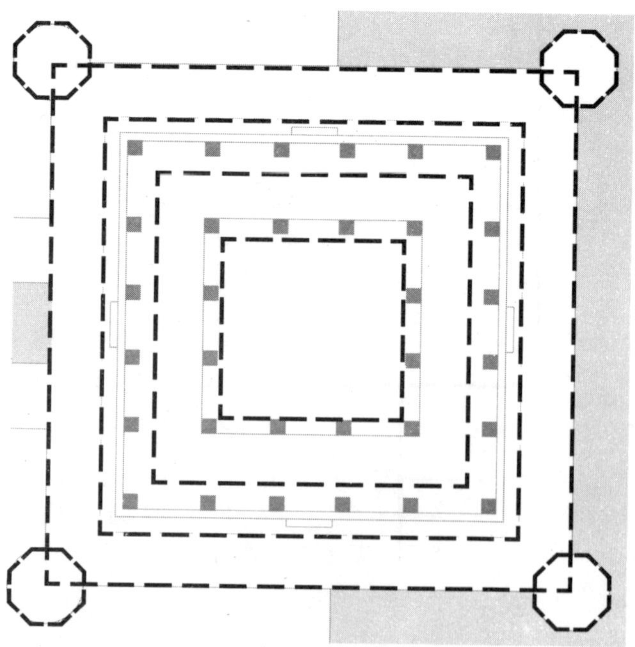

Figure 140 — *Keshav Badon, Bagh Mahal,* Deeg, indicating a *śilpa śāstra* ideal overlayed (— — —)

Plate 57 — *Deeg-garh* (*Garden Palace*), plan detail indicating multiple perpendicular axiality

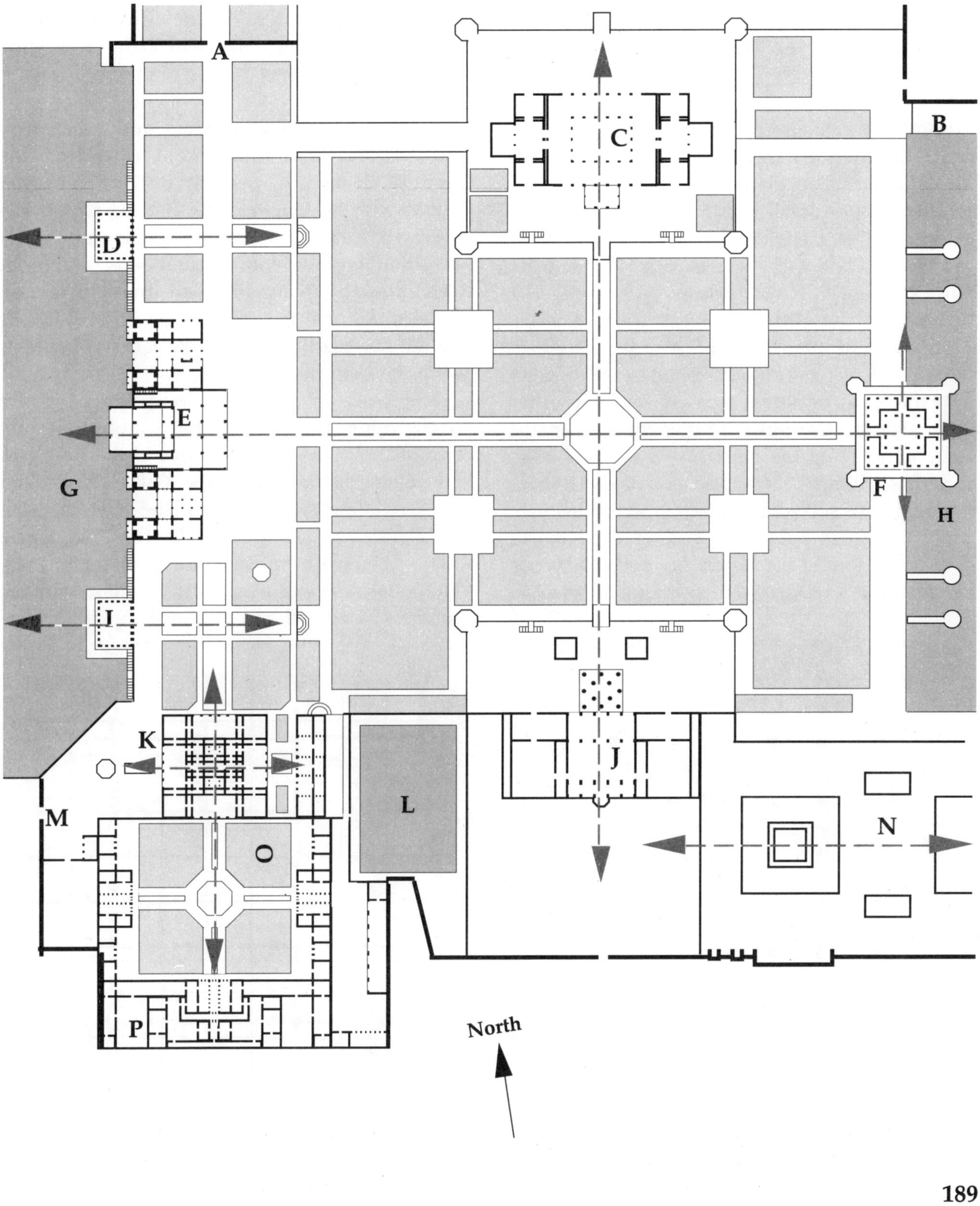

Deeg-garh (*Garden Palace*) (Continued)

Basically the *garh mahal* is oriented east to west (See: **Plate 56**). The major *bhawans* of the *Deeg-garh* follow this orientation or they face north to south — i.e., multiple perpendicular axiality. The major structures which are north-south oriented are four: the *Nand Bhawan* and *Kishan Bhawan* (See: **Plates 56** & **57 — C** & **J**) both on the major north south axis through the garden, and the complex consisting of: *Sūraj Mahal* and *Hardev Bhawan* (See: **Plates 56** & **57 — K** & **P**). The latter — i.e., *Hardev Bhawan* — is considered by some to have been the *zenānā*.

It is of interest to note that the *Deeg-garh* (*Bagh Mahal* or *Garden Palace*) is not clearly divided into the areas of access that one finds in other *garh mahals*. Certainly, either of the major structures facing the garden — i.e., the *Keshav Badon, Nand Bhawan, Kishan Bhawan* and *Gopal Bhawan* — could have served as a place in which the Raja could have held public audience (*diwān-i ām*) or *darśana*. Further, if the *Hardev Bhawan* was indeed the *zenānā*, it would have been unusually small in relative comparison to others within the region. It may have been that when the Jats were "elevated" they retained some of their old ways.[148] Within the lower castes, womenfolk were to be protected from the public, not necessarily isolated and or confined, kept away from the sight of all men. It was only in the Rajput *garh mahals* and the Mughal *qilās* that the *zenānā* was elevated to a space of major size and virtual isolation and/or confinement was practiced. Therefore, the requirements or divisions seen in more traditional or tradition-bound *garh mahals* do not necessarily apply to the Jats of Bharatpur or to the *Deeg-garh*.

Coming from a traditional Hindu background, it is interesting to note that only two of the numerous structures of the *Deeg-garh* are square, *en plan* — i.e., the *Keshav Bhawan* and the *Sūraj Mahal* (*Sūraj Bhawan*). The latter, the *Sūraj Mahal*, faces its own, small *chahar bagh* (See: **Figure 139**) — i.e., the *Sūraj Bagh* (See: **Figure 139 — O**). The *Keshav Bhawan* is an open pavilion with six columns along each face.[149] It rests upon a terrace

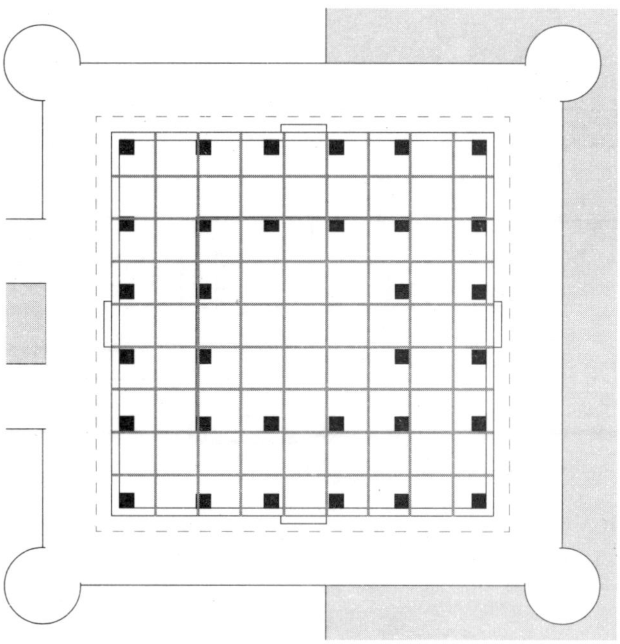

Figure 141 — *Keshav Badon, Bagh Mahal*, Deeg, indicating a *Paramaśayika Maṇḍala*

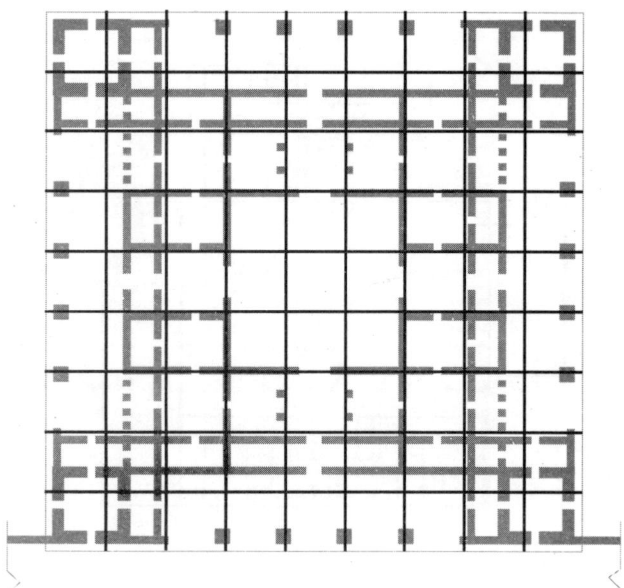

Figure 142 — *Sūraj Mahal, Deeg-garh*, Deeg, indicating a *Paramaśayika Maṇḍala*

with circular terminations at the four corners, following the tradition set down by the *śilpa śāstras* (See: **Figure 140**). The *Keshav Bhawan* is the only pavilion at *Deeg-garh* that is open, in the form of a *baradari*. To the east is the large tank, the *Rup Sagar* and to the west one of the two main axes of the formal garden which is laid out in a modified *chahar bagh*. It is seen in **Figure 141** that the plan of the *Keshav Bhawan* finds its genesis in a *Paramaśayika Maṇḍala*. In addition, this pavilion assumes additional importance since it is the eastern pavilion of the four — i.e., the others being the *Nand Bhawan, Kishan Bhawan* and the *Gopal Bhawan*. In Indian temple architecture, the entrance is generally towards the east — i.e., the sun and the masculine direction — while the sanctuary is in the west — i.e., the moon and the feminine direction. Here, at the *Deeg-garh*, the major group of pavilions are the *Gopal Bhawan*, flanked by the *Sawan Bhavan* and the *Bhadon Bhawan*. Therefore, one might assume that the *Keshav Bhawan* assumes the masculine role and the group of the *Sawan, Gopal* and *Bhadon Bhavans* assume the feminine role in this complex.

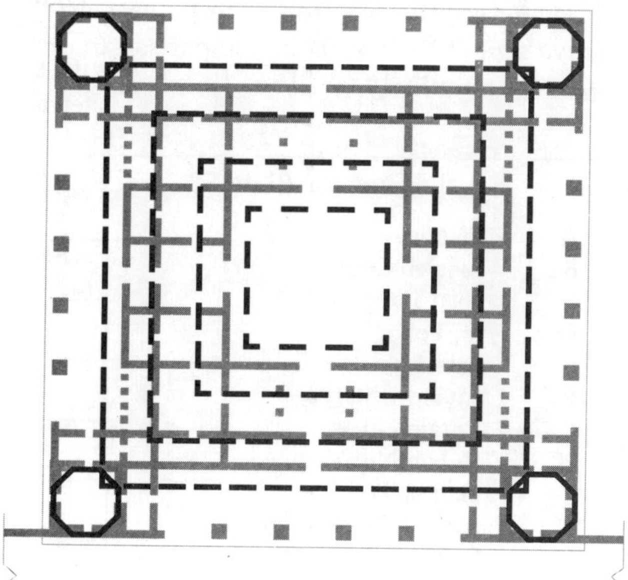

Figure 143 — *Sūraj Mahal, Bagh Mahal*, Deeg, indicating a *śilpa śāstra* ideal overlayed (— — —)

The *Sūraj Mahal* also appears to be based upon a *Paramaśayika Maṇḍala* (See: **Figure 142**). The major divisions fall within the ranks and files of this *maṇḍala's pada*. Likewise, this *mahal* also appears to be based upon the *śilpa śāstra* ideal (See: **Figure 143**), although, here, the octagonal towers of the ideal are replaced by square pavilions. It is also to be noted that the *Sūraj Mahal* and the *Hardev Mahal* are adjacent to a tank (See: **Plates 56 & 57 — L**).

The *Deeg-garh* exemplifies, in the early eighteenth century, what later becomes a standard in the palaces of the ruling families of India. Warfare had technically advanced to the point that *garh mahal*s such as Jodhpur, Udaipur and even Bharatpur were no longer impenetrable from modern artillery. Further, the princely states of India had become firmly established and territorial aggrandizement was better accomplished through diplomatic channels. The days of bitter struggles, the machismo of hand to hand battle no longer was terribly appealing. In this atmosphere, lavish pleasure palaces, or even grand palaces of rule were to be found with only rudimentary fortification. The *Jag Mandir* and the *Jag Nivās* of Udaipur, along with the *Deeg-garh* became viable in their lack of impenetrable fortification. Later, such palaces as the *Chau Mahalla* of Hyderabad, the *Falaknama* near Hyderabad or the *Jai Vilas* at Gwalior were constructed without the expense of massive fortifications.

City Palace

Jaipur (1727- a. 1733 CE)

For the Kachwaha Rajputs, the *Rāj Mahal* at Amber was no longer a tenable capital — furthermore, it was too small! In 1727 CE, Sri Sawai Mahārājā Jaya Singh II (r. 1727-1743 CE) (See: **Appendix B**), having considered himself too important for the "small" *Rāj Mahal*, decided to move his regnal city to Jaipur. The perceived import of this powerful ruler demanded, in his mind, a more expansive and magnificent palace; expansion of Amber was not a consideration. Jaipur, one of the most notable capital cities of the Rajputana, was constructed by this puissant monarch. The move was accomplished in the year 1733.

Based upon a *Pīṭha Maṇḍala*, with the palace complex occupying the *brahmāsthāna*, the city grew as did the *City Palace* (See: **Figure 144**). Not a *garh mahal* in the traditional sense since the fortifications were minimal, the *City Palace of Jaipur* as designed, constructed and fortified was singularly undefendable to a concerted direct attack or a prolonged siege. This made it unique amongst the *garh mahal*s of the rulers of the Rajputana to that date. Two substantially defensive forts overlooked the city on high ground which might have allowed for the palace to assume its present character — i.e., the *Nahargarh* and the *Ambargarh*.

There are a number of ways in which *City Palace of Jaipur*[150] differs from other *garh mahal*s within India. First, Jaipur was initially designed on a grid with wide avenues along the *pada* markers and gates at the termini (See: **Figure 144**). In part, due to the lay of the land, a strict *Pīṭha Maṇḍala* of nine squares was not employed, but was modified as seen in **Figure 144**. Further, the orientation of Jaipur is 15^0 from true north-south. It is supposed that this was because Jai Singh oriented the city to the Lion of the Zodiac — the lion being the family symbol of the Kachwahas of Jaipur.

A second variation is to be seen in the relative size of the *zenānā* in comparison to other areas, particularly within the residential-

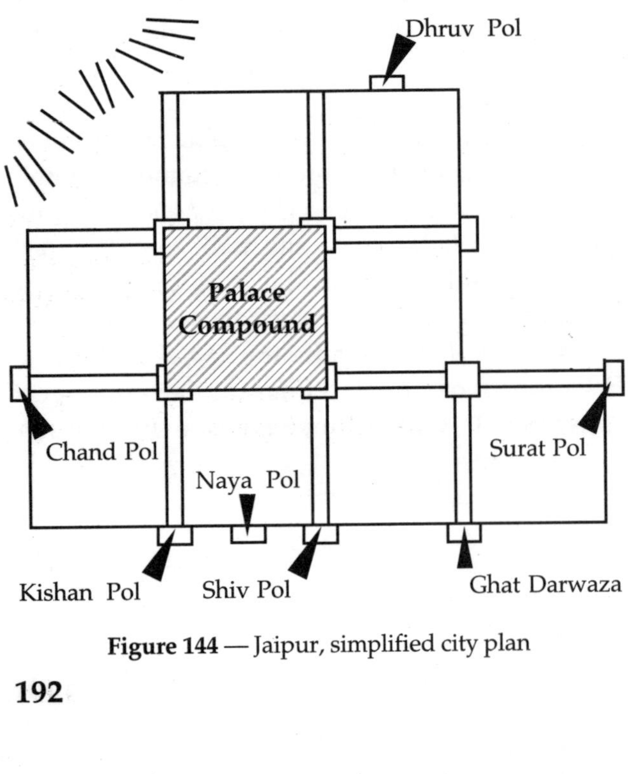

Figure 144 — Jaipur, simplified city plan

Legend for **Plate 58**

A	Jai Nivās
B	to Jaleb Chowk
C	Vijay Pol
D	Jay Pol
E	Sabhā Nivās Chowk
F	Chandra Mahal
G	Pritam Nivās
H	Pritam Nivās Chowk
I	Ganesh Pol
J	Sarvato Bhadra Chowk
K	Sarvato Bhadra (Diwān-i Khās)
L	Ambā Pol
M	Sabhā Nivās (Diwān-i Ām)
N	Anand Mahal
O	Rajendra Pol
P	Mubārak Mahal Chowk
Q	Mubārak Mahal
R	to Jantar Mantar
S	Zenānā
T	to Tripolia

Plate 58 — *City Palace*, Jaipur, plan of ceremonial and residential area (partial)

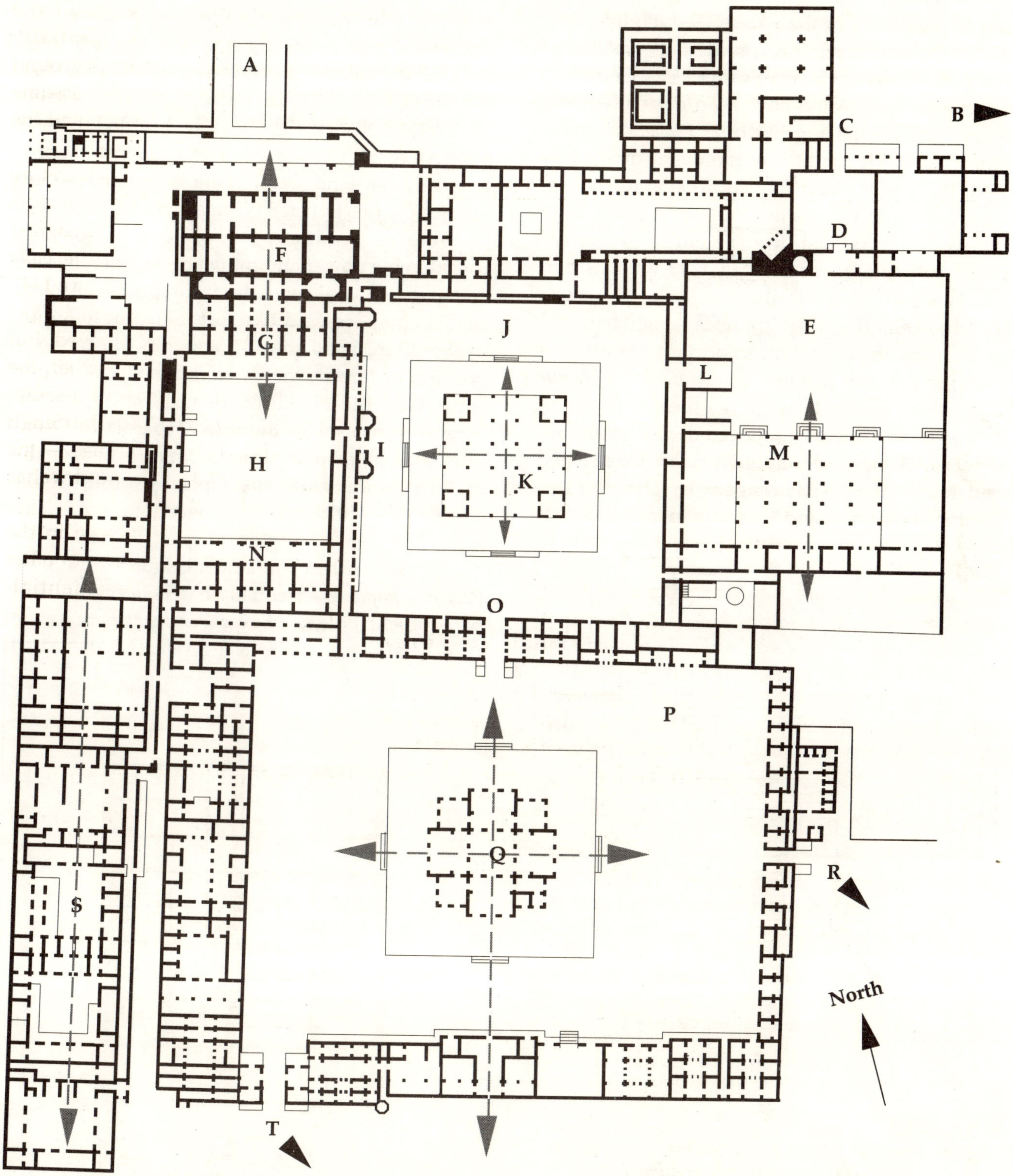

ceremonial areas of the palace (See: **Figure 145**). In *City Palace of Jaipur* it is considerably smaller, in comparison as seen in other *garh mahals*. Certainly, the comparison would have been more favorable if one removes the large *Mubārak Mahal Chowk*, as indicated in **Figure 145** by the dash-square (— —). This *chowk* was a later addition to the whole. As a possible compensation, the famed *Hawa Mahal* (Palace of the Winds) (to the right of the partial plan of **Plate 58**) was built in 1799 with its two courts was assigned to the women of the court, thereby, enlarging their confines somewhat.

The third, and an important variation is found in the clear fact that the *City Palace of Jaipur* was not as easily defended as the *Rāj Mahal* of Amber. Other rulers had moved their capitals, but only when their original *garh mahal* was sieged and fell — e.g., Vijayanagara to Chandragiri, Chittor to Udaipur, and Mandore to Jodhpur. This was not the case with the move from the impressive bastion of Amber's *Rāj Mahal* to Jaipur! By 1733 the tribal feuds between the Rajputs and the wars with Muslim rulers had not ceased completely. Nonetheless, they had settled to such a degree that the construction of a *garh mahal* upon relatively flat land was not altogether untenable. Many view this transfer as unusual but it "indicates Jai Singh's boldness"[151] not to mention his considerable power and influence. Further, he still had tight control over the impregnable Amber citadel and possessed two forts adjacent to Jaipur — should the need arise. To underline the tenuous position of Jaipur, the Sawai Mahārājā of Jaipur supported the elevation of the *Thakur* Badan Singh's successor to the title Mahārājā of Deeg. This was obviously done to insure his north-eastern border from the rapacious and highly effective agriculturalist-cum-warriors — i.e., the Jats.

Set within the central square, the *City Palace of Jaipur* is essentially based upon multiple perpendicular axes.[152] Several of its structures are cross axial — e.g., the *Sarvato Bhadra* (*Diwān-i Khās*)

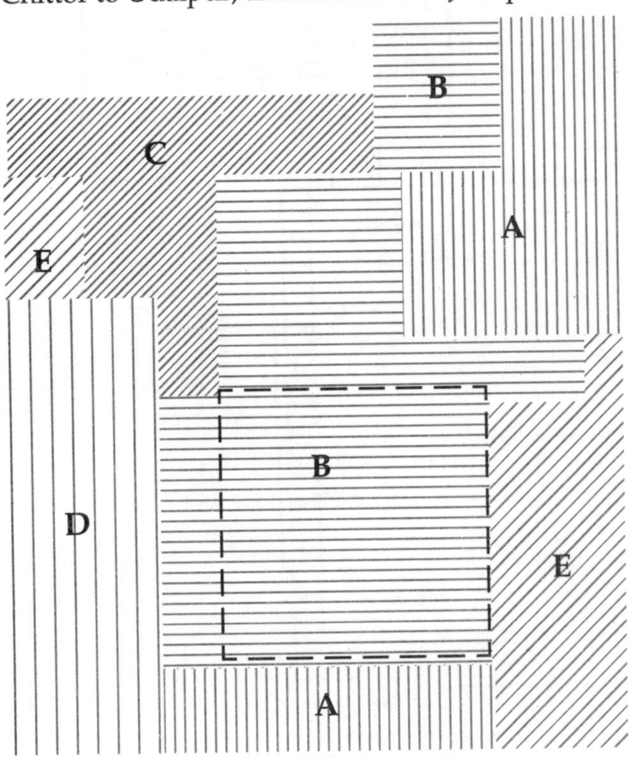

Figure 145 — Distribution of areas, *City Palace, Jaipur*; public areas (**A**), limited access areas (**B**), restricted (**C**), *zenānā* (**D**), attendents and military (**E**)

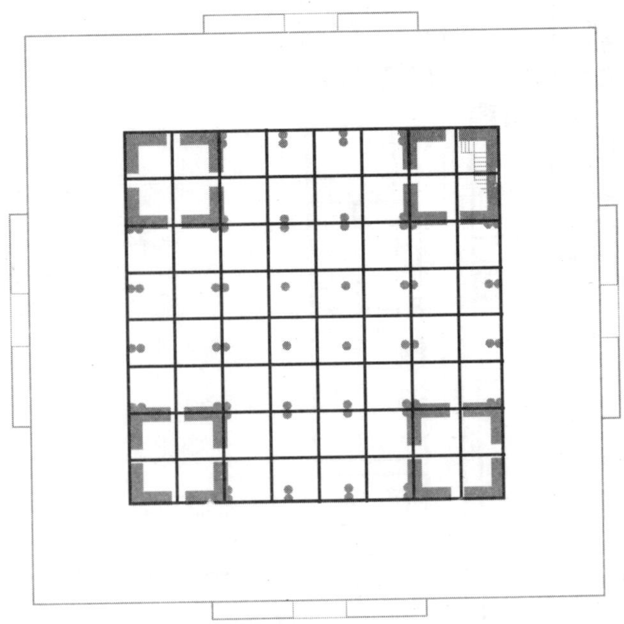

Figure 146 — *Sarvato Bhadra, City Palace, Jaipur*; indicating *Maṇḍūka Maṇḍala*

City Palace of Jaipur (Concluded)

(See: **Plate 58 — K**) and the *Mubārak Mahal* (See: **Plate 58 — Q**). There are five major courtyards or *chowks* associated with the *City Palace of Jaipur* — e.g., *Jaleb Chowk* (See: **Plate 58 — B**), *Sabhā Nivās Chowk* (See: **Plate 58 — E**), *Pritam Nivās Chowk* (See: **Plate 58 — H**), *Sarvato Bhadra Chowk* (See: **Plate 58 — J**), and *Mubārak Mahal Chowk* (See: **Plate 58 — P**). Additionally, there are the traditional seven gates (Indic: *pol*). Four are indicated in **Plate 58** — i.e., the *Vijay Pol* (See: **Plate 58 — C**), the *Jay Pol* (See: **Plate 58 — D**), the *Ambā Pol* (See: **Plate 58 — L**) and the *Ganesh Pol* (See: **Plate 58 — I**) — the latter leading into the *Pritam Nivās Chowk*, or the inner confines of the palace. Access to the ruler would have had to follow this circumlocutious route. Unlike the *Mān Mandir* at Gwalior, *Rāj Mahal* at Amber, or the *City Palace* of Udaipur, all of which assumed an elongated plan due to their geographic locale; the *City Palace of Jaipur* tends to be more compact, nearly square in area, again due to its locale and the unique design of the city.

Two structures are of interest: the *Sarvato Bhadra*, sometimes referred to as the original *Diwān-i Ām* (*c.* 1733) (See: **Figure 146**), and the *Mubārak Mahal* (a. 1875 CE) (See: **Figure 147**). They are of interest as both appear to conform to the standards established in the *śilpa śastras*. As indicated in the **Figures**, both appear to be designed with the *Maṇḍūka Maṇḍala* in mind. The podium upon which both rest is two *pada* wider. This, then forms a *Deśiya Maṇḍala* (See: **Figure 148**). This is particularly interesting when considering the *Mubārak Mahal* which was designed in the late nineteenth century by the British architect S. S. Jacob.

Unique in many aspects, common in others,[153] the *City Palace of Jaipur* is, nonetheless a most interesting *garh mahal*. The term *garh mahal* may no longer apply to this palace, as it is more residence (*mahal*) than fort (*garh*). In many ways it is parallel to its contemporary neighbour — i.e., the *Deeg-garh* (*Bagh Mahal* or *Garden Palace*) — a relatively short distance to the north-east. The *City Palace of Jaipur* also indicates the character of its founder: the proud Sri Sawai Mahārājā Jaya Singh II.

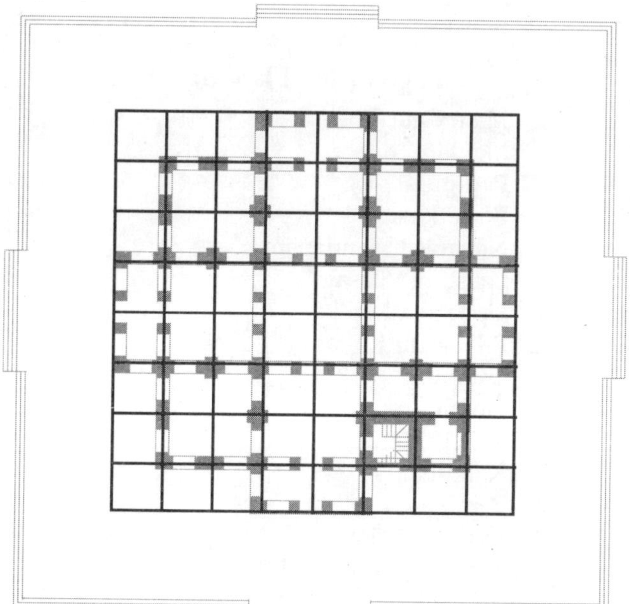

Figure 147 — *Mubārak Mahal, City Palace, Jaipur;* indicating *Maṇḍūka Maṇḍala*

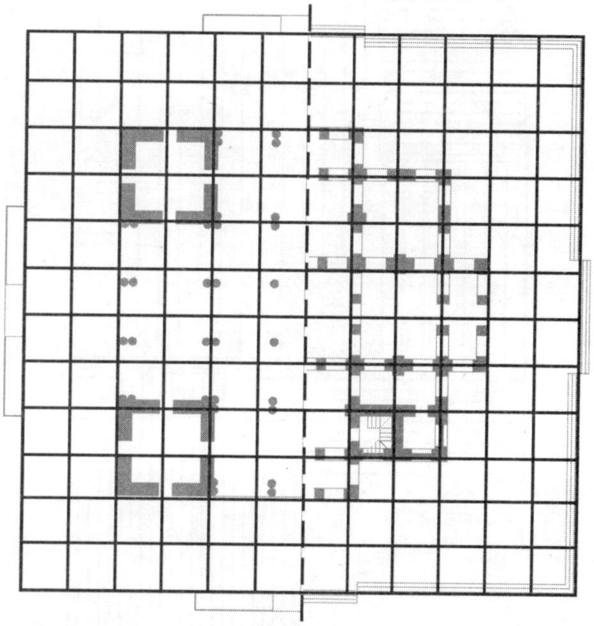

Figure 148 — *Sarvato Bhadra* (left) & *Mubārak Mahal* (right), *City Palace, Jaipur;* indicating *Deśiya Maṇḍala* over platform

Padmanabhapuram

Kanyakumari, (1729-1758 CE)

Far away from the maddening crowd and the political upheavals of the Deccan region, Rajputana and imperial Delhi, the Travancore Rajas, later elevated to Mahārājā status, of south Kerala reigned. The Rājā Martanda Varma III (r. 1729-1758 CE) (See: **Appendix B**) the second of the Cheraman (Kulashekhara) Dynasty constructed a new *garh mahal*, the *Padmanabhapuram*[154] (City of Vishnu Padmanabha). The Cheraman Dynasty reigned in Kanyakumari until 1790 when the capital was moved to Trivandrum by Rājā Rama Varma II (r. 1758-1798). *Padmanabhapuram* then became the summer palace of the rulers of Travancore.

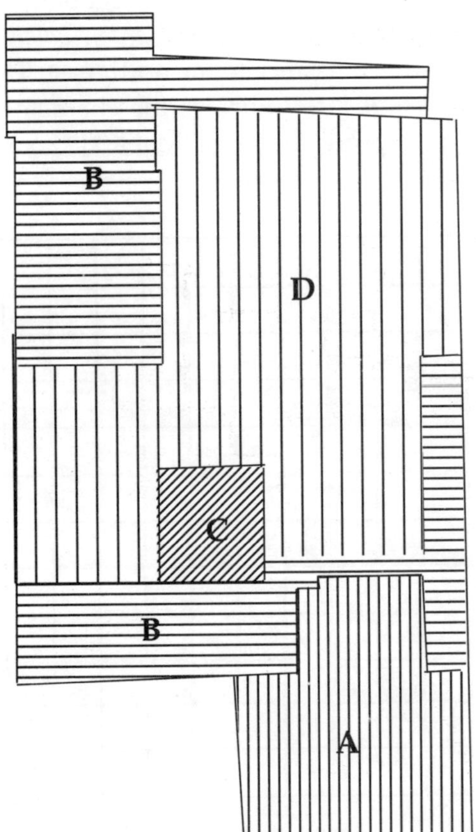

Figure 149 — Distribution of areas of access, *Padmanabhapuram*; public areas (**A**), limited access areas

Of all the *garh mahals* of India, the major structures of *Padmanabhapuram* are singular in that they are primarily constructed of wood rather than the more permanent stone or masonry. Prior to the late Thirteenth Century, the vast majority of royal residences were constructed of wood. Little wonder that there are no examples of *garh mahals* prior to that period. It is probably due to the fact that this region of India did not suffer the strife that the central and northern states suffered. In addition, the *Padmanabhapuram* was retained as a summer residences by the Rajas of Travancore which may have added to its fine state of preservation.

As with most *garh mahals*, there are distinct areas of access. These areas at *Padmanabhapuram* include: public access (See: **Figure 149 — A**), limited access (See: **Figure 149 — B**), restricted areas (See: **Figure 149 — C**), and the *zenānā* (See: **Figure 149 — D**).

Padmanabhapuram is further divided into four distinct courts (See: **Plate 59 — I - IV**). The *First Court* (**I**) is entered after passing through the *Main Gate*, crossing a *maidān* and then through

Legend for **Plate 51**

A	Main Gate (Pol)
B	Maidān
C	Padipura
D	Pumukham
E	Navarātrī Maṇḍapam
F	Lakshmi Vilāsam
G	Upparika Malika
H	Pilamuttu Kottaram
I	Uttapura
J	Homapura
K	Thai Kottaram
L	Kalkulam
M	Temple
N	Indra Vilāsam
I	1st compound
II	2nd compound
III	3rd compound
IV	4th compound

Plate 59 — *Padmanabhapuram*, plan (partial)

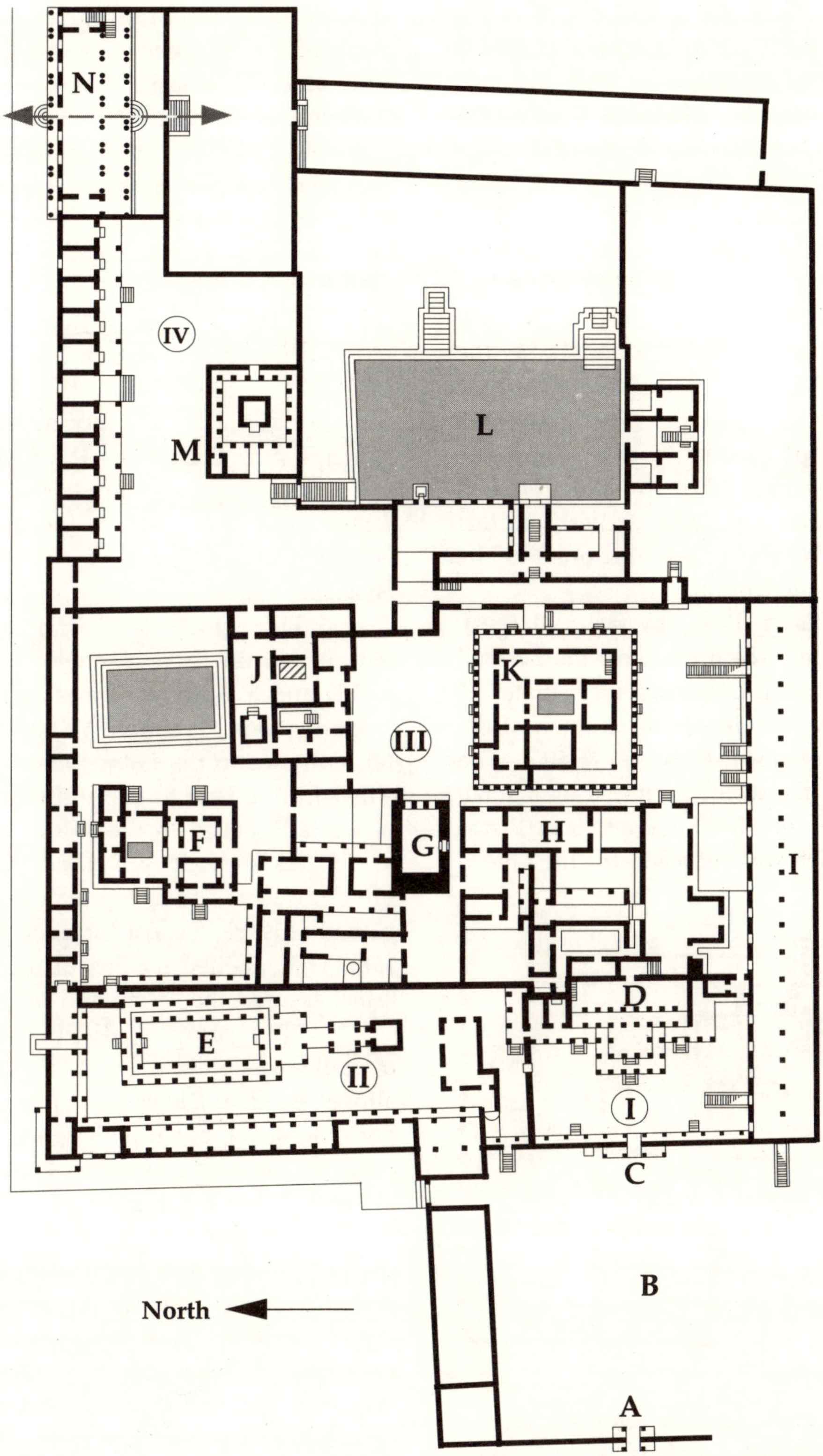

the *Padipura* (See: **Plates 59 & 60 — A, B & C**). This court is the smallest of the four enclosed spaces and holds the *Pumukham* or Hall of Public Audience (*diwān-i ām*) (See: **Plates 59 & 60 — D**). Here the open space in front of the Audience Hall is more limited than has been seen in other *garh mahals* in this study.

The *Second Court* (**II**) is entered either from the *maidān*, the *First Court* or from a gate at the northern end. This court consists of a long rectangle running south to north and holds the *Navarātrī Maṇḍapam* (Dance Hall) (See: **Plates 59 & 60 — E**). This large, open pavilion possesses support columns of carved stone around the inner rectangular area with a floor of polished gypsum. Named after the Navarātrī festival, this pavilion allowed lavish celebrations to be witnessed by a limited public.

The *Third Court* (**III**) is by far the largest. It contains the *zenānā* which contains: the *Lakshmi Vilāsam* and the *Pilamuttu Kottaram* (See: **Plates 59 & 60 — F & H**) two residences for women of the *zenānā*, the *Homapura* (See: **Plates 59 & 60 — J**) a ritual structure for the women with its own small tank and a temple, the *Thai Kottaram* (See: **Plates 59 & 60 — K**) which was set aside for the Queen Mother and her entourage, a small tank to the north of the *Homapura*, the *Kalkulam* (See: **Plates 59 & 60 — L**), a large tank or reservoir, and the *Upparika Malika* (See: **Plates 59 & 60 — G**). It is the *Upparika Malika*, the tallest structure at *Padmanabhapuram* that was the residence of the Raja. It contained four storeys. The ruler's bedroom was on the third and a bed chamber assigned to the Lord Vishnu Padmanabha occupied the uppermost floor. The walls of this structure were constructed of masonry unlike the walls of any of the other buildings in this complex. Finally, the strangely proportioned *Uttupura* (See: **Plate 59 — I**) a two storey structure for dining may be entered from the *Third Court* either into the first or second storeys. An entrance to the first storey is also found in the *First Court*.

Figure 150 — *Padmanabhapuran*, Kanyakumari, indicating path from *Padi Pura* to *Upparika Malika*

The *Fourth Court* (**IV**) contained a small temple within its own enclosure (See: **Plate 59 — M**) and a suite of offices and a residence for foreign visitors, the *Indra Vilāsam* (See: **Plate 59 — N**). Entrance to the *Indra Vilāsam* may be gained either from a lane to the north or through a series of walled spaced to the south.

As with all *garh mahal*, direct, unimpeded physical access to the ruler's residence is to be gained only via a most tortuous path (See: **Figure 150**). This, abetted by the fortification of the *garh mahal* assured the safety and security of the ruler.

"The complex displays no evidence of overall axial planning. . . ."[155] This quote is not altogether true. *Padmanabhapuram* is neither axial, nor cross axial, but it is designed around multiple perpendicular axiality (See: **Plate 60**), the temple of the *Homapura* being oriented towards the east.

Padmanabhapuram conforms to virtually all the parameters of a royal complex. It is further noteworthy in that as an essentially wooden structure which has been maintained it offers us a rare glimpse into what older wooden *garh mahals* might have resembled. Its basic wood fabrication does not diminish its importance.

Plate 60 — *Padmanabhapuram*, plan detail, compound I, II & III indicating multiple perpendicular axiality

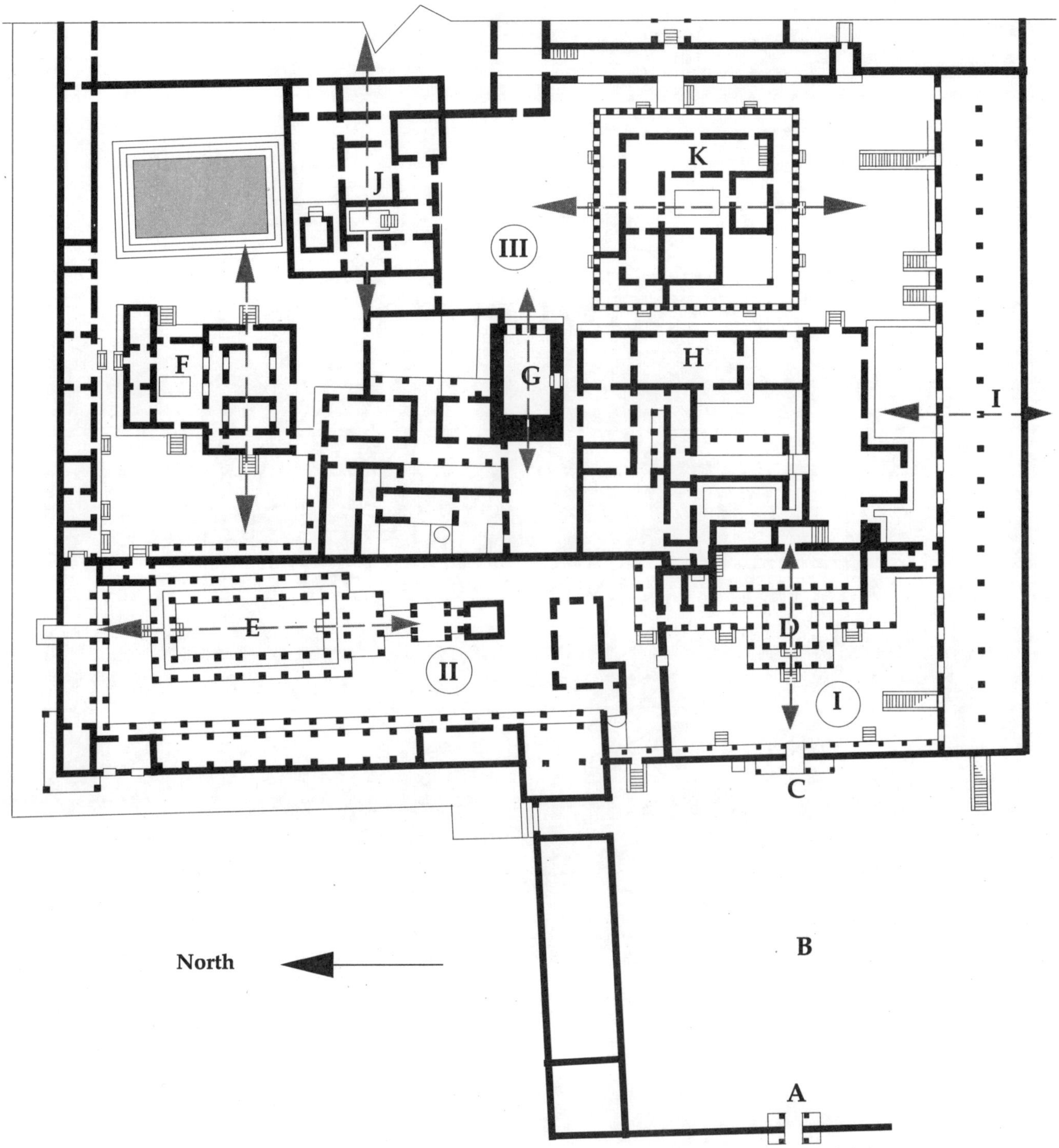

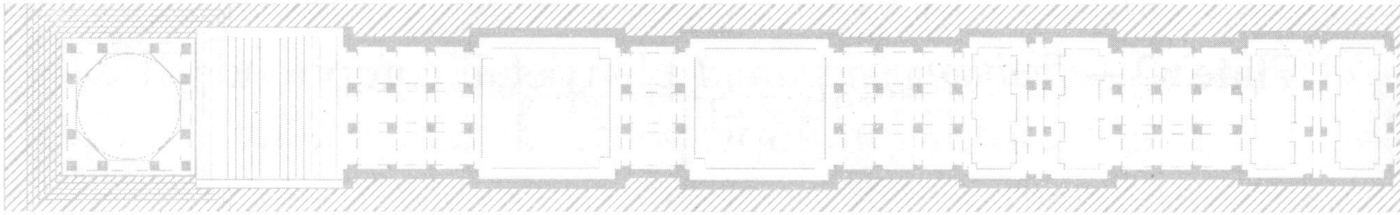

Conclusions

The immensely powerful and wealthy Sangamas, the *Rāyas* of Vijayanagara constructed a vast *garh mahal* (fortified citadel/palace) after 1350. The *Vijayanagara Kotla* stood in lordly splendour near the Tungabhadra River for nearly two centuries. In 1459 the Marwar, *Rao* Jodha transferred his capital from Mandore to Jodhpur, and raised one of the most impregnable fortresses in India. This transfer was due to the fact that the ruler saw a need for a more defensible capital. The Mewars under the rule of the *Maharana* Udaya Singh II, shifted their capital from the highly fortified Chittor to the more pleasing prospects of Udaipur in 1567. Thus, the move created a city of some security as well as one containing some of the most aesthetically pleasing palaces in India. In 1565 the *Vijayanagaran* Empire suffered a stunning defeat and the Tuluva Rāya Sadashivarāya moved his capital to Penukonda. He was quickly followed by the Saluva Rāya, Tirumala I, who again moved in 1569; this time to the relative remoteness of Chandragiri. The Jat Badan Singh of Sinsini, who had raised from the rank of a *vaiśya* farmer to ruler and *Rājā* of Deeg, constructed the palatial ensemble — i.e., the *Deeg-garh* (Garden Palace) — after 1722. *Mahārājā* Sawai Jai Sing transferred his capital from Amber to Jaipur in 1727, far less defensible, merely because he wanted a larger capital.

The citadels, *garh mahals*, palaces and royal pavilions of India are myriad. Their size, elaborateness of design and employment of costly materials is second to none in panoply of world cultures. Europe may have had defensible forts or castles — e.g., Chinon, Heidelberg, Warwick, Edinburgh, Segovia, Salzburg or Urbino — but they do not compare in size or luxury or elaborateness to many of the *qilā* or *garh mahals* of India.

From the thirteenth century through the eighteenth century the growth and development of royal structures utilizing more permanent materials is noteworthy. That is not to say that earlier periods did not employ such permanent materials as fired brick and/or stone in the raising of their various structures. However, the invading Turko-Afghani-Persio Muslims brought with them the predilection for the employment of more permanent material. Certainly, sun-baked bricks and wood which had been employed for millennia in the vast subcontinent could be fashioned into suitable royal structures of stunning beauty. One merely needs to look at impressive *Padmanabhapuram* at Kanyakumari (1729-1758 CE) to understand that elegant luxury does not depend solely on fired bricks and stone.

The royal palaces, residences and pavilions of India in the elemental design of their plans are unique. This uniqueness, in great part, is based upon the employment of ancient treatises of design — e.g., the *Manasara*, *Mayamatam* and *Arthaśāstra*. These treaties, the *śilpa-śāstra*, were instituted, developed, codified and finally found their way into written form over a period of centuries. Certainly, rudimentary forms were devised soon after the Indo-European (Āryan) invasion, BCE

For the Hindu, the most perfect, preferred plan was based upon the immutable square. This can be seen employed even by the early Muslim invaders as well — e.g., the *Tomb of Firuz Shah* attached to the *Haus Khas* (See: **Plate 1**; see also: **Figure 18**); the *Kotla Firuz Shah*, Delhi (See: **Plate 2**); various pavilions of *Vijayanagara*, such as: the *100-Columned Pavilion, Mahavanami Platform* or the *Square Water Pavilion* (See: **Plate 3**); the *Palace of Baz Bahadur* at Maṇḍu (See: **Plate 6**); the *Bathing Tank, Kalyāṇa Mahal* and the *Royal Residence* at

Gingee (See: **Plate 14**); the entrance pavilion of the *Wav Dādā Harir* (Baoli Bāi Hari) at Asarwa (See: **Plates 15** & **16**); the Square Pavilion of the Water Pavilion at Kumatagi (See: **Plate 18**; and **Figure 55**); the Bundelkhand's *Rāja Mandir* of Orchha (See: **Plates 19-21**); *Fatehpur-Sikri* possesses the *Diwān-i-Khās*, and the *Anup Talao* (*Char Chaman*) (See: **Plates 26** & **27**); the *Amar Vilas* of the *City Palace* of Udaipur (See: **Plate 38**; and **Figures 98** & **99**); the *Farah Bagh* (aka *Feria Bagh*) at Ahmadnagar (See: **Plate 39**); the *Jahangir Mandir* of Orchha (See: **Plates 42** & **43**); the *Govind Mandir* of Datiya (See: **Plates 44-46**); the *Shahi Bagh* of Ahmadabad (See: **Plate 49**); the various gardens of the *Lāl Qilā, Shahjahanabad* of Delhi (See: **Plate 50**); *Deeg-garh's Keshav Badon* and the *Suraj Bagh* (See: **Plates 56** & **57**; and **Figures 138-141**); and the *Sarvato Bhadra* (*Diwān-i-Khās*) as well as the *Mubārak Mahal* of Jaipur (See: **Plate 58**; and **Figures 147** & **148**). Other structures deviate from the square, but adhere to other *śilpa-śāstra* designs — e.g., the *Rāja Mahal* of the *Chandragiri Palace* is an example of the *dandaka* design.

Many of the Muslim royal palaces, residences and pavilions do not, understandably, conform to the *śilpa-śāstra* design elements. What is interesting is the structures and ensembles of the Hindu rulers which appear to deviate dramatically from these treatises — e.g., the *Kumbhalgarh* (aka *Rānā Kumbha Mandir* or *Kumbhalmer*) of the Sisodias Rajput at Chittor (See: **Plate 10**); the highly eccentric *Meherangarh* of Jodhpur (See: **Plate 11**); the *Mān Mandir* of *Rājā* Man Singh Tomar at Gwalior (See: **Plate 12**); the *City Palace* of Udaipur (with the exception noted above) (See: **Plate 38**); the *Rāj Mahal* of the Kachwaha Rajput at Amber (See: **Plate 40**); the *Jag Mandir* of Udaipur (See: **Plates 47** & **48**); the *Nāyaka Mahal* of Madurai (See: **Plate 55**); the major structures of the *Jat's Deeg-garh* at Deeg (with the exception noted above) (See: **Plate 56**); the *City Palace* of Jaipur (with the exception noted above) (See: **Plate 58**); and the complex *Padmanabhapuram* at Kanyakumari (See: **Plate 59**). It must be noted, however, that the majority of those cited immediately above were constructed after the mid sixteenth century — after the establishment of the highly influential and incredibly powerful Mughal Empire.

The royal palaces, pavilions and residences must all be viewed as not mere residences or dwellings of the particular rulers or collateral families. They are clear and manifest indications of rule. The luxury of rare and/or costly materials employed and the vast spaces, both enclosed and open air, underline the right of rule. These are dwellings, edifices of and for the ruling elite of the various kingdoms, sultānates and empires.

The predominant design element of the various royal palaces, residences and pavilions throughout the region (including the Mediterranean region) indicates a tendency towards axiality (See: **Plates 63, 64, 65, 66, 67, 72, 82, 84** & **92**). Of course the Hindu predilection for the square implies cross-axiality (See: **Plate 114**). However, where the square is not applied, axiality reigns. There are examples of rotating axiality (See: **Plate 111**), but they are few compared to the first two design parameters noted above. Frequently, multiple perpendicular axiality (See: **Plate 112**) tends to be the norm, particularly where an ensemble has been added on to over successive generations — e.g., the *Haus Khas* of Delhi (See: **Plate 1**); the *Shadiabad Mandir* at Mandu (See: **Plate 6**); elements of the *Bidargarh* of Bidar (See: **Plate 9**); the Kumbhalgarh at Chittor (See: **Plate 10**). Gwalior's *Mān Mandir* (See: **Plate 12**); elements of the Mughal's *Lāl Qilā* at Agra (See: **Plate 23**); Akbar's *Fatehpur Sikri* (See: **Plate 26**); the *Chandragiri Palace* ensemble near Tirupati (See: **Plates 35** & **36**); the vast *City Palace* of Udaipur (See: **Plate 38**); the Kachwaha Rajput's *Rāj Mahal* at Amber (See: **Plate 40**); the

Conclusions (Continued)

elegant *Jag Mandir* of Udaipur (See: **Plates 47 & 48**); the sumptuous *Lāl Qilā, Shahjahanabad* of Delhi (See: **Plate 50**); the Thirumala Nāyaka Dynasty's Nāyaka Mahal at Madurai (See: **Plate 55**); the *Deeg-garh* (Garden Palace) at Deeg (See: **Plate 56**); the *City Palace* of Jaipur (See: **Plate 58**); and the *Padmanabhapuram* at Kanyakumari (See: **Plate 59**). Strict adherence to the *śilpa-śāstras* may not have been followed, however, axiality or multiple perpendicular axiality was, almost without exception, the rule. The major exception, and one may add, an exception with a vengeance, is the *Meherangarh* of Jodhpur (See: **Plate 11**). The *Meherangarh* may be characterized as the only *garh mahal* within this study that exhibits multiple non-perpendicular axiality (See: **Plate 113**).

With axiality symmetry tends to follow. Even in a *garh mahal* where multiple non-perpendicular axiality exists, individual structures often times are symmetrical — e.g., the *Shish Mahal*, the *Fateh Mahal*, the *Zenānā Mahal*, and the *Moti Mahal* all of the *Meherangarh* of Jodhpur (See: **Plate 11**). Numerous multiple perpendicular axial ensembles which are essentially asymmetrical, possess structures which are symmetrical — e.g., the *Kumbhalgarh* at Chittor (See: **Plate 10**): the *Tripolia*, and the *Reception Area*; the *Mān Mandir* of Gwalior (See: **Plate 12**): the *Second Court* and the *Reception Area*; the *Bidargarh* (See: **Plate 9**) of Bidar: the *Diwān-i Ām*; the *Shadiabad* (See: **Plate 6**) at Mandu: *Lal Mahal* and the *Mosque of Dilwar Khan*; as well as numerous structures found in the *Lāl Qilā* of Agra (See: **Plate 23**).

The sacred structures of the major world religions tend to be found in specific orientations or alignments. Buddhist and Hindu sacred temples generally tend to be aligned east to west. Major and important Christian churches, specifically cathedrals, are to be found oriented west to east, and all Muslim mosques are aligned towards Mecca. The powerful Genghis Khan made sure that his *yurt* faced south as he believed that all good news and fair winds came from that direction. The *Forbidden City* of Beijing faces south, the direction of the sun at its zenith; the Emperor was often referred to as the "Son of Heaven." So too, the majority of the Ming Tombs faced south. The megalithic *Stonehenge* near Salisbury was aligned to the solstice.

The royal palaces, residences and pavilions tend to be oriented, for the most part towards the cardinal points of the compass. East-west alignment tends to appear most often in the ensembles under consideration. Doubtless this is, in part, due to the *śilpa śāstras* — e.g., *Kumbhalgarh* at Chittor (See: **Plate 10**); *Aināpur Mahal* at Aināpur faces east (See: **Plate 17**); the *Rāja Mandir* at Orchha faces east (See: **Plate 19**); *Lāl Qilā* of Agra is oriented east-west (See: **Plate 23**); the *Rānā Mahal* at Chandragiri (See: **Plate 36**); the *Jahangir Mandir* of Orchha (See: **Plate 42**); the *Govind Mandir* at Datiya (See: **Plate 44**); *Jag Mandir* of Udaipur faces east (See: **Plate 47**); the *Shahi Bagh* of Ahmadabad (See: **Plate 49**); *Lāl Qilā, Shahjahanabad* of Delhi (See: **Plate 50**); the *Daulat Kothi* of Bijapur faces east (See: **Plate 53**); the *Athar Mahal* (aka: *Dad Mahal, Ashar Mahal, Mubārak Mahal, Athar Sharif*) of Bijapur (See: **Plate 54**); and the *Nāyaka Mahal* at Madurai (See: **Plate 55**). The north-south alignment is less frequently encountered — e.g., *Hauz Khas* at Delhi (See: **Plate 1**); *Shadiabad* at Mandu, except the mosque (See: **Plate 6**); the *Mān Mandir* at Gwalior (See: **Plate 12**); the *Gingee Mandir* at Gingee tends to be south to north (See: **Plate 14**); the *Gagan Mahal* at Bijapur faces north (See: **Plate 22**); the *Rāja Mahal* at Chandragiri (See: **Plate 35**); the *City Palace* of Udaipur (See: **Plate 38**); and the *City Palace* of Jaipur (although not strictly aligned) (See: **Plate 58**). Many of the larger, more complex *garh mahal* tend to be oriented to the various cardinal points — e.g., *Vijayanagara Kotla,* Vijayanagara (See: **Plate 3**); *Bidargarh* (*Qilā* and *Mandir*) at Bidar (See: **Plate**

9); the *Meherangarh* at Jodhpur (See: **Plate 11**); *Fatehpur Sikri* (See: **Plate 26**); the *Deeg-garh* (Garden Palace) at Deeg (See: **Plate 56**); and the *Padmanabhapuram* at Kanyakumari (See: **Plate 59**). Finally, an anomaly found within the various royal palaces, residences and pavilions is the *Rāj Mahal* of Amber which is oriented northeast-southwest (See: **Plate 40**). This, in part, may be due to its geographical locale.

With the exception of the pavilions under consideration — i.e., the *Kotla Firuz Shah*, Delhi (See: **Plate 3**); the *Gujari Mahal* at Gwalior (See: **Plate 13**); the *Wav Dādā Harir* (*Baoli Bai Hari*) at Aswara (See: **Plate 15**); the *Aināpur Mahal* at Aināpur (See: **Plate 17**); the *Water Pavilion* at Kumatagi (See: **Plate 18**); the *Gagan Mahal* at Bijapur (See: **Plate 22**); the *Farah Bagh* at Ahmadnagar (See: **Plate 39**); the *Jag Mandir* at Udaipur (See: **Plate 47**); and the *Shahi Bagh* at Ahmadabad (See: **Plate 49**) — the majority of the *garh mahal* were constructed upon hills, islands or rocky escarpments. The exceptions were the *City Palace* of Jaipur (See: **Plate 58**) and the *Deeg-garh* at Deeg (See: **Plate 56**). The high place was not merely defensive, it literally raised the ruler above the populous — i.e., separating the ruler physically and iconographically. The palaces, the *garh mahal* of the Bundelkhand (See: **Plates 19, 40 & 44**), Jodhpur (See: **Plate 11**) and Udaipur (See: **Plate 38**) are salient examples of the residence upon high ground.

Many of the royal palaces and/or residences possessed a labyrinthine character. Not only the larger *garh mahal*s which had developed over generations — such as, the *City Palace* at Udaipur (See: **Plate 38**) — but many of the smaller residences possessed a complex maze of rooms, corridors and stairways as well as hidden passageways. A prime example of the latter is the *Rāja Mandir* at Orchha (See: **Plates 19-21**), a smaller residence by contemporary standards. The *Rāja Mandir* not only had a bewildering assortment of rooms and stairways within its three storeys, it also possessed hidden passageways on every level (See: **Plates 19 & 20**). The labyrinth, as the high place, was a defensive iconograph, protecting the ruler by allowing him secret or, at least, quick egress particularly in times of trouble.

Virtually all the rulers of India, as well as other cultures, wrested their realms from others. Many of these rulers were not even sons of the soil.[156] The need to legitimize their reigns was fertilized in the concept of the "right to rule," or rule "by the Grace of God." This right, they attempted to justify by rule "by the Grace of God." Rulers are, or have been, an accepted practice around the world. Buddhist teachings listed the qualities associated with a Universal Monarch (Ind.: *chakravartin*) and this concept — i.e., the *Chakravartin* — was soon applied to Hindu rulers as well. However, few approached these laudable qualities. One may assert that a number of the forgoing iconic principles are tangentially related to the right to rule — i.e., the palace, the high place and the labyrinth. It must be assumed that the right to rule was highly coveted, hence the need to protect the person. Rule "by the Grace of God" must have been underlined by a basic paranoia which festered and caused, in part the raising of many of these impressive structures. The right to rule was never considered sacrosanct! Virtually every ruler, even the Great Akbar, was subject to assassination attempts. In the case of the Khaljiz, Nasir-ud-din Khusrav (See: **Appendix B**), among many, assassination was successful! Yet most rulers clung to the concept of rule by Divine Right.

Nothing could confirm the Right to Rule more than a lasting dynasty — i.e., one that spanned many generations. A well fortified palace that protected the ruler, hence the dynasty, became *de rigueur*. If a *garh mahal* proved defensively suspect the seat of rule was shifted

— e.g., the Rathor Rajputs of Marwar began in Kannauj, then shifted to Pali, then shifted to Mandore and finally shifted to Jodhpur where one of the most impressive and impregnable citadels was constructed. Many realms saw brief dynastic reigns — e.g., the Ganesh-Shahi Dynasty of Bengal lasted a mere twenty-two years (1415-1437 CE) (See: **Appendix B**). Few were as long lasting as the Sisodia Rajput Rawals of the Ahra Guhilot Dynasty of the small state: Dungarpur (1197-1948 CE) (See: **Appendix B**). It must be noted that those realms which saw frequent shifts of dynasties were frequently the richest or the largest — those which were the most coveted.

A number of physical elements were necessary for a royal palace or residence — i.e., royal accoutrements. Part of the right of the populous was to be able to ascertain on a regular, daily basis that the ruler was still in control, hence, the practice of *darśana*. This public viewing required a suitable venue that allowed both the common folk to view as well as a certain degree of security for the ruler. Often times this took the form of a viewing platform as seen in the *Vijayanagara Qilā* (See: **Plate 3 [N]**), or a physically separated and raised throne as seen in the *Diwān-i Ām* of the *Shahjahanabad, (Lāl Qilā)*, Delhi (See: **Plate 50 [R]**; see also: **Figure 132**). Similarly, ritualized or required bathing required rather elaborate structures within the *garh mahals* for this purpose. Again, the *Vijayanagara Qilā* possessed several tanks — e.g., the elaborate *Square Water Pavilion* (aka the *Queen's Bath*) (See: **Plate 3 [R]**; see also: **Plate 4** [bottom]); or the *Geometric Tank,* (See: **Plate 3 [O]**; see also: **Appendix A, Plate 93**); and, the *Hammam* of the *Shahjahanabad, (Lāl Qilā)*, Delhi (See: **Plate 50 [I]**; see also: **Plate 52 [Type F]**). Large areas were required and utilized for festivities, parades and military assemblies — e.g., the *Outer Court* of the *Shadiabad*, Mandu (See: **Plate 6 [C]**); the *Manek Chowk* of the *City Palace* at Udaipur (See: **Plate 38 [F]**); or the *Maidān* of *Padmanabhapuram* (See: **Plate 59 [B]**). These, and various other structures and areas were seen as requisite of a royal palace in India.

*Zenānā*s were certainly a royal accoutrement, but more than that they were a necessity for rule. The Muslim invaders, culturally found a need to segregate, to protect the women of the court, especially the wives and concubines. Apparently, the Indo-European (Āryan) rulers, at first, did not. Nonetheless, by the fifteenth Century, in the larger complexes (*garh mahal*s), this area became physically important and in some cases dominated the total area(s). The *zenānā* finds its way into the earliest examples of the *garh mahal*s under consideration. Both the Hindu *Vijayanagara Qilā* (See: **Plate 3**) and the *Shadiabad Mandir* (See: **Plate 6**) both possessed areas that may well have served this purpose of segregation although much of both *garh mahal*s are in such a state and extant literature is such that a specific area, a *zenānā* has not been precisely defined. In the *Kumbhalgarh* at Chittor the *zenānā* consisted of a large, complex court upon which numerous suites opened (See: **Plate 10 [H]**). At *Fatehpur Sikri*, the area restricted to women was large, indeed (See: **Plate 26, & Figures 70 & 78**) as was the *zenānā* at *Shahjahanabad* (*Lāl Qilā*) at Delhi (See: **Plate 50, & Figure 123**). The *City Palace* at Jaipur possessed a *zenānā*, but one which was not as important, area-wise, as those of the Muslim rulers noted above (See: **Plate 58, & Figure 145**). The royal palaces of the Bundelkhand rulers — i.e., the *Rāja Mandir* (See: **Plates 19 & 20**), the *Jahangir Mandir* (See: **Plates 40 & 41**),) and the *Govind Mandir* (See: **Plates 44-46**) are interesting in that there is no clear segregated area(s) or *zenānā* within these unique palaces.

The iconography of the royal palaces, residences and pavilions of India is complex and, in many areas, unique to this subcontinent. The evolution of rule, a universal development, was

Conclusions (Concluded)

influenced not only by the geography of the region, but also by the various invasions, particularly the Indo-European (Āryan)[155] and the Turko-Afghani (Mughal). By the Common Era numerous realms or areas of rule had developed and by the 11th century, clearly defined states had emerged. Their lust for power and aggrandizement created ever-changing borders. By the 13th century two clear modes emerged — one Hindu-based and one Muslim-oriented. Each possessed its own basis of power and by the 17th century, the reign of the Mughal Jahangir (r. 1606-1627), there was an assortment of Hindu and Muslim States existing cheek by jowl. This uneasy existence was, nonetheless, fertile ground and allowed for an intermixing of apparent cultural imperatives and ideas.

It is this mixing, this existence of two or even three religious cultures within a single region that makes the royal palaces, residences and pavilions of India truly unique. As a group the royal palaces, residences and pavilions appear to resemble one of the intricate fountain or waterways of Islam. A waterway or fountain in which the interlocking of positive and negative spaces is so complete, it is difficult to separate, to isolate either without irreparable damage to the whole, becomes an icon.

A final comment! These, the royal palaces, residences and pavilions, these brilliant structures, these aesthetically compelling monuments that, in part, define India's cultural past, came at an incredibly high cost to treasuries of the individual realms and an even higher price in human life. The separation (economic, social and physical) between the rulers and the populous became so vast as to be unbelievable! The royal palaces, residences and pavilions are monuments of the past that may best be laid in the past. But, without their existence, we would be somehow lessened, even bereft.

Notes

Iconography

1 Parmono Atmadi, *Some Architectural Design Principles of Temples in Java*. Yogyakarta: 1994, pp. 218-220.

2 *Ibid.*, these concepts have been shown by Atmadi to apply to temples of Java before and during the period in which *Borobudur* was constructed. See: specifically pp. 181-226; 314-318; 320-322, 352, and 381-382. It is also to be noted that the Indianized states of South-east Asia also utilized these proportions to greater or in the case of Thailand to lesser degrees.

3 Sterlin, Henri, ed. *Architecture of the World: India*. Lausanne: n. d. , pp. 15-19. Henri Sterlin is used extensively in this section.

4 Fredrick W. Bunce, *The Iconography of Plans: A Study of the Influence of Buddhism and Hinduism on Architectural Plans of South and South-east Asia*, New Delhi: 2002, pp. 11-13.

5 The terms referring to dwelling plans differ from the *Manasara* to the *Mayamatam*. The terms: *ekśālā, dviśālā, triśālā* and *caturśālā*, are those used in the *Manasara* to denote dwellings with one, two, three or four units. However, the *Mayamatam* utilizes the term: *dandaka* in referring to a dwelling of a single unit (*ekśālā*). Further, the *Mayamatam* denotes a number of roof-line variations within this *dandaka* plan — e.g., *maulika* type A & B, *svāstika* type, and *caturmukha* type A & B. Bruno Dagens (ed.) *Mayamatam: Treatise on Housing, Architecture and Iconography*. Delhi: 1994, vol. 2, pp. 517-529; and illustrated in vol. 1, p. lxxv.

6 The term *dviśālā* is referred to as *langala* (plough share) in the *Mayamatam*. This plan has three types of roof-line variations — e.g., the *dandavaktra* type, *svāstika* type and *caturmukha* type. *Ibid.*, vol. 2, pp. 529-531; and illustrated in vol. 1, pp. lxxvi-lxxvii.

7 The term *triśālā* refers to that dwelling which consists of three connected units forming a block "U" shape. In this plan there are but two types of roof-line variations — e.g., the *merukanta* type and the *maulibhadra* type. *Ibid.*, vol. 2, pp. 531-533; and illustrated in vol. 1, pp. lxxviii-lxxix.

8 The term *caturśālā* is applied to a dwelling with four connecting units forming an open court in the centre. There are five types with numerous variations — e.g., *sarvatobhadra, vardhamāna, svāstika, nandyavarta* and *rucaka*. *Ibid.*, vol. 2, pp. 533-61; and illustrated in vol. 1, pp. lxxx-lxxxiii.

9 *Ibid.*, vol. 2, p. 561.

10 *Ibid.*, vol. 1, p. lxxxiii.

11 BD, vol 2, p. 527. The "*maulika* (type) has a hipped roof or it has only one gable.[26]" Footnote 26 states: "An (sic) hipped roof . . . has no gable, while a single-gable roof is probably a single-hip-roof, that is to say an apsidal one. . . ." An "apsidal one" makes no sense in this context. Where the gable is constructed is 'up in the air!' This author believes that there are two possibilities. The first is illustrated in "maulika type A."

12 *Ibid.*

13 *Ibid.* The *Mayamatam* states "there is a forepart (?) at the back like the one in the front; (would this not be a 'back-court?') this makes four gables: . . ." Yet, the *ekśālā* is generally seen as a single, rectangular structure with a "forecourt" and not with a corresponding backcourt, although the possibility exists.

14 *Ibid.*, p. 539. It is to be noted that in the other types the number of dormers are listed. This may give rise to ***sarvatobhadra* type D**.

15 *Ibid.*, p. 555.

16 *Ibid.*, p. 559.

17 *Ibid.*, p. lxxxiii.

18 *Ibid.*, p. lxxxiv.

19 *Ibid.*, pp. lxxxvi, 627-39.

20 These numbers and the plan are taken from: *Ibid.*, p. lxxxvi.

21 Dwarfs and hunchbacks were also "collected" by the Courts of Europe. Foremost was the Courts of Spain where certain dwarfs were elevated to high positions within the government. Also, due to constant inbreeding with Southern European, Catholic royalty, many of the Austrian and Spanish Hapsburgs were dwarfish themselves.

22 BD, *op. cit.*, pp. lxxxviii (illus.), & 649-55. It is interesting to note that this palace plan resembles the *Temple of Śiva and Mīnākṣī* (See:).

23 The six rulers, from highest to lowest are: *chakravartin* (emperor); *adhirāja* who is a ruler of seven

kingdoms; *narendra* who rules three kingdoms; the *parshinika* who rules a single kingdom; a *pattadhara* who rules half a kingdom; the *mandalesha* who is the ruler of a province; the *pattabhaj* or *prabaraka* who is in charge of any of the four classes; and the *astragriha* the lowest of the six.

24 BD, *op. cit.*, pp. 645-49 and 655-61.

25 BD, *Ibid*, p. 645, states in note 77 that "it seems to comprise two enclosures only, in spite of the lengthy description . . . of a five enclosure arrangement." On the other hand, a five enclosure palace is stated to be that of an emperor (Ind.: *chakravartin*). It, therefore seems unlikely that this palace would contain five enclosures. **Figure 15** is conjectural, and indicates the two enclosure that Dagens refers to as well as what seems to be the possibility of a rectangular three enclosure palace.

26 Bruno Dagens, ed. & tr., *Mayamatam, Treatise of Housing, Architecture & Iconography* (2 vols.), New Delhi: 1994, Chapter 29, pp. 623-79.

27 In *Fatehpur Sikri*, the women's area(s) was vast in comparison to the public areas and the *mardānā*. Likewise, the *zenānā* of the *City Palace* of Udaipur was considerably larger than the *mardānā*. The fact that the *garh mahals* of the various rulers were generally only used for special festivals and *darbārs* made them less occupied by the ruler who frequently was at war or preferred other pleasure palaces to the *garh mahal*.

28 For example, the *Gingee Mandir*'s stables were, indeed, vast. They were proportionally larger than those found in many Indian palace complexes.

29 One may encounter axial arrangements in other Asian cultures — e.g., the *Forbidden City*, Beijing, or the *Kondo*, Nara — and, indeed, even in a number of European cultures as well — e.g., the central pavilion of the *Palace of Versailles* is essentially axial, or *Blenheim Palace*, Oxfordshire, or the *Amalienburg*, Munich. Cross-axiality is another matter. With the exception of the Renaissance and High Renaissance in Europe — e.g., *Santa Maria delle Caceri*, Prato, or *Tempietto*, Rome — cross-axiality is generally eschewed by the West. India, on the other hand, is literally a hotbed of cross-axiality in which examples spring up in every sphere — i.e., palaces, tombs, temples and *masjid*.

30 For example: the *Ladh Khan*, Aihole, the *garbhagṛha* of the *Subrahmanya Temple*, Manjeri, of the *Kitali Śiva Temple*, Thiruvanchikula, of the *Brahmeshvara Temple*, Bhubaneswar, to name but a few.

31 For example: the *Śiva Temple*, Indore; the *Śiva Temple*, Trichur; the *Śiva Temple*, Masaon (See: **Appendix A, Plate 61**); or the *Śiva Temple*, Chandrehe.

32 For example: the *Stūpa I*, Sanchi, the *Thuparama Dagoba*, Anuradhapura, or the fabulous *Borobudur*, Java. Although, Buddhist Pagan (Burma) employed the square in preference to the circle. This may have been due to the fact the Hindu brāhmaṇas were active members — i.e., the majordomos and *factotums* — of the Pagan Court.

33 The *Palace of the Louvre*, Paris, as well as *Buckingham Palace*, London, are two examples to which a structure was "added on" over a period of years.

34 GT 2, p. 36.

35 The Christian orientation tends to be from East to West — i.e., the sanctuary being in the East. Buddhist orientation depends upon a number of factors. Foremost being the preference of Theravada Buddhism to orient their temples towards water and preferably towards the East.

36 This orientation is based upon the alignment of the main entrance or the emperor's apartments, and additionally in the case of *Fatehpur Sikri*, the alignment of a number of the more important structures within this eclectic compound.

37 FWB, *Ibid*., pp. 31-32.

38 See: Fredrick W. Bunce, *Numbers, Their Iconographic Consideration in Buddhist and Hindu Practices*, New Delhi: 2002, pp. 19-21.

39 The concept of isolation within a labyrinth may be encountered in the *Palace of Knossos*, Crete, or in the *Great Zimbabwe*, or *Versailles*. It was carried to such extremes that in the *Forbidden City*, Beijing, the Emperor was confined to one of a series of inner apartments in a huge compound that was closed off to all men after dark. The exception were the small army of eunuchs who served the emperor and due to their physical mutilation were not considered "men."

40 The concept of Divine Right or "By the Grace of God" finds numerous parallels throughout the world — e.g., in Malaysia, as Sultān is so "*dengan keizinan Nya (Allah)*." Here, "with God's permission" is a bit more forceful or positive than is "By the Grace of God." To the Islamic world a Sultān or King is so "with God's permission."

Notes (Continued)

[41] This concept, *le droit de seigneur,* was practised by many lords (*seigneurs*) of medieval Europe — i.e., the right to deflower a young maiden on her wedding night. This was done, particularly in areas that were newly conquered as a means of the assertion of the conqueror's right, might and prerogative. In particular, the Normans-English claimed *le droit de seigneur* particularly in Scotland. Because of religious and cultural exigencies the practice of *le droit de seigneur was* not exercised within India.

[42] In the animal world a layered or hierarchial work system is to be found among ants and bees.

[43] England, in the eighteenth and nineteenth centuries was ruled by a number of inept, self indulgent and clearly mad kings most of whom were not even English. Yet, their position "by the Grace of God" placed them so far above the common folk that their ineptitude to rule or their patrimony never came into question. They may have been mad, but, they were the Kings! They may have been German, but, they were the Kings! It was only when a ruler and his excesses affected the common folk directly that his right to rule came into question. The French Revolution was so abhorrent to the reigning heads of Europe, not because a king was deposed by the ruling elite, but because he was deposed and executed by the commoners, thereby, setting aside a centuries old practice — "by the Grace of God."

[44] This palatine law was promulgated by King Borom Trailok (aka Paramatrailokanatha) (r. 1424-1448) of Ayutthaya and practised ever since. It was, in part, for this reason that the death of King Ānanda, Rāma VIII was so traumatic to the Thai ethos as his death by gunshot was outside the accepted tradition.

[45] The concept of death resulting from looking upon the face of the *devarāj* also finds a parallel in the *Old Testament* where the early Hebrews also felt the same when confronting the real presence of God, Almighty. Moses shielded his eyes when confronted by the Burning Bush which exemplified the real presence of The Almighty, in order to preserve his life. In addition, the concept of looking on the face of the ruler, particularly in the East, may have carried the concept of the "evil eye." One could curse or cause evil by harboring such intense desires in one's heart and directing these feelings towards the one from which these feelings originated. Thus the king, the *devarāj*, protected himself from malevolent intentions by forbidding people to look upon his face. Even today, the act of staring in the orient is ground for strong, physical counter measures.

[46] Thailand employed the Wang Na, the heir designate to the throne who had his own palace and court. In Thailand the concept of primogeniture did not exist prior to the present reign. Often in Thailand the kingship passed laterally from brother to brother rather than father to son. Additionally, in Thailand the right to rule was endowed upon an individual by the Grand Council.

[47] For example famous women rulers were: Raziyya (Radiyya Begum) (1236-40) of the Mamluk Dynasty, India; Thao Mae Ku (Queen) (1551), Lan Na; Chamma-Devi of Lamphun (*c.* 800-825); and, of course the Dowger Empress of China, Tsu Hsi.

[48] Even though Kublai Khan installed many of his own bureaucrats upon his usurpation of the Chinese throne as well as that of the Manchus centuries later both saw conquerors dominated by the laborious governmental processes or accepted bureaucracy that had long been institutionalized in China, as well an numerous other accoutrements that were associated with rule in China.

[49] The most sacred and important rite during the coronation of English rulers is the procedure of anointing. During this rite a golden canopy is held over the ruler-to-be and he or she is anointed. This is the moment that they are elevated "by the Grace of God." It is interesting to note that Malaysia has a rotating kingship in which each of the nine, anointed sultāns assume the title of "agong" (king) for five years. However, they are not anointed to the kingship! Their rule is temporary. They are anointed to their particular Sultānates and once anointed only death can "un-anoint!"

[50] GT 2, p. 9, makes the statement: "A Rajput palace was a symbol of dynasty. . . ." Certainly, this may be said of all palaces.

[51] Generally, in Asian kingdoms and empires the ruler picked his successor and named him before his death. Frequently, as in Thailand, the successor was elevated during the reign of the former and became the Second King residing in the Wang Na Palace adjacent to the royal palace. His right to rule was confirmed by a

council. The Chinese emperor chose his replacement from amongst his many children, ostensibly picking the most able replacement. Asia's rulers were in a position, due to multiple wives and concubines, to have a relatively large pool from which to pick. Generally, but not always, the successor was picked from the wives, although concubines' sons were elevated to the throne.

52 GM 2, Oleg Grabar, "The Architecture of Power: Palaces, Citadels and Fortifications," pp. 48-79. Grabar, in the "Chapter 2" of *Architecture of the Islamic World*, specifically considers the architecture of power as it applies to Islam. However, his hypothesis applies to non-Islamic architecture as well, and particularly to the palaces of India, whether Hindu, Muslim or Sikh.

53 Biblical scholars see the story of Onan (Genesis 38:1-11) not so much as a repudiation of pre-orgasmic withdrawal, and certainly not as any condemnation of masturbation, but as not giving the patriarch Judah his right in supplying him with a grandchild through Onan's sister-in-law, his brother Er's widow, Tamar. The "seed" he spilled on the ground was by extension the property of Judah, and therefore, by wasting the property, he was wasting the property of Judah. This concept of patristic property is not just Judaic, but is found throughout the world.

54 It is interesting to note that within Judaism, traditionally, any child born of a Jewish — i.e., Hebrew — mother was Jewish — since she was of that group. However, a child born of the union of a Jewish father and a gentile mother did not enjoy the same status since, in the past, paternity could not be absolutely proven. Within Hinduism, similar strictures also apply. You must be born Hindu and of a Hindu mother.

55 In Malaysia, this item of apparel is a *tudung*, and is generally and currently worn by all Muslim women. There are exceptions. Sultānas of the Malaysian sultānates, generally do not wear a *tudung*. They may wear a diaphanous scarf lightly covering their head, but revealing much of their hair. An exception to this was the wife of a former sultān who was not royal by birth, but a commoner. She wore a *tudung*.

56 Mongkut, Rāma IV, was 47 when he ascended the throne of Thailand in 1851, having spent all his adult life as a monk. Until his death in 1868 he fathered 82 children via 39 wives — 39 sons and 43 daughters — as if it was his royal duty. Indeed a busy man!

Palaces, Residences and Pavilions

57 The plan of the *Haus Khas* seen in **Plate 1** was redrawn from: SG, p. 33.

58 The plan of the *Kotla Firuz Shah* seen in **Plate 2** was redrawn from: HS, p 141, and SG, p. 50.

59 The *Mayamatam*, BD, *op. cit.*, pp. 451-714; devotes six chapters in the description of houses, palaces and their details.

60 Hindu temples, particularly the *garbhagṛha*, were based on one of two sacred *maṇḍalas* — i.e. the *Maṇḍūka Maṇḍala* of sixty-four *pada*, and the *Paramaśayika Maṇḍala* of eighty-one *pada*.

61 Seven is a masculine number often seen as sacred. It is seen as the number of creation. Forty-nine is also a masculine, sacred number, whose Ü is seven. It is also interesting to note that it equals the number of cells found in the third storey of the *Lohaprasad*, Wat Thepidaram, Bangkok.

62 FWB III, pp. 279-282.

63 The plan of the *Vijayānagāra* seen in **Plate 3** was redrawn from: GM, p. 186, and GM 3, p. 88.

64 GM, pp. 186-187, refers to this structure as "the Queen's Bath." However, he in a singular study, GM 3, pp. 17-19, identifies it as "Square Water Pavilion."

65 EH, Vol II, p. 185, states: "'the Elephant Stables,' which I take to be a mosque built by Deva Raja II for his Muhamadan troops." This cannot be! The orientation is wrong by 180^0. The entrance(s) are in the west where the *qibla* should have been.

66 The plan of the *Shadiabad Mandir* at Mandu seen in **Plate 6** was redrawn from: GM, p 83.

67 The massiveness of the *Hiṇḍolā Mahal* is parallel to the *Tomb of Hushang Shah* (*c.* 1440) which is typically square, but ponderous in aspect and lacks the more delicate, even airy design of so many of the Islamic tombs which were contemporaneous. See: FWB 3, pp. 72-75.

68 The plan of the *Bidargarh* as seen in **Plate 9** was redrawn from: GM, p 85.

69 SG, *op. cit.*, p. 87. The construction of a round column involves either a lathe-like mechanism to form

Notes (Continued)

the pillar, or even more laboriously formed by hand. Square pillars or columns were far easier to construct. Further, they were easier to embellish with numerous forms.

70 The plan of the *Kumbhalgarh* at Chittor seen in **Plate 10** was redrawn from: GM, p 83 and GT, p. 43.

71 The *Kumbhalgarh* was also sacked in 1303 by the Delhi Sultān 'Ala-ud-din Muhammad Khaljiz (r. 1296-1316), yet it remain the premier Rajput stronghold for eight centuries. Further, GT, pp. 40-55, entitles the chapter dealing with Chittor: "In Media Res." Truly, Chittor physically was situated in the middle of Rajputana. However, they — i.e., the Sisodia Rajputs — were for a long period of time in the forefront of Rajput development and finally settling in Udaipur.

72 RHo, pp 12-27. The writings of Mandan include: *Vāstu Maṇḍan, Rūpa Maṇḍan, Prasāda Maṇḍan, Raja Vallabh Mandan, Vāstusaar, Vāstushastra, Apatattva* and *Devata Murti Prakarṇam*. These works, RHo asserts were highly influential in Rajputana and are even employed today in traditional building. Certainly there is evidence of his theories in a number of *garh mahals* of the Rajputana — e.g., the *City Palace* of Udaipur. On the other hand the *Meherangarh* of Jodhpur appears to disregard Mandan's ideas completely.

73 The plan of the *Meherangarh* at Jodhpur seen in **Plate 11** was redrawn from: GT, p 134.

74 The *Diwān-i Ām* or similar use areas of most *garh mahals* are easily accessible, often at the end of broad avenues, prospects or bordering large courts — e.g., the *Kumbhalgarh* at Chittor, the *Lāl Qilā* at Agra, *Fatehpur Sikri*, or the *Rāj Mahal* of Amber. This form was an important part of any royal residence as it provided an appropriate space for the *darśana*.

75 GH, pp. 35-39, describes, as a stylistic quality of the Rajput palaces, their asymmetry. In truth, strict symmetry is to be found in few palaces in India, Hindu or Muslim. The notable exception being the palaces of the Bundelas in Orchha and Datiya, or the *Rājā Mahal* (*Chandragiri Palace*) near Tirupati. However, virtually all the *garh mahals* of India tend towards multiple perpendicular axiality. There are those complexes which do not strictly adhere to this principle — e.g., *Bidargarh, Gingee Mandir*, or *Lāl Qilā* at Agra — but they all indicate a strong tendency or preference towards multiple perpendicular axiality. Only the *garh mahal* of Jodhpur is based upon multiple non-perpendicular axiality. It is totally, absolutely, unremittingly asymmetrical!

76 The plan of the *Mān Mandir* at Gwalior as seen in **Plate 12** was redrawn from: GM, p 154 and GT, p. 57.

77 Yet rule was not limited to either the brāhmaṇas or the kṣatriya. The Jats, the powerful rulers of Bharatpur were from a farming caste, the vaiśya. Also, the Nāyakas of Southern India were not necessarily drawn from either the brāhmaṇa or kṣatriya castes, initially.

78 The plan of the *Gujari Mahal* at Gwalior seen in **Plate 13** was redrawn from: GM, p 154.

79 GM, p. 154.

80 The plan of the *Gingee Mandir* as seen in **Plate 14** was redrawn from: GM, p 188. Further the term "*mandir*" is here applied to the palace complex and not the whole fortification.

81 Bathing for purposes of bodily cleanliness and its salient health benefits in Europe was not regularly practised until the twentieth century, even among the royals. It is acknowledged that Louis XIV bathed once a year; Peter the Great was by all standards, filthy and constantly befouled; and the French Queen Maria Guiseppina of Savoy reeked so bad that she was asked to at least wash her neck and brush her teeth before her marriage to Louis XVIII — and this in the late Nineteenth Century.

82 The plan of the *Wav Dada Harir* or the *Baoli Bai Hari* as seen in **Plate 15** was redrawn from: SG, p 70.

83 EH, vol II, pp. 142-43.

84 SG, pp. 70-71.

85 The plan of the *Aināpur Mahal* of Bijapur as seen in **Plate 17** was redrawn from: HC, **Plate CIX**.

86 This plan with the triple arched verandah appears to have been a form favored by the rulers of Bijapur, the Turkish 'Adil Shahi. There is considerable evidence that this form — i.e., an arched or arcaded verandah before a narrow, wide series of rooms (See: **Appendix A, Plate 68**) — may have been brought to Bijapur and adapted to residential use. Certainly the deep, covered verandah would have been imposing as well as giving a cooling effect to the interior. Also, similar plan is seen in Iran (See: **Appendix A, Plate 78**) and Palermo (See: **Appendix A, Plate 64**).

Notes (Continued)

[87] The plan of the *Water Pavilion* (*Hammam*) of Kumatagi as seen in **Plate 18** was redrawn from: HC, **Plate CXII**.

[88] This referent to water and Paradise is further underlined by the *chahar-bagh*s associated with major Islamic tombs — e.g., the *Tomb of Humayun*, the *Tāj Mahal*, and the *Tomb of Jahangir* — as well as the famous *Shalimar Bagh* of Lahore and the *Shalimar Bagh* of Srinagar. See: FWB 3, pp. 240-56.

[89] The plan of the *Rām Mandir* of Orchha as seen in **Plate 19** was redrawn from: GT, p. 73.

[90] The *maṇḍala* shown in the ideal plan in **Plate 21** is the *Paramaśayika Maṇḍala* (See also: **Appendix D, Plate 87**). Both this *maṇḍala* and the *Maṇḍūka Maṇḍala* were considered to be ideal, especially for temple design. They were also considered as auspicious for palaces and other constructions as well. However, this did not preclude the application of other *maṇḍalas*. **Figure 60** indicates the application of the *Bhadramahasana Maṇḍala* to the *Rāja Mandir*. This *maṇḍala* would have had some mystical importance as it was based upon the sacred numeral seven — i.e., although seven is a masculine number, it is associated with the moon as seven times four is the cycle of this feminine orb.

[91] The Bundela *garh mahals* often carried the descriptive term "*mandir*." Although this term is generally applied to a temple, it is also applied in some areas to fortified palaces.

[92] FWB 2, pp. 47-51 and 96-97.

[93] The plan of the *Gagan Mahal* of Bijapur as seen in **Plate 22** was redrawn from: HC, **Plate XVII**.

[94] See note: 86, above.

[95] The plan of the *Lāl Qilā* of Agra as seen in **Plate 23** was redrawn from: GM, p. 116.

[96] The plan of the *Jahangiri Mahal* of the *Lāl Qilā* at Agra as seen in **Plate 25** was redrawn from: HS, p. 77.

[97] HS, pp. 136-138

[98] The plan of the *Fatehpur Sikri* as seen in **Plate 26** was redrawn from: HS, p. 130, and GM, p. 114.

[99] SG, P. 134.

[100] It may be suggested that "symmetry around multiple axes" (SG, P. 134) as applied to *Fatehpur Sikri* would be more aptly defined as: "symmetry around multiple perpendicular axes," as indeed it is. On the other hand, the same descriptive phrase could also be applied to the *Meherangarh* of Jodhpur (See: **Plate 11**), but the confusing plan would be more aptly defined as: "symmetry around multiple non-perpendicular axes." Refer to **Appendix D, Plates 81-86**.

[101] The plan of the *Ekastambha Prasāda* (aka *Diwān-i-Khās*) at *Fatehpur Sikri* as seen in **Plate 27** was redrawn from: HS, p. 38. In addition, RN2, vol II, pp. 251-269; and RN4, pp. 37-44, asserts that the *Ekastambha Prasāda* (aka *Diwān-i-Khās*), the "House of (the) Unitary Pillar" was a purely nonfunctional structure. He states that some Mughal structures "were either commemorative or symbolic" the "latter were built to convey a metaphysical or spiritual idea." (RN4, p. 37). He provides an example of a "commemorative" architectural example — i.e., the *Buland-Darwāzāh*. In truth, this is a monumental gateway which extols the greatness of the dynasty and his reign. But, it is utilitarian in that it is a gateway, albeit "commemorative" and unusually massive. However, to categorize the *Ekastambha Prasada* (aka *Diwān-i-Khās*), the "House of (the) Unitary Pillar" as purely "symbolic" is a leap of logic. If it is, then it is a "unitary" example with few, if any, other examples! An *ekastambha* is not unique to India, and certainly not a Mughal concept. The emperor Ashoka erected numerous pillars (*ekastambha*) across his realm. In cities in India, whether square or circular, *en plan*, in the inception, one generally finds a tree or post (*ekastambha*) in the centre around which the elders might gather. Special holy men, when they died, sometimes were not cremated, but were buried in a seated position around a stake (*ekastambha*) driven into the ground symbolizing an *axis mundi* and a tumulus was raised over them — a rudimentary *stūpa*. The Buddhist *stūpa* in which the hemispherical *anda* was seen as a representation of the celestial sphere, and the implied half that was not seen, consists, in part, of a *chattravali* (*ekastambha*) which symbolically was the *axis mundi*. The *Vajrayana chorten* was also constructed with an implied or real (*ekastambha*) in the centre. Even, the central part of a *garbhagṛha's* foundational preparation contained an axis of sorts. (See: **Appendix A, Plate 94**).

[102] FWB 2, pp. 120-121 & 36-40. The possible use of the numeral seven would have been most understandable as it is a numeral which is universally considered to be sacred — i.e., sacred to Islam, Buddhism, Hinduism, Judaism and Christianity — and

Notes (Continued)

associated both with the masculine sun and the feminine moon.

103 The plan of the *Birbal Bhavan* (*House of Rājā Birbal*) at *Fatehpur Sikri* as seen in **Plate 28** was redrawn from: HS 58-59 and SG, p. 139.

104 The plan of the *Jodh-Bai Mahal* (aka *Jodha Bai Mahal*) at *Fatehpur Sikri* as seen in **Plate 29** was redrawn from: EH II, p. 173.

105 The plan of the *Jodh-Bai Mahal* is sometimes referred to as a *mardānā* plan. GM, p. 154 applies it to the plan of the *Gujari Mahal* — i.e., a series of apartments around an inner court. The term is also applicable to the *Jodh-Bai Mahal*. Although there are other separate residences within the *zenānā* — i.e., the *Birbal Bhavan* and the *Sunahrā Makān* — it would seem that this structure was the primary residence for the majority of the women of the court.

106 The plan of the *Sunahrā Makān* or *Golden House* at *Fatehpur Sikri* as seen in **Plate 31** was redrawn from: EH II, p. 173.

107 The plan of the *Pañch Mahal* as seen in **Plates 32 & 33** was redrawn from: EH II, p. 173; SH, p. 37.

108 Refer to: FWB 2, *op. cit.*, pp. 118-119, 83-86, 41-46, 19-21 & 16. "If there is smoke there must be fire." I called the Department of Mathematics at the University of Malaya and was put in touch with Professor Dr. G. L. Chia. In a phone conversation to my 'unmathematical' mind, he pointed out to me that the number of bays in storeys one (1) through four (4) were the squares of prime numbers, minus one (1) — i.e., $7^2 = 49 - 1 = 48$, $5^2 = 25 - 1 = 24$, $3^2 = 9 - 1 = 8$ and $2^2 = 4 - 1 = 3$. Of course, $1^2 = 1 - 1 = 0$ which simply doesn't work! However, "one is generally considered neither an odd nor an even number. It is seen as an absolute, and, as an absolute it is beyond all, therefore, divine. It denotes the first principle, The Absolute One, The Primordial One, *Allah*, *Brahmā*, *Devī*, *Adi-Buddha* (Tib.: *Thog-mahi Sangs-rgyas*), *Buddha Sāmanta-Bhadra* (Tib.: *Kun-tu-bzang-po*) and *God*. It is the source, the monad and 'non-dualism' (Ind.: *advaita*). Further it represents unity, spiritual balance, the divine sign of universal life." (FWB 2) As such, it is, therfore, not untoward that the integer one (1) would stand alone, insoluble, indivisible and indestructable. In a brief table at the end of this section of "Notes" (p. 216) is to be seen some interesting prospects. However, it must be left for some later researcher to ferret out this interesting conundrum.

109 RN2, vol II, pp. 251-69; and RN4, pp. 37-44.

110 RN2, vol II, pp. 262-67; and RN4, p. 45.

111 There is considerable discrepancy as to when the *Rāja Mahal* was constructed. Some say soon after their move to this region — i.e., a. 1565 (EH, vol II, p. 213) or: a. 1584 (GM, p. 187). Others place the date well into the seventeenth century — i.e., *c.* 1620 (GT 2, p. 206). The plan of the *Rāja Mahal* or *Chandragiri Palace* at Tirupati as seen in **Plate 34** was redrawn from: EH II, p. 213.

112 BD, vol. II, pp. 623-679.

113 *Ibid.*, p. 525.

114 The plan of the *City Palace* at Udaipur as seen in **Plate 35** was redrawn from: GM, p. 159; & GT, pp. 91 & 106.

115 Udaya Singh's reign of Mewar was actually 1537-1572, but only the last few years in Udaipur after the capital was moved.

116 Unlike the *Kotla Firuz Shah* (See: **Plate 2** & **Figure 23**) the outcropping at Udaipur's *City Palace* was utilized as an adjunct to the defensive measures of the *garh mahal* and not as a means of cooling — i.e., providing a flywheel effect for the warm days and cool nights.

117 See: FWB 3, pp. 34-37, 60-63, 168-75 & 176-81.

118 The plan of the *Farah Bagh* (aka *Feria Bagh*) at Ahmadnagar as seen in **Plate 36** was redrawn from: HS, p. 96.

119 The plan of the *Rāj Mahal* at Amber as seen in **Plate 37** was redrawn from: GT, p. 93, & GM, p. 163.

120 *Baradari* is a descriptive term. Traditionally it referred to an open, square pavilion raised upon a podium or base and composed of sixteen columns in four equal ranks of four columns, all supporting a roof. The term later came to be applied to any square, columned , roofed structure — e.g., the *Keshav Bhawan* at Deeg is referred to as a *baradari*-type pavilion although it has thirty-two columns, twice the traditional number.

121 See: FWB 2, pp. 120-121.

122 The plan of the *Jahangir Mandir* (*Jahangiri Mahal*) at Orchha as seen in **Plates 39 & 40** was redrawn from: GT, p. 75.

123 GT 2, pp. 79-84, discusses the application of the *Paramaśayika Maṇḍala* and the manner in which it is applied to the Bundela *mandirs*, particularly the *Govind*

Notes (Continued)

Mandir. Although the *maṇḍala* he illustrates differs from that seen in the BD, Figure 6, p. liv, it is essentially similar.

124 The plan of the *Govind Mandir* (*Bir Singh Judeo Mahal*) at Datia as seen in **Plates 41 - 43** was redrawn from: HS, p. 141, & GT, p. 76.

125 FWB 2, pp. 47-51.

126 Tillotson's discussion of the *Paramaśayika Maṇḍala* is quite complete, but he fails to show the actual imposition of the *maṇḍala*. Further, it is true that in some of the *śilpa śāstra* the *Paramaśayika Maṇḍala* is considered as the preferred form. The *Paramaśayika Maṇḍala's* application to temples, particularly the *garbhagṛha* is absolutely preferred. Other of the *śilpa-śāstra* do not place such a caveat upon the plan of a palace. The *Mayamatam*, for example accepts numerous plans and applies them to the various levels and castes of rulers.

127 Tillotson reproduces the *Manasara Paramaśayika Maṇḍala* on: GT 2, p. 81. It differs somewhat from the *Mayamatam Paramaśayika Maṇḍala*: BD, **Figure 6**, p. liv, but is essentially the same.

128 The plan of the *Gul Mahal* of the *Jag Mandir* as seen in **Plate 45** was redrawn from: GM, p. 161.

129 The plan of the *Shahi Bagh* at Ahmadnagar as seen in **Plate 46** was redrawn from: CA, p. 136.

130 The plan of the *Shahjahanabad* at Delhi as seen in **Plate 47** was redrawn from: AM, p. 16; GM, p. 119; HS, p. 138; SG, p. 169.

131 SG, p. 169. Although Grover states this as a backhanded compliment, it is true, and it is a compliment! The *Shahjahanabad* is not experimental as was *Fatehpur Sikri*, and may be seen as 'marble tent architecture" (p. 179), however, no tent was ever so glorious! *Shahjahanabad* is the synthesis of the Great Mughals' architectural *oeuvre* and a refined monument to a refined ruler.

132 EH, Vol II, p. 209. Havell's comment is also somewhat backhanded, but he hits the mark!

133 The plan of the *Lāl Qilā, Shahjahanabad* as seen in **Plate 48** was redrawn from several figures found in: AM, especially the use of the grid, which was of enormous aid. However, AM, p. 128-129, displays the configuration of the *Chowk Hawd Nahr* and shown in **Plate 47**, but after citing two sources who refer to a square *chowk* (Gordon Sanderson, *Delhi Fort: A Guide to its Buildings and Gardens*, Calcutta: 1914, p. 8; and Jaipur City Palace Museum, F -122, [*c.* 1750]) and two who refer to a rectangular *chowk* (Syed Ahmed, *Monuments of Delhi*, trans. R. Nath, New Delhi: 1979, p. 11; and Zafar Hasan, *List of Monuments of the Delhi Circle*, vol. I, *Shahjahanabad*, [1916] repro. New Delhi: 1997, p. 10), he casts his lot with the latter — i.e., the rectangular *chowk*. Further he states: "The stability and sense of equal importance in all four directions suggested by a square shape is at variance with the primary function of this forecourt" (*Chowk Hawd Nahr*), p. 128. This makes no sense and does not take into account that this *chowk* was at the intersection of the *Chhatta Chowk* and the *Rastah Delhi Darwāzā* which would naturally entail a square space. Therefore, **Plate 47** indicates a square *chowk*.

134 AM, pp. 122-155, in the chapter "*Imperial Domains*," presents a thorough discussion regarding the layout of *Lāl Qilā, Shahjahanabad*, and sees this axis as the main ceremonial access and axis. He rightly states that before the addition of the rubicon to the *Lahore Darwāzā* (and the *Delhi Darwāzā*) there was a clear, symbolic line of sight from the Chandni Chowk (Lahori Bazaar), through the *Lahore Darwāzā*, the *Chhatta Chowk*, across the *Chowk Hawd Nahr*, through the *Naqqār Khānā*, across the *Chowk Diwān-i Ām* and to the Imperial throne of the *Diwān-i Ām* and the person of the emperor. This, in both a real and symbolic sense, allowed the public visual access to the imperial person, especially during *darśana*. It also implied the reverse — i.e., the emperor's regard of his subjects — although in actuality the latter was of minimal import.

135 AM, p. 118.

136 Movement is an important concept in any extensive ensemble. It is paramount in *Lāl Qilā, Shahkahanabad*.

137 See: FWB 3, pp. 240-46, for a brief discussion of the *chahar-bagh* and its significance.

138 It is noted that the *Moti Masjid* was completed in 1659, hardly enough time for the commencement of construction during Aurangzeb's reign. AM, pp. 147-147, suggest, and rightly so, that the *masjid* had to have begun during the reign of Shah Jahan, probably around the year 1552.

139 AM, p. 106.

140 FWB 3, p. 148.

Notes (Continued)

[141] The plan of the *Daulat Kothi* at Bijapur as seen in **Plate 48** was redrawn from: HC, Plate CIX.

[142] HC, p. 118, is referred to as a "hall."

[143] The plan of the *Athar Mahal* (*Dad Mahal*) at Bijapur as seen in **Plate 49** was redrawn from: GM, p. 86.

[144] GM, p. 86, although he shows the plan at the bottom of the page, it is erroneously labeled as "*The Gagan Mahal* at Bijapur." HC, pp. 89-95, states that it was originally constructed as a "Hall of Justice" then converted into the "Palace of the Relic." Further, he states that it was the site of Sultān Muhammad 'Adil Shah's (r. 1626-1656) court for a period of time.

[145] The plan of the *Nāyaka Mahal* at Madurai as seen in **Plate 50** was redrawn from: GM, p. 189.

[146] The use of squat, circular shaft columns which are of the Roman Doric order indicate the obvious European influence.

[147] The plan of the *Deeg-garh* as seen in **Plates 51** & **52** was redrawn from: GM, p. 166, & GT, p. 189.

[148] It is of interest to note that frequently when a throne is usurped, the usurper generally assumes a most conservative attitude and also assiduously assumes all the previously established accoutrements of rule. For example, the general Thong Duang Chaophraya Chakri, after the assassination of King Taksin of Thonburi, assumed the kingship as Rāma I. As Rāma I, he was most careful to follow the long established rites of kinship. In addition, the German Princess who became Catherine II of Russia, known as The Great, was quick to establish a tenuous hold on the throne by following all the ancient Russian prerogatives of rule after the murder of her husband. However, the Jats of Bharatpur were not "usurpers" in the traditional sense. They were conquerors, and they established their state by conquest. This may have been a reason why they apparently did not follow established tradition in the forming of a distinct *zenānā*, especially as practised by the Rajputs and as seen in most of the *garh mahal* of Rajputana.

[149] GT, p. 189, identifies this form as an "open *baradari*." However, earlier he describes this form — i.e., a *baradari* — as a pavilion with four columns across each face.

[150] The plan of the *City Palace of Jaipur* as seen in **Plates 51** was redrawn from: VS, p. 62, & GT 2, p. 179.

[151] GT 2, p. 167.

[152] In redrawing the plan of the *City Palace of Jaipur* from VS (p. 62), it was noted that some of the elements were not in direct or strict perpendicular alignment with the major structures — i.e., the *Sarvato Bhadra*, the *Sabhā Nivās* (*Diwān-i Ām*) or the *Chandra Mahal*. The illustration in VS may be accurate and these elements may well vary, or the plan may have suffered a technical abnormality in its transfer. Nonetheless, **Figure 51** is essentially accurate and mirrors the reproduced plan in VS, p. 62.

[153] Several scholars have viewed the *City Palace of Jaipur* with what might be termed as a jaundiced eye! GM, pp. 164-65, merely gives a cursory description of this palace and makes no comment as he had done with other *garh mahal*s within his tome. GT 2, pp. 167-85, devotes a chapter to this palace. He extols the design of the city and some of the elements of the palace proper, but ends by saying: "the decline of design is not . . . (the) Mughal influence but the weakness of the design . . . ." (p. 185) of the *City Palace of Jaipur*. The backhand comments continue in: VS, pp. 61-73, doubtless due to Tillotson's coauthoring.

[154] The plan of the *Padmanabhapuram* at Kanyakumari as seen in **Plates 53** & **54** was redrawn from: GM, p. 190.

[155] GM, p. 191.

[156] The Mughals, *in toto*, were Turko-Afghanis, the Sultāns of Bijapur were initially pure Turkish, etc. The rulers of England, since William the Conqueror, have not been English, but French and then, as now, German. Queen Elizabeth II is actually a Wettin/Saxe-Coburg-Gotha, called Windsor; and her husband, Prince Philip is a Schleswig-Holstein-Sonderburg-Glucksburg, called Mountbatten.

[157] R. Eisler's thesis, although keeping it specifically to Europe, may well find some applicability to India; pp. 42-58. The Indo-European invaders — i.e., the Aryans displaced the older and somewhat peaceful Dravidian culture and imposed its own system which included a rigid hierarchial system (caste).

Notes (Concluded)

Storey	Bays	Reduction Bays	š - 1	Columns	Reduction Columns	Bays + Columns	Reduction Bays + Col.
1st storey	48	4+8=12= 1+2=**3**	7	**84**	8+4=12 2+1=**3**	32	3+2=**5**
2nd storey	24	2+4=**6**	5	56	5+6=11 1+1=**2**	80	8+0=**8**
3rd storey	8	**8**	3	20	2+0=**2**	28	2+8=10 1+0=**1**
4th storey	3	**3**	2	12	1+2=**3**	15	1+5=**6**
5th storey	1	**1**	(1)	4	**4**	5	**5**
Total	**84**	21	(18)	184	14	260	25

Pañch Mahal, Fatehpur Sikri, plan, storeys 1-5 and numerical considerations

Bibliography

Bibliography

Acharya, P.K. *An Encyclopaedia of Hindu Architecture*. London: 1927-46.

__________., *Architecture of Manasara*, translated from the original Sanskrit. London: 1932.

Alfieri, Bianca Maria. *Islamic Architecture of the Indian Subcontinent*. London: 2000.

Asher, Catherine B. *Architecture of Mughal India*. New Delhi: 1995.

Atmadi, Parmono. *Some Architectural Design Principles of Temples in Java*. Yogyakarta: 1994.

Auboyer, Jeannine; and others. *Oriental Art: A Handbook of Styles and Forms*. Trans. Elizabeth and Richard Bartlett. New York: 1980.

Banerje, Jitendranath N. *The Development of Hindu Iconography*. 2nd ed. , Kolkata: 1956.

Banerjee, P. , *et al. Buddhist Iconography*. New Delhi: 1989.

Bary, Theodore de. *Sources of Indian Tradition*, vol. I. New York: 1958.

Batley, C. *Design Development of Indian Architecture*. Bombay: 1934.

__________. *Indian Architecture*. London 1934.

Begde, P.V. *Forts and Palaces of India*. Delhi: 1982.

Bell, Eric T. *Numerology*. Baltimore: 1933.

Bhattacharyya, Benoytosh. *The Indian Buddhist Iconography Mainly Based on the Seadhanamealea and other Cognate Tantric Texts of Rituals*. Calcutta: 1958.

Bhattacharyya, Dipak Chandra. *Studies in Buddhist Iconography*. New Delhi: 1978.

Bhattacharya, K. "Les religions Brahmāniques dan l'ancien Cambodge, d'après l'épigraphie et l'iconographie," *Cahiers de l'École Française d'Extrême-Orient*; XLIX. Hanoi: 1961.

Blurton, R.T. "Palace Structures at Vijayanagara: the Archaeological Evidence," *South Asian Archaeology* 1985, ed. K. Frifelt and P. Sorenson. London: 1989.

Brand, M. and Lowry, Glenn D., eds. *Fatehpur Sikri: A Sourcebook*. Cambridge: 1985.

Brown, Percy. *Indian Architecture* (*Buddhist and Hindu Periods*). Bombay: n. d.

__________. *Indian Architecture* (*Islamic Period*). Bombay: n. d. (1965-1968).

Brunes, Tons. *The Secrets of Ancient Geometry and Its Use*; vols. I-II. Copenhagen: 1967.

Bunce, Fredrick W. *A Dictionary of Buddhist and Hindu Iconography — Illustrated — Objects, Devices, Concepts, Rites and Related Terms*, New Delhi: 1996.

__________. *Numbers Found in Buddhist & Hindu Practices: an Iconographic Consideration*, New Delhi: 2002.

__________. *The Iconography of Plans: A Study of the Influence of Buddhism and Hinduism on Architectural Plans of South and South-east Asia*, New Delhi: 2002.

__________., *Islamic Tombs in India: The Iconography and Genesis of Their Design*. New Delhi: 2004.

Burgess, J. *Muhammadan Architecture in Gujarat*. Varanasi: 1971.

Bussagli, Mario; John Shepley, trans. *Oriental Architecture/ 1: India, Indonesia, Indochina*. New York: 1989.

Carr, Stephen. *Archaeology and Monumental Remains of Delhi*. Allahabad: 1967.

Chopra, P.N., T.K. Ravindran, N. Subrahmanian, *History of South India*, 3 vols. New Delhi: 1979.

Coedès, George. *The Indianized States of South-east Asia*. Honolulu: 1968.

__________. "Les Etats hindouises d'Indochine et d'Indonesie," *Histoire du Monde*, vol. III. Paris: 1948.

__________. "Arte dell'Indonesia," *Civiltā dell'Oriente*, vol. IV. Rome: 1962.

Commissariat, Manekshah Sorabshah. *A History of Gujarat: Including a Survey of its Chief Architectural Monuments and Inscriptions*. Mumbai: 1938.

Coomaraswamy, Ananda Kentish. "Symbolism of the Dome," *Indian Historical Quarterly*; XIV. Kolkata: 1938, pp. 1-56.

__________. *Early Indian Architecture: Palaces*, repr. Delhi: 1975.

Cousens, Henry. *Bijapur and Its Architectural Remains: With an Historical Outline of the Adil Shahi Dynasty*; (Archeological Survey of India, vol. XXXVIII, Imperial Series). reprint. Delhi: 1996.

Creswell, K.A.C. *A Short Account of Early Muslim Architecture*. Beirut: 1958.

Critchlow, Keith. *Islamic Patterns: An Analytical and Cosmological Approach*. London and New York: 1976.

Crowe, S. and Hawood, S. The *Gardens of Mughal India: a History and a Guide*. London: 1972.

Crump, Thomas. *The Anthropology of Numbers*. Cambridge: 1990.

Dagens, Bruno, ed. & tr. *Mayamata, Traite Sanskrit d'architecture, Premiere Partie*. Paris (?): 1970.

__________, ed. & tr. *Mayamata, Traite Sanskrit d'architecture, Deuxeme Partie*. Paris (?): 1970.

__________, ed. & tr. *Mayamatam, Treatise of Housing, Architecture & Iconography* (2 vols.). New Delhi: 1994.

Davies, P. The *Penguin Guide to the Monuments of India, II, Islamic, Rajput, European*. London: 1989.

de Bary, Wm. Theodore (ed.) *et al. Sources of Indian Tradition*, vol. I. New York: 1958.

Deva, Krishna. *Temples of India*, 2 vols. New Delhi: 1995.

Dieulafoy, M. *L'art antique de la Perse*. Paris: 1884-85.

Edwardes, M. *Indian Temples and Palaces*. London: 1959.

Fass, V. *The Forts of India*. London: 1986.

Fergusson, James, *et al. History of Indian and Eastern Architecture*, 2 vols. Delhi: 1967.

Fritz, J. M., Michell, G. and Nagarājā Rao, M. S. *Where Kings and Gods Met: the Royal Centre at Vijayanagara*. Tucson: 1983.

Gaekwad, F. and Fass, V. *The Palaces of India*. London: 1980.

Ghurye, G.S. *Rajput Architecture*. Mumbai: 1968.

Gollings, J. Fritz, J.M. and Muchell, G. *Vijayanagara: City of Victory, a South Indian Hindu Capital*. New York: 1991.

Goodwin, Godfrey. *A History of Ottoman Architecture*. London: 1971.

Grover, Satish. *Islamic Architecture in India*. New Delhi: 1981.

Grube, Ernst, *et al.* George Mitchell, ed. *Architecture of the Islamic World: Its History and Social Meaning*. London: 1978.

Haig, Wolseley, ed. *The Cambridge History of India*. Delhi: 1958.

Bibliography (Continued)

Hambley, G. *Cities of Mughal India*. London: 1968.

Havell, E.B. *Encyclopaedia of Architecture in the Indian Subcontinent*, reprint. New Delhi: 2000.

Hill, D. and Grabar, O. *Islamic Architecture and Its Decoration*, AD. 800-1500. Chicago: 1964.

Hillenbrand, Robert. *Islamic Art and Architecture*. London: 1999.

__________., *Islamic Architecture: Form, Function & Meaning*. Edinburgh: 1994.

Hoag, John D. *Islamic Architecture*. Milan: 1975.

Hooja, Rima. "Of Buildings and Books: The Theory and Practice of the Architect Mandan," *Marg: A Magazine of the Arts*, vol. 52, no. 4; Mumbai: 2001.

Husain, A.B.M. *Fatehpur-sikri and its Architecture*. Dacca: 1970.

Issam El-Said and Parman, Ayse, *Geometric Concepts in Islamic Art*. London: 1976.

Jain, J. and Jain-Neubauer, J., eds. *Rajput Art and Architecture*. Wiesbaden: 1966.

Jung, C.G. *Maṇḍala Symbolism*, trans. R.F.C. Hull. Princeton: 1973.

Koch, Ebba. *Mughal Architecture: An Outline of Its History and Development* 1526-1858. London: 1991.

Krishna Murthy, K. *Early Indian Secular Architecture*. Delhi: 1987.

Lalou, M. *Iconographie des etoffes peintes d'apres le Manjusrimulakalpa*. Paris: 1930.

Lehrman, J. *Earthly Paradise: Garden and Courtyard in Islam*. London: 1980.

Liebert, G. *Iconographic dictionary of the Indian Religions*. Leyden: 1976.

Lim Jee Yuan. *The Malay House: Rediscovering Malaysia's Indigenous Shelter System*. Pulau Pinang: 1987.

Luce, G. H. *Old Burma, Early Pagan*, 3 vols. New York: 1969.

_________. "The Greater Temples of Pagan; The Smaller Temples of Pagan; Fu-kan-tu-lu; The Tan and the Ngai;Countries Neighboring Burma; The Ancient Pyu; Economic Life of the Early Burman." *Burma Research Society*, Fiftieth Anniversary Publication, no. 2. Rangoon: 1960.

Majumdar, R.C., ed.*The Delhi Sultanate*. Bombay: 1960.

Mani, Vettam. *Puranic Encyclopaedia*. Delhi: 1996.

March, Lionel, *et al.*, *The Geometry of Environment*. Cambridge: 1974.

Marchal, H. *L'Architecture comparṛe dans l'Inde et l'Extrême-Orient*. Paris: 1944.

Mehta, Rustam. *Masterpieces of Indo-Islamic Architecture*. Bombay: 1976.

Michell, G., ed., *Architcture of the Islamic World*. London: 1978.

_________. "Courtly Architecture in Gingee under the Nāyakas," *South Asian Studies*, 7: 1991.

_________. *The Royal Palaces of India*. London: 1998.

_________. *The Vijayanagara Courtly Style*. New Delhi: 1992.

Misra, B.D. *The Forts and Fortresses of Gwalior and its Hinterlands*. New Delhi: 1993.

Mohammad al-Asad, *et al.* Martin Frishman and Hasan-Uddin Khan, eds. *The Mosque: History, Architectural Development & Regional Diversity*. London: 1994.

Morgan, W.S. *Kisah Tanah Melayu*. Singapore: 1949.

Muhammad Rabi 'ibn Muhammad Ibrahim. *The Ship of Sulaiman*. New York: 1972.

Mukherji, Anisha Shekhar. *The Red Fort of Shahjahanabad*. New Delhi: 2003.

Bibliography (Continued)

Nath, R. *Fatehpur Sikri and its Monuments*. Agra: 2000.

_________. *History of Mughal Architecture*. New Delhi: 1985.

_________. *History of Sultanate Architecture*. New Delhi: 1978.

_________. *Islamic Architecture & Style in India*. New Delhi (?): 1982.

__________, *Indigenous Characteristics of Mughal Architecture.* New Delhi:2004.

Nayeem, M.A. *The Splendour of Hyderabad : The Last Phase of an Oriental Culture* (1591-1948 AD), reprint. Hyderabad: 2002.

Nilakanta Sastri. *South Indian Influences in the Far East*. s. l. : 1949

Pereira, Jose. *Islamic Sacred Architecture: A Stylistic History*. New Delhi: 1994.

Prabhakar Apte, June. "Vāstu-Puruṣa Maṇḍala: Dramatic Architectural and Artistic Study of Vāstu-Puruṣa Maṇḍala in Vāstu-Vedic, Agamic and Puranic Tradition with Special Reference to Mayamata." 1993 *Seminar on Mayonic Science & Technology*, Madras (unpublished: Library of the American Institute of Indian Studies, Gurgaon, Haryana).

Prochazka, Amjad Bohumil. *Architecture of the Islamic Cultural Sphere.* Zurich: 1986.

Rapson, E. J. , *et al.* (eds.). *The Cambridge History of India*, 6 vols. Delhi: 1955.

Reuther, Oscar. *Indische Palaste und Wohnhauser*. Berlin: 1925.

Rowland, Benjamin. *The Art and Architecture of India: Hindu, Buddhist, Jain*. Baltimore: 1967.

Sachdev, Vibhuti and Tillotson, Giles. *Building Jaipur: The Making of an Indian City*. New Delhi: 2002.

Safrani, Shehbaz H. *Golconda and Hyderabad*. Bombay: 1992.

Sartono Kartodirdjo, ed. 700 *Tahun Majapahit* (1293-1993) *Suatu Bunga Rampai*. Surabaya: 1993.

Sarkar, H. *Some Contributions of India to the Ancient Civilization of Indonesia and Malaysia*. Calcutta: 1970.

_________. *Studies in Early Buddhist Architecture of India*. Delhi: 1966.

Schotten, Merklinger, E. *Indian Islamic Architecture: The Deccan* 1347-1686. Warminster: 1981.

Sevcenko, Margaret, ed. *Theories and Principles of Design in the Architecture of Islamic Societies*. Cambridge: 1988.

Sharma, P.K. *Mughal Architecture of Delhi*. New Delhi: 2000.

Sinclair, W.B. "Monasteries of Pagan," *Burma Research Society*, Fiftieth Anniversary Publication, no. 2. Rangoon: 1960.

Singh, A.P. *Forts and Fortifications of India*. Delhi: 1993.

Sivaramamurti, C. *The Art of India*. New York: 1977.

Soucek, Pricilla P. *Content and Context of Visual Arts in the Islamic World*. University Park: 1988.

Soundara Rajan, K.V. *Ahmadabad*. New Delhi: 1980.

_________., *Islam Builds in India*, Delhi: 1983.

Stierlin, Henri, ed. *Architecture of the World: India*. Lausanne: n. d.

__________., *Architecture of the World: Islamic India*. Lausanne: n. d.

_________., *Hindu India: From Khajuraho to the Temple City of Madurai*. Köln: 2002.

_________. *Turkey: From thr Selçuks to the Ottomans*. Köln: 2002.

Bibliography (Continued)

Sthapaka Miranjana Mahapatra. *Silpararnakosa: A Glossary of Orissan Temple Architecture*. New Delhi: 1994.

Strachan, Paul. *Imperial Pagan: Art and Architecture of Burma*. Honolulu: 1989.

Stuart, C.M. Villiers. *Gardens of the Great Mughals*. New Delhi: 1983.

Tadell, C. *The History of Architecture in India*. London: 1990.

Tewari, S. P. *Hindu Iconography*. New Delhi: 1979.

Tillotson, G.H.R. *Mughal India*. London: 1990.

__________., *The Rajput Palaces*. New Haven and London: 1987.

__________., *The Rajput Palaces : The Development of an Architectural Style, 1450-1750*. London: 1999

Toy, S. *Strongholds of India*. London: 1957.

__________., *The Fortified Cities of India*. London: 1965.

Vatsyayan, Kapila. *Buddhist Iconography*. New Delhi: 1989.

__________., *The Square and the Circle of the Indian Arts*. New Delhi: 1983.

Volwahsen, A. *Living Architecture: Islamic-Indian*. London: 1970.

Waliullah Khan, Mohammad. *Lahore and its Important Monuments*. Karachi: 1973.

Wheeler, M., ed. *Splendors of the East: Temples, Tombs,Palaces and Fortresses of Asia*. London: 1965.

Wilson, G. *et al. Geometry for Architects*. Champaigne: 1962.

Yazdani, Ghulam. *Bidar, Its History and Monuments*. London: 1947.

__________., *Mandu: The City of Joy*. Oxford: 1929.

Appendices

A — Miscellaneous Plans & Maps
B — Major Rulers of India
C — Chronology of Major Indian Monuments
D — Glossary

Appendix A:
Miscellaneous Plans and Maps

Notes to Miscellaneous Plans

Plate 61 — *Palace of Minos* (*c.* 1600-1400 BCE), Knossos, Crete, p. 233. The Palace at Knossos, frequently known as the "Palace of Minos," reputed to be the home of the Minotaur of Perseus fame. The complex, convoluted plan of the palace would appear to give rise to the labyrinth myth. Whether this labyrinthine quality was a result of numerous additions, or as a symbol of the wealth and power of the Knossos Court, or as a means of security is conjectural. Nonetheless, it stands, and stood as an example of a palace complex of considerable scale. With the possible exception of the "Pillar Hall" (**F**), axiality was not a concern here.

Plate 62 — *Temple of Amen-Re* (*c.* 1500-1280 BCE), Karnak, Egypt, p. 234. Unlike the *Palace of Minos* , the *Temple of Amen-Re* does indicate a debt to an axial arrangement. Nonetheless, its vastness, and the multiple, pillared areas do create a labyrinthine quality. This temple was not open to the general public. Its "elevated" status plus its vastness would have stood as a paradigm for later temples — i.e., palaces of the gods.

Plate 63 — *Kasr Kharana* (*c.* 710 CE), Amman, Jordan, p. 235. Constructed during the beginnings of Islamic architecture, the *Kasr Kharana* indicates a debt to the Roman *castrum* — i.e., a military encampment or barracks (Ger.: *kaserne*) (See: **Figure 151**). The *Kasr Kharana* is a desert palace which obviously possesses defensive capabilities and can be seen, *en plan*, to be a form adapted by mosques as well. Here an open courtyard is surrounded by rooms, also a hallmark of many civilian residences of the Mediterranean. The strict cross-axiality is obvious, and must have been influenced by the cross-axial *castrum*.

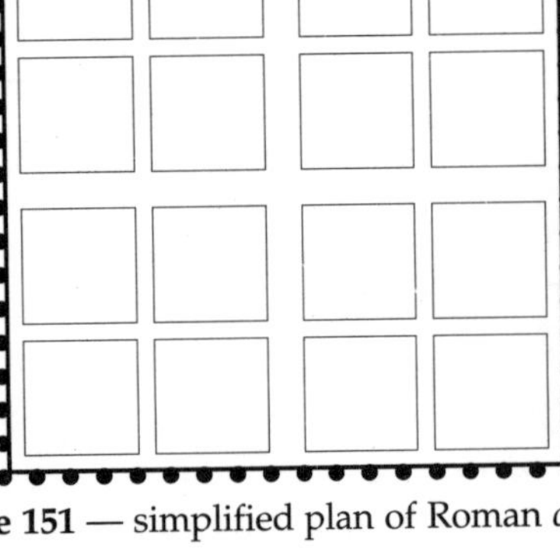

Figure 151 — simplified plan of Roman *castrum*

Plate 64 — *Kasr Amman* (a. 750 CE), Amman, Jordan, p. 236. Here the strict cross-axiality is again employed. However, the open court in the centre has been replaced by a domed space in this smaller residence. It seems that the square implied order and also possessed some social imperative.

Plate 65 — *Palace of Ukhaydir* (a. 750 CE), Ukhaydir, Iraq, p. 237. Set within developed perimeter, defensive battlements, the *Palace of Ukhaydir* indicates an axial plan for the residential complex which is virtually mirror-axial. Even the supposed *Diwān-i-Khās* (**F**), set to the south of the residence is mirror-axial. Additionally, the size and scope of the various elements of this palace creates a labyrinthine atmosphere.

Plate 66 — *Bulkawara Palace* (*c.* 850-860 CE), Samarra, Iraq, p. 238. The axis of this vast palace complex is oriented towards Mecca. Further, it is to be noted that the general layout is cruciform. The main axis of the compound is roughly north-east-south-west, bisecting three baghs. Within the cross arm, particularly in the southern area, the majority of the structures rest perpendicular to the north-east-south-west axis. This creates a plan with multiple, perpendicular axes.

Plate 67 — *Diwān-i Ām & Diwān-i-Khās of Abdul al-Rahman III, Palace* (Detail) (*c.* 936 CE), Cordoba, Spain, p. 239. The famous Cordoba Moorish palace is complex and asymmetrical compound. Yet elements of this palace exhibit a strict axiality. Here the *Diwān-i-Khās* with its flanking pools is set with a bagh and axially aligned to the *Diwān-i-Ām*.

Plate 68 — *Śiva Temple* (*c.* 950), Masaon, India, p. 240. The uniqueness of this temple is to be found in the circular plan. Generally, the circle was considered sacred to the Buddhists and the square to the Hindu. In addition, it is noteworthy that this plan is uterine in shape.

Plate 69 — *Ananda* (*c.* 1105 CE), Pagan, Burma, p. 241. The magnificent *Ananda* of Pagan stands at the apogee of temple architecture in this kingdom. The major temples of Pagan all tended to be cross-axial. There are, however, examples of axial temples, but they are smaller in scale and size.

Plate 70 — *Angkor Wat* (*c.* 1113-1150 CE), Angkor, Kamboja, p. 242. The peerless *Angkor Wat* indicates, on the outset, the impression of cross-axiality. However, the whole is axial, only the sanctuary area is strictly cross-axial. This seems to underline the Hindu *śilpa śāstra* adherence to the square. Only the incomparable *Bayon* deviates from this norm.

Plate 71 — *Neak Pean* (a. 1175 CE), Angkor, Kamboja, p. 243. Within the vast area of Angkor, the *Neak Pean* is virtually lost. Yet, it was a most important site within the vast Angkorian Empire. Various god-kings (Ind.: *devaraj*) raised their own temples, but they all came to *Neak Pean* to make offerings on special, yearly occasions. The mirror cross-axiality establishes a feminine swastika, an important symbol to both Buddhists and Hindu alike.

Plate 72 — *Ziza Palace* (1185 CE), Palermo, Sicily, p. 244. This palace in Sicily is nearly mirror axial in its plan. Rectangular, rather than square, it indicates a model that was to be seen in the smaller palaces and pavilions of Bijapur, for example. Here the triple openings of the façade are minimized, but in Bijapur, this feature is extended to include the whole front.

Plate 73 — *Bayon* (*c.* 1200 CE), Angkor Thom, Kamboja, p. 245. The incomparable Bayon exhibits axiality as well as a labyrinthine character. The central, circular sanctuary is, likewise axial, rather than cross-axial. Only the pavilions proper at the corners and the cardinal points are cross-axial.

Plate 74 — *Temple of Śiva and Mīnākṣī* (13th-17th *c.* CE), Madurai, p. 246. This vast temple, also referred to as the *Mīnākṣī Sundareśvara* Temple, was constructed over centuries and indicates the employment of multiple perpendicular axiality. The only anomaly in this important complex is the large tank near the southern *gopuram*, which is more closely oriented to north than the whole. The major and minor temples are oriented east to west. However, the "Great Thousand Pillared Hall" is oriented south to north.

Plate 75 — *Tomb Ghiyas-ud-din Tughluq I* (a. 1325 CE), Tughluqabad; and *Sayyid Usman Rausa* (*c.* 1460 CE), Usmanpur, p. 247. Both of these square early tombs are cross-axial. Virtually all the Islamic tombs of India are similarly cross-axial.

Plate 76 — *Firuz Bey Çami* (*c.* 1394 CE), Milas, Turkey (above); and *Hatuniye Çami* (*c.* 1489 CE), Manisa, Turkey (below), p. 248. Both of these mosques utilize a simple rectangular plan. Additionally, they are both fronted by an arcaded verandah.

Plate 77 — Brunelleschi, *Santa Maria degli Angeli* (abandoned) (1434-37 CE), Florence, p. 249. Brunelleschi's elegant proposal for *Santa Maria degli Angeli* finds antecedents in the circular-type temples of the Greco-Roman period. Further the *Santa Costanza*, Rome, (*c.* 350 CE) also serves as a precursor. As a church based upon an octagon, the *Temple of the Palace of Diocletian*, Split, Croatia (450 CE) as well as the *Qubbat as-Sulaybiyya*, Samarra, Iraq (*c.* 892 CE) also serve as cogent forerunners. The octagon becomes an important form in the plans of Islamic architecture. Its appearance in *garh mahals* is considerably less. In Hindu architecture its employment is generally relegated to corner towers.

Plate 78 — *Mahmet Pasha Çami* (1464 CE), Istanbul, p. 250. Many of the early palaces and or residences of Islam tended towards the square. Virtually all the tombs were either octagonal, round or square. Yet, the most important and largely visible Islamic structure — i.e., the mosque (Arab.: *masjid*) — is almost

Notes to Miscellaneous Plans (Continued)

always rectangular. Even the very earliest, extant mosques were rectangular. This may have had something to do with the congregational quality of Islam. The *Mahmet Pasha Çami* exhibits this penchant for the rectangle and, further the axial quality of the whole. In addition, the domes of the roof line make a clear statement that the Renaissance architects sought — i.e., squaring the circle or circling the square.

Plate 79 — Bramante, *Proposed New St. Peter's* (1505 CE), Rome, p. 251. Cross-axiality was not a favoured form in the West. However, Bramante's proposed plan for the new *St. Peter's* is an exception on a grand scale. The employment of a great dome, and multiple subsidiary domes would have been gleefully accepted by Islamic builders.

Plate 80 — *Tomb of Sher Sur* (1540 CE), Saseram; and *Tomb of Isa Khan* (1547 CE), Delhi, p. 252. By the time of the Mughals, the octagon has all but supplanted the square as the preferred form for Islamic tombs. Still, cross-axiality reigned.

Plate 81 — *Tomb of Humayun* (1565 CE), Delhi; and *Tāj Mahal*, Agra (1632-54 CE), p. 253. The two major tombs of the Mughals — i.e., the *Tomb of Humayun* and the *Tāj Mahal* — both appear to be based upon the square. They do fit within a square, however, this design is based upon the *muthamman baghdadi* and the *Tāj Mahal's* debt to the octagon is more apparent. Nonetheless, they are both cross-axial.

Plate 82 — Palladio, *Villa Rotunda* (*c.* 1566-70 CE), Vicenza, Italy, p. 254. Palladio's design for the *Villa Rotunda* was seen as revolutionary during his period. Nonetheless, there are numerous Buddhist/Hindu/Islamic antecedents to this elegant residence — e.g., the *Ruvanveliseya Dagoba*, Anuradhapura, Sri Lanka (II-I *c.* BCE) or the *Chendebji Stūpa*, Bhutan (central), a. 8th *c.* CE; the *Tomb of the Samanids* (plan), Bukhara, Uzbekistan (*c.* 920 CE) or the *Chandi Kalasan*, Java, a. 778 CE; the Tomb of Firuz Shah Tughluq, Delhi, *c.* 1389 CE, or the Tomb of Muhammad Ghaus, Gwalior, *c.* 1565 CE.

Plate 83 — *Masjid-i Jami* (1644-1658 CE), Delhi, p. 255. As stated above, mosques tended to be rectangular, *en plan*. The exception being the *Masjid-i Jami* of Delhi. Vast in scale, this mosque, adjacent to the Lāl Qilā (Shahjahanabad) is a fitting exponent of imperial wealth and power. It is square, but not cross-axial. It is unremittingly axial.

Plate 84 — *Chihil Sutun* (b. 1666 CE), Isfahan, Iran, p. 256. It may have been a symptom of the times, but square, cross-axial plan for residences was not strictly adhered to. The *Chihil Sutun* is an elegant example of an axial plan, *in toto*. The area to the west of the covered vestibule — i.e., the enclosed area — is square. The total is strictly axial.

Plate 85 — *Topkapisaray* (a. 1326-1900 CE), Istanbul, p. 257. The *Topkapisaray* is a prime example of a palace that had been added on to over the centuries. It exhibits a plan with non-perpendicular axes, although it tends towards a north-east orientation.

Plate 86 — ***Viṭṭhala* (*Vithoba*) *Temple*** (1509-30 CE), Hampi, p. 258. Although not part of the Vijayanagara complex, it sits a short distance to the north. The *vimana* (**A**) and *maṇḍapa* (**B**) are traditionally designed. However, the *mahāmaṇḍapa* (**C**) is rather erratic in its design.

Plate 87 — ***Chandragiri Palace*** (*Rājā Mahal*), proportional elevation and 1st storey plan, p. 259. Axial (mirror axial) this palace is related to the Bundela palaces.

Plate 88 — *Jahāz Mahal* (1st half 16th *c.* CE), Bijapur, p. 260. Although strictly axial, the *Jahāz Mahal* is based upon a five-square model.

Plate 89 — *Rāja Mandir*, proportional elevation & half plan (a. 1554 CE), p. 261. Square, *en plan*, it follows the standard set in the *śilpa-śāstras*. Its elevation is rather uninteresting, especially when compared to other Bundela palaces.

Notes to Miscellaneous Plans (Continued)

Plate 90 — *Jahangir Mandir*, proportional elevation & half plan (a. 1605 CE), p. 262.

Plate 91 — *Govind Mandir* (*Bir Singh Judeo Mahal*), proportional elevation & half plan (a. 1620 CE), p. 263. The most developed Bundela *garh-mahal*, *en plan*, and the most elaborate elevation, this palace is considered to be the last of the true Hindu palaces.

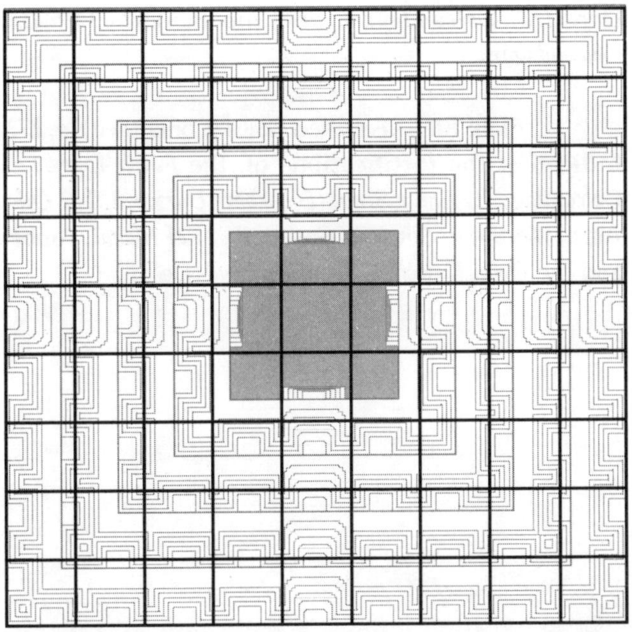

Figure 152 — *Geometric Tank* with *Paramaśayika Maṇḍala*

Plate 92 — *Hesht Behest* (*c.* 1669), Isfahan, p. 264. Roughly contemporaneous with the *Shahi Bagh* of Ahmadabad (*c.* 1623 CE), the *Hesht Behest* is a standard for a pleasure pavilion of Persia that had existed for centuries. An open pavilion with private rooms it was adapted to India which had similar weather conditions — i.e., hot and dry during the dry season.

Plate 93 — *Geometric Tank* (a. 1400), *Vijayanagara*, India, p. 255. This stepped tank, to the north of the Great Tank (See: **Plate 3**) is believed by some to have been constructed for the Raya's consecration rites. Constructed of green chlorite, it reflects the high level of technical and design capabilities of that empire. The progression of step elements per face from the centre out is: 1, 3, 5, 7 and 9. The treatment of the central step elements per face is such that an emphasis is placed upon the cardinal points of the compass. In addition, the imposition of a *Paramaśayika Maṇḍala* over the stepped elements finds that each of the top steps per element rests within a *pada* (See: **Figure 152**).

Plate 94 — Axis (*axis mundi*), p. 266. implied and real. R. Nath refers to the *ekastambha* of the *Ekastambha Prasada* (aka *Diwān-i-Khās*) at Fatehpur Sikri as a Mughal presentment. However, there are numerous other examples — e.g., the implied axis of a *stūpa's chattravali*, the real axis of a Tibetan *chorten*, and implied axis within a *garbhagṛha*'s foundational preparation.

Plate 95 — Fortified Gates (line of fire), p. 267. Entrance to the outer and inner precincts of an Indian citadel, whether pre- or post-Mughal, followed similar parameters. Entrances were generally limited to the width and height of a single elephant, a 90° turn slowed down progress, serpentine access was also a feature, and an incline upwards from the exterior was, defensibly, a most desirable feature. A number of the barbicans were truly impressive.

In *Lāl Qilā, Shahjahanabad*, Delhi, Shah Jahan threw tradition to the wind by constructing both the *Lahore* and *Delhi Darwāzā* with direct access to the interior. His bigoted son, Aurangzeb, with obvious paranoid concern, constructed two massive barbicans for his protection. The fortifications of Gingee hinged upon three hills or outcroppings. Here protected cross-fire could be employed to repel any invader. There were a number of impressive gateways along the outer perimeter. However, the *Tripolia*, giving access to the inner precincts, was an impressive structure (See: **Plate 96**).

Before and after the introduction of guns, the entrances were so constructed so that intense cross-fire could be employed by the defenders upon any invading force. The *Fateh Darwāzā* of the *Golcondagarh* (below) indicates a design in which withering cross-fire was possible. The height of these barbicans and/or gates, made defence easier. It is notable that few citadels were not breached during the long history of warfare in India.

Notes to Miscellaneous Plans (Concluded)

Plate 96 — *Gingee Mandir*, Gingee (a. 1490 *c.* CE), p. 268. The garh-mahal is found on a high plateau between three high outcroppings. Suitably fortified, it presented a formidable citadel for the *Nāyakas*.

Plate 97 — *Devagiri* (*Daulatabad*), Maharashtra (a.1187 CE), p. 269. The *Devagiri* or *Daulatabad*, depended upon a height to insure proper fortification. However, here, not three outcroppings but a single, precipitous rise was utilized (See: **Plate 97**) with successive rings of defence. It was so well designed that it never succumbed to siege. It did fall, however, to internal intrigue.

Plate 98 — Fortified Gates, p. 270. Indicating the fortifications of: the *West Gate, Gulbargagarh*, the *Hāthī Pol, Shadiabad*, the *Tarapura Darwāzā, Shadiabad* and the *Delhi Darwāzā, Shadiabad.*

Plate 99 — Fortified Gates (Continued), p. 271. Indicating the fortifications of: the *Gumbad Darwāzā, Bidargarh*, the *Fateh Darwāzā, Bidargarh*, the *Tripolia, Kumbhalgarh* and the *Zohrahpur Darwāzā*, Bijapur.

Plate 100 — Fortified Gates (Continued), p. 272. Indicating the fortifications of: the *Arh Kila Darwāzā*, Bijapur, the *Tripolia, Gingee Mandir*, the *Bala Hissar Darwāzā, Golcondagarh* and the *Banjari Darwāzā, Golcondagarh.*

Plate 101 — Fortified Gates (Concluded), p. 273. Indicating the fortifications of: the *Fateh Darwāzā, Golcondagarh, Amar Singh & Akbarī Darwāzā, Lāl Qilā*, Agra, the *Sūraj, Singh & Ganesh Pol, Rāj Mahal*, Amber and the *Delhi Darwāzā, Shahjahanabad*, Delhi .

Plate 61 — *Palace of Minos* (*c.* 1600-1400 BCE), Knossos, Crete, indicating a labyrinthine layout

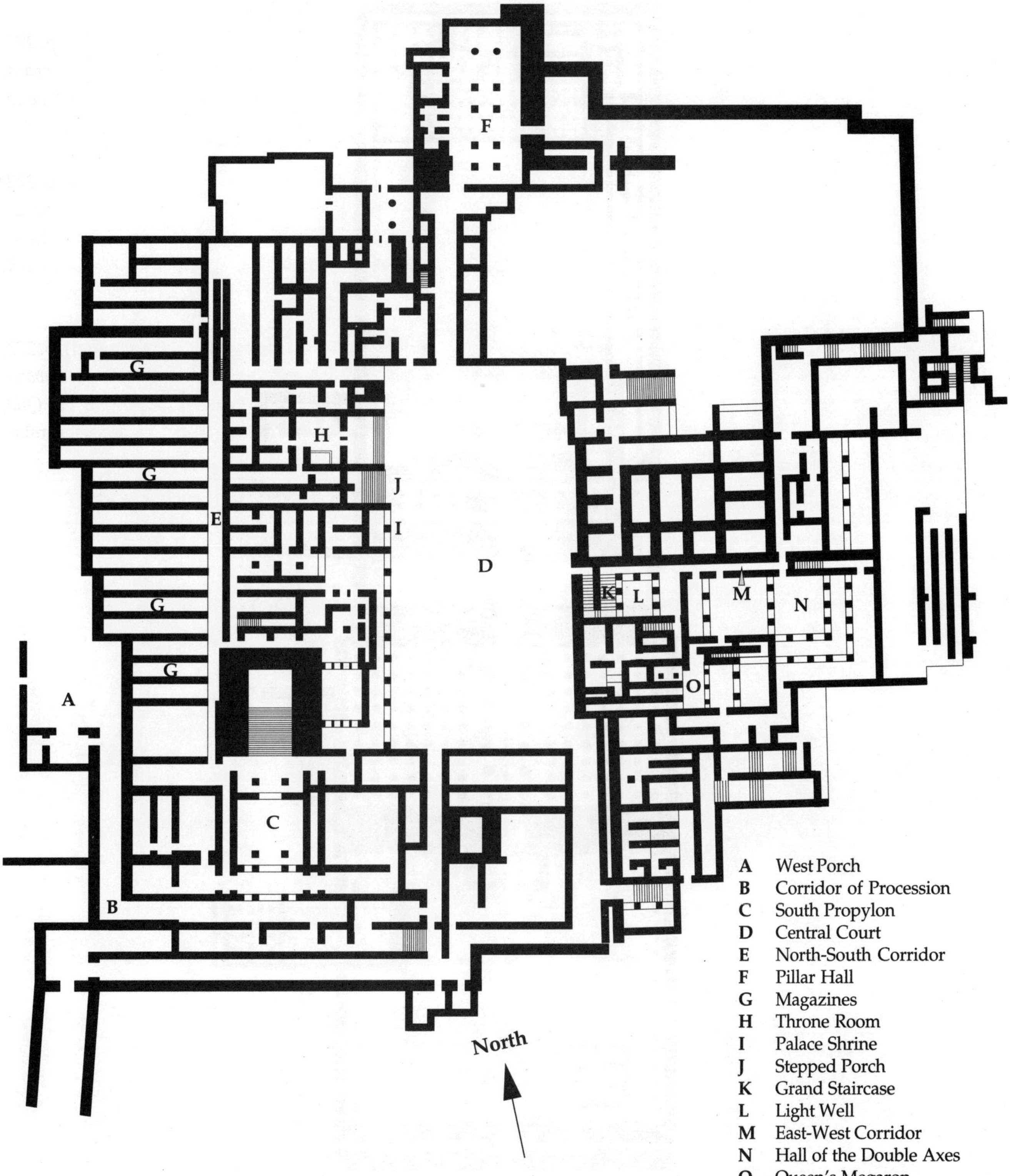

A West Porch
B Corridor of Procession
C South Propylon
D Central Court
E North-South Corridor
F Pillar Hall
G Magazines
H Throne Room
I Palace Shrine
J Stepped Porch
K Grand Staircase
L Light Well
M East-West Corridor
N Hall of the Double Axes
O Queen's Megaron

Plate 62 — *Temple of Amen-Re* (*c.* 1500-1280 BCE), Karnak, Egypt, indicating an axial alignment & labyrinthine layout

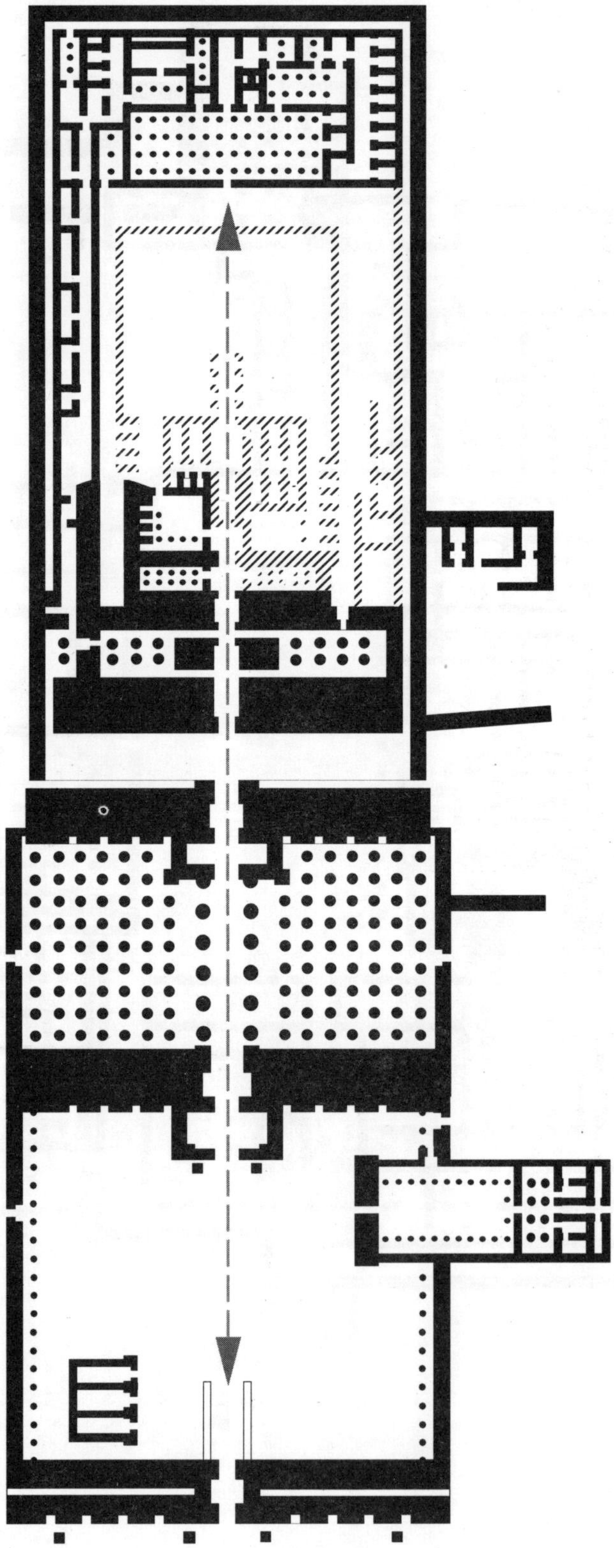

Plate 63 — *Kasr Kharana* (*c.* 710 CE), Amman, Jordan, indicating cross axial alignment

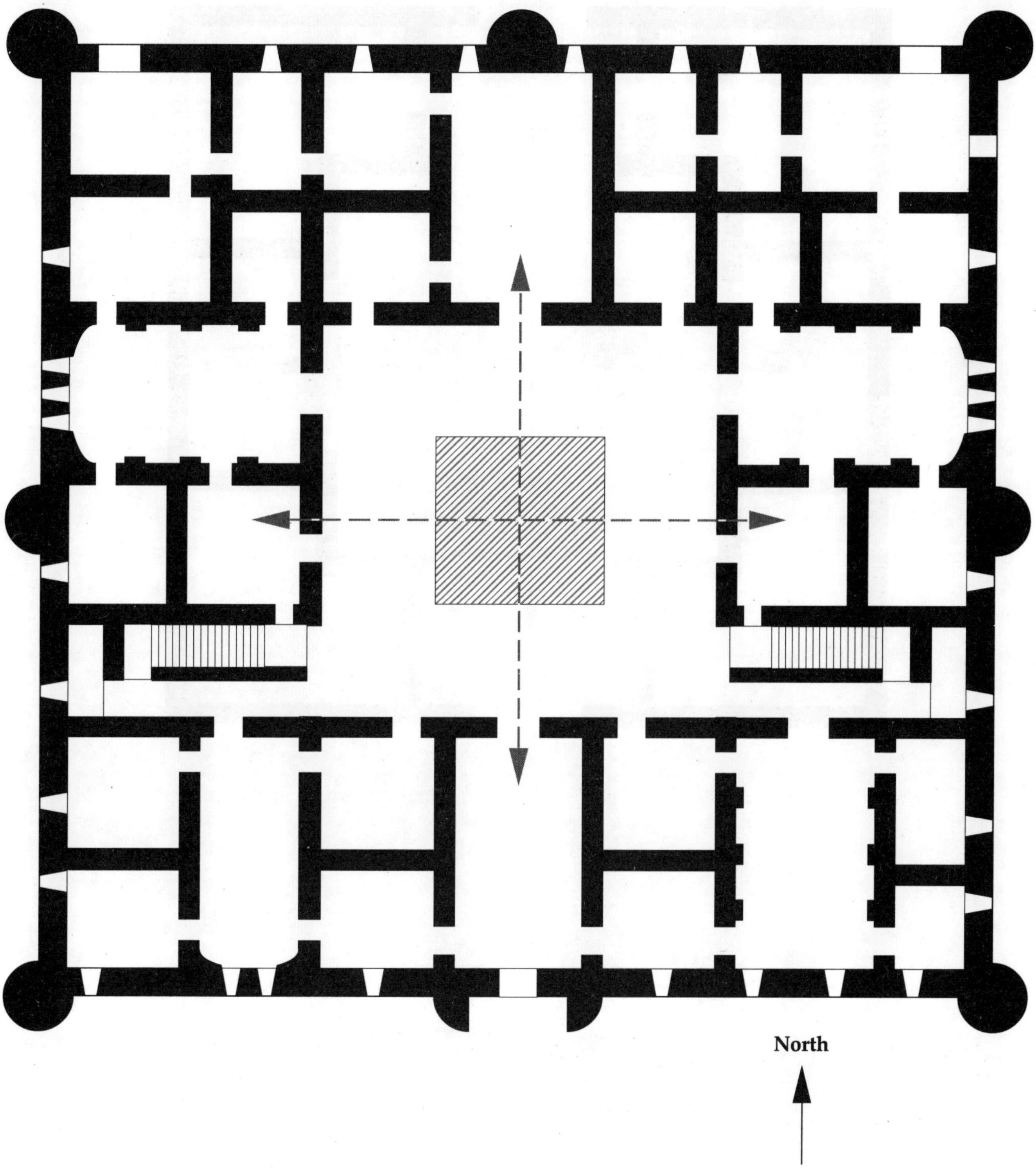

Plate 64 — *Kasr Amman* (a. 750 CE), Amman, Jordan, indicating cross axial alignment

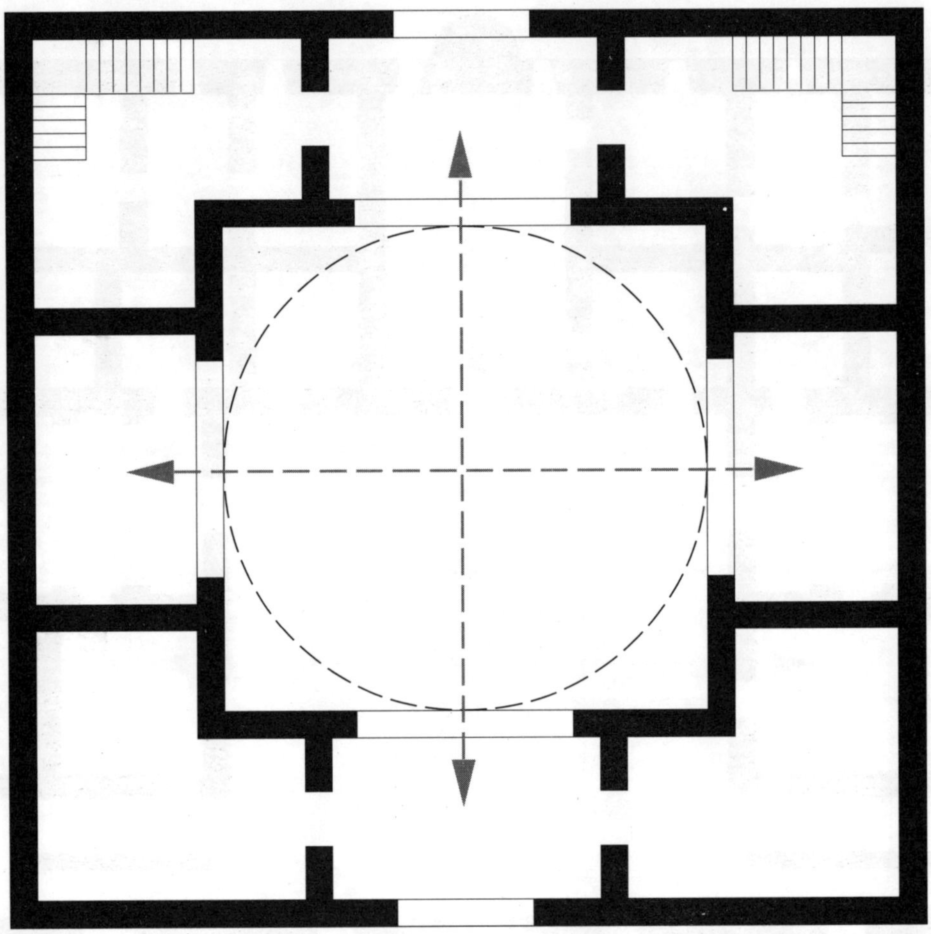

Plate 65 — *Palace of Ukhaydir* (a. 750 CE), Ukhaydir, Iraq, indicating axial alignment & labyrinthine layout

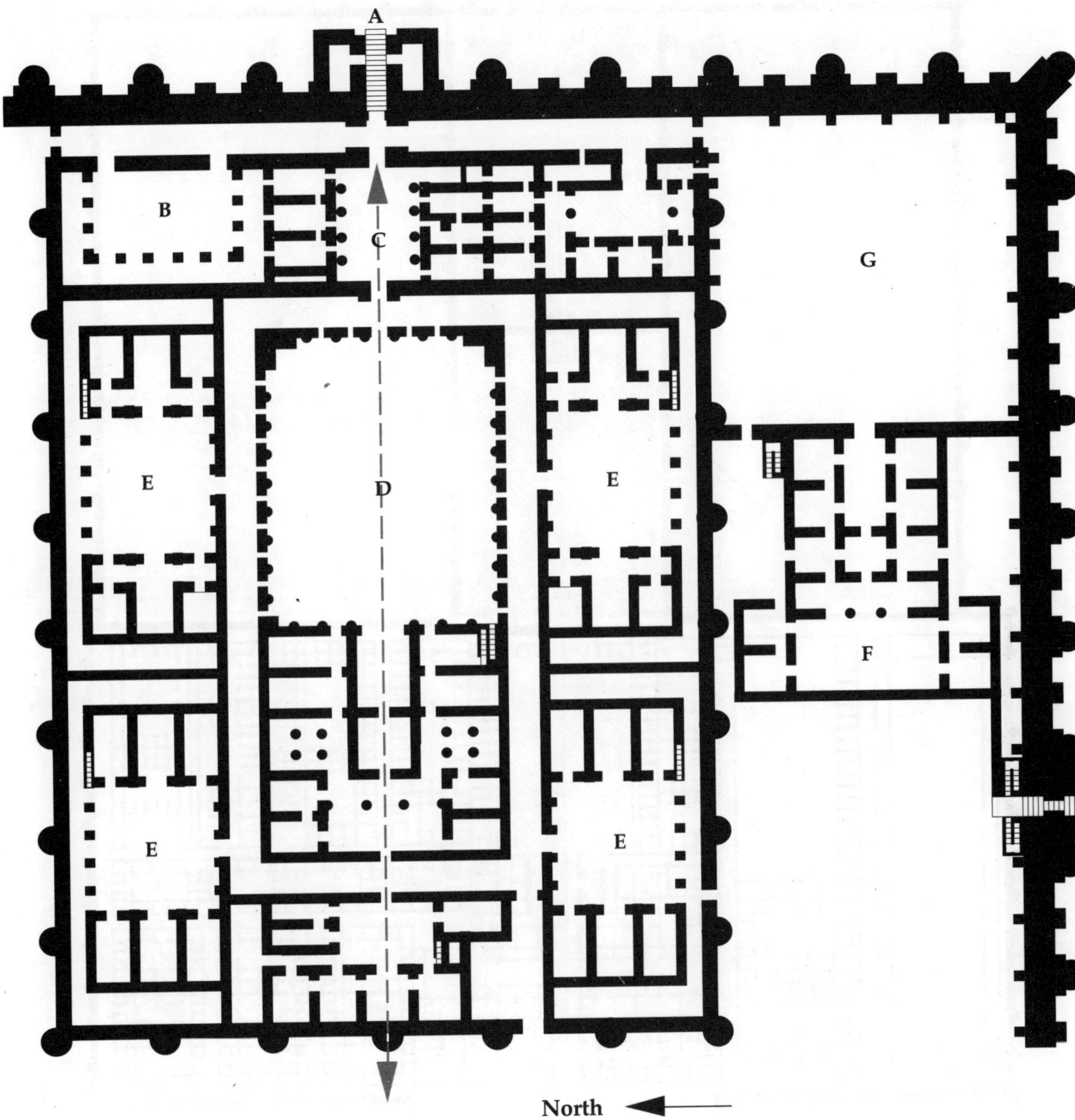

A Main Entrance
B Mosque
C Great Hall
D Inner Court
E Residences
F *Dewān-i-Khās* (?)
G Court

Plate 66 — *Bulkawara Palace* (*c.* 850-860 CE), Samarra, Iraq, indicating axial alignment

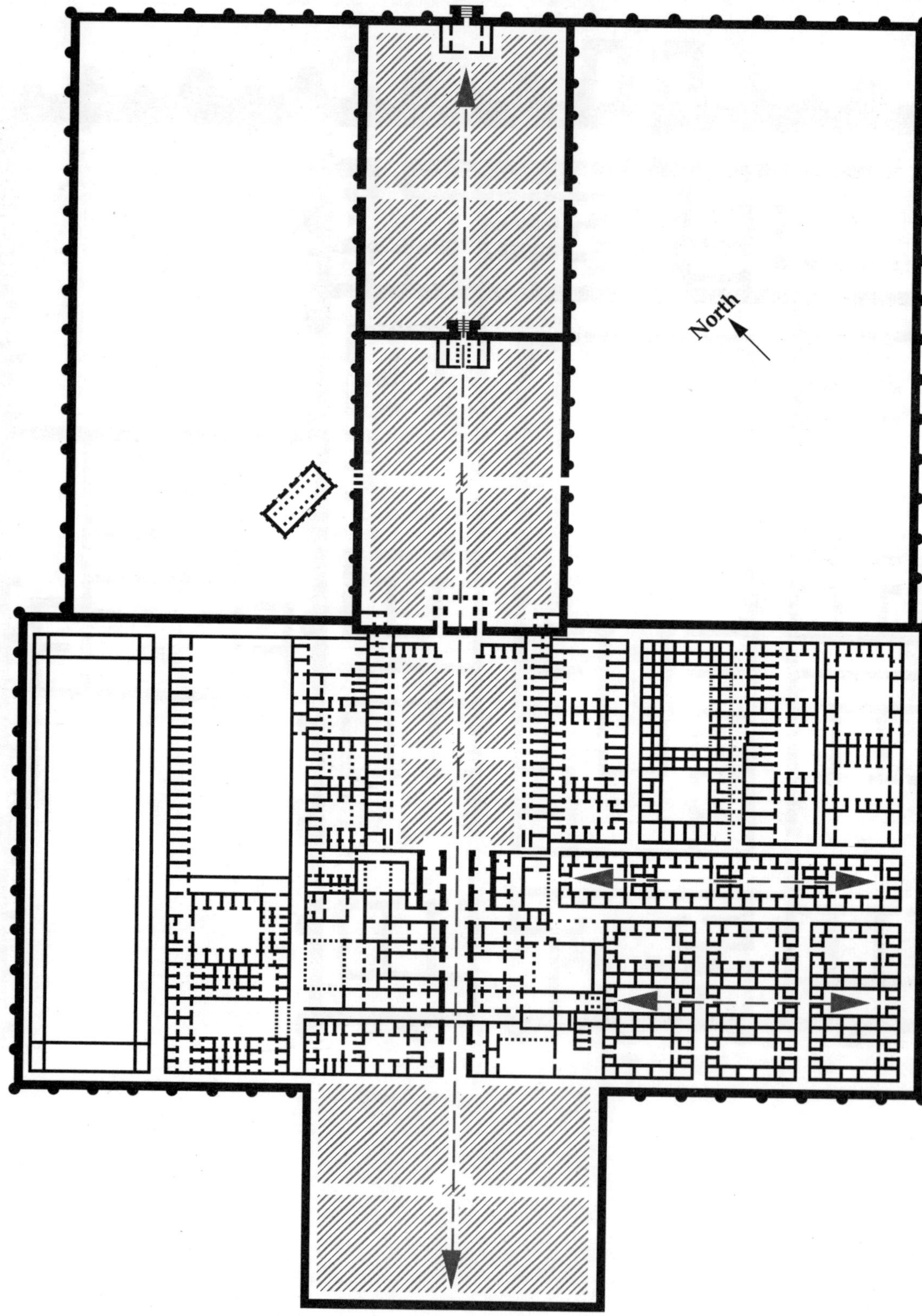

Plate 67 — *Diwān-i-Ām & Diwān-i-Khās of Abdul al-Rahman III, Palace* (Detail) (*c.* 936 CE), Cordoba, Spain, indicating axial alignment

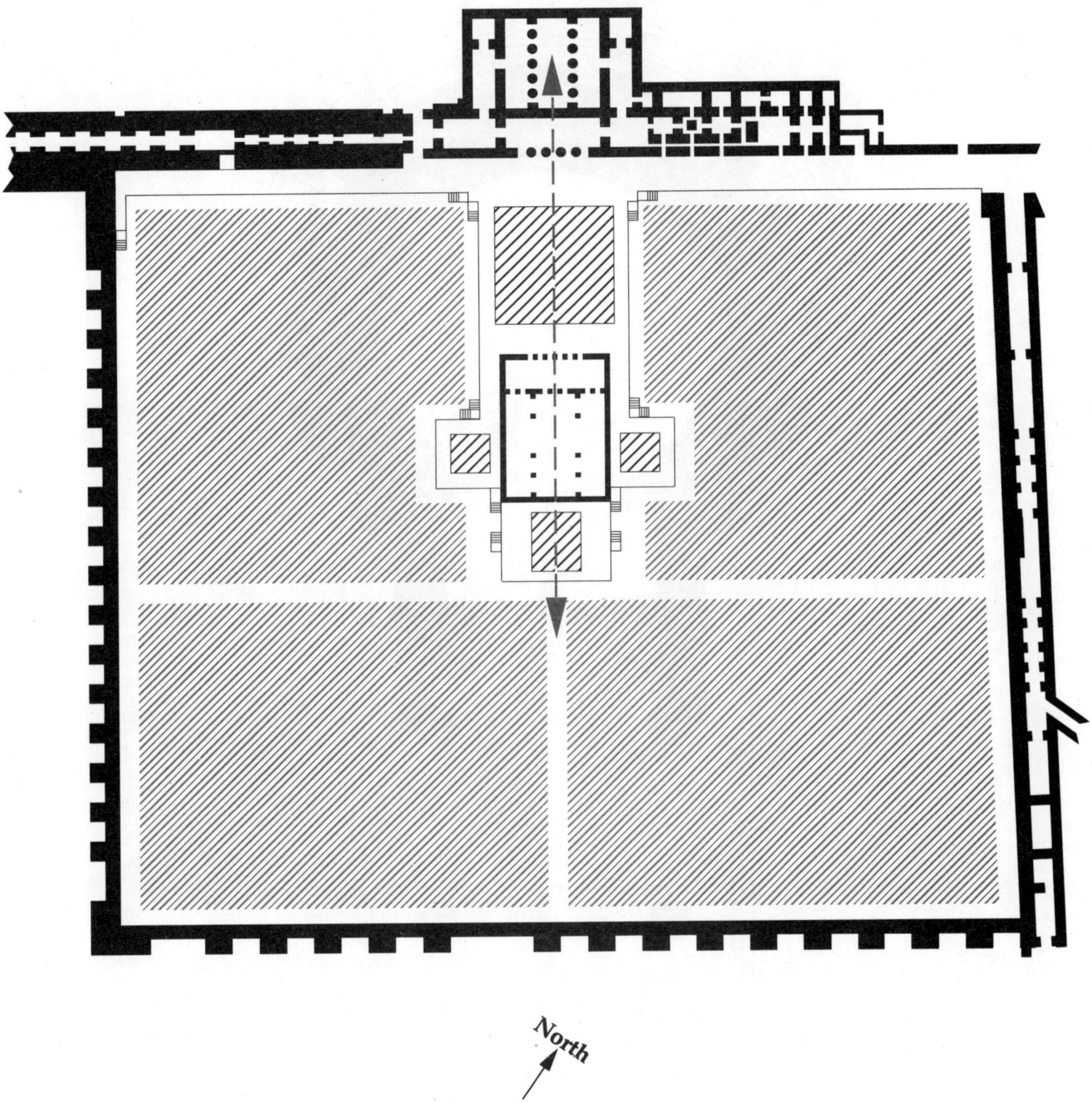

Plate 68 — *Śiva Temple* (*c.* 950 CE), Masaon

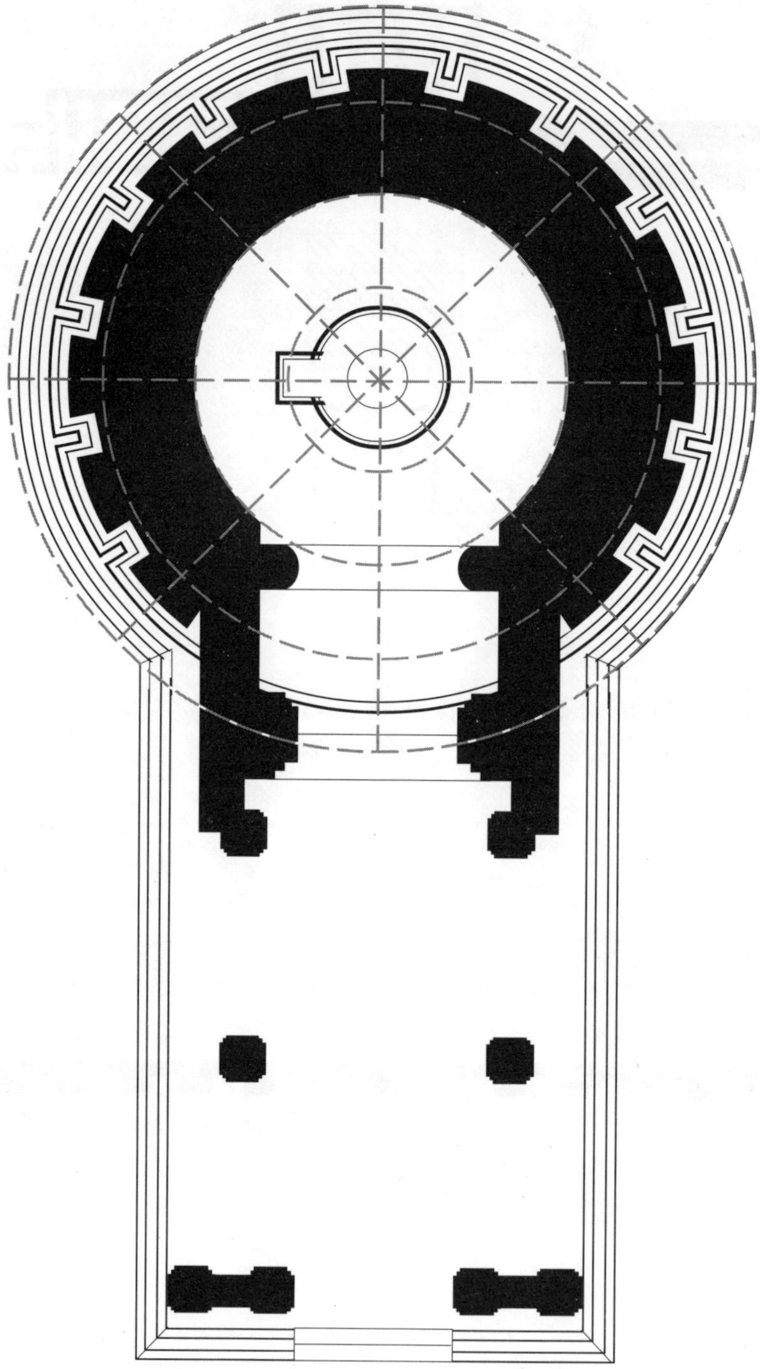

Plate 69 — *Ananda* (*c.* 1105 CE), Pagan, Burma, indicating a cross axial & labyrinthine layout

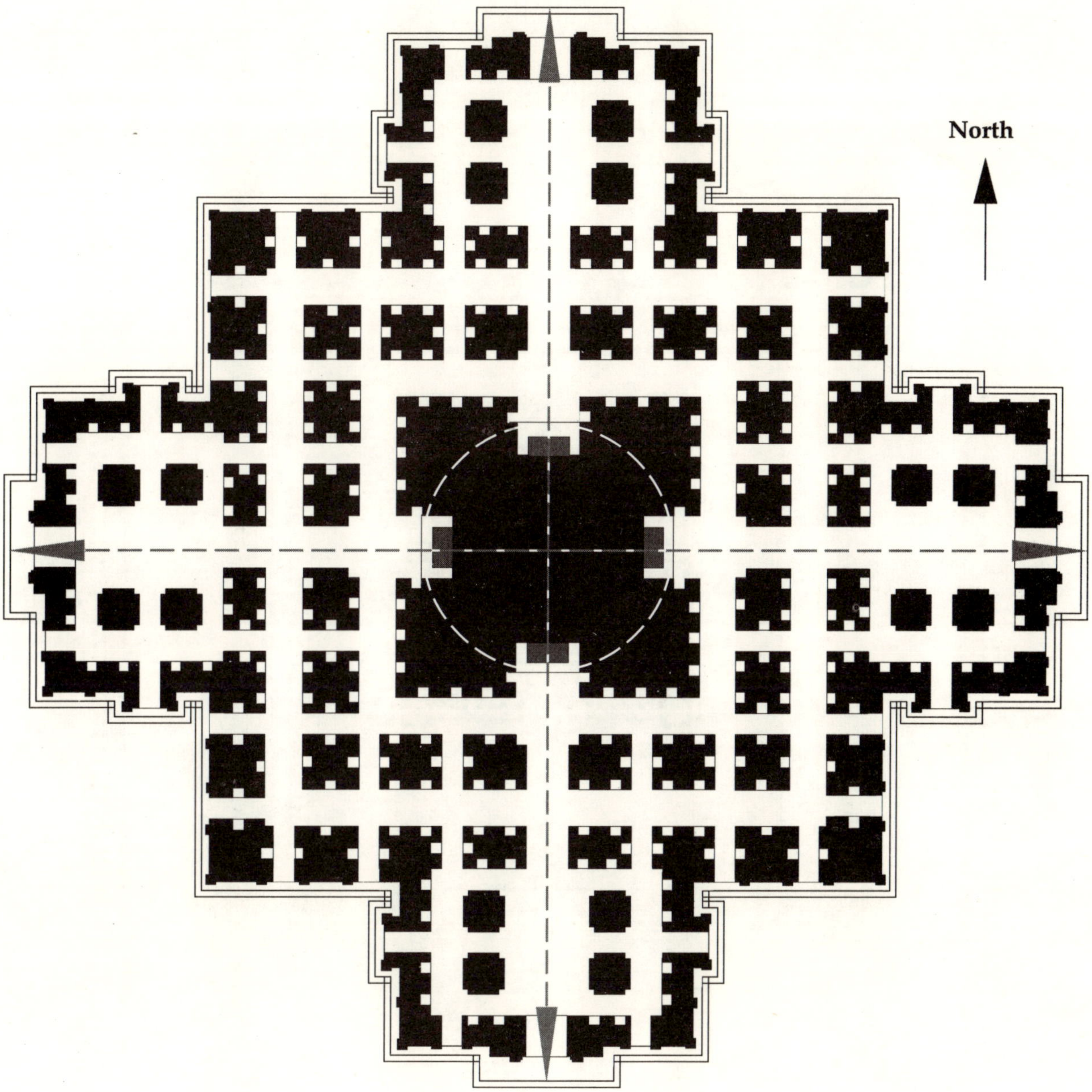

Plate 70 — *Angkor Wat* (*c.* 1113-1150 CE), Angkor, Kamboja, indicating a cross axial alignment of sanctuary

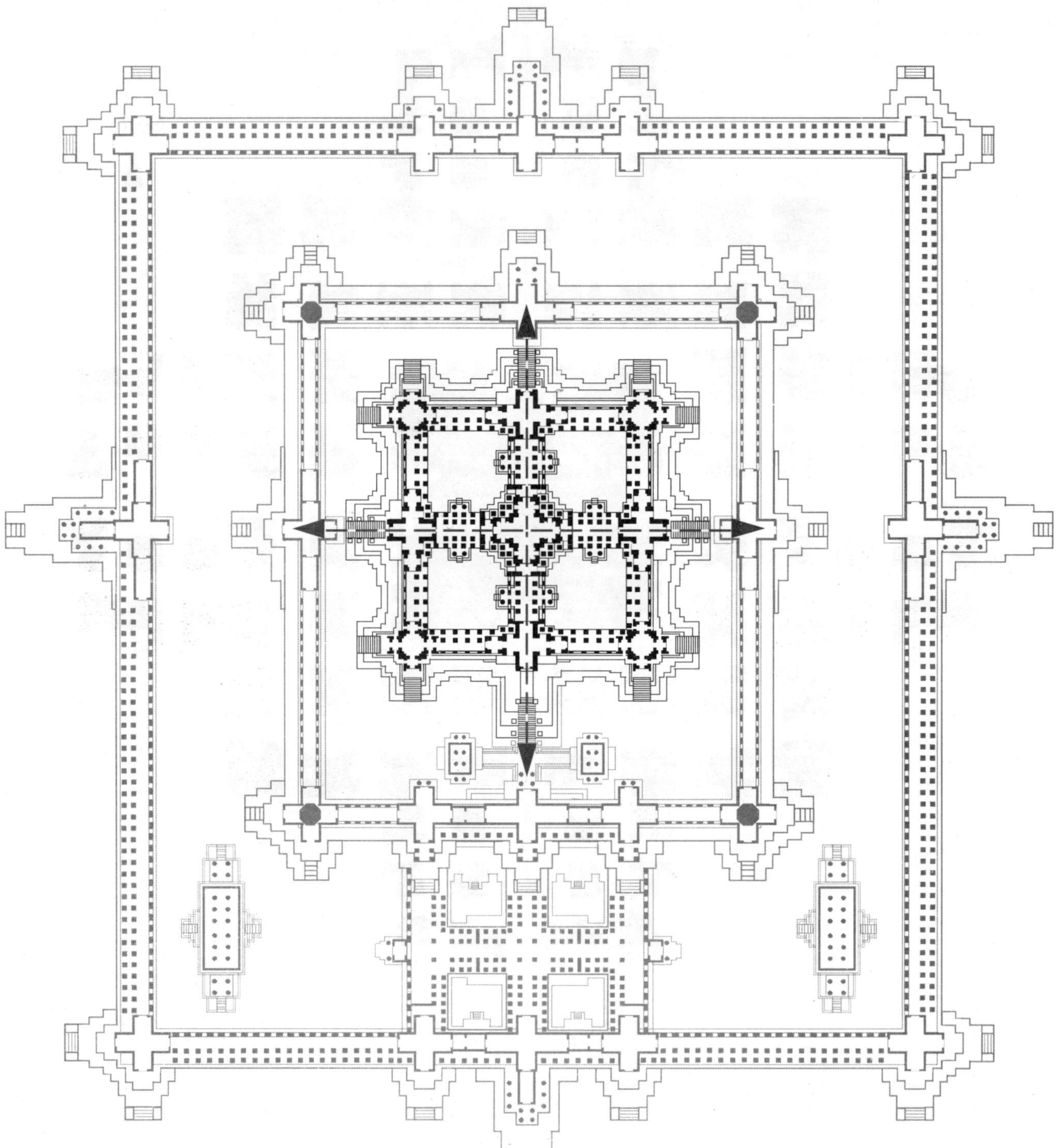

Plate 71 — *Neak Pean* (a. 1175 CE), Angkor, Kamboja, indicating mirror cross-axiality and female swastika

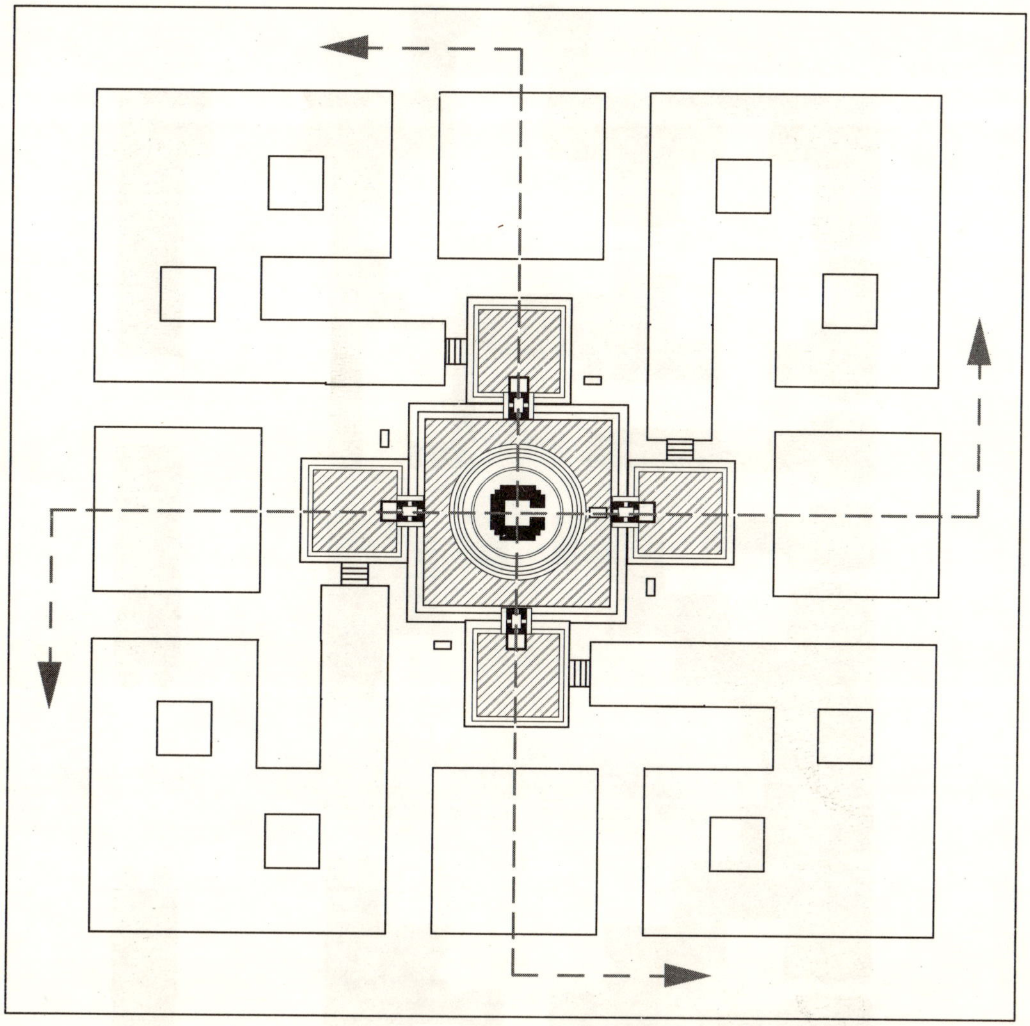

Plate 72 — *Ziza Palace* (1185 CE), Palermo, Sicily, indicating an axial alignment

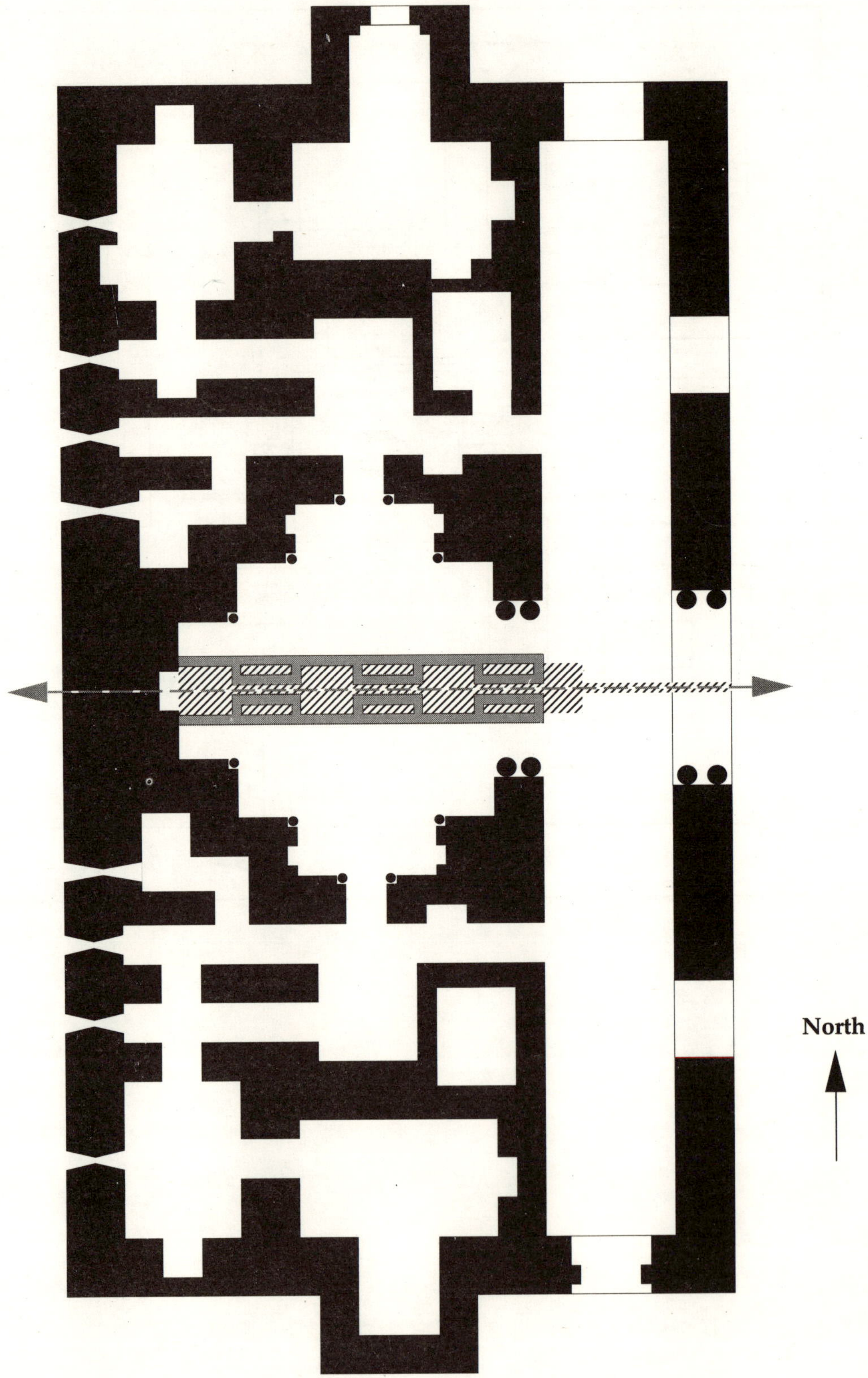

Plate 73 — *Bayon* (*c.* 1200 CE), Angkor Thom, Kamboja, indicating an axial alignment & labyrinthine layout

Plate 74 — *Temple of Śiva and Mīnākṣī (Mīnākṣī Sundareśvara)* (13th-17th *c.* CE), Madurai, indicating a labyrinthine layout & axial alignments

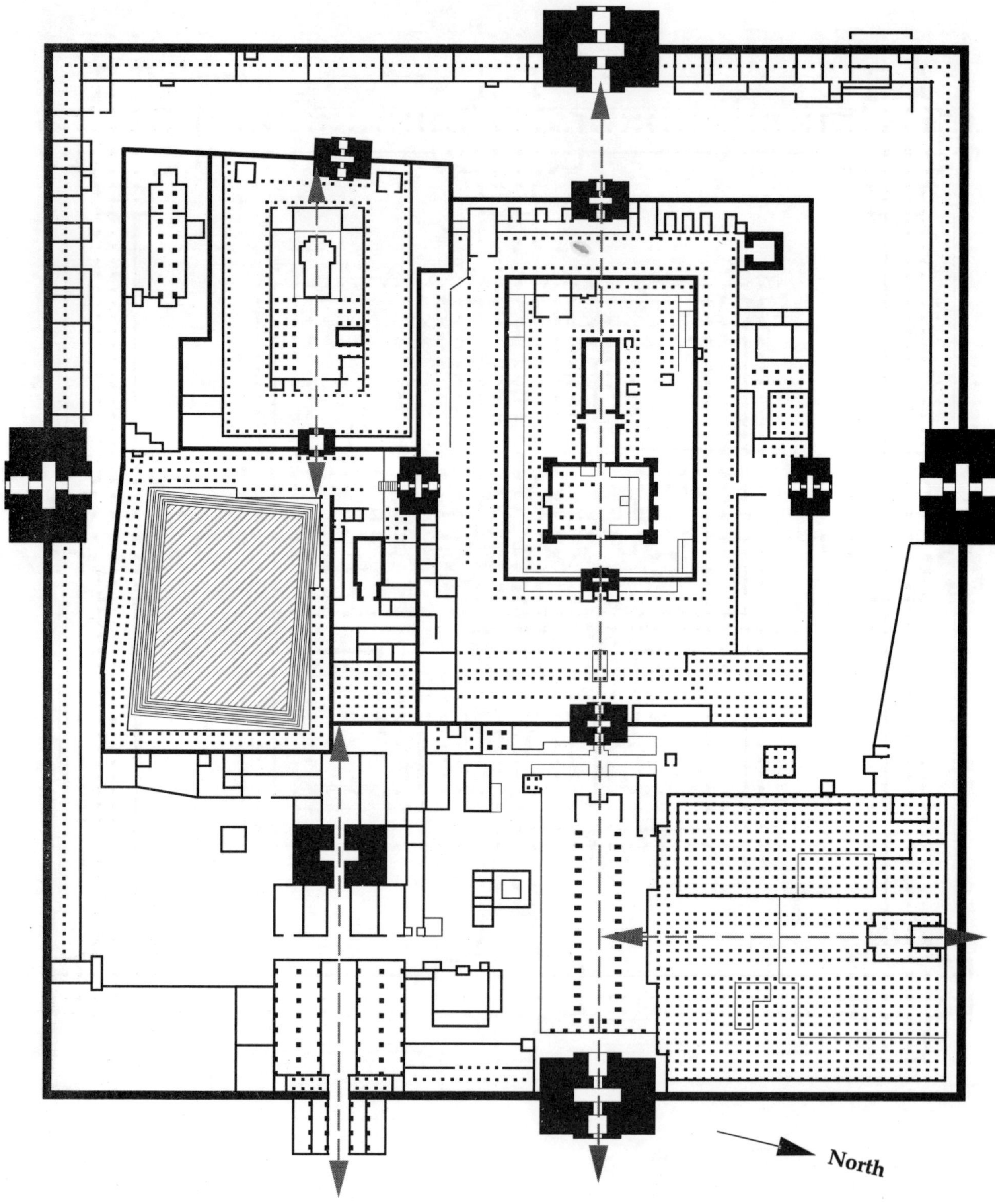

Plate 75 — *Tomb Ghiyas-ud-din Tughluq I* (a. 1325 CE), Tughluqabad, (above); and *Sayyid Usman Rausa* (*c.* 1460 CE), Usmanpur, (below) indicating cross-axial alignment

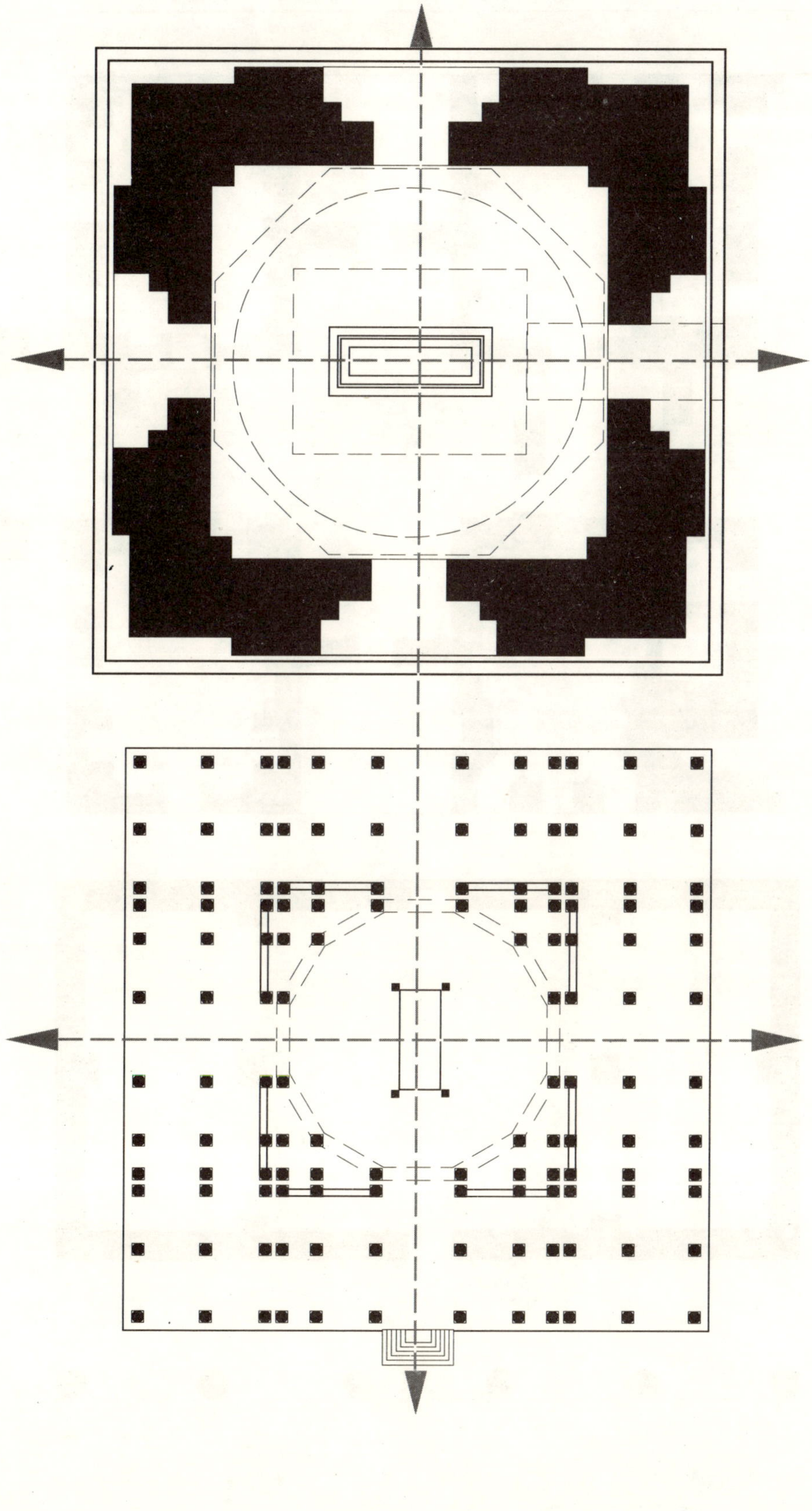

Plate 76 — *Çinili Kiosk* (*c.* 1473 CE), Istanbul (above); and *Hatuniye Çami* (*c.* 1489 CE), Manisa, Turkey (below)

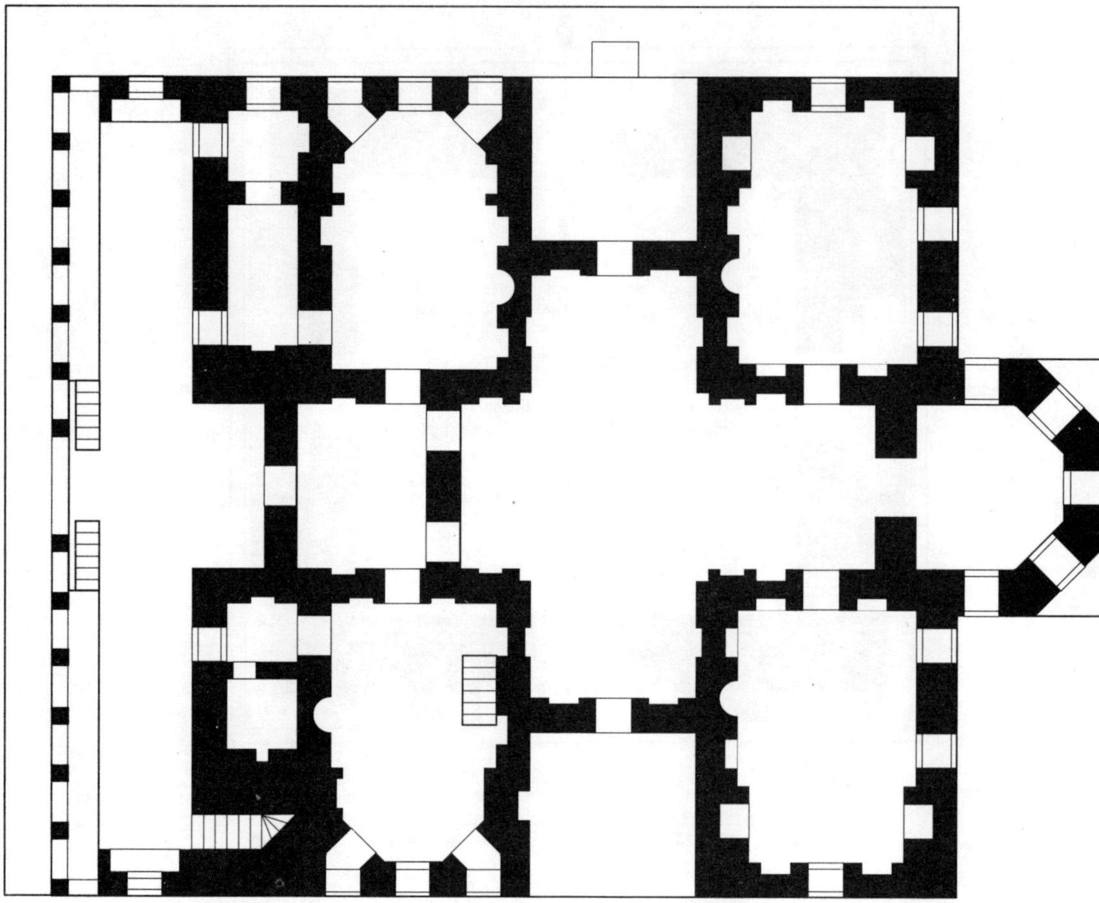

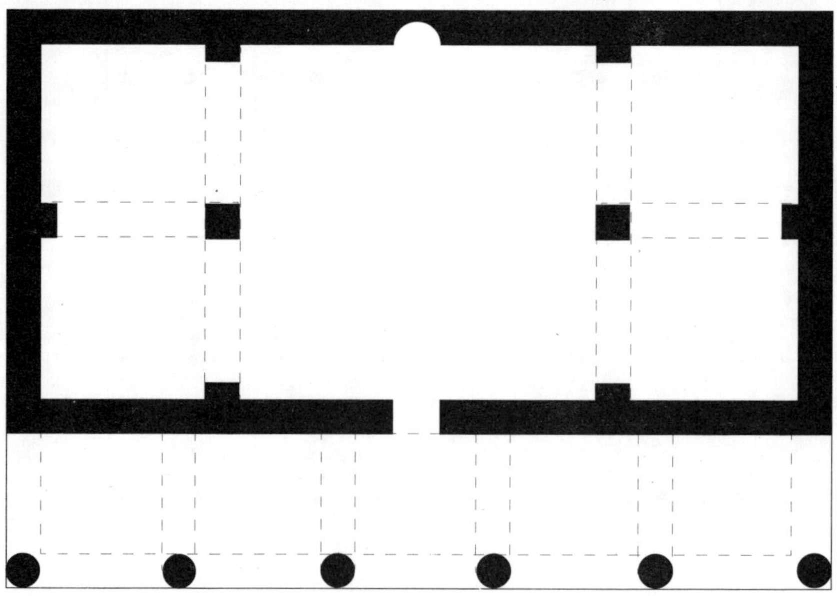

Plate 77 — Brunelleschi, *Santa Maria degli Angeli* (abandoned) (1434-1437 CE), Florence, indicating cross axial alignment

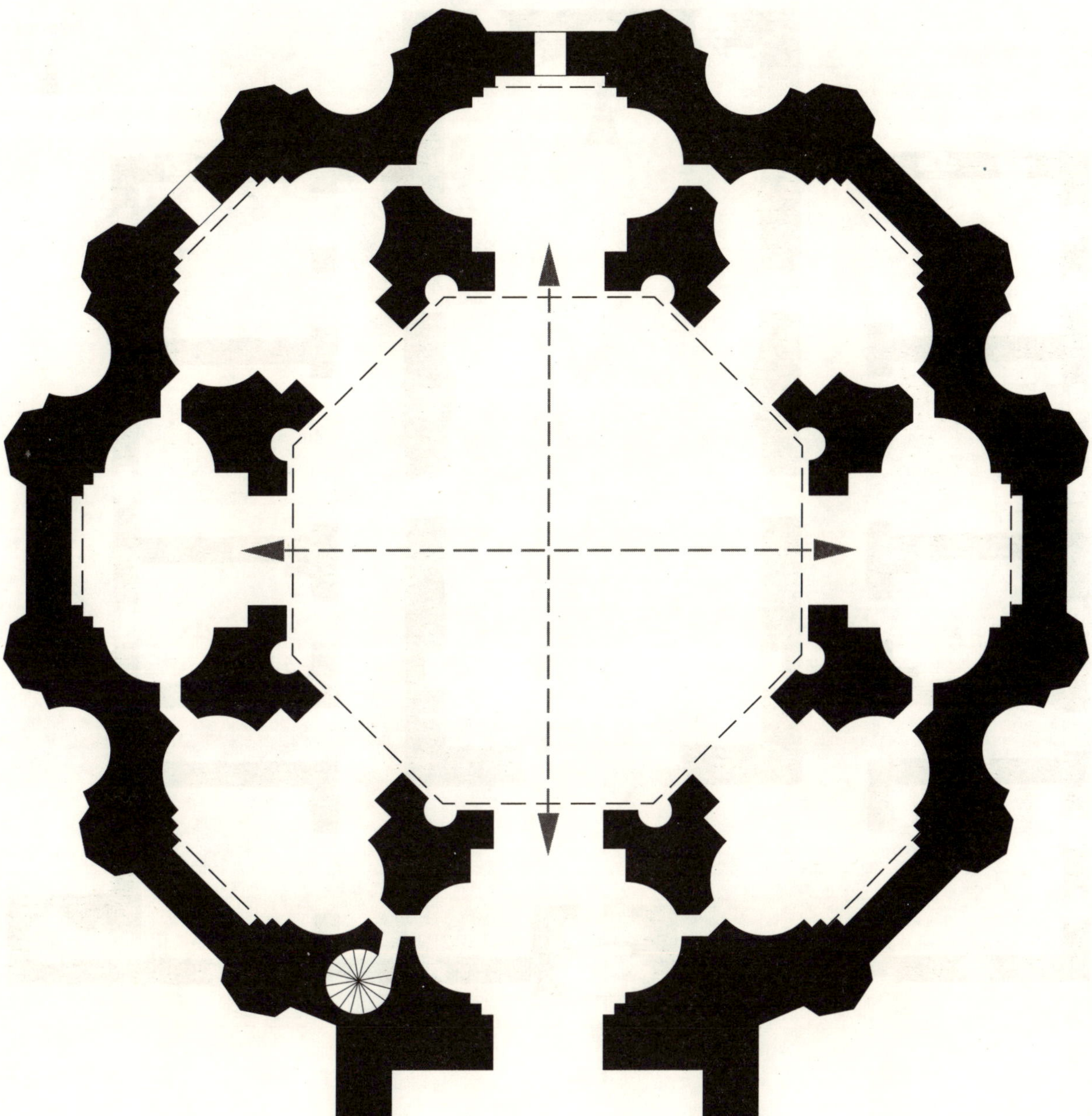

Plate 78 — *Mahmet Pasha Çami* (1464 CE), Istanbul, indicating axial alignment

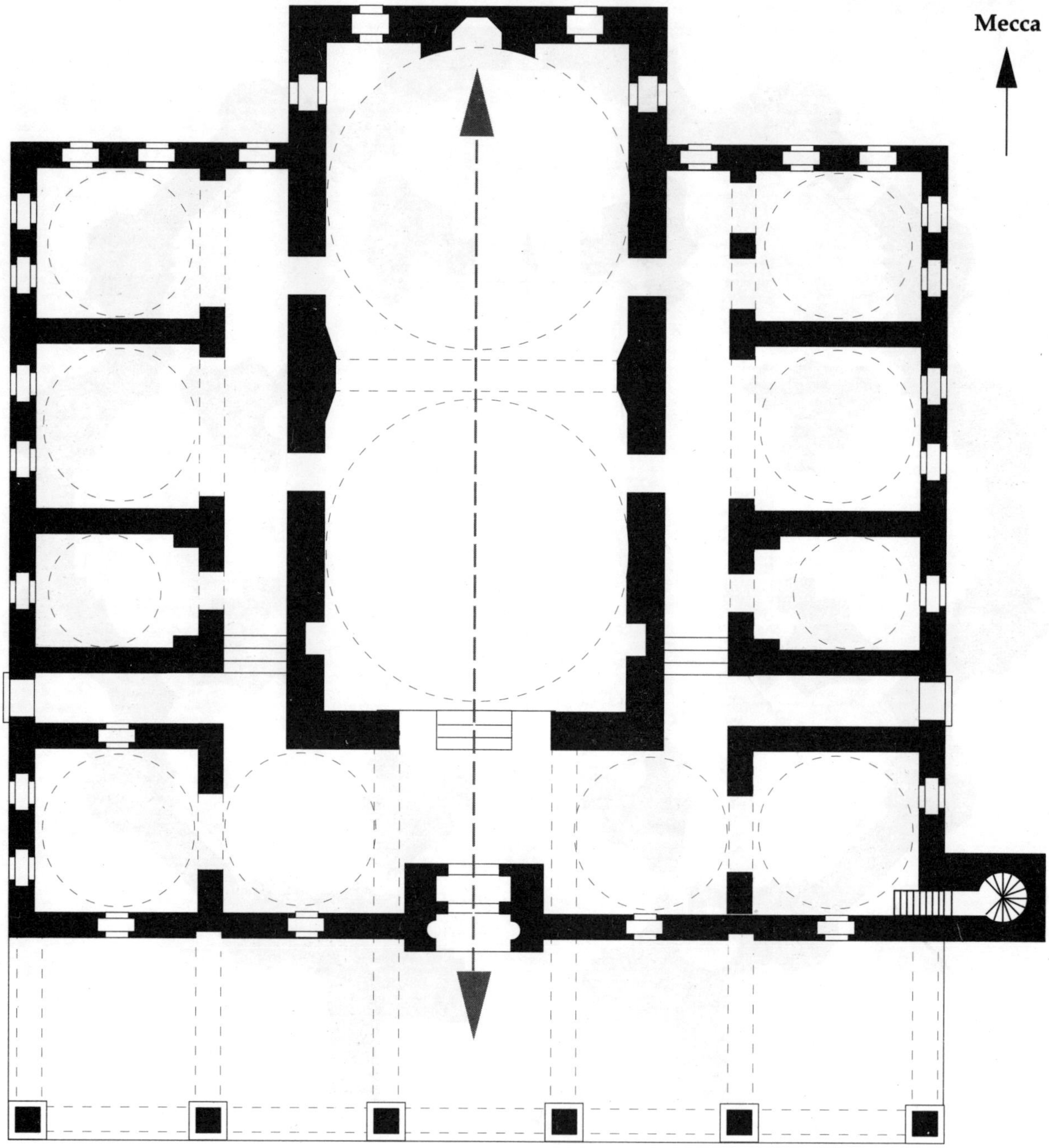

Plate 79 — Bramante, *Proposed New St. Peter's* (1505 CE), Rome, indicating cross axial alignment

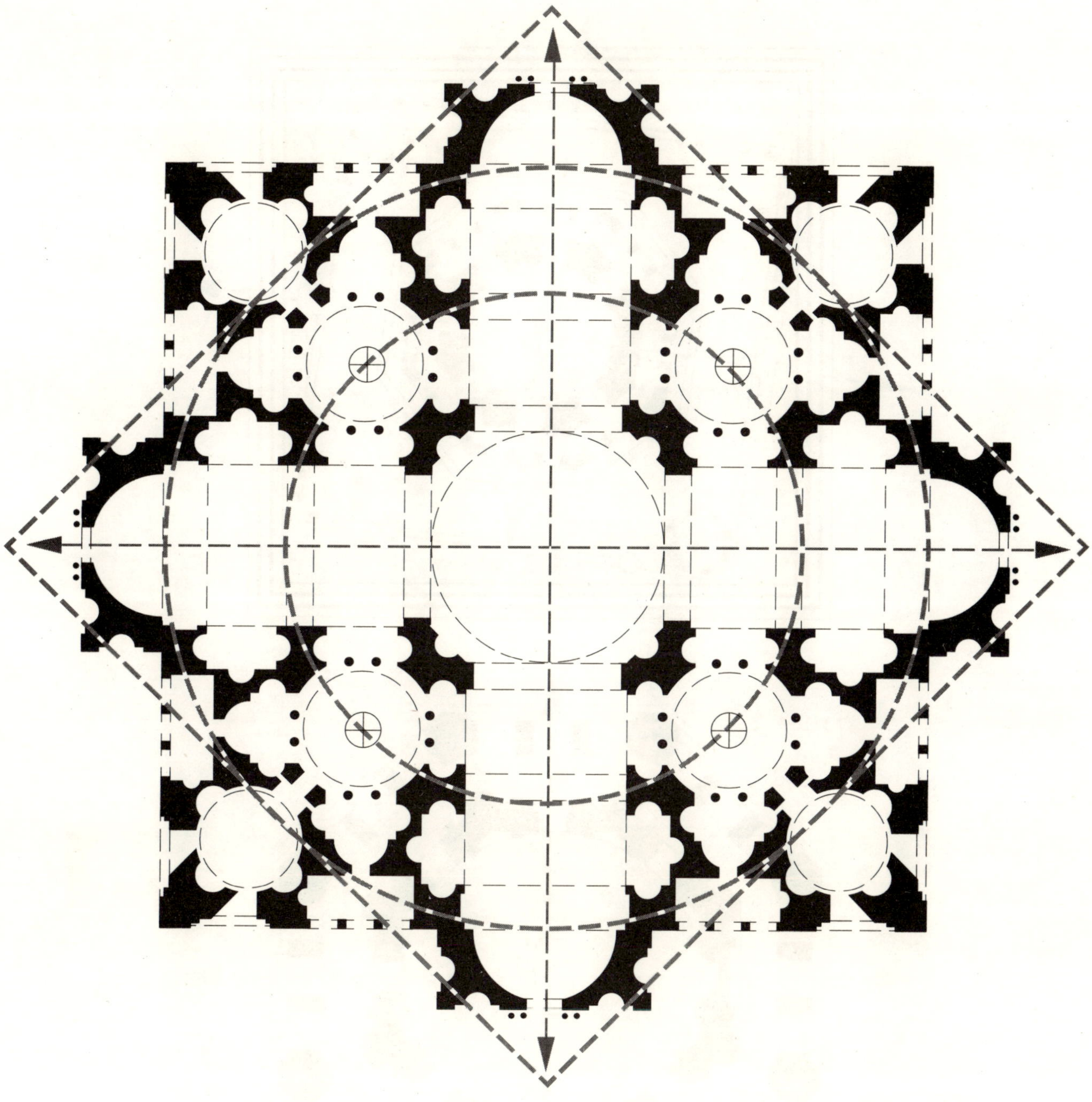

Plate 80 — *Tomb of Sher Sur* (1540 CE), Saseram, (above); and *Tomb of Isa Khan* (1547 CE), Delhi, (below) indicating cross-axial alignment

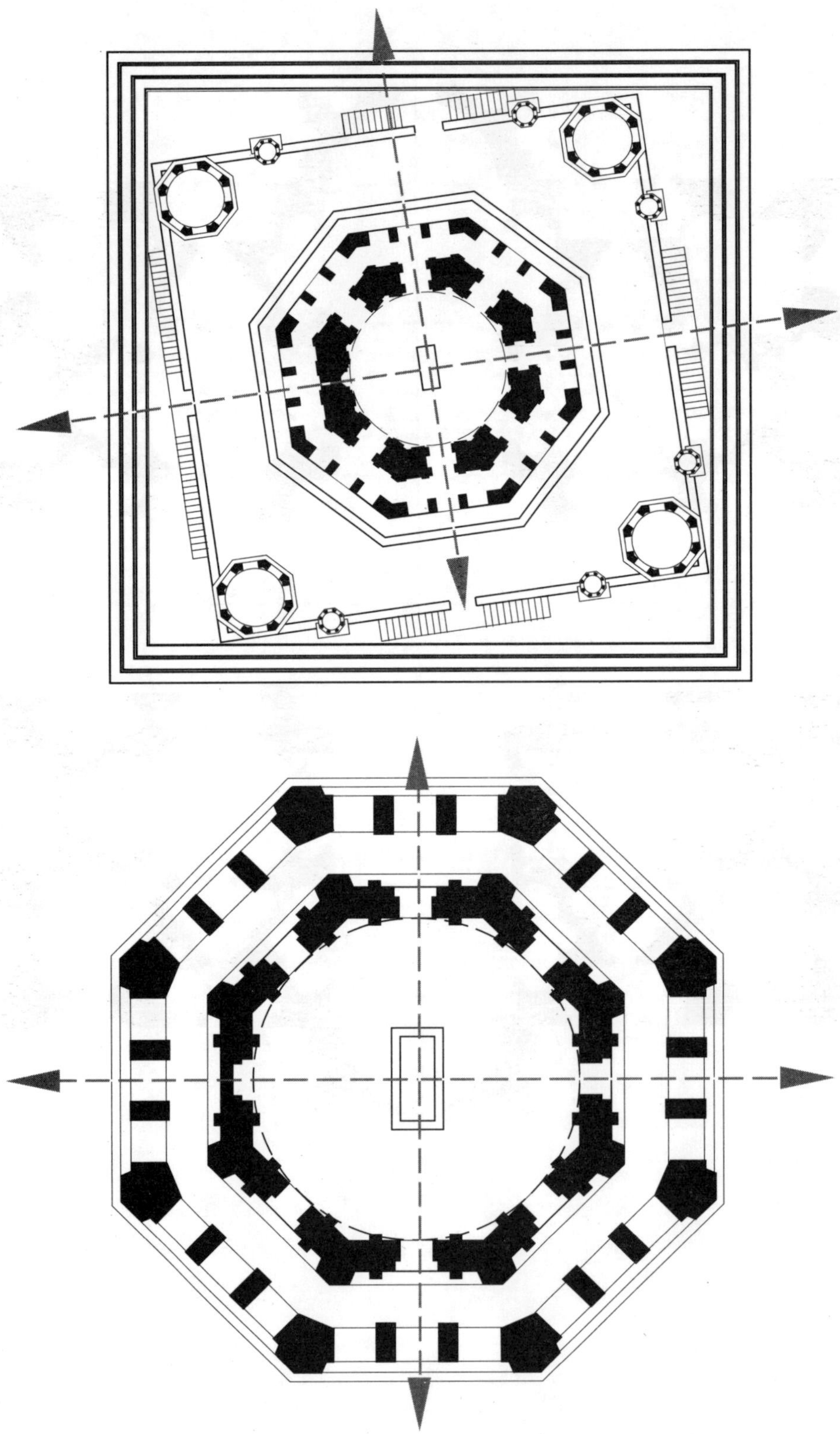

Plate 81 — *Tomb of Humayun* (1565 CE), Delhi, (above) and *Taj Mahal*, Agra (1632-1654 CE), (below) indicating cross-axial alignment (*muthamman baghdadi*)

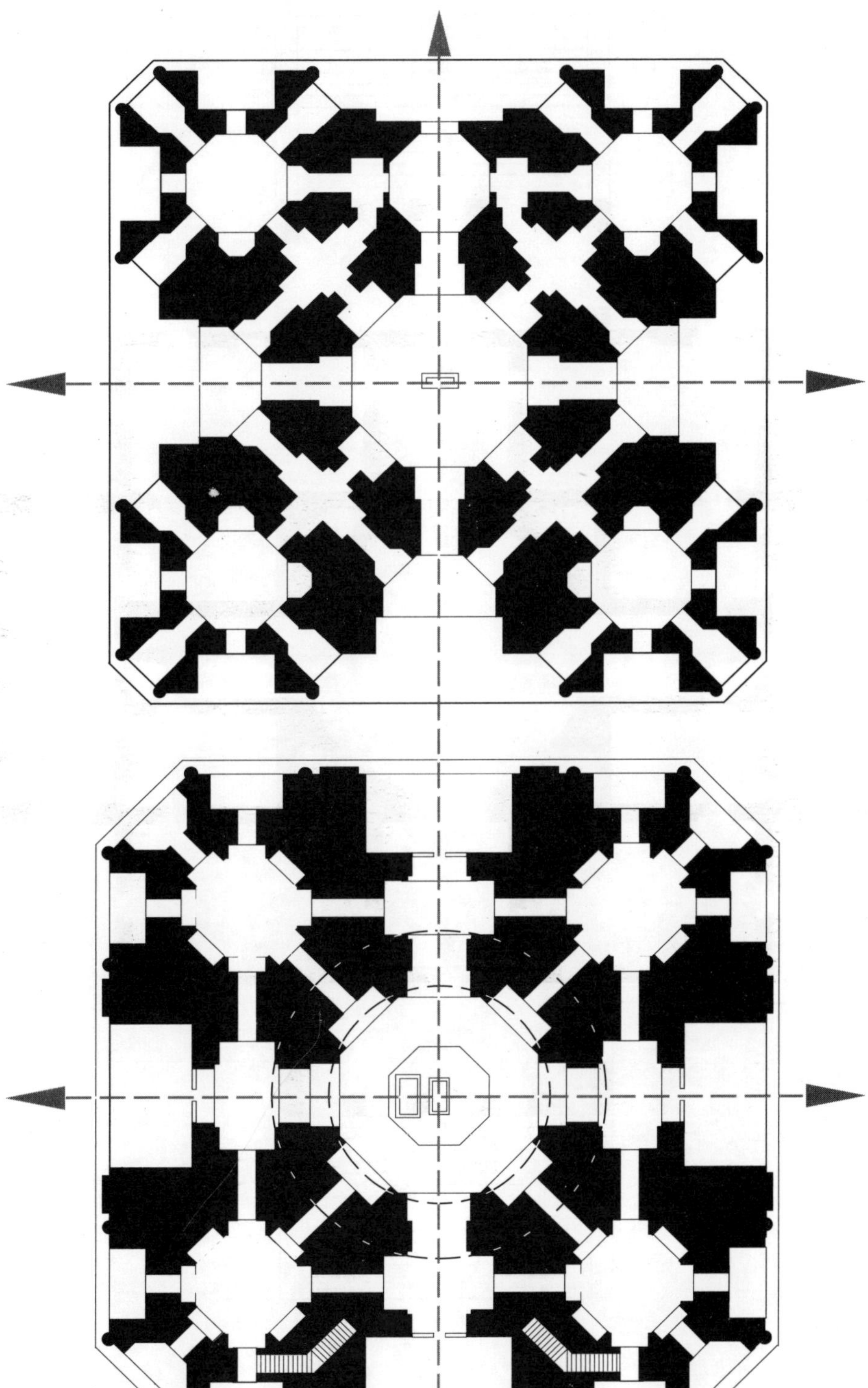

Plate 82 — Palladio, *Villa Rotunda* (*c.* 1566-1570 CE), Vicenza, Italy, indicating cross axial alignment

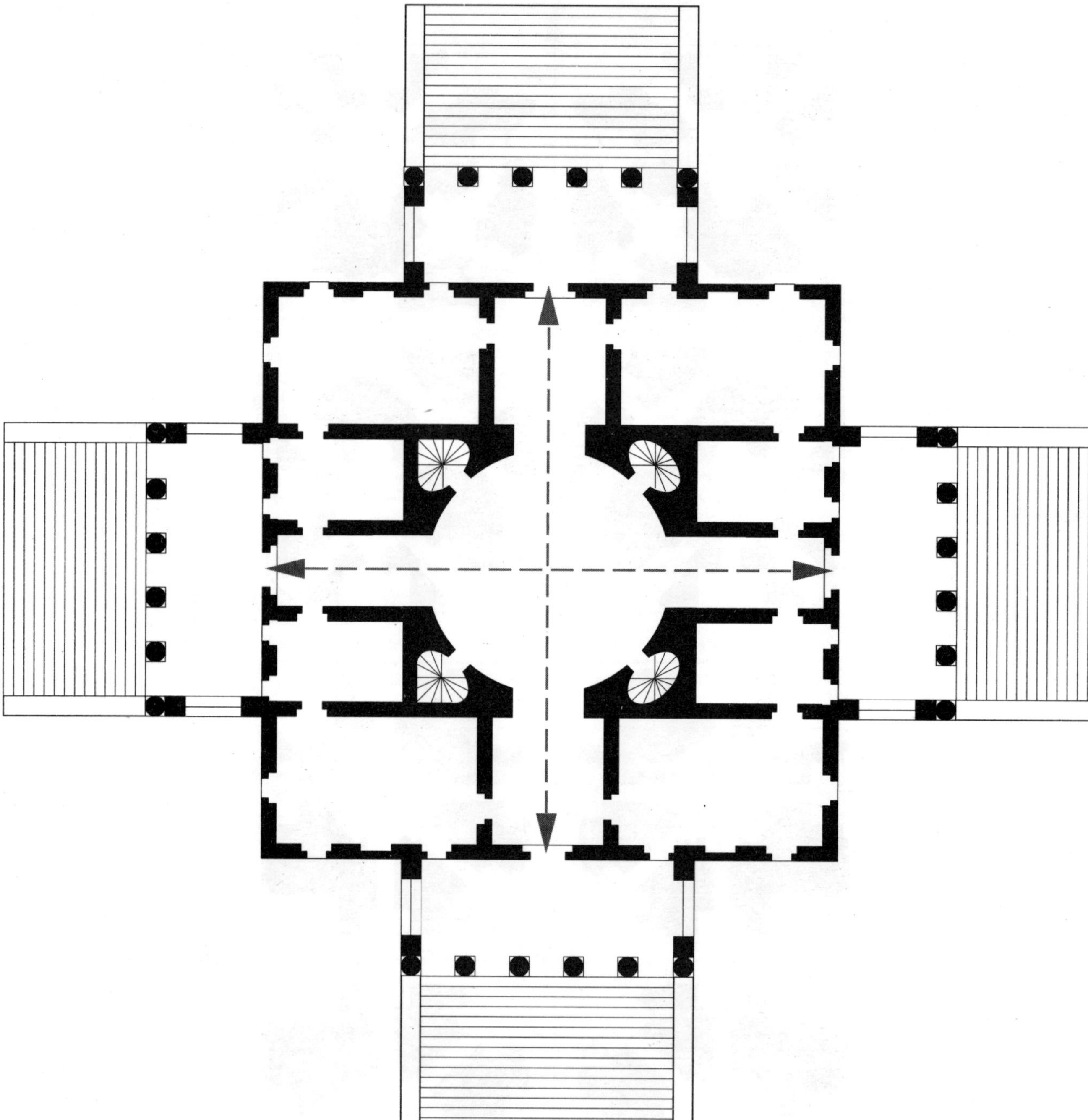

Plate 83 — *Masjid-i Jami* (1644-1658 CE), Delhi, indicating axial alignment

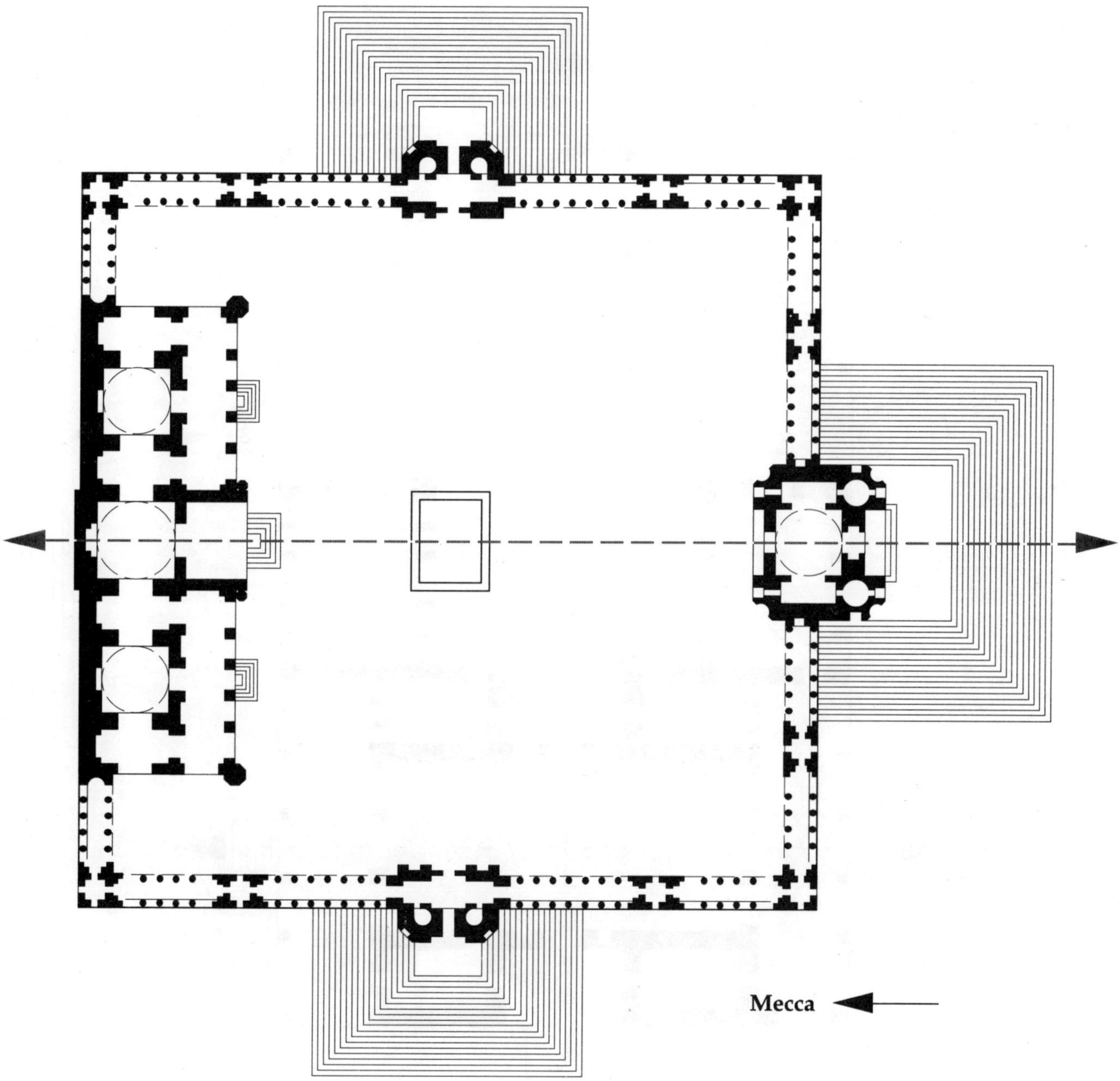

Plate 84 — *Chihil Sutun* (b. 1666 CE), Isfahan, Iran, indicating axial alignment

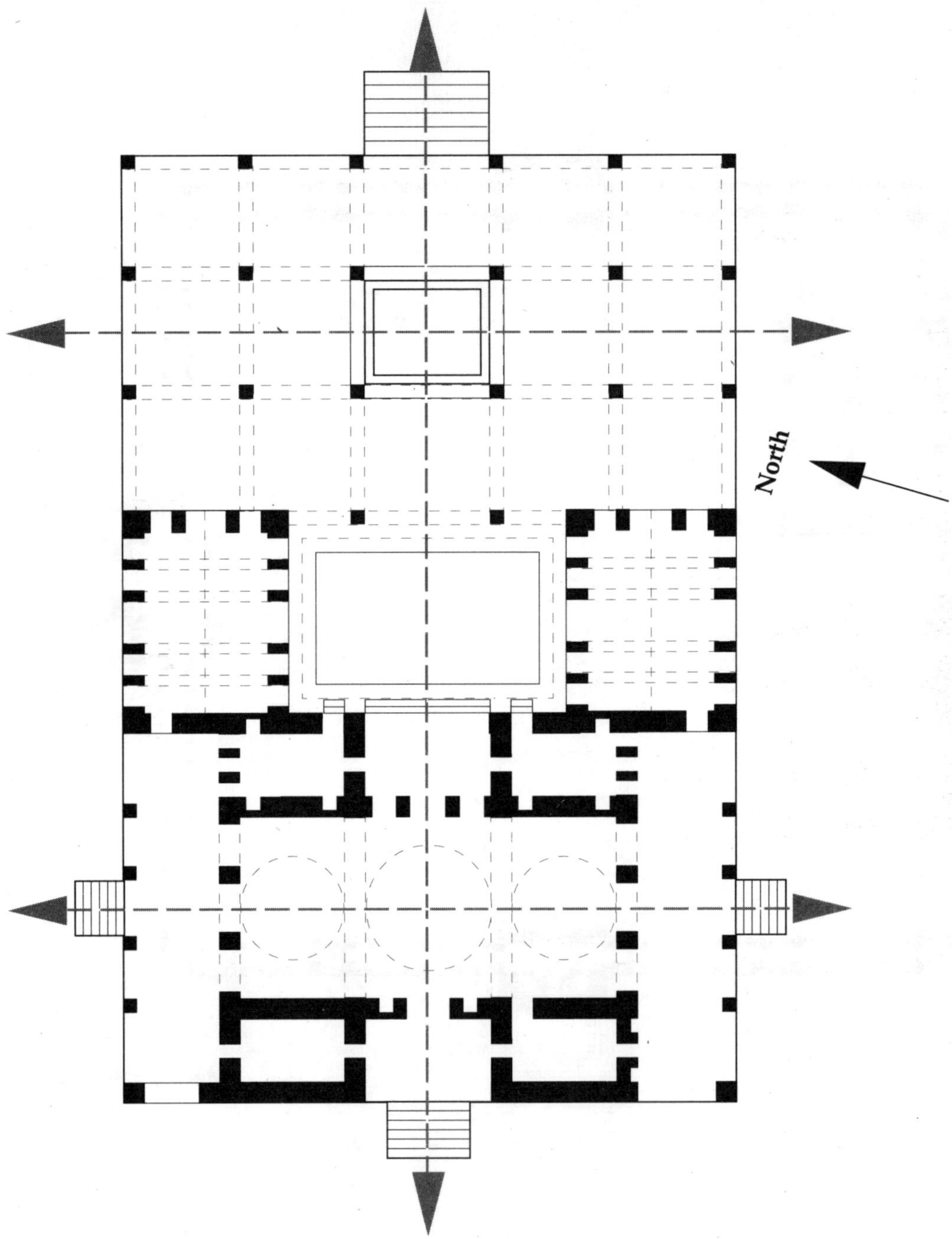

Plate 85 — *Topkapisarayi* (a. 1326-1900 CE), Istanbul, indicating asymmetrical plan with multiple non-perpendicular axes

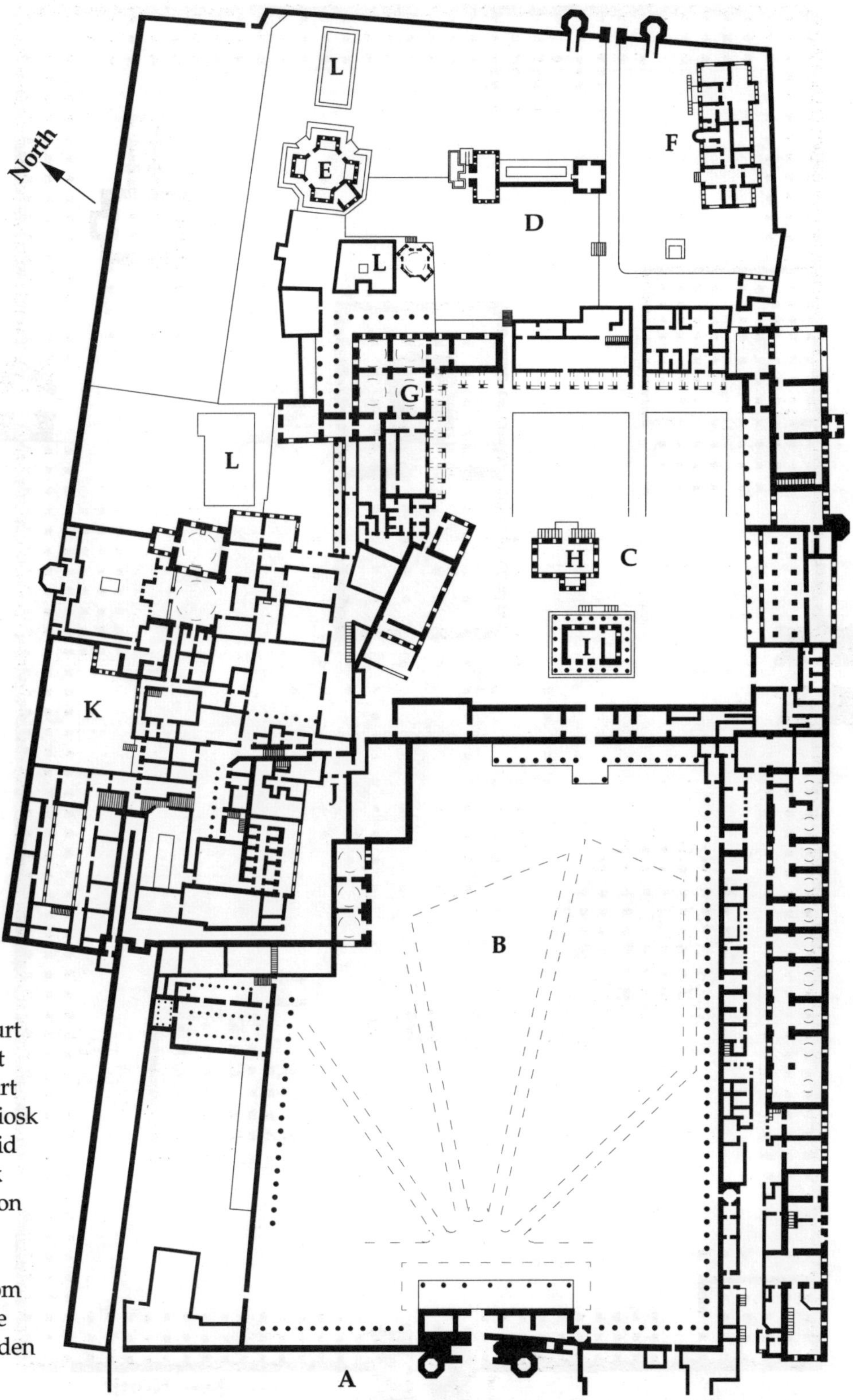

A First Court
B Second Court
C Third Court
D Fourth Court
E Baghdad Kiosk
F Abdul Mecid Kiosk
G Robe Pavilion
H Ahmet III Library
I Throne Room
J Harem Gate
K Harem Garden
L Pools

Plate 86 — *Viṭṭhala* (*Vithoba*) *Temple*, Hampi

(1509-1530 CE)

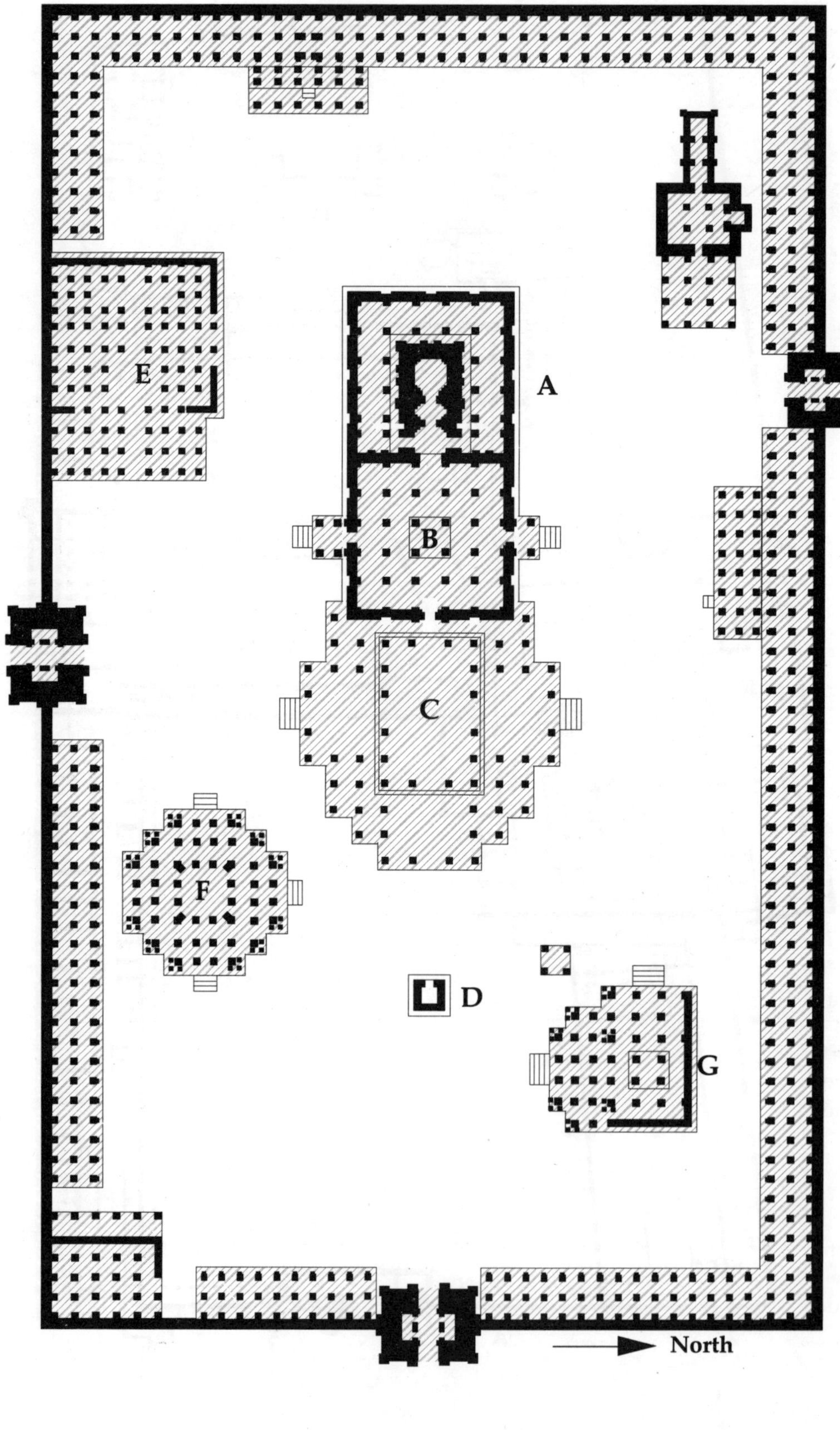

Plate 87 — ***Chandragiri Palace*** **(*Rājā Mahal*),** proportional elevation and 1st storey plan (a. 1565 CE)

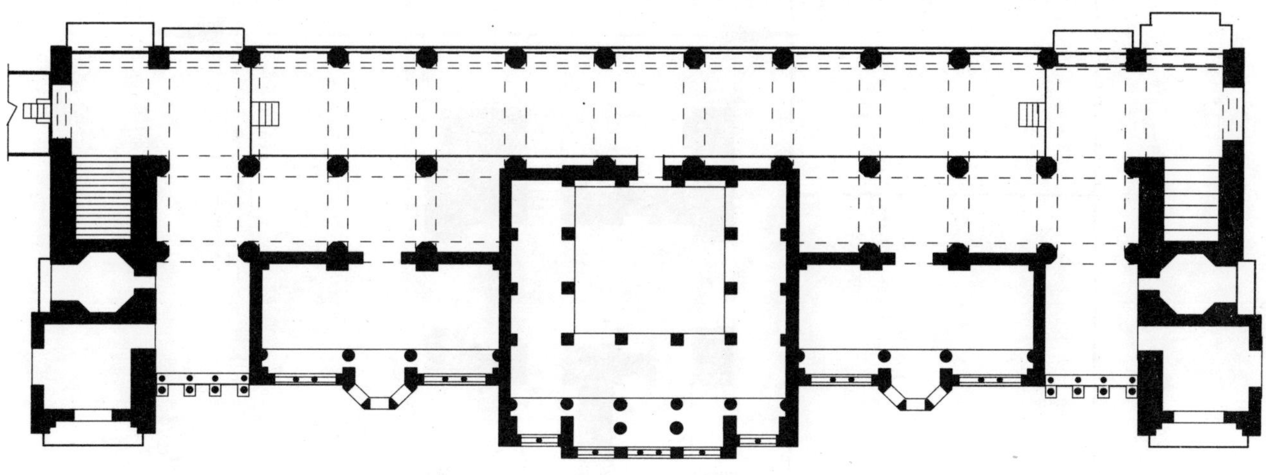

Plate 88 — *Jahāz Mahal* (1st half 16th *c.* CE), Bijapur, plan, indicating five square plan

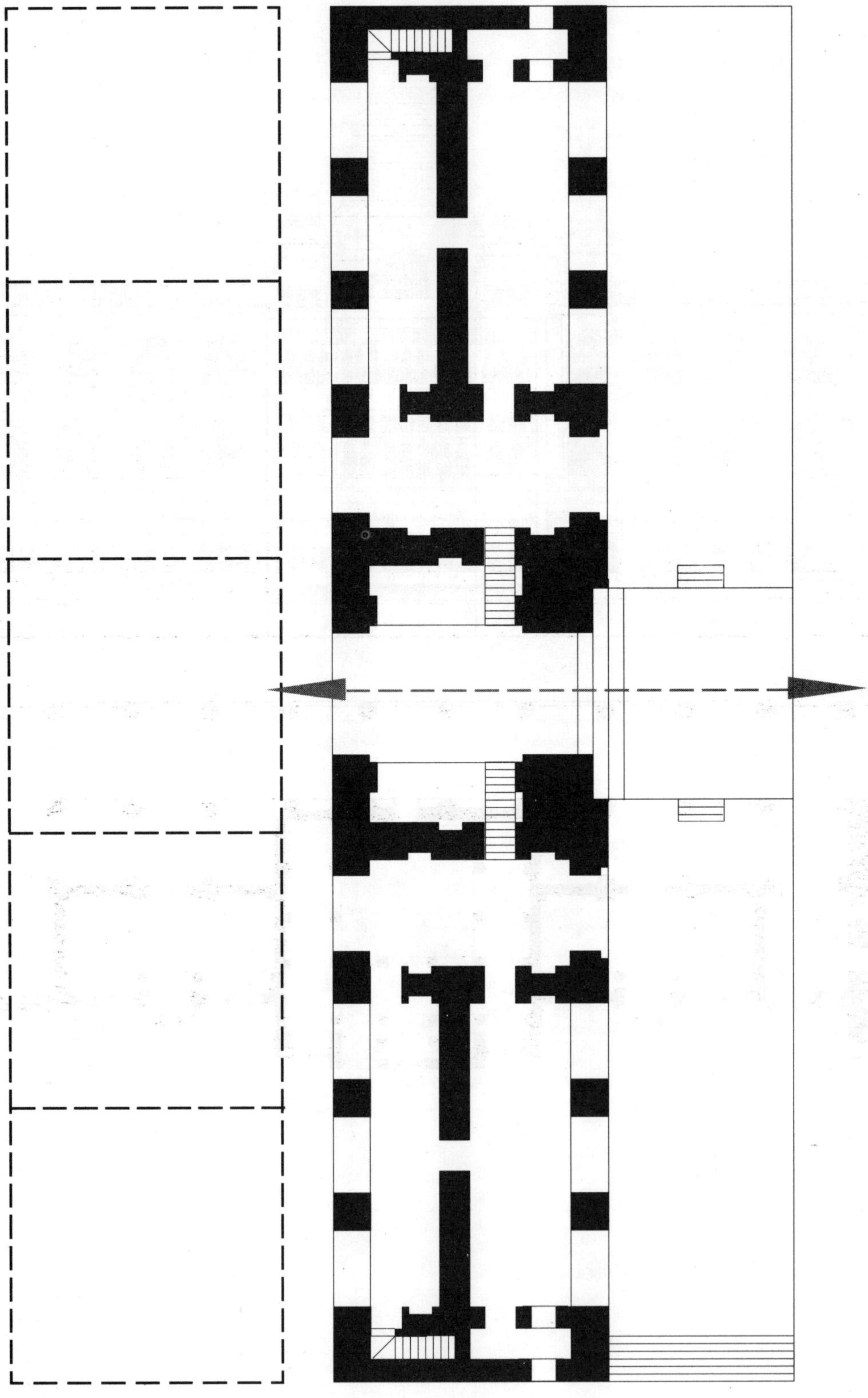

Plate 89 — *Rājā Mandir*, proportional elevation & half plan

(a. 1554 CE)

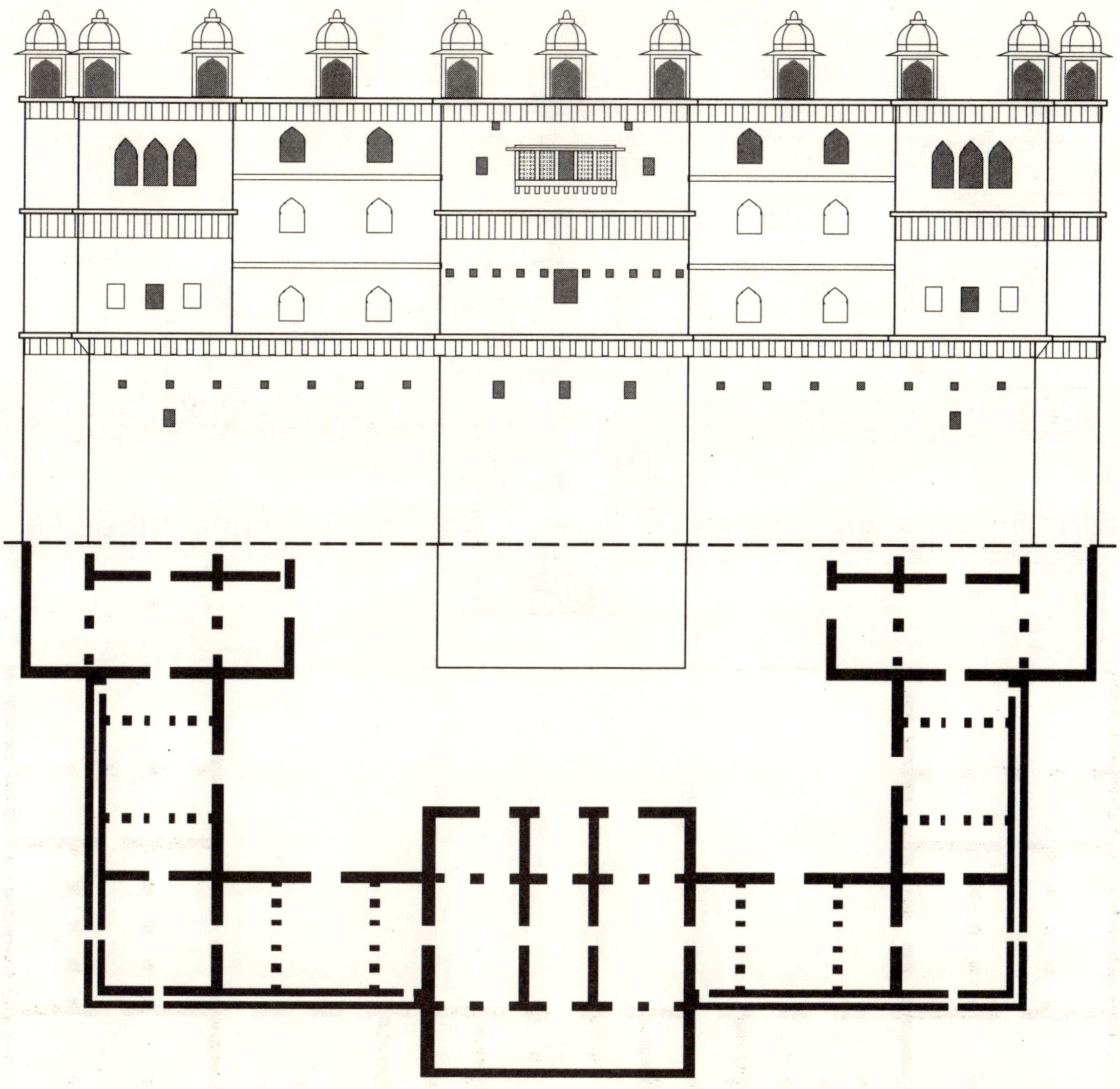

Plate 90 — *Jahangir Mandir*, proportional elevation & half plan

(a. 1605 CE)

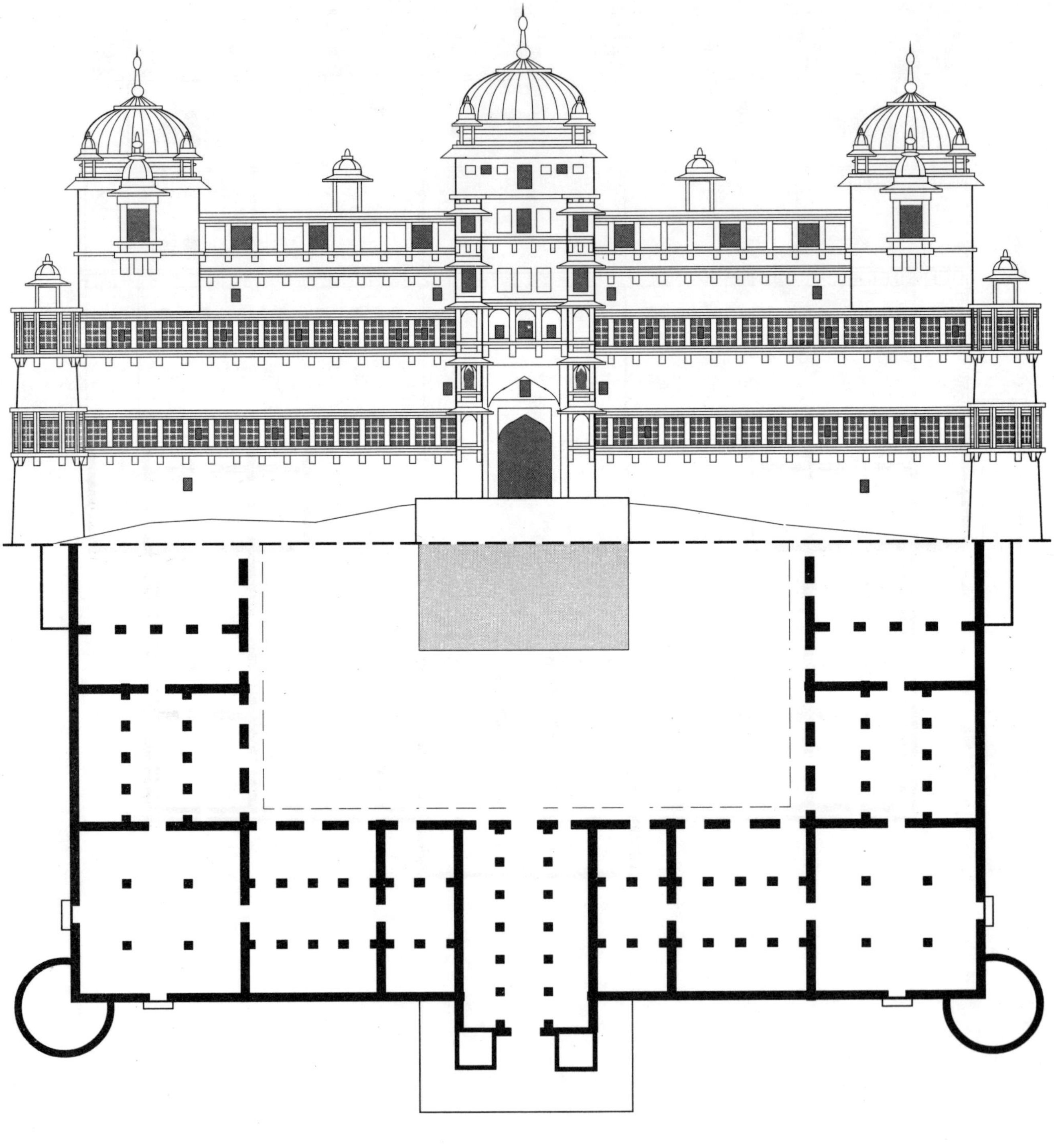

Plate 91 — *Govind Mandir* (*Bir Singh Judeo Mahal*), proportional elevation & half plan (a. 1620 CE)

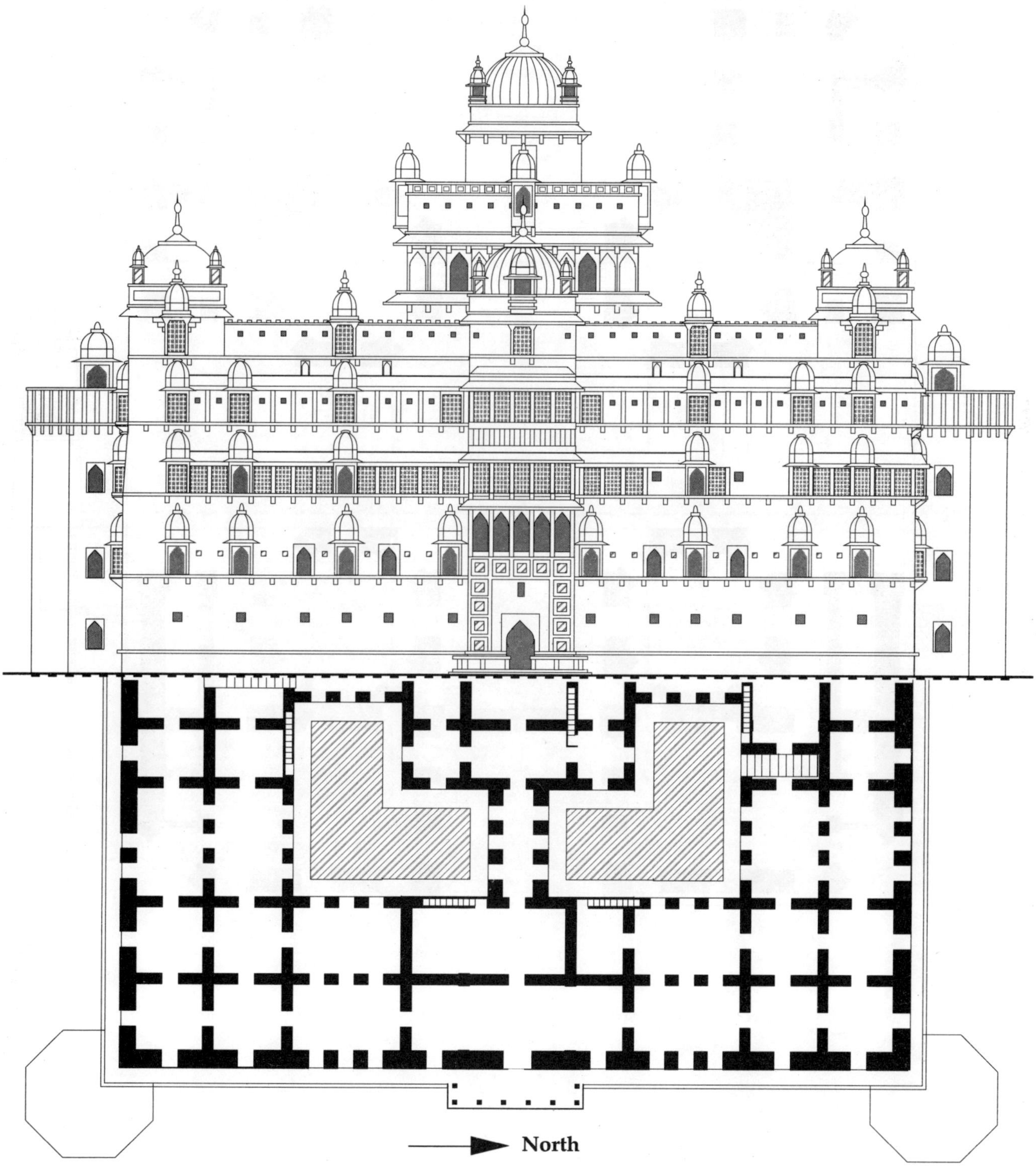

Plate 92 — *Hesht Behest*, Isfahan, *c.* 1669

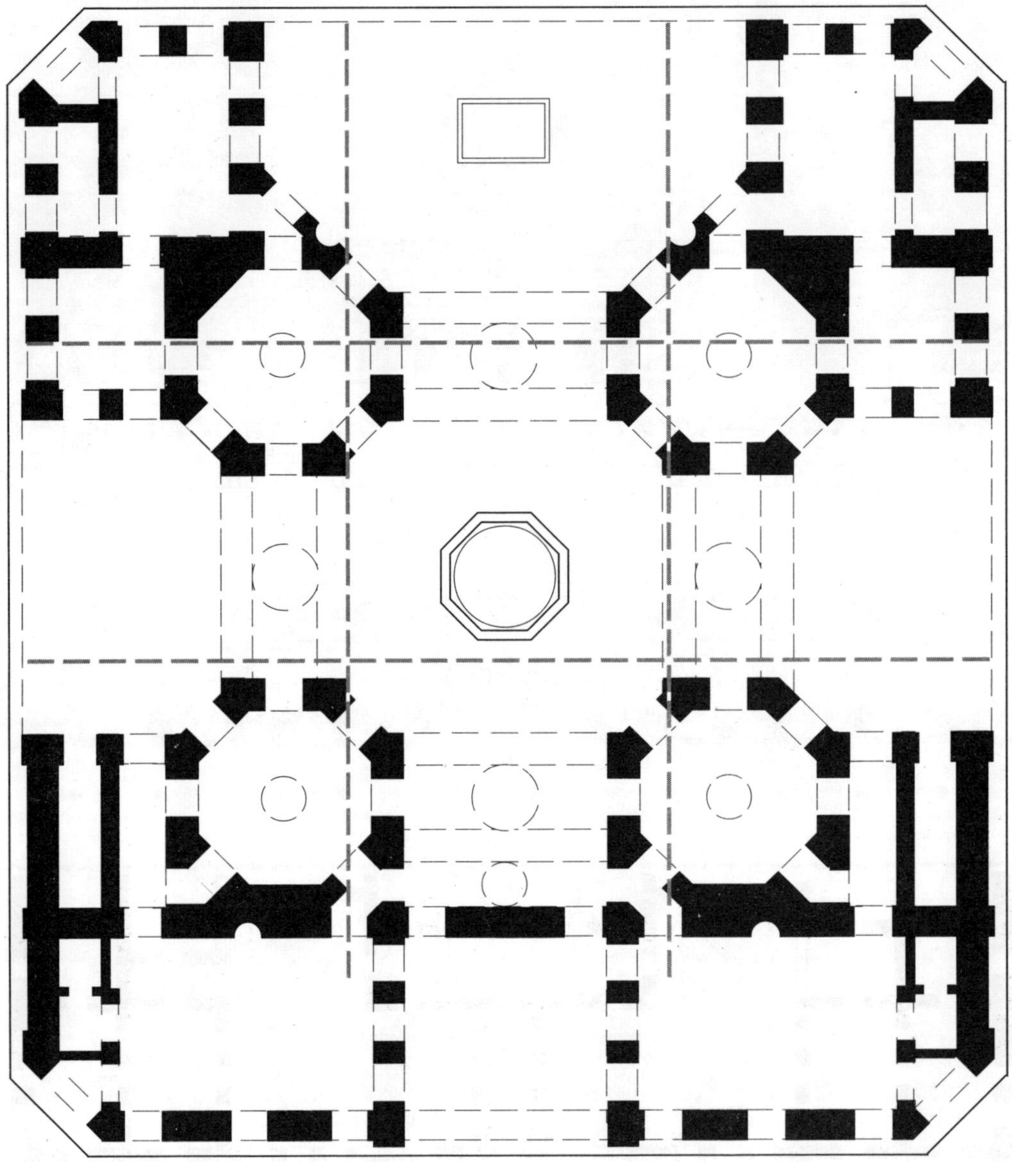

Plate 93 — *Geometric Tank*, Vijayanagara, a. 1400

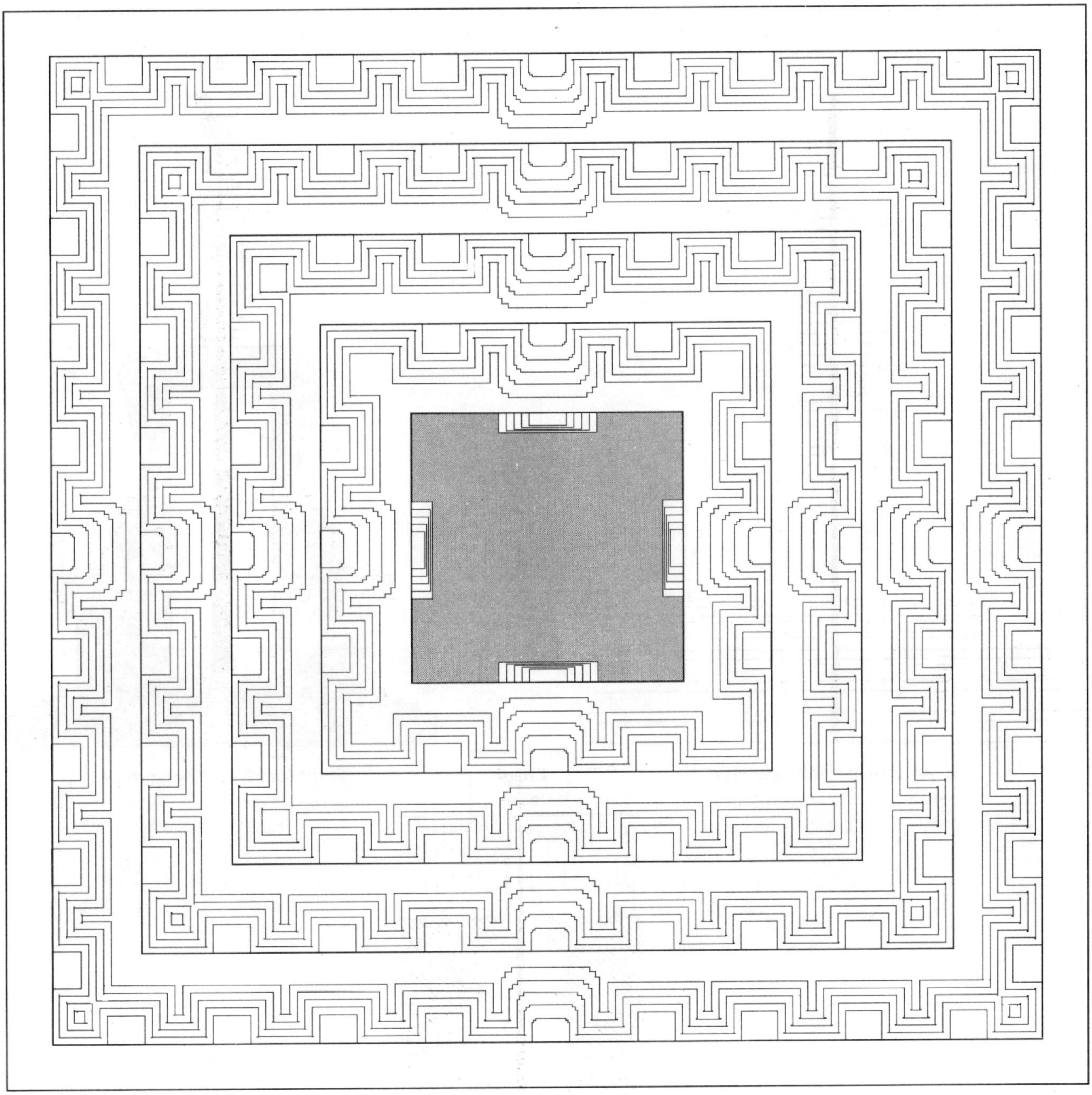

Plate 94 — Axis (*axis mundi*) implied and real

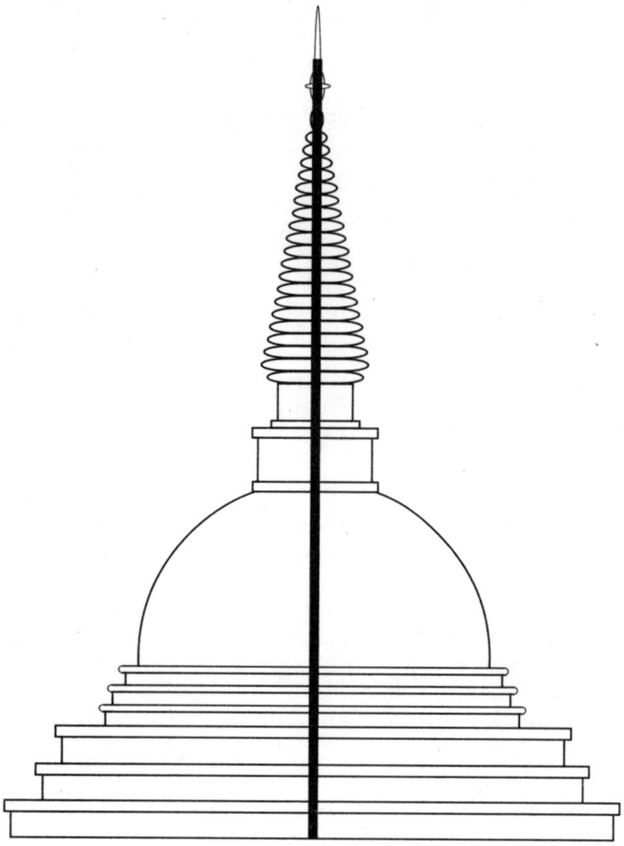

Stupa, Indian/Sinhalese type

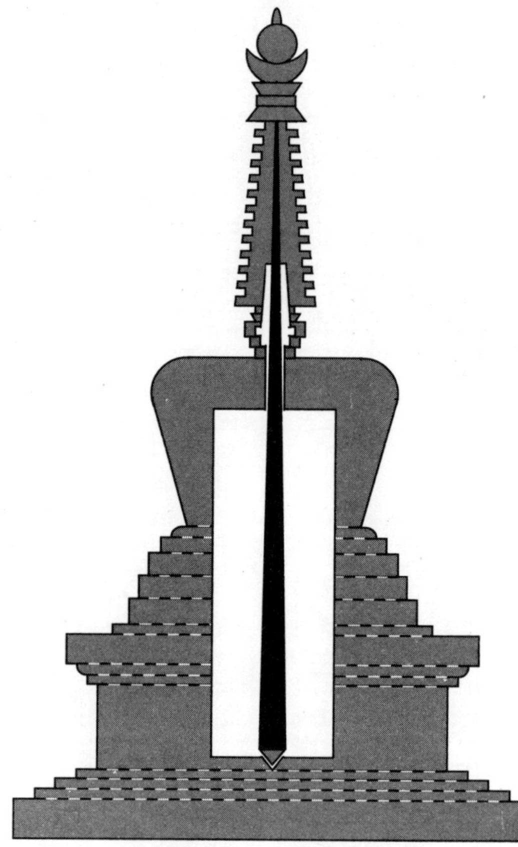

Stupa (*chorten*), Tibetan type

Garbha-griha foundation preparations

Plate 95 — Fortified Gates (line of fire)

Fateh Darwāzā, Golcondagarh, Golconda, indicating overlapping lines of fire

Plate 96 — *Gingee Mandir*, Gingee (a. 1490 *c.* CE)

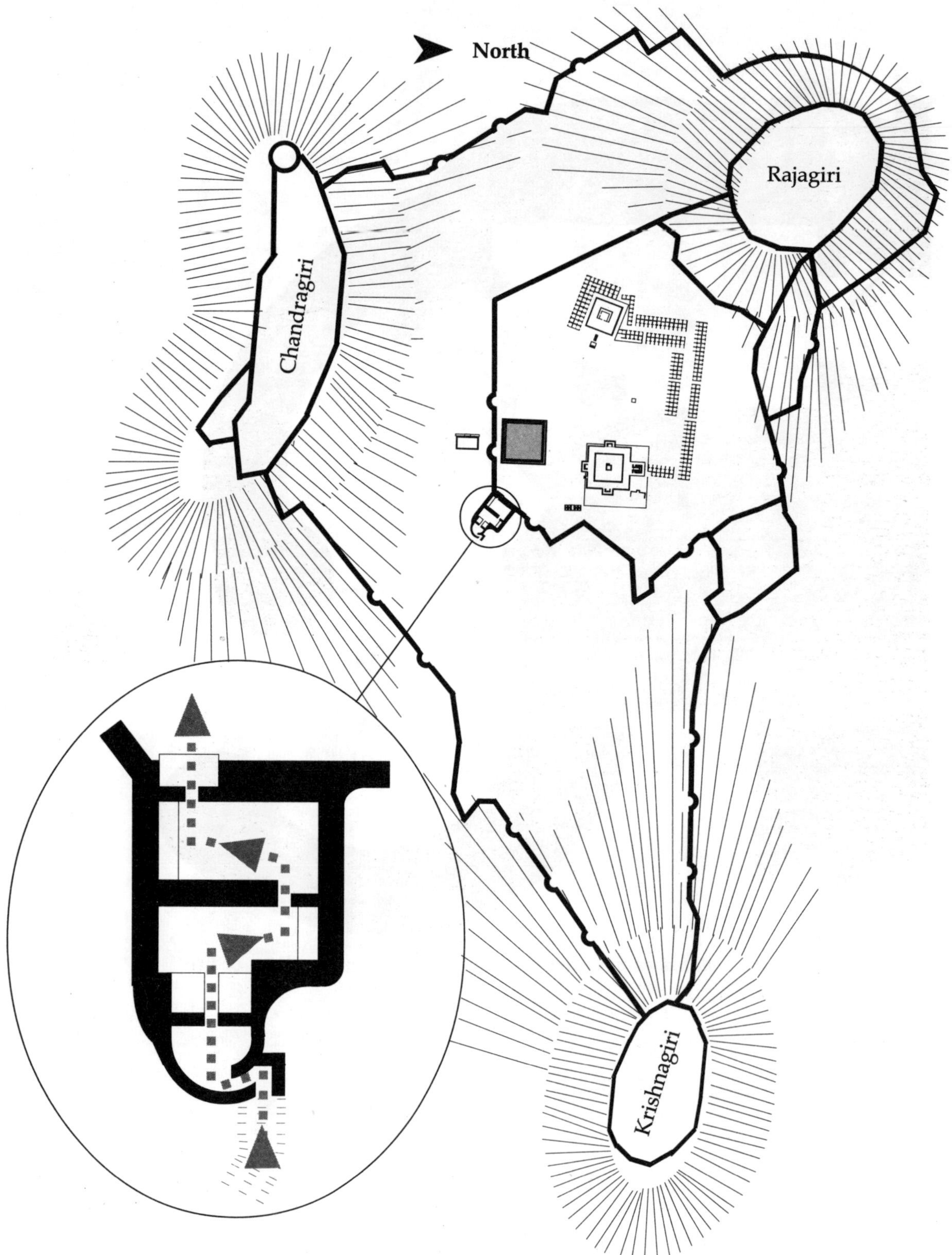

Plate 97 — *Devagiri* (*Daulatabad*), Maharashtra (a. 1187 CE)

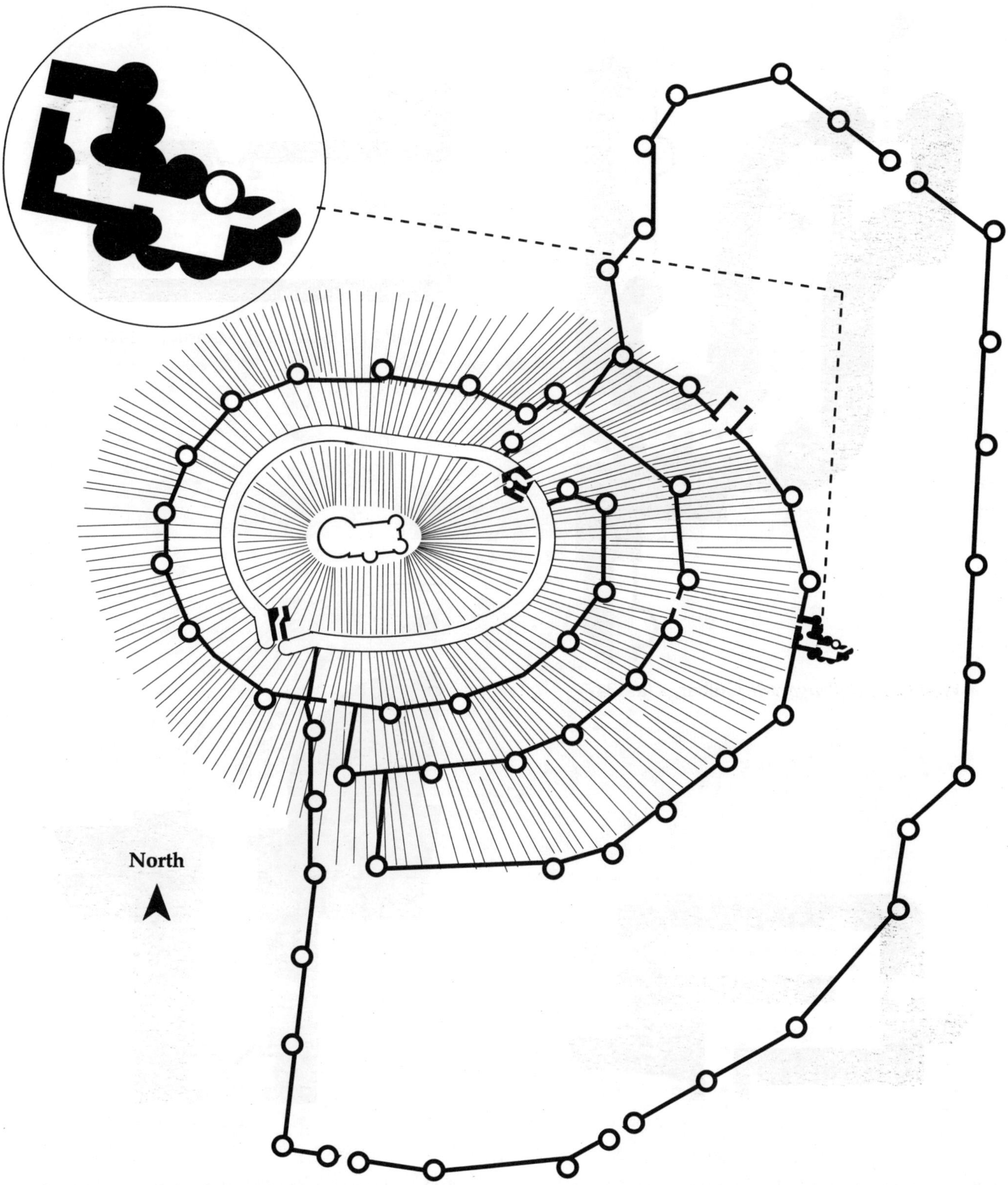

Plate 98 — Fortified Gates

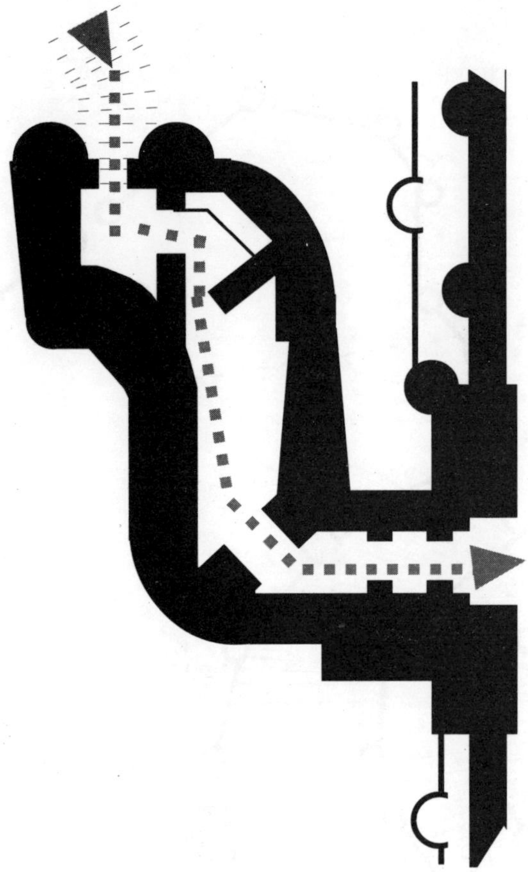

West Gate, Gulbargagarh, Gulbarga (a. 1347)

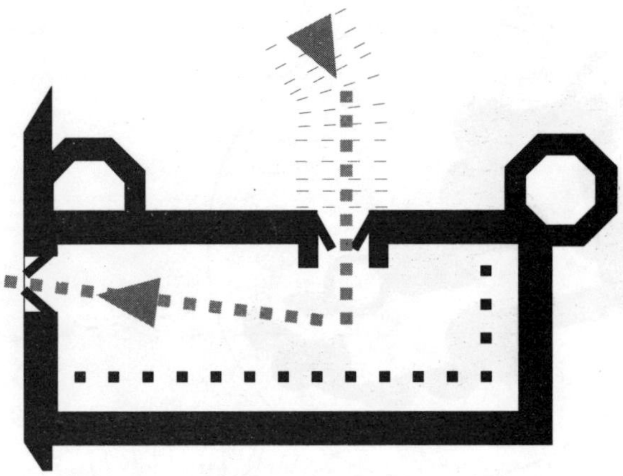

Hāthī Pol, Shadiabad, Mandu (a. 1410 CE)

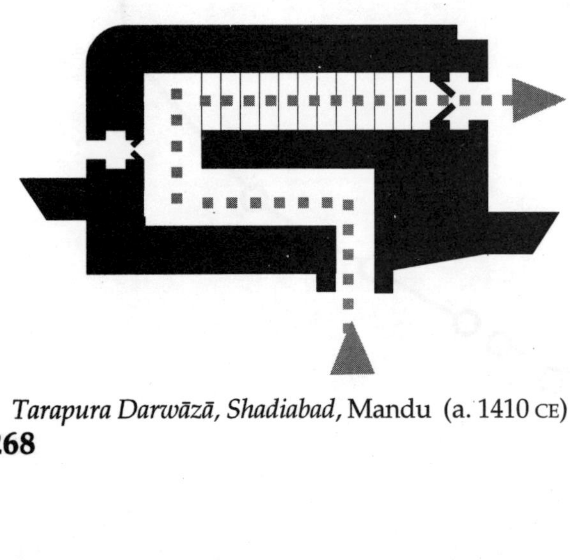

Tarapura Darwāzā, Shadiabad, Mandu (a. 1410 CE)

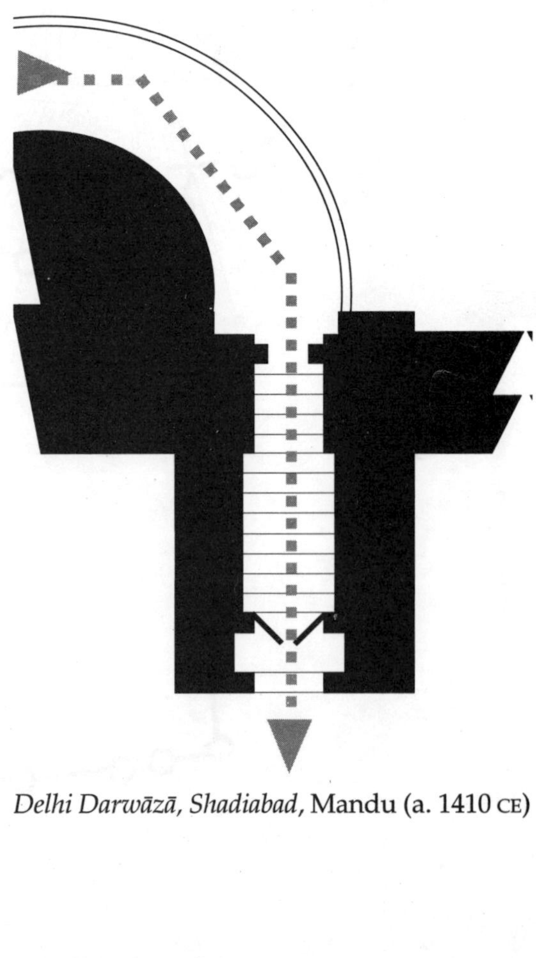

Delhi Darwāzā, Shadiabad, Mandu (a. 1410 CE)

Plate 99 — Fortified Gates (Continued)

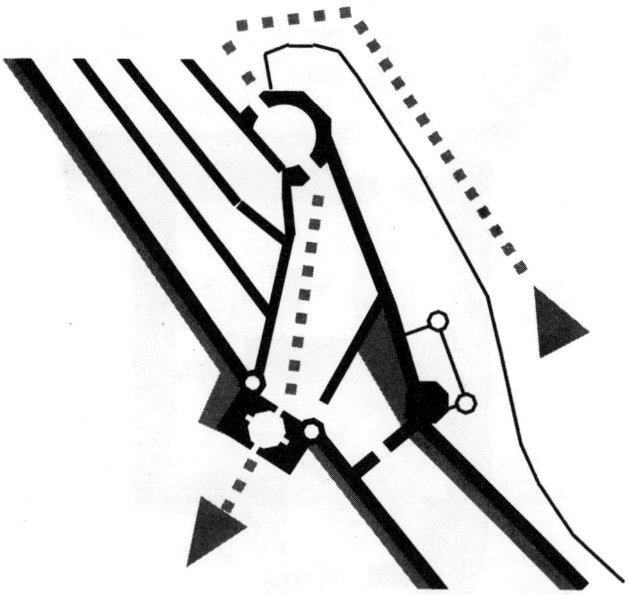

Gumbad Darwāzā, Bidargarh, Bidar (a. 1424 CE)

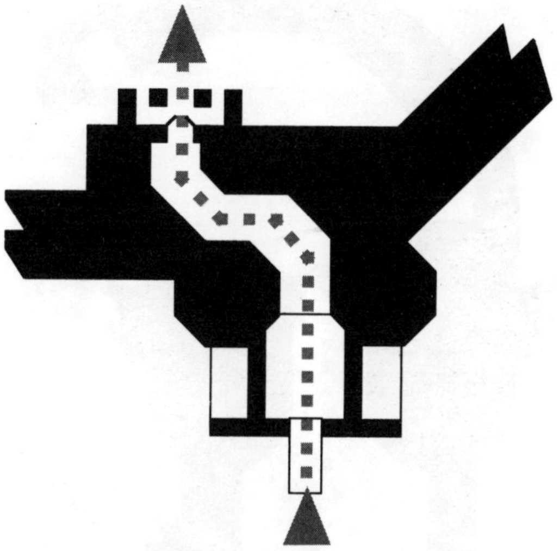

Fateh Darwāzā, Bidargarh, Bidar (a. 1424 CE)

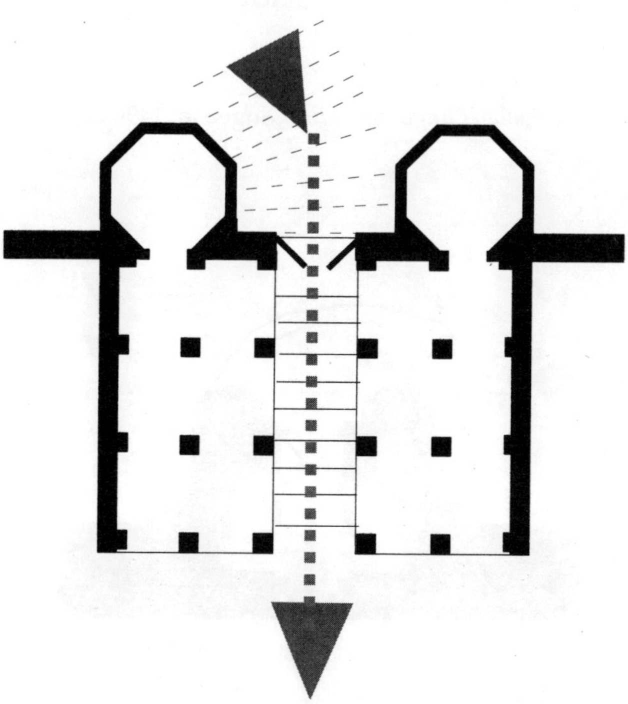

Tripolia, Kumbhalgarh, Chittor (a. 1433 CE)

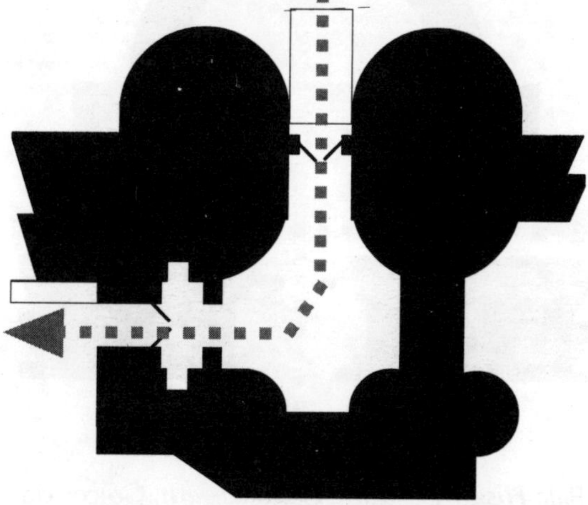

Zohrahpur Darwāzā, Bijapur (a. 1489)

Plate 100 — Fortified Gates (Continued)

Arh Qilā Darwāzā, Bijapur (a. 1489)

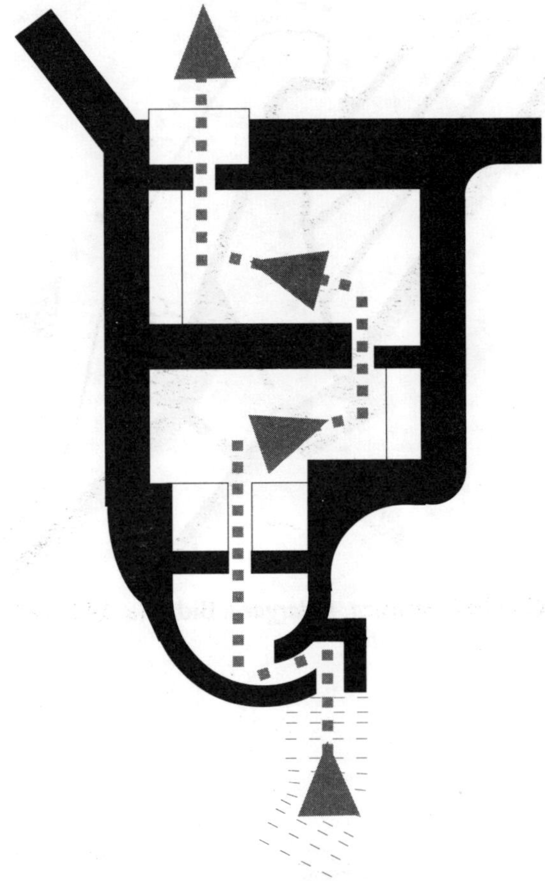

Tripolia, Gingee Mandir, Gingee (a. 1490 CE)

Bala Hissar Darwāzā, Golcondagarh, Golconda (a.1540)

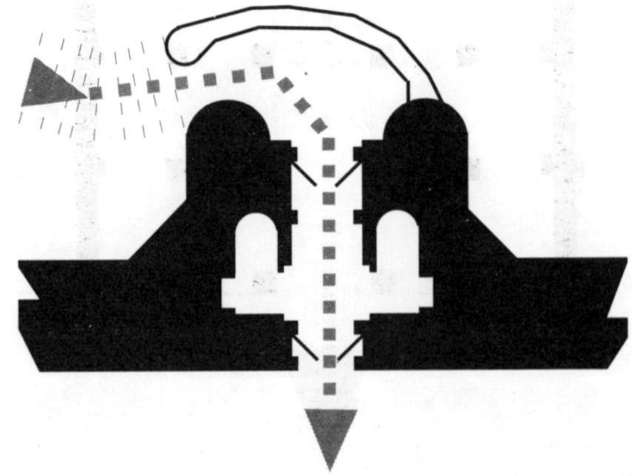

Banjari Darwāzā, Golcondagarh, Golconda (a.1540)

Plate 101 — Fortified Gates (Concluded)

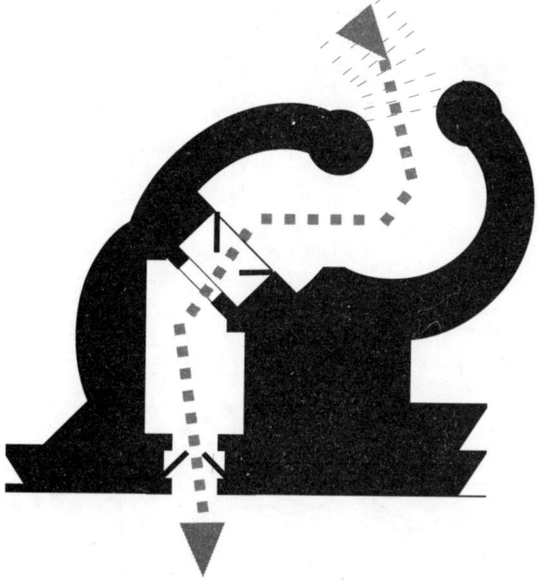

Fateh Darwāzā, Golcondagarh, Golconda (a.1540)

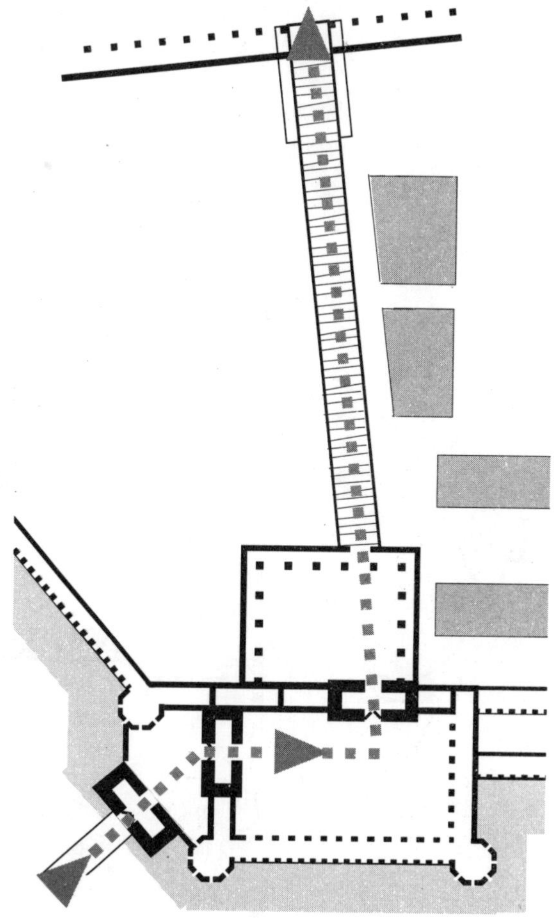

Amar Singh & Akbari Darwāzā, Lal Qila, Agra (*c.* 1565)

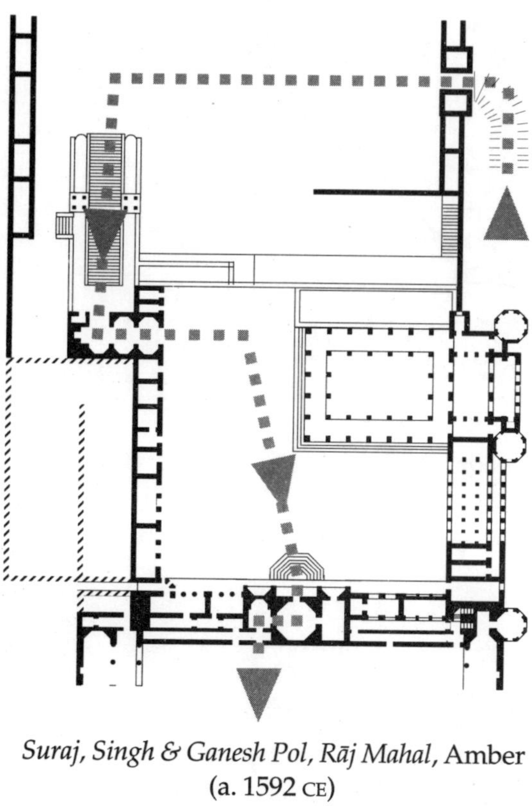

Suraj, Singh & Ganesh Pol, Rāj Mahal, Amber (a. 1592 CE)

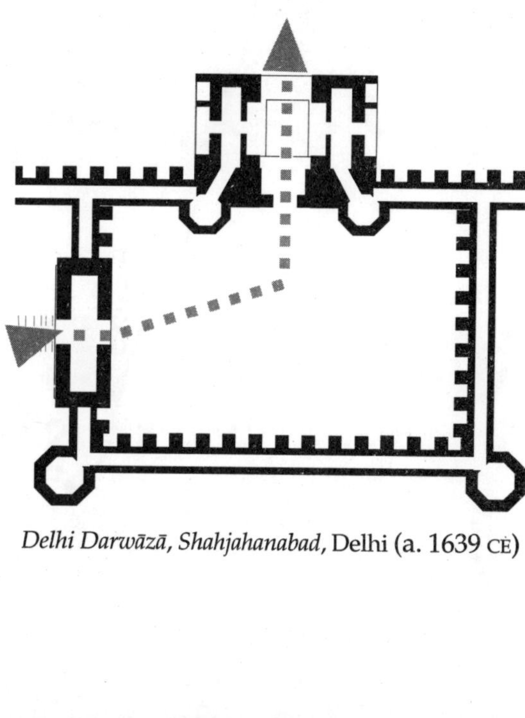

Delhi Darwāzā, Shahjahanabad, Delhi (a. 1639 CE)

Plate 102 — India, 250-200 BCE

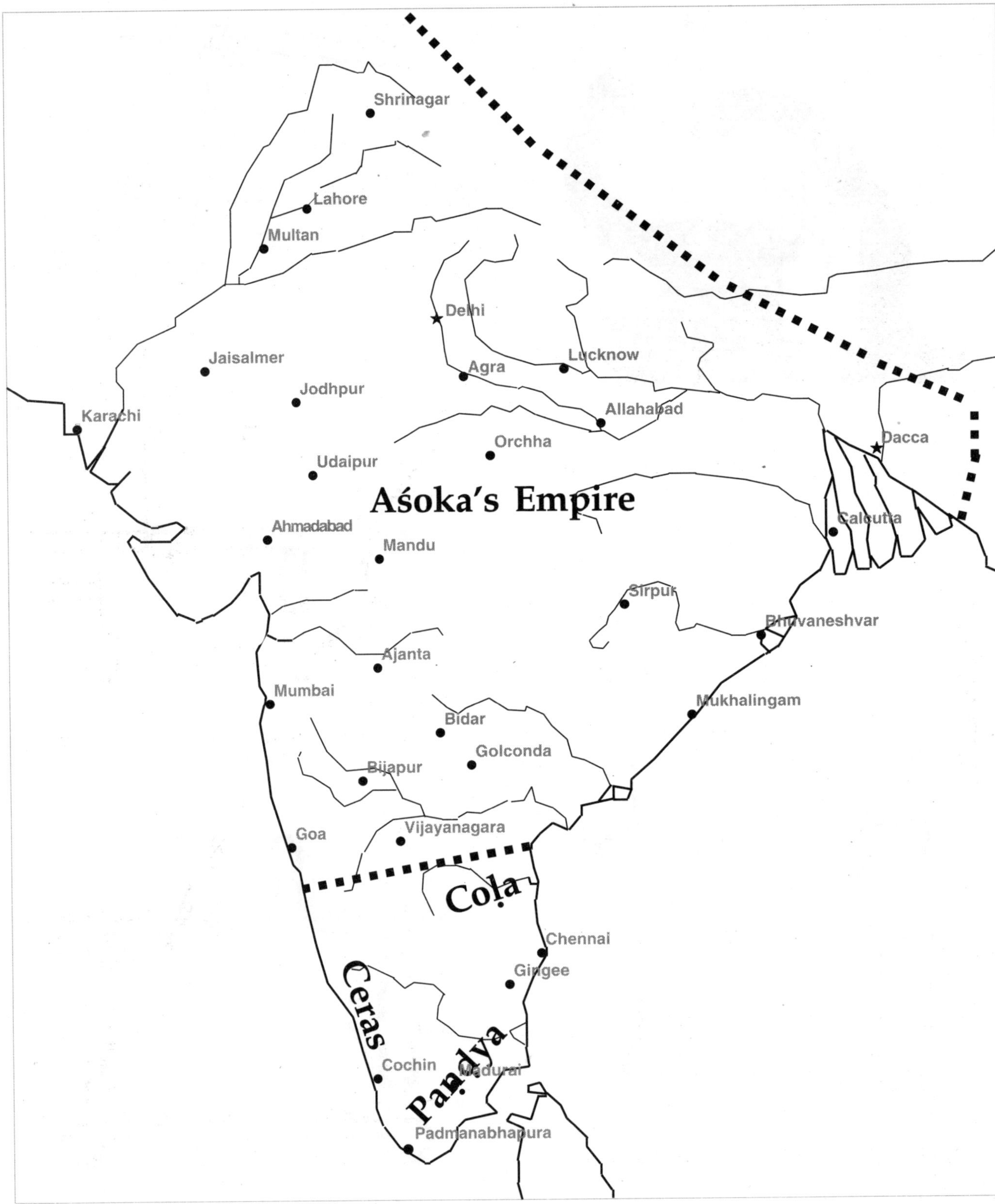

Plate 103 — India, 100 CE

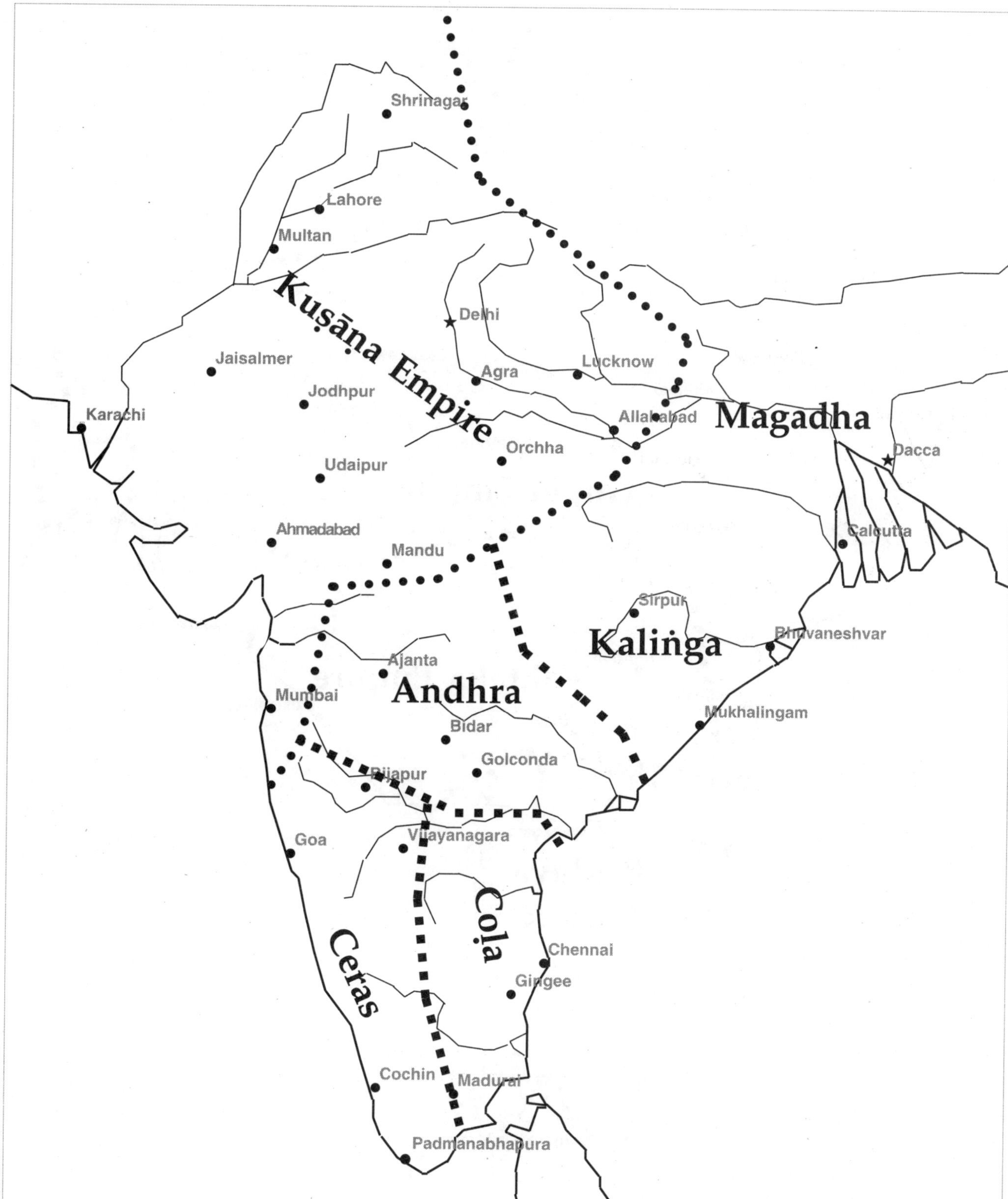

Plate 104 — India, 450 CE

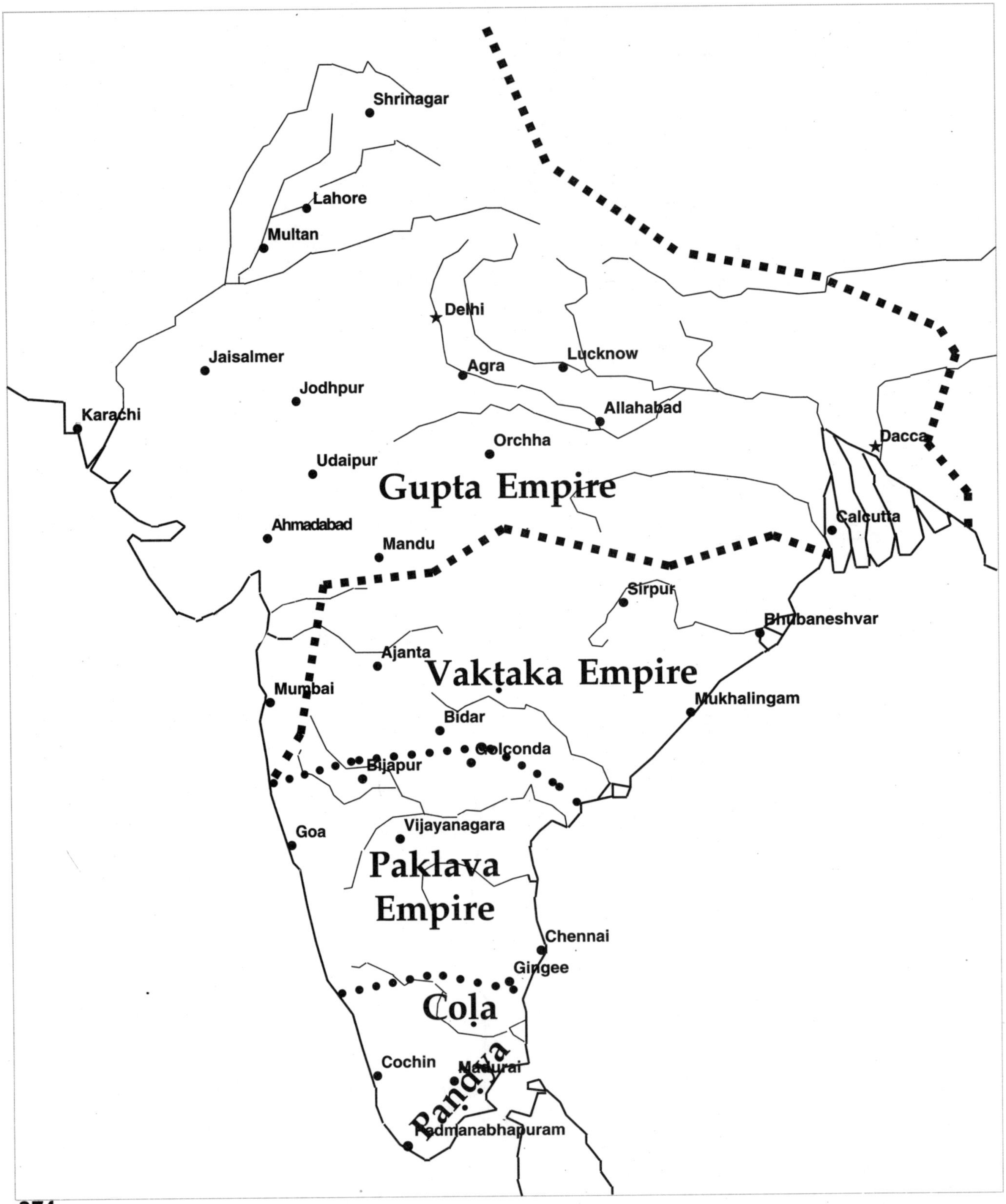

Plate 105 — India, 6th - 8th *c.* CE

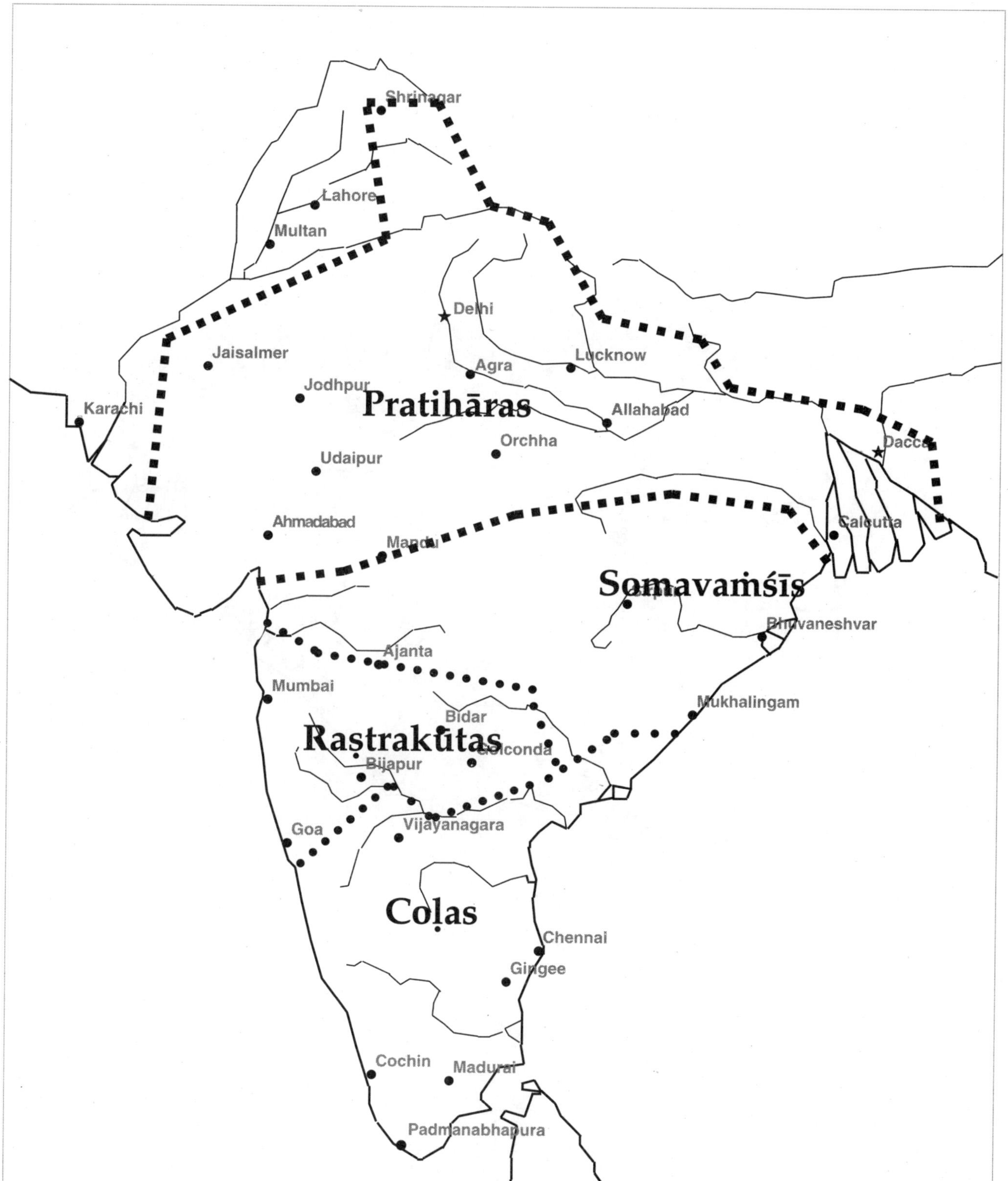

Plate 106 — India, 5th - 13th *c.* CE (various)

Plate 107 — India, empires after 1200 CE

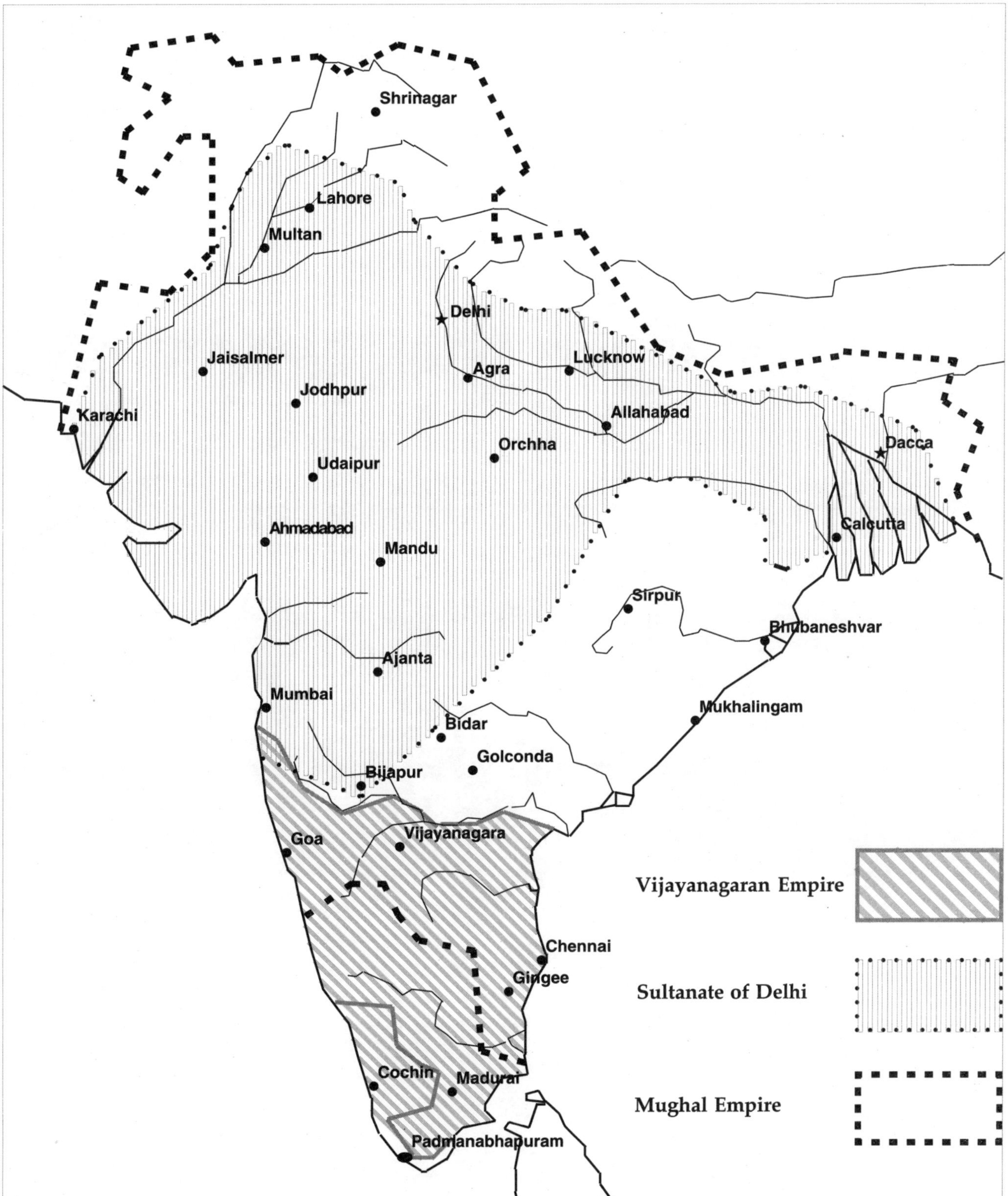

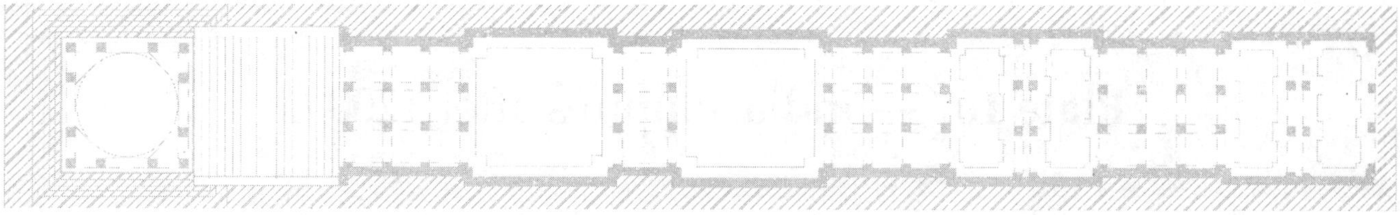

Appendix B:
Major Rulers of India

Listed Alphabetically
by
City and/or State

(In the following, all dates shown are
CE (Common Era),
and italicized names are of female rulers.)

Major Rulers of India

Ahmednagar

(Muslim)

(1490-1680)

Ahmednagar Sultanate

Nizam Shahi Dynasty

(from Bhamani Sultanate)

Nizam-ul-Mulk Bahri.	1490
Malik Ahmad, Ahmad Nizam Shah I	1490-1509
Burhan Nizam Shah I	1509-1553
Hussain Nizam Shah I	1553-1565
Murtaza Nizam Shah I	1565-1586
Hussain Nizam Shah II	1586-1589
Isma'il Nizam Shah	1589-1591
Burhan Nizam Shah II	1591-1595
Ibrahim Nizam Shah	1595-1596
Bahadur Nizam Shah	1596-1603
Murtaza Nizam Shah II	1603-1610
Burhan Shah III	1610-1631
Hussain Nizam Shah III	1631-1633
to Mughal Empire	1633

Amber

(Kachwahas Rajput)

(*c.* 1128-1727)

Rājas (Mirza Rājas, Sri Sawai Mahārājās) of Amber

Kachwaha Dynasty

(capital moved from Dundhar. See: Dundhar)

Rāja Prithvi Singh I	1502-1527

Puran Mal	1527-1534
Bhima Singh	1534-1537
Ratan Singh	1537-1547
Baharmalla	1547-1547
Bhagwan Das	1547-1592
Mirza Rāja Man Singh I	1592-1615
Jagat Singh I	1615
Bhao Singh	1615-1622
Jaya Singh I	1622-1667
Rāma Singh I	1667-1688
Bishan Singh	1688-1700
Sri Sawai Mahārājā Jaya Singh II	1700-1743

(Capital moved to Jaipur. See: Jaipur)

Awadh (Oudh)

(Muslim)

(*c.* 1080-1857)

Awadh Nawābs

Sa'adatid Nawābs (1720-1857)

Burhan ul-Mulk Mohammed sa'adat Khan	1720-1739
Abu'l Mansur Khan Safdar Jang	1739-1754
Shuja ud-Dawlah Haidar	1754-1775
Asaf ud-Dawlah	1775-1797
Wazir 'Ali	1797-1798
Sa'adat 'Ali Khan	1798-1814
Ghazi ud-Din Haidar	1814-1827
Nasr ud-Din Haidar	1827-1837
Mohammed 'Ali Shah	1837-1842
Amjad 'Ali Shah	1842-1847
Wajid 'Ali	1847-1856
to England	1856

Bahmani Sultanate

(See: Gulbarga/Deccan)

Baroda (Vadodara)

(Muslim)

(1391-1938)

Gujarat Sultanate

Muzaffarid Shahi Dynasty (1391-1583)

Muzaffar (Khan) Shah I	1391-1411
Shams-ud-Din Muzaffar Shah I	1411-1442
Mohammed Karim Shah	1442-1451
Nasir-ud-Din Ahmad Shah I	1442-1451
Qutb-ud-Din Ahmad Shah II	1451-1458
Da'ud Shah	1458-1459
Nasir-ud-Din Mahmud Shah I Beghara	1459-1511
Shams-ud-Din Muzaffar Shah II	1511-1526
Nasir-ud-Din Sikandar Shah	1526
Nasir-ud-Din Mahmud Shah II	1526
Qutb-ud-Din Bahadur Shah	1526-1535
Humayun occupies Gujarat	(1535-1536)
Qutb-ud-Din Bahadur Shah	1536-1537
Miran Muhammad Shah III	1537
Nasir-ud-Din Mahmud Shah III	1537-1554
Ghiyath-ud-Din Ahmad Shah III	1554-1561
Shams-ud-Din Muzaffar Shah III	1561-1573
Akbar occupies Gujarat	(1573-1583)
Shams-ud-Din Muzaffar Shah III	1573-1583
to Mughal Empire	1583

(Maratha Confederacy)

(1721-1948)

Mahārājā Gaekwads of Baroda

Gaekwad Dynasty

Mahārājā Gaekwad Pilaji Rao	1721-1732
Damaji Rao	1732-1768
Govind Rao	1768-1771
Sayaji Rao	1771-1789
Manaji Rao	1789-1793
Govind Rao (restored)	1793-1800
Anand Rao	1800-1818
Sayaji Rao II	1818-1847
Ganpat Rao	1847-1856
Khande Rao	1856-1870
Malhar Rao	1870-1875
Sayaji Rao III	1875-1939
Pratap Singh Rao	1939-1948
to India	1948

Bengal

(Hindu)

(*c.* 750-1948)

Sena Dynasty (1161-1282)

Ballalasena	*c.* 1161-1178
Lakshamanasena	*c.* 1178-1205
Vishvarupasena	*c.* 1205-1220
Keshavasena	*c.* 1220-1250
(vacant)	1250-1282

(Muslim)

(1282-1576)

Bengal Sultanate

Iliyas Shahi Dynasty (1282-1415)

Nasir-ud-din Bughra	1282-1291
Rukn-ud-din Kaukaus	1291-1301
Shams-ud-din Firuz Shah	1301-1322

Major Rulers of India (Bengal Concl'd)

Shihab-ud-din Bughra Shah	1322-1324
Ghiyas-ud-din Bahadur Shah	1324-1336
Fakhr-ud-Din Mubarak Shah	1336-1340
Ali Mubarak , Ala-ud-din Ali Shah	1341-1342
Malik Iliyas Haji, Shams-ud-din Iliyas Shah	1342-1348
Ikhtiyar-ud-din Gaji Shah	1349-1352
Sikandar Shah	1358-1390
Ghiyas-ud-din Azam Shah	1390-1410 or 1396?
Sultān-ud-Salatin Saif-ud-din Hamza Shah	1412 or 1396-1405?
Shihab-ud-din Bayazid Shah	1412-1414 or 1405-1415?
Ala-ud-din Firoz Shah	1414?-15

Ganesa-Shahi Dynasty (1415-1437)

Rāja Ganesh	1415-1418
Jalal-ud-din Muhammed Shah	1419-1431 or 1432?
Shams-ud-Din Ahmad Shah	1431 or 1433? - 1435? 1437?

Ilyas-Shahi Dynasty (1435-87)

Nasir-ud-din Mahmud Shah	1435 or 1437?-1459
Rukn-ud-din Barbak Shah	1455-1476
Shams-ud-din Yusuf Shah	1474-1481 or 1483?
Sultān Sikandar Shah II	1482
Jalal-ud-Din Fateh Shah	1482-1484 or 1487

Habshis Dynasty (1486-1494)

Barbak II	1486-1487
Firuz III	1487-1489
Mahmud II	1489-1490
Muzaffar	1490-1494

Hussain-Shahi Dynasty (1494-1538)

Alauddin Hussain Shah	1494-1519
Nasib Shah, Nasir-ud-Din Nusrat Shah	1519 -1533
'Ala-ud-Din Firuz Shah II	1533
Ghiyas-ud-din Mahmud Shah	1533-1538

Shir Shah Sur Dynasty (1538-1563)

Farid-ud-din Abul Muzaffar Shir Shah Sur	1538-1545
IslĀm ShĀh	1545-1553
Firuz Shah	1553
Muhammad Mubariz Khan, Muhammad Shah Adil	1553-1555
Ghiyas-ud-din Bahadur Shah	1555-1560
Jalal-ud-din, Ghiasuddin II Abul Muzaffar	

Jalal Shah	1560-63
Ghiasuddin III	1563

Taj Karrani Dynasty (1563-1576)

Taj Khan Karrani	1563-65
Sulaiman (II) Khan Karrani	1565 -72
Bayazid Karrani	1572
Daud Khan	1572-76
to Mughal Empire	1576-1757

(1703-1770)
Nawābs of Bengal

Mueshid Quli Djafar Khan	1703-1727
Shoja ud-din	1727-1739
Safaraz Khan	1739-1741
Ali Vardi Khan	1740-1756
Siraj ud-Daula	1756-1757
Mir Djafar	1757-1760
Mir Qasim	1760-1763
Mir Djafar (restored)	1763-1765
Najim ud-Dawlah	1765-1765
Saif ud-Dawlah	1765-1770
to England	1856
to India	1948

Berar

(Muslim)
(1490-1574)
Berar Sultanate

'Imad Shahi Dynasty
(from Bhamani Sultanate)

Fath-Allah 'Imad ul-Mulk Shah	1490-1504
'Ala-ud-Din' Imad Shah	1504-1529
Darya 'Imad Shah	1529-1562
Burhan 'Imad Shah	1562-1568

Tufal Khan Dakhni	1568-1572
to Ahmadnagar	1572

Bharatpur/Deeg

(Sinsini Jats)

(1722-1948)

Mahārājās of Bharatpur

Sinsini Jat Dynasty

Thakur Badan Singh	1722-1733
Mahārājā Suraj Mal	1733-1767
Jawahar Singh	1767-1768
Ratan Singh	1768-1769
Kesri Singh	1769-1771
Newal Singh	1771-1776
Ranjit Singh	1776-1806
Randhir Singh	1805-1823
Baldeo Singh	1823 -1825
Balwant Singh	1825 -1853
Jaswant Singh	1853 -1893
Ram Singh	1893-1900 (Exiled)
Girraj Kaur (regent)	1900-1918
Vrijendra Sawai Kishan Singh	1900-1928 (Exiled)
Vrijendra Singh	1929-1947
to India	1948

Bidar

(Muslim)

(1492-1687)

Bidar Sultanate

Barid Shahi Dynasty

(from Bahamani Sultanate)

Amir Qasim Barid Shah I	1492-1504
Amir Barid Shah I	1504-1542

'Ali Barid Shah I	1542-1579
Ibrahim Barid Shah	1579-1587
Qasim Barid Shah II	1587-1591
'Ali Barid Shah II	1591
Amir Barid Shah II	1591-1600
Mirza 'Ali Barid Shah	1600-1609
Amir Barid Shah III ('Ali Shah II)	1609-1618
to Bijapur	1619

Bijapur

(Muslim)

(1489-1686)

Bijapur Sultanate

'Adil Shah Dynasty

(from Bahamani Sultanate)

Yusuf 'Adil Shah	1489-1512
Ismail 'Adil Shah	1512-1534
Mallu 'Adil Shah	1534-1535
Ibrahim 'Adil Shah I	1536-1557
Ali 'Adil Shah I	1557-1580
Ibrahim 'Adil Shah II	1580-1626
Muhammad 'Adil Shah	1626-1656
Ali 'Adil Shah II	1656-1672
Sikandar 'Adil Shah	1672-1686
to Satara	1686

Bikaner

(Rathor Rajput [junior line])

(1465-1948)

Raos (Rājas & Mahārājās) of Bikaner

Rathor Dynasty

(from Rao Jodha of Jodhpur)

Rao Bika (Rao Bikaji)	1465-1504
Naroji Singh	1504-1505
Lunkaranji	1505-1526
Jetsiji Singh	1526-1542
Kalyan Singh	1542-1571
Rāja Raj Singh I	1571-1612
Dalpat Singh	1612-1613
Sur Singh	1613-1631
Karan Singh	1631-1669
Mahārājā Anup Singh	1669-1698
Sarup Singh	1698-1700
Sujan Singh	1700-1736
Zorawar Singh II	1736-1745
Gaja Singh	1745-1787
Raj Singh II	1787
Pratap Singh	1787
Surat Singh	1787-1828
Ratan Singh	1828-1851
Sardar Singh	1851-1872
Mahārājā Shri Dungar Singh	1872-1887
Mahārājādhiraj Raj Rajeshwar Narendra Siromani	
Mahārājā Shri Ganga Singh	1887-1943
Sadul Singh	1943-1948
to India	1948

Bundelkhand

(See: Datiya, Orchha)

Bundi

(Harachauhan Rajput)

(1342 - 1658)

Raos of Bundi

Harachauhan Dynasty

Rao Suraj Mal	?-1531
Narbud Singh	1531-1555
Arjun Singh	1555

Surjan Singh	1555-1585
Bhoj Singh	1585-1607
Rao Rāja Ratan Singh	1607-1631
(gave Kota to Madho Singh, 1625)	
Maharao Chattar Sal Singh	1631-1658
to Mughal Empire	1658
Rao Rāja Bhao Singh	1658-1682
Anirudh Singh	1682-1696
Budh Singh	1696-1735
Dalel Singh	1735-1749
Umaid Singh	1749-1770
Ajit Singh	1770-1773
Umaid Singh	1773-1804
Bishen Singh	1804-1821
Maharao Rāja Ram Singh	1821-1889
Raghubir Singh	1889-1927
Ishwari Singhji	1927-1945
Bahadur Singh	1945-1948
to India	1948

Chittor (Mewar)

(Sisodias Rajput)

(1213-1567) [18]

Rawals (Rājas & Maharanas) **of Mewar**

Guhila Dynasty

Rawal Karan Singh I	1158-1168
Kahem Singh	1168-?
?	
Rāja Jaitra Singh	*c.* 1213-*c.*1260
Teja Singh	*c.* 1260-*c.*1273
Samara Singh	*c.* 1273-*c.*1302
Ratna Singh I	*c.* 1302-*c.*1303
Lakhana Singh	*c.* 1303-*c.*1314
Maharana Hammir I Singh (Junior Line)	*c.* 1314-*c.*1378
Kshetra Singh	*c.* 1378-*c.*1405
Laksha Singh	*c.* 1405-*c.*1420
Mokala Singh	*c.* 1420-1433
Kumbhakarna Singh	1433-1468

Udaya Karna	1468-1473
Rayamalla (Raimal) Singh	1473-1509
Sangrama Singh I	1509-1528
Ratna Singh II	1528-1532
Bikramajit	1532-1535
Ranbir	1535-1537
Udaya (Udai) Singh	1537-1567

(Sacked by Akbar (1567) capital to Udaipur. See: Udaipur)

Datiya

(Bundela Rajput)

(1626-1948)

Raos (Rājas & Mahārājās) **of Datiya**

Bundela Dynasty

(Datiya given by father Bir Singh Ju Deo of Orchha)

Rao Bhagwan Rao	1626-1656
Subha Karan	1656-1683
?	?
Rāmachandra Singh	1706-1733
Indrajit Singh	1733-?
?	?
Rāja Parichhat Singh	1802-1839
Bijai Singh	1839-1857
Mahārājā Bhawani Singh	1857-1907
Mahārājā Lokendra Govind Singh	1907-1948
to India	1948

Major Rulers of India (Delhi)

Delhi

(Muslim)

(1206-1526)

Delhi Sultanate

Slave or Mamluk Dynasty (1206-1320)

Qutb-ud-din Aibak, 1st Sultān of Delhi	1206 -1210
Aram Shah	1210-1211
Shams-ud-din Iltutmish	1211-1236
Rukn-ud-din Firuz	1236
Raziyya (Radiyya Begum)	1236-1240
Mu"izz-ud-din Bahram	1240-1242
'Al-ud-din Mas'ud	1242-1246
Nasir-ud-din Mahmud	1246-1266

House of Balban

Ghiyas-ud-din Balban	1266-1287
Mu'izz-ud-din Kaiqubad	1287-1290
Kaiumarth	1290

The Khaljiz

Jalal-ud-din Firuz Khaljiz	1290-1296
Rukn-ud-din Ibrahim (II)	1296
'Ala-ud-din Muhammad Khaljiz	1296-1316
Shihab-ud-din 'Umar	1316
Qutb-ud-din Mubarak	1316-1326
Nasir-ud-din Khusrav	1320

Tughluq Dynasty (1320-1414)

Ghiyas-ud-din Tughluq Shah I	1320-1325
Muhammad Shah Tughluq Shah (II)	1325-1351
Mahmud Ibn Mohammed	1351
Firuz Shah Tughluq	1351-1388
Ghiyas-ud-din Tughluq Shah II	1388-1389
Abu Bakr Tughluq	1389-1390
Mohammed Tughluq Shah (III)	1390-1393
Sikandar Tughluq Shah I	1393
Mahmud Tughluq Shah II	1394-1396
	interregnum
Mahmud Tughluq	1399-1413
Daulat Khan Lodi	1413-1414

Sayyid Dynasty (1414-1450)

Khizir Khan Sayyid	1414-1421
Mu'izz-ud-din Mubarak Shah II Sayyid	1421-1434
Muhammed Shah Sayyid (IV)	1434-1444
'Ala-ud-din Alam Shah Sayyid	1444-1451

Lodi Dynasty (1451-1526)

Buhlul Lodi	1451-1489
Nizam Khan, Sikandar Lodi	1489-1517
Ibrahim Shah Lodi (II)	1517-1526
to Mughul Empire	1526

Deeg

(See: Bharatpur/Deeg)

Dhundhar

(Kachwahas Rajput)

(1197 - 1527)

Rājās of Dhundhar

Kachawaha Dynasty

Rāja Dulha Rao	1093-1136
Kankal	1136-?
Maidal Rao	?
Hunadeva	?
Kantal I	?-1185
Punjanadeva	1185-1191
Malesi	1191-?
Byala	?
Rājadeva	?
Kilhan	?-1276
Kantal II	1276-1317
Jansi	1317-1367
Udayakarna	1367-?
Nara Singh	?-1413
Banbir Singh	1413-1424

Udha Rao	1424-1453
Chandrasena	1453-1502
Prithvi Singh I	1502-1527

(moved capital to Amber). See: Amber)

Dungarpur (Mewar)

(Sisodias Rajput Junior Line [from Chittor])

(1197 -1948)

Rawals (Maharawals & Rai-i-Rayan Maharawal Shris) **of Dungarpur**

Ahra Guhilot Dynasty

Rawal Samwat Singh	1197-1209
Jatant Singh	1209-1218
Sinhad Deo	1218-1248
Jai Singh Deo	1248-1251
Deopali Deo	1251-1278
Virsinh Deo	1278-1303
Bhu Chand	1303-1331
Dungar Singh	1331-1363
Karan Singh I	1363-1384
Jai Krishna	1384-1386
Mahipal Singh I	1386-1398
Kanhad Deo	1398-1403
Pratap Singh I	1403-1423
Gopinath Singh	1423-1447
Soma Das	1447-1479
Ganga Das	1479-1497
Udai Singh I	1497-1527
Prithviraj Singh	1527-1549
Askaran Singh	1549-1580
Sahas Mal	1580-1606
Karan Singh II	1606-1609
Punjaraj Singh	1609-1657
Girdhar Das	1657-1661
Jaswant Singh	1661-1691
Khuman Singh	1691-1702
Ram Singh	1702-1730

Shiv Singh	1730-1785
Vairi Sal	1785-1790
Fateh Singh	1790-1808
Maharawal Jashwant Singh II	1808-1845
Udai Singh II	1846-1898
Rai-i-Rayan Maharawal Shri Bijay Singh	1898-1918
Lakshman Singh	1918-1948
to India	1948

Gingee

(Nāyakas)

(1490-1750)

Nāyakas (Rāja) of Gingee

Nāyaka Tubaki Krishnappa	1490-1521
?	1521-1529
Vishvanatha	1529-1564
Krishnappa I	1564-1572
Virappa	1572-1595
Krishnappa II	1595-1601
Muttu Krishnappa	1601-1609
Muttu Virappa I	1609-1623
Tirumala	1623-1659
Muttu Virappa II	1659-1682
to Maratha Confederation	1676
to Mughals	1691
Rājā Sarup Singh	1691-1714
Desingh	1714
to Nawāb of Arcot	1714
to France	1750
to England	1761

Golconda

(Muslim)

(1512-1687)

Golconda Sultanate

Qutab Shahi Dynasty

(from Bhamani Sultanate)

Quli Qutub Qutbul-mulk Shah	1512-1543
Jamsheed Quli Qutub Shah	1543-1550
Subhan Quli Qutub Shah	1550
Ibrahim Quli Qutub Shah	1550-1580
Muhammad Quli Qutub Shah	1580-1612
Muhammad Qutub Shah	1612-1626
'Abdullah Qutub Shah	1626-1672
Abdul Hasan (Qutub) Tana Shah	1672-1687
to Mughal Empire	1687

Gujarat Sultanate

(See: Baroda)

Gulbarga/Bahmani

(Muslim)

(1337-1347)

Gulbarga Sultanate

Shihab-i-Sultāni Nusrat Khan	1337-1347
Ismail Mukh (Afghani)	1347

(1347-1527)

Bahmani Sultanate

Bahmani Dynasty (1347-1527)

Sikandar-uth-thani Ala-ud-din Hasan Bahman Shah al-wali. ('Ala-ud-din I)	1347-1358
Muhammad Shah I	1358-1377
Mujahid Shah	1377
Daub Khan	1377
Muhammad Shah II	1377-1397
Yaj-ud-din Firoz Shah	1397-1422
Ahmad Shah	1422-1435
(Capital moved to Bidar, 1424)	
'Ala-ud-din II	1436-1458
Humayun	1458-1461
Nizam Shah	1461-1463
Muhammad Shah III Lashkari	1463-1482
Mahmud Shah	1482-1518
Ahmad Shah III	1518-1521
'Ala-ud-Din	1521-1522
Wali-Allah Shah	1522-1525
Kalim-Allah Shah	1525-1527
to Bijapur	1489
to Ahmednagar	1490
to Berar	1490
to Bidar	1492
to Golconda	1512
to Mughals	1527

Gwalior

(Tomar Rajput)

(1398-1948)

Rājas (Mahārājās, Mahārājā Scindias) of Gwalior

Tomar Dynasty

from Delhi Sultanate	1398
Rāja Bir Singh Deo Tomar	1398 — ?
Man Singh	1486-1516
Vikramaditya	1516-1518

to Mughals	1518-1751

(Maratha Confederacy)
Sindha (Scindias [Shinde]) Dynasty

Mahārājā Scindia Ranojirao	1726-1745
Jayappa Rao	1745-1755
Jankoji Rao I	1755-1762
Madhava Rao I	1761-1794
Daulat Rao	1794-1827
Jankoji Rao I	1827-1843
Jayaji Rao	1843-1858
to England	1858-1886
Madhava Rao II	1886-1925
Jivaji Rao	1925-1948
to India	1948

Hyderabad

(Qamarid Muslim)

(1724-1948)

Nizams of Hyderabad

Asaf Jahi Dynasty

Mir Qamar ud-Din (Asaf Jah)	1724-1748
Mohammed Nasir Jung	1748-1750
Muzaffar Jang	1750-1751
Ghazi-ud-Din	1751-1752
Asaf ud-Dawlah Salabat Jang	1752-1761
Nizam 'Ali Khan	1761-1803
Sikandar Jah	1803-1829
Nasir ud-Dawlah	1829-1857
Afzal ud-Dawlah	1857-1869
Mahbub 'Ali Khan	1869-1911
Uthman 'Ali Khan Bahadur Jang	1911-1948
to India	1948

Indore

(Maratha Confederacy)

(1728-1948)

Mahārājās of Indore

Holkar Dynasty

Mahārājā Malhar Rao Holkar I	1728-1764
Malle Rao	1764-1766
Ahalya Bai	1765-1795
Tukoji	1795-1798
Jaswant Rao I	1798-1811
Malhar Rao II	1811-1834
Hari Rao	1834-1843
Tukoji Rao II	1843-1886
Sivaji Rao	1886-1903
Tukoji Rao III	1903-1926
Jaswant Rao II	1926-1948
to India	1948

Jaipur

(Kachwahas Rajput)

(*c.* 1128-1948)

Sri Sawai Mahārājās (Saramand-i-Rājah-i-Hindustan Raj Rajindra Sri Maharajdhiraj Sawais) of Jaipur

Rājawat Dynasty

(capital moved from Amber. See: Amber)

Sri Sawai Mahārājā Jaya Singh II	1727-1743
Ishwari Singh	1743-1750
Madhu Singh I	1750-1768
Prithvi Singh I	1768-1778
Pratap Singh	1778-1803
Jagat Singh II	1803-1818

Man Singh II (usurper)	1818-1819
Jaya Singh III	1819-1835
Rāma Singh II	1835-1881
Saramand-i-Rājah-i-Hindustan Raj Rajindra Sri Maharajdhiraj Sawai Madhu Singh II	1881-1922
Man Singh II	1922-1948
to India	1948

Jaisalmer

(Bhatti Rajput)

(1156-1948)

Rawals (Maharawals & Mahārājādhiraj Maharawal) **of Jaisalmer**

Bhati Dynasty

Rawal Jaisal	1156-1168
Salivahan I	1168
Bai Jal	1169-1200
Kailan	1200-1219
Chachick Deo	1219
Karan Singh I	1219-1251
Kakhen Sen	1251-1275
Punpal	1275-1276
Jait Singh I	1276-1294
Mulrājā I	1294-1306
Dudu	?
Gharsi	?
Kehan	?
Maharawal Nunkuran	1528-1550
Malla Dev	1550-1561
Harraj	1561-1577
Bhim Singh	1577-1613
Kalyan Das	1613-1650
Manohar Das	1650
Sabal Singh	1650-1661
Amar Singh	1661-1702
Jaswant Singh	1702-1707

Jagat Singh	1707-1722
Budh Singh	1707-1721
Tej Singh	1721-1722
Sawai Singh	1722
Akhai Singh	1722-1762
Mulraj Singh II	1762-1820
Haj Singh	1820-1846
Ranjit Singh	1846-1864
Bairai Sal	1864-1891
Salivahan Singh	1891-1914
Maharawaldhiraj Maharawal Jawahir Singh	1914-1948
to India	1948

Jammu/Kashmir

(Sikh)

(850-1822)

Rājas (Mahārājā) of Jammu

Dogra Dynasty

Rāja Suraj Dev	850-920
Bhoj Dev	920-987
Avtar Dev	987-1030
Jas Dev	1030-1061
Sangram Dev	1061-1095
Jasaskar	1095-1165
Brij Dev	1165-1216
Narsing Dev	1216-1258
Arjan Dev	1258-1313
Jodh Dev	1313-1361
Mal Dev	1361-1400
Hamir Dev (Rai Bhim)	1400-1423
Ajab Dev	?
Bairam Dev	?
Khokhar Dev	(d. 1528)
Kapur Dev	1530-1570
Samil Dev	1570-1594
Sangram	1594-1624
Bhup Dev	1624-1650
Hari Dev	1650-1686
Gujai Dev alias Gujja Singh	1686-1703
Dhruv Dev	1703-1725

Ranjit Dev	1725-1782
Brij Raj Dev	1782-1787
Sampuran Singh	1787-1797
Jit Singh	1797-1816
under Punjab rule	
Kishore Singh	1820-1822
Mahārājā Gulab Singh, Mahārājā of Jammu and Kashmir	1822-1846

(1822-1948)
Mahārājās of Jammu/Kashmir

Dogra Dynasty

Mahārājā Gulab Singh,	1822-1857
Ranbir Singh	1857-1885
Pratap Singh	1885-1925
Hari Singh	1925-1948
to India	1948

Jaunpur

(Muslim)

(1394-1476)
Jaunpur Sultanate

Sharqi Dynasty

Malik Sarvar (Sharqi)	1394-1399
Malik Qaranful, Mubarak Shah	1399-1402
Shams-ud-Din Ibrahim Shah	1402-1440
Nasir-ud-Din Mahmud Shah	1440-1457
Muhammad Shah	1457-1458
Husen (Husain) Shah	1458-1476
to Mughal Empire	1559
to England	1775

Jodhpur (Marwar)

(Rathor Rajput)

(1438-1948)

Raos (Rājas, Sawai Rājas, Mahārājās, Mahārājā Dhiraj Mahārājās, Raj Rajeshwar Saramand Raj-hai Hindustan Mahārājā Dhiraj Mahārājās, Raj Rajeshwar Mahārājā Dhiraj Mahārājās, & Raj Rajeshwar Mahārājādhiraj Shri) of Jodhpur

Rathor Dynasty

(capital moved from Mandore. See: Kannauj/Pali/Mandore)

Rao Jodha	1438-1489
Satal	1488-1491
Suja	1491-1515
Ganga	1515-1532
Malladeva	1532-1584
Rāja Udaya Singh Rāja	1584-1595
Sawai Rāja Sura Singh	1595-1620
Mahārājā Gaja Singh	1620-1638
Jaswant Singh I	1638-1678
to the Mughals	1678-1707
Ajit Singh	1707-1725
Abhaya Singh Mahārājā	1725-1750
Rāma Singh	1750-1751
Bakht Singh	1751-1752
Vijaya Singh	1752
Rāma Singh (restored)	1752-1773
Vijaya Singh (restored)	1773-1792
Bhim Singh	1792-1803
Man Singh	1803-1843
Takht Singh	1843-1873
Jaswant Singh II	1873-1895
Mahārājā Dhiraj Mahārājā Sri Sardar Singh	1895-1911
Raj Rajeshwar Saramand Raj-hai Hindustan Mahārājā Dhiraj Mahārājā Sumer Singh	1911-1918
Raj Rajeshwar Mahārājā Dhiraj *Mahārājā* Umaid Singh	1911-1947

Raj Rajeshwar Mahārājādhiraj Shri Hanwant Singh	1947-1948
to India	1948

Kannauj/Pali/Mandore (Marwar)

(Rathor Rajput)

(1170-1438 CE)

Rājas (Raos) of Marwar

Rājas at Kannauj

Rāja Jai Chand	1170-1194
Kumar Harish Chand	1194-1226

Raos at Pali

Rao Sheoji (Siha?)	1226-1273
Asthan	1273-1292
Doohad	1292-1309
Raipal	1309-1313
Kanhpal	1313-1323
Jalansi	1323-1328
Chada	1328-1344
Tida	1344-1357
Kanha Dev	1357-1374
Biram Dev	1374-1383

Raos at Mandore

Rao Chanda (Chonda)	1383-1424
Kanha	1424-1427
Ranmal	1427-1438
Jodha	1438-1488

(Capital moved to Jodhpur. See: Jodhpur)

Kashmir

Major Rulers of India (Kashmir)

(Muslim)

(1346-1589)

Kashmir Sultanate

Shahmir Dynasty (1346-1555)

Shah Mirza (Shah Mir), Shams-ud-Din I	1346-1349
Jamshid	1349-1350
'Ali Sher, 'Ala-ud-Din	1350-1359
Shirashamak Shihab-ud-din	1359-1378
Hindal Qutb-ud-Din	1378-1393
Sikandari	1393-1413
'Ali Shah	1413-1420
Zainal-'Abidin	1420-1470
Haidar Shah	1470-1472
Hasan Shah	1472-1484
Muhammad Shah	1484-1487
Fath Shah	1487-1499
Muhammad Shah (2nd reign)	1499-1505
Fath Shah (2nd reign)	1505-1514
Muhammad Shah (3rd reign)	1514-1515
Fath Shah (3rd reign)	1515-1517
Muhammad Shah (4th reign)	1517-1528
Ibrahim Shah I	1528-1529
Nazuk Shah, Nadir	1529-1530
Muhammad Shah (5th reign)	1530-1537
Shams-ud-Din II	1537-1538
Isma'il Shah I	1538-1540
Ibrahim Shah II	1540
Nazuk Shah, Nadir (2nd reign)	1540-1546
Haidar Dughlat	1546-1550
Nazuk Shah, Nadir (3rd reign)	1550-1551
Ibrahim Shah II (2nd reign)	1552-1554
Isma'il Shah II	1554
Habib Shah, Mahmud	1555

Chakk (Ghazi) Dynasty (1555-1589)

Muhammad Ghazi Shah	1555-1562
Nasir-ud-Din Husain Shah	1562-1570
Muhammad 'Ali Shah	1570-1579
Muhammad Yusuf Shah	1579
Mubarak Shah	1579
Lohar Shah	1580
Muhammad Yusuf Shah (2nd reign)	1580-1586
Muhammaad Ya'qub Shah	1586-1589

to Mughal empire	1589
to Afghanistan	1747

(Sikh)

(1819-1948)

Rājas of Kashmir

Sukerchukia Dynasty

Rāja Ranjit Singh	1819-1839
Kurruk Singh	1839-1840
Sher Singh	1840-1843
Dulip Singh	1843-1846
to England	1846

Dogra Dynasty (1846-1948)

Gholab Singh	1846-1856
Ranbir Singh	1857-1885
Rertab Singh	1885-1925
Hari Singh	1925-1948
to India	1948

Kolhapur

(Maratha Confederacy)

(1700-1948)

Rājas (Rāja Chhatrapati, Mahārājā) of Kolhapur

Bhonsle Dynasty

Rāja Sivaji I	1700-1712
Rāja Chhatrapati Shambhuji	1712-1760
Sivaji II	1760-1812
Shambhu	1812-1821
Shahaji I	1821-1837
Sivaji III	1837-1866
Rājaram I	1866-1870
Sivaji IV	1870-1883

Mahārājā Shahu Yashwantrao	1883-1922
Rājaram II	1922-1940
Shahaji Chhatrapati II	1940-1948
to India	1948

Kotah

(Harachauhan Rajput)

(1625-1948)

Raos (Maharaos, Maharao Mahendra Shris) of Kotah

Harachauhan Dynasty (junior line)

(from Ratna Singh of Bundi. See: Bundi)

Rao Madho Singh	1625-1656
Mokund Singh	1656-1658
Jagat Singh	1658-1669
Kishore Singh I	1669-1685
Ram Singh I	1685-1707
Maharao Bhim Singh I	1707-1720
Arjun Singh	1720-1724
Durgan Sal	1724-1756
Ajit Singh	1756-1759
Chhatar Sal	1759-1766
Guman Singh	1766-1771
Umaid Singh I	1771-1819
Kishore Singh II	1819-1828
Ram Singh II	1828-1866
Chhatar sal II	1866-1889
Maharao Mahendra Shri Umaid Singh II	1889-1940
Maharao Bhim Singh II	1940-1948
to India	1948

Madurai

(Nāyaka)

(*c.* 850-1948)

Nāyakas of Madurai

Thirumala Nāyaka Dynasty

Vishvanatha	1529-1564
Krishnappa I	1564-1572
Virappa	1572-1595
Krishnappa II	1595-1601
Muttu Krishnappa	1601-1609
Muttu Virappa I	1609-1623
Tirumala	1623-1659
Muttu Virappa II	1659-1682
Chokkanatha	1659-1678
Muttu Linga	1678-1682
Muttu Virappa III	1682-1689
Mangammal	1689-1706
Vijayaranga Chokkanatha	1706-1732
Mīnākṣī	1732-1736
to France	1736-1763
to England	1763-1948
to India	1948

Malwa (Mandu)

(Muslim)

(1392-1531)

Malwar Sultanate

Ghuri Dynasty (1392-1436)

Dilvar Khan Ghuri	1392-1405
Husam-ud-Din Hushang Shah	1405-1435
Ghazni Khan, Muhammad Shah I	1435-1436
Masud Khan, Masud Shah	1436

Khalji Dynasty (1436-1531)

Mahmud I, Khalji	1436-1469
Ghiyath Shah	1469-1500
Nasir Shah	1500-1510
Mahmud II	1510-1531
Muhammad Shah II (pretender)	c 1511-1516
Hushang Shah II (pretender)	1511
to Gujarat Sultanate	1531
to Mughul Empire	1535

Maratha Confederacy

See: Gaekwar, Mahārājās of Baroda; Gwalior Sindhia Dynasty; Indore Holkar Dynasty; Kolhapur Bhonsle Dynasty; Nagpur Bhonsle Dynasty; Poona (Pune) Peshwa Dynasty; Satara Bhonsle Sisodia Dynasty; & Tanjore (Thanjavur) Bhonsle Sisodia Dynasty

Marwar

(See: Kanauj/Pali/Mandore, Jodhpur)

Mewar

(See: Chittor, Dungarpur, Udaipur)

Mughal India (Empire)

(Muslim)

(1526-1876)

Timurud Dynasty (1526-1540) (See Timur/Genghisid Descent, p. 306)

Zahir-ud-din Muhammad Babur, King of Ferghana, "the Great Mughul"	1526-1530
Nasir-ud-din Humayun	1530-1540

Major Rulers of India (Mughal Empire Concl'd)

Suri Dynasty (1540-1555)

Sher Khan (Sur Sher Shah)	1540-1545
Islam Sur Shah	1545-1553
Firuz	1553
Mohammed Adil	1553-1555
Sikandar	(opposition) 1554-1555
Ibrahim	(opposition) 1554-1555

Timurud Dynasty (1555-1876)

Nasir-ud-din Humayun	1555-1556
"Rāja" (General) Himu (Hindu)	1556
Jalal-ud-din Akbar the Great	1556-1605
Nur-ud-din Jahangir	1606-1627
Dawar Bakhsh	1627-1628
Shihab-ud-din Shah Jahan	1628-1658
Murab Bakhsh	(1657)
Shah Shuja'	(1657-1658)
Muhiy-ud-din Aurangzib	1658-1707
A'zam Shah	1707
Kam Bakhsh	1707
Qutb-ud-din Shah Alam Bahadur	1707-1712
'Azim-ush-Shan	1712
Mu'izz-ud-din Jahandar Shah	1712-1713
Muhiy-ud-din Farrukh-siyar	1713-1719
Rafi'-ud-Darājāt	1719
Rafi'-ud-Daula Shah Jahan II	1719
Nasir-ud-din Muhammad Shah	1719-1748
Mujahid-ud-din Ahmad Shah Bahadur	1748-1754
'Aziz-ud-din 'Alamgir II	1754-1759
Shah Jahan III	1759
Jalal-ud-din Shah 'Alam II	1759-1788
Bidar Bakht	1788-1806
Mu'in-ud-din Muhamad Akbar II	1806-1857
Siraz-ud-din Bahadur Shah II	1857-1876
to England	1876

Mysore

(Wadiyar/Hindu)

(1399-1948)

Mahārājās (Shri Mahārājās) of Mysore

Wadiyar (Wodeyar) Dynasty (1399-1796)

Mahārājā Yadu Raya	1399-1423
Hiriya Bettada Chamarājā Wadiyar I	1423-1459
Timmarājā I	1459-1478
Hiriya Chamarājā II	1478-1513
Hiriya Bettada Chamarājā III	1513-1553
Timmarājā II	1553-1572
Bola Chamarājā IV	1572-1576
Bettada Devarājā	1576-1578
Rāja Wadiyar	1578-1617
Chamarājā V	1617-1637
Immadi Rāja	1637-1638
Kanthirava Narasarājā I	1638-1659
Kempa Devarājā	1659-1673
Chikkadevarājā	1673-1704
Kanthirava Narasarājā II	1704-1714
Krishnarājā I	1714-1732
Chamarājā VI	1732-1734
Krishnarājā II	1734-1766
Nanjarājā	1766-1770
Bettada Chamarājā VII	1770-1776
Khasa Chamarājā VIII	1776-1796

Haidarid Dynasty (1762-1799)

Haodar 'Ali Khan	1762-1782
Tipu Sultān	1782-1799

Wadiyar Dynasty (1799-1948)

Krishnarājā III	1799-1831
to England	1831-1881
Shri Mahārājā Chamarājā IX	1881-1894
Krishnarājā IV	1894-1940
Jayachamarajendra Bahadur	1940-1948

to India	1948

Nagpur

(Maratha Confederacy)

(1738-1948)

Mahārājās of Nagpur

Bhonsle Dynasty

Bhakt Buland of Gond	17??-17??
Chand Sultān	17??-1738
Mahārājā Raghuji Bhonsle I	1738-1755
Janoji	1755-1772
Mudhoji I	1772-1788
Raghuji II	1788-1816
Mudhoji II	1816-1818
Raghuji III	1816-1853
to England	1853
to India	1948

Orchha (Bundela)

(Bundela Rajput)

(1501-1948)

Rājas (Mahārājās & Saramad-i-Rajha-i-Bundelkhand Mahārājā Mabindra Sawai Shri) of Orchha

Bundela Dynasty

Rāja Rudra Pratap Singh	1501-1531
Bharti Chand	1531-1554
Madhukhar Shah	1554-1577
defeated by the Mughals	1577

Ram Shah	1591-1605
Bir Singh Ju Deo	1605-1627
Jhujhar Singh	1627-1635
Devi Singh	1635-1641
Pahar Singh	1641-1653
Sujan Singh I	1653-1672
Indramani	1672-1675
Jashwant Singh	1675-1684
Bhagwat Singh	1684-1689
Udwat Singh	1689-1735
Prithivi Singh	1735-1752
Sanwat Singh	1752-1765
Hati Singh	1765-1768
Man Singh	1768-1775
Bharti Singh	1775-1776
Vikramajit	1776-1817
Dhram Pal	1817-1834
Tej Singh	1834-1842
Sujan Singh II	1842-1848
Mahārājā Hamir Singh	1848-1874
Saramad-i-Rajha-i-Bundelkhand Mahārājā Mabindra Sawai Shri Pratap Singh	1874-1930
Vir Singh	1930-1948
to India	1948

Orissa

(Hindu)

(*c.* 915-1703)

Rājas (Mahārājās) of Orissa

Gajapati Dynasty (1434-1541)

Kapilendra	1434-1467
Purushottama	1467-1497
Prataparudra	1497-1540
Kaluadeva	1540-1541
Kakharudeva	1541

Govindarājā Dynasty (1541-1703)

GovindarājāVidyadhara	1541-1549
Chakrapratapa	1549-1557

Narasimha Jana	1557-1558
RaghuramaChhotra	1558-1560
Mukundadeva Harichandana	1560-1568
to Bengal	1568
to Mughal Empire	1576
to Nagpur	1738
to England	*c.* 1850
to India	1948

Patiala

(Sikh)

(1762-1948)

Rājas (Mahārājās) of Patiala

Phulkian Dynasty

Rāja Ala Singh	1762-1765
Amar Singh	1765-1781
Sahib Singh	1781-1813
Karam Singh	1813-1845
Mahārājā Narindar Singh	1845-1862
Mohindar Singh	1862-1876
Rajindar Singh	1876-1900
Bhupindar Singh	1900-1938
Yadavindar Singh	1938-1948
to India	1948

Poona (Pune)

(Maratha Confederacy [Bhonsle])

(1713-1818)

Peshwas of Poona

Peshwa Dynasty

Peshwa Balaji Vishvanatha	1713-1720
Balji Rao I	1720-1740

Thorala Balaji Baji Rao Peshwa	1740-1761
Madhava Rao Ballal	1761-1772
Narayana Rao	1772-1773
Raghunath Rao	1773-1774
Madhava Rao Narayan	1774-1796
Chimnaji Appa	1796
Balji Rao II	1796-1818
to England	1818
to India	1948

Punjab (Lahore)

(Sukerchukia)

(1799-1849)

Mahārājās of Punjab (Lahore)

Sandhanwalia Dynasty

Mahārājā Ranjit Singh Bahadur, Sher-i-Punjab,	1799-1839
Kharak Singh	1839-1840
Nao Nehal Singh	1840
Chand Kaur	1840-1841
Sher Singh	1841-1843
Duleep Singh	1843-1849
to England	1849
to India	1948

Rajput Clans

Early Clans

(Deccan & Malwa, 6th *c.* CE)

Chauhan (Chahamana)
Solanki (Chaulukya)
Parihar (Pratihara)
Pawar (Paramara)

Middle Clans

Guhilots (Sisidias) (Chittor, 8th *c.* CE)
Chandels (Chandalas) (Khajuraho, 9th *c.* CE)
Tomars (Delhi, 11th *c.* CE)

Later Clans

Sisodias (Nagda, 7th *c.* & Chittor, 8th *c.* CE)
Sisodias (senior) Udaipur, *c.* 1550 CE)
Sisodias (junior) (Dungarpur *c.* 1350 CE)
Kachwahas (Amber, 967 CE & Jaipur, 1727 CE)
Bhattis (Jaisalmer, 1156 CE)
Rathors (Pali 1226 CE, Mandore 1383 CE, Jodhpur, 1438 CE)
Rathors (junior) (Bikaner, 1485 CE)
Harachauhans (Bundi, 1342 CE & Kota, 14th *c.* CE)
Tomars (Gwalior, 1398 CE)
Bundelas (Orchha, 1501 CE)
Bundelas (junior) (Datiya, 1626 CE)

Satara

(Maratha Confederacy)

(1674-1848)

Mahārājās of Satara

Bhonsle Sisodia Dynasty

Mahārājā Sivaji I (The Great)	1674-1680
Shambhuji I	1680-1689
Rājaram	1689-1700
Tara Bai	1700-1708
Shahu Sivaji I	1708-1749
Rāmarājā	1749-1777
Shahu II	1777-1808
Pratap Singh	1808-1839
Shahji Rāja	1839-1848
to England	1848
to India	1948

Sisodia

(Guhilot Rajput)

(b.1168—1314)

Rānās (Maharanas) of Sisodia

Guhilot Dynasty (Junior line)

(from Rawal Karan Singh I of Mewar [Chittor])

Rānā Rahap Singh	a.1168-?
Narpat Singh	?
Dinkaran Singh	?
Jaskaran Nagpa Singh	?
Puran Pal Singh	?
Prithi Pal Singh	?
Bhuvan Singh	?
Bhim Singh	?
Jai Singh	?
Lakhana Singh	*c.* 1303-*c.*1314
Maharana Hamir Singh I, *Rānā* of Sisodia and Mewar	1303-1378

Tanjore (Thanjavur)

(Nāyaka)

(1549-1855)

Nāyaka Dynasty (1549-1673)

Sevappa	1549-1572
Achyutappa	1572-1614
Raghunatha	1614-16??
Vijaya Raghava	16??-1673

Rājas of Tanjore

(Maratha Confederacy)

Bhonsle Sisodia Dynasty (1674-1855)

Rāja Venkaji Rao I	1674-1686
Shahji Rao	1686-1711

Sarabhoji Rao I	1711-1727
Turkoji Rao	1727-1735
Venkaji Rao II	1735-1736
Sujana Bai	1736-1738
Sawai Shahji Rao	1738
Sayaji Rao	1738-1739
Pratap Rao	1739-1763
Tusalji Rao	1763-1787
Amar Rao	1787-1798
Sarabhoji Rao II	1798-1824
Sivaji Rao	1824-1855
to England	1855
to India	1948

Travancore

(Kulashekhara)

(*c*.1110-1948)

Rājas (Mahārājās) of Travanvcore

Cheraman (Kulashekhara) Dynasty

Rāja Rāma Varma I	1724-1729
Maṛtanda Varma III	1729-1758
Rāma Varma II	1758-1798
Bala Ram Varma I	1798-1810
Rāma Varma III (q.v.)	1810-?
Martanda Varma IV (q.v.)	?-1815
Rani Ghauri Parvati Bai (Regent)	1815-1829
Rāma Varma III	1829-1846
Martanda Varma IV	1846-1860
Mahārājā Rāma Varma IV (q.v.)	1860-?
Rāma Varma V (q.v.)	?
Rāma Varma IV	1860-1880
Rāma Varma V	1880-1885
Bala Rāma Varma II	1885-1924
Bala Rāma Varma III	1924-1948
to India	1948

Udaipur (Mewar)

(Sisodias Rajput)

(1567-1948)

Maharanas (Mahārājādhiraj) **of Udaipur**

Guhila Dynasty

(capital moved from Chittor. See: Chittor)

Maharana Udaya (Udai) Singh II	1567-1572
Pratap Singh I	1572-1597
Amar Singh I	1597-1620
Karan Singh	1620-1628
Jagat Singh I	1628-1652
Rāja Singh I	1652-1680
Jaya Singh	1680-1699
Amar Singh II	1699-1711
Sangrama Singh II	1711-1734
Jagat Singh II	1734-1752
Pratap Singh II	1752-1754
Rāja Singh II	1754-1761
Ari Singh II	1761-1773
Hammir II	1773-1778
Bhim Singh	1778-1828
Jawan Singh	1828-1838
Sardar Singh	1838-1842
Sarup Singh	1842-1861
Sambhu	1861-1874
Sujjan Singh	1874-1884
Mahārājādhiraj Fateh Singh	1884-1930
Bhopal Singh	1930-1948
to India	1948

Vijayanagar
(1336-1565)
Rājas of Vijayanagara

Sangama Dynasty (1336-1485)

Harihara I	1336-1356
Bukka I	1366-1377
Harihara II	1377-1404
Virupaksha I	1404-1405
Bukka I	1405-1406
Devaraya I	1406-1422
Rāmachandra	1422-1430
Devaraya II	1422-1446
Vijaya II	1446-1447
Mallikarjuna	1446-1465
Virupaksha II	1465-1485

Saluva Dynasty (1485-1505)

Narasimha Saluva	1485-1490
Timma	1490-1491
Immadi Narasimha Rao	1491-1505

Tuluva Dynasty (1505-1576)

Vira Narasimha (Naresh Tuluva)	1505-1509
Krishnadevaraya	1509-1530
Achyutadevaraya	1530-1542
Venkata	1542
Sadashivaraya	1542-1576

capital moved to **Penukonda** (1565)

Aravidu Dynasty (1569 -1664)

Tirumala I	1569-1572
Shrirangaraya (Krishnadeva Ranga II)	1572-1585
Venkata (Vencattapatti Rayalu)	1586-1614

capital moved to **Chandragiri** (*c.* 1601)

Ranga III (Chikka Raya)	1614
Ranga IV	1614-?
Rāmaraya	1629-1634
Pedda Venkata II	1634-*c.*1642
Ranga (V) (Sri Rangaraya)	1642-1681

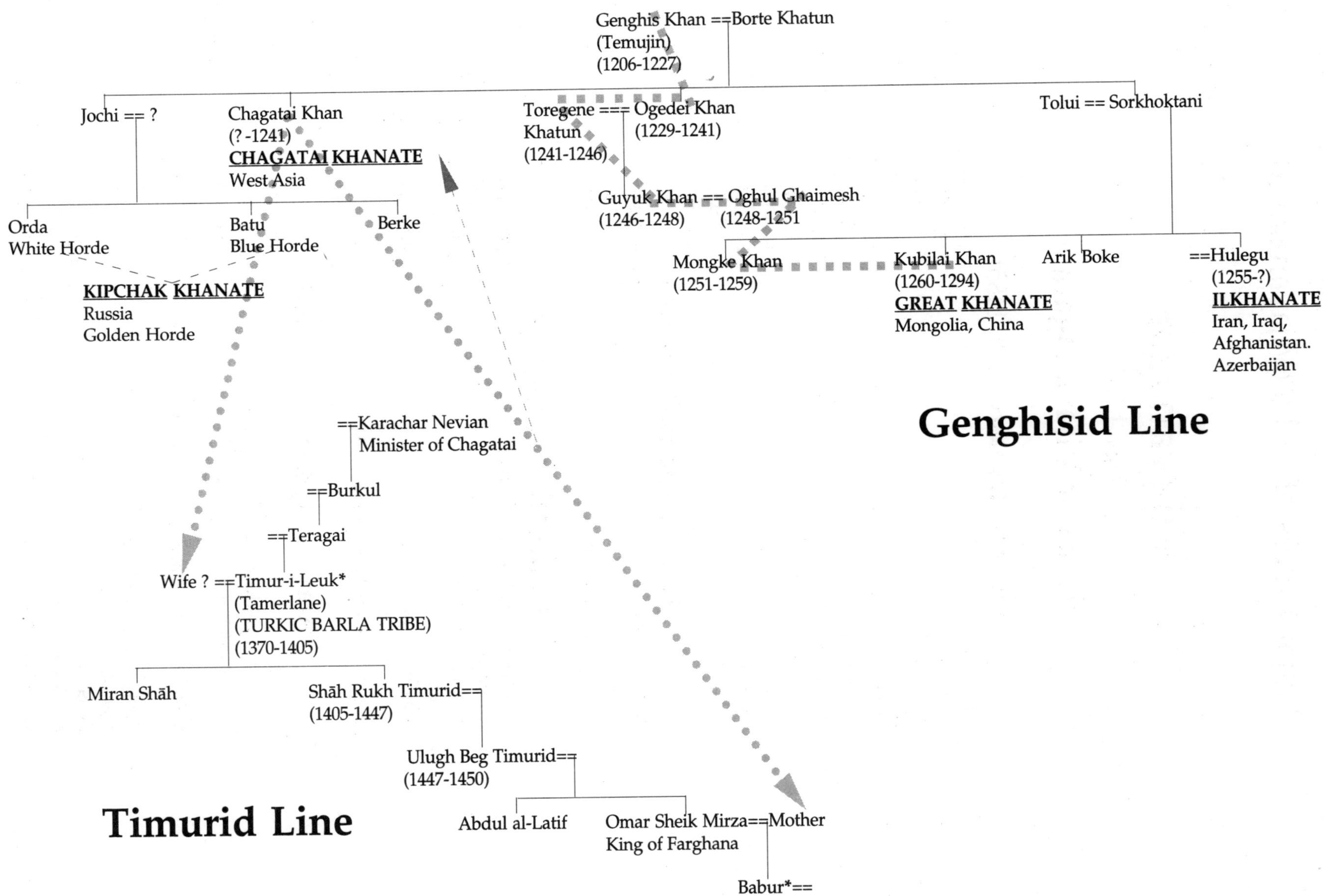

*Timur-i-Leuk æs wife and Babur's mother trace their lineage to Chagatai Khan

Appendix C:
Chronology of Major Indian Monuments

	Palaces, Pavilions and Residences	OTHER
1200		**Qutb Minar**, Delhi
		Tomb No. 36, Delhi
		Tomb of Sultān Iltutmish, Delhi
1250		**Surya Temple**, Konarak
		Keshava Temple, Somnathpur
	Hauz Khās, Delhi (*c*. 1290- a. 1388 CE)	
1300		
		Tomb of Sheikh Rukn-i 'Alam, Multan
	Vijayanagara Kotila (a. 1350)	
1350	***Kotila Firuz Shāh***, Delhi (a. 1351)	
		Tomb of Khan-i Jihan Tilangani, Delhi

	Palaces, Pavilions and Residences	OTHER
1400		**Jami' Masjid**, Srinagar
	Mandu Mandir, Mandu (a. 1410 CE)	
	Rānā Kumbha Mandir, Chittor (a. 1433 CE)	Tomb of Mubarak Shāh Sayyid, Delhi, 1434 CE
1450		Tomb of Hushang Shāh, Mandu, 1440 CE
	Jahāz Mahal, Mandu (*c.* 1460 CE)	Sayyid Usman Rauza, Usmanpur, *c.* 1460 CE
	Wav Dada Harir (Baoli Bai Hari), Asarwa (1499 CE)	
1500	***Mān Mandir*** (Palace of Man Singh), Gwalior (*c.* 1500 CE)	
	Gujari Mahal, Gwalior (1510 CE)	Tomb of Sikandar Lodi, Delhi, *c.* 1518 CE
	Daulat Kothi, Bijapur (1st half 16th *c.* CE) ***Aināpur Mahal***, Aināpur (1st half 16th *c.* CE) ***Water Pavilion*** (*hammam*), Kumatagi (1st half 16th *c.* CE) ***Jahāz Mahal***, Bijapur (1st half 16th *c.* CE)	
1550		Tomb of Sher Shāh, Saseram, a. 1540 CE
	Gagan Mahal, Bijapur (1561 CE)	
	Lal Qilā (Red Fort), Agra (1565-a. 1600 CE)	
	Jahangiri Mahal, Red Fort, Agra (1570 CE)	Tomb of Humayun, Delhi, 1565 CE
	Fatehpur Sikri, (1569 -1574 CE): ***House of Rāja Birbal*** (a.1569); ***Diwan-i-Khās*** (a.1569); ***Jodh-Bai Mahal*** (a.1569); ***Sunahra Makan*** (a.1569)	
	Gingee Mandir, Gingee (16th-17th *c.* CE)	
	Rājā Mahal, (Chandragiri Palace), Tirupati (a. 1585 CE)	

Palaces, Pavilions and Residences

Year	Palaces, Pavilions and Residences		OTHER
1600	*Feria Bagh*, Ahmadnagar (a. 1600 CE)		
	Govind Mandir, (*Bir Singh Judeo Mahal*), Orchha (a. 1605 CE)	**Rānā Mahal, Chandragiri**	Tomb of Akbar, Sikandra
	Udaipur Mandir (City Palace), Udaipur (1614-18th *c.* CE)		
	Shāhi Bagh, Ahmadabad, (*c.* 1623 CE)		Ibrahim Rauza, Bijapur Gol Gumbaz, Bijapur
	Lal Qilā (*Shāhjahanabad*), Delhi (1639-1648 CE)		Tomb of Jahangir, Lahore
	Rāj Mahal, Amber, (1639-1668 CE)		Tāj Mahal, Agra
1650	*Nāyaka Mahal*, Madurai (*c.* 1650 CE)		**Jami' Masjid**, Delhi
			æ**Pearl Mosque**,' Red Fort, Delhi Tomb of Ali 'Adil Shāh II, Bijapur *Badshahi Mosque*, Lahore
1700			
	Suraj Mal Mandir (*Jats of Bharatpur*), Deeg, (1722-1763 CE)		
	Padmanabhapuram, Kanyakumari, (1729-1758 CE)	**Jag Nivās, Udaipur**	
	Gul Mahal, Jag Mandir, Udaipur, (a. 1734 CE)	**Jaipur Mandir (City Palace), Jaipur**	
1750		**Chau Mahalla, Hyderabad**	Tomb of Safdar Jang, Delhi

Palaces, Pavilions and Residences

OTHER

	Palaces, Pavilions and Residences	OTHER
1800		
	Palace of Padmini, Chittor Falaknama, Hyderabad	
1850		
	Lakshmi Vilas, Baroda Jai Vilas, Gwalior	
1900		
	Lal Bagh, Indore Jagatji, Kapurthala Mysore Mandir, Mysore	
1950		
	Umaid Bhavan, Jodhpur Morvi Mandir (New Palace), Morvi	

Appendix D:
Glossary

Related terms that are to be found within the text. "Indic" refers to those terms which are derived from any or many dialects and languages indigenous to the Indian sub-continent. "Arabic" refers to those terms which are derived from Arabic root words and include: Iranian & Turkish.

Plate 108 — Axiality

(*Kilatali Śiva Temple,* Thiruvanchikula)

Axiality refers to: the symmetrical arrangement of the elements of a plan along a given axis. In the case of the *Kilatali Śiva Temple*, that axis is the east-west axis. The northern half is a duplicate of the southern half.

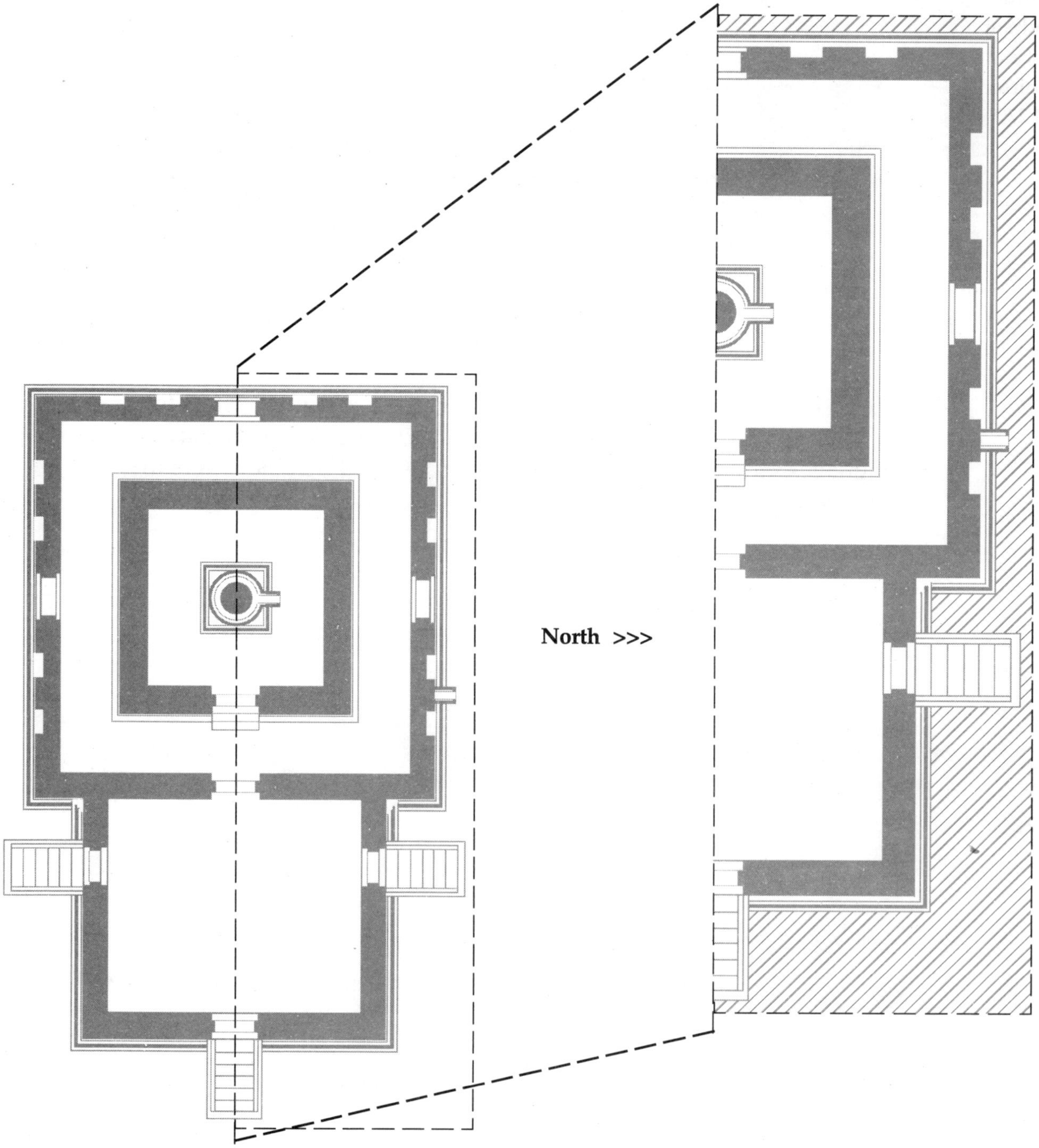

Plate 109 — Cross-Axiality

(*Ananda*, Pagan)

Cross-Axiality refers to: the symmetrical arrangement of the elements of a plan along both axes, precisely duplicating each quadrant. This term is not applied to rectangular plans. In the case of the *Ananda*, the north-south and east-west axes divide the form. The north-west quadrant is seen as a duplicate of the north-east, south-west and south-east quadrants. This quadrant can either be mirrored in any of the other three, or rotated 90°, 180°, and 270° to achieve the whole.

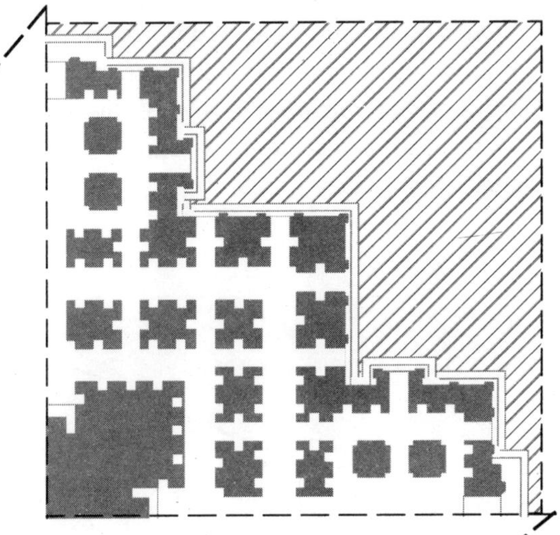

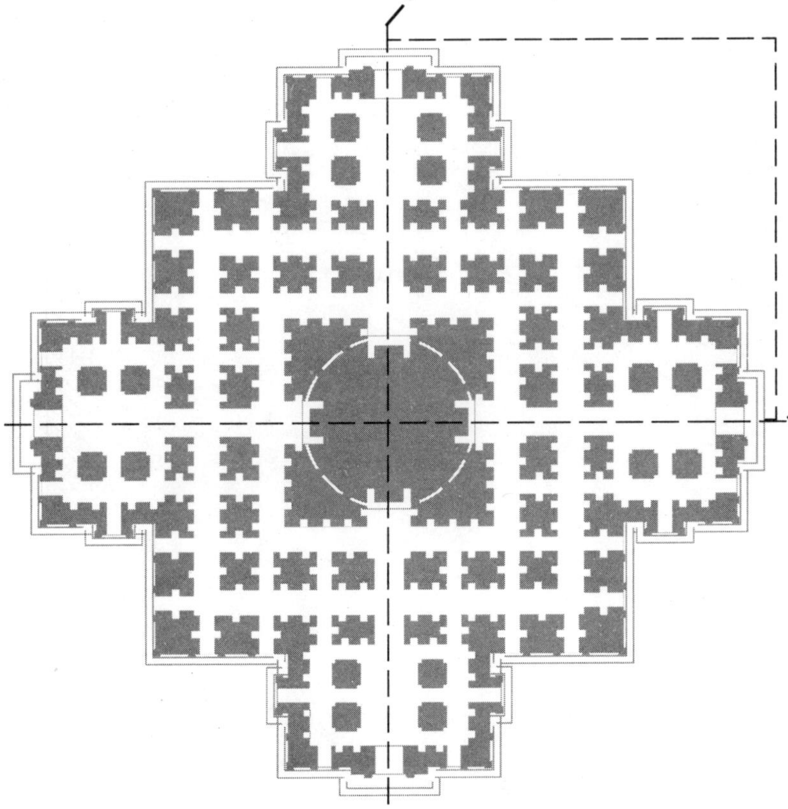

North >>>

Plate 110 — Mirror Cross-Axiality

(*Library, Angkor Wat*, Angkor)

Mirror Cross-Axiality refers to: the symmetrical arrangement of the elements of a plan along both axes, mirroring each quadrant. This term is applied to rectangular plans. In the case of the *Library, Angkor Wat*, the north-south and east-west axes divide the form. The north-west quadrant is seen as a mirror duplicate of the north-east, south-west and south-east quadrants. This quadrant can be mirrored in any of the other three. It cannot be rotated to achieve the whole as can be seen in the cross-axial plan.

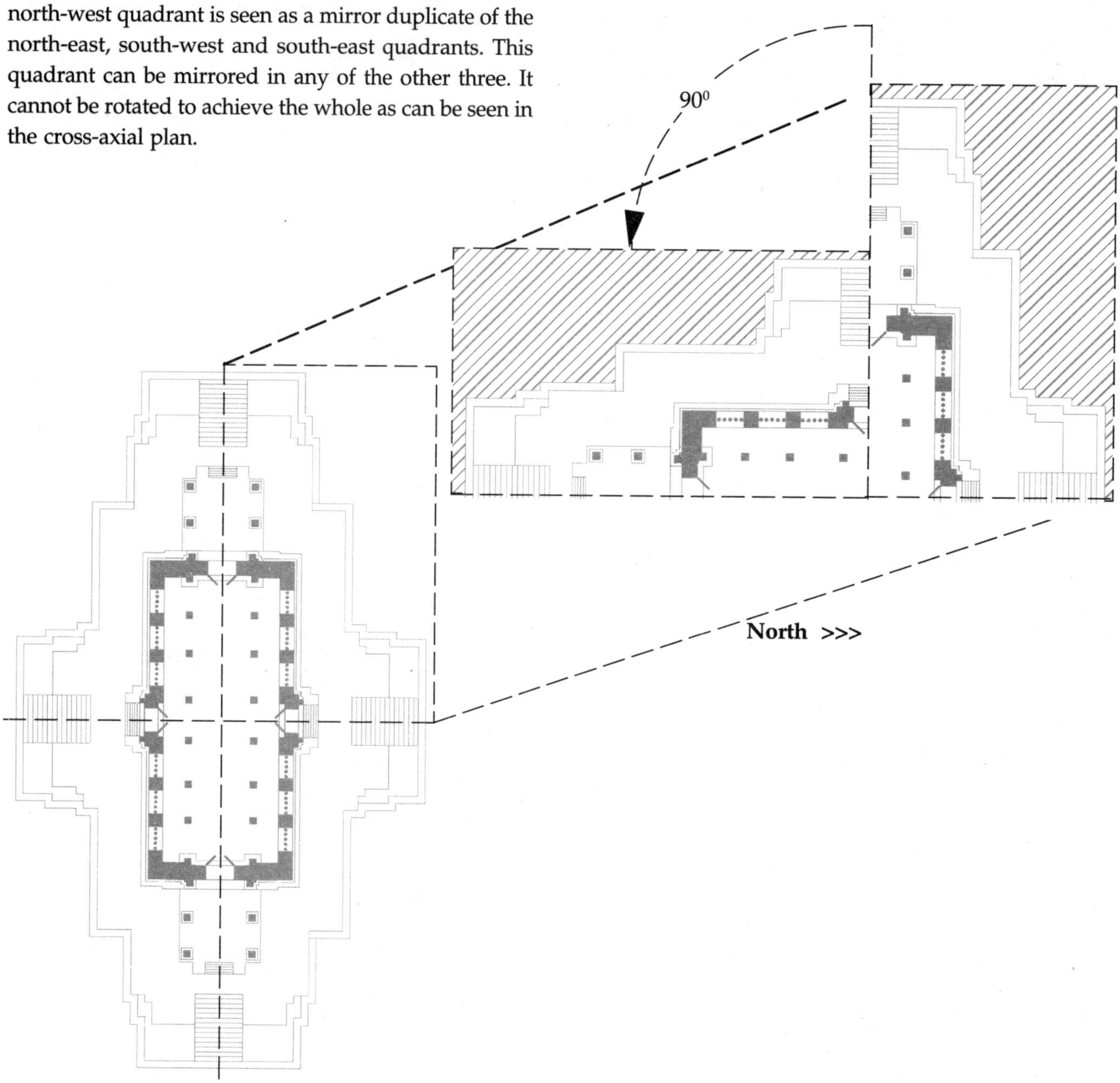

Plate 111 — Rotating Axiality

(House of Rājā Birbal, Fatehpur Sikri)

Rotating Axiality refers to: the arrangement of the elements of a plan along a single axis in which half the plan is rotated 180^0. This term is applied to rectangular plans. In the case of the *House of Rājā Birbal*: the north-south axis divides the form and that half-plan is rotated 180^0 arriving at the complete plan.

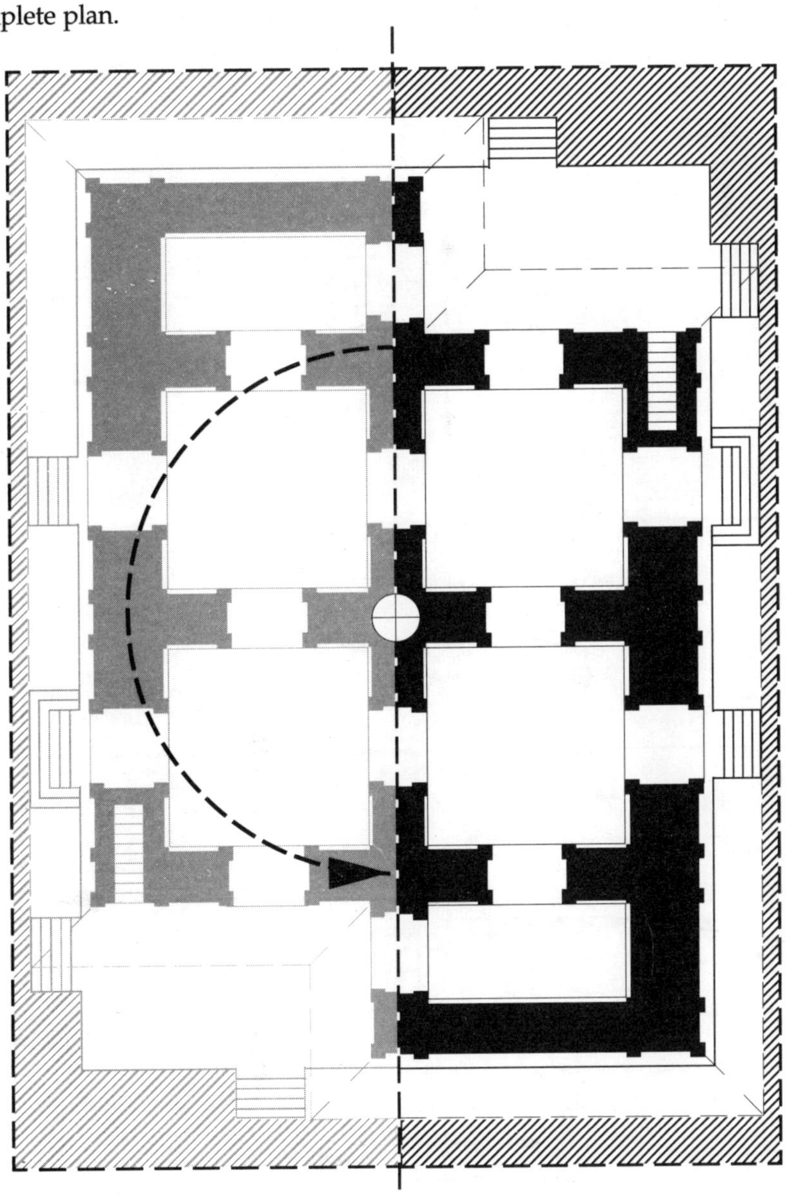

Plate 112 — Multiple Perpendicular Axiality

(Fatehpur Sikri)

Multiple Perpendicular Axiality refers to: the arrangement of the elements of a plan based upon an axis or axes oriented to a specific point and other axes perpendicular to the main axis or axes. In the case of the *Fatehpur Sikri*: the main axis appears to be north, while other structures are oriented perpendicular to this axis — i.e., east-west.

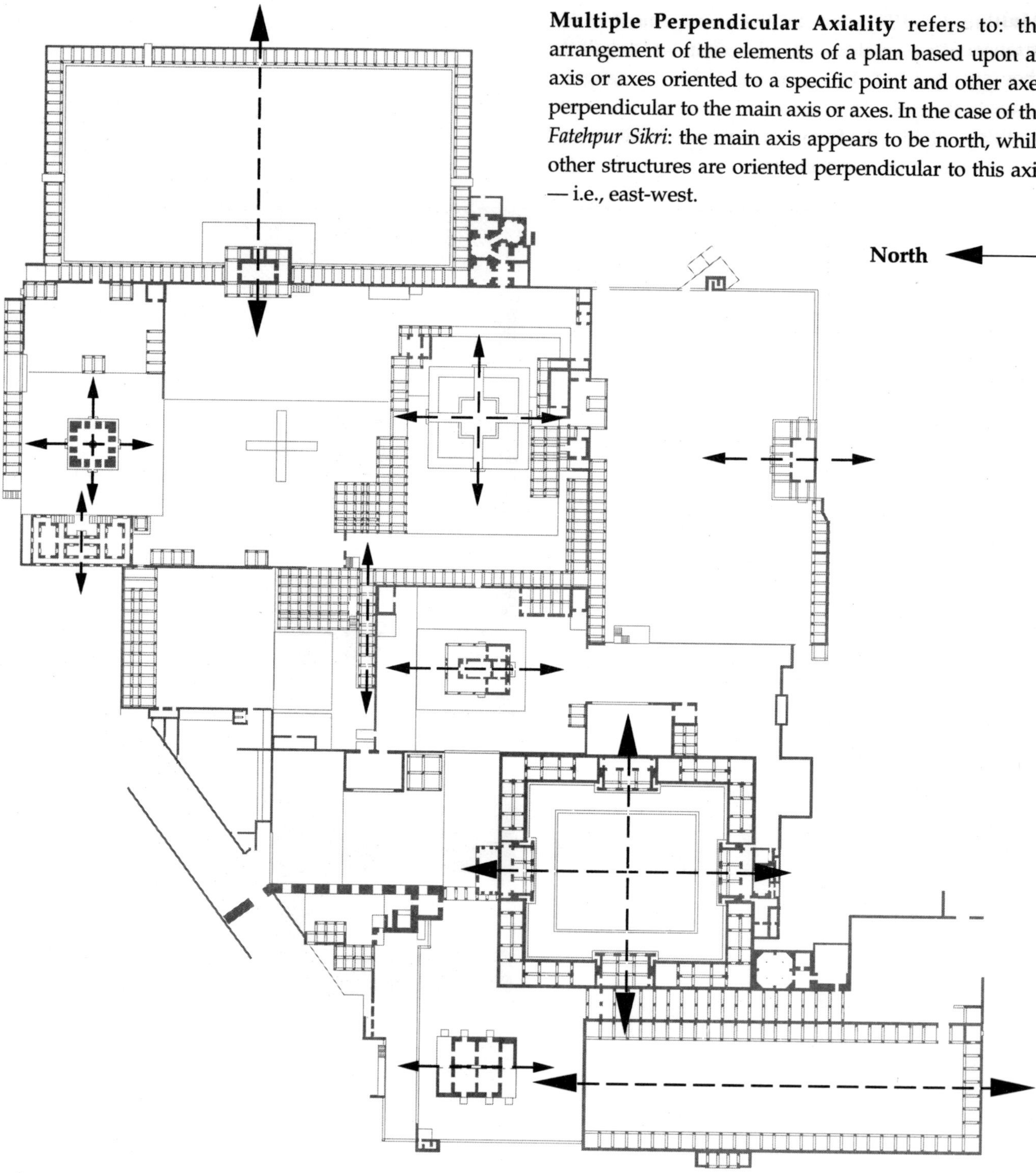

Plate 113 — Multiple Non-Perpendicular Axes

(*Meherangarh*, Jodhpur)

Multiple Non-Perpendicular Axiality refers to: the arrangement of the elements of a plan based in which there are many different axes, oriented to various points of the compass. In the case of the *Meherangarh of Jodhpur*: few structures are on the same or perpendicular axes.

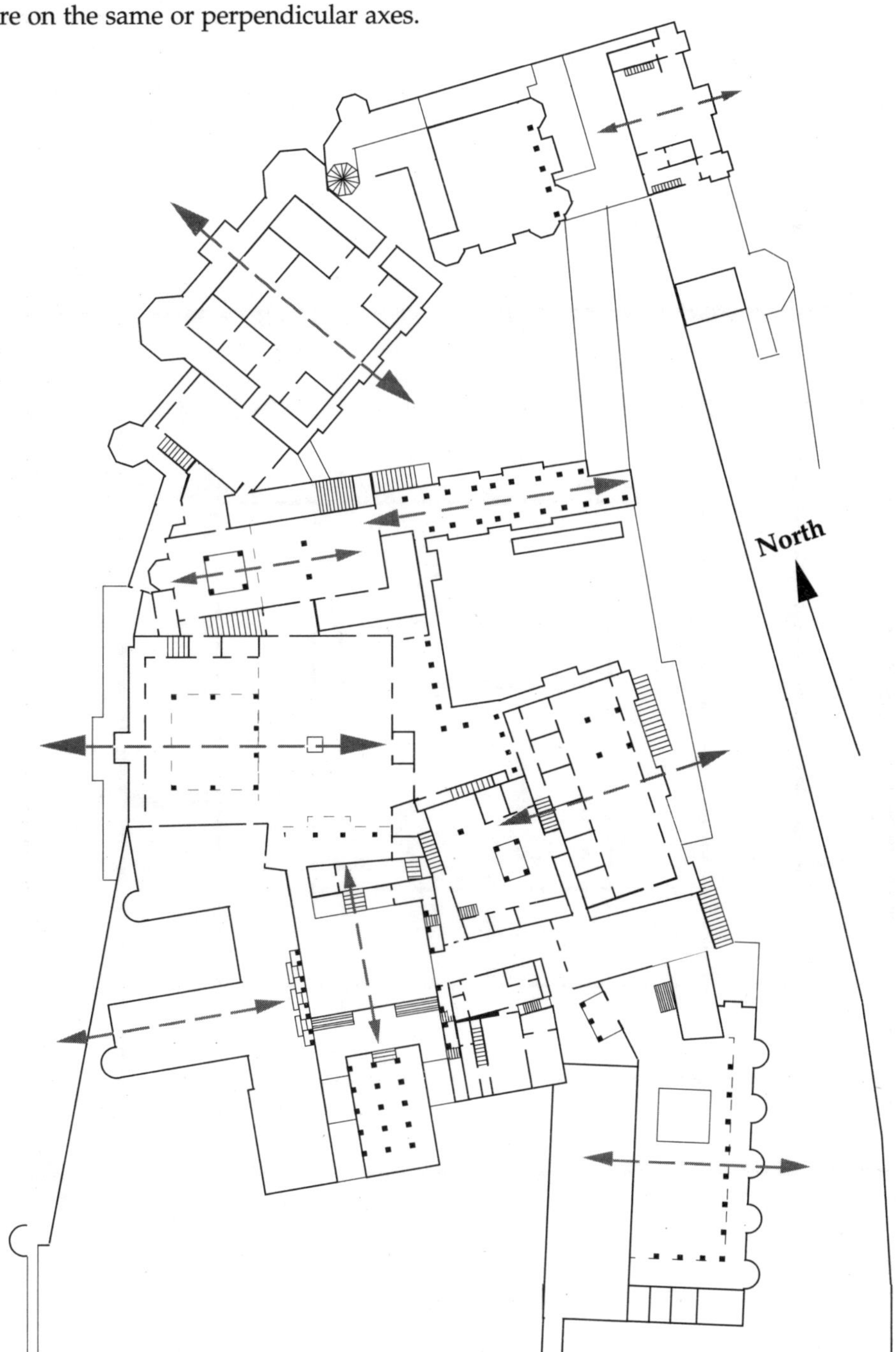

Plate 114 — Hindu Ideal Based on a *Paramaśayika Maṇḍala*

(*Govind Mandir*, Datiya)

The Hindu ideal is based upon the *Paramaśayika Maṇḍala* of eighty-one *pada*. When applied to a *garh mahal*, towers of approximately one and one-half *pada* in diameter are placed at the four corners, the intercardinal points. The inner square corresponds with the *brahmāsthāna*. In the case of the *Govind Mandir* of Datiya: the central tower is within the nine *pada* of the *brahmāsthāna*, and the inner border of the *bagh* rests upon this square. The other internal divisions fit regularly within the subsequent squares.

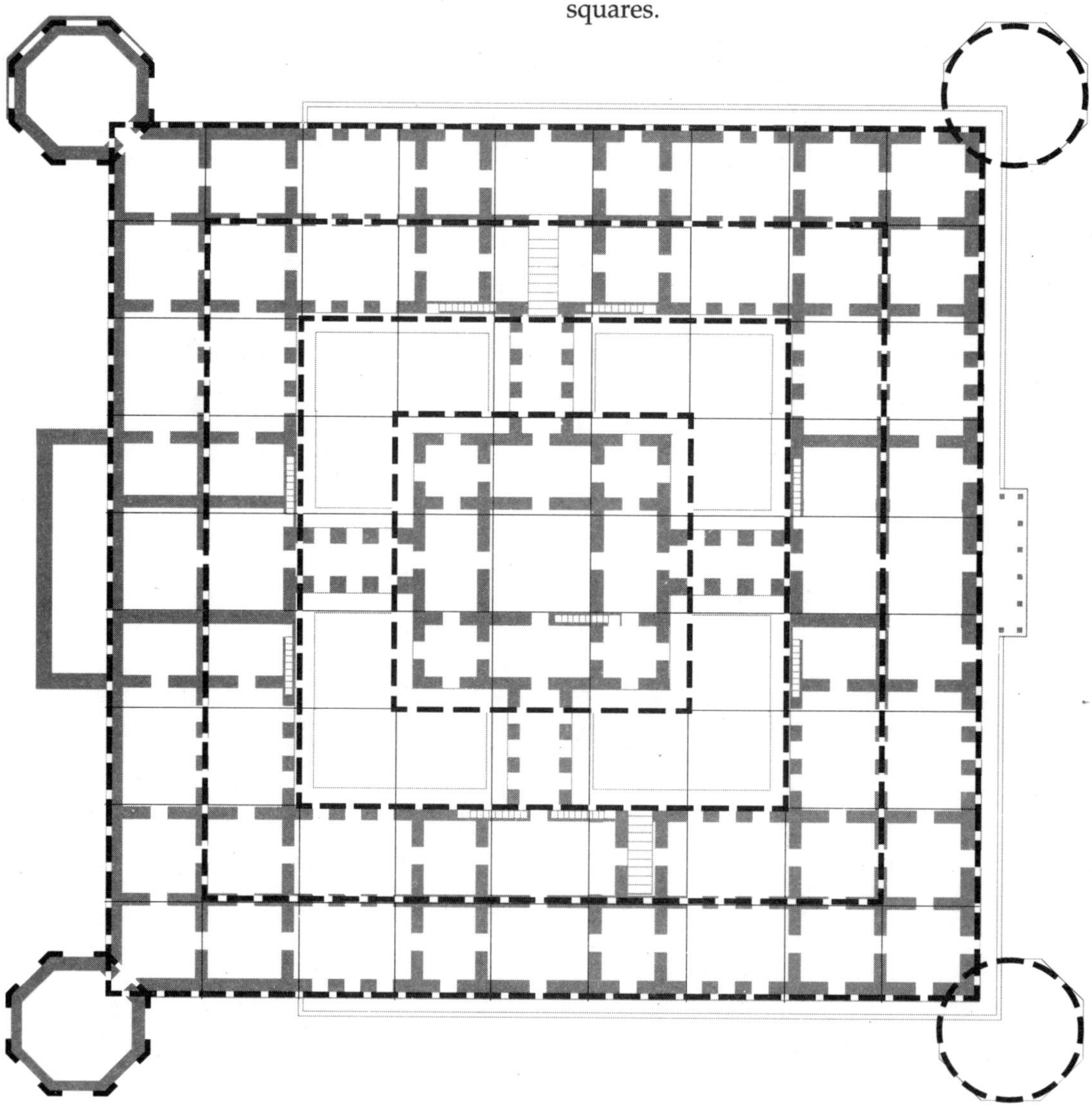

Glossary

A

abhiṣeka — The term refers to a ritual bathing ceremony. When applied to an Indian monarch, it is the moment of elevation to the position of ruler.

amir — The term refers to a commander or prince of the Islamic world.

aṇḍā — (aka *dhatu-garbha, garbha, gaeba*) The term refers to an egg-shape, more specifically to the hemispherical form of a stupa. It is also referred to as: *garbha* and *gaeba*.

aśvamedha — The term refers to the sacrifice of a horse, originally performed by Hindu rulers on ascending the throne.

axiality — The symmetrical arrangement of the elements of a plan along a given axis. If that axis is the east-west axis, then the northern half is a duplicate of the southern half. See: **Plate 000**.

B

bagh — The term refers to a garden, usually square or made up of square components. It may also refer to a pleasure palace.

bagh mahal — The term refers to a garden palace, and may be applied to the *Deeg-garh* of Deeg.

bangaldar — The term refers to the roof-form derived from the Bengali, curved or 'humped' bamboo or thatched roofs; the form is usually employed in smaller structures.

baoli — (aka *bauli, wav*) The term refers to well or reservoir which has been given architectural embellishment consisting of descending steps.

baradari — The term refers to a columned, open pavilion, similar to a śālā. Traditionally, *baradari* possessed sixteen columns — i.e., four ranks of four — however, the term is often compared to any columned pavilion.

bauli — (aka *baoli, wav*) See: *baoli*.

bhavan — (aka *bhawan*; Indic: *mahal*) The term refers to an internal hall for assembly. The term may also refer to a house as a structure or an enclosed pavilion.

bhawan — (aka *bhavan*) See: *bhavan*.

birka — (aka *fisqiya, haud, saqaya, sihrij*) The term refers to an ablution tank.

Brāhmaṇic — Here, referring to the religious practice which includes both Vedic and post-Vedic or Hindu beliefs.

brahmāsthāna — The term refers to the central area of a Hindu *maṇḍala* in which the prime deity, Brahmā, resides.

burj — The term refers to a fortified tower or bastion.

C

caravansari — (aka *han*) The term refers to a resting place for travellers or caravans. Generally found on trade routes and may be fortified to protect the travellers and their goods.

cardak — The term refers to a reception room generally employed during the summer months.

chahar-bagh — (aka *charbagh*) The term refers to a plot of land, generally square, that is divided into four equal sections.

chajjā — (aka *cajja*) The term refers to the overhanging eaves-stone that generally encircles a temple or mausoleum above the level of the doors.

charbagh — (Arabic: aka *chahar-bagh*) See: *chahar-bagh*.

chatrī — (aka *chhatrī, chhatta*) See: *chatrī*.

chaturśālā — The term refers to a plan in which rooms appear on all four sides of a courtyard.

chatrī — (aka *chhatrī, chhatta*) The term refers to a kiosk with a dome usually supported by four or eight, slender pillars. It also refers to a royal, ceremonial umbrella held over a ruler to protect for Hindu rulers.

chatta — (aka *chhatrī, chatrī*) See: *chatrī*.

chitra mahal — The term refers to a hall with painted scenes.

cross-axiality — The symmetrical arrangement of the elements of a plan along both axes, precisely duplicating each quadrant. This term is not applied to rectangular plans. The north-south and east-west axes divide the form. The north-west quadrant is a duplicate of the north-east, south-west and south-east quadrants. This quadrant can either be mirrored in any of the other three, or rotated 90°, 180°, and 270° to achieve the whole. See: **Plate 000**.

Glossary (Continued)

D

dad mahal — The term refers to a hall of justice.

dandaka — The term refers to a rectangular house-form which is divided into three equal sections.

darbār — (aka *durbar*) The term refers to a royal audience which may include large numbers of people or relatively private audiences.

dargah — The term refers to an entrance or portal.

darih — The term refers to a tomb.

darśana — The term refers to the public viewing of a ruler, usually in the morning.

darwāzā — The term refers to an entrance gate, usually elaborate and ceremonial.

daulat khana — The term refers to a treasury room or structure.

diwān — The term refers to a royal reception chamber or enclosure. It may also refer to a ministry of the government.

diwān-i ām — (aka: *sabhā nivās*) The term refers to a hall or court where public audience or *darbārs* are held.

diwān-i khās — The term refers to a hall or court where private audience are held.

durbar — (aka *darbār*) See: *darbār*.

durg — (aka *garh, kot, kotla, kotila*) See: *garh*.

dviśālā — The term refers to a plan in which rooms appear on two sides of a courtyard, forming an 'L.'

E

ekśālā — The term refers to a plan in which rooms appear on but one side of a courtyard.

F

file — The term refers to a vertical (length) line in which individual elements are equally spaced. It is related to "rank" as in "rank and file."

fisqiya — (aka *birka, haud, saqaya, sihrij*) The term refers to an ablution tank.

funduq — The term refers to an inn or warehouse.

G

gaddi — The term traditionally refers to a cushioned seat upon which a ruler sat. It has come to refer to "a throne" proper within the Hindu/Indian context. It may also refer to "the throne" of a particular state.

gagan mahal — The term refers to a room or pavilion elevated above other structures.

garbhagṛha — The term refers to the sanctuary or *sañctum sanctorum* of a Hindu temple (*devālaya*). Within the *garbhagṛha* is found the primary image of the temple or shrine. Horizontally, the various segments of the temple symbolize parts of the body cosmic.

Ganesh pol — (aka *hāthī pol*) The term refers to an elephant gate, usually the first gate into a fort and often decorated with elephants.

garh — (aka *durg, kot, kotla, kotila, qilā*) The term refers to a fort or a heavily fortified, defensive structure — e.g., *Kumbhalgarh* of Chittor, the *Meherangarh* of Jodhpur, or the *Deeg-garh* of Deeg.

garh mahal — The term that is employed herein refers to any palace or royal residence that is within and/or part of a fort or fortified, defensive structure.

ghat — The term refers to a broad stepped way leading to a river or tank for bathing.

ghazi — The term refers to a holy warrior, one who defends the faith.

giri — (aka *ghat*) The term refers to a hill, usually defensive.

gumbad — (aka *qubba*) The term refers to a dome.

H

hammam — The term refers to a pavilion or structure where bathing takes place.

han — (aka *caravansari*) The Turkish equivalent for *caravansari*. See: *caravansari*.

harem — (aka *zenānā*) The term refers to private quarters in a home or mosque. Generally, it refers to women's quarters or locale within a palace compound. See also *zenānā*.

hasht bihisht — The term refers to the eight paradises. In architecture it refers to the eight rooms or areas around a central space. See also: *muthamman baghdadi*.

hāthī pol — (aka *Ganesh pol*) See: *Ganesh pol*.

haud — (aka *birka, fisqiya, saqaya, sihrij*) The term refers to an ablution tank found in a *sahn*.

Glossary (Continued)

hujra — The term refers to a small chamber or cell.

I

intarsia — (aka *pietra dura*) See: *pietra dura* .

iwan — The term refers to a roofed hall exposed at one end.

J

jabana — (aka *maqbara*, *qabrstan*) The term refers to a cemetery.

jālī — The term refers to a thin, stone screen with a perforated design. See also: *maśrabiya.*

jahaz mahal — The term refers to a pavilion or *mahal* that is situated on a lake, literally "ship" *mahal*.

jai mahal — The term refers to a ceremonial pavilion, literally: pavilion or *mahal* of victory.

jai mandir — (aka *jas mandir*) The term refers to a ceremonial structure or palace, literally: palace of victory or palace of glory.

jami' — The term refers to a large mosque where Friday prayers are held and a sermon is preached.

jas mandir — (aka *jai mandir*) See: *jai mandir*.

jharoka — The term refers to a throne or balcony containing a *gaddi* at which the ruler would appear during the *darśana*.

K

Kalyāṇa maṇḍapa — The term refers to a ceremonial hall, frequently referred to as a marriage hall. In southern India, the name given to a *zenānā*.

khan — The term refers to a man of high rank, either a lord or a prince.

khanaqah — The term refers to a monastic-like structure that may also contain a mausoleum.

khās mahal — The term refers to a private pavilion or structure within a palace complex.

khwabgah — The term refers to the private sleeping quarters of a ruler.

kiosk — The term refers to a summer house or a pavilion of open construction. It also refers to a small, often domed architectural form supported by pillars that appears as a major ornamental unit, usually at the corners of larger structures. See: *chatrī*.

kot — *(aka durg, garh, kotila, kotla, qilā)* See: *kotila*.

kotla — (aka *kotila, kot, durg, garh, qilā*) See: *kotila*.

kotila — (aka *kot, kotla, durg, garh, qilā*) The term refers to a fort or fortified area.

ksar — The term refers to a fortified village.

kṣatriya — The term refers to the Hindu caste, second to the brāhmaṇas, the warrior caste and one from which many of the rulers emerged.

L

lahd — The term refers to a burial vault. It may also refer to a niche. See also: *madfam*.

M

madfam — (aka *lahd*) The term refers to a burial vault or mausoleum.

madrasa — The term refers to a Muslim school or institution in which orthodox sciences are taught, generally associated with a *masjid*.

maidān — The term refers to a square or plaza or ceremonial enclosure.

mahal — (aka *mandir*) Originally, the term referred to any hall or ceremonial room, pavilion or apartment within a palace or other notable structure. See: *bhavan*. By extension it is now commonly applied to a palace — e.g., *Gagan Mahal* of Bijapur, the *Rāja Mahal* of Tirupati, or the *Rāj Mahal* of Amber. See: *garh mahal*.

Mahārājāh — The term refers to a great king, may also refer to a Hindu emperor. See: *nawāb, nāyaka, nizām, rājāh, rao, raya, sultān*.

maidān — The term refers to an open area where parades or military manoeuvres occur.

manabhat-kari — The term refers to stone inlay or *pietra dura*.

maṇḍala — The term refers to a sacred Buddhist/ Hindu diagram. Certain *maṇḍalas* were employed as the basis for architectural plans. The two preferred forms for temple designs were the *Maṇḍūka Maṇḍala* with sixty-four *pada* and the *Paramaśayika Maṇḍala* with eighty-one pada.

Glossary (Continued)

maṇḍapa — The term refers to a covered structure attached to a *garbhagṛha* of a Hindu temple which serves as an assembly hall.

mandir — (aka *mahal*) Generally, herein, the term refers to a palace or royal residence — e.g., *Mān Mandir* of Gwalior, or *Rājā Mandir* of Orchha. However, it is generally applied to a temple in its more common usage. It also applies to a room.

Maṇḍūka Maṇḍala — The term refers to a *maṇḍala* of sixty-four *pada* — i.e., eight in either direction. See: *maṇḍala*.

maqbara — (aka *jabana, qabrstan*) The term refers to a cemetery.

mardānā — The term refers to a design, originally square, a fortified men's quarters with a central court. Later, the term is used to describe a residence with an inner court generally for men and separate from the *zenānā*.

marmas — The term refers to the perpendicular crossing of lines within a *maṇḍala*, created by the conjunction of four or more *pada*. In the Hindu tradition, it is considered inauspicious for any line delineating the form of the structure to fall upon a *marmas*. See: *maṇḍala*.

mashrabiya — The term refers to a grilled window or screen usually of wood. See also: *jālī*.

masjid — (aka *mosjid, cami*) The term refers to a mosque; literally 'a place of prostration.'

masjid-i jami' — The term refers to a mosque specifically for Friday prayers.

mazar — The term refers to a mausoleum.

merlon — The term refers to a solid element often on a battlement between two openings (crenels). Within Indo-Islamic architecture these tend to be more decorative than functional.

mihrab — (aka *mikhrab*) A variant of *mikhrab*. See: *mikhrab*..

mikhrab — (aka *mihrab*) The term refers to the "prayer niche" found in mosques in the wall facing Mecca (*qibla*). The *imam* preaches or recites the *Qur'an* from the *minbar* adjacent to the *mikhrab* during the prayers.

mirror cross-axiality — The term refers to: the symmetrical arrangement of the elements of a plan along both axes, mirroring each quadrant. See: **Plate 000**.

mosjid — (aka *masjid)* The term refers to a variation on the term *masjid*. See *masjid*.

multiple perpendicular axiality refers to: the arrangement of the elements of a plan based upon an axis or axes oriented to a specific point and other axes perpendicular to the main axis or axes. In the case of the *Fatehpur Sikri*: the main axis appears to be north, while other structures are oriented perpendicular to this axis — i.e., east-west. See: **Plate 000**.

multiple non-perpendicular axiality refers to: the arrangement of the elements of a plan in which there are many different axes, oriented to various points of the compass. In the case of the *Meherangarh of Jodhpur*: few structures are on the same or perpendicular axes. See: **Plate 000**.

musalla — (*surau*) See *surau*.

musamman burj — The term refers to an octagonal tower.

muthamman baghdadi — The term refers to a square plan to which the corners have been sheared off forming an irregular octagon. See also: *hasht bihisht*.

N

Naqqār khana — The term refers to a drum house or pavilion within a palace complex which was used to announce visitors and/or times of the day.

naubat khana — The term refers to a guard house.

nawāb — The term refers to or is a title of a governor or ruler. See: *Mahārājāh, nāyaka, nizām, rājāh, rao, sultān*.

nāyaka — The term refers to a governor or ruler. It is especially applicable to southern India where the governors (*nāyakas*) of Gingee, Thanjavur and Madurai declared independence from the beleaguered Vijayanagara. After the independence from Vijayanagara, *nāyaka* then assumed the definition of 'ruler.' See: *Mahārājāh, nawāb, nizām, rājāh, rao, sultān*.

nivās — (aka *niwas*) The term refers to a palace. Specifically a smaller palace within a larger or also an abode.

nizām — The term refers to a ruler. See: *Mahārājāh, nawāb, nāyaka, rājāh, rao, sultān*.

P

pada — The term refers to a single square found within a *maṇḍala*. See: *maṇḍala*.

Pañcharatha — The term refers to two separate extensions, generally in the middle portion of the surface of a wall, creating five surfaces per face. See: *ratha* & *triratha*.

Paramaśayika Maṇḍala — The term refers to a *maṇḍala* of eighty-one *pada* — i.e., nine in either direction. See: *maṇḍala*.

Pathan — The term frequently refers to a style of Indo-Islamic architecture which finds its roots in Afghanistan (Pashtun tribe) and Iran (Persia).

pietra dura — (aka *intarsia*) The term refers to the inlaying or fitting of small, often complexly formed, pieces of stone, both precious and semi precious, into a larger stone matrix which has been carefully carved out to receive the smaller pieces. It differs from the technique employed in an inlaid stone floor in which larger pieces of stone are fitted together in a pattern and set in concrete or other cementing agent.

pishtaq — The term refers to a tall arch which frames an *iwān*. It may also refer to a large, impressive portal.

pol — The term refers to a gate.

purdah — The term refers to the practice of isolating or hiding the women of a household, particularly from men outside of the close family group. It may also be applied when women appear veiled in public.

putra — The term refers to a son or a prince. When used as in Mandan *putra* Kshetra, it means: "son of."

Q

qabrstan — (aka: *jabana, maqbara*) The term refers to a cemetery.

qasaba — The term refers to a citadel or capital.

qasr — The term refers to a fortified residence, castle or a palace.

qibla — The term refers to a wall which is perpendicular to the direction in which prayers are offered — i.e., always towards the *Ka'ba* in Mecca.

qilā — (aka *durg, garh, kot, kotla, kotila*) The term refers to a fort.

Qur'an — The term refers to the holy book of Islam.

R

rājāh — The term refers to king or ruler. See: *Mahārājāh, nawāb, nāyaka, nizām, rana, rao, raval, sultān.*

rana — The term refers to king or ruler. See: *Mahārājāh, nawāb, nāyaka, nizām, rājāh, rao, raval, sultān.*

rank — The term refers to a horizontal (width) line in which individual elements are equally spaced. It is related to "file" as in "rank and file."

rao — (aka *Mahārājāh, nawāb, nāyaka, nizām, rājāh, raya, sultān*) The term refers to king or ruler. See: *Mahārājāh.*

ratha — (aka *puṣpaka*) The term refers to an extension of a wall surface, generally on all four sides. If there is a single extension, the form is called *triratha* — creating three surfaces per face. If there are two extensions, the form is called *Pañcharatha* — creating five surfaces per face. The term also refers to a celestial conveyance. See: *Pañcharatha* & *triratha*. Also, a variant of the term *pushpaka*. See: *pushpaka*.

raval — The term refers to king or ruler. See: *Mahārājāh, nawāb, nāyaka, nizām, rājāh, rana, rao, sultān.*

rawala — See: *zenānā.*

raya — The term refers to an emperor. See: *Mahārājāh, nawāb, nāyaka, nizām, rājāh, rao, sultān.*

ribat — The term refers to a fortified Islamic monastery or hermitage. It may also refer to a frontier settlement.

rotating axiality — The term refers to: the arrangement of the elements of a plan along a single axis in which half the plan is rotated 180^0. This term is applied to rectangular plans. In the case of the *House of Rājā Birbal*: the north-south axis divides the form and that half-plan is rotated 180^0 arriving at the complete plan. See: **Plate 000**.

S

sabhā nivās — (aka: *diwān-i ām*) The term refers to an assembly hall or pavilion where public *darbārs* may be held

śālā — The term refers to a small structure with an elevated floor, open on four sides, and a roof supported by narrow columns.

Glossary (Concluded)

samand — The term refers to a reservoir or tank for bathing or storing water.

sardar — The term refers to a nobleman or lord, but not a ruler.

saqaya — (aka *birka, haud , fisqiya, sihrij*) The term refers to an ablution tank.

serai — The term refers to a pavilion, often open on four sides and is used for relaxation and other pleasurable activities. It is similar to the Thai *śālā*.

shaikh — (aka sheik) The term refers to a leader, usually a tribal chief.

shari'a — The term refers to Islamic law or code.

shikhara — The term refers to a towerlike superstructure over the *garbhagṛha* of a temple or any part thereof. It is made up of various sculptural devices and its form can vary. It also is often applied to any towerlike form upon a temple or palace.

shila khana — The term refers to an armoury.

shish mahal — The term refers to a pavilion or room with many mirrors. The surface may be covered with mirrors.

sihrij — (aka *saqaya, birka, haud , fisqiya*) The term refers to an ablution tank.

śilpa-śāstras — The term refers to ancient treatises of design — e.g., the *Manasara, Mayamatam* and *Arthaśāstra*.

sthapati — The term refers to an architect-builder, who in the Indian Hindu tradition was what the 'master builder' was to the European Medieval tradition.

suffa — The term refers to a stone platform usually as a base for tombs.

sultān — The term refers to an Islamic ruler with the rank equivalent to a king. Although, a *sultān* is referred to as 'His Highness' rather than 'His Majesty.' See: *Mahārājāh, Nawāb, Nāyaka, Nizām, Rājāh, Rao.*

suraj pol — The term refers to a gateway, specifically the "sun gate" which is ceremonial and refers to the ruler.

T

tank — The term refers to a small reservoir or artificial pool of water. Generally they are square and used for bathing. See: *hammam*; see also: *samand*.

thakur — The term refers to a leader, it is a non-royal title, but a *thakur* may hold considerable power and prestige..

tin darwāzā — The term refers to a triple gate. See: *tripolia*.

tripolia — The term refers to a triple gate. See: *tin darwāzā*.

triratha — The term refers to a single extension, generally in the middle portion of the surface of a wall, creating three surfaces per face. See: *ratha* & *Pañcharatha*.

triśālā — The term refers to a plan in which rooms appear on three sides of a courtyard, forming a 'U.'

tudung — The term refers to a scarf worn by Muslim women of Malaysia and Indonesia. It may be simple, but must cover the hair of the woman and may extend downward covering all to the fingertips of the woman. This serves the same purpose as the traditional Indian sari.

turba — The term refers to a mausoleum

turbe — The term refers to a mausoleum.

V

vilas — The term refers to a space or room for retreat or privacy.

visir — (aka *vizier, wazir*) See: *wazir*.

vizier — (aka *visir, wazir*) An alternate spelling for *visir*. See: *visir*.

W

wav — (aka *baoli, bauli*) See: *baoli*.

wazir — (aka *visir*) The term refers to a high governmental official, the Minister of State.

Z

zanana — (aka *zenānā*) See: *zenānā*.

zenānā — (aka *rawala, zanana*) The private area for the women, particularly in a Muslim palace, as opposed to the men's area — the *mardānā*. See: *harem*.

ziyara — The term refers to a tomb.

Acknowledgements

Professor Dr. G. L. Chia, Department of Mathematics, University of Malaya.